日本の特撮映画

特撮の男たち

JAPANESE SPECIAL EFFECTS CINEMA: GODFATHERS OF TOKUSATSU VOL. 1

by J.L. Carrozza

Foreword by Norman England

Additional articles by Tyler Martin and Patrick Galvan

© Orochi Books, 2022. All Rights Reserved

All trademarks and brands referred to in this book are for illustrative purposes only, are the property of their respective owners and not affiliated with this publication in any way. Any trademarks are being used without permission, and the publication of the trademark is not authorized by, associated with or sponsored by the trademark owner.

DEDICATED TO
GUY MARINER TUCKER
(1969-2006)
&
AKIRA TAKARADA
(1934-2022)

SPECIAL THANKS

SEAN BARRY	KIEFER BEELMAN
MATT BURKETT	MICHAEL CALLARI
FRANÇOIS COLOUMBE	KEVIN DERENDORF
NORMAN ENGLAND	STUART GALBRAITH IV
PATRICK GALVAN	ED GODZISZEWSKI
CODY HIMES	BRETT HOMENICK
TED JOHNSON	DAVID KALAT
JOHN LEMAY	PATRICK MACIAS
TYLER MARTIN	JAKE MCDANIEL
TOSHIO MIIKE	DAVID MILNER
OKI MIYANO	RICHARD PUSATERI
AUGUST RAGONE	ANTHONY ROMERO
STEVE RYFLE	DAISUKE SATO
TAKAO YOSHIBA	

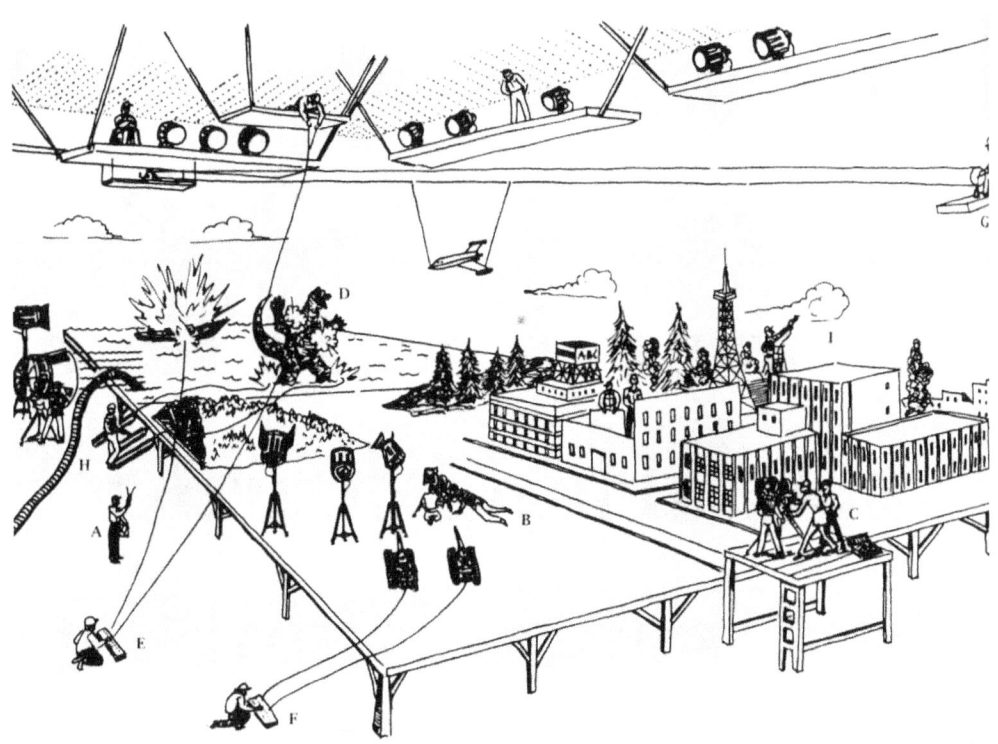

FOREWORD by Norman England..................4

INTRODUCTION............7

I.. **1901-1936**................13

II. **1937-1945**..............32

COLOR FILM IN JAPAN by Patrick Galvan..............49

III. **1945-1954**..............52

IV. **1954**..............67

SHOOTING TOKUSATSU................85

V. **1955-1956**..............91

VI. **1957-1959**.............108

VARAN: SHINICHI SEKIZAWA AND GENRE TROPES by Patrick Galvan..............133

VII. **1960-1961**.............135

VIII. **1962-1963**.............157

IX. **1964**.................181

X. **1965**................195

XI. **1966** (1)............214

XII. **1966** (2)...........233

XIII. **1967**..............259

XIV. **1968**.............283

THE MUSIC OF TOKUSATSU by Tyler Martin....................309

XV. **1969-1970**...........317

XVI. **1971** (1)...........341

XVII. **1971** (2)..........357

XVIII. **1972**.............371

XIX. **1973**............389

XX. **1974**............413

XXI. **1975-1976**..........437

XXII. **1977**.............460

XXIII. **1978-1979**..........483

GLOSSARY..............505

BIBLIOGRAPHY...........511

ABOUT THE AUTHOR.........516

"In Japan, the special effects director is a really special kind of artist who is always thinking about better ways to shoot film."

- Kinji Fukasaku, *Monsters Are Attacking Tokyo!* (1998) by Stuart Galbraith IV., Feral House.

FOREWORD

by Norman England

Few and far between are English books detailing the fascinating history of Japanese special effects cinema. The reason is not a lack of Western interest; it's more a case of the daunting effort the research effort entails. Additionally, few releases on the subject demonstrate to publishers that a large enough market for this material exists. Making matters worse are the Japanese companies themselves. Satisfied within the confines of their nation's borders, Japanese people in the entertainment business are notoriously lackadaisical when dealing with the world outside Japan.

Making a grassroots effort to fill in this lack of information, *Godfathers of Tokusatsu Vol. 1* by Jules Carrozza aims to unravel the complex history of Japanese special effects cinema. It's a book I can marvel at; when my interest in Japanese FX cinema began via a 1965 TV broadcast in the New York area of *Godzilla, King of the Monsters*, information of this kind didn't exist. At best, we got snippets of information from *Famous Monsters of Filmland* gleaned from sparse press releases issued by US distributors of Japanese sci-fi films. Obtaining hard information on how these Japanese FX films were made and by whom would involve traveling to Japan and conducting (and translating) interviews with the filmmakers, something beyond the scope of any US movie magazine at the time. (In many ways, it still is.) Compounding this was (and still exists) a general dismissal of Japanese film effect techniques by the Western public. I believe this bias persists today due to a lack of early information on how Japanese FX films were made. The reputation of their being "cheesy" was established decades ago by clueless writers who may have had a racial bias, something common in the decades following World War II.

As a child of the '60s, I was enamored by fantastic cinema. Weekend TV gave me the sci-fi films of the '50s, with theaters offering the latest FX films: *Fantastic Voyage, 2001, Planet of the Apes*, etc. TV, too: *Star Trek, The*

Invaders, and anything by Irwin Allen. Mixed in with this was the output by Japanese studios, mainly Toho (Godzilla and company) and Daiei (Gamera). Even to a kid, the aesthetic of the Japanese-produced films was noticeably different from those of Western studios. Whereas Westerners seemed preoccupied with reproducing reality, the Japanese seemed to be after a middle ground between reality and the hyper-reality one encounters when gazing at an intricately detailed HO train set.

While I loved the films from my own country, they seemed to lack the ballsiness of those coming out of Japan. Take 1961's *Mothra*. When flying over New Kirk City, miniature cars whip around the air and crash into store windows in ways that look in no way real. Did I care? Hell, no! It looked cool! While the major American studios were sweating it out not to be accused of releasing films that looked "fakey," the Japanese studios were making film after film filled with the most mind-boggling and fun effects.

One of the greatest moments in my childhood cinema-viewing history was seeing *The War of the Gargantuas* in 1970. 11 at the time, I could hardly believe what I was seeing: a giant octopus, maser tanks, volcanoes springing out of nowhere, and two behemoth creatures that, to me, emoted on a non-verbal level the equal of Karloff in the first *Frankenstein*. I was so enchanted by the film that I made my mom drive me to see it three times, making it the first film I saw in a theater more than once. I wasn't alone in my feelings. All my friends my age got it. We'd rather see miniature tanks rattling down a miniature highway than the grainy stock footage of military equipment or rocket launches you'd get in US films. Honestly, only the adults seemed to have an issue with the FX out of Japan.

Alas, the glory days of the so-called *Showa* era were short-lived. Cinema in the late '60s was entering a new phase. Special effects in America were reaching new heights of realism, and the audience for authenticity in both acting and visuals was growing. The Japanese studios were hard-pressed to keep up. Even their own audiences abandoned them as foreign FX films outperformed domestic homegrown FX films at the box office. Reduced budgets and movies aimed at a less discriminating younger audience meant Japan lost even more of its edge. It's been this way more or less ever since.

I began visiting Japan in 1990 and made the move here in 1993. One of the ways I curbed my homesickness was to enjoy the things my new home had to offer. One way was taking in the sporadic domestic releases of FX films. Like anything, some were better than others. Although I enjoyed the Heisei Godzilla films, I found them a little rough around the edges. It wasn't as if I was losing the faith, but it did feel like the best was behind us.

One day at the top of '95 a writer friend invited me to a screening of Daiei's new Gamera film. Although I'd loved Gamera as a kid, as an adult, I wouldn't list any of them among my favorite films. In fact, now that I was living in Japan, one thing I did was check out Gamera VHS tapes of the films I hadn't seen. Less than impressed with them, I can't say I had high hopes for a new Gamera film. So, visiting the Daiei office in Osaka, my friend and I joined a preview screening.

Whoa!

From the get-go the film excelled in every department: story, direction, acting, you name it! Best of all, *Gamera: Guardian of the Universe* came stocked with special effects as good as anything out of Hollywood. Soon after and through fortuitous circumstances, I was given work by *Fangoria* magazine to visit sets and conduct interviews with filmmakers in Japan. This began a new chapter in my life. During this time I learned how the studio system worked in Japan and the kind of people who take on the difficult task of filmmaking. Eventually, I switched careers and today make a living doing various tasks for the film industry in Japan.

In addition to *Fangoria*, I also wrote for various Japanese publications: *Eiga Hiho*, *Hobby Japan*, *The Japan Times*, etc. I also directed a few films. Of relevance to this book was *Bringing Godzilla Down to Size* (2008), a documentary exploring the art of Japanese miniature effects. Working with writers Steve Ryfle and Ed Godziszewski, I strove to put a face on many of the unsung artisans who have defined Japanese FX cinema. More recently is my book *Behind the Kaiju Curtain: A Journey Onto Japan's Biggest Film Sets*, in which I share my journal during the productions of *Gamera 3* through *Godzilla, Mothra and King Ghidorah: Giant Monsters All-Out Attack*.

I feel an affinity with Jules and what he's set out to do with *Godfathers of Tokusatsu Vol. 1*, and that is to bring attention and much-needed knowledge to the often neglected world of Japanese *tokusatsu* filmmaking. Now that he has, I can hardly wait for *Vol. 2*!

序論
INTRODUCTION

Japanese Special Effects Cinema: Godfathers of Tokusatsu provides a comprehensive history of the **tokusatsu** genre and art of Japanese special effects filmmaking. Its legacy stretches from wartime propaganda films such as *The War at Sea From Hawaii to Malay* (1942) to the recent *Shin Ultraman* (2022). These two volumes will examine the lengthy chronology of Japan's tokusatsu industry and the careers of the hardworking people who made it possible. Through the personal connections they forged, the reader will see how the medium has evolved and been passed from one generation of artisans to the next.

The word tokusatsu translates to "special filming". Employed in a plethora of Japanese films and television shows including the Godzilla, Ultraman and Kamen Rider franchises, along with anime it has become a national post-war art form. The medium's greatest luminary and the man almost single-handedly responsible for its creation was **EIJI TSUBURAYA** (1901-1970). The process he devised involves a myriad of cinematic techniques. These range from performers in monster suits and meticulously crafted miniature models to pyrotechnics and optical animation.

In 1896, French trailblazer Georges Méliès was filming a Parisian street scene when his camera jammed. When he projected the footage, a bus changed into a hearse and women turned into men. This happy accident paved the way for a revolution in cinematic technique and all future trick photography. The art of special effects cinema was born. Méliès had numerous spiritual successors: America's Willis O'Brien and Ray Harryhausen, Italy's Ricardo Freda and Mario Bava, and of course, Japan's Tsuburaya, born a few years after the fated incident. A year after Tsuburaya's birth, Georges Méliès' *A Trip to the Moon* was released, effectively the first science fiction and special effects picture ever made.

Our cast of characters. From left to right: Ishiro Honda, Eiji Tsuburaya, Tomoyuki Tanaka, Shinji Higuchi, Tomio Sagisu, Noriaki Yuasa, Akio Jissoji, Sadamasa Arikawa, Teruyoshi Nakano, Koichi Kawakita, Keita Amemiya, Hideaki Anno, Koichi Takano, Nobuo Yajima, Shotaro Ishinomori, Kenpachiro Satsuma, Katsuro Onoue, Tsutomu Kitagawa, Kiyotaka Taguchi, Makoto Kamiya, Shusuke Kaneko, Haruo Nakajima, Teizo Toshimitsu, Yasuyuki Inoue, Eizo Kaimai, Nobuyuki Yasumaru, Keizo Murase, Toshio Miike, Shinichi Wakasa, Fuyuki Shinada, Tomoo Haraguchi and Daisuke Sato

Unlike in other countries, in Japan, a film's special effects sequences were seldom supervised by the main director. FX heavy movies were typically shot with two units, one helmed by the main director who directed the actors. The other was led by the special effects director. Eiji Tsuburaya was so well regarded at Toho that he was eventually given a special credit right before the name of the main unit directors he worked under.

His special effects set was like a cross between a classical Renaissance workshop and a mad scientist's laboratory. Under him, craftspeople perfected innovative high-speed filming techniques, sculpted model cities and warships, constructed monster suits from scratch and rigged gunpowder-laced pyrotechnics with electrical charges - all while chain smoking cigarettes. On each film, Tsuburaya's team went through miles of piano wire, a favorite tool of theirs for hanging flying props, and metric tons of gelatin, used for thickening water to make it resemble the ocean as seen from a plane.

The hours on Tsuburaya's sets at the Toho studios were long. The work was hard and at times dangerous to a degree that would violate many labor laws today. Suit actors like Haruo Nakajima got off the worst, suffering tortures of the damned inside giant rubber skins that became hellish saunas under the burning lights. These stuntmen like Nakajima and his protege Kenpachiro Satsuma suffered burns, electrocutions and near drownings in Toho's giant special effects pool. Teruyoshi Nakano, who started off as an assistant director for Tsuburaya before inheriting his mantle, minced no words about the brutal working conditions. In an interview for the books *Monsters Are Attacking Tokyo* and *Japan's Favorite Mon-star,* Nakano said "It was a very hard job. They used the term '3-K' for the crappiest jobs. '3-K' stands for *kitsui*, a hard job, *kitanai*, a dirty job, and *kurushi*, a stinky job. But special effects work was more like a 7-K or 8-K job!" Yet these men persevered and made strikingly beautiful cinematic images as they sweated under searing tungsten lights. Many were Imperial Army veterans who bore the scars of World War II. Yet, like many men in post-war Japan, they were determined to build a better world. They had seen the horrors of war firsthand and lived through their country's bitter defeat. Some of these craftsmen even went to other East Asian countries to help Japan's former enemies with their special effects productions, putting aside bitter national grudges for the art of cinema.

In some Western film criticism of Japanese genre films, there's an uninformed tendency to give too much credit to their main unit's directors. In general, the most memorable and spectacular moments of Toho's special effects pictures were the work of Eiji Tsuburaya. While directors like Ishiro Honda, Jun Fukuda or Seiji Maruyama contributed a human element, it was ultimately Tsuburaya's unit who dominated the films and got people into theater seats on both sides of the Pacific. In the United States, Tsuburaya's pictures were surprisingly profitable, with *Rodan* the top grossing sci-fi movie of 1957. Many in the U.S. saw and still see Japanese special effects films as "cheap" and poor in quality. Stop motion pioneers like Ray Harryhausen thumbed their noses at Tsuburaya's work. Harryhausen was said to be jealous that Tsuburaya could make movies more quickly than him. What is poorly understood is that the art form of tokusatsu is intended to have an unreal, theatrical pantomime beauty. In Hollywood, special effects are created to be as photorealistic as can be achieved. In Japan, they like to have a little more fun. While the models and monster suits integral to tokusatsu are seen as unconvincing by Western eyes, in Japan, this pantomime quality is viewed in a similar light to the work of Jim Henson.

Tokusatsu films and television also often boast ingenious filmmaking. Special effects directors like Eiji Tsuburaya and his many successors and rivals were adept at image-based storytelling. Their unique style of cinema hearkens back to silent film directors such as D.W. Griffith, Abel Gance, Sergei Eisenstein and F.W. Murnau. Eisenstein, his distinct aesthetic and editing style inspired by Japanese linguistics, was an influence on and personal friend to Tsuburaya's mentor, director Teinosuke Kinugasa. It was while acting as a shooting assistant on Kinugasa's *A Page of Madness* (1926) that Tsuburaya began to develop his dynamic visual style.

Tsuburaya later founded his own company, pioneering special effects television shows like *Ultraman*. By the late 1960s Japanese airwaves were swarming with colorful pantomime beasts. Of course, even as Tsuburaya's proteges came into their own, many rivals sprang up. Competing studios began producing their own special effects extravaganzas for theaters and television. Some included Daiei's Noriaki Yuasa and Yoshiyuki Kuroda, Toei's Nobuo Yajima and P-Productions' Tomio Sagisu. Tokusatsu filmmakers were surprising trailblazers in commercial cinema. Eiji Tsuburaya and manga artist-turned-showrunner Shotaro Ishinomori were among the first to develop live action cinematic and television universes. The Godzilla, Ultraman and Kamen Rider franchises predated Lucasfilm, Warner Brothers or Disney in having some continuity between each film and show. And like DC, Marvel or Star Wars, these franchises persist to the present. Tsuburaya and Ishinomori's strong marketing of their characters as toys also predated George Lucas' by years. Japanese anime and tokusatsu films and television, spearheaded by Tsuburaya, Ishinomori and Osamu Tezuka, would spark "toy culture" in Japan and perhaps abroad.

Like Renaissance sculptors or samurai sword makers, a major part of the tokusatsu art form involves the training of the next generation of craftspeople. In Japan, there's a stronger social dynamic among professionals, called the *kohai-senpai* relationship. In workplaces and academic environments, an older student or worker, the senpai, will take the younger one, the kohai, under their wing. In the Japanese film world, this dynamic is particularly prevalent, as one generation of filmmakers and craftspeople mentors the next. The tokusatsu art form has thus been passed down from one modern generation to another, from the early years of *Showa* to the new *Reiwa* era. Much as in the anime industry, wherein most professional animators working in Japan today can be directly traced to Osamu Tezuka's Mushi Production, every modern tokusatsu technician can be connected to Eiji Tsuburaya.

Tsuburaya left the world sooner than he should have. His direct successor, Sadamasa Arikawa, departed Toho soon after his death, leaving Teruyoshi Nakano in charge of the special effects division. Nakano was younger than either and known for his love of pyrotechnics and no-holds-barred '70s directing style. Another protege of Tsuburaya, Arikawa and Nakano was Koichi Kawakita, who was first given the opportunity to supervise the special effects on the war epic *Zero Pilot* (1976). Kawakita, who had the soul of an engineer and loved his mechanics, succeeded Nakano as head of Toho's FX unit in the late 1980s. On Kawakita's unit for *Bye Bye Jupiter* and Nakano's set for *The Return of Godzilla* (both 1984), a teenage boy named Shinji Higuchi worked as an uncredited production assistant. Higuchi would, of course, go on to become a titan of modern tokusatsu cinema, helming the FX unit for the stunning 1990s Gamera trilogy and co-directing 2016's *Shin Godzilla*.

Yet this isn't just about the special effects directors. Film is a collaborative art form, especially in Japan. A good director knows how to assemble and handle the best talent. The below-the-line folks who designed the monsters, built the suits, painted the set backdrops, constructed the miniatures and rigged the explosions are seldom written about in English. This is just as much their story. You will learn about cinematographers like Motoyoshi Tomioka and Fujio Morita, suit builders such as Nobuyuki Yasumaru, Keizo Murase and Fuyuki Shinada, art directors like Yasuyuki Inoue and Toshio Miike and even pyrotechnicians like Kyuzo Yamamoto, Tadaaki Watanabe and Izumi Negishi.

The two volumes of **Japanese Special Effects Cinema: Godfathers of Tokusatsu** trace the creative lineage of Eiji Tsuburaya directly to Shinji Higuchi and beyond. Today, especially with some proficiency in Japanese, rare materials and films previously inaccessible or even unknown can be imported with the click of a key. Japanese information straight from the front lines can be accessed and given a readable AI translation in seconds. Japanese data and names can also be cross referenced for deeper research. This book takes advantage of these technological leaps to give the reader what is hoped to be the most in-depth look at the Japanese special effects film industry in English.

Tokusatsu is a national art form that, for the sake of historical criticism, needs an academic definition. Tokusatsu is not merely "Japanese special effects" per se. Old school Japanese horror films like *Ghost of Yotsuya* (1959) and *Onibaba* (1964) have heavy use of special effects makeup and many other films contain process shots. Movies with entirely computer generated FX like Takashi Yamazaki's live action *Space Battleship Yamato* (2011) have also been misclassified as tokusatsu. The definition of classical tokusatsu in this book is the cinematic technique and production style created by Eiji Tsuburaya distinguished by its own unit devoted to "special filming". While not a black and white definition, but for the purposes of the text: if a work was produced in Japan, used a "special filming" unit separate from the main director's and features heavy use of practical effects such as miniatures, puppets and monster suits, it qualifies as tokusatsu. There are subtle exceptions to this. These include certain independent movies along with films and shows where the distinction between the units was weaker like *The Human Vapor* (1960) or *Kamen Rider* and tokusatsu-style films produced by Japanese technicians in other Asian countries.

As you read this first volume of **Japanese Special Effects Cinema: Godfathers of Tokusatsu,** try to imagine how a schoolboy in Japan felt in the 1960s and '70s, when one tokusatsu production after another was released to theaters and they could watch an assortment of colorful monster shows after school. Also envision how, at any given time in the '60s-70s, there were multiple tokusatsu film and television units simultaneously shooting in Tokyo and creating their distinct brand of visually beautiful cinematic mayhem. In addition to being an obsessed historian, I am a filmmaker myself. As someone who has directed independent films, the special effects end of these movies has always held a particular fascination for me. This is a book, first and foremost, about filmmaking; indeed, one of the most special forms of filmmaking in the world.

I.
<u>1901 - 1937</u>
明治三十四 - 昭和十二

Aodo Denzen (Eiji Tsuburaya's ancestor) by Endo Denichi

The 20th century dawned in Japan.

Legend has it that a child named Eiichi was born on July 7th, 1901 in the village of Sukagawa in Fukushima Prefecture to parents Isamu and Sei Tsumuraya. This was at the start of the *Tanabata* festival. During this festival, children make wishes to hone their talents. The narrative of Eiji Tsuburaya's birth coinciding with the start of *Tanabata* is seen as a testament to his natural talent. The truth is that he was most likely born on July 10th. Regardless of what Tsuburaya's genuine birthday was, his talent would come to be legend. This boy was also a descendent of legendary Tokugawa-era painter and engraver **AODO DENZEN** (1748-1822) via his grandmother Natsu.

Fittingly, young Eiichi Tsumuraya entered a changing world burgeoning with new technology. Only eight years prior, Thomas Edison had patented the Kinetoscope, the first working motion picture camera. Then in 1895, brothers Auguste and Louis Lumière perfected their own movie camera. Their first film screening was held in Paris that year and the art of cinema was born. In 1896 to early 1897, films by Edison and the Lumière Brothers were screened in Japan. The concept of a motion picture was not entirely new to the Japanese. The magic lantern had been introduced to Japan in the Edo period by the Dutch. Phantasmagoria-style magic lantern shows or *utsushi-e* were extremely popular. The first Japanese films were made months after the Lumières' and similarly depicted daily life in Tokyo. In the silent era, Japanese theatrical screenings boasted live narration by a performer called a *benshi*. Adding an element akin to Japanese theater like *kabuki* and *No*, the benshi became an integral part of the cinematic experience. To Japanese audiences, the benshi themselves often had more draw than the films and actors they narrated. Moviegoers would even travel from other regions to see the most famous.

A Trip to the Moon (1902)

Only a year after Tsumuraya's birth, **A TRIP TO THE MOON [Director: GEORGES MELIES** (1861-1938) - **Release Date (France):** September 1st, 1902] was premiered in Paris. The Parisian born Méliès pioneered early cinematic technique, largely inventing the very process of cinematic special effects. *A Trip to the Moon* was not only one of cinema's first real science fiction films but also an early complex special effects picture. Earlier special effects films had been created, such as a film from the Lumière Brothers called *The Mechanical Butcher* (1895). In it, an entire pig is fed to a turn-of-the-century futuristic machine that transforms it into sausages. However, until Méliès, special effects in cinema were crude, often consisting of simple transitions from one image to another. As Eiji Tsuburaya would later draw influence from his country's native kabuki theater, Méliès drew upon France's *feerie* style theatrical traditions. He created imaginative props while using innovative camera techniques. The following year, another revolutionary film was released in the United States by Thomas Edison's fledgling film company: **THE GREAT TRAIN ROBBERY** [**Director:** Edwin S. Porter - **Release Date (U.S.):** December 7th, 1903]. *The Great Train Robbery* was another of the first elaborate narrative films and contained innovative cinematic techniques, such as an early use of kinetic editing. This revolution in narrative filmmaking would soon make its way to Japan.

When Tsumuraya was only three, his young mother tragically passed away giving birth to her second son. His father, who had just divorced her, abandoned the family and went to China for business. Tsumuraya was thus raised by his grandmother Natsu. His uncle Ichiro was only five years older than him and treated him as his younger brother. Eiichi got the nickname "Eiji" from him. Young Tsumuraya began primary school at the age of seven. An introverted boy, he loved making watercolor paintings. His first obsession was with locomotives and Tsumuraya thought he might become a train engineer.

Shozo Makino

At the same time, the fledgling cinematic art form continued to advance in Japan. Inspired by Méliès, director **SHOZO MAKINO** (1878-1929) made some of the first sophisticated narrative films for an early Japanese film studio, Yokota Shokai, founded by industrialist

EINOSUKE YOKOTA (1872-1943). Makino began making films in 1908 and is regarded today as the D.W. Griffith of Japan. It was Makino who pioneered the *jidai-geki* (period film) genre. Just as early European cinema was shot in an artless "proscenium" style, Japanese silents were largely kabuki plays on film. Yet Makino was one of the first Japanese filmmakers to incorporate sophisticated cinematic technique. His early trick photography predated the work Eiji Tsuburaya would someday be known for.

A few years after Tsumuraya's birth, another budding technology came into the world. In the United States, brothers Orville and Wilbur Wright completed the first successful airplane flight in December of 1903. The science of aviation, which would captivate young Tsumuraya, had taken wing. In late 1910, Imperial Army captains Yoshitoshi Tokugawa and Kumazo Hino conducted the first successful manned flight in Japan. Young Tsumuraya's interest was piqued. He dreamed of being an aviator and constructed his own model planes as a hobby, often out of bamboo and Japanese lanterns.

In 1911, the ten-year-old Tsumuraya saw his first film, documentary footage of a volcanic eruption on Sakurajima Island. Tsumuraya was once again captivated, not so much by the film itself but by the projection equipment. Legend has it that, with his allowance, he bought a children's projector and used paper to simulate film stock with stick figure drawings as frames. This early aptitude and talent in technical trickery would go on to define much of Eiji Tsuburaya's legacy.

On July 30th, 1912, Mutsuhito, the *Meiji* Emperor, passed away. His son Yoshihito succeeded the Chrysanthemum Throne, ending the *Meiji* era and ushering in *Taisho*. The *Taisho* era would be short-lived and marked by a tumultuous world stage, rapid economic development, democratic reforms and a terrible natural disaster. Japan's first major film studio, Nikkatsu, was founded in September. Tsumuraya, meanwhile, built a particularly impressive miniature plane at the age of 11. This got him interviewed in a local newspaper. He wasn't, however, always a perfectly behaved child. Young Eiichi once threw a temper tantrum so his family would let him get in the cockpit of a plane.

In June 1914, a hemisphere away, Archduke Franz Ferdinand was assassinated in Sarajevo. In a month, the globe was plunged into its first World War. The *Taisho* Japanese government sided with the Allies against Imperial Germany and entered the war in August. With World War I came the dawn of air combat. Young Tsumuraya's desire to become a flying ace no doubt swelled as he heard accounts of American and German biplanes waging war in the skies. In 1916, he read about aviator Art Smith's acrobatic flight over Tokyo in his Curtis biplane. Though his grandmother and uncle were dead-set against it, Tsumuraya begged them. He wanted to move to Tokyo and attend the Japan Flying School. They relented and he began his training under young aviator Seitaro Tamai. The entrance fee was a-then appalling 600 yen, but his uncle Ichiro begrudgingly took care of it.

Sadly, Tsumuraya's dreams of aviation were crushed by tragedy. On May 20th, 1917, Tamai was killed during an unsuccessful flight demonstration over Tokyo. His plane experienced engine failure and crashed. The Japan Flying School was closed and young Tsumuraya abandoned his dream. This passion for aviation, however, would no doubt go on to influence the miniature cinematography techniques he would one day pioneer. Tsumuraya instead enrolled in the Tokyo Engineering School.

While attending school, Tsumuraya worked at Utsumi Toy Works, a toy manufacturer. With his engineering skills, Tsumuraya was quite successful and designed a tricycle and battery powered phone. These toys were some of Utsumi's best-selling. Later, in November of 1918, World War I concluded as the deadly Spanish flu epidemic raged and a communist revolution was in process in nearby Russia. Japan was at first not hit by the pandemic as hard as other countries, but suffered significant disruptions in infrastructure and economy by 1919. In spite of this, that year was critically significant in young Tsumuraya's life and career.

In spring 1919, Tsumuraya attended a party at a tea house in Tokyo during the cherry blossom viewing festival. A drunken fistfight broke out between some of Tsumuraya's friends and a second group. Tsumuraya talked to one of his ostensible foes, who turned out to be none other than **YOSHIRO EDAMASA** (1888-1944), another pioneering film director at the studio Tenkatsu. Edamasa, born in Kujima at Hiroshima Prefecture, had studied under another one of early Japanese cinema's great pioneers: **KICHIZO CHIBA** (1874-1927). Chiba and Edamasa were rivals to Shozo Makino. While Edamasa liked the visual effects pioneered in Makino's films, he also felt the movies themselves were sloppily produced.

Yoshiro Edamasa

Edamasa strived to create Japanese films that rivaled anything made abroad. In 1917, he had been the cinematographer for a full length adaptation of the Chinese classical novel **JOURNEY TO THE WEST** [**Director:** Jiro Yoshino - **Release Date (Japan):** January 10th, 1917], He made early use of moving trick photography for shots of Son Goku, the monkey god, flying on his nimbus. *Journey to the West* also contained more scene transitions than any Japanese film prior. Edamasa was impressed with Tsumuraya's technical skills and offered him a job as a cameraman. Tsumuraya at first refused, but the eccentric Edamasa was persistent, often visiting the young man at his boarding house. Tsumuraya accepted Edamasa's offer and joined Tenkatsu. It would be Edamasa's protege who would one day fulfill his goal of creating Japanese films that rivaled Hollywood's productions.

Yoshiro Edamasa enthusiastically taught Tsumuraya the basics of filmmaking which the young man quickly proved adept in. His first job was helping shoot the title sequence for **A SORROWFUL SON** [**Director:** Yoshiro Edamasa - **Release Date (Japan):** October 18th, 1919]. As Japan suffered through another wave of the Spanish flu pandemic in early 1920, Tenkatsu was soon bought out by Kokukatsu, a bigger studio. In March, Edamasa traveled to Hollywood to research film techniques. Tsumuraya stayed behind and worked on more pictures. He did aerial photography when other assistant cameramen were afraid to, impressing the higher ups and earning him a promotion.

In 1920, the Mitchell Camera Company, founded the year prior in the United States by George Mitchell, introduced the Mitchell Standard 35mm camera. This then state-of-the-art camera would further revolutionize the worldwide film industry. Japanese film studios would use Mitchell cameras until the 1970s. Cheaper German cameras were also used, especially during the coming World War when trade with the United States was halted. Japanese cinematographers often struggled to decipher the instruction manuals of these foreign cameras, printed only in English or German. Also in 1920, kabuki theater company Shochiku would branch into film production and become Japan's next major movie studio.

A proto-tokusatsu monster battle in *Jiraiya the Brave* (1921)

At the same time, Shozo Makino created perhaps the first extant Japanese genre picture and proto-tokusatsu film: **JIRAIYA THE BRAVE [Director:** Shozo Makino - **Release Date (Japan):** February 1st, 1921]. Released on February 1st, 1921, the film was an early adaptation of the folktale *Jiraiya Goketsu Monogatari*. Featuring popular kabuki actor turned film star Matsunosuke Onoe in the title role, *Jiraiya the Brave* features some impressive optical effects for its time such as Jiraiya appearing and disappearing through double exposure. Most interestingly, for the transformations of Jiraiya and nemesis

Orochimaru (Suminojo Ichikawa), puppets and monster suits were used. These creations look forward to those employed in the tokusatsu productions of the coming mid-century. A large puppet and suit were built for Jiraiya's giant toad form. The puppet featured a moving mouth which devoured enemy samurai onscreen.

Meanwhile, Tsumuraya's fledgling career as a cameraman was cut short by conscription. He served in the Imperial Army's fifth division and was assigned to communications thanks to his technical engineering degree. Tsumuraya was discharged in 1923. He returned to his hometown to recuperate. His grandmother Natsu pleaded with him to abandon filmmaking and take on the family's lucrative general store business. Yet Tsumuraya was eager to return to Tokyo and make films again. His uncle Ichiro allowed him to go to Tokyo and would take over the family business himself.

On September 1st, 1923 at close to noon, the city of Tokyo violently shook as the Great Kanto earthquake took place. The city was reduced to rubble and ravaged by hellish firestorms. It was one of the most appalling natural disasters in modern history. The earthquake left close to 150,000 people dead, Japan's economy in ruins and incinerated much of its cinematic history up to that point. The political aftershocks caused by the quake would reverberate well into the *Showa* era. The 22-year-old Tsumuraya was not in the city when this happened, but film production in Japan was severely affected. Tsumuraya took some work at Kokukatsu that year, one of the last surviving Japanese movie studios. With Tokyo in ruins, Kyoto would become a temporary production hub for the Japanese film industry. It remains a popular film town in Japan to the present day. Its old school architecture and rural population density in its surrounding areas particularly made it ideal for shooting authentic-looking *jidai-geki* or period pieces. Tsumuraya reluctantly went to Kyoto in 1924 and began work on productions there.

In the United States a pioneering film would soon be released: **THE LOST WORLD [Director:** Harry Hoyt - **Release Date (U.S.):** February 2nd, 1925] based on the novel by Sir Arthur Conan Doyle. It featured groundbreaking stop motion animated dinosaurs by the pioneering **WILLIS O'BRIEN** (1886-1962) that stunned audiences. *The Lost World* even features cinema's first sequence of a monster destroying a city, in this case a brontosaurus rampaging through London. Also containing an early cinematic usage of miniature sets, the

DNA of every urban monster rampage that came afterwards can be seen here. This includes O'Brien's upcoming *King Kong* (1933), his protégé Ray Harryhausen's *The Beast From 20,000 Fathoms* (1953) and the visions of destruction young Eiichi Tsumuraya would one day create in films like *Godzilla* (1954).

One of cinema's earliest monster rampage sequences in *The Lost World* (1925)

In late 1925, an iconic and influential propaganda film was released in Soviet Russia: **BATTLESHIP POTEMKIN** [Director: **SERGEI EISENSTEIN** (1898-1948) - **Release Date (Russia):** December 21st, 1925]. Eisenstein and his classmate **LEV KULESHOV** (1899-1870) believed that the aesthetic foundation of cinema lay in editing and montage. Eisenstein was inspired by D.W. Griffith, who had also begun to employ montage-style editing; in Griffith's case, it was inspired by the storytelling of Charles Dickens. Eisenstein also strived to make the art of cinema a powerful sensory experience, something he called *synaesthesia*. *Battleship Potemkin* would meld cinematic imagery in the most dynamic way yet.

Like Griffith's *Birth of a Nation* (1915) or Leni Riefenstahl's later *Triumph of the Will* (1934), *Potemkin* is blatant propaganda: in this case to drum up support for Stalin's regime which was rising to power. The most famous and powerful sequence, the Odessa Steps Massacre, is a partial fabrication brilliantly sold with visceral images ingeniously combined. Yet just as the genuine *Potemkin* sparked off a Marxist revolution in Russia, the film would ignite a cinematic revolution of its own. Despite being a propagandistic fiction, the Odessa Steps sequence was the most dynamically staged and cut in cinema yet. *Battleship Potemkin*'s finale is also the first masterful action sequence in cinema. *Potemkin*'s aesthetic influence stretches as far as Christopher Nolan's *Dunkirk* (2017). *Potemkin*'s stylistic DNA can also be seen in Japan's fervent propaganda and fatalistic war epics in the decades to come.

Battleship Potemkin (1925) - the visceral editing style employed by Eisenstein was derived from his obsession with the pictorial nature of Japanese text

Sergei Eisenstein had actually developed his style of cinematic montage through his obsessive study of Japanese aesthetics. Eisenstein loved kabuki theater in particular and its staging was influential on his visceral style of storytelling. The use of revolving stages and folding background screens, which looked forward to the miniatures and painted backdrops used by Eiji Tsuburaya, particularly impressed him, as did the dramatic gestures made by kabuki actors. Eisenstein would go on to see some of the very first kabuki performances held outside Japan in Moscow, including *Chushingura*: the beloved story of the 47 Ronin. Eisenstein's kinetic and visual editing rhythm was inspired by his obsession with Japanese text and kanji characters. The pictograph-based nature of the Chinese characters used in the Japanese language and how they link together in a sentence strongly informed his editing techniques as did the laconic and sequential nature of haiku. Eisenstein, however, disliked most

Japanese cinema as he felt it copied the commercial films of Hollywood instead of utilizing the genius of Japan's cultural aesthetic. Nevertheless, several Eisenstein-influenced filmmakers would soon arise in Japan, the most famous was **TEINOSUKE KINUGASA** (1896-1982).

Kinugasa, to be best known for *Gate of Hell* (1953), was born in Mie Prefecture and originally a female impersonator (*onnagata*) in kabuki plays. Branching out into Nikkatsu films with such roles, he switched to directing. Shozo Makino would take young Kinugasa under his wing. Makino hired Kinugasa to direct films for his company. Kinugasa soon went independent however and made the avant-garde **A PAGE OF MADNESS** [**Director:** Teinosuke Kinugasa - **Release Date (Japan):** September 24th, 1926]. To assist his cinematographer **KOHEI SUGIYAMA** (1899-1960), Kinugasa hired the young cameraman Eiichi Tsumuraya. Sugiyama would be another mentor to Tsumuraya and one day the greatest DP in Japan. *A Page of Madness* would likewise go on to become one of the most iconic Japanese silent films. Set in a mental hospital, the picture's opening images are arresting: as a rainstorm takes place outside, a costumed woman (Eiko Minami) does a surrealistic dance before a spinning, striped ball. It turns out that she's a mental patient, pathetically dancing in her cell.

A Page of Madness (1926)

A Page of Madness combines the haunting phantasmagoria of Robert Weine's *The Cabinet of Dr. Caligari* (1920) with the ingenious montage of Eisenstein's *Battleship Potemkin*. It is as complex in its cinematic technique as

Eisenstein, if not more so, featuring images that take the fledgling medium of Japanese film to new heights. The picture also boasts expressionistic flair akin to F.W. Murnau, best known for his unauthorized Dracula adaptation *Nosferatu* (1922) and *The Last Laugh* (1924). *A Page of Madness* is both experimental yet one of the most masterfully directed Japanese films to date. Seen in a darkened theater with a benshi shouting at the audience, it must have been majestic but unsettling.

Strikingly shot, the surreal, disturbing images in *A Page of Madness* also look forward to Luis Buñuel's scandalous *Un Chien Andalou* (1929). The influence of *Page*'s moody monochrome visuals can be seen in Japanese cinema for decades hence; including the horror films of Nobuo Nakagawa, Kaneto Shindo's *Onibaba*, Hiroshi Teshigahara's *Woman in the Dunes* (both 1964) or even Shinya Tsukamoto's *Tetsuo: The Iron Man* (1989). Eiichi Tsumuraya, who mainly acted as camera operator, no doubt had a hand in its atmospheric imagery. The film even features some of the first elaborate moving shots in Japanese cinema. It was with mentors Kinugasa and Sugiyama that Tsumuraya truly began to learn the art of visual storytelling. *A Page of Madness* even features one of Japanese cinema's earliest complex uses of the optical printing methods which Tsurumaya would one day be known for using. On the set, he was nicknamed "Zuburaya", another nickname that would stick. *A Page of Madness* was believed lost until a print was discovered by director Kinugasa in his Kyoto storehouse in 1971.

On December 25, 1926, the sickly Emperor Yoshihito died at the young age of only 47. Thus ended the *Taisho* era. His son, Hirohito, ascended the Chrysanthemum Throne the same day and the *Showa* era began. The *Showa* era would wind up being the most eventful in Japan's long history. It was marked by the rise of militarism, another World War ending in humiliating defeat for Japan and a decades-long postwar economic miracle.

In January 1927, the most iconic science fiction film yet made was released in Weimar Germany: **METROPOLIS** [Director: **FRITZ LANG** (1890-1976) - **Release Date (Germany):** January 10th, 1927]. *Metropolis* featured some of the most elaborate visual effects in cinema to date. Created by cinematographer **EUGEN SCHUFFTAN** (1893-1977), Eiji Tsuburaya would later employ many of these techniques himself. This influential picture also contained a pioneering use of miniature cityscapes to create the titular dystopia. In Japan meanwhile, Tsumuraya worked on his first film as a full fledged DP: **CHILDREN'S SWORDPLAY** [**Director:** Minoru Inuzuka - **Release Date (Japan):** March 19th, 1927]. It was the debut vehicle for up-and-coming superstar Kazuo Hasegawa and a huge hit. Tsumuraya was now on the map as one of Japan's rising talents in cinematography. He would shoot several more films that year. In 1928, Teinosuke Kinugasa's company, the Kinugasa Motion Picture League, was incorporated into the larger Kyoto branch of Shochiku and with it Tsumuraya. He would shoot the drama **CROSSROADS** [**Director:** Teinosuke Kinugasa - **Release Date (Japan):** May 11th, 1928] with Kohei Sugiyama that same year.

A young Eiji Tsuburaya uses a camera crane of his own invention

In early 1929, Tsumuraya met a set designer freshly graduated from art school: **AKIRA WATANABE** (1909-1999). Tsumuraya took Watanabe under his wing, teaching him how to paint set backgrounds on sheets of glass, which layered in-camera created a sense of depth. Tsumuraya also began development of a wooden camera crane. Inspired by the crane used for D.W. Griffith's *Intolerance* (1916), Tsumuraya would craft an affordable and practical version for the thrifty Japanese industry. While using the crane, Tsumuraya fell to the ground and injured himself. Rushing to his aid was a young woman named **MASANO ARAKI** (1910-19??) who was on a tour of Shochiku Kyoto. The 19-year-old Araki went to visit Tsumuraya while he recuperated in the hospital. On February 27th, 1930, the two married, buying a house behind the Shochiku Kyoto studio. Eiichi Tsumuraya soon changed his name to **EIJI TSUBURAYA**.

At the same time, director Teinosuke Kinugasa returned to Japan after a lengthy trip to Europe where he had met with his Soviet idols **VSEVOLOD PUDOVKIN** (1893-1953) and Sergei Eisenstein. In 1931, Tsuburaya helped Kohei Sugiyama shoot Kinugasa's first film upon the director's return to Japan: **BEFORE THE DAWN** [**Director:** Teinosuke Kinugasa - **Release Date (Japan):** May 5th, 1931]. Though Tsuburaya spent half of his salary on the research of novel photographic technology, his fledgling family was now in a better financial state. In April, they welcomed their first son, **HAJIME TSUBURAYA** (1931-1973), into the world.

By this time, the 30-year-old Tsuburaya was one of the most respected cinematographers in the pre-war Japanese film industry. He was the first DP in Japan to use "day-for-night" shooting techniques, sheets of painted glass to create depth-filled backgrounds and "push processing" for underexposed film, along with a new style of cyclorama backdrop for better rear projection effects. He became known as "Smoke Tsuburaya" due to his notorious frequent use of smoke machines. Of course, not everyone understood Tsuburaya's almost experimental techniques. Certain actors, particularly Kazuo Hasegawa, were frustrated by his realistic approach to filming them. They felt that Tsuburaya made them look ugly as they were used to stylized traditional shooting techniques in line with the kabuki plays many their careers began in. Other cameramen who worked under him sometimes found his methods puzzling. His rivals coined the biting nickname "Tsuburaya Who Doesn't Know What He's Doing." Eiji Tsuburaya, however, persevered and continued on his course as a rising star behind the camera.

As Tsuburaya's career advanced, so did Japan's colonial ambitions and unrest on the world stage. In Mukden (now Shenyang) in Northern China, the Japanese military staged the "918

Incident". They placed explosives on a railway, drumming up support at home by blaming it on the Chinese. The Imperial Japanese Army proceeded with a full-scale invasion of Manchuria. By February of 1932, the Japanese had effectively annexed Northeastern China, establishing a puppet state to be known as Manchukuo. Tsuburaya, meanwhile, in May of 1932, formed the Japan Cinematographers Association with mentors and colleagues such as Kohei Sugiyama, Hiroshi Sakai and Masao Tamai. That same year, he transferred from Shochiku to Nikkatsu Studios.

A King Kong-related display in Imperial Japan

By 1933, the world stage continued to destabilize. Adolf Hitler cemented his rise to power and became German chancellor in January. Japan withdrew from the League of Nations in March over international anger due to the establishment of Manchukuo. That spring, a highly influential new monster film would be released in the United States that revolutionized special effects cinema: **KING KONG** [**Directors:** Merian C. Cooper, Ernest Schoedsack - **Release Date (U.S.):** April 7th, 1933]. Featuring a giant gorilla created through groundbreaking stop motion animation by Willis O'Brien, *King Kong* also contained synergistic use of miniature sets, matte paintings and rear projection.

As influential as *Star Wars* 45 years later, *King Kong* would establish cinematic conventions in monster movies both in its images and tropes. In the picture's most stunning scene, Kong battles an Allosaurus as ingenue Ann Darrow (Fay Wray) looks on. Once again, every monster duel staged by every filmmaker to come owes something of its DNA to this astounding scene. Tsuburaya himself would one day recreate it. Kong's escape and rampage through New York City before scaling and falling from the Empire State Building, is another one of cinema's most influential sequences. Despite being a monster gorilla portrayed by two-foot jointed models, Kong had a surprising pathos. Audiences felt a degree of pity for this creature upon his death.

A new generation of filmmakers on both sides of the Pacific were inspired by *King Kong*. Upon seeing the film, a 13-year-old boy named **RAY HARRYHAUSEN** (1920-2013) was inspired to follow in O'Brien's footsteps, eventually becoming his protégé. *King Kong* was released in Japan in September. Eiji Tsuburaya was also captivated by this amazing new Hollywood film which he saw in Kyoto. Even as a veteran cinematographer, he could not believe his eyes at the incredible imagery on display. Tsuburaya acquired a personal print which he watched obsessively. He studied the film frame by frame to learn the secrets of Willis O'Brien's revolutionary techniques. Tsuburaya would quickly apply what he learned to his work. Decades later, in an interview with the Associated Press during the production of *Mothra* (1961), Tsuburaya would confess: "The change in my life came when I saw *King Kong*, that inspired me. At the time, Japanese trick photography was very backward. I started working in that field and by 1937 I began to accomplish some of the things I wanted to do."

That fall, Shochiku capitalized on the release of *King Kong* in Japan with the short silent comedy **WASEI KING KONG** [**Director:** Torajiro Saito - **Release Date (Japan):** October 5th, 1933]. Like *King Kong*'s own spider pit scene, it is now lost. Believed by many to be a Japanese *King Kong* ripoff, the picture was in fact not a monster movie, though it did feature a proto-tokusatsu ape suit. In it, a vagabond (Isamu Yamaguchi) dresses up as King Kong on a vaudeville stage. In February 1934, Tsuburaya had a spat with Nikkatsu's brass, who were starting to grow frustrated with his unorthodox methods. The final straw came when he used a low-angle, expressionistic lighting set-up on actor

Momonosuke Ichikawa. Ichikawa felt the lighting scheme was unflattering and was incensed. Tsuburaya thus quit his position at Nikkatsu.

Meanwhile, Tsuburaya's former mentor, Yoshiro Edamasa, created the first *kaiju* (Japanese giant monster) film: **THE GREAT BUDDHA ARRIVAL** [**Director:** Yoshiro Edamasa - **Release Date (Japan):** September 14th, 1934]. Drawing influence from *King Kong*, the picture concerned a *Daibutsu* (giant Buddha statue) coming to life. Rather than wrecking destructive havoc like later tokusatsu giants, however, the Buddha merely tours the countryside. Remade in 2019 by independent filmmaker Hiroto Yokokawa, it is once again, sadly, a lost film. It was planned to be the start of a series and was director Edamasa's final picture.

The Great Buddha Arrival (1934)

At the same time, entrepreneur **YOSHIO OSAWA** (1902-1966) invited Tsuburaya to join his fledgling J.O. Studios. At J.O., Tsuburaya was made chief of the Cinematography Research Division. By late 1934, with Osawa's investment, Tsuburaya had completed an improved metal version of his camera crane. It was first used on the J.O. production **THE CHORUS OF A MILLION** [**Director:** Atsuo Tomioka - **Release Date (Japan):** January 13th, 1935]. The Tsuburaya family suffered tragedy shortly after, as their infant daughter Miyako died. That year, however, Tsuburaya would make his directorial debut on the propaganda documentary **THREE THOUSAND MILES ACROSS THE EQUATOR** [**Director:** Eiji Tsuburaya - **Release Date (Japan):** January 15th, 1936]. To shoot the film, Tsuburaya took a five month voyage on the warship *Asama* to Hawaii, the Philippines, Australia and New Zealand. While he was away, his second son, **NOBURU TSUBURAYA** (1935-1995) was born.

Upon his return to Japan, Tsuburaya collaborated with **KENZO MASAOKA** (1898-1988), an early pioneer of Japanese anime. Masaoka had made *The World of Power and Women* (1933), the first anime short to employ cel animation. His project with Tsuburaya would be entitled **PRINCESS KAGUYA** [Director: Yoshitsugu Tanaka - **Release Date (Japan):** November 21st, 1935], an adaptation of the famed folktale *The Tale of the Bamboo Cutter*. Its story being as iconic in Japanese culture as Charles Perrault in the West, it revolves around Kaguya (Kazuko Kitazawa), a princess from the moon who comes to ancient Japan as an infant.

The first miniature sets in Japanese cinema appear in *Princess Kaguya* (1935)

Princess Kaguya used revolutionary miniature and stop motion photography that Tsuburaya had learned from studying *King Kong*. The picture contains dream-like images throughout and features phantasmagorical process shots employing similar rear projection to that used in *Kong*. There's a sequence depicting a ship caught in a storm at sea, created in miniature, that foreshadows much of Tsuburaya's future work in its aesthetic. *Princess Kaguya* was pivotal for Tsuburaya in the development of his cinematography techniques. It sparked an interest in pursuing visual effects and trick photography as a career. The classic tokusatsu filmmaking style stems from this picture, including the use of miniatures and painted backdrops. Believed lost for decades, film material for *Princess Kaguya* was discovered in England.

The following year, Tsuburaya took part in **THE DAUGHTER OF THE SAMURAI**, a co-production with Nazi Germany [**AKA: THE NEW EARTH** - **Directors: ARNOLD FANCK** (1889-1974), Mansaku Itami - **Release Dates:** February 4th (**Japan**) - March 23rd, 1937 (**Germany**)]. Commissioned by Joseph Goebbels, it was an anti-communist piece, a stylistic mix of the *jidai-geki* and popular German "alpine film" and directors Fanck and Itami had creative differences. Despite the ugly politics, Tsuburaya pioneered improved rear projection. Fanck, known for his mountaineering pictures with Leni Riefenstahl, was impressed by Tsuburaya's ingenuity. Eiji Tsuburaya's contributions are mainly prevalent in the final reel. Mitsuko (Setsuko Hara) contemplates throwing herself into the active Mount Mihara as her fiancee has fallen in love with a German girl (Ruth Eweler). The volcano then erupts - the first sequence of tokusatsu destruction staged by Eiji Tsuburaya. This scene is a fair tour-de-force of elaborate miniature work, process shots and trick shooting such as studio-made bubbling lava. With crumbling models, it looks ahead to the many sequences of destruction to come from the special effects director, predating *Godzilla* (1954) by nearly two decades. Tsuburaya worked on another film with Fanck entitled *A History of Japanese Skiing*, but for reasons unknown, it was not completed. *The Daughter of the Samurai* would be far from Eiji Tsuburaya's last work in the propaganda field. In the forthcoming war, Tsuburaya would refine his special effects processes on pictures made to promote the Empire's agenda.

II.
1937 - 1945
昭和十二 - 二十

Imperial Japanese forces invade Shanghai in July 1937

The following summer, Japan mounted a full scale invasion of China after the Marco Polo Bridge incident in Beijing. By July 1937, the Imperial Japanese Army had seized Beijing and then moved onto Shanghai by August and Nanjing by November. Eiji Tsuburaya's brother-in-law, **SHUZABURO ARAKI** (1913-1961), was sent to the war front as a news and combat photographer by the *Domei* (Federated) News Agency. By the time the Imperial Japanese Army got to Nanjing, they began engaging in scorched earth campaigns. These only further alienated Japan abroad and increased Chinese resistance. Throughout the coming war, Japan's general public would be kept in the dark about the army's brutality in the countries they conquered, believing their military to be liberating them from Western colonial influence. The up-and-coming Toho would release a propaganda documentary on Nanjing's "liberation" in early 1938.

Ichizo Kobayashi (left) and Iwao Mori (right)

That same fall, railroad industrialist **ICHIZO KOBAYASHI** (1873-1957) merged several companies, including J.O. and PCL (Photochemical Laboratories) into Japan's biggest movie studio: Toho Company Ltd. Eiji Tsuburaya was absorbed into this conglomerate as Kobayashi built an enormous production facility in Tokyo. One of his executive managers was **IWAO MORI** (1899-1979). Mori, who had been a film school instructor, had visited Hollywood. He understood the importance of special effects better than the average Japanese executive. Mori wanted Tsuburaya as the head of Toho's cinematography department, but the company's DPs were opposed. Tsuburaya's methods were too unconventional for them.

Mori thus gifted Eiji Tsuburaya the "special effects" division of Toho. Tsuburaya was hesitant, but decided to accept the position. He was granted a research budget by Mori and experimented with an optical film printer. Used to print celluloid elements together to create visual effects composites, the use of optical printers would become a major trademark of Tsuburaya's. By December, as Japanese forces conquered Nanjing, Tsuburaya had moved into a new home in Tokyo with his wife Masano and sons Hajime and Noboru.

Tsuburaya's first work with Toho would be creating process composites in the *jidai-geki* **THE ABE CLAN** [**Director:** Hisatora Kumagai - **Release Date (Japan):** March 2nd, 1938], based on a popular short story by Ogai Mori. At the same time, poverty row company Zensho produced a two-part silent period picture called **KING KONG APPEARS IN EDO** [**Director:** Soya Kumagai - **Release Dates (Japan):** March 18th (**Part 1**) - April 5th, 1938 (**Part 2**)]. Despite talkies now dominating the industry worldwide, many Japanese films in the 1930s were still silent. This was because live *benshi* performances remained popular in Japan. The *benshi* would not fall out of favor until the Pacific War. *King Kong Appears in Edo*, featured another proto-tokusatsu gorilla suit. Contrary to popular belief, the monster was human-sized and only shown gigantic in publicity shots to draw in curious audiences. The suit was fabricated and worn by actor and special effects modeler **FUMINORI OHASHI** (1915-1989). Also known as Ryunosuke Kabayama, he had risen to fame playing a Japanese Tarzan. Sadly, like *The Great Buddha Arrival*, *King Kong Appears in Edo* is lost.

King Kong Appears in Edo (1938)

In June of that year, another industrialist in the railroad industry, **KEITA GOTO** (1882-1959), also had ambitious plans to expand his empire into the movie biz. Goto founded a Japanese movie company and theater chain of his own. Called Toyoko Eiga, it would soon be Toho's biggest rival. The company would be renamed Tokyo Film Distribution and later Toei Company Ltd. Another proto-tokusatsu monster costume, in this case a robot, can be seen in **THE THREE INVINCIBLE SWORDSMEN** [**Director:** Masao Yonezawa - **Release Date (Japan):** July 28th, 1938], released by Far East Kinema. Also lost, this picture is among the first to combine the *jidai-geki* and sci-fi genres. It predates future works like *Time Slip* (1979) and *Moon Over Tao* (1997) by decades.

Another monster robot suit can be seen in the noirish two-part **TERROR OF THE MYSTERIOUS RADIO WAVES** [Director: Toshihide Yamanouchi - **Release Date (Japan)**: September 9th (**Part 1**), September 14th, 1939 (**Part 2**)]. Produced by Daiei's precursor Daido Films, these two movies are still in existence, though little seen in Japan outside of rare screenings.

A proto-tokusatsu robot suit in *Terror of the Mysterious Radio Waves* (1939)

Eiji Tsuburaya, meanwhile, took on an early apprentice in May 1939, a teenage boy named **TOMIO SAGISU** (1921-2004), later known as Soji Ushio. Young Sagisu helped Tsuburaya with his optical composites, learning a great deal. He had been forced to drop out of college at Kogakuin University due to beriberi, a thiamine deficient condition common in Japanese men at the time due to their white rice-heavy diets. While recuperating at home, Sagisu had seen a job posting for positions at Toho's special effects department in the newspaper. This young protege was to one day become a rival to Tsuburaya.

The same year, at the request of the Imperial government, Eiji Tsuburaya shot a handful of educational training films for the Kumagaya Flight School in Saitama. Tsuburaya's aerial photography on these films impressed the Imperial military. He was awarded an honorary master's certification in aviation for his efforts: the fulfillment of his lifelong dream. This footage would come in handy for use in the forthcoming propaganda pictures. Shooting these aviation films would be an invaluable reference in developing the miniature photography that Tsuburaya continued to pioneer.

Later in 1939, Tsuburaya would take in more apprentices for his special effects unit and significantly build up his staff. These new recruits included **KEIJI KAWAKAMI** (1912-1973), **HIROSHI MUKOYAMA** (1915-198?), **YOSHIO WATANABE** (191?-199?) and **SADAO UEMURA**. Kawakami was a cameraman from Tokyo who would lend his shooting skills to the fledgling venture, becoming Tsuburaya's first DP. Mukoyama and Watanabe were optical engineers who would help Tsuburaya refine and improve his trademark compositing process. Unlike in Hollywood films, where the director chose the camera angles for the effects scenes, in Japan Tsuburaya got to run a separate unit with his own special effects staff. This arrangement would be the standard in tokusatsu film production for decades hence. The world stage, meanwhile, grew even more precarious as Nazi Germany invaded Poland in September.

In 1940, Tsuburaya shot the propaganda documentary **THE IMPERIAL WAY OF JAPAN** [**Director:** Taisuke Aoki - **Release Date (Japan):** April 24th, 1940]. Tsuburaya would also direct the effects unit on two dramatic films at Toho. First was **NAVAL BOMBER SQUADRON** [**Director:** Sotoji Kimura - **Release Date (Japan):** May 22nd, 1940]. It would be his first on-screen "special effects" credit. *Naval Bomber Squadron* was also believed lost until an incomplete print was discovered in Japan in 2006. The second was **THE BURNING SKY** [**Director: YUTAKA ABE** (1895-1977) - **Release Date (Japan):** September 25th, 1940]. In both, Tsuburaya pioneered eye-catching effects shots with meticulously constructed miniature planes.

An impressive sequence of miniaturized aerial bombardment in *The Burning Sky* (1940)

With *The Burning Sky*, Tsuburaya creates visually stunning aerial sequences on par with anything being done concurrently in Hollywood. There are impressive rear projection shots and miniature planes bombing realistic facsimile landscapes. Shooting the bombardment sequence was difficult as the German camera used by Tsuburaya's unit could only expose 20 seconds of film at a time. The final images, comprising a cavalcade of (miniature) bombers flying in formation, are hauntingly beautiful. Three days prior to the release of *The Burning Sky*, the Imperial Japanese Army had invaded Indochina (now Vietnam), seizing it from Vichy France. A day afterward, Japan signed the Tripartite Pact with Nazi Germany and Benito Mussolini's fascist Italy. Japan was now a member of the Axis. The demand for wartime propaganda increased in Japan; accordingly, so did Tsuburaya's work assignments.

Pearl Harbor is attacked by Imperial Japanese aviators - Tsuburaya would go on to recreate this on film in miniature form twice

Tsuburaya would next work on **SON GOKU** [Director: **KAJIRO YAMAMOTO** (1902-1974) - **Release Date (Japan):** November 6th, 1940].

Son Goku is a fanciful adaptation of the classical Chinese novel *Journey to the West;* Tsuburaya's mentor Edamasa had previously shot an adaptation in the silent era. *Son Goku* contains the first use of matte paintings in Japan, created by Tsuburaya's apprentice Tomio Sagisu. The picture is a lavish Imperial Japanese equivalent to an old school Hollywood musical with scenes that evoke *Footlight Parade* (1933) and *The Wizard of Oz* (1939). There are comically anachronistic flourishes. Instead of his "flying nimbus", Sun Wukong/Son Goku flies around in a Zero-like fighter plane, a nod to the increasing war effort on the Chinese front. There's even an aerial dogfight looking forward to Tsuburaya's coming wartime propaganda. The villains are futuristic robots with imagery reminiscent of Fritz Lang's *Metropolis*; a rare pre-war science fiction flourish. In the final act, the effects division delivers extensive miniature work. Eiji Tsuburaya next created an impressive miniature tidal wave on **SHANGHAI MOON [Director: MIKIO NARUSE** (1905-1969) - **Release Date (Japan):** July 1st, 1941].

On December 7th, 1941, the Japanese Empire launched its infamous attack on the American naval base at Pearl Harbor in Hawaii, soon bombed by Mitsubishi Zeros. Since Japan's withdrawal from the League of Nations and the Nanjing Massacre, relations with America were in freefall. At Nanjing, the Japanese had even destroyed an American ship, the *USS Panay*. After Japan's invasion of French Indochina, the U.S. halted export of supplies to the Japanese. By July 1941, the United States prohibited the sale of petroleum to Japan. Diplomatic measures to bring peace between the two countries failed and Japan launched its attack without a formal declaration of war. On December 8th, the U.S. declared war on Japan. With the entrance of the United States into hostilities, World War II was now in full swing. Japan began invasions of the Philippines, Hong Kong and Malaysia that same day. CBS correspondent John Daly reported, widely heard on American radios: "Here is the Far East situation as reported to this moment. The Japanese have attacked the American naval base at Pearl Harbor, Hawaii and our defense facilities at Manila, capital of the Philippines."

With the war now raging, the production of propaganda pictures to boost civilian morale ratcheted up. In early 1942, several film companies including Shinko Kinema and Daido Films were merged to produce propaganda supporting the war effort. This company, called Dai Nippon (Great Japan) Film Company, would become another rival to Toho. Run by mogul **MASAICHI NAGATA**

(1906-1985), it would be better known as Daiei.

At Toho meanwhile, Eiji Tsuburaya did extensive miniature shooting for **BOUQUET OF THE SOUTH SEAS** [**Director:** Yutaka Abe - **Release Date (Japan):** May 21st, 1942]. The effects work, all but absent in early scenes, comes into play in a beautifully executed later sequence showing a naval bomber crashing into a stormy sea with lightning bolts vividly striking the water's surface. These animated bolts foreshadow later Tsuburaya monster films such as *Ghidorah, the Three-Headed Monster* (1964). A teenage boy named **SADAMASA ARIKAWA** (1925-2005) would see *Bouquet of the South Seas* and be inspired to join the military as a pilot. Unbeknownst to him, he would one day become the special effects director's right-hand man and successor.

Eiji Tsuburaya's next assignment put him on the map as Japan's leading special effects pioneer. In May 1942, to promote the war effort to the public and commemorate the attack on Pearl Harbor, Toho commissioned **THE WAR AT SEA FROM HAWAII TO MALAY** [**Director:** Kajiro Yamamoto - **Release Date (Japan):** December 3rd, 1942]. It was Japan's biggest-budgeted film to date and was allotted a lengthy production schedule. Yamamoto's end of *The War at Sea From Hawaii to Malay* is a Riefenstahl-like piece of propaganda indicative of Japan's dark collective state, a window into its Imperial fanaticism. As the picture was being shot, numerous military officials and members of the Imperial family, including Prince Yasuhiko Asaka, visited the set.

A miniature Pearl Harbor is constructed to restage the attack for *The War At Sea From Hawaii to Malay* (1942)

There were production problems on Tsuburaya's end as he clashed with the Imperial military's brass. Tsuburaya and director Yamamoto wanted to tour the navy's newest ships but were not allowed to. They were only given a tour of the outdated vessel *Honsho*. The Imperial Navy was also incensed that Tsuburaya, as he had been refused access to blueprints of Japanese aircraft carriers, relied on a captured American ship as a reference for miniature building. Tomio Sagisu was often sent as liaison to deal with the military officials. Sagisu also interviewed the airmen who participated in the attack. These accounts would help Tsuburaya give his impressive sequence realism and aided in construction of the miniatures.

The War at Sea From Hawaii to Malay becomes more interesting in its second half as the miniature shooting starts to take stage. With his optical printer perfected, Tsuburaya's team integrates shots of genuine planes and battleships with models. It can often be hard to tell the difference between Tsuburaya's work and genuine aerial shots. One highlight is a near-seamless process shot combining miniatures, actual ships and actors as impressive as anything in *King Kong*. Tsuburaya's lifelong love of aviation played a major part in his enthusiasm for creating *The War at Sea*'s effects sequences. Yamamoto and Tsuburaya's units had to closely coordinate to maintain continuity, foreshadowing the effects director's future collaborations with Ishiro Honda, Shue Matsubayashi and Seiji Maruyama.

Tsuburaya recruited his old friend Akira Watanabe from Shochiku to serve as art director. Watanabe and company created full-scale miniature sets that were the most expensive and expansive yet built in Japan. For obvious reasons, Tsuburaya and Watanabe could not visit Pearl Harbor. Thus Tsuburaya's wartime unit had to work from intelligence used to plan the attacks six months prior, recollections from naval officers and pilots who took part and scant photos of aircraft carriers in a smuggled-in copy of American LIFE magazine. Tsuburaya and Watanabe's team fabricated an extensive replica of Pearl Harbor, mathematically calculating the size of its battleships, planes and terrain from available photographs. On Tsuburaya's post-war genre classics, Akira Watanabe would go on to handle many iconic monster and mechanical designs.

An important future member of Tsuburaya's crew was brought on board for this film: **TEIZO TOSHIMITSU** (1909-1982). A shy and reserved Osaka native with incredible sculpting skills, Toshimitsu was tasked with the production of miniatures. As small-scaled Mitsubishi Zeros were flown, a miniaturized Pearl Harbor would be unceremoniously blown up to simulate the attack. The tokusatsu pyrotechnic process typically involved the rigging of small metal beads filled with gunpowder. These would then be detonated with electrical charges. This technique would be used for decades hence. While shooting the heavy pyrotechnics, the camera would often be protected by a wooden partition with a hole cut in it for the lens.

Tsuburaya's wartime apprentice Tomio Sagisu on the set of *The War At Sea From Hawaii to Malay* (1942)

Tsuburaya's Pearl Harbor attack in *The War at Sea* is an amazing sequence. It is an Eisensteinian symphony of destruction with pioneering miniature work, dynamically shot by Keiji Kawakami. The scene's large-scale mass demolition very much looks forward to *Godzilla* (1954). A climactic sequence where naval bombers attack the British fleet and sink the ships HMS *Repulse* and *Prince of Wales* is another triumph.

Tsuburaya's work on the film is overall a cinematic marvel and makes an otherwise forgettable piece of propaganda memorable. Having been mentored by Eisenstein acolyte Teinosuke Kinugasa, Tsuburaya was obsessed with editing and his distinct cutting style would form the aesthetic basis for the tokusatsu medium. According to later script supervisor Keiko Suzuki, Tsuburaya "thought in cuts". That is, he was able to envision the editing style of his sequence as he was planning and shooting it.

The War at Sea From Hawaii to Malay was released close to a year after the attack on Pearl Harbor. It was the top-grossing film ever released in Japan and Tsuburaya's reputation as a special effects wizard was now firmly secured. Aboard the bridge of the *Yamato*, the Combined Fleet's Chief of Staff Matome Ugaki was shown the film and loved it. Many audience members in Japan and in colonies like Manchuria thought Tsuburaya's end was documentary footage shot by the bombers. Rumors that the U.S. Navy's film division believed Tsuburaya's footage in *The War at Sea* to be genuine documentary shots of the attack are likely false. It was, however, used by Frank Capra's film unit for his propaganda documentaries.

By the time *The War at Sea* was released, however, the tides were turning against Japan in the Pacific War. In June 1942, Japan lost its first major engagement with U.S forces at Midway. A brutal battle on the South Pacific island of Guadalcanal was now raging. It would be lost to the United States in February of 1943. The beloved Admiral Isoroku Yamamoto was killed two months later; his plane covertly shot down by American forces.

Eiji Tsuburaya next provided miniature and process work for **THE OPIUM WAR** [Director: **MASAHIRO MAKINO** (1909-1993) - **Release Date (Japan):** January 14th, 1943]. A Toho propaganda epic about the first Opium War in 19th century China, it amusingly used Japanese actors as British navalmen. As it was filmed on Japanese soil and Japan was now at war with most of the West, Caucasian actors were all but impossible to find.

That same year, Shochiku, in the wake of the success of *The War at the Sea From Hawaii to Malay*, decided to form their own special effects division. Executive **SHIRO KIDO** (1894-1977) offered members of Tsuburaya's unit higher pay in exchange for moving to Shochiku. Keiji Kawakami and a handful of others accepted this offer. Kawakami's first job with Shochiku was miniature work on **ENEMY AIR**

RAID [Directors: Minoru Shibuya, Hiromasa Nomura, Kozaburo Yoshimura - **Release Date (Japan):** April 1st, 1943]. Kawakami would soon be drafted into the Imperial Navy the following year. Upon his return, he would remain the head of Shochiku's FX division for decades to come. Despite Kawakami's defection to Shochiku, he and Tsuburaya would remain friends. Tsuburaya would also lose Tomio Sagisu early in 1943. Sagisu was drafted into the Imperial Army, where he would serve as a combat and aviation photographer.

Eiji Tsuburaya's next project was **DECISIVE BATTLE IN THE SKIES** [Director: **KUNIO WATANABE** (1899-1981) - **Release Date (Japan):** September 16th, 1943]. Tsuburaya was disappointed, however, in the miniature photography his unit produced, feeling it was a major step down from his work on *The War At Sea*. The challenge for Tsuburaya's unit on *Decisive Battle in the Skies* was that materials for model building were becoming scarce due to the war. Thus they could not produce miniatures at the scale and level of realism as *The War At Sea From Hawaii to Malay*. Only days prior, fortunes for Imperial Japan grew ominous as Italy would be the first member of the Axis to formally surrender to the Allies on September 8th, though pockets of fascist resistance continued.

As the war's outlook grew bleaker for Japan in 1944, Tsuburaya kept busy with propaganda. His third son, **AKIRA TSUBURAYA** (1944-) was born in February. Tsuburaya's next major propaganda film was **DAWN OF FREEDOM** [Directors: Yutaka Abe, Gerardo de León - **Release Date (Japan):** February 19th, 1944]. A co-production shot in the Philippines, large swaths of the picture are in English and Tagalog. A less tragic consequence of Japan's conquest of Asia is that the Japanese heavily modernized the film industries of the countries they conquered in the interest of producing propaganda. The work of Eiji Tsuburaya, with support from **EIZO MITANI**, in *Dawn of Freedom* is subtle and limited to miniature shots filmed in Japan.

The film's battle sequences are well staged, akin to Stanley Kubrick's *Paths of Glory* (1957). *Dawn of Freedom* features American and British characters played by prisoners of war along with the use of captured American military equipment. One of the POWs, Burt Leroy, was executed by the Japanese Imperial Army after appearing in this film. The captured soldiers were made to run through dangerous pyrotechnics when shooting the battle scenes. *Dawn of Freedom*'s cinematographer, Yoshio Miyajima, later felt such shame over his involvement that he attempted to destroy every single print. Miyajima missed one and so the film is still extant. It was General Douglas MacArthur himself who saved the picture's Filipino version upon America's liberation of the Philippines from Japanese control. The Filipino co-director de León was nearly executed for his part in the film's creation.

Colonel Kato's Falcon Squadron (1944)

COLONEL KATO'S FALCON SQUADRON [**Director:** Kajiro Yamamoto - **Release Date (Japan):** March 9th, 1944] was Toho's following propaganda epic. A better directed film than *The War At Sea*, it is a commemorative biography of Tateo Kato, a flying ace who had been killed in action two years prior as portrayed by wartime heartthrob Susumu Fujita. Yamamoto's assistant director on the film was a younger man named **ISHIRO HONDA** (1911-1993). The son of a Buddhist monk from a mountain village in Yamagata Prefecture, Honda's career had been interrupted by military service on the Chinese front. His commanding officer had been the late Yasuhide Kurihara, who led the 1936 military coup against the government infamously known as the February 26th Incident. As punishment for his commander's insurrection, Honda was continuously sent to the front. He was close friends with another Yamamoto protege, the up-and-coming director **AKIRA KUROSAWA** (1910-1998).

Tsuburaya would meet Honda for the first time on *Colonel Kato's Falcon Squadron*. Honda, who had seen *The War at Sea From Hawaii to Malay* while stationed in Wuhan, helped with coordination between Yamamoto and Tsuburaya's units. To create the effect of miniature planes soaring in formation below clouds, Tsuburaya liked to hang the planes upside down above a base made of cotton. This technique would continue to be used in tokusatsu films for decades to come. A shot that Honda prepared drew Tsuburaya's ire. The younger assistant was hurt, but director Yamamoto soothed Honda's nerves. Neither Honda nor Tsuburaya knew that they would one day be iconic collaborators. Honda was sent back to the war front only a few months later. By the war's end, Honda had spent eight years in the army, far more time than he did at Toho. In his own words in an interview by Yoshimitsu Banno in 1990: "When would I be able to go home? When would I be able to make films again? Those things gave me hope."

After the success of *The War at Sea From Hawaii to Malay*, the Imperial Army provided more material support to Yamamoto and Tsuburaya's units for *Colonel Kato's Falcon Squadron*. This included aircraft for full-scale aerial photography. Tsuburaya once again creates uniquely stunning images. It is again difficult to tell the difference between genuine aerial shots and Tsuburaya's miniature work. There are impressive aerial dogfights, often imitated in subsequent war films. A sequence depicting the bombing of Rangoon is nearly on par with *The War At Sea*'s Pearl Harbor attack in spectacle and splendid miniature work. The film made early use of novel compositing techniques such as track mattes and "masking". Track mattes allowed for visual effects composites to be made with the camera moving, a rarity at that time even in Hollywood. Masking involves blacking out an area of the frame of one shot to allow another shot to be printed in the black area. This was typically done through multiple exposure on the internegatives of the films. The technique would go on to be used frequently by Tsuburaya's unit. Such a method is impressive when one remembers that most cameras back then were cranked by hand.

At the same time, the Pacific War situation grew increasingly desperate as Japanese-held island after island fell to American forces like dominos. First the Marshalls were lost to the Allies, followed by the Marianas. Saipan fell in July. It was a horrific battle that ended in *gyokusai* - mass suicide. Then Guam and Tinian fell in August. Tsuburaya's next major propaganda production would be called **BATTLE TROOP** [**Director:** Kajiro Yamamoto - **Release Date (Japan):** December 7th, 1944]. It featured more impressive miniature aircraft, ships and fiery pyrotechnics. Though the film was meant to boost morale, director Yamamoto could not hide the dire circumstances of the war.

In retrospect, *Battle Troop* is regarded as something of an anti-war film in Japan today. Intended to show the frontline soldiers' and aviators' heroic sacrifices, it includes scenes of *tokko (kamikaze)* attacks, depicting the desperate lengths the Japanese Imperial military was going to with surprising earnestness. Regardless, *Battle Troop* is another picture that features Tsuburaya's most innovative miniaturized effects which formed the basis for what he created post-war. By this time, the average Japanese had faith that the grim situation at the war front could be turned around by their "Yamato spirit". These hopes would be dashed by the events of the following eight months.

Battle Troop (1944)

1945, or *Showa* 20 as often called in Japan, would be possibly the most eventful year in Japan's history. By February, American forces were on Japan's doorstep preparing to mount a full-scale invasion of the archipelago. The battle of Iwo Jima commenced. American forces would also conduct a massive fire-bombing raid on Tokyo in March. During the worst of it, Eiji Tsuburaya himself had to hide in a bomb shelter with his family. In typical Tsuburaya fashion, he told his sons fanciful tales to calm them. The chaos felt like a monster was laying waste to the city. If Tsuburaya survived this war, he hoped he'd get to make a monster movie someday.

As the bombs fell, flesh seared and entire neighborhoods of Tokyo were engulfed in flame. The fire-bombings, which became a frequent occurrence for the Japanese in the final months of the war, had another unfortunate side effect. Old nitrate film stock was infamous for how easily it burned. The fire-bombings would thus rob Japan of much of its cinematic history. The

Imperial Army's fanaticism also contributed. Desperate for more material for munitions, the army destroyed numerous film prints for their metal. For the IJA, winning the war was now far more important than preserving Japan's filmic legacy. It is estimated that 99% of Japan's pre-war cinematic history is lost.

By late March, U.S. forces were landing on nearby Okinawa. As the Battle of Okinawa raged, Nazi Germany also fell under American and Soviet control and Adolf Hitler committed suicide. Japan was now the last Axis member standing. The *Yamato*, Japan's naval pride and joy, soon lay at the bottom of the Pacific Ocean, along with other warships and aircraft. The battle for Okinawa would continue until July with horrific civilian casualties amounting to a third of the island's population and the mass suicide and death of over 100,000 Japanese troops. Soldiers and civilians, brainwashed by Imperial propaganda, holed up in Okinawa's caves and refused to surrender. Many died horrific deaths as American troops shot flamethrowers into the entrances. The fighting in Okinawa was so savage it made the U.S. military rethink its decision to mount an invasion of the Japanese mainland. Only two weeks after its victory at Okinawa, the United States would test a fearsome new weapon in New Mexico. At the end of July, the Allies issued the Potsdam Declaration to Japan calling for its "prompt and unconditional surrender."

U.S. forces invade Okinawa

Times were tough in Japan, but its people persevered. Food was strictly rationed but most Japanese tried to make the best of the situation. Tsuburaya and his protégés would work on several more propaganda pictures in 1945. His final wartime effects job was **THREE OF THE**

NORTH [Director: Kiyoshi Saeki - Release Date (Japan): August 5th, 1945]. *Three of the North* would be the first film produced by **TOMOYUKI TANAKA** (1910- 1997), a young producer and apprentice of Iwao Mori. Featuring wartime siren Setsuko Hara as a radio operator for the Imperial airforce in Manchuria, Tsuburaya's contributions are subtle but the miniature shooting is well crafted as usual. Shots of warships sailing amidst miniature icebergs look forward to future Tsuburaya films like *Gorath* and *King Kong vs. Godzilla* (both 1962). The work of Tsuburaya's unit mainly comes into play in the picture's visually stunning climax, with miniaturized aircraft set against some of Tsuburaya's best facsimile high-altitude vistas.

While a fairly routine propaganda picture, *Three of the North* has a darker significance. Distributed to what few theaters still stood in Japan's firebombed cities, it's a picture stirring up false hope in an empire that was literally hours from its defeat. Indeed, most Japanese who saw the picture did so after the surrender while they waited for the Americans to arrive; it was the only film showing in most theaters. Tsuburaya himself was called up for the draft in early August as the Japanese people were expected to defend their motherland to the last. Before he got the chance to do any fighting, however, a momentous event took place.

The new weapon the Americans had been testing, the atomic bomb, was deployed against the Japanese people. On August 6th, the U.S. airship *Enola Gay* dropped "Little Boy" on Hiroshima. In a blinding flash, human flesh was burned from bone, metal reduced to slag, buildings imploded and an entire city was wiped from the map, its land poisoned by radioactive fallout. On August 8th, the *Bockscar* dropped another atomic bomb, nicknamed "Fat Man", on Nagasaki, destroying another city in the blink of an eye. A day later, the Soviet Union declared war on Japan and Russian troops poured into Japanese-held Manchuria. Emperor Showa thus decided to surrender to the Allies. On August 15th, Japanese around the country choked back tears as his voice, previously considered too sacred to meet the ears of commoners, was broadcast on the radio. Hirohito announced the surrender of the Empire and urged capitulation. Japan had been defeated and was now obliged, in the emperor's words, to **"endure the unendurable."**

日本映画のカラーフィルム
COLOR FILM IN JAPAN

by Patrick Galvan

The proliferation of color film in Japan was decades in the making. As early as the 1900s, camera-armed businessmen were experimenting with additive hues for black and white movies. They manually colored scenes frame by frame. Shots of cherry blossoms exploded with pink and gloomy night scenes became drenched in shades of orange. In the 1910s, the short-lived film studio Tenkatsu adopted a British projection technique called Kinemacolor. Black and white footage was projected through alternating filters of red and green to create the tacky illusion of color. While the novelty factor was exciting, these pseudo-color films didn't sell enough to make up for their expensive techniques. With fewer Hollywood films imported in the years leading to World War II, the Japanese had less opportunity to study Western photographic developments. *Gone With the Wind* (1939), for instance, was not released in Japan until 1952. Consequently, Japanese studios defaulted to black and white for the next few decades, awaiting a film stock designed to shoot color images.

Interest resuscitated in 1946 with the release of Motoyoshi Oda's *Eleven Girl Students*. An occupation-era film whose title sequence was the first public demonstration of Fujicolor, Oda's movie paved the way for further experimentation. Over the next four years, the Japanese utilized Fujicolor in shooting newsreels, select scenes of feature-length movies and *kabuki* performances. The perception of color as a technique for limited use persisted though. The otherwise black-and-white *The Rainbow Man* (1949) would feature a color rainbow pattern on-screen for its horror sequences, created by none other than Eiji Tsuburaya. This effect was shocking to Japanese audiences at the time.

In 1951, Shochiku produced Keisuke Kinoshita's *Carmen Comes Home*, now remembered as Japan's first full-color movie. Kinoshita worked with two different cameras on this production: one shooting in Fujicolor, the other in traditional black and white. Two versions of the movie were released. Despite *Carmen Comes Home*'s significance, it was the black and white version that played in most Shochiku theaters when the film was new. The studio had only printed eleven copies of the color version.

Historically, 1953 was a significant year for Japanese color films. This was when most of the major studios tried to capitalize on the trend, encouraged by the recent success of imports from Hollywood. Two years after *Carmen Comes Home* and one year after its black and white sequel, *Carmen's Innocent Love*, Shochiku took another stab at Fujicolor with *Natsuko's Adventure,* directed by Nobuo Nakamura. Toho followed suit with Kajiro Yamamoto's *Girls in Flowers* (also 1953). Toei also tested a new brand of Japanese film stock in making Kunio Watanabe's *The Sun* (also 1953). Nikkatsu, often last to catch up on the latest fads, was a few years away from their first Konicolor release. Yet it wasn't until Daiei imported Eastman stock from the West that color Japanese film really caught on.

With opulent costumes and photographed on Eastman color stock, Teinosuke Kinugasa's *Gate of Hell* (1953) promptly went overseas. Its lush color cinematography won praise in the New York Times; "In color of a richness and harmony that matches that of any film we've ever seen". It also snatched the Palme d'Or at the 1954 Cannes Film Festival and took home the Best Foreign Language Film prize at the 1955 Academy Awards. Beloved Danish filmmaker Carl Theodor Dreyer even applauded the film. The timing was perfect. Akira Kurosawa's *Rashomon* (1950) and Kenji Mizoguchi's *Ugetsu* (1953) had won numerous awards and Japanese cinema was at last making waves internationally. Tantalized by *Gate of Hell*'s success, the major studios set out to prepare "export-worthy" films in the lushest manner they could afford.

This was most evident at Toho. They invested $500,000, the second highest budget for a Japanese movie at that time, into Hiroshi Inagaki's *Musashi Miyamoto* (1954). Inagaki's crew constructed huge sets, cast hundreds of extras and followed Daiei's example of shooting in Eastman color. All of this required a longer production schedule:

six months for a 93 minute film. While *Musashi Miyamoto* was getting attention at the Academy Awards, the studio searched for another international hit. They joined forces with Hong Kong's Shaw Brothers, producing Shiro Toyoda's *Madame White Snake* (1956). Based on a Chinese legend, it was a lavish supernatural fantasy that climaxes with an Eiji Tsuburaya typhoon. This same legend would be re-adapted into *The Tale of the White Serpent* (1958), the first feature length anime. Daiei, however, had been first in getting a color tokusatsu film to the public. The sci-fi spectacular *Warning from Space* had premiered a few months before *Madame White Snake*. Toho was determined to catch up and surpass them. Having pioneered the *kaiju eiga* sub-genre, it was only a matter of time before Tsuburaya and director Ishiro Honda pointed color cameras at city-wide mass destruction. While *Madame White Snake* failed to strike international gold, Honda and Tsuburaya's *Rodan* performed well at home and spectacularly abroad.

1957 was a pivotal year for Japanese special effects cinema. Anamorphic widescreen films were finally taking off thanks to renovated theaters now equipped to show their elongated images. It was in this year that Toho added 'scope to their itinerary. They debuted their version of Cinemascope with *On Wings of Love*, the latest color musical starring idol Hibari Misora. The film ended up becoming the studio's biggest moneymaker that year. Yet there was another Tohoscope film released in 1957 that is now more iconic. *The Mysterians* was an ambitious alien invasion spectacular that would revolutionize tokusatsu and implement genre tropes followed for generations to come. While black-and-white films continued to be produced in Japan until the early 1970s, by the mid '60s, the majority of movies were being made in color.

III.
<u>1945 - 1954</u>
昭和二十・二十九

Japanese foreign minister Mamoru Shigematsu signs the Instrument of Surrender aboard the USS *Missouri*

The American Occupation forces began to arrive on August 28th. Their leader, General Douglas MacArthur, came to Tokyo two days later. Aboard the USS *Missouri* on September 9th, Japan formally surrendered to the Allies. Japan renounced its control of the countries it had occupied and its soldiers abroad began to retreat. What few survived or escaped Soviet captivity were traumatized, battle-scarred, malnourished and exhausted as they boarded cramped ships and trains with only the clothes on their backs to their defeated homeland.

One of these men was Ishiro Honda, Kajiro Yamamoto's protege. Honda had an especially painful experience on his final deployment. The fighting in China was brutal. He had watched many of his friends die and was nearly killed by a grenade. In the end, Honda was taken as a prisoner of war by the Chinese. Allowed to return to Tokyo in March 1946, his spirits darkened more as the train he was on passed through the ruins of Hiroshima. Honda became a fervent pacifist and his emotional war scars came to influence his coming work upon promotion to director.

For now, Eiji Tsuburaya remained at Toho. He worked on a handful of projects in 1946 including **THE DESCENDANTS OF TARO URASHIMA** [**Director:** Mikio Naruse - **Release Date (Japan):** March 28th, 1946]. Due to Toho's reduced production slate, Tsuburaya did a lot of experimentation with optical printing, mattes and glass work in his spare time. In the following year of 1947, Toho would be hit with union disputes, a communist purge and a labor strike from March until October. The labor union formed a picket line around Tsuburaya's office at Toho. The union supporters had taken one of Tsuburaya's special effects fans, powered by the engine of a Mitsubishi Zero fighter, and were using it to keep the police away. Tsuburaya grabbed the fan and with it fought his way through. The union supporters wound up breaking off from Toho and forming yet another rival company: Shin Toho (New Toho). Tsuburaya's optical engineer Hiroshi Mukoyama was among those to defect, but he would return to Toho in the early 1950s.

Later in 1947, Tsuburaya received an unexpected visit from a young fan: Sadamasa Arikawa, who had been working at Toho as an audio engineer. Arikawa had been a pilot at the war front and avoided being sent to his death as a kamikaze. Throughout the hardships of battle, Tsuburaya's war films and their dazzling effects sequences had kept him going; he had seen many of them while stationed in Taiwan. Arikawa had particularly loved *Battle Troop*. The two shared stories and bonded over their mutual love of aviation until the late night. This young man would become Tsuburaya's most trusted associate in the years to come. As a former aviator, Arikawa had a trained eye that would come in handy as Tsuburaya made him his top cameraman. Tsuburaya told Arikawa in their meeting: "We Japanese may never fly Zeroes again, but we can still fly planes in the movies.". Tsuburaya then asked Arikawa "Why don't you join us?" and the young man was hired on the spot.

In March of 1948, however, Tsuburaya found himself targeted by U.S. occupation forces. When the war ended, Tsuburaya had destroyed the surviving miniatures used in his propaganda films such as *The War At Sea From Hawaii to Malay*. Tsuburaya knew the American occupiers would be unamused that he took part in a film celebrating the attack on Pearl Harbor and worried he might find himself tried as a war criminal. This may have delayed the inevitable, but the films themselves survived. To U.S. forces, the detailed miniatures seen in *The War at Sea* were just too realistic for comfort and had to have been created through espionage. Executive Iwao Mori had also been forced from his post Toho with the arrival of American forces and may have received criminal charges. From the Allies' perspective, Toho's propaganda films had been socially harmful and aided in the indoctrination of the Japanese populace.

Though he had been patriotic during the wartime years, Eiji Tsuburaya was by now quite ashamed at having taken part in propaganda films. He realized they had convinced teenage boys to sign up as kamikaze pilots, though Tsuburaya would pilfer them for stock footage in decades hence. Remorse wasn't enough for the Americans, however. Tsuburaya was thus released from his position at Toho - throwing him into dire financial straits. He started the Tsuburaya Visual Effects Institute with Sadamasa Arikawa, along with his son Hajime and brother-in-law Shuzaburo Araki, who had returned from the front at New Guinea alive. They did freelance work for a variety of studios in 1948 and '49. Akira Watanabe would hold down the fort as head of Toho's FX staff for now.

During his years in exile from Toho, Tsuburaya often worried about providing for his family. Composer Akira Ifukube ran into Eiji Tsuburaya while drinking with actor Ryunosuke Tsukigawa. They did not recognize Tsuburaya and bought the cash-strapped special effects director a few drinks.

One of Tsuburaya's first freelance jobs post-exile was uncredited work on **THE RAINBOW MAN** [Director: Kiyohiko Ushihara - **Release Date (Japan):** July 18th, 1949] at Daiei. The aforementioned Akira Ifukube provided the film's musical score. *The Rainbow Man* is a good Japanese potboiler with moments of strong atmospheric spookiness. The picture also features an interesting look at a post-war Japan just beginning its economic recovery. Tsuburaya's contributions are subtle, consisting of occasional miniatures and process shots. Subtle, that is, save for one effect: the titular "Rainbow Man" appears via hallucinogenic color opticals placed into the otherwise black and white film. These consist of a variety of animated patterns. This presented a technical difficulty in distribution and preservation as many reels had to be printed on color stock. *The Rainbow Man* was preserved in black and white, however and the original color excerpts are lost.

The Adventures of Tobisuke (1949)

As Tsuburaya struggled to regain his footing, an early production from the fledgling Shin Toho to employ tokusatsu-style special effects was **THE ADVENTURES OF TOBISUKE [Director: NOBUO NAKAGAWA (1905-1984) - Release Date (Japan):** September 20th, 1949]. Nakagawa would be better known for his horror-themed ghost story films in later years and *The Adventures of Tobisuke* is an early example with some tokusatsu flourishes that take hold in the last few reels. The special effects were supervised by Sadao Uemura, a former apprentice of Eiji Tsuburaya. Uemura had left Toho for Shochiku with Keiji Kawakami and then moved to Shin Toho to become its FX department head.

This rare film, a musical, boasts an unreal theatrical aesthetic throughout with set paintings designed to look like puppet show backdrops. Nakagawa gives the picture the funhouse-like phantasmagoria he would one day be known for with his *kaidan eiga* (ghost story films). There's a demonic spider woman (Heihachiro Nakamura) staged with similar ghoulishness to female ghosts in future Nakagawa films such as Oiwa in *Ghost of Yotsuya* (1959). There are several giant *oni* (demonic Japanese ogres), executed similarly to Bert I. Gordon's later *The Cyclops* (1958). They could be considered the first giant monsters in Japanese cinema. There's a beautifully staged miniature flood and a well-executed sequence where little girl Fuku-chan (Yukie Daigo) tricks a giant oni (Teruko Asahi) into falling to his death. In the "Valley of Death" which Fuku-chan and protagonist Tobisuke (Kenichi Enomoto) must cross in the climax, fanciful creatures abound. These include monster mushrooms predating *Matango* (1963), pantomime monster alligators and frogs and a giant serpent looking forward to *Atragon*'s Manda. The final moments in *The Adventures of Tobisuke* feature impressive optical animation. The exiled Iwao Mori surreptitiously ghost-produced the film and the script was written by *The War At Sea*'s Kajiro Yamamoto.

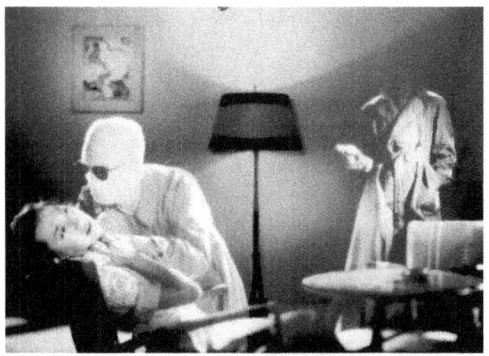

The Invisible Man Appears (1949)

Eiji Tsuburaya's next project, also at Daiei, was **THE INVISIBLE MAN APPEARS** [Director: **NOBUO ADACHI** - Release Date (Japan): September 26th, 1949]. Confusingly plotted, the production values are high quality for a film made in a Japan still recuperating from the Pacific War. Tsuburaya took the project to heart as he was quite fond of James Whale's *The Invisible Man* (1933) with Claude Rains. Indeed, his subtle practical effects are the highlight. Tsuburaya's inventive visual trickery is on par with anything in the Invisible Man films made in Hollywood by Universal. Intriguing images include an invisible cat wreaking havoc in a home and the titular invisible man (Kanji Koshiba) sitting in a chair smoking a cigarette, driving a police moped and firing a pistol. Close-ups of the villain's eyeline strongly evoke Bela Lugosi in *White Zombie* (1932).

After *The Invisible Man Appears*, Daiei offered Eiji Tsuburaya the chance to head their special effects department. Tsuburaya turned them down and chose to remain freelance for the time being. He left a mark there as he mentored two younger protégés; teaching them much of what he knew. These two men were **TORU MATOBA** (1920-1992) and **YONESABURO TSUKIJI** (1923-2012). Matoba was a veteran of the Imperial Army who had also made his way back from China in 1946. The son of painters, he graduated from the Tokyo University of the Arts in 1938. Matoba joined Nikkatsu in 1939 before his career was interrupted by conscription. Tsukiji was a graduate of the Tokyo Electric School and had joined Shinko Kinema in '39, soon merged into Dai Nippon in 1942. Tsukiji did location shooting and optical work for the propaganda film *Hong Kong Strategy: Day of Britain's Defeat* (1942). Matoba and Tsukiji would head the special effects division of Daiei's Tokyo branch in the years to come and employ numerous techniques learned from Tsuburaya on future productions.

Claws of Iron (1951)

Another post-war production with tokusatsu elements is **CLAWS OF IRON [Director:** Nobuo Adachi - **Release Date (Japan):** February 24th, 1951], released by Daiei. If Adachi's previous *The Invisible Man Appears* evoked H.G. Wells, *Claws of Iron* resembles a Japanese take on Robert Louis Stevenson's *The Strange Case of Dr. Jekyll and Mr. Hyde*. Other elements recall *Murders in the Rue Morgue* (1932), *King Kong* and Universal's *The Wolf Man* (1941). A remake of a film made pre-war, *Claws of Iron* concerns a man named Tashiro (Joji Oka) who, thanks to a bite from a gorilla beast sustained during the war, transforms into an ape-like monster whenever he drinks alcohol. The ape who bit him and Tashiro's monster form are both created via tokusatsu-style methods. It is not known who supervised the special effects, but Toru Matoba is a possible candidate.

On September 8th, 1951, The Treaty of San Francisco was ratified and signed, effectively ending the U.S. Occupation of Japan. The war raging in nearby Korea took priority for American military forces. By this time, Eiji Tsuburaya's team were quietly allowed to do uncredited commissions at Toho. He would create an impressive typhoon and landslide for **THE SKIN OF THE SOUTH** [**Director:** Ishiro Honda - **Release Date (Japan):** February 28th, 1952]. This sequence again looks forward to the mass destruction Tsuburaya would come to create in future collaborations with director Ishiro Honda.

The U.S. Occupation forces departed on April 28th, 1952. Japan's bombed-out cities had been rebuilt and its post-war economic miracle began to manifest. With the Americans gone, Iwao Mori was permitted to return to Toho and soon appointed general manager. Mori invited Eiji Tsuburaya back as well, once more crowning him head of Toho's special effects department. Though his ragtag team of apprentices were regarded as so many eccentric misfits, they were soon given their own building in which to set up shop.

Tsuburaya's first official post-war project as a contracted Toho employee was **THE MAN WHO CAME TO PORT** [**Director:** Ishiro Honda - **Release Date (Japan):** November 27th, 1952]. Concerning the lives of Japanese whalers, Tsuburaya's contributions consisted mainly of miniature and process work. That same year, Tsuburaya pitched a proposal to Toho for a movie involving a monster whale attacking Tokyo. Mori's protégé Tomoyuki Tanaka was interested as *King Kong* had done well in re-release in Japan that year. Toho's brass, however, were not yet completely swayed. Tsuburaya would resubmit the proposal the following year with a giant octopus as its antagonist. Incidentally, Tsuburaya's Hollywood rival Ray Harryhausen would create a stop motion octopus in *It Came From Beneath th Sea* (1955) only a few years later.

With the occupying American troops now gone, the Japanese film industry was free to make war movies again. Absolutely forbidden during the Occupation years, fatalistic films dealing with Japan's World War II defeat became oddly cathartic for a country still processing its trauma. One of the first was **TOWER OF LILIES** [**Director:** Tadashi Imai - **Release Date (Japan):** January 9th, 1953]. The true story of a group of high school girls who worked as army nurses during the Battle of Okinawa, it featured process shots by Tsuburaya's unit. That year, former Tsuburaya protégé Keiji Kawakami worked on a similar film and one of Shochiku's first major post-war special effects productions: **LAST STUDENT OF OKINAWA** [Director: Tsuruo Iwama - Release Date (Japan): September 30th, 1953]. *Last Student of Okinawa* revolves around a group of male students pressed into military service at Okinawa. Kawakami's effects unit contributed realistic miniature and process shots on par with Toho's at the time.

Next for Eiji Tsuburaya was **THE SUNDAY THAT JUMPED OUT** [Director: **TAKEO MURATA** (1907-1994) - **Release Date (Japan):** April 22nd, 1953]. A ten minute short subject, it was Japan's first movie shot in 3-D. Toho's filmmakers had been studying 3-D shooting techniques during the war and a process called "Touvision" was created. With Japan's defeat, the technology was abandoned. The success of *Bwana Devil* (1952) in the U.S., however, inspired Toho to attempt a 3-D film, though experimentally as a brief short. The "Touvision" process was dusted off and employed. Although Tsuburaya enjoyed the challenge of working in 3-D, he was overall disappointed with the results.

The newly founded Shin Toho would produce another early post-Occupation Japanese war picture, **BATTLESHIP YAMATO** [Director: Yutaka Abe - **Release Date (Japan):** June 15th, 1953]. *Battleship Yamato* boasts solid production values though Abe's direction feels pedestrian. Far removed from the mournful fatalism of Ishiro Honda's *Eagle of the Pacific* later that year, it feels closer to the wartime propaganda director Abe had been involved in such as *Dawn of Freedom*. It pays strong homage to propaganda masters like Sergei Eisenstein and Leni Riefenstahl as certain images strongly evoke *Battleship Potemkin* and *Triumph of the Will*. *Battleship Yamato* takes on glimmers of antiwar sentiment with its Eisensteinian finale, an explosive assault on the senses with a high body count. The closing visuals, of the Imperial Japanese naval flag floating beneath the ocean's surface, feel heavy handed.

Battleship Yamato was Shin Toho's first film to use extensive special effects and miniature work. These were supervised by Sadao Uemura, now head of Shin Toho's effects department with art direction by Yoshio Watanabe, another wartime Tsuburaya apprentice. Uemura's work on *Battleship Yamato* feels below Tsuburaya-quality. Major highlights are impressive process shots combining actors, the miniature *Yamato* deck and matte paintings. The numerous miniaturized warships are not photographed as effectively as similar images by Tsuburaya and company. High-speed photography, a "secret weapon" of Eiji Tsuburaya's, is not employed. The miniature battleships are thus stripped of the realistic illusion of weight and call attention to themselves. There are some visually arresting shots of the *Yamato* firing its cannons, however, achieved with numerous gunpowder rounds. The *Yamato* itself would be depicted more majestically in later films like *Attack Squadron* (1963), *Imperial Navy* (1981) and *Yamato* (2005).

Miniature warship construction

Despite its failings, some members of Tsuburaya's future *Godzilla* crew got their start on this film. *Battleship Yamato* was an early job for a young craftsman named **YOSHIO IRIE** (1928-2013) who helped build the enormous 1/44th and 1/70th scaled miniatures of the ship. Irie, a graduate of the Nihon University College of Art, was a skilled miniature builder who had just begun his career at Shin Toho. Irie had seen *The War At Sea From Hawaii to Malay* during the war and was inspired to get into miniature effects. A perfectionist, he made a point to craft his miniatures as beautifully as he could. Both Irie and Inoue would join Eiji Tsuburaya's unit the following year.

A second unit was run by a young, newly promoted director named **SHUE MATSUBAYASHI** (1920-2009). Both an ordained *Jodo-Shinshu* Buddhist monk and proud ex-navalman, he had joined Toho as an assistant director in 1942. Matsubayashi yearned to make films that reflected Buddhist teachings. Like Ishiro Honda, he had to interrupt his career with military service, in his case in the Imperial Navy. Matsubayashi had seen *The War At Sea* and been an assistant director on *Decisive Battle in the Skies* before he was sent to serve aboard the *Akishima-Maru* in the South China Sea. Unlike Honda, he had been a fiercely patriotic soldier. Matsubayashi, indeed, went on to specialize in directing World War II films.

Matsubayashi was not, however, a nationalist. He saw the Imperial Navy as a personal Buddhist monastery and felt his naval service had helped him mature. In his own words in his memoir: "I was beaten half to death as a Naval cadet, endured the horrors of war as a commissioned officer and was demobilized after the war, my life strangely spared. Although accused of being 'right wing' and 'demobilized scum' after Japan lost the war, I have never spoken badly of the Imperial Navy nor regretted enlisting in it. Even today, I feel what I learned from the Navy was very important. This attitude, of course, stands in a position that is absolutely against war itself." His first war picture would be **HUMAN TORPEDOES** [**Director:** Shue Matsubayashi - **Release Date (Japan):** January 9th, 1955], released by Shin Toho. A huge hit in Japan, it would cement Matsubayashi's reputation. A bleak film about manned *kaiten* underwater suicide vessels, *Human Torpedoes* also includes miniature work from Sadao Uemura's effects unit.

In the United States, also in June, came a new monster picture entitled **THE BEAST FROM 20,000 FATHOMS** [**Director:** EUGENE LOURIE (1903-1991) - **Release Date (U.S.):** June 13th, 1953]. It featured visual effects by Ray Harryhausen, now a protege of *King Kong*'s Willis O'Brien. Outside of Harryhausen's stunningly realized visual wizardry, the film is fairly routine. Inspired by the short story *The Fog Horn* by **RAY BRADBURY** (1920-2012), *The Beast* lacks the pathos of the upcoming *Godzilla* (1954) which it would heavily inspire. Harryhausen's visual effects sequences are astonishing, however. Like *Godzilla*, it features a dinosaurian monster rampaging through a major city. The Rhedosaurus' New York rampage is a masterfully executed visual effects sequence with shots brilliantly blending Harryhausen's fluidly animated stop motion model with Lourie's live action plates. Harryhausen would come to call his visual effects process "Dynamation".

Yet the scene also lacks the haunting, tragic poignancy of Godzilla's Tokyo raid as staged by Eiji Tsuburaya the following year.

Released by Daiei in Japan, *The Beast From 20,000 Fathoms* would do good business and make Toho's Tomoyuki Tanaka begin to contemplate putting a similar Japanese film into production. Director Lourie would return to the genre with *The Giant Behemoth* (1959), featuring effects by Willis O'Brien and *Gorgo* (1961) which used Japanese-style suitmation. For *Gorgo*, Toho's FX staff were courted to handle the effects work but unable to commit for reasons unknown.

Japanese poster for *The Beast From 20,000 Fathoms* (1953)

With the success of *The Day the Earth Stood Still* (1951), George Pal's *The War of the Worlds* (1952) and *The Beast From 20,000 Fathoms*, Hollywood began a genre movie Renaissance of its own, fueled by atom-age anxieties. With the exception of Harryhausen's work and classics like *Invaders From Mars* (1953) or *Forbidden Planet* (1956), many of these Hollywood sci-fi films were low grade. They tended to be independently produced by smaller firms like the up-and-coming American Releasing Corporation, soon to be called American International Pictures. Their production values were below those of Japan's studio genre pictures. AIP, headed by moguls **JAMES H. NICHOLSON** (1916-1972) and

SAMUEL Z. ARKOFF (1918-2001), would itself become a major distributor of Japanese genre films in American theaters and TV.

Eiji Tsuburaya's next project would be **EAGLE OF THE PACIFIC [AKA: OPERATION KAMIKAZE - Director:** Ishiro Honda - **Release Date (Japan):** October 21st, 1953]. Director Honda was at first hesitant to take on a war film due to his personal trauma, but decided to center the film around Admiral Isoroku Yamamoto (played by Danjiro Okochi). Admiral Yamamoto was a figure Honda related to. The admiral had been against the invasion of China and alliance with Nazi Germany but was obligated to serve his motherland nonetheless. Honda's tone is fervently anti-war and *Eagle of the Pacific* boasts a fatalistic self-awareness to its military spectacle not present in wartime propaganda.

Tsuburaya's end of the film is fairly bloated with stock footage from *The War at Sea From Hawaii to Malay* and *Colonel Kato's Falcon Squadron*. The Pearl Harbor attack and bombing of Rangoon from those films are reused wholesale. The use of stock shots from earlier productions would become a familiar though maligned trademark of the Toho effects department and *Showa*-era Japanese filmmaking in general. *Eagle of the Pacific* also mixes in a great deal of wartime combat footage. Much of the Battle of Midway sequence is newly filmed, however, though some *Battle Troop* footage is mixed in. The Midway segment is the film's highlight, an explosive symphony of nautical carnage. To create it, Tsuburaya and art director Akira Watanabe, with the help of builder Yoshio Irie, constructed their most intricate Imperial warships to date. As the war had long since ended, the layouts of these ships were no longer a closely guarded secret and there was a lot of historical material to work from. The numerous miniature ships and planes took three months to construct. Watanabe had them built from wood and coated in tin. Most impressive were his replicas of the aircraft carriers *Akagi* and *Hiryu*. These goliath miniatures were over 80 and 40 feet long, respectively. Powered by diesel engines, they had to be filmed on the open seas.

Eagle of the Pacific was also Tsuburaya's first film to use storyboards, a Hollywood-style practice that allowed his team to meticulously plan their shots, pyrotechnics and effects. Toho executive Iwao Mori liked the process of storyboarding as it could be used to stay on budget: identifying cuts that could be removed or replaced with stock shots. For tokusatsu production, storyboards would soon become the standard. Tsuburaya's team would also gain a few new recruits with *Eagle of the Pacific*: **YOICHI MANODA** (1935-), **SABURO DOI** (1929-) and Yoshio Irie. Manoda, only 17 years old, would come to be a valued camera assistant and cinematographer. Doi would assist Hiroshi Mukoyama in the creation of the Tsuburaya unit's dynamic composite shots.

Akira Watanabe - Tsuburaya's art director and master of miniatures

Next for Eiji Tsuburaya at Toho was **FAREWELL RABAUL** [Director: Ishiro Honda - **Release Date (Japan):** February 10th, 1954]. Honda was given more creative leeway this time around. Rabaul is thus a fervently anti-war film which condemns Imperial Japan's battle tactics. More Honda's film than Tsuburaya's, *Farewell Rabual* is very much a post-war deconstruction of Imperial propaganda films like *Colonel Kato's Falcon Squadron*. Lead Ryo Ikebe, an Imperial Army veteran himself, even plays a similar role but with more realism and pathos. Tsuburaya once again contributes stunning aerial dogfights and pyrotechnic sequences. Much of Tsuburaya's footage is newly shot though some American-filmed combat material and scenes from *Colonel Kato* are peppered in. A segment where Ikebe's Zero fighter passes through a storm cloud is stunning. The climactic dogfight is also impressive with superb miniature work and process shooting nearly on par with *The War at Sea From Hawaii to Malay*.

With the help of Hiroshi Mukoyama, Tsuburaya refined his unit's optical photography processes even more. By this time, to project background plates, Tsuburaya's team used Mitchell Projectors. The work of his team comes into play more in the hauntingly beautiful final act. They went through more gunpowder than ever on *Farewell Rabaul*. While shooting the aerial bombardment of Rabaul by American forces in the dead of night, the booms from the effects set were so deafening that residents living nearby complained to the authorities. Largely responsible for this disturbance was pyrotechnician and gunpowder specialist **KYUZO YAMAMOTO**. Yamamoto would work on most of Tsuburaya's forthcoming projects which tended to require his talents. He sometimes overdid his explosions, resulting in a lot of "NGs" - "no good".

 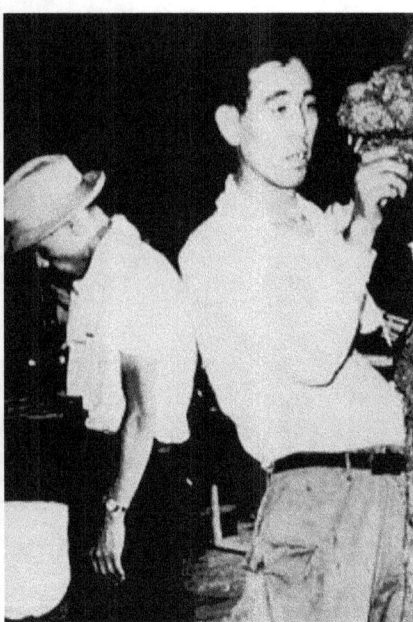

Ishiro Honda (left) - Eizo Kaimai (right)

On the production of *Farewell Rabual*, Tsuburaya picked up two new team members: **FUMIO NAKASHIRO** (1918-199?) and **EIZO KAIMAI** (1929-2020). The older Nakashiro was a special effects engineer and would be known for his intricate hanging and manipulation of miniatures with wire. Nakashiro had also worked for Mikio Naruse's art department. Over the course of his career, he developed a cunning technique to hide his wirework: Nakashiro would have the wires painted to obscure them. For shots where they needed to rotate, Nakashiro would hang model planes from cranes. Kaimai, known for his height, had worked at an amusement park creating the various pantomime horrors in its haunted house. This early experience came in handy; Kaimai would become one of Tsuburaya's most trusted modeling assistants and a "materials expert". Both men would go on to be invaluable members of Tsuburaya's unit. *Farewell Rabaul* is a notable Honda/Tsuburaya collaboration which foreshadows their next project in a number of interesting ways, from its moral and visual themes to cast, even concluding similarly with a mournful, female vocal-led song. The two directors could not have known the impact their next joint effort would have on their respective careers.

IV.
<u>1954</u>
昭和二十九
(Part 2)

Tomoyuki Tanaka

Toho's next major production, which Tsuburaya would likely have taken part in, was to be a lavish color war drama called *In Glory's Shadow*. The picture was to be a co-production with Indonesia's Perfini Studios directed by **SENKICHI TANIGUCHI** (1912-2007). The Indonesian Foreign Minister, however, harbored bitterness toward the Japanese for their country's wartime occupation. He sabotaged the project by denying work visas to the cast and crew. Producer Tomoyuki Tanaka was thus left scrambling for a replacement project. On the flight back from Jakarta, he remembered the proposal that Tsuburaya had brought him: a film about an aquatic monster. It was soon greenlit and codenamed *Project G*. In the finished film, the salvage ship first destroyed by Godzilla is called the *Eiko-Maru*. This was likely a production in-joke as *eiko* is Japanese for "glory", the first word of the scrapped film's title.

On March 1st, 1954, the U.S. military conducted the Castle Bravo hydrogen bomb test in the Bikini Atoll, ironically wrested from Japanese control a decade prior. More terrible than the atomic bombs that laid waste to Hiroshima and Nagasaki, it was the most powerful human-made explosion in history. As this apocalyptic weapon detonated, Japanese fishing vessel *Daigo Fukuryu Maru* (*Lucky Dragon No. 5*) saw a flash in the sky. This vessel was outside of the danger zone declared by U.S. authorities, but the explosion was twice as powerful as expected. Radioactive ash fell upon the *Lucky Dragon No. 5* like snow. The fishermen became violently ill from radiation sickness and the radioman died. Some of their catch, contaminated by radioactivity, even reached Japanese seafood markets, prompting a recall of tuna. By summertime, it was a hot-button issue, with members of the press calling it "The third atomic bombing of Japan".

The *Lucky Dragon No. 5*

This news story influenced producer Tomoyuki Tanaka and soon-to-be director Ishiro Honda on *Project G*'s direction. Tanaka decided to make a darker, allegorical picture channeling Japan's Cold War anxieties. Eiji Tsuburaya was of course hired as special effects director. It was a dream project for him. Tsuburaya had wanted to make a monster movie since he had seen *King Kong* over two decades prior. The nature of the film's monster required development. Tsuburaya was keen on a giant octopus. Tanaka, however, decided on a more dinosaurian monster, likely influenced by Hollywood's recent *The Beast From 20,000 Fathoms*.

Ishiro Honda was selected as director after Senkichi Taniguchi turned the film down. Honda did not intend to make just any old monster movie, but a picture tapping into his own painful war experiences and evoking Japan's collective trauma. Drawing from a treatment written by novelist **SHIGERU KAYAMA** (1904-1975), a script was soon co-written by Honda and Takeo Murata. The two would frequently consult with Eiji Tsuburaya to make sure their vision was executable. The majority of the time, Tsuburaya said yes. At one point during this pre-production stage, Honda, his assistant director **KOJI KAJITA** (1923-2013), Tsuburaya and FX art director Akira Watanabe all went to the rooftop of the Matsukaya Department Store in Ginza to plan out the geography of the monster's rampage. They casually discussed which buildings would be destroyed and where fires would break out. Concerned authorities confronted them and made them show proof that they worked for Toho.

With the script for *Project G* completed, design and storyboard work commenced. Manga artist Kazuyoshi Abe created an early design for the monster with a head like a mushroom cloud which was rejected. Akira Watanabe wound up creating the monster's now classic design. He once again turned to an issue of LIFE Magazine, putting together the creature's distinct look using illustrations of a Tyrannosaurus Rex, Iguanodon and Stegosaurus. The creature was scaled at about 160 feet, as Tsuburaya wanted the monster to destroy the similarly sized Wako clock tower in Ginza. Watanabe made a point to keep the design practical rather than outlandish. The creature's face in particular went through many incarnations in the art and modeling departments until Tsuburaya was happy with it. Watanabe also storyboarded the effects scenes. His extensive storyboards contained 306 shots. Teizo Toshimitsu sculpted the first two-foot clay prototype of the monster. The creature soon had an official name: **GODZILLA** [Director: Ishiro Honda - **Release Date (Japan):** November 3rd, 1954]. So far, executive Iwao Mori was pleased with producer Tanaka's progress on *Godzilla*'s development. Mori could sense Toho had a hit on their hands.

Eiji Tsuburaya had wanted to create Godzilla through stop motion animation but the process was far too time consuming for Toho's fast-paced production style. As a nod to Willis O'Brien, however, several stop motion shots were inserted into the film. Tsuburaya instead opted to bring the creature to life by way of a monster suit. Teizo Toshimitsu and brothers **KANJU YAGI** and **YASUEI YAGI** thus began construction on a suit with assistance from Eizo Kaimai and **YOSHIO SUZUKI** (1935-). Toshimitsu's modeling shop was located off-site at Tokyo Seijo Academy. It was brutally hot and stank of latex and ammonia, yet there was a strong family atmosphere. The Yagis had a long history making dolls for Japanese festivals before they started modeling for films.

To wear the suit, two stuntmen were auditioned. The first was former baseball player **KATSUMI TEZUKA** (1912-198?). The second was **HARUO NAKAJIMA** (1929-2017). Nakajima, from Sakata in Yamagata Prefecture, had an athletic background and loved swimming. The son of a butcher, as a teenager he was drafted into the Imperial Navy's flight training program. Luckily for Nakajima, the war ended before he could be sent to his death as a kamikaze pilot. After the war, Nakajima, while working as a driver for the Occupation, stumbled upon a newspaper ad. It was a call for new acting talent at Toho. His physical fitness and ability was noted and got him work as a stuntman. Tsuburaya knew Nakajima was dependable and tough with a can-do attitude. On *Eagle of the Pacific*, Ishiro Honda needed an actor for the first fire stunt ever performed in Japan. Only the fearless Nakajima volunteered. Eiji Tsuburaya showed Nakajima his personal print of *King Kong* for inspiration and reference. Nakajima also made frequent visits to the zoo to study the movement of animals. His performance as Godzilla was particularly influenced by bears.

When Eizo Kaimai was brought aboard *Godzilla*, Tsuburaya showed him Toshimitsu's maquette and the plans for making a monster suit with an actor inside. Kaimai was bewildered as Tsuburaya told him to look closely, but also inspired. Given that Toho's new monster was one of the first elaborate creature suits built in Japan, the modeling team was quite green and the process rather experimental. It would take two entire months to construct the first Godzilla suit. Toshimitsu and the Yagi Brothers' monster suit making process originated with this project and would become the norm for future films. First, a full-sized sketch of the planned suit would be made on plywood using Watanabe's design. Next a wire armature was constructed. This armature was then coated in rice paper and fabric. A light coat of latex was then applied. At the same time, the monster's outer form was sculpted from clay and used to make a plaster mold. Latex was then poured into the plaster mold. The mold was then baked and dried in a kiln powered by infrared lamps. The dried latex skin was then molded to the armature and cleaned up, decorated and painted. Once everything was dry, the armature would be removed through a small incision in the rubber. Wall plaster was frequently used to make the monsters' scales. Godzilla's trademark dorsal fins were modeled with a wire mesh armature followed by a layer of papier mache and a rubber finish. The creature's fangs were sculpted from rubber and the eyes were painted wooden balls. Tsuburaya paid visits to the modeling division several times a week to check on progress. He respected his artisans and gave them frequent encouragement.

Godzilla was one of the first Japanese films to heavily use synthetic petrochemical-based rubber, employed as the main material to build the suit. Eizo Kaimai was in charge of procuring materials for the modeling department and his requests for better, more expensive ones were often denied by Toho's brass. Getting synthetic rubber, imported in blocks from the United States, was a hard won battle. The rubber had to be treated with oil before it could be used. Teizo Toshimitsu and the Yagi Brothers had difficulty with the rubber skin tearing and had to often resculpt it.

This first suit wound up weighing around 220 pounds. Katsumi Tezuka put the suit on and was only able to walk about 10 feet before passing out. Nakajima, however, managed close to 40 feet. Tsuburaya thus decided to use Nakajima for the bulk of the Godzilla scenes and for another, lighter suit to be made. Toshimitsu and the Yagi Brothers built the leaner suit more quickly this time as they had gotten their rubber sculpting down to a science. Fuminori Ohashi, thanks to his past experience making ape costumes, was brought on board to assist in the modeling for this second suit.

Haruo Nakajima - here flattening buildings with the bottom half of the suit

The rejected first suit would wind up in the finished film, however. It was cut into two halves. The bottom half was used for shots of Godzilla's feet trampling buildings and its top for water sequences. As became usual for Tsuburaya's unit, Toshimitsu built the heads of the suits and the Yagi Brothers constructed the bodies. According to recollections of set staff, including DP Sadamasa Arikawa and modeler Eizo Kaimai, the suits were a dark tan in color. Tsuburaya maintained strict secrecy on his sets, particularly in the modeling department. This was to the point that family members of crew were not allowed to visit. He was also insecure about screening his effects footage. At first, he would not allow composer Akira Ifukube to watch any of it. After repeated requests, however, the composer was finally able to talk Tsuburaya into showing it to him. When Ifukube went into Tsuburaya's editing room to see the footage for the first time, he noticed a peculiar sight: disassembled blenders everywhere. By this time, Tsuburaya loved to use the motors from blenders in the engineering of his effects sequences, particularly for powering the model tanks and making buildings collapse.

The shoot for *Godzilla* commenced in August of 1954, divided into three units. "A" was run by director Ishiro Honda and shot the dramatic sequences with the actors. "B" was run by Eiji Tsuburaya and lensed the monster and miniature sequences. Anticipating digital effects, an auxiliary "C" unit run by Tsuburaya's optical specialist Hiroshi Mukoyama helped create the film's impressive composites using mattes, background plates and even double exposure. Honda and Tsuburaya's units had to coordinate to make sure their footage conformed to continuity and cut together seamlessly. Sadamasa Arikawa was often sent as liaison to advise Honda's unit on how to shoot footage that matched the FX team's end. The gaffer, or lighting director, who joined the "B" unit on *Godzilla* was named **KUICHIRO KISHIDA** (1907-1996). Kishida would become an essential, valued member of Tsuburaya's FX unit, working very closely with Arikawa. A native of Kyoto, he had gotten his start at Toho when it was still PCL in 1936. Kishida not only often worked for Eiji Tsuburaya but also for Akira Kurosawa and Hiroshi Inagaki, including on the former's *I Live in Fear* (1955) and *Throne of Blood* (1957) with DP Asakazu Nakai.

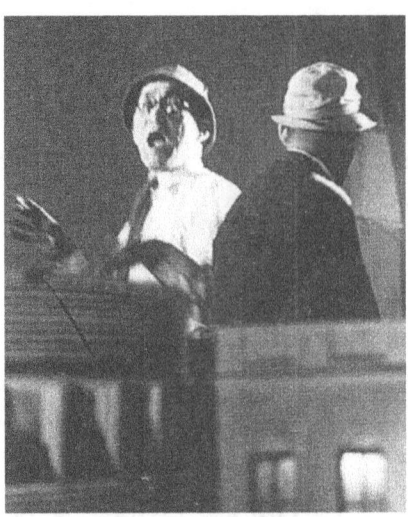
Eiji Tsuburaya (left)

An essential skill for a good director is knowing how to bring together a quality team. Eiji Tsuburaya was adept at this. In Japan, he was often compared to legendary Chinese horse tamer Bo Le, or Hakuraku. Tsuburaya would add more new members of his team for *Godzilla*'s shoot. These included **YASUYUKI INOUE** (1922-2012), **TORU NARITA** (1929-2002) and **SADAO IIZUKA** (1934-).

Inoue, a native of Fukuoka and known as "Taiko" to his friends, had been an Imperial Navy veteran, serving aboard the transport ship *Munekata*. In late 1944, his left leg was hit with shrapnel during an air attack in China. After an agonizing operation with no aesthetic, Inoue survived but lost his left foot in the process. Inoue returned home in August of 1945 where he was admitted to an army hospital and learned to walk with a prosthetic. He developed a love of furniture making in a rehabilitation program for disabled veterans run by famed architect and Bauhaus alumnus **IWAO YAMAWAKI** (1898-1987). While visiting Shin Toho's lot in early 1954, the impoverished Inoue was given a free meal. When it was discovered that he was an Imperial Navy veteran and a skilled craftsman, he was hired on another early war picture: **SUBMARINE RO HAS NOT SURFACED** [**Director:** Hiromasa Nomura - **Release Date (Japan):** July 13th, 1954]. *Godzilla* was Inoue's first film at Toho. He was at first overwhelmed by the studio's enormous facilities and numerous staff compared to Shin Toho's, but Inoue would one day become Toho's top art director.

Toru Narita, from Kobe, had learned sculpture at Musashino Art University. A natural southpaw, as an infant, his left hand was burned in an accident and he learned to skillfully draw with his right. Narita assisted with the miniatures for now, but would become one of Tsuburaya's favorite monster and mecha designers. Iizuka was only 19 at the time. A skilled draftsman, he assisted Akira Watanabe in the production of the film's storyboards. On set, he was mainly tasked with helping paint the miniatures, making them look more "lived-in". The finishing touches on the models, including the final painting and gluing of cardboard roof tiles, were often done by groups of uncredited women.

Building a miniaturized Tokyo to be destroyed by a soon-to-be iconic monster

Godzilla's miniature work is a technical marvel. The larger size of the actor-driven Godzilla suit allowed Tsuburaya's unit to build bigger miniatures than if they had used stop motion. Akira Watanabe's team of carpenters and builders, headed by **KINTARO MAKINO** and including Yoshio Irie, Yasuyuki Inoue and Toru Narita, constructed over 500 miniature buildings at 1/25th scale. They went around Tokyo and took extensive photographs of the various neighborhoods they planned to destroy. Inoue, in particular, was tasked with this and traveled around Tokyo with a young woman named Toriko Kawabe. She held a striped pole that helped the art department determine the buildings' scales. Kawabe grew tired of this fairly quickly as Inoue took numerous photos of every structure from multiple angles. He went back to the Diet Building alone three times. These were then used to make the 1/100th scale blueprints of the miniature sets. As the special effects department under Tsuburaya was still being reestablished at Toho, they did not yet have an FX soundstage. The crew had to build the miniature sets gradually and slowly assemble them to better make use of the stage's space. The biggest wide shots of the model city had to be shot outdoors as Toho's then-current stages weren't large enough to house them.

Readying the miniature Diet (Parliament) for shooting

Watanabe's department faced a unique challenge. They had to make their miniatures both practical to build and assemble but also as life-like as they could. Like the suit modeling department, they struggled to find decent materials in post-war Japan. Miniatures were often built so intricately as to contain working doors and electric lighting. A mixture of plaster and chalk was used to improve their integrity. Structural weaknesses were engineered into the buildings to be destroyed by Godzilla, so they would crumble more realistically. The small streets were made from sawdust and plaster so as to crack and break apart under the Godzilla suit's feet. Buildings that weren't destroyed in some scenes were saved and reused in others. The miniatures seen in the horizon of shots were often built at a smaller scale to create the effect of forced perspective. This was a tokusatsu industry trademark: used since *The War At Sea From Hawaii to Malay* and for decades hence. It was Toru Narita who built the miniature Wako clock tower. His scaling was off and Akira Watanabe ordered it redone. Amusingly, the owners of the Matsukaya department store and Wako clock tower were furious that their buildings were unceremoniously destroyed in *Godzilla*. Toho would be unable to shoot in much of Ginza for years.

The miniature team also built ten model Sherman and Chaffee tanks and ten miniaturized Howitzer cannons. Blender motors were installed in the tanks to make them move, but they often had to be steered with fishing line. Fifty F-86 Saber jets measuring two feet were built out of wood for an impressive scene, reminiscent of Tsuburaya's war film work, where Godzilla battles the SDF's airforce in Tokyo Bay against a smoky sky. Yoshio Irie built most of the military vehicles in Tsuburaya's films as he had engineering skills. For the train Godzilla destroys in its first attack on Shinagawa district, a model was borrowed from the Transportation Museum in Chiyoda. To shoot it realistically, cameraman Sadamasa Arikawa had to lay low on his stomach.

Tsuburaya's unit refined FX techniques on *Godzilla* that they would use in future productions. One striking scene involves Godzilla melting high-voltage towers erected to defend Tokyo. These were built with a mix of wax and lead. They were made to melt using strong lights and hot air. Miniatures to be blown up were often built from wafer crackers as they exploded similarly to concrete on film. The explosives were more effectively placed inside them rather than on their exteriors. Models that needed to burn brilliantly were sprayed with gasoline. The water sequences in *Godzilla* made heavy use of agar, a Japanese variation of gelatin. Thousands of sticks of agar were shipped to Toho. This, along with aquarium conditioner, was mixed into the effects pools to make them look more like the ocean as seen from a plane for wide shots. This technique, first experimented with on *Battle Troop* and *Eagle of the Pacific*, became another standard for Tsuburaya's team in the future.

To make the monster look heavy and the miniatures crumble realistically, the FX sequences were shot "overcranked" at a high frame rate, typically 120 to 240 frames per second. Sometimes Tsuburaya and his cameramen would employ a hand-cranked Parvo camera for such effects. Played back at 24 fps, this high speed shooting created a better illusion of weight and scale. For *Godzilla*, Tsuburaya and his cameramen Sadamasa Arikawa, **MOTOYOSHI TOMIOKA** (1924-2011) and Shuzaburo Araki refined their shooting style. They often covered Tsuburaya's setups with two or three cameras. Arikawa typically manned "A" and Tomioka "B". On camera, the main Godzilla suit tended to look better from the front, which made shot selection tricky. Tsuburaya was fairly particular about composition and for master shots, he decided on framing and gave guidance to Arikawa and company for lens usage. Keeping the focus and depth of field deep so the miniatures looked good was often challenging for Arikawa. As a cameraman, Arikawa had a very perfectionistic attitude, always being a little disappointed that he didn't get as much coverage as he wanted. In the cutting room, Honda, Tsuburaya and the editors would then decide which portions of the cameras' footage looked the best and these bits would be edited together.

Shooting a miniaturized version of Tokyo's Shinagawa ward

The first day of shooting on Tsuburaya's "B" unit for *Godzilla* was not auspicious. The sawdust streets were extremely delicate. A crew member making final touches on the Diet Building fell through the surface of one of these streets. The models had to be repaired which wasted several hours. When filming began and Nakajima came onto set in the Godzilla suit, he immediately fell over in the exact same spot, damaging the miniatures yet again. By the time everything was repaired and Tsuburaya's unit was ready to shoot again, the sun had set. Tsuburaya pushed his team hard; they were motivated to do the best job they could so they wouldn't have to do each shot over again. The crew, in turn, put their faith in Tsuburaya as they had little idea how the finished picture would look.

Preparing miniature electrical towers; built from a leaded wax

For the special effects crew, *Godzilla's* shoot was a brutal one. They would start preparations for shooting at 9 am. Thanks to the shoot's complex variables resulting in production snags like the aforementioned incident, Tsuburaya's unit often weren't ready to film until the early evening. They would then go through the night, often not wrapping until 4 or 5 am in the morning. *"Goji"*, the first two syllables of *"Gojira"*, also means 5 AM in Japanese. This became an on-set joke among the exhausted crew. The greatest torments, however, were suffered by suit actor Nakajima. Inside the suit, under the hot studio lights, temperatures would rise to around 130 degrees fahrenheit. This was made even more harsh by Tsuburaya's high frame rate shooting style, which required Nakajima to move quickly in the heavy monster skin. Even with his athletic abilities, Nakajima often fainted if a take ran too long. He could generally only manage a few minutes at a time before losing consciousness. Eizo Kaimai provided assistance and first aid to Nakajima and Katsumi Tezuka when they were in the suit. The Yagi Brothers would haul the Godzilla suit back to Toho's storage each morning in a rickshaw cart. Toho's brass, taking pity, eventually got them a truck. The cotton lining inside the suit absorbed Nakajima's sweat and a cup of it had to be drained out after every night of shooting. The suit also needed frequent repairs as it was often damaged by pyrotechnics and stunts

According to Eizo Kaimai, Godzilla's breath was created in some shots by a gas torch placed inside the suit. The suit's mouth was lined with tin foil to protect it and the torch was angled, but the teeth would get burned and Kaimai often had to replace them. Shooting with the torch was terrifying for actor Nakajima, whose eyes had to be shielded from it. In other shots, it was created by optical animation courtesy of Mukoyama and Sadao Iizuka. For the effect of the suit's spines lighting up, an in-camera process using light bulbs was attempted but proved unwieldy. Thus optical animation by Iizuka was used, who came to specialize in animating monster rays. Strings from a Japanese harp, or *koto,* were used to crudely create the effect of the Godzilla suit's mouth opening and closing without mechanical parts. Fishing line controlled Godzilla's tail, soon to be supplanted with the stronger piano wire, which at the time was hard to obtain in Japan. The fishing line was painted by Fumio Nakashiro to disguise it better against the set backdrops. For a shot where the monster's foot breaks through the ceiling of a warehouse's interior, a larger miniature was built at double scale. A Godzilla foot prop, also at double scale, was dropped with a crane onto the warehouse model. It took two takes to get right. Inoue needed to weaken the walls upon repairing the miniature so they would realistically smash.

For expressive close-ups of Godzilla, a hand puppet was used, constructed by Teizo Toshimitsu and puppetered by Fumio Nakashiro. Shots using the puppet include Godzilla's first appearance on Odo Island, the creature biting a radio tower and the monster snapping its jaw at the Wako clock tower. The use of *bunraku*-style puppets (called "Guignols" in Japan) to augment the suitmation footage would become another trademark of Tsuburaya's unit for their monster pictures.

As with many films, a few special effects shots wound up on the cutting floor. There was to be a sequence with Ogata (Akira Takarada) and Emiko Yamane (Momoko Kochi) seeing Godzilla's tail on the beach of Odo Island, though only Honda's half of the scene was likely shot. Also unused was an alternate take of Godzilla's first appearance on Odo Island. In these shots, Godzilla holds a cow in its mouth. Tsuburaya thought the scaling on the cow was off and so redid his elements with the Godzilla puppet's mouth empty. Like *King Kong*'s spider pit sequence, these scenes no longer exist save for a few scant stills. Tsuburaya's unit would start saving their unused special effects footage in later years, however. He was quite story conscious and allowed directors he worked with to edit out any special effects shots that didn't serve the movie's narrative. He keenly understood the idea, later articulated by George Lucas, that "A Special effect without a story is a very boring thing".

The special effects sequences in *Godzilla* stand among Eiji Tsuburaya's greatest cinematic triumphs. Shot on the silvery splendor of old-school nitrate film, his smoky, atmospheric monochrome images are phantasmagorical, unforgettable and iconic. They are every bit as polished and powerful as a contemporary Hollywood picture. The most impressive shots were done with the perfect coordination of Honda, Tsuburaya and Mukoyama's units. In its first appearance on Odo Island, Godzilla pokes its head out over a hill, letting out a deafening roar as frightened villagers flee down the summit. Tsuburaya used the Godzilla puppet and a miniature hill, while Honda shot local extras fleeing in Mie Prefecture. This was created through timed double exposure with the top of Honda's half and the bottom of Tsuburaya's half masked out.

Later on, Godzilla, looking like a hulking goliath, trudges toward Tokyo's Shinagawa ward as residents flee. Aided by Akira Ifukube's thundering musical score, this shot was also created through masking a top half filmed by Tsuburaya and a bottom portion from Honda or Mukoyama. Another strikingly realistic shot features Godzilla's foot stepping onto a street as hapless pedestrians flee, combining a miniature street with a genuine one via masking. In yet another gorgeous shot, Godzilla's head ominously looms from behind a residential building before a smoke-filled sky. The observant viewer will note the building's terrified tenants in the windows. This was also accomplished through masking and optical printing.

Then there's an iconic close-up of Godzilla as it lets out a frenzied roar. It has the puppet, shot by Tsuburaya's unit, framed inside an aviary filled with horrified birds shot by Honda or Mukoyama. Another beautiful composite features the Godzilla puppet hovering above a flaming commercial district in Tokyo as a light-up tower display blares brightly. Yet another stunning wide shot features Godzilla advancing from behind the Diet Building, Japan's House of Parliament, before another smoky sky. In the movie's final moments, Godzilla, exposed to the Oxygen Destroyer, falls to the bottom of the seabed in defeat. Through superb optical fading, the creature turns into a set of bones which then vaporize. Godzilla's skeleton in its final on-screen moments was made by

Teizo Toshimitsu with wire, cotton and rubber. Even in today's digital age, Tsuburaya's images impress. They have a unique ability to stay with the moviegoer and burrow their way into one's subconscious. Moreover, these deathless images serve a story replete with tragic subtext courtesy of Ishiro Honda. Iwao Mori says it best in the documentary *The Father of Ultra Q* (1966): "(*Godzilla*) is not just a monster film. There's something else to it, there's more depth to its content despite it being about a monster."

A miniature replica of the Kachidoki Bridge is readied for shooting

Godzilla was completed in late October. Toho arranged a Shinto ceremony to pray for the film's success at the box office. With the Godzilla suit present, actor Akihiko Hirata served as the priest and Momoko Kochi the *miko* (shrine maiden). A formality, this was hardly needed as their advertisement campaign for *Godzilla* was quite clever. Iwao Mori had banned journalists from setting foot on either Tsuburaya or Honda's sets, maintaining an air of mystery. The members of Tsuburaya's unit were, for a time, sworn to secrecy about their techniques and could not share them with reporters. It would not be officially acknowledged that Toho's kaiju menagerie were created through actors in suits until the 1960s. Toho advertised the film in Tokyo with a full-sized Godzilla doll driven around on the back of a truck and a giant, Godzilla-shaped balloon. American newspapers took notice of this. What was likely the first piece of Godzilla-related press in the United States ran in local papers in late 1954 to early '55. It reads: "**H- BOMB MONSTER**: This huge balloon monster is moored over Tokyo, Japan. It was made to advertise a movie called *'Gojira'*, which means half gorilla and half whale (sic). The creature supposedly came into being after the U.S. H-Bomb test at Bikini. It then swam into Tokyo Bay, clambered ashore, destroying several large buildings including the Diet." Released on November 3rd, *Godzilla* became an unprecedented blockbuster. While critical reviews were mixed, lines of spectators stretched across the block with audience members waiting hours to see it. Celebrities praised it, including author Yukio Mishima and beloved manga artists **OSAMU TEZUKA** (1928-1989) and **SHIGERU MIZUKI** (1922-2015). It wound up raking in similar cash to *Seven Samurai*. Kurosawa would incidentally make a Cold War anxiety-driven film of his own the following year: *I Live in Fear*.

A balloon made to promote the film in late 1954 and a stateside promotional trail for *Godzilla! King of the Monsters* (1956)

The first English language review for *Godzilla* was written by ex-pat film historian and journalist **DONALD RICHIE** (1924-2013) in *The Japan Times* on November 4th. Richie both praised and criticized Tsuburaya's special effects: "As monsters go, he's (Godzilla's) quite well done. Though apparently several hundred feet high, he is actually a man inside a suit carefully crunching delicately constructed miniatures. This method is much more realistic than others which have been used from time to time." He goes on, however, to say "The implicit fault in the method used in *'Gojira'* (sic) is that no matter how well made the miniatures are they still look unreal." Another early English language review was written by Albert D. Ricketts, an American sergeant stationed in Japan, for the military periodical *Pacific Stars and Stripes* a day later. It reads: "'*Gojilla*' (sic), Japan's first venture into the science-fiction field, bears a close resemblance to '*The Beast From 20,000 Fathoms*', an American production released about a year ago. If nothing else, Toho Studios can lay claim to producing a movie no worse than '*The Beast*'. A dubious distinction but a distinction nonetheless." Ricketts continues, "The Japanese seem to get quite a kick out of the whole picture, breaking into riotous laughter as Gojilla lumbers past the Matsuzakaya Department Store and the Nichigeki Theater (where the picture is playing) and onto the Diet Building. The special effects, all done in miniature, are about as good as special effects in miniature can ever be."

Godzilla would also be one of the first post-war Japanese films to be extensively exported in international markets. When Iwao Mori decided that the film should be sold internationally, he was presented with three names for its title's Romanization: Gojira, Gozila and Godila. Mori chose the last one as he liked that it had "God" in it. On the advice of a foreigner, he had the syllable "zi" added. In the U.S. in early 1956, the film was retitled *Godzilla, King of the Monsters!* and heavily re-edited, featuring new scenes with Hollywood hunk Raymond Burr. It was also extremely successful stateside and played to packed movie houses and drive-ins from the East to West coasts. While Akira Kurosawa's films played to arthouses in the big cities, Honda and Tsuburaya's work began to gain a more populist appeal stateside. In 1957, *Godzilla, King of the Monsters!* would, amusingly, be reverse exported back to Japan. Scenes involving a translator played by Japanese-American actor Frank Iwanaga were said to elicit laughter from Japanese moviegoers.

Eiji Tsuburaya and his special effects team were now on the map both at home and abroad. The success of *Godzilla* gave them a lot more bargaining power at Toho. The brass began to take them more seriously and realize the value of their work. In the wake of *Godzilla*'s success, Toho's special effects department was formally reestablished. There would be little rest for the special effects wizard as Tsuburaya swiftly moved on to his next project: **THE INVISIBLE AVENGER**

[**Director:** MOTOYOSHI ODA (1909-1973) -, **Release Date (Japan):** December 29th, 1954]. Tsuburaya would act as both special effects supervisor and main DP with help from Shuzaburo Araki.

As with *The Invisible Man Appears*, Tsuburaya creates inventive images much akin to Universal's films and refines them even further. Particularly impressive is the titular invisible man playing an accordion. These effects were mainly accomplished through a mix of objects suspended by wire and optical printing. Haruo Nakajima wore a suit that was completely black to assist in this process. Actor Seizaburo Kawazu portrays Nanjo, the titular invisible man and victim of a wartime experiment. Nanjo hides his invisibility by playing a circus clown. *The Invisible Avenger*'s most impressive shot involves Nanjo removing his clown makeup and vanishing. This was accomplished through a mix of actor Kawazu smearing black ink onto his face, Nakajima's stand-in black suit and an optically printed background plate. *The Invisible Avenger* also contains striking miniature and pyrotechnic work including a finale at an oil refinery akin to his and Oda's following *Godzilla Raids Again*. As Akira Watanabe was not involved in *The Invisible Avenger*, Yasuyuki Inoue designed and built these miniatures. Eiji Tsuburaya's career was on track again after a trying period of exile. The next few years would further cement his place in Japan's post-war studio system as the industry creatively and financially blossomed.

特撮のシネマトグラフィ
SHOOTING TOKUSATSU

Cinematography is the art of creating moving cinematic images for film and TV. Charged with the creation of these images is the DP, or director of photography. As someone who has made films and done a bit of DP work, I can say with confidence that understanding camera lenses, how to use them and how they work is of fundamental importance in mastering cinematography. This is particularly the case when shooting complicated Japanese-style special effects sequences. Eiji Tsuburaya's background as DP was pivotal to his development of the tokusatsu aesthetic. Tsuburaya keenly understood the art of camera positioning, exposure, lighting and lens selection. It's a complicated equation for the layman, but with practice it can become such second nature that one can practically see an image just looking at its histogram. It often helps to have experience in still photography, though cinematography is trickier as it involves shooting many images per second rather than one at a time. In this competitive industry, it is essential to make every frame shot look as good as possible.

Thankfully, things have come a long way in both Hollywood and Japan since Tsuburaya got started in the Imperial era. In those days, cameras had to be operated and cranked by hand. Japanese DPs often learned their craft through trial-and-error and instinct as they struggled to decipher English camera manuals. To maintain scene continuity, they often looked at their unexposed negatives in a dark room with colored flashlights before sending them off. Today, we have powerful digital cameras that are approaching film quality. Even independent filmmakers have quite a selection at their disposal, from DSLRs (digital single-reflex lens cameras) that shoot video to heavier-duty cameras like the Blackmagic and RED series.

These images were taken with lenses of a variety of focal lengths from the same position and distance. From left to right (top): 17mm, 35mm; (bottom): 58mm, 140mm

Lenses are the most important aspect of cinematography; film or digital. They are measured in millimeters in what's called focal length. Shorter focal lengths produce a wider view, have deeper depth of field and are called wide lenses. 12mm, 18mm, 24mm and 35mm are all commonly used lenses on the wider side. Mid-length "normal" lenses are popular for wide close-ups of actors and include 50mm and 58mm. Over 60mm we start to get into long lenses: 70mm, 85mm and 135mm lenses are popular for shooting close-ups of actors' faces. Longer focal lengths produce a narrower, closer view and a shallow depth of field. Depth of field is the sense of how much of a shot is in focus. Lenses with shallow depth of field keep less of the image in focus.

The lens' iris or F-stop measurement also helps determine the depth of field. A low F-stop number means an open iris and the higher the number, the more the iris is closed. An open iris gives you a shallow DOF, while a closed one deeper. Additionally, there's a major difference between prime and zoom lenses. A prime lens is locked to a single focal length while a zoom lens allows its shooter to choose from a short to a long focal length and everything in between. Professional DPs tend to prefer primes as they are sharper in their imaging and more attractive in their DOF.

There's also the difference between spherical and anamorphic lenses. An anamorphic lens typically compresses an image into a "scope" widescreen format. Even for digital mounts, there are anamorphic lenses available. I tend to prefer spherical lenses as there is a wider variety of focal lengths available for them and a "scope" format can be easily matted/cropped in post-production. Another thing a shooter must be mindful of is that different cameras have different sized "mounts" where the lens is attached to the camera's "body". Know your camera's mount style before you buy lenses. There are adapters, but lenses do not work as well on a mount they weren't designed for.

The first image was taken with an open iris (f/5.4) and the second closed (f/22). The focal lengths are identical (69mm). Note the major difference in depth of field

Per my directorial style, I typically like to shoot scenes with actors using longer lenses and special effects sequences with wide/short ones. Wide lenses tend to have distortion around their edges, so they are less flattering towards the human face than long lenses. When it comes to shooting monsters, miniature cities and planes, however, wide lenses placed from a low or sometimes very high angle are recommended, coupled with a closed iris. Their sense of size distortion actually aids in making monster suits look giant and their low depth of field makes miniature sets and models more life-like.

If you want to shoot suitmation and miniatures like Tsuburaya, you should also look into a camera that records at a high frame rate. Tsuburaya and others typically shot their FX sequences at around 120 frames per second and many higher range "prosumer" cameras shoot at these rates. With any NLE (non-linear editing) software, you can then slow the footage down to 24 frames. When you watch the footage, you will notice that the miniatures and suits have more weight like genuine buildings and monsters. With a high frame rate, shutter speed becomes incredibly important. The shutter allows light into the aperture for a fraction of a second. A slow shutter creates a motion blur effect. That works for an art film like *Koyaanisqatsi*, not so well for Japanese-style special effects photography. A fast shutter shows clearer motion. Shooting at 120 frames per second, you want your shutter speed to be very fast: "1/120" or over. A lower shutter speed will actually decrease the frame rate. The combination of fast shutter and high f-stop makes strong lighting essential, especially if you are shooting indoors. These two factors, combined with the low sensitivity of Eastman color stock, was why Tsuburaya's sets were brutally hot saunas.

To paraphrase Goldilocks: one image is overexposed, one is underexposed and the last one's *just right*

Other basics of cinematography include resolution, ISO setting, white balance and shooting linear vs. log. I generally like shooting in 4K for a 1080p export. Many cameras cut the resolution at higher frame rates. Using a variety of resolutions is actually quite useful for tokusatsu-style special effects photography. Shinji Higuchi and Katsuro Onoue's team has done this since making the leap to digital. For films like *Attack on Titan* or *Shin Godzilla*, they often shoot very high resolution background plates and then their miniatures at a lower resolution so the flaws in them aren't as apparent. A digital camera's ISO setting is equivalent to the "speed" or light sensitivity of film stock. A low ISO gives you low light sensitivity and a high one greater. I generally advise shooting at the lowest ISO you can without losing picture information. Just as high-speed film stock tends toward graininess, high ISOs tend to reveal digital noise, especially in the image's shadows. One does not want their footage awash in digital noise - consumers hate it and it can get one fired from a DP job fast. Exposing your footage properly is important whether shooting special effects or actors. Overexposed, washed-out images are considered "unusable" in this industry. Noisy images are similarly regarded, though noise reduction applications can occasionally salvage footage.

The first image was shot with a slow shutter speed and the second with a fast one. Note the marked difference in motion blur

Always get a camera with a histogram and learn to understand it. A digital image consists of data ranging from the whitest whites to the highlights, midtones and shadows and then the blackest blacks. A histogram allows you to see how the data is dispersed in the image akin to an audio waveform. Unlike film cameras, digital cameras can be wildly different and good exposure on one may not be so good on another, so like a new car, you'll need a little time to ease into your camera and its quirks and settings. Generally though, a DP keeps his histogram in the midrange, preserving the most data for post-production image processing. Possibly even more important than resolution is dynamic range. Dynamic range, measured in "stops", is the amount of variation an image has from its whitest whites to its blackest blacks. If given the choice between a camera that shoots at a higher resolution vs. a higher dynamic range, you want the latter. One of the most popular cameras in Hollywood is the Arri Alexa which was also used on *Shin Godzilla*. Despite only shooting at just over 2K (2000 pixels), it has a film-like dynamic range that DPs love.

Shooting in "log" (or logarithmically) is great for getting a film-like image with high dynamic range. In log footage, pixels are organized in a logarithmic rather than standard linear fashion, more like the grain structure of film stock. It also shoots footage with very low saturation and contrast, which preserves more color and highlight/shadow data. In camera, log footage looks bland. When you get it into an NLE or color grading software like DaVinci Resolve, however, you're in for a surprise. Well exposed and properly graded log footage is pretty stunning and combined with a film grain overlay can fool laymen into thinking it was shot on film. LUTs (or "Look Up Tables") are sort of color grading templates that can be quite effective and many log formats have LUTs designed to work with them. The challenge with shooting in log is that it can be harder to expose as its data doesn't register on the histogram in a linear fashion. With some cameras that shoot in log, you may want to push it just a nudge toward overexposure. Many DPs even use LUTs on set to calibrate their monitors, giving them a better idea of what the footage will look like. Overall, experiment with what looks good in your spare time and you will begin to master an effective shooting style.

The first image was shot linear, the second is ungraded log and the third is graded log. The black-and-white printing obscures this, but note the more film-like dynamic range in image #3

V.
1955 - 1956
昭和三十・三十一

Eiji Tsuburaya

At the end of *Godzilla*, the stoic Professor Yamane (Takashi Shimura) says "If we keep conducting nuclear tests, who's to say another Godzilla won't show up somewhere else in the world?". The moment is Honda's somber equivalent to the question mark at the end of a contemporary American sci-fi B flick - a classic monster movie trope that echoes all the way to *Shin Godzilla* (2016). Yamane's prophecy proved true. After the success of *Godzilla*, Iwao Mori ordered Tomoyuki Tanaka to make him a sequel immediately. **GODZILLA RAIDS AGAIN [AKA: GIGANTIS, THE FIRE MONSTER** - Director: Motoyoshi Oda - **Release Date (Japan):** April 24th, 1955] would commence production early in 1955. Ishiro Honda was occupied with other assignments, so Motoyoshi Oda was hired as director. Oda's half of *Godzilla Raids Again* features among the most pedestrian direction in a Japanese programmer. Eiji Tsuburaya's portions are the saving grace of an otherwise inferior sequel.

Tsuburaya gained two new recruits for the shooting of *Godzilla Raids Again*: **TORU SUZUKI** (1930-2012) and **KOICHI TAKANO** (1935-2008). Hajime Tsuburaya also began to take a bigger part in his father's productions. Hajime's education in physics gave him a knowledge of materials that was often helpful to Eiji. Suzuki was a special effects engineer who had already worked on several Shin Toho films including *Battleship Yamato*. He would assist Fumio Nakashiro in the wirework for now, but would go on to have one of the most storied careers in the tokusatsu industry, working for nearly every FX team.

Teizo Toshimitsu inspects a maquette

Godzilla Raids Again features kaiju cinema's first monster battle with a new Godzilla going up against novel foe Anguirus. Both designed by Akira Watanabe, Godzilla and Anguirus suits were again built by Teizo Toshimitsu and the Yagi Brothers. Synthetic liquid latex was specially ordered from the United States this time around. The suits' paint was changed from oil to water-based. This new Godzilla suit even had electrical components installed for the first time to move its eyes and mouth. These were powered by a car battery placed at the base of the tail. Hand puppets of both monsters were made for expressive close-ups. A small miniature doll about a foot in height was used for very wide shots, particularly for the finale on Miko Island. The motor of a wind-up penguin toy that Tsuburaya purchased was repurposed to make the doll move. Eiji Tsuburaya had a particular obsession with motors and how they worked. He had a massive collection of them in his house and always tried to implement them into his FX scenes.

Tinkering with miniaturized military equipment - the Rocket Launchers were loaded with gunpowder-filled rounds

In the film's credits, Eiji Tsuburaya would be listed for the first time as "special effects director" before main director Oda, rather than just as head of the special effects staff. This was an unprecedented honor in the Japanese film industry. His unit would also be granted their own, larger soundstage to film their sequences. This stage, Studio 10, was built from granite. This allowed for better soundproofing as complaints from residential neighbors were commonplace. The granite walls also stood up better to Tsuburaya's explosive stunts.

Eiji Tsuburaya's half of *Godzilla Raids Again* features atmospheric miniature work recalling his wartime pictures along with a kinetic monster battle. Akira Watanabe's team went to Osaka and once again took photographs of the city, which they recreated in miniature form at around 1/25th scale. The largest and most expensive miniature was Osaka Castle, intended to be toppled by Godzilla and Anguirus mid-battle. It was built too well by Watanabe's team and Haruo Nakajima and Katsumi Tezuka could barely damage it. The crew decided to pull the model down from the back with piano wire. Unfortunately, when the first take was shot, the timing was off and the miniature crumbled too quickly. It would take two weeks to rebuild the Osaka Castle miniature and execute a retake. Taking this as a painful but valuable lesson, the team got it right this time.

The effects work on *Godzilla Raids Again* is not as polished as in *Godzilla* or the coming *Rodan* (1956) and a little more experimental. There are some visually arresting shots, however, such as the two monsters sparring against a flaming cityscape and smoke-filled sky. In the film, the city of Osaka, having learned from Tokyo's fate the previous year, is ordered to turn off all its lights to avoid attracting Godzilla. The blacked-out city environment strongly evokes the World War II fire-bombings, for which Japanese cities had to do the same thing to avoid American bombardment.

Destroying the Osaka Castle miniature

Another highlight is a stunningly staged miniature subway flood. As water cannot be miniaturized, this set was built at surprisingly large size by Yasuyuki Inoue: 1/5th scale. Though Tsuburaya was known for his kindness and generosity, he also had a strong personality and was particular in his vision. Inoue had his first of many arguments with Tsuburaya during production of *Godzilla Raids Again*. The special effects director wanted Inoue to quickly build him a miniature set of Osaka in ruins. Inoue suggested that they wait to build it until after the monster sequences were shot as they'd have already smashed models to work with.

The battle between Godzilla and Anguirus was planned to be shot, like the original *Godzilla*, overcranked at around 120 frames per second.

Assisting Arikawa and Tomioka as "C Cameraman", Koichi Takano accidentally undercranked camera C and shot it in fast motion instead. When the footage was viewed by Tsuburaya, Takano burst into tears with shame. Tsuburaya, however, liked the effect which reminded him of two wild animals fighting. He ordered most of the battle to be shot undercranked. From this technical "happy accident", Tsuburaya's unit began mixing and matching camera speeds on subsequent films. often combining overcranking and undercranking. Tsuburaya's monster battles received minimal storyboarding and their shot sequence was largely decided in editing. Sadamasa Arikawa and Motoyoshi Tomioka tended to cover the scenes with two cameras and leave them running for as much coverage as possible.

The finale, wherein Godzilla is buried under the ice by aerial bombardment, is reminiscent of Tsuburaya's wartime propaganda and the film's best sequence. It was extremely dangerous to film. Pyrotechnician Kyuzo Yamamoto was given a lot to do: mixing his heavy pyrotechnics with several tons of genuine ice and snow acquired from a skating rink. Both Haruo Nakajima and Eizo Kaimai were, at various points, buried alive in the snow, though neither was injured.

By the time it was rushed to release, both Toho's brass and Tsuburaya's effects crew saw that *Godzilla Raids Again* lacked the impact of the original. According to Sadamasa Arikawa in Steve Ryfle's *Japan's Favorite Mon-Star*: "Something was missing when we wrapped *Godzilla Raids Again*. At the staff screening, people were talking about the first Godzilla movie."

Stateside, ABC's film subsidiary AB-PT was to have created a full-scale Americanization of *Godzilla Raids Again* that used only the special effects sequences entitled *The Volcano Monsters*. The project was scrapped and new Godzilla and Anguirus suits shipped to Hollywood for extra shooting were never returned. *Godzilla Raids Again* wound up released stateside in an extensively re-edited version on a double bill with the independent sci-fi opus *Teenagers From Outer Space* (1959). In the dubbing script, Godzilla's name was changed to "Gigantis".

The Tsuburaya unit's next major job, which somewhat overlapped with *Godzilla Raids Again*, would be on **HALF HUMAN [AKA: ABOMINABLE SNOWMAN - Director:** Ishiro Honda - **Release Date (Japan):** August 14th, 1955]. Unlike

Honda's previous monster picture which featured a giant creature, *Half Human* concerns a man-sized Yeti living in the Japan Alps. Construction of the Snowman suit would be overseen by Fuminori Ohashi. With a passion for both playing apes and making suits of them, Ohashi would portray the Snowman as well. Working closely with Teizo Toshimitsu and the Yagi Brothers, it took around six months for Ohashi to build the suit. Ohashi wanted to add lifts to the costume to make himself appear larger, but he was forbidden due to safety concerns. The suit was coated with goat hair and an intricate mask was made. The mask was designed to fit closely to Ohashi's face, showing his eyes and moving with his facial muscles. When Ohashi first tried the suit on at an inn, he gave the maid a real fright. The Abominable Snowman suit in *Half Human* is one of the best monster ape suits in an old-school tokusatsu film. Ohashi was also friendly with Akira Kurosawa. Years later, he would create the severed hand hanging out of the dog's maw in the early moments of *Yojimbo* (1961).

U.S. poster for *Half Human* - it was shown in a double-bill with *Monster From Green Hell* (1958)

On "regular size" monster films like *The Invisible Avenger* or *Half Human*, Eiji Tsuburaya worked more closely with the drama directors. Many sequences would be co-directed by Honda and Tsuburaya, though *Half Human* feels dominated by Honda's unit. Tsuburaya's presence is absent in early scenes. His work overall is a mixed bag. There are impressive process shots and occasional spooky, atmospheric images akin to Italian horror directors like Ricardo Freda or Mario Bava. Matte paintings are used splendidly to extend sets through masking. The Snowman is shown climbing a cavern with stop motion animation, a clear nod to *King Kong*. There are also a lot of clunky shots of miniatures and dolls being thrown down the walls of cliffs, along with the very worst optical composites in Tsuburaya and Hiroshi Mukoyama's careers.

Half Human is at its best when depicting the Abominable Snowman with a tragic, Kong-like pathos. It's at its worst in scenes featuring a grotesque portrayal of the *burakumin*, a Japanese minority group comparable to India's dalits; a surprisingly hateful representation from the socially conscious Honda. For this reason, Toho has suppressed the film. Like Disney's *Song of the South* (1946), it is under a self-imposed studio ban. *Half Human* has never been given an official video release in Japan and the closest one can get to legally watching its original version is through a "drama CD" containing only the film's audio. *Half Human* was released in the U.S. in 1958 and distributor DCA took a similar approach to *Godzilla, King of the Monsters!* This time, sequences with horror stalwart John Carradine were added. One sequence features Carradine examining the dead baby snowman's corpse. For filming, Toho sent the actual suit to Hollywood. These scenes were directed by Kenneth G. Crane, who would later co-direct the more interesting U.S./Japanese co-production *The Manster* (1959).

Japan's next major genre and special effects production would be produced by Daiei's Tokyo branch: **WARNING FROM SPACE [AKA: THE COSMIC MAN APPEARS IN TOKYO - Director:** Koji Shima - **Release Date (Japan):** January 29th, 1956]. A *Day the Earth Stood Still*-like story of benevolent aliens helping humanity destroy a destructive rogue planetoid, it is intelligently written by Kurosawa scribe **HIDEO OGUNI** (1904-1996). The film features starfish-like space creatures designed by **TARO OKAMOTO** (1911-1996). Okamoto, educated in Paris, was often called Japan's answer to Picasso.

Building miniatures in *Warning From Space* (1956)

Warning From Space would be notable as Japan's first color tokusatsu film. Just as Daiei beat out rival Toho's *Musashi Miyamoto* (1954) with 1953's *Gate of Hell* for the first color *jidai-geki*, their *Warning From Space* preceded Toho's effects releases that year by six months. Eastman color film stock, developed in the U.S. in 1950, would be a pivotal tool for tokusatsu filmmaking in the years to come. The Eastman stock's tones give *Warning From Space* a dream-like quality. The spirited special effects work was supervised by Toru Matoba with assistance from Yonesaburo Tsukiji and **SHINSUKE KOJIMA** (1935-2013). It is almost as polished as the contemporaneous work Tsuburaya was doing for Toho. Certain miniature shots in particular are nearly Tsuburaya grade. These include the aliens' satellite hovering before a vast starfield, the glowing "Planet R" approaching Earth and some impressively staged miniaturized coastal flooding. There's also an imaginative transmutation sequence using stop motion animation and optical fading. Hollywood auteur **STANLEY KUBRICK** (1928-1999) was said to be quite fond of *Warning From Space*.

Toho was quick to put a color special effects picture of their own into production: **MADAME WHITE SNAKE [Director:** Shiro Toyoda - **Release Date (Japan):** June 22nd, 1956]. The film, an adaptation of the Chinese folktale *The Legend of the White Serpent*, was a co-production with Hong Kong's Shaw Brothers, headed by Chinese businessman **RUN RUN SHAW** (1907-2014). Shaw was fond of Japanese filmmaking and based the operation of his soon-to-be monolithic Hong Kong movie factory on studios like Toho. It was cinematographer **TADASHI NISHIMOTO** (1921-1997) who would help Shaw modernize his studio in the late 1950s to mid '60s. There's a bit of both companies in *Madame White Snake*. It has the unreal, soundstage-based recreation of Ancient China that Shaw's films were known for with Toho's production values and sets which look and feel "lived-in".

For *Madame White Snake*, Tsuburaya worked in color for the first time. Early Eastman stock was extremely "slow" (not light sensitive) and required harsher lighting set-ups than the crew was used to. The special effects sets in particular on early color Toho films were described as being like a sauna. *Madame White Snake* was also the very first Japanese film to use blue-screen technology for its matting and compositing. Tsuburaya had used the color black for matting and masking on prior black-and-white films. Shooting elements in front of blue screens allowed for better element separation in the composites. Tsuburaya would continuously research and improve these effects throughout the remainder of his career. When exhibited theatrically in Japan, the prints of special effects films tended to receive heavier chemical timing than the average color movie.

In *Madame White Snake*, Tsuburaya's FX end is subtle until the final reel where his unit lets loose with a beautifully executed whirlpool and flood sequence. This scene is quite jaw-dropping with solid composite and miniature work. *Madame White Snake* was successful in both Japan and Hong Kong. The production and success of *Madame White Snake* would inspire Toei's president **HIROSHI OKAWA** (1896-1971) to produce an animated version of the story. *The Tale of the White Serpent* (1958) was the first post-war anime feature and would kickstart Japan's animation industry. At the same time, on the premises of his home and out of pocket, Eiji Tsuburaya would reopen his Visual Effects Institute. When he wasn't working hard on films for Toho, Tsuburaya experimented with trick photography techniques including optical processing and stop motion animation.

At the same time, Keiji Kawakami's unit at Shochiku was enlisted to create the climatic typhoon sequence in the French/Japanese co-production **TYPHOON OVER NAGASAKI** [**Director:** Yves Ciampi - **Release Dates:** September 15th, 1956 (**Japan**) - February 6th, 1957 (**France**)]. *Typhoon Over Nagasaki* is a routine romantic tragedy featuring a French engineer (Jean Marais) working for the Nagasaki shipyard who falls for a Japanese woman (Keiko Kishi). Kawakami's contributions are only seen in the climax where an enormous typhoon apocalyptically floods Nagasaki. Kawakami won a "Special Technology Award" for his work on *Typhoon Over Nagasaki* and it's an impressive sequence that looks ahead to disaster films like *Submersion of Japan* (1973).

French poster for *Typhoon Over Nagasaki* (1956)

Kawakami's apprentice on *Typhoon Over Nagasaki* was **NOBUO YAJIMA** (1928-2019). Born in Saitama, Yajima had been enraptured by John Ford's *The Hurricane* (1937), which gave him a passion and interest in special effects. He wound up dropping out of chemistry studies in college to join Shochiku in 1949. Eiji Tsuburaya had tried to recruit Yajima to his unit for *Godzilla*. Yajima, loyal to Shochiku and his mentor Kawakami, politely declined. He would himself soon become a major creative force in Japanese special effects cinema.

One of Japan's first independent special effects productions was **FEARFUL ATTACK OF THE FLYING SAUCERS** [Director: **SHINICHI SEKIZAWA** (1920-1992) - **Release Date (Japan):** November 7th, 1956]. Produced by Kokumotsu, it was released by Shin Toho after Toho and Daiei passed on distributing it. The special effects work was handled by Shin Toho's FX staff, headed by Sadao Uemura. Featuring one of actor Tadao

Takashima's first roles, it parallels and draws influence from Hollywood's recent *Earth vs. the Flying Saucers* (also 1956) featuring visual effects by Ray Harryhausen. The picture features heavy miniature photography via flying saucers and rockets and a human-scaled monster robot suit. The evil aliens are from the M87 Nebula, later influential on Sekizawa when developing *Ultraman*, who hails from M78.

Actors Tadao Takashima and Junko Ebata pose with miniatures from *Fearful Attack of the Flying Saucers* (1956)

Sekizawa, a native of Kyoto, like his contemporaries suffered painful experiences at the Pacific War front as a young man in the Imperial Army. After the war, he worked as an assistant to director Hiroshi Shimizu, best known for *Children of the Beehive* (1948). Sekizawa was also a protégé of Osamu Tezuka, under whom he studied manga. After directing *Fearful Attack of the Flying Saucers*, Sekizawa would join Toho as a screenwriter. Starting with 1958's *Varan*, Sekizawa would become one of Ishiro Honda's favorite writers for his monster pictures with Tsuburaya. *Fearful Attack of the Flying Saucers* was believed to be lost until a 16mm print was discovered and put up for action in 2010.

A little known film series outside Japan that employed tokusatsu flourishes is **THE BOYS DETECTIVE CLUB [Director: TSUNEO KOBAYASHI (1911-1991) - Release Dates (Japan):** November 7th **(Part 1)** - November 14th, 1956 **(Part 2)]**, put out in nine short serial-style episodes by Toei. The films are based on a series of junior detective novels by transgressive author **RAMPO EDOGAWA** (1894-1965), Japan's own Agatha Christie. In them, genius detective Kogoro Akechi (Eiji Okada), after the fashion of Sherlock Holmes and Hercule Poirot, uncovers the nefarious schemes of a criminal mastermind known as the Fiend With Twenty Faces. This is with the help of his Boys Detective Club, a group of kids akin to Doyle's Baker Street Irregulars who aid him in gathering information. Occasionally in these films, Akechi would come up against a threat created with tokusatsu effects. The third and fourth installments, **THE MONSTER BEETLE** [Director: Hideo Sekigawa - **Release Date (Japan):** May 20th, 1957] and **THE PHANTOM OF STEEL TOWER** [Director: Ibid - **Release Date (Japan):** May 28th, 1957], would feature an oversized monster beetle and some sci-fi elements.

Toho and Eiji Tsuburaya's next major effects spectacle was the monster picture **RODAN** [Director: Ishiro Honda - **Release Date (Japan):** December 26th, 1956]. As with *Godzilla*, its inception drew influence from a news headline. In January of 1948, a young National Guard pilot in Kentucky named Thomas Mantell was ordered to pursue an unidentified flying object in his P-51 Mustang jet. He never came back, This event would be directly reenacted in one of *Rodan*'s best scenes. The concept of a winged monster was possibly a carryover from Hideo Unagami's scrapped 1955 script *Bride of Godzilla*. Akira Watanabe's early designs for the monster Rodan were much closer to the *Archaeopteryx*, which appeared in Unagami's script. Eventually, a more *Pteranodon*-like design was created, its maquette sculpted by Teizo Toshimitsu.

Rodan lacks the novelty of *Godzilla*, but is a stellar, if formulaic monster picture. Ishiro Honda's half of the movie boasts an effective horror movie flourish, though *Rodan* is elevated particularly by strong work from Tsuburaya's unit. Honda's unit dominates the first half of *Rodan*. Early sequences with the human-sized Meganuron insect monsters have a fright film flair reminiscent of Warner Brothers' *Them!* (1954) and would be influential on future productions. The main Meganuron suit was a hulking 15 feet long. It was played pantomime horse-style by Haruo Nakajima, Katsumi Tezuka and **SHOICHI HIROSE** (1918-199?). The Meganuron is one of the more effective suits using multiple performers from the *Showa* era.

In the film's final act, *Rodan* switches gears from a middling Honda picture to a stupendous Eiji Tsuburaya film as his unit takes command. For *Rodan*, Tsuburaya added another young member to his team: **MICHIO MIKAMI** (1935-). Mikami, born in Tokyo, had studied to be a painter but in 1954 failed his entrance exam at the Tokyo University of the Arts. Mikami then volunteered for some part-time work on *Godzilla*. *Rodan* was his first full-time job with Tsuburaya and he mainly assisted in miniature building. Mikami would go on to work for nearly every FX unit in Japan and be a close collaborator of manga and tokusatsu luminary Shotaro Ishinomori. By this time, Tsuburaya's unit consisted of about 50 people. His on-set staff numbered around 30. The crew again had to contend with the slowness of early Eastman stock. As *Rodan* was shot in the peak of summer, the heavy studio lights made the working conditions especially brutal. They often had to shoot at night on the hottest days as the stifling midsummer heat combined with searing tungsten lights made being on set unbearable. The sweat of the technicians as they worked on the scaffolding above was known to pour down like rain.

Eiji Tsuburaya

The scene in which Shigeru (Kenji Sahara) witnesses Rodan hatching in a grotty underground cavern is a highlight. It feels like Ishiro Honda and Eiji Tsuburaya in perfect creative synergy. A hand puppet was used to portray the baby monster. The Meganuron being devoured by the hatchling Rodan is a nightmarish little moment tinged with a certain existential horror. It was a suggestion from none other than Honda's colleague Akira Kurosawa and his touch of genius shows.

Yasuyuki Inoue - future head of Toho's FX art department and another master of miniatures

The main Rodan suit was once again constructed by Teizo Toshimitsu and Kanju and Yasuei Yagi. Toshimitsu's modeling department was particularly proud of their work on Rodan; especially the wings: made partially from foam rubber. A variety of flying Rodan props were built at various scales for the aerial sequences. Haruo Nakajima was nearly killed playing Rodan. Throughout the shoot he was suspended in the air inside the suit with wire and cables. As the monster was shot rising from the sea before wrecking the Saikai Bridge, the cables snapped and Nakajima fell 20 feet into the water. Luckily the rubbery skin of the suit broke his fall. The Saikai Bridge itself had just been built only a year prior in 1955. The model, built at 1/20th scale, had been painted red. When Tsuburaya's crew realized that the bridge was actually silver, they frantically repainted it overnight. The bridge's destruction is a particularly memorable sight. Thanks to its appearance in *Rodan*, the Saikai Bridge itself is a popular tourist attraction in Japan to this day. The miniature F-86 Saber jets were again constructed by Yoshio Irie, also at varying scales. For the largest, Irie gained access to designs and mechanical parts from the U.S. Air Force at Yokota.

Rodan contains stunning optical compositions, executed in the more challenging medium of color. A wide shot of Rodan emerging from its lair in front of a crowd of horrified onlookers placed near the bottom of the frame is one of Tsuburaya and Hiroshi Mukoyama's finest. Rodan's rampage through Kyushu's Fukuoka is another of Tsuburaya's best-executed monster sequences, on par with *Godzilla*'s Tokyo scenes but in broad daylight and luminous color. The elaborate miniature work is remarkable. Yasuyuki Inoue, a native of the Fukuoka area, took creating the miniatures for this sequence particularly to heart. As usual, a hefty amount of reference photos were taken. Inoue supervised the construction of model power lines, street lights, road signs and train tracks. Realistic and impressive shots of tiles flying off rooftops were inspired by a crewman's childhood memories of a typhoon. These tiles were made from cardboard so they would blow off easily. Rodan's powerful gusts were created with a modified airplane engine. An interior shot of the military brass running as the building they're inside is destroyed was accomplished by reflecting footage of the actors with a mirror placed in a model building. Tsuburaya's unit includes a self-referential Easter egg for sharp-eyed viewers: a camera shop called "Tsubumeya" is destroyed during this sequence.

In *Rodan*'s final ten minutes, pyrotechnician Kyuzo Yamamoto ferociously lets loose on the explosions with a rapid fire of missiles. These shots involved the heaviest and most sophisticated pyrotechnics Tsuburaya had used yet and were extremely dangerous for the crew to stage. Firing the miniature missiles was difficult and hazardous as they had to be pulled along piano wire in a quick and coordinated fashion. The "24-Rocket Launcher" trucks introduced in *Godzilla Raids Again* and seen more prominently in *Rodan* are not, in fact, authentic military hardware. Inspired by Soviet launchers, they were designed by Akira Watanabe with modeling assistance from Yasuyuki Inoue. The miniatures were loaded and primed with fuses and gunpowder by Yamamoto and various effects staff.

The ending makes a sharp turn for pathos as the two Rodans are immolated in a fiery volcanic eruption. For this scene, an enormous, over 30-foot wide Mount Aso model was built from plaster. Tsuburaya's team used molten iron from a blast furnace brought over from Kawaguchi as realistic lava and puppets were used for the dying Rodans. A happy accident occured when, due to the intense heat, one of the wires on a puppet snapped. A stagehand, perhaps Toru Suzuki, was operating the puppet and his quick thinking gave the impression that the monster, which had been trying to save its mate, was now making a last desperate bid to save itself. Tsuburaya ordered Sadamasa Arikawa, who was about to stop the camera, to keep rolling. This impressive finale sets *Rodan* apart.

Rodan did solid business and Honda and Tsuburaya were now dubbed "The Golden Duo". Despite their now iconic association with each other, they were never strong friends. At least, not like Honda was with Akira Kurosawa.

They both, however, respected each other in their fields. In the documentary *Toho Special Effects Outtake Collection* (1986), Honda would say: "He (Tsuburaya) had a firm grasp of special effects: the cameras, the film... He could bring out the best in everything. He was always investigating means of expression only possible in cinema."

Child actor Tomoko Matsuhima (center) holds a model while meeting directors Ishiro Honda (left) and Eiji Tsuburaya (right)

Exported to the U.S. months later, *Rodan* would be that country's top grossing science fiction film in 1957. It outperformed domestic fare like *The Black Scorpion* (with effects by *Kong*'s Willis O'Brien), Harryhausen's *20 Million Miles to Earth* or *The Monster That Challenged the World*. An American newspaper article in The Galveston Daily News dated November 12, 1957 heaped heavy praise upon Tsuburaya's effects work: "'The color and the effects are breathtaking!' This is a frequently heard comment among audiences who have seen *Rodan*." It continues: "The picture gains tremendously in its impact by stunning Technicolor photography and unique production of Academy Award stature." It ends with "Of equal stature with the striking use of color is the memorable work of Eiji Tsuburaya, deemed the best director in the 'special photographic effects field' in Japan, and the creator of the unusual photography in the chilling *Godzilla* - a feat which many feel he has more than surpassed with the incredible supermonster, Rodan. As another Hollywoodite put it 'The monsters dreamed up by Tsuburaya are enough to frighten Lon Chaney." With Japanese monster films and science-fiction spectaculars rapidly gaining popularity at home and abroad, it was clear that there would be no rest for the wicked now.

VI.
1957 - 1959
昭和三十二 - 三十四

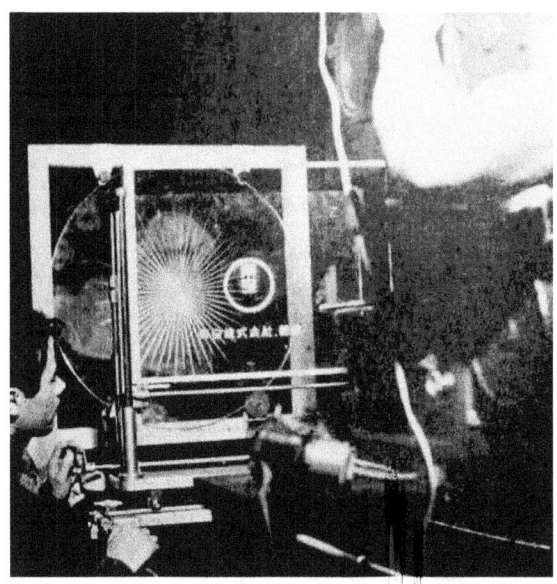

Creating one of the Toho logos circa the 1950s

The contributions of Tsuburaya's special effects unit can be seen in more Toho films than he was given credit for. The team was often called upon to assist in rear-projection and composite shots on films otherwise devoid of special effects. His unit created all the Toho logos from 1950 to 1965, using spinning sheets of painted glass with light projected through them. **PARADISE ISLAND STORY [Director: Kozo Saeki - Release Date (Japan):** January 29th, 1957], especially bears his distinct fingerprints. A darkly comedic musical featuring Imperial Japanese soldiers stranded on a tropical island, it boasts unmistakable Tsuburaya miniatures and process shots. The art direction of the island setting itself looks forward to Tsuburaya's work on films like *Mothra* (1961) and *King Kong vs. Godzilla* (1962). There is even a surprisingly good ape suit, clearly the work of Toho's SFX modeling department. *Paradise Island Story* is capped in a volcanic eruption that is quintessentially Tsuburaya.

The next major Japanese film to use tokusatsu effects was the color historical epic **EMPEROR MEIJI AND THE GREAT RUSSO-JAPANESE WAR** [Director: Kunio Watanabe - **Release Date (Japan):** April 29th, 1957]. Supervised by Sadao Uemura, the effects work mainly comes into play for spirited recreations of the Battle of the Yellow Sea and Battle of Tsushima, which feature extensive use of miniature ships and pyrotechnics. It was also one of the first Japanese movies shot in anamorphic Cinemascope. A "standard" version was filmed simultaneously with spherical lenses, however, so the film could be exhibited in more theaters.

Mitsugu Okura

Shin Toho, now under the command of executive **MITSUGU OKURA** (1899-1978), had been daring enough to make *Battleship Yamato*, one of Japan's first war movies after the Occupation. *Emperor Meiji and the Great Russo-Japanese War* contains the similarly bold first onscreen depiction of an emperor. The Meiji Emperor is portrayed by Kanjuro Arashi, marking the first time an actor was allowed to play a member of the Imperial family. This was considered sacrilege by some Japanese. As such, *Emperor Meiji and the Great Russo-Japanese War* was shockingly controversial and enraged Japan's right-wing factions. Such controversy only fanned the flames of anticipation and the film was a massive blockbuster. Okura was pleased with the picture's success and it would keep his company afloat for several more years.

Later that year, Okura also created one of Japanese earliest superhero pictures for Shin Toho with **SUPER GIANT** [Director: **TERUO ISHII** (1924-2005) - **Release Date (Japan):** July 30th, 1957]. Played by Ken Utsui, the character was inspired by DC Comics' Superman and named after Japan's premier baseball team, the Yomiuri Giants. The Super Giant films were under an hour long each. They were released in serial style with the first two parts debuting in July and August of 1957. Ishii directed the first six installments. Then a child, pretending to be Super Giant and wearing a blanket as a cape, jumped off his family's apartment balcony in Tokyo. The boy badly injured himself and Ishii was unsettled. He wound up quitting the series, leaving the last three episodes in the hands of other directors. The final three Super Giant films, released in April 1958 and March and April of 1959, were separate stories helmed by Akira Mitsuwa and Chogi Akasaka. Actor Utsui was so embarrassed by the role that he refused to talk about it in interviews.

Super Giant: The Space Mutant Appears (1958) - released stateside as *Evil Brain From Outer Space*

The special effects on the Super Giant series were handled by Sadao Uemura, though little is known about their production. **EIZO YAMAGIWA** (1932-) would direct the effects shots as well on later entries. Director Ishii's style is pedestrian, though there are occasional glimmers of the Rampo-like *ero-guro* madness he was later known for. The miniature work on Uemura's end tends toward clunkiness. The flying scenes, mainly created through the rear-projection processes Uemura learned from Tsuburaya are generally good. There are some major hiccups, however, that ruin the suspension of disbelief. Most of the time, they are on par with similar scenes in American serials like *King of the Rocketmen* (1949) or the *Adventures of Superman* TV show with George Reeves.

These surprisingly influential mini-movies boast a breathless atmosphere akin to the Hollywood serials of old. They recall *Flash Gordon* (1936) or *Buck Rogers* (1939) more than *Godzilla* with furious pacing, goofy but eclectic costume design and art direction and gravity-defying stunt silliness. In the United States, the Super Giant films were released in a quartet of feature length compilations with the character renamed "Starman". Somehow, the final three installments were edited into an incoherent mess entitled *Evil Brain From Outer Space*. Teruo Ishii would come to be known for his works of exploitative grotesquery such as in Toei's *The Joy of Torture* (1968) and *Horrors of Malformed Men* (1969).

Daiei, meanwhile, next produced **THE INVISIBLE MAN VS. THE HUMAN FLY [Director: MITSUO MURAYAMA (1920-1979) - Release Date (Japan): August 25th, 1957]**. *The Invisible Man vs. the Human Fly* is by far the most interesting Japanese take on H.G. Wells' classic story. Though used sparingly, the visual effects by Toru Matoba are consistently imaginative and effective. A memorable moment features the titular human fly (Shizuo Chujo) crawling on the voluptuous body of a scantily clad dancer (Ikuko Mori). The optical invisibility effects are impressive and nearly on par with Tsubruaya's work in *The Invisible Avenger*. Like Toho's coming "transformed human" films such as *The H-Man* (1958) and *The Human Vapor* (1960), *Invisible Man vs. the Human Fly* alternates between noirish pot-boiler and sci-fi with horror flourishes.

Back at Toho, Tomoyuki Tanaka had big plans for another sci-fi extravaganza: **THE MYSTERIANS [Director: Ishiro Honda - Release Date (Japan):** December 28th, 1957]. In October, the Soviet Union had launched the first artificial satellite, *Sputnik-1*, into the Earth's atmosphere. The release of *The Mysterians*, Toho's first alien invasion picture, was well timed as science fiction was on everyone's mind. Like *Godzilla*, *The Mysterians* is another standout 1950s Toho film, holding its own against similar Hollywood productions such as *The War of the Worlds* (1952) and *Earth vs. the Flying Saucers* (1956). Bearing strong influence from the works of George Pal, *The Mysterians* combines Tsuburaya's distinct visuals with humanist subtext from Honda. Unlike Hollywood's typically jingoistic science fiction pictures, in *The*

Mysterians, humanity puts its Cold War differences aside to battle the titular alien threat. Such themes were timely as Japan had formally joined the United Nations only a year prior. *The Mysterians* was also Toho's first special effects film in Cinemascope. Having researched Hollywood's style of anamorphic cinematography, Toho had debuted their version, Tohoscope, earlier that year.

Tsuburaya's unit prepares to shoot a miniature set

The Mysterians features impressive retro-futuristic designs of the aliens' flying saucers, orbiting satellite and dome-shaped base, as well as a medley of high-tech weapons invented by humanity to combat them. These *mecha* were created by **SHIGERU KOMATSUZAKI** (1915-2001). A Tokyo native, Komatsuzaki was trained as a painter. During World War II, his illustrations and mechanical drawings of military hardware began to draw notice and were published in several magazines. The 1945 firebombings of Tokyo destroyed his home, art supplies, and much of his pre-war work and left him destitute. In 1948, he skyrocketed to fame with his illustrated story *Earth SOS*, which was published in the manga magazine *Shonen Gaho*. Komatsuzaki's lavish illustrations would come to grace numerous model kit boxes over the years, particularly Japanese kits of the vehicles in Gerry Anderson's *Thunderbirds*. The futuristic miniature ships designed by Komatsuzaki for *The Mysterians* predate and strongly look forward to those in Anderson's shows. The Mysterians themselves were also designed by Komatsuzaki. Their ranks differentiated by color, the helmets were made of plexiglass and inspired by the *daruma* doll. The plexiglass tended to fragment and irritated the actors' skin. Replicas of the Mysterians' pistols also became a popular toy in Japan.

The Mysterians features Mogera, the first giant robot in Japanese cinema. Added at the request of producer Tomoyuki Tanaka, it was likely included to cash in on the recent popularity of Mitsuteru Yokoyama's manga *Tetsujin No. 28* (*Gigantor*). Hideo Unagami's recently scrapped *Bride of Godzilla* script had also featured an enormous robot. Designed by Akira Watanabe, Mogera was first conceived as a mole-like creature. Teizo Toshimitsu sculpted a rough maquette and once again built the head of the suit. The Mogera suit, each part made from latex poured into plaster molds, was built in multiple pieces that had to be fitted to actor Haruo Nakajima one at a time. The inside of the suit was cushioned with foam rubber. The Mogera costume was finished with a layer of polyester-based resin paint, giving the impression of metal. Construction also began on a two-foot moving mechanical puppet. The robotic puppet proved too difficult to engineer and was scrapped midway through building. For Mogera's rampage, a miniature bridge was built on the Segawa river outside Toho's backlot. It was then blown up to create the sequence where the bridge is booby-trapped to halt the robot's advance.

The miniature work in *The Mysterians* is extraordinary. A motorized model of the Mysterians' satellite was constructed, the camera placed on a mechanical rail in front of it. The Mysterian dome was one of the first tokusatsu miniatures made from plastic, found to be cheaper than glass. The plastic used for the dome was the same material later used to make the tips of the first *shinkansen* (bullet train). The seven-foot miniature featured extensive mechanical enhancements and internal lighting. Shots of melting tanks were made by the classic technique, also used on *Godzilla*, of blowing hot air onto wax models.

Akira Watanabe's modeling team, headed by Yasuyuki Inoue, kept quite busy during *The Mysterians'* production crafting numerous miniaturized *mecha* from wood. The modeling team's wood supply quickly exhausted and Inoue had to beg

Kintaro Makino for more. The Earth Defense Force's ships, *Alpha* and *Beta*, had two separate four-foot miniatures constructed each. Several Markalite FAHP ray cannons were built in large and small scales. Also constructed were two miniatures for the Markalite GYRO ship along with multiple scaled Mysterian saucers. These were also built from FRP by Inoue and Yoshio Irie.

Filming the launch of the Markalite GYRO ship and its ascension into the sky was challenging. The studio's ceiling was too low for the shot of it soaring high into the air, making it necessary to film outdoors. The breeze proved a problem as it made the miniature to sway in an unrealistic fashion, resulting in numerous "NGs". The problem was finally solved by holding the miniature ship still with piano wire suspended from a bridge. Miniaturized dolls were also created by the modeling department for the scene where ingenues Etsuko (Yumi Shirakawa) and Hiroko (Momoko Kochi) are kidnapped by the Mysterians and taken to their saucers.

Rigging pyrotechnics - gunpowder-filled metal balls to be detonated with electric charges

Eiji Tsuburaya's special effects sequences in *The Mysterians* best Pal's production of *The War of the Worlds*. Tsuburaya takes the tokusatsu craft to a more ambitious height than on *Godzilla* or *Rodan*. Aided by the novelty of the Cinemascope ratio, his images, impressively shot by Sadamasa Arikawa and Shuzaburo Araki and set to the driving music of Akira Ifukube, are dynamic throughout. *The Mysterians* featured the most elaborate use of superimposed ray beams to date. It was here that Sadao Iizuka finally found his niche on Tsuburaya's team: the various hand-animated death rays seen in the film are his work. Tsuburaya was inspired by *The Ten Commandments* (1956) to include elaborate optical animation. Iizuka was nicknamed "Den-san" after his resemblance to a newspaper manga character called Densuke. It was Eiji Tsuburaya who arranged his marriage to a female assistant. The two had a close relationship in the years hence. In Iizuka's words Tsuburaya "asked for the impossible". In response, the optical animator would often think "Damn him". Whenever Iizuka presented him with an animation cut he found "NG", Tsuburaya would crumble the film up in a grouchy fashion.

Certain shots in *The Mysterians* are astoundingly creative. A striking, seamless composite features a crowd of concerned villagers gathered on a riverbank as a forest fire, courtesy of Tsuburaya, burns on the other side of it. Another stunning shot is a wide view of a fire brigade as they prepare to battle the fires caused by the robot, meanwhile projecting death-rays from its eyes off in the distance. The work of Hiroshi Mukoyama, this shot combined human elements shot by Honda, the monster suit shot by Tsuburaya plus pyrotechnics, masking and animated rays. Inside the Mysterian dome from a high angle, alien soldiers scurry along a walkway crossing through a cylinder-like space age elevator shaft, another arresting composition combining live elements and miniatures. A Markalite FAHP death ray cannon, on the right side of the 'scope frame, projects its immense beam at the Mysterian dome in the center. The beam was created by filming an oxygen cylinder's gas emptied in a water tank which was then turned sideways and superimposed onto the film. There are sequences of landslides early on and a massive flood at the climax that boast miniaturized engineering of astounding quality.

At the very end of *The Mysterians'* principal photography, *Sputnik-1* was launched. In response, Ishiro Honda and Eiji Tsuburaya decided to include a last-minute addition to the picture. In the final moment, shot by Tsuburaya's unit, a Sputnik-inspired artificial satellite is launched by the Earth Defense Force to monitor Earth's orbit for future attacks. *The Mysterians* did solid business at the Japanese box office and science fiction-themed special effects productions would continue in earnest at Toho. Tsuburaya's work on *The Mysterians* went on to win the "Special Technology Award" from the Japan Movie Association. Amusingly, when *The Mysterians* was released in the United States in 1959, Ishiro Honda's egalitarian themes came under the scrutiny of J. Edgar Hoover's FBI. In a declassified letter sent to Hoover on October 1st, *The Mysterians* was accused of communist sympathy and promoting a "one world" government to child audiences.

Meanwhile, advertising agency Senkosha and TV station KRTV (soon to be TBS) were inspired by the success of Shin Toho's *Super Giant*. Writer **KOHAN KAWAUCHI** (1920-2008) was hired to create a superhero for the fledgling medium of television. Kawauchi's career had started when he joined Toho in 1941. In around 1942 or '43, he scripted a short puppet film called **RAMAYANA**, based on the famed Indian epic. *Ramayana* had featured special effects photography by none other than Eiji Tsuburaya. For Senkosha, Kawauchi created **MOONLIGHT MASK [Television Run (Japan):** February 24th, 1958 - July 5th, 1959], a Japanese answer to Zorro and Batman. With his identity never fully revealed, Moonlight Mask was decked out in a cape, gloves, turban and sunglasses. He battled nefarious evildoers on the back of a motorcycle, foreshadowing Shotaro Ishinomori creations like *Kamen Rider*. *Moonlight Mask* was Japan's first television superhero and tokusatsu TV series, as well as being only the second Japanese show shot on film stock.

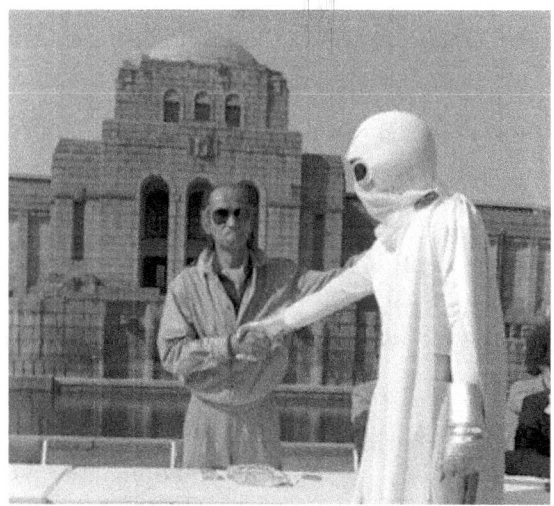

Kohan Kawauchi (left)

Due to the show's low budget, early episodes were shot on a 16mm camera that could only expose 28 seconds at a time. This forced the staff to keep cuts short and tight which wound up benefiting the action sequences. *Moonlight Mask* would go on for a whopping 131 episodes with six story arcs over the next year and a half. *Moonlight Mask* was enormously popular with children. By 1958, television sets were mainly owned by wealthy Japanese, Eiji Tsuburaya included. Local kids would often crowd around TVs at well-to-do friends' houses to catch episodes of *Moonlight Mask*. In one story arc, Moonlight Mask would even battle Mammoth Kong, a giant gorilla and the first *kaiju* on Japanese airwaves. Little is known about who was involved in the special effects; the show's staff tended to be young and underpaid.

Moonlight Mask (1958-59) title card

Toho and Eiji Tsuburaya's next major special effects film was **THE H-MAN** [**Director:** Ishiro Honda - **Release Date (Japan):** May 28th, 1958]. One of the first tokusatsu horror movies, *The H-Man*'s premise is a more pointed reference to the *Lucky Dragon* incident than *Godzilla*. (The incident would itself receive a film adaptation the following year by Kaneto Shindo.) *The H-Man* is Honda's film more than Tsuburaya's but the latter's contributions are striking. A highlight where both units are in synergy is an unsettling flashback wherein a group of fishermen encounter a derelict boat poisoned by radiation. It is a masterfully directed sequence with impressively grotesque FX work combining the aesthetic of Japan's native ghost stories and modern atomic terror. The atmospheric lighting schemes courtesy of Honda's gaffer

Tsuruzo Nishikawa elevate *The H-Man*. Nishikawa went on to frequently work with director Kihachi Okamoto.

For *The H-Man*, Tsuburaya would add yet another new recruit to his team, **KEIZO MURASE** (1935-). Murase would assist Teizo Toshimitsu, the Yagi Brothers and Eizo Kaimai in the modeling department. Murase grew up in Hokkaido, the son of dairy farmers. He developed a skin condition and had to move to Tokyo, where the climate was more favorable. His brother, who was working at Shin Toho, got him involved in movies. Murase had no formal art school training but showed a talent for craftsmanship. He lived in abject poverty for his first year on Tsuburaya and Toshimitsu's modeling team but soon rose through the ranks to become a respected artisan in his own right. On *The H-Man*, Murase would make buckets of the liquid monsters, created from a seawood solution used in cosmetics, and carry them to the set. The solution was colored with "aotake", a pigment made from bamboo. The liquid would be left overnight to thicken.

Tsuburaya's effects work for *The H-Man* is consistently inventive. Shots of the monsters oozing down walls were achieved via a rotating set with the camera bolted to it. Other shots were created by dripping the seaweed mixture and printing the frames in reverse. The disturbing shots of the creatures dissolving their victims were done by deflating balloon dummies dressed in characters' wardrobe. *The H-Man* was released the same year as Jack Harris and Irvin Yeaworth's *The Blob*, another film about a liquid monster dissolving human victims. Yet Tsuburaya's work bests the special effects in *The Blob* by a wide margin. Tsuburaya takes command in *The H-Man*'s climax with his penchant for phantasmagorical spectacle. The atmospheric sewer finale, featuring an effective synergy between Honda and Tsuburaya's units, was shot on sets left over from Akira Kurosawa's *Drunken Angel* (1948). The final images, with miniatures of Tokyo's sewers and bay alight in a green-orange conflagration, are hauntingly beautiful and pure Tsuburaya.

Toei, meanwhile, began production on a series of *Moonlight Mask* films. The first, **MOONLIGHT MASK** [**Director:** Tsuneo Kobayashi - **Release Date (Japan):** July 30th, 1958], was soon followed by a second part, **DUEL TO THE DEATH IN DANGEROUS WATERS** [**Director:** Ibid - **Release Date (Japan):** August 6th, 1958]. The special effects staff is unknown, but four more *Moonlight Mask* films would follow into mid-1959. These serial-style entries, an hour each, tended to be condensed versions of the story arcs on the simultaneously running TV show. *Moonlight Mask* wound up being prematurely canceled, its final episode airing on July 5th, 1959. As with *Super Giant*, another boy pretended to be Moonlight Mask and imitated the character's stunts. This time, the child was killed. Creator Kohan Kawauchi then filed a defamation suit against the conservative tabloid *Shukan Shincho* for unflattering coverage. Both contributed to the show's cancellation.

Shooting the finale of *Nichiren and the Great Mongol Invasion* (1958) in Daiei Kyoto's newly constructed special effects pool

At Daiei's Kyoto branch, executive Masaichi Nagata, a devout Nichiren Buddhist, spearheaded a historical epic called **NICHIREN AND THE GREAT MONGOL INVASION** [**Director:** Kunio Watanabe - **Release Date (Japan):** October 1st, 1958]. To direct, he brought *Emperor Meiji and the Great Russo-Japanese War*'s Kunio Watanabe over from Shin Toho. Yonesaburo Tsukiji was put in charge of the special effects unit. *Nichiren and the Great Mongol Invasion* is the Japanese studio equivalent to a Hollywood biblical epic and is dominated by Watanabe's side. Kazuo Hasegawa plays Nichiren, a famed Buddhist monk who, according to legend, brought about the "Divine Wind" that sank Kublai Khan's Mongol fleet. Tsukiji's contributions come into play with a well executed miniature fleet of Mongol ships. His unit takes the stage with the final

"Divine Wind" sequence which, indeed, evokes Moses' parting of the Red Seas in *The Ten Commandments* (1956). To shoot this sequence, a special effects pool was constructed on Daiei's Kyoto lot. The Mongolian warship miniatures were built by a local art school at a variety of scales. With the largest miniatures placed closest to the camera and the smallest furthest away, it created an impressive illusion of depth.

The assistant director to Tsukiji on *Nichiren* was a younger man named **YOSHIYUKI KURODA** (1928-2015). Kuroda, from Ehime Prefecture, had been a child actor. Graduating from Ritsumeikan University with a degree in mathematics, he was a high school math teacher for a time. Kuroda's immense knowledge of engineering would help him stage in atmospheric special effects sequences in years hence. Suddenly, a communist purge had left Daiei's Kyoto branch understaffed and looking for assistant directors. Kuroda was thus able to take an AD job at Daiei Kyoto in 1950. By this time, Kuroda had been an assistant director on main units. *Nichren and the Great Mongol Invasion* was his first assignment as AD on the special effects unit. Here Kuroda would discover a passion for tokusatsu filmmaking as it was Kuroda who largely directed the "Divine Wind" sequence with supervision from Tsukiji. Right out of the starting gate, Yoshiyuki Kuroda shows an immense talent for helming special effects sequences. The "Divine Wind" scene in *Nichiren* foreshadows a water-based sequence Kuroda would one day stage in *Return of Majin* (1966).

Toho's next monster picture with Tsuburaya was **VARAN [AKA: VARAN THE UNBELIEVABLE - Director:** Ishiro Honda **- Release Date (Japan):** October 14th, 1958]. The film was originally intended as a four-part TV miniseries co-produced with American ABC subsidiary AB-PT. Tomoyuki Tanaka thus had *Varan* made at a lower budget than prior films and shot in black and white at full frame with spherical lenses.

By this time, Toho's modeling department had moved into a log cabin on the backlot. Toshimitsu and the Yagi Brothers once again directed construction of the Varan suit with help from Eizo Kaimai and Keizo Murase. Made mostly from latex as usual, it was built with a softer texture than Godzilla to allow Haruo Nakajima more freedom of movement. The skin's bumpy texture was achieved with the use of crushed peanut shells; these were modeled onto the clay used to make the plaster molds. Varan's spines were made by Murase and cut from a transparent hose. They were sewn to the suit with the seams covered with latex, as the glue then available was not sufficient for the task. Varan's tail was fragile and tended to damage easily. The inside of the tail was molded from sponges and its edges were softened with a grinder before latex skin was added. Varan's claws were made with latex shaped around wire; Murase could never get them as sharp as he wanted. Additionally, the suit had a small motor installed, with mechanical mouth controls and light up eyes. A Varan puppet was built as usual for certain close ups and a half-sized model was made for the creature's flying scenes. Murase would help Akira Watanabe's team build miniatures as well; he proved adept at creating farms from memory, as he had lived and worked on one.

Keizo Murase

The water scenes in *Varan* were shot in Studio 10's pool. The monster's entrance is augmented by whirlpool effects, which were created with multiple running hoses placed under the water. This became a common Toho FX technique. These hoses were hooked up to nearby air cylinders and run under the water with the tips placed near the surface. The miniature sets feature quite a few prop rocks. These were made by coating tin with a layer of plaster. The modeling crew often wore straw hats on set to keep the plaster out of their hair. In the finale, an impressive miniature of Tokyo's Haneda airport was constructed, mainly by Yasuyuki Inoue, who built the set bigger than Tsuburaya had wanted. *Varan* is perhaps most notable as having given Nakajima the worst injury of his career. While shooting the explosive climax with pyrotechnics detonated directly on the costume,

Nakajima sustained nasty burns to his groin that required hospital treatment.

Unfortunately, well into shooting, AB-PT pulled out, leaving Toho holding the bag. *Varan* was thus retooled into a Japanese theatrical release as Tanaka did not want to scrap an almost completed film. Problem was, the film had been mostly shot and Toho did not want to release the film in standard "Academy" ratio. *Varan*'s footage was thus cropped to 'scope and billed as "TohoPanScope". The practice of shooting a film intended for anamorphic projection with spherical lenses was already being used in Hollywood and particularly Europe as "Superscope" and the similar "Techniscope".

Overall, *Varan* is not a particularly high-quality *kaiju eiga* opus and possibly Honda and Tsuburaya's single weakest collaboration. That *Varan* started out made for television and became a theatrical film is part of its problem. If it had been a television oddity not compared to the Honda/Tsuburaya team's theatrical films, *Varan* would have been more successful. Tsuburaya's effects end is decent though pales in comparison to his work on *Godzilla, Rodan* and *The Mysterians*. His unit cut some corners knowing their work was intended for the small screen. Varan itself is one of the least interesting of Toho's monster menagerie and the suit looks majestic in some shots, clunky in others. Due to its unusual construction, the monster's back flops about, an unsightly and distracting technical issue. The footage is also weakened by an overabundance of stock shots from *Godzilla* and Ishiro Honda's direction is unusually pedestrian. *Varan* was a box office failure and Toho put a stop to their monster-centered pictures temporarily as a result. Though the Japanese version of *Varan* is an unremarkable if mildly entertaining film, the U.S. version, called *Varan the Unbelievable* and not released until 1962, makes it look like a masterpiece. It is a Jerry Warren-style bastardization that is among the very worst Westernizations of a kaiju film.

Inspired by the success of *Moonlight Mask*, Toei partnered with Senkosha and began production on their very first tokusatsu TV program: **PLANET PRINCE** [Television Run (Japan): November 11th, 1958 - September 4th, 1959]. The first work of writer **MASARU IGAMI** (1931-1991), *Planet Prince* was also strongly influenced by *Super Giant*. Toei put out a contest for children's sci-fi TV scripts and the winner was Igami, who had just graduated from Meiji University. *Planet Prince* concerned the adventures of an alien prince (Fujio

Murakami) defending Earth from a variety of nasty extraterrestrial invaders. Once again, it was popular with children.

By 1959, ownership of television sets was becoming commonplace in post-war Japan. The royal wedding of Crown Prince Akihito and Michiko Shoda was broadcast on TV in April. Millions of Japanese families bought television sets to watch it. Another, lesser-known tokusatsu TV program was a live action adaptation of Osamu Tezuka's beloved manga **MIGHTY ATOM [AKA: ASTRO BOY - Television Run (Japan):** March 7th, 1959 - May 28, 1960]. Produced by Mainichi Broadcasting (MBS), *Mighty Atom* starts with an animated prologue created by Tezuka himself that looks ahead to the coming anime adaptation in 1963.

The live-action *Mighty Atom/Astro Boy* (1959), played by child actor Masahito Segawa

The special effects work is stellar for television and was supervised by none other than Eiji Tsuburaya himself. Producer Keiji Matsuzaki, a friend and former collaborator of Tsuburaya's, wanted the effects director to handle the unit on *Mighty Atom* himself but Tsuburaya was too occupied with his slate of work at Toho. Instead, he advised the production on effects techniques and his staff at the Visual Effects Institute worked on the show. The medium of television was a more experimental one. This allowed the staff to use techniques that might be considered too risky for films. The tokusatsu effects in *Mighty Atom* are surprisingly lavish for television and feature elaborate miniature work. The flying scenes involving Atom (Masahito Segawa) are the most impressive and best the *Super Giant* films from Shin Toho. Though obscure, *Mighty Atom* is notable as being one of the very first live-action manga adaptations, as well as the sole (semi-) collaboration between the titans of anime and tokusatsu: Osamu Tezuka and Eiji Tsuburaya.

The show's art director was **RYOSAKU TAKAYAMA** (1917-1982). The son of a carpenter from Yamanashi Prefecture, Takayama aspired to be a painter from youth. He worked on Tsuburaya's wartime unit as a miniature builder after a stint in the Imperial Army at the Chinese front. In 1946, Takayama joined the Japanese Communist Party and helped paint protest signs and street art during the union disputes. He left Toho soon afterwards and went freelance, helping model miniatures and monster suits on a variety of productions. Takayama would go on to become an influential modeler for tokusatsu television.

Eiji Tsuburaya's next film at Toho was **MONKEY SUN** [**Director:** Kajiro Yamamoto - **Release Date (Japan):** April 19th, 1959]. Another adaptation of *Journey to the West* directed by Yamamoto, *Monkey Sun* is surprisingly different from the director's earlier version, though a few scenes are copied. Once again it boasts an unreality akin to *The Wizard of Oz* (1939). Heavily comic, it is shot on deliberately theatrical sets with painted backdrops. At several points, Monkey god Son Goku (Norihei Miki) rides a "flying nimbus" into battle, the effect being scratched directly onto the film stock. Another impressive sequence features a giant tornado. Tsuburaya created this by pouring paint into a water tank and swirling it around with an apparatus at the bottom. He was inspired to create the effect while swirling a bowl of miso soup his wife had served him for breakfast; much to the fascination and occasional frustration of those around him, Eiji Tsuburaya seldom stopped thinking about his visual effects sequences. Using colored paints in water, often to create mushroom clouds and volcanic eruptions, would become a Tsuburaya unit trademark from here on. *Monkey Sun*'s demon villains disintegrate at the climax in a manner akin to UK studio Hammer's then-recent *Dracula* (1958). This was done by deflating balloon mannequins. As with *Madame White Snake*, Toei produced an animated rival production, *Alakazam the Great*. It was released the following year, though both were in production around the same time.

Toei next produced a two-part film version of **PLANET PRINCE** [**Director:** Eijiro Wakabayashi - **Release Date (Japan):** May 19th (**Part 1**) - May 25th, 1959 (**Part 2**)]. Here, Planet Prince (Tatsuo Umemiya) battles a gaggle of pointy-nosed space imps. The special effects, supervised by **SHOZO HIRAI**, are a mixed bag, though there's some quality miniature work. The tokusatsu FX mainly consist of the aliens' and hero's spaceships and optically animated rays. Some of these miniatures are interestingly engineered with moving parts. Like *Super Giant*, the two films are breathlessly paced and unrelentingly goofy. *Planet Prince* is, however, far more tolerable in its original Japanese form than its recut, disjointed and poorly dubbed English iteration shown on *Mystery Science Theater 3000*.

Around this time, Kohan Kawauchi would create another tokusatsu hero show, this time for Toei, **SEVEN COLOR MASK** [Television Run (Japan): June 3rd, 1959 - June 30th, 1960]. The show was given a bigger budget by Toei and filmed in 35mm. Actor Susumu Namijima played the role in the show's first half. The program was retitled *New Seven Color Mask* for its second half, with Namijima being replaced by a soon-to-be famous young actor and martial artist named Shinichi Chiba. This program would prove surprisingly influential, inspiring, among numerous others, a teenage artist named **GO NAGAI** (1945-).

Shue Matsubayashi

Toho's next major special effects production was their first big-budget war film since *Farewell Rabaul*, **SUBMARINE I-57: WILL NOT SURRENDER** [Director: Shue Matsubayashi - **Release Date (Japan):** July 5th, 1959]. In 1957, Matsubayashi had moved from Shin Toho to Toho, where he became known for his comedies, particularly the *Company President* series. At Toho, Matsubayashi became as closely associated with the Company President franchise as Ishiro Honda was to Godzilla. *Submarine I-57* marks Matsubayashi's first collaboration with Eiji Tsuburaya. He respected Tsuburaya to such a degree that he gave him very little direction. *Submarine I-57* belongs more to Matsubayashi, but features the Tsuburaya unit's always stellar miniature work, used for scale shots of the titular submarine. A 20-foot miniaturized I-57 was built.

Tsuburaya's end was shot at the then-current special effects pool at Studio 10. Unusually, the underwater shots were not filmed on dry sets with lighting effects as in later films. The modeling staff put together a realistic seabed for underwater photography with rocks and coral. A small, aquarium-like window was constructed on the side of the pool to allow the crew to shoot underwater shots without submerging the camera. Despite the film being in black and white, Tsuburaya's unit used superior blue-screen elements for compositions. These were shot on color stock and then printed in black and white after composition. Tsuburaya's FX unit takes command in the final minutes of the picture, which evoke Eisenstein's *Battleship Potemkin*, but depicting fatalistic defeat instead of victorious revolution. *Submarine I-57* was a massive hit for Toho and more war epics directed by Matsubayashi would follow.

Toei, meanwhile, decided to expand their special effects division with the increasing production of tokusatsu shows and films. President Hiroshi Okawa welcomed Shin Toho's Sadao Uemura into the fold, along with Nobuo Yajima, as Keiji Kawakami's unit at Shochiku was cutting staff. Toru Narita from Toho was also quietly brought on board as an art director. Toei's special effects division was smaller in staff and given a lot less time and money to work with than Toho's. Yajima initially had trouble with Toei's production practices, which were fast-paced compared to Shochiku's, but he adjusted. Yajima learned to heavily storyboard his sequences ahead of time. This helped him determine the editing rhythm and be more economical with shooting. Yajima's unit then only filmed shots that were necessary for the edit; helping them stay on budget and schedule. Yajima's first work with Toei was miniature shooting in **ALTITUDE 7,000 KM: FOUR HOURS OF HORROR** [Director: Tsuneo Kobayashi - **Release Date (Japan):** September 30th, 1959].

Eiji Tsuburaya

For their thousandth production, Toho had special plans. **THE THREE TREASURES [AKA: THE BIRTH OF JAPAN- Director: HIROSHI INAGAKI** (1905-1980) - **Release Date (Japan):** October 25th, 1959] was something of an Eastern cross between a biblical epic and a Harryhausen-style mythological fantasy movie. A three-hour prestige picture based on Japan's Shinto myths, it boasts an all-star cast headed by Toshiro Mifune as Susano-o and his descendant Yamato Takeru. As usual, Eiji Tsuburaya handled the lavish effects work and on *The Three Treasures* pioneered new optical printing technology. *The Three Treasures* boasts a stunning opening with heavy optical work and practical FX making heavy use of paint, chemicals and dry ice.

Inagaki's unit dominates the middle portions set in prehistoric *Jomon*-era Japan. In one marvelous sequence, Susano-o, akin to Heracles, Saint George and Marduk, slays the eight-headed mythological dragon Yamata no Orochi. Inventively shot, it is similar to Harryhausen's Hydra scene in *Jason and the Argonauts* (1963), but staged in a classically Tsuburaya manner. It also resembles a sequence in the Soviet production *Ilya Muromets* (1956) or *The Sword and the Dragon*. There were two Orochis built: a smaller puppet and an enormous suit. Both were difficult to construct. Every single scale was crafted one-by-one and the puppet required difficult wire work. The necks would often twist so a bellows-like mechanism was installed in the main suit to keep them from tangling. The mouths were moveable by radio control. The scene of Orochi emerging from the lake was achieved by moving the suit on a rail under the water. The giant suit was operated from within by eight people. As the passionate Mifune kept stabbing its hide with a sword, the stuntmen and effects staff huddled inside in terror. Yasuyuki Inoue and Tsuburaya had another falling out while this scene was being filmed. Tsuburaya had ordered Inoue to build a lakebed set filled with reeds that swayed as Yamata no Orochi approached. The lakebed set took longer than Inoue expected to build - the entire floor had to be coated in clay so that the reeds would stand still. By afternoon, the set was still not yet complete which enraged Tsuburaya. He called off shooting for the day and stomped away. Inoue wryly joked to a producer manager: "Looks like Tsuburaya doesn't feel like shooting a movie today."

On *The Three Treasures*, Tsuburaya's team gained several new young members, including **MINORU NAKANO** (1939-2021) and **KAZUO SAGAWA** (1939-). Both were talented college students who had studied at Tsuburaya's Visual Effects Institute and were eager to learn all they could from the man himself. Another recent recruit for Tsuburaya's unit was script supervisor **KEIKO SUZUKI** (1937-). The script supervisor oversees a film's continuity and Suzuki would be a valuable member of Tsuburaya's team for the next decade. For years, Suzuki, her maiden name Keiko Hisamatsu, would be Tsuburaya's only female crew member. In group photos, she's a sole feminine face amongst a sea of male technicians. Suzuki started out as an assistant editor in 1958 and transitioned to script supervision. At first, Suzuki was disappointed to be assigned to Tsuburaya's effects unit as she wanted to work with the main crew. Suzuki decided to take a positive attitude, however. In her words: "I knew there was a reason that these men had worked so hard for so many years on these special effects films, so I observed them closely. I tried and tried to get interested in special effects."

In time, Keiko Suzuki realized that the editing and shooting of special effects sequences was a pure form of cinema and from thereon began to enjoy her work. She loved that, unlike in many other films where the crew changed from production to production, Tsuburaya used the same team for each movie. As a result, she began to feel at home as despite the hard work and dangerous stunts, Tsuburaya's unit had a family atmosphere. Suzuki even called Sadamasa Arikawa *"O-nii-san"* or "big brother". According to Suzuki, on bad days dealing with complicated visual effects shots, Tsuburaya's unit would get a single cut filmed. On good, busy days, they'd sometimes manage to lens 40 shots.

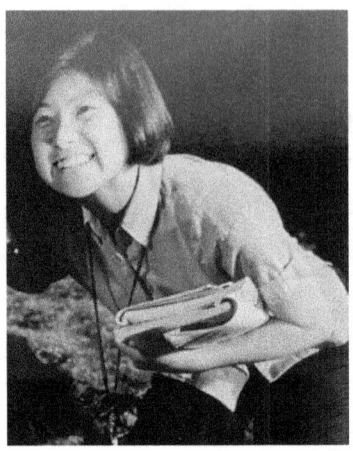

Keiko Suzuki

On *The Three Treasures,* Tsuburaya and company refined their fantastical effects techniques introduced in prior films like *Madame White Snake* and *Monkey Sun* with many arresting images. Similarly to the recent *Nichiren and the Great Mongol Invasion*, Yamato Takeru's fleet is nearly wiped out by a storm at sea. *The Three Treasures* features a biblical finale where the eruption of Mount Fuji and a gigantic flood wipes out an army, a top notch sequence. For this climax, seven tons of molten iron and ten tons of water were used. Panoramic composite vistas of the armies fleeing the apocalyptic destruction are among the finest process shots Tsuburaya's unit ever produced. The closing shots of Yamato Takeru turning into a swan were created with cel animation by Sadao Iizuka. *The Three Treasures* went on to win another "Special Technology Award" for Eiji Tsuburaya.

Toho's final special effects production of the 1950s was **BATTLE IN OUTER SPACE [Director:** Ishiro Honda - **Release Date (Japan):** December 26th, 1959]. *Battle in Outer Space* is a loose semi-sequel to *The Mysterians* where humanity unites once again to stop an even nastier army of extraterrestrials. Though the theme of human brotherhood is strong and there are striking moments of pathos, the picture belongs more to Tsuburaya than Honda. The plot is thin with the characters developed little. Yet Tsuburaya utterly commands the special effects sequences. There's a stronger George Pal vibe, with many scenes recalling *Destination: Moon* (1950) and *The War of the Worlds*.

Tsuburaya refers to exhaustive storyboards, in his own words: "Here, production kinks are worked out in advance."

Shigeru Komatsuzaki once again created the striking retro-futuristic mechanical designs, with the miniatures modeled by Yoshio Irie and Yasuyuki Inoue. The two SPIP spaceships were built at both one-foot and three-foot scale, mainly out of balsa wood and tin. Some engineering was installed into the larger miniatures, including moveable hatches and landing gears. Similarly to the Markalite GYRO in *The Mysterians*, the shot of the SPIPs flying high into the sky had to be filmed outdoors. The lunar expedition vehicles were also built in both one and three-foot scales. For the shots of the lunar rovers levitating like a hovercraft, Tsuburaya's unit suspended the models in the air with piano wire and placed the set on a moving platform. The exhaust was aerosolized steam. The alien saucers were reused, repainted miniatures from *The Mysterians*. The leftover

Mysterian dome miniature was even used to build the main saucer. Numerous one-foot miniatures for the Earth fighter rockets were also made by Irie.

Preparing the miniaturized decimation of Tokyo with buildings made of delicate materials

While *Battle in Outer Space* was in principal photography, the unmanned Soviet craft Luna 3 took the first photographs of the dark side of the moon on October 4th, 1959. These would be used by Honda and Tsuburaya's units as a reference for the production design. Three-foot, globe-like miniatures of the Earth and moon were also built for the landing and launch sequences. They would be kept and reused in future productions. The gorgeously unreal lunar battle sequences feature the early painted backdrop work of **FUCHIMU SHIMAKURA** (1940-). Shimakura, from Niigata Prefecture, was a talented painter from youth, his first exhibition having taken place when he was in junior high school. By 17, he was already employed as a set painter for an independent production company. Shimakura was hired by Toho while visiting the set of *The Three Treasures* and worked on that film's optical composites. It was Shimakura, soon to be called "The God of Clouds," who painted the striking starfield "horizont" backdrops for the miniature sets in *Battle in Outer Space*.

With miniatures and Sadao Iizuka's animated rays, Tsuburaya takes the sci-fi aesthetic pioneered in *The Mysterians* to greater heights. Iizuka's main influence for certain beams came from tracer bullets - used in World War II for making gun fire more visible.

Aided by a thundering medley of Ifukube themes, *Battle in Outer Space* comes alive in its finale - among Tsuburaya's grandest displays of spectacle. A highlight is an eye-popping sequence where Tokyo is destroyed by an anti-gravity beam. To create this scene, miniature buildings were made with soft materials like paraffin and styrofoam. With the help of mathematical calculation, a compressed air bomb was detonated under the miniatures which were shot in high frame rate while being blown apart by powerful electric fans. Another stunning shot features rocket fighters being rapidly fired from Earth's space port. The set's ceiling was too low to properly execute it, so assistant art director Yasuyuki Inoue dug a large hole into the ground of the studio. A guard caught him and Inoue was nearly fired, but an amused Tsuburaya defended him.

Battle in Outer Space was Toho's first film to be pre-sold to an American distributor. Before shooting had even wrapped, it was picked up by Columbia. The picture would be more influential than given credit and its visuals and tropes can be seen in a wide variety of films. *Battle in Outer Space*'s images of interstellar, fighter-pilot like spacecraft exchanging laser projectiles and alien bases destroyed likely influenced the iconic space dogfights in *Star Wars* (1977). The 1950s were the most pivotal decade in the development of Japanese special effects. During this time, Eiji Tsuburaya rose from a pariah in the industry to become its godfather. In the coming years, he became a Walt Disney-like institution to himself.

VARAN: SHINICHI SEKIZAWA AND GENRE TROPES

by Patrick Galvan

This is a reprint of an article originally published on Toho Kingdom
(tohokingdom.com)

To describe Ishiro Honda's *Varan* (1958) as a lesser entry in the director's science fiction oeuvre is something of an understatement. In a genre career packed end to end with highs and lows, this ill-conceived venture about a giant reptile who — for reasons never adequately explained — rises from his lair to threaten civilization resides near the bottom of the spectrum. Flatly directed by Honda and headed by bewildering characters, the picture manages only a few pockets of fun in its first forty-five minutes. After the surreal moment wherein the monster spreads his "wings" and flies away, *Varan* devolves into impersonal monster-versus-military skirmishes and dreadful scenes that showcase Honda trapped in situations he was seldom proficient at. These include static boardroom meetings photographed in the most pedestrian manner; an abominable "suspense scene" wherein the hero drives a truck of explosives up to the monster and runs — lightly jogs — to safety.

Initially contracted to shoot a TV movie before being told mid-production to make something for Japanese cinemas, Honda years later looked back on this picture as "a work I am not happy with." His sentiments are understandable. Yet there is a certain aspect to the 1958 misfire that makes it worthy of acknowledgment in the history of *kaiju eiga*. *Varan* marked Ishiro Honda's first collaboration with Shinichi Sekizawa, the wordsmith later responsible for the fun, witty scripts of such classics as *Mothra* (1961), *King*

Kong vs. Godzilla (1962), and *Invasion of Astro-Monster* (1965) — not to mention several of Jun Fukuda's science fiction home runs à la *The Secret of the Telegian* (1960) and *Son of Godzilla* (1967). Although the original story for Varan came from writer Ken Kuronuma, it was up to Sekizawa to develop concept into script. While the results certainly don't launch his partnership with Honda in a particularly auspicious manner, one can see rudimentary forms of tropes that would define their later films.

In *Varan*, we see: a trio of bantering protagonists — among them the aforementioned plucky female reporter: a progenitor of Yuriko Hoshi's heroine from *Ghidorah, the Three-Headed Monster* (1964). The remote forest where Varan resides is explored by researchers encountering untrusting natives who worship a monster — reminiscent of *Half Human* (1955), written by Takeo Murata, while pointing the way to Sekizawa's work on *Mothra* and *Mothra vs. Godzilla* (1964). Even the picture's agonizingly dull climax exhibits a few action patterns now iconic for the genre. As Varan approaches Tokyo, the military enacts strategy after strategy in a vain effort to stop him; this came to mind repeatedly during my most recent viewings of *King Kong vs. Godzilla* and *Mothra vs. Godzilla*. In the end, the monster's defeated via a solution made possible by scientists and civilians — a recurring trope in such pictures of the 1960s as *Dogora* (1964) and *Invasion of Astro-Monster*.

Also worth noting is that the original script included an unfilmed scene of children pretending to be Varan, indicating Sekizawa was already shrewdly aware of — and interested in reflecting — youngsters' interest in kaiju. This, too, would continue as the genre developed into the following decade. In *King Kong vs. Godzilla*, a child pleads with his mother to take him to see a rampaging Godzilla. In *Ghidorah, the Three-Headed Monster*, two boys on a talk show answer "Mothra!" when queried who they'd like to meet. And in 1969's *All Monsters Attack*, Sekizawa took youthful fascination with monsters to a new and very personal level, with its young protagonist fantasizing about kaiju to escape the harsh realities of everyday life.

These plot threads and devices didn't necessarily all begin with *Varan*, but Sekizawa's merging of them here nonetheless makes this otherwise unremarkable movie worthy of some acknowledgment — even if as a forerunner of better things to come.

VII.
1960 - 1961
昭和三十五・三十六

Demonstrators mob outside the Diet, once destroyed by Godzilla on film, in protest of the ANPO Security Treaty

It is for good reason that the 1960s are called the "Golden Age" of Japanese special effects cinema. As Japan entered 1960, it was rocked by ongoing protests over the U.S/Japan ANPO Security Treaty that allowed the American military to maintain a presence on Japanese soil. By summer, the ANPO protests would become violent enough that a student was killed and a planned visit by President Eisenhower canceled. The protests could not stop the treaty from going into effect, but they did result in the resignation of Prime Minister Nobusuke Kishi and his cabinet. On the airwaves, Hitachi and Matsusaki Productions produced a live-action adaptation of the beloved manga **TETSUJIN NO. 28 [AKA: GIGANTOR** - **Television Run (Japan):** February 1st - April 25th, 1960] by **MITSUTERU YOKOYAMA** (1934-2004). This 13-episode miniseries is notable as another early take on a popular manga. Little is known about the staff of *Tetsujin No. 28* and the effects work is crude compared to the earlier *Mighty Atom*. Tetsujin itself is far closer to human size than future tokusatsu robots. There's the occasional miniature and the use of printing in negative. As with *Mighty Atom*, the coming 1963 anime adaptation would be far more successful.

Next from Daiei's Kyoto branch came **THE INVISIBLE DEMON [AKA: INVISIBLE TENGU** - **Director:** Mitsuo Hirotsu - **Release Date (Japan):** March 1st, 1960]. *The Invisible Demon* combines the aesthetic of the two Invisible Man films made at the Tokyo branch with the *jidai-geki* theatrics Daiei Kyoto was known for. Veteran Chishi Makiura served as cinematographer; assisting him was the up and coming **FUJIO MORITA** (1927-2014). Morita had worked under Eiji Tsuburaya for *The Invisible Man Appears*. On *The Invisible Demon*, Morita puts to the test the techniques Tsuburaya taught him. The titular demon, a *tengu* (Ryuzo Shimada) was given a white kimono which made the invisibility effects easier to execute. A technique called two-time processing was employed by Makiura and Morita which involved processing the film between exposures. The main drawback was that it darkened the first layer (typically the background behind the invisible tengu). Fujio Morita would soon be promoted to full-fledged cinematographer; in this capacity he would continue to advance innovative shooting techniques at Daiei Kyoto.

The studios' release slate for the month of April 1960 was a busy one for tokusatsu cinema. First came **THE SECRET OF THE TELEGIAN [Director: JUN FUKUDA** (1923-2000) - **Release Date (Japan):** April 10th, 1960] from Toho. The second "transformed human" film, Ishiro Honda was originally to direct but was busy putting the finishing touches on *Battle in Outer Space*. Honda vouched for Jun Fukuda as replacement; he had served Honda well as AD on *Rodan* and had recently made his debut with *It's Dangerous Playing with Fire* (1959). Fukuda, with a more energetic directing style, dominates the picture with occasional Nobuo Nakagawa-like J-Horror flourish. Shinichi Sekizawa's script features intriguing subtext about Japan's wartime misdeeds returning to haunt the country in its post-war prosperity, fitting for a picture released as ANPO protesters mobbed outside the Diet. A group of wealthy businessmen left their army comrade, Sudo (Tadao Nakamaru), for dead at the war's end. Sudo survived and can now project himself electronically thanks to research by an Imperial Army scientist. Naturally, he uses this novel means to exact vengeance.

Export poster for *Secret of the Telegian* (1960)

The contributions of Eiji Tsuburaya's unit are subtle but notable, in part because his team were already deep in preparation for the upcoming war epic *Storm Over the Pacific*. The special effects work on *The Secret of the Telegian* was done while Tsuburaya was on vacation from *Storm*'s production during the New Years holiday. The optical work in *Telegian* is impressive, with Sudo's appearance being distorted by TV signal-like interference whenever he transmits himself to take murderous revenge. To create this, Tsuburaya studied CRT television signals and interference. Though given much to do, optical animator Sadao Iizuka disliked working on the transformed human films, particularly this one, amusingly calling them "evil".

The unit's miniature photography can mainly be seen in an exploding train midway and volcanic eruption at the end of the picture. American television prints of *The Secret of the Telegian* were in black and white, giving it a noirish quality that oddly benefits it.

The next Toho special effects release would be the aforementioned **STORM OVER THE PACIFIC [AKA: I BOMBED PEARL HARBOR - Director:** Shue Matsubayashi - **Release Date (Japan):** April 26th, 1960], a prestige war picture. To stage the film's extensive recreations of nautical warfare, a giant pool was constructed on Toho's backlot. Called the "Big Pool" and measuring over 80,000 square feet, it was engineered by Yasuyuki Inoue. Toho's was even bigger than the massive pool used in many a *peplum* (sword and sandal picture) at CineCitta in Rome. Inoue had wanted it even larger and pushed Toho's brass to buy additional property to build it, but they refused so he had to scale it down. This pool would become an integral part of Toho's special effects productions and be used by generations of tokusatsu directors. Matsubayashi was at first skeptical that such an enormous pool could be built successfully. He was in awe when he saw the newly constructed "Big Pool", calling it the Toho effects unit's "dojo". The pool was not without its logistical problems, however. Fish and water insects often bred in it during summer and the pool quickly filled with mold and algae. To make matters worse, busy crew members would often use it to cop the occasional bathroom break. Shooting in the pool was frequently done in the dead of winter which was brutal for the effects crew.

Constructing another miniaturized Pearl Harbor in Toho's newly built special effects pool

At first glance, *Storm Over the Pacific* is a color remake of *The War at Sea From Hawaii to Malay*. Yet the two films, one made during the height of the Pacific War and the other post-war, could not be more night-and-day in their approach. Matsubayashi directs with a sense of tragic inevitability. Eiji Tsuburaya, meanwhile, creates a nearly cut-for-cut recreation of his Pearl Harbor sequence in *The War at Sea* close to two decades later in color, Tohoscope and with more manpower, money and technology. It doesn't quite have the pioneering novelty of *The War at Sea*'s version and there are historical inaccuracies, but it's impressive nonetheless. Note that it is placed in the first reel of the film rather than near its end like with *The War at Sea*. Years later, Tsuburaya would visit Pearl Harbor during the making of *None But the Brave* (1965). He was impressed by how much it resembled the miniature sets his craftsmen built in *The War at Sea* and *Storm Over the Pacific*.

Around a thousand model planes are constructed

The miniature work in *Storm Over the Pacific* is among the Tsuburaya unit's finest to date. Outdoing their work on *Eagle of the Pacific*, around 500 model ships and a thousand miniature planes were constructed by the modeling team. Some were only a few inches long and used in the arresting god's-eye view shots of the Imperial Fleet. Tsuburaya's team mixed over 5,000 pounds of agar into one of the effects pools. This created a glistening ocean like would be seen from high up in the sky. The *Hiryu*, *Akagi* and *USS Yorktown* miniatures were dozens of feet long each with built-in motors. FX staff, typically headed by Toru Suzuki, steered them from inside. These scenes were shot on the open seas off the Miura peninsula. Trouble was, the mammoth miniatures were too gigantic to be transported, even with Toho's largest trucks. They had to be sailed to the location: down the Sumida River and through Tokyo Bay.

In one scene, as a squadron of Zeros take off from the *Hiryu*, the crew of the ship waves from its deck. In wide miniature shots, the assembled navalmen are portrayed by six-inch dolls. Made by Keizo Murase, fishing line was tied to their hands and they were puppeteered from inside the miniature ships. Pyrotechnics were executed by switches placed inside the miniature boats, which was extremely dangerous. Kyuzo Yamamoto was given a lot to do as one miniature ship was blasted after another. Young **NOBUYUKI YASUMARU** (1935-2022) would join the modeling team with *Storm Over the Pacific*. Yasumaru was a student at Musashino Art College and would soon become a full-time employee.

Eiji Tsuburaya

For the Battle of Midway, which occupies the final hour, Tsuburaya's unit is in as good a synergy with Matsubayashi's as with Ishiro Honda's in *Godzilla*. *Storm Over the Pacific*'s last half presents one stunning naval bombardment sequence after another paired with a mournful fatalism from Matsubayashi. The aerial dogfights feature the addition of vivid tracer flare rendered by Sadao Iizuka, evoking the space battles in *Battle in Outer Space* which their real life counterpart inspired. A bombardment scene early on in the Battle of Midway is particularly thrilling in its execution. There are stunning optical composites, among Hiroshi Mukoyama's best work, capturing the battle's scope.

Storm Over the Pacific was one of Toho's biggest hits of 1960. It was also among Toho's first war films to be released in the United States. Years later, its effects work would be pilfered for Universal's *Midway* (1976). *The Japan Times* covered the film in an article dated January 5th, 1961 and titled "**Toho Raking in Profits On World War II Movie**". "The Toho Film Co. is reaping a neat profit from its production of *The Storm of the Pacific,* a film story of the Japanese imperial navy during the Second World War from the Pearl Harbor attack to the disastrous Battle of Midway." It continues: "The film, which cost Toho about $730,000 to produce, has brought in about 60 per cent profit since it was released less than eight months ago. By Japanese standards, the film was a very expensive production." Producer **SANEZUMI FUJIMOTO** (1910-1979) was quoted as saying "If an American producer had produced an identical film in the United States, I am sure the expense would have been triple what we spent, and this was one of the 10 most expensive films ever produced in Japan."

Daiei Kyoto's **THE DEMON OF MOUNT OE** [Director: **TOKUZO TANAKA** (1920-2007) - **Release Date (Japan):** April 27, 1960] was released a day later. The picture is a lavish color costume drama with stunning cinematography by premier DP Hiroshi Imai. Its titular antagonist is Shuten Doji, a shape-shifting demon of Japanese folklore. The effects unit was headed by **SHOZO HONDA**, who mainly served as a DP on Daiei Kyoto pictures, including on several entries in the iconic Zatoichi series. *The Demon of Mount Oe* features several elaborate FX sequences and well-executed monsters modeled by Fuminori Ohashi. These include a flying demon head, monster ox and an impressively constructed giant spider. The spider sequence, using a full-scale mechanical puppet, is not quite executed to perfection but a highlight. Another standout is the ox scene, which fares better. *The Demon of Mount Oe* is an early melding of *jidai-geki* theatrics with tokusatsu monster effects looking forward to future Daiei Kyoto productions like *Majin* (1966) and *One Hundred Monsters* (1968).

Masano and Eiji Tsuburaya attend Catholic mass (left)
Tomio Sagisu, the soon-to-be founder of P-Productions (right)

Kohan Kawauchi's next show with Toei was the 26 episode **MESSENGER OF ALLAH** [**Television Run (Japan):** July 7th - December 27th, 1960]. Like *New Seven Color Mask*, *Messenger of Allah* starred Shinichi Chiba. It was inspired by Kawauchi's love of Islamic culture; he had converted to Islam the previous year. Amusingly, the show is rife with product placement for confectionery giant Kabaya Foods. Another major figure in the tokusatsu industry would convert to an Abrahamic faith around this time: Eiji Tsuburaya himself. Years prior, his wife Masano had been converted to Catholicism by her younger sister. In 1960, Masano persuaded her husband to receive baptism, his baptismal name being "Peter". Despite his grinding work schedule at Toho and later his own company, Tsuburaya would still find time to attend mass every Sunday.

Also in July 1960, Tsuburaya's former wartime apprentice Tomio Sagisu would establish P-Productions. After the war and union disputes at Toho, Sagisu had focused on drawing manga rather than working on live-action tokusatsu films but decided to return to the medium. Sculptor Ryosaku Takayama and former Tsuburaya optical technician Yoshio Watanabe were also founding members. At first, P-Productions did freelance commissions for the Japanese studios including animated title cards for Daiei movies and process shots. In the coming years, they would become influential in tokusatsu television.

On the feature film front, Toei produced the nuclear war drama **WORLD WAR III BREAKS OUT** [**AKA: THE FINAL WAR** - **Director:** Shigeaki Hidaka - **Release Date (Japan):** October 19th, 1960]. A timely film as the U.S/Japan ANPO treaty had gone into effect on June 23rd, *World War III Breaks Out* was released under the brief "Shin Toei" outfit. Director Hidaka had previously written the scripts for Toho's *The Invisible Avenger* and *Godzilla Raids Again*. The effects footage by Nobuo Yajima is confined to the picture's final ten minutes where the world's landmarks are blown to smithereens by nuclear hellfire.

Yajima's unit pulls off impressive miniature shots. These include nuclear missile launches and the destruction of San Francisco's Golden Gate Bridge and the Diet and Tokyo Tower in Tokyo. Like Tsuburaya, Yajima uses the classic method of pouring paint into a water tank for the apocalyptic mushroom clouds. The work of Yajima's team wound up documented in none other than LIFE Magazine. For years, *World War III Breaks Out* was an elusive holy grail for Japanese cinema collectors, unavailable on home video in Japan or the States. Toei would finally air the film on their movie channel in the early 2010s, putting it back in circulation.

Miniature cities are ready to be blasted to smithereens

Toho and Eiji Tsuburaya's next special effects production was **THE HUMAN VAPOR** [Director: Ishiro Honda - Release Date (Japan): December 11, 1960]. *The Human Vapor* is a picture that belongs far more to Honda than Tsuburaya. The film is one of Honda's bleakest, scripted by **TAKESHI KIMURA** (1911-1987). Known for writing scripts with darker themes than his contemporary Shinichi Sekizawa, Kimura was such a reclusive figure that no publicly available photographs of him are known to exist. A fervent Japanese Communist Party member, he had been imprisoned as a dissident during World War II. *The Human Vapor* concerns Mizuno (Yoshio Tsuchiya), an air force pilot-turned-librarian who, by volunteering for a top-secret experiment, develops the ability to transform himself into a gaseous state. He uses his newfound power to commit robberies and woo Fujichiyo (Kaoru Yachigusa), a *No* dancer he's infatuated with. Tsuburaya's impressive optical and practical effects work begins to take the stage midway.

To create the effect of Mizuno dissolving himself into a gas decades before computer-generated imagery, Tsuburaya and his team developed an imaginative process. An inflatable rubber doll was built in the likeness of actor Tsuchiya and outfitted in his wardrobe. The figure was suspended with piano wire and dry ice was put inside it. Underneath the inflatable mannequin was placed a bucket of hot water. The doll was deflated and the piano wire was lowered. As the mannequin sank into the bucket of water, the dry ice dissolved and dispersed into the air. In post-production, this was frosted with optical animation. The result is a cinematic illusion that rivals anything being done in Hollywood. *The Human Vapor* is capped with a suspenseful, stunning finale well directed by both Honda and Tsuburaya ending in double suicide-style betrayal and conflagration. In Japan, *The Human Vapor* is considered a stand-out in Ishiro Honda's oeuvre.

Stateside, *The Human Vapor* was released by Brenco in 1964 with its plot structure rearranged and a new narration track by Tsuchiya's Mizuno (voiced by James Hong)

The next major film at Toho to employ Eiji Tsuburaya's services would be **DAREDEVIL IN THE CASTLE [AKA: THE TALE OF OSAKA CASTLE - Director:** Hiroshi Inagaki - **Release Date (Japan):** January 3rd, 1961], a period vehicle starring Toshiro Mifune. Besides some early miniature and process work, Tsuburaya's unit brings its forces to bear in the final ten minutes of this high-concept *jidai-geki* picture. The battle, siege and burning of Osaka Castle features spectacular model work and evokes the burning of Atlanta in *Gone With the Wind* (1939). Tsuburaya's art department made a large-scale recreation of the castle for this sequence and used the small pool in Studio 10 for its moat.

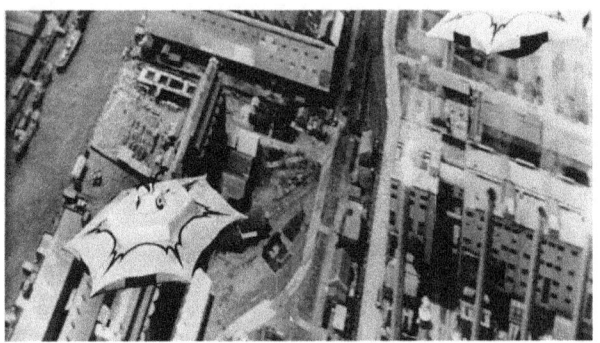

Iron Sharp (1961)

Rival Toei's next foray into tokusatsu film production was **IRON SHARP [AKA: INVASION OF THE NEPTUNE MEN - Director:** Koji Ota - **Release Date (Japan):** July 19th, 1961]. It was again released under the brief "Shin Toei" subsidiary. Starring *Messenger of Allah*'s Shinichi Chiba, *Iron Sharp* is similar to the *Planet Prince* films but a step up in production value. Nobuo Yajima's explosive sequences of destruction in the film's final 20 minutes are its highlight. Having cut his teeth on *World War III Breaks Out,* Yajima delivers spirited miniature work that is nearly Tsuburaya grade with stock footage from the former picture peppered in. A peculiar shot to Western eyes shows a building with a display of Adolf Hitler being blasted by the film's aliens. This was actually depicting a movie theater screening a then-popular *Mein Kampf* documentary. *Iron Sharp*'s spaceship designs were created by an uncredited Toru Narita.

By this time, at Toho, producer Tomoyuki Tanaka was eager to make another monster picture. Tanaka wanted to make a different kind of creature feature: the story of a feminine beast with elements of magical realism. With the help of writers Shinichiro Nakamura, Takehiko Fukunaga and Yoshie Hotta, along with screenwriter Shinichi Sekizawa, a story was fleshed out. This became **MOTHRA [Director:** Ishiro Honda - **Release Date (Japan):** July 30th, 1961]. Honda and Eiji Tsuburaya were given one of their biggest budgets yet for a monster movie and there's a lavishness to *Mothra* reminiscent of old Hollywood.

Associated Press correspondent Bob Thomas would visit Tsuburaya's unit during *Mothra*'s pre-production in early 1961 and write an article that ran in American papers entitled **"All Out Shock Film Due From Japan"**. The writer observes: "Tsuburaya was sitting at the Toho commissary, which was just like those in Hollywood - noisy and bustling. The filmmaker is a quiet, unassuming man who wears glasses and a slouch hat." Thomas goes on: "[Tsuburaya] visited tents on a soundstage in which miniature jet planes suspended by wire were flown against a mammoth blue backdrop. He showed other playthings in his workshop - three foot tanks, rockets and more jets that will be used to attack the monster. In another shop, several workers were laboring over a foam rubber mock-up of the beast. Visitors were sworn to secrecy, lest Toho's competitors steal the designs for their own horror epics." Tsuburaya told Thomas that he'd like to visit Hollywood and meet John Fulton, George Pal and Walt Disney. The article concludes with Tsuburaya sighing, in a self-deprecating fashion: "American trick techniques are still the best in the world."

Eiji Tsuburaya

For *Mothra*, Eiji Tsuburaya's special effects sequences are indeed beautifully executed, boasting one phantasmagorical image after another. As Tsuburaya began work on *Mothra*, he suffered a personal tragedy with the death of his colleague and brother-in-law Shuzaburo Araki in February. **YUKIO MANODA** and **YOSHIYUKI TOKUMASA** (1935-) would thus take over Araki's position on Tsuburaya's unit, assisting Hiroshi Mukoyama in optical photography. The optical composites in *Mothra* are among the Tsuburaya and Mukoyama's team's finest. Shots miniaturizing the Twin Fairies, played by pop identical twin duo The Peanuts (Emi and Yumi Ito), are extremely effective. Keizo Murase constructed the doll facsimiles of the Ito Sisters used as on-set doubles by Honda's unit and in brief cutaways. The actors spoke to the dolls on set and the Fairies' lines were fed to them with a tape player.

Eiji Tsuburaya

Three different versions of Mothra's larval form were constructed. This included a smaller, mechanical puppet, used for long shots, the attack by Self Defense Forces at sea and the Tokyo Tower scene. Electronic toy tank components were put inside the larva puppet to make it move. The maritime attack was filmed in Toho's Big Pool. One of *Mothra*'s very best sequences features the larval monster attacking Yokota air base with dazzling aerial shots and life-like miniature destruction throughout. A particularly striking special effects cut mixing both units in *Mothra* is a composited vista. The Mothra larva hatches atop its altar on Infant Island, with a matte painting extending the set below as the natives pay homage at the bottom of the frame.

The demolition of Kurobe Dam is another impressive scene. The dam was recreated at 1/50th scale and Tsuburaya was planning to destroy and flood it with water pumped from four large tanks. However, assistant art director Yasuyuki Inoue knew that four water tanks wouldn't be enough. The volume of water used needed to burst the miniature dam and create a realistic-looking deluge. Inoue thought sixteen tanks would get the job done, but Toho had only eight on their backlot. The brilliant Inoue constructed four more water tanks for twelve in total. This at first irritated Tsuburaya, who was frustrated that Inoue's rigging of the tanks made camera placement difficult. It took multiple takes to destroy the dam, but Tsuburaya was impressed with the results and Inoue's ingenuity.

Eiji Tsuburaya (bottom right) and some core members of his effects unit on the set of *Mothra* (1961)

For use in much of larval Mothra's Tokyo rampage, an almost 40-foot suit was crafted by Teizo Toshimitsu and the Yagi Brothers with help from Keizo Murase and Eizo Kaimai. Murase did heavy work on the costume to make it look "lived in" and Tsuburaya was pleased with these touches. Murase added a barnacle to the head along with hand-painted veins. A vinyl coating was added and the suit dried with a blowtorch. The vinyl, however, made the Mothra suit very flammable. It had to be frequently repaired and repainted. There were eight people in total inside the pantomime horse-style suit, headed by Haruo Nakajima and Katsumi Tezuka. Younger members of the special effects staff were placed in the back. This sequence is another of the Tsuburaya unit's very best. The miniature work is stunning and, thanks to the gigantic suit, could be built larger than usual. Some of the models were built as big as 1/20th scale. Once again, the crew took photos around Tokyo to build them.

The original story and Akira Watanabe's storyboards called for Mothra to cocoon herself on the Diet Building. Eiji Tsuburaya likely realized this was redundant as they had already demolished it in *Godzilla*. Tsuburaya liked to destroy different landmarks in each film to give his sequences novelty. He opted to go with the recently built Tokyo Tower instead. Tsuburaya's staff petitioned the local government to use Tokyo Tower's blueprints for building a miniature but were declined. Undaunted, they took extensive photographs of the tower and made their own. These came in handy for future films featuring Tokyo Tower. Mothra's cocoon silk was made from a liquid polystyrene substance, a recipe that would continue to be used for decades. It was sticky and highly corrosive. Protection was required for the camera equipment and it tended to burn the skin of crew members.

The miniature Atomic Heat Ray Cannon that attacks Mothra in cocoon form was designed by Watanabe and built by Inoue. Its distinctive ray was drawn by Sadao Iizuka. As Mothra's cocoon is assaulted by the death ray, placed against a background plate of Tokyo, one of Hiroshi Mukoyama's most lifelike composites. As with larval Mothra, three versions of the adult imago Mothra prop were built. The largest and most elaborate was 18 feet long and had lightbulbs placed in its eyes to make them glow. These props were suspended from a moving rig with piano wire. The wires were attached to the center of the wings, giving them a realistic flapping motion. Typically it took ten crew members to operate the imago Mothra puppet. The wings on all three props were constructed from sturdy bamboo and the patterns on them created by painter Fuchimu Shimakura. The prop was used soon after in the comedy *Cheers! Mr. Awamori*, released later in 1961.

Toho's brass had wanted an ending set in the volcanic mountains of Kyushu where villain Clark Nelson (Jerry Ito) is blown into a volcano by Mothra. Columbia, however, had bought the rights to *Mothra* before shooting had begun. Their contract stipulated that the film's finale take place in an American-style city to make it more marketable overseas. Toho petitioned Columbia for their less expensive ending in Kyushu and Ishiro Honda's half of the scene was even shot while they waited for approval. Columbia wouldn't budge. The alternate ending's footage was discarded without even being developed and a new ending was filmed taking place in "New Kirk City," the capital of Rolisica: a fictional amalgamation of Russia and America.

Mothra's climatic attack on the city is another stupendous sequence with jaw-dropping miniature work. New Kirk City was designed by Akira Watanabe and his team, working from pictures of various American cities like New York and Chicago. As Mothra beats its wings, multitudes of cars sail through the air like leaves in the wind, with some smashing through storefront windows; miniaturized bridges collapse and boats capsize in the stormy harbor.

Mothra plays at Toho's Nichigeki Theater in Yurakucho, Tokyo

Mothra's most stunning composite appears at its end as the kidnapped Twin Fairies are returned to the beast. Mothra sits on an airport tarmac at the top of the frame as a large crowd gathers before her on the bottom. This is possibly the single greatest image Tsuburaya and Honda ever created as filmmakers. *Mothra* wound up the 10th highest-grossing domestic film in Japan that year. With its spirited performance, Tomoyuki Tanaka began to contemplate reviving Godzilla. The producer also took note of the fact that *Mothra* drew a surprising amount of children to theaters. Indeed, a six-year-old Tokyoite named **SHUSUKE KANEKO** (1955-) would see the film and be enraped by its flurry of monster spectacle.

On August 31st, 1961, Shin Toho went bankrupt. The company had fallen into financial hardship with Nobuo Nakagawa's *The Sinners of Hell* (1960) being its final production. Powerhouse producer Mitsugu Okura resigned not long before due to a union strike. Okura had planned to merge the struggling Shin Toho with Toei's television branch, but negotiations broke down. With Shin Toho dissolved, there was now one less player in the post-war Japanese film arena.

The remaining movie studios, Toho, Daiei, Toei, Shochiku and Nikkatsu, became known as "The Big Five" throughout the 1960s. With five major studios pumping out movies on a near-weekly basis and much of Hollywood and Europe's output also being released in Japan, the Japanese theatrical window during this time was swift. There were only so many screens, many owned by Toho, so films tended to come and go in a few weeks.

Eiji Tsuburaya's next assignment at Toho was a nuclear war drama produced in competition with Toei's *World War III Breaks Out*: **THE LAST WAR** [**Director:** Shue Matsubayashi - **Release Date (Japan):** October 10th, 1961]. Its original script by **SHINOBU HASHIMOTO** (1918-2018) was based on the popular novel *The First 41 Hours of World War III*. The Okadas at Toei managed to scoop up the rights before Toho and made *World War III Breaks Out*. Executives Iwao Mori and Tomoyuki Tanaka thus ordered the script reworked to remove more overt similarities to Toei's film. Like *Fail-Safe* and *Dr. Strangelove or How I Learned to Stop Worrying and Love the Bomb* (both 1964) or *The Day After* (1983) and *Threads* (1984), *World War III Breaks Out* and *The Last War* are rival nuclear war-themed productions that take wildly different approaches.

The Last War was to be directed by Kurosawa protege Hiromichi Horikawa, who was replaced by Shue Matsubayashi as Horikawa did not want to make an effects-heavy film. Matsubayashi directs with the same dour fatalism as *Storm Over the Pacific*, but this time, it's the entire world who "loses the war", not just Japan. Predating *Threads*, *The Last War* focuses on a Japanese family whose lives are doomed to be cut short by the foolish ambitions of ruthless few. It is one of the greatest speculative films about thermonuclear war, shuttling towards its devastating finale with tragic inevitability. In this way, *The Last War* sees Matsubayashi channeling the Buddhist concept that all things are transient. In his own words: "When the bombs hit Tokyo, every living thing dies and everything that has any shape changes and become something else. This is the kind of Japanese philosophy that we have inherited throughout our history - that everything changes and does not last forever."

Tsuburaya's staff poses for a photo on the set of *The Last War* (1961)

Once again, Eiji Tsuburaya crafts numerous inventive sequences of spectacular destruction; *The Last War* features no fewer than 700 effects cuts. Certain images again stand among his very finest: one a squadron of bombers flying low against a miniaturized coastal area. When Tsuburaya visited the United States, a Hollywood producer would mention these shots and ask him "How many planes did you fly?". Another of *The Last War*'s most arresting visuals features a nuclear missile fired from underwater by a submarine in the Arctic. This was accomplished by miniatures and remote-controlled pyrotechnics placed under the water of the effects pool and shot at a very high frame rate. Miniature flying bombers from early in the picture were created with radio-controlled models filmed outdoors.

Shooting miniaturized mayhem

The Last War features two fictionalized stand-ins for the United States and Soviet Union armed with miniaturized, retro-futuristic *mecha* realized via miniatures. These mechanical designs were headed by Akira Watanabe with support from Yasuyuki Inoue and a young designer named **MUTSUMI TOYOSHIMA**. Toyoshima would go on to become one of the Toho special effects unit's most trusted mecha designers. *The Last War*'s nuclear holocaust finale was heavily storyboarded by Shigeru Komatsuzaki with uncredited assistance from Tomio Sagisu. For shots of the world's landmarks being destroyed, blasts of compressed air were blown at inverted miniatures made from wafer crackers, which then exploded skywards, so it appears in the finished film. Tsuburaya's team had been using wafer models since *Godzilla;* filmed at high speed they exploded like concrete. Mice would often nibble on the model cities, much to the annoyance of the crew.

The most iconic shots of *The Last War* show a smoldering Diet Building in post-nuke Tokyo surrounded by hellish rivers of melting steel. For these shots, the miniatures were made from lead and charcoal to produce an eerie glow like immolated concrete. Similarly to *Rodan* and *The Three Treasures*, molten iron was poured onto the miniatures to create the effect of lava-like melted steel flowing through Tokyo's ruins. *The Last War*'s production used a whopping 30 tons of iron. Again, Tsuburaya borrowed an industrial blast furnace from a metalworking factory. It had to be disassembled, transported on three trucks and put back together at Toho's backlot. This process alone took ten days. Tsuburaya wanted more footage, so the crew went to shoot at two steel mills in Chiba and Kawasaki. While shooting this sequence from high up on a platform he had built, DP Sadamasa Arikawa ran the camera for a little too long and was almost injured by the intense heat emanating from the burning slag. The camera became too hot to touch and Arikawa almost passed out before jumping off the platform.

The Tokyo mushroom cloud was created through the classic technique of paint poured into a water tank and the resulting image inverted. Tsuburaya's inspiration for this ghastly sight had come from an ominous cloud of conflagration created during a Self-Defense Force exercise he had attended. Titanium tetrachloride was used for the first time by Tsuburaya's unit on *The Last War* to create the effect of smoldering, scorched cities and earth at the film's climax. They had used a mix of ammonia and sulphuric acid to create fake smoke before. The team also began to add titanium tetrachloride to the miniatures' flame burners to create more realistic smoke which soon became their standard practice. A sign of its pedigree is that *The Last War* became the Toho FX division's favorite work to pilfer for stock footage. Its fiery images would reappear in a large number of films as recent as *Godzilla vs. Destoroyah* (1995).

The Last War was Toho's second highest grossing film of 1961. It proved relevant to the Cold War tensions at the time and Japan's feeling of helplessness in the face of them. Less than three weeks after *The Last War* was released, the Soviet Union tested Tsar Bomba, the most powerful nuclear weapon in history. A year later, the Cuban Missile Crisis took place and nearly brought *The Last War*'s speculations to reality.

Masaichi Nagata's Daiei, meanwhile, was at work on **BUDDHA [Director: KENJI MISUMI** (1921-1975) - **Release Date (Japan):** November 1st, 1961]. *Buddha* was a prestige production and the first Japanese film to be exhibited in 70mm. Nagata was inspired by the success of *Nichiren and the Great Mongol Invasion* along with Hollywood biblical epics such as *Ben Hur* (1959) and the currently-in-production *King of Kings*. As Daiei had been the trend-setter with color film, Nagata wanted to beat the other companies in making the first Japanese 70mm picture.

Beginning principal photography in April of 1961 at Daiei's Kyoto branch, *Buddha* was not shot in 70mm. Cinematographers Hiroshi Imai and

Kazuo Miyagawa used a 35mm VistaVision camera bought from Hollywood with an anamorphic lens attached. As VistaVision's pulldown (see glossary) is vertical rather than horizontal and uses a larger portion of the frame, the quality is almost as sharp as shooting in 70mm. The footage was then shipped to England for printing to 70mm, as no labs in Japan were equal to the task. The shoot was tense as even one "NG" was costly. According to Fujio Morita, who assisted the two cinematographers, the prints for *Buddha* were not processed properly and less sharp than they should have been. The British lab also handled the prints' sound mixes with unfortunate results, much to composer Akira Ifukube's consternation.

The special effects in *Buddha* were handled by Toru Matoba with optical contributions from Tomio Sagisu's P-Productions. Yoshiyuki Kuroda acted as Matoba's assistant and Michio Mikami also took part. Mikami had left Tsuburaya's unit and moved to Daiei two years prior. The effects shots are subtle for much of the picture and limited to process work. The most memorable sequence is the iconic moment where Siddhartha (Kojiro Hongo) sits beneath the Bodhi tree, featuring optical compositions by P-Productions and demonic minions modeled by Fuminori Ohashi. These look forward to the *yokai* creatures in future Daiei films like *Spook Warfare* (1968). There is the occasional use of miniatures and dolls as doubles. Matoba's unit finally takes stage in the final reel of the two-and-a-half hour epic with a sequence featuring an earthquake destroying a temple and city, liberating Buddha's followers in a way that foreshadows the *Majin* films. This splendid scene, which features superb miniatures, nearly matches Tsuburaya's work in quality.

Buddha's final shots are visually stunning and make use of optical effects courtesy of P-Productions and technician Yoshio Watanabe. The Nagatas and Daiei's brass did not want to trust the optical shots of this prestigious production to an upstart company. They planned to create the effect of flowers blooming thanks to the miracle of Buddha practically using a motor. This could not be effectively pulled off. Thus Sagisu and Watanabe were allowed to create the final shots mixing live-action elements with animation. To create these cuts, the physical shooting was done first and the undeveloped film double exposed with the animated effects. It was a difficult process that had to be timed with a stopwatch. These shots were praised by none other than Sagisu and Watanabe's former mentor Eiji Tsuburaya, who was impressed with how beautifully they had combined animated and live-action elements. P-Productions' work on *Buddha* put them on the map as a force to be reckoned with in the tokusatsu industry. Japan's special effects cinema was now experiencing an impressive ascent in popularity. The following year, the industry would continue this trend by pitting monster moviedom's two greatest behemoths against one another in a now-legendary blockbuster.

VIII.
__1962 - 1963__
昭和三十七・三十八

Tsuburaya (left) and Sadamasa Arikawa (right) inspect a model

At Toho, the next special effects extravaganza was the sci-fi spectacular **GORATH [Director:** Ishiro Honda - **Release Date (Japan):** March 21st, 1962]. Another film which sees Honda and Tsuburaya's units in perfect balance, *Gorath* features the former's most earnest humanist elements and the latter's finest miniature work. As in *Mothra*, Eiji Tsuburaya was given one of his biggest budgets and longest shooting schedules yet. His unit's work is consistently inventive. When *Gorath* comes alive, it is a tautly made picture that puts Pal's *When Worlds Collide* (1951) to shame. Ishiro Honda took this project to heart as he had a longstanding interest in scientific study. During scripting, Honda and his assistant Koji Kajita conducted earnest research for nearly a month at Tokyo University's astronomy department, consulting with astrophysics professor Takeo Hatanaka and his assistant Genichiro Horii.

The eponymous Gorath, a planet-destroying star that threatens Earth, was made from fire-proof acrylic cloth with a powerful lighting mechanism placed inside it. The miniatures for the spaceships *Hayabusa* and *Otori* were sleekly designed by Akira Watanabe and built by Yasuyuki Inoue. Around three feet tall, they were equipped with propane burners for their launch scenes. The space shots are stunningly composed, besting the team's previous work on *Battle in Outer Space*. Certain images of sprawling space station infrastructure even look forward to visuals in Stanley Kubrick's *2001: A Space Odyssey* (1968). The *Otori* features a docking bay with a rectangular door akin to Station V. It is known that during *2001*'s lengthy pre-production, Kubrick obsessively watched space films from all over the world, including Japan.

FX art staff tend to miniature ships in seas of styrofoam

For miniature shots of the Antarctic, icebergs were crafted from styrofoam, then a novel material. The miniature Antarctic base set, designed and engineered by Yasuyuki Inoue, was the largest constructed at Toho to date - taking up the entire floorspace of its biggest soundstage. This at first annoyed Tsuburaya, who had trouble finding a position for DP Arikawa to put the camera. He said to Inoue: "You built it like this to amuse yourself, didn't you?". The atomic-powered propulsion rockets placed on Antarctica to move the Earth from Gorath's path were in reality fueled by propane. It took 200 cylinders worth, making the set brutally hot. The male crew members often shed their shirts on the effects set as the temperature shot up to 120 degrees. Poor Keiko Suzuki, however, as a woman on an otherwise male crew, did not have this luxury. She dealt with the set's brutal heat by wearing light shirts and jeans which she often cut into makeshift shorts. In her own words: "I couldn't think of myself as a woman or I couldn't work".

One shot, a wide canvas of the moon gliding across a miniature sky and landscape towards collision with Gorath, is downright painterly. The flooding sequences at the climax of *Gorath* are among the most impressive staged by the Tsuburaya unit. For shots at the end of the picture depicting submerged cities, the crew placed miniatures in the nearby Arakawa river. As the models were made of wood and lightweight, they would often float away, much to everyone's annoyance. An Osaka Castle miniature left over from *Daredevil in the Castle* was used for this sequence.

Gorath's flaws are mildly superfluous elements. Tomoyuki Tanaka insisted that the picture include a giant monster: a prehistoric walrus called Maguma, awakened by the propulsion units. Maguma's suit was constructed by Teizo Toshimitsu and the Yagi Brothers with assistance from Eizo Kaimai and Keizo Murase. Murase built Maguma's tusks out of the then-novel FRP (Fiber Reinforced Plastic). Tsuburaya praised him, believing the tusks to be made of ivory. A small puppet version, built by Kaimai, was used for pyrotechnic shots of the creature's death. Ishiro Honda was opposed to the inclusion of Maguma. While a lavish, quality monster sequence from Tsuburaya's team, it stops the picture in its tracks. Honda would later say that *Gorath* was his favorite film he ever directed "except for that monster".

On *Gorath*, Tsuburaya gained a pair of new apprentices: **TERUYOSHI NAKANO** (1935-) and **KOICHI KAWAKITA** (1942-2014). Nakano, nicknamed "Shokei", was born in Japanese-occupied Manchuria. He started work at Toho as an AD for the main units. Coordinating with Tsuburaya's unit on *Submarine I-57: Will Not Surrender*, Nakano was inspired by their creativity and developed an interest in special effects. Nakano was finally allowed to join Tsuburaya's team as second assistant director with *Gorath*. His job as AD was mainly to coordinate the different departments within the unit and make sure they all were on schedule. It was a challenging job that came with pressure. If one department fell behind, the entire shoot could be delayed. In Nakano's own words in *Monsters Are Attacking Tokyo:* "At first, I hated what I was doing, but later on I realized special effects are the core of movie-making." The young Kawakita, as a teenager in Tokyo, had seen *The*

Mysterians and was captivated, longing to follow in his idol Tsuburaya's footsteps. Koichi Kawakita had interned at Toho and dropped out of college to become part of the special effects department with *Gorath*. For now, Kawakita worked as an assistant on the optical shots. Under the tutelage of Tsuburaya and Sadamasa Arikawa, both young men would become luminaries of the tokusatsu medium in the decades to come.

By this time, Eiji Tsuburaya was known by younger members of his staff as *"Oyaji-san"* which can be translated as "Pops" or "The Old Man". Tsuburaya wore a suit, tie and fedora to his special effects set. It was joked that he had no fashion sense, though Tsuburaya was respected to the point that he was never called *oyaji* to his face. Nonetheless, this affectionate nickname stuck. Once the sound of Tsuburaya's car could be heard in the Toho backlot, his crew would jump into action knowing he would soon be on set. They could even smell him walking onto the set, as Tsuburaya was a notoriously heavy smoker. Like many Japanese directors in his day, he chain-smoked pack after pack while helming his cinematic mayhem.

Eiji Tsuburaya often withdrew inward when brainstorming ideas for sequences. Once, according to Teruyoshi Nakano, he was so deep in thought about a current film project as he returned home from Toho's lot that he didn't recognize his wife Masano. Despite his age, it was as if he never tired. Tsuburaya was so obsessed with editing that he would often bring a mobile Moviola, to view film footage on set. Whenever his crew were busy setting up complex shots, he'd sit in a makeshift editing booth and start cutting the previous day's footage together with the editing staff and script supervisor Keiko Suzuki. Oftentimes, Tsuburaya would decide to shoot additional coverage as he looked at and edited the footage. He would even bring the Moviola to locations from time to time.

Tsuburaya soon took a vacation to the United States and visited Los Angeles. He would tour several of the studios and meet with none other than **GEORGE PAL** (1908-1980) himself along with Hollywood special effects guru **A. ARNOLD GILLESPIE** (1899-1978). Tsuburaya would also become fascinated with a state-of-the-art piece of technology employed by only one Hollywood studio: Disney. This was the Oxberry optical printer, which could composite up to six layers of film with a clarity and versatility that stunned Tsuburaya.

Moving the full-sized Whale God prop took a crane

Back in Japan, **THE WHALE GOD** [**Director:** Tokuzo Tanaka - **Release Date (Japan):** July 15th, 1962] was released, another underrated gem combining the period film and tokusatsu genres. Produced at Daiei's Tokyo branch, it was based on a novela by Koichiro Uno, a controversial writer known for his erotica. *The Whale God* strongly evokes Herman Melville's classic *Moby Dick* and is a well-produced maritime monster flick with dramatic focus. The stark monochrome images and sense of nautical horror lend a haunting beauty to *The Whale God*. The character development is engaging and its special effects sequences are well executed and plentiful.

The effects scenes were supervised by Toru Matoba. Originally, Yonesaburo Tsukiji was to work on *The Whale God* and Matoba was to helm the FX unit on the historical epic *The Great Wall* which was in production simultaneously. Their roles were switched at the last minute. *The Whale God* features elaborate whaling sequences in which Matoba's unit takes center stage. These superb scenes are nearly Tsuburaya quality and equal Augie Lohman's work on John Huston's *Moby Dick* (1956). Most spectacular is the climax where rival spearmen Shaki (Kojiro Hongo) and Kishu (*Zatoichi*'s Shintaro Katsu) attempt to slay the titular beast on the open seas.

The Whale God itself was built in three sizes. A full-sized hundred foot whale prop was constructed by Fuminori Ohashi, mainly used for shots of the actors climbing on and spearing it. Another, close to twenty-foot whale was also built by Ohashi, along with a smaller miniature version with a puppet snout by Ryosaku Takayama. The large whale props had to be moved with cranes. Matoba's sequences could not be filmed in Tokyo as Daiei had no FX pool there. They were thus mainly shot at Daiei's Kyoto facility in the special effects pool built for *Nichiren and the Great Mongol Invasion*. The Melvillian touch of seabirds circling in the skies to herald the Whale God's appearance was created through cel and optical animation. This and other visual effects were handled by Tomio Sagisu and P-Productions.

The next special effects release was a much-ballyhooed monster picture from Toho: **KING KONG VS. GODZILLA [Director:** Ishiro Honda **- Release Date (Japan):** August 11th, 1962]. Godzilla, after seven years of absence, was brought back to the screen in Tohoscope and Eastman color and pitted against Hollywood's most celebrated monster titan, King Kong. *King Kong vs. Godzilla* actually owed its genesis to *King Kong*'s own special effects wizard, Willis O'Brien. By 1960, O'Brien had developed a proposal entitled *King Kong and Prometheus*, pitting Kong against a Frankenstein-like creature. O'Brien partnered with a producer named John Beck, who hired screenwriter George Worthing Yates to flesh out a screenplay. The project was nearly greenlit with Nathan Juran, best known for programmers like *Attack of the 50 Foot Woman* and the Harryhausen fantasy film *The 7th Voyage of Sinbad* (both 1958), at the helm.

What happened next is the stuff of cinema legend. As the project would employ costly stop motion, Hollywood studios were hesitant to give it the go-ahead. Beck began shopping it around overseas and found one interested buyer in Japan: Toho. Tomoyuki Tanaka and company jumped at the chance to make a King Kong film on the heels of *Mothra*. To use the character, Toho had to pay an exorbitant 80 million yen to RKO. This alone equaled the cost of about three average Toho productions and gave them the rights to King Kong for five years. The project's script, however, would be rewritten from scratch by Shinichi Sekizawa. The Frankenstein monster, "Ginko", would be supplanted by Toho's own monster king Godzilla. Merian C. Cooper, director of the 1933 *King Kong*, was bitterly opposed to his brainchild starring in Japanese films. A year later, Cooper would sue Beck, Toho and distributor Universal to prevent the American release, but the suit was thrown out.

One of the first kaiju films made with a child audience in mind, *King Kong vs. Godzilla* is far from the finest Honda/Tsuburaya collaboration. Perhaps its major flaw is the infamously poor Kong suit, but there are superb sequences. Making a King Kong film was a passion project for Eiji Tsuburaya. To take part in it, he even postponed work on another pet project: a new adaptation of *Tale of the Bamboo Cutter*. Tsuburaya opted to take the Toho kaiju cycle in a lighter-hearted direction than previous entries. Godzilla and King Kong's climactic battle would not be staged as a death match but with a comic flair akin to professional wrestling. An influence was beloved pro-wrestler Rikidozan's 1958 match against Hungarian Lou Thesz. Such light-hearted monster theatrics were a controversial decision among the special effects staff and opposed by Ishiro Honda. Tomoyuki Tanaka, however, was in favor. *Mothra*'s box office receipts had shown him that children were a viable audience for these pictures. Honda would infuse a comic self awareness into his half of the film, creating a cunning satire mocking post-war consumerism and channeling Toho's popular *Company President* series.

The film's maligned King Kong suit was created by Teizo Toshimitsu and the Yagi Brothers. The modeling team had a difficult time creating a suit that Tsuburaya was happy with and the first one was rejected. One of RKO's stipulations for Toho using the Kong character was that the design was not allowed to resemble the 1933 version. Thus Toshmitsu sculpted the masks using a Japanese macaque as influence rather than gorilla. One Kong head was made for expressive close-ups with a moving mouth and facial expressions and the other for wide shots requiring less facial movement. The Yagi Brothers as usual built the body with assistance from Eizo Kaimai. The body was covered in yak hair which Kaimai hand-dyed brown. Two sets of arms were also built for Kong, one pair longer to emphasize an ape-like posture, operated by small rods inside the suit. The other pair were normal sized and used for shots requiring more dexterity from suit actor Shoichi Hirose, such as hand-to-hand combat with Godzilla. Hirose had to be sewn directly into the costume to keep the zipper from appearing on screen. As a result, he had to spend long periods of time inside. Hirose also nearly drowned while shooting the ending where

Godzilla and Kong plummet into the Pacific Ocean. An upper body hand puppet of Kong with marionette enhancement was built. This was along with two smaller full-body models, one for a brief stop motion cutaway and the other for scenes of Kong being airlifted. A full-sized prop of Kong's hand was also built for use on Honda's unit for a scene where the monster kidnaps ingenue Fumiko (Mie Hama). In Hama's own words in Stuart Galbraith's *Monsters Are Attacking Tokyo:* "I didn't know what was going on. I had no idea what it was all going to look like."

Eiji Tsuburaya (right) shoots with a live octopus

Godzilla's design was heavily altered and a new suit was built. In order to give it a more dinosaur-like appearance, the head was reworked with the ears no longer included. The feet were given three toes instead of four and the dorsal fins were enlarged. This would become the standard for all the Godzilla suits until 1984. For the first time, the suit was made entirely from plaster molding with no usage of a bamboo or metal skeleton. State-of-the-art materials were employed including silicone and urethane, the latter used to make Godzilla's outer skin and tail. The suit's color was finished with an ink coating. This was also the first Godzilla suit with a mouth that could open and close via radio control. The eyes and nails were made from a vinyl polyester resin. In addition, a full-body miniature was built for wide and stop motion shots, as well as a Guignol puppet, footage of which was largely discarded save for a single close-up in the Arctic base attack. For a shot of Godzilla breaking out of the iceberg, Katsumi Tezuka briefly took over the role from Haruo Nakajima.

The work of Tsuburaya's unit on *King Kong vs. Godzilla* is brought down by the quality of the Kong suit but is otherwise exuberant. The Earth miniature from *Battle in Outer Space* is comically used in the film's first shots and the iceberg scene with submarine "*Seahawk*" were shot in Toho's Big Pool. Godzilla's attack on a Soviet Arctic base is a quality scene and there are stunning process shots in the Faro Island segments. *King Kong vs. Godzilla*'s strongest segments are midway. The highlight is a well-staged sequence where a giant octopus attacks Faro Island and is fended off by Kong. Tsuburaya had long wanted to make a film with a giant octopus and took this scene to heart. It's a tour de force combining Honda's actor footage, miniatures, two octopus puppets and numerous live cephalopods procured from local fishermen. These proved difficult to control and were, unfortunately, prodded around the models with pokes from cigarettes, blasts of heated air and bright lamps. After shooting, they were cooked and devoured by Tsuburaya and his crew. The best shots feature the Faro natives, armed with spears, standing before the enormous octopus.

Eiji Tsuburaya stands before a model of tourist resort Atami Castle

Akira Watanabe and Yasuyuki Inoue's miniature team was kept busy as usual. By this time, Toho's FX art department worked in a building on the far side of Toho's backlot. At peak, a staff of 30-40 designers and carpenters all worked under Watanabe and Inoue. One of the biggest miniatures they built for *King Kong vs. Godzilla* was the *Venture*-style freighter that attempts to bring Kong to Japan. This model was over 30 feet long and, like the miniature ships in Toho's war films, powered by its own motor. While shooting a stunt with an exploding helicopter during Godzilla and Kong's first battle, the Tsuburaya unit had one of its worst on-set accidents. The pyrotechnics flew out of the miniature and went off in the face of camera operator **TAKAO TSURUMI** (1939-). Thankfully, he was able to wet his face using a nearby miniature river, thus avoiding injury.

Tsuburaya blocks a shot before a miniaturized Tokyo

A segment where Godzilla attacks a train in Hokkaido is also quality. There are numerous beautifully-executed miniature shots such as King Kong advancing to Tokyo during the night. What appears to be a seamless composite shot features Self-Defense Force soldiers standing in the foreground as Godzilla advances during a military operation. This was not a process shot; it was in fact done in-camera with the actors on the special effects stage. The scene where Kong is airlifted from Tokyo to Mount Fuji to battle Godzilla is another standout. Tsuburaya hired P-Productions to rotoscope silhouettes of Self-Defense Force soldiers for the composite shots. Footage of Godzilla encountering the Daikannon statue at Takasaki was filmed but unused; it was decided that having the statue, made in the likeness of a revered Buddhist deity, menaced in a monster film could be considered sacrilegious.

For Godzilla and Kong's final confrontation, a single cut of stop motion was used as a nod to Willis O'Brien. This was animated by Koichi Takano with support from Sadao Iizuka. Suit actors Nakajima and Hirose choreographed Godzilla and Kong's brawl themselves, using elements taken from pro wrestling. During the shooting of *King Kong vs. Godzilla*, an American producer visiting Toho's lot, perhaps John Beck, offered Nakajima a contract as a Hollywood stuntman. Nakajima was tempted but Tsuburaya talked him out of it, telling him, according to an interview in Steve Ryfle's *Japan's Favorite Mon-Star*, "I cannot make Godzilla movies without you".

The climax is another memorable segment as Godzilla and Kong destroy Atami Castle. Despite its appearance, this castle is not a historical relic but a then-recently built tourist attraction adjacent to a seaside resort. The miniature was close to ten feet tall and its set was built outdoors near Toho's Big Pool. Godzilla and Kong ferociously destroying such a brazen tourist trap is a fitting capstone for in a film satirizing post-war consumerism. Of course, the outcome of the picture's ending was kept a closely guarded secret at Toho, though most moviegoers figured it would be a tie. *King Kong vs. Godzilla* was a massive blockbuster, drawing in the biggest crowds for a domestic film since *Emperor Meiji and the Great Russo-Japanese War*. To date it remains the most attended Godzilla entry in Japan. The massive box office success of *King Kong vs. Godzilla* was the point where the Godzilla series formally began.

Having gained considerable momentum themselves, Daiei released **THE GREAT WALL [Director: SHIGEO TANAKA** (1907-1992) - **Release Date (Japan):** November 1st, 1962]. Made at the Tokyo branch, the picture is another prestigious 70mm production a la *Buddha* and came about thanks to that film's success. *The Great Wall* revolves around legendary Chinese emperor Qin Shi Huang (Shintaro Katsu) who brutally unified China and fortified the titular wall.

The special effects work, handled by Yonesaburo Tsukiji, is all but absent in the picture's first hour save for the occasional process shot. His unit mainly comes into play for a single extravagant sequence where, ala the biblical Tower of Babel, the Great Wall is struck by lightning and broken. The miniature work in this scene is stupendous and even better than Toru Matoba's in *Buddha*. Only two days later, Toho would release a prestige picture of their own entitled **CHUSHINGURA** [**Director:** Hiroshi Inagaki - **Release Date (Japan):** November 3rd, 1962]. Based on the fabled folktale of the "47 Ronin" who avenged their former master, it contained a number of process shots created by Eiji Tsuburaya.

Eiji Tsuburaya stages nautical warfare aboard a miniature replica of the legendary battleship *Yamato*

Tsuburaya's next major effects spectacle was the war film **ATTACK SQUADRON** [**AKA: WINGS OF THE PACIFIC** - **Director:** Shue Matsubayashi - **Release Date (Japan):** January 3rd, 1963] from Toho. *Attack Squadron* is set this time during the doomed final months of Pacific War, giving Matsubayashi plenty of opportunity to infuse the film with his usual mournful fatalism. While the budget was lower than *Storm Over the Pacific*, *Attack Squadron* is still a lavish production with some of the Tsuburaya unit's very finest war movie work. The miniature photography is impressive with a stronger emphasis on aircraft than ships. The SFX modeling team built around 300 miniature planes for the film and many were flown through RC and control line techniques.

Rather than the Mitsubishi Zero, the main aircraft featured are of the lesser known but more fearsome Kawanishi Shiden class. To shoot the extensive scenes of the Shiden fighters taking off, one of Toho's effects pools was drained and turned into a makeshift runway. The miniature planes were pulled forward with wires attached to a truck. Tsuburaya's team also built an enormous 1/15 scale model of the iconic battleship *Yamato*. Close to 60 feet long, it was so large it had to be photographed at Lake Yamanaka in Yamanashi Prefecture instead of the Big Pool. Aerial shots of the miniature *Yamato* were taken by Sadamasa Arikawa with a helicopter. Tsuburaya was insecure about these shots as he felt the lake water had a different opacity than the ocean and only a bit of the helicopter footage was used.

Tsuburaya's aerial sequences are his most stunning yet. An American attack on a transport plane and a dogfight over the Japanese mainland are particularly impressive scenes. There's a stunning wide composite shot of Iwo Jima hit by American bombers. Other superb images include an eagle's-eye view in midair of fighter planes flying against the landscape from above and swarming like flies as they battle. For shots of the Shiden fighters flying in formation, operator Fumio Nakashiro hung piano wires and miniature planes from a small, cut-down tree. Only the tree was moved during shooting, giving the effect of miniature planes flying through the air in formation. For Nakashiro's first time rigging this effect, he and his assistant worked through the night. The following morning, the perfectionistic Tsuburaya had Nakashiro redo the rigging. *Attack Squadron* is capped in a hauntingly beautiful and creatively executed finale and is among Tsuburaya's finest work on a war picture. *Attack Squadron* would also be Teruyoshi Nakano's first film as Tsuburaya's main assistant director.

On April 12th, 1963, Eiji Tsuburaya finally realized his long-held dream of founding his own company. For years, he had hoped to expand Tsuburaya Visual Effects Institute into its own firm, doing freelance effects work for the studios, producing television programs and mentoring a new generation of artisans. Thanks to his clout, Tsuburaya was able to cancel his exclusive contract with Toho, though he would, of course, continue as the principal director of the special effects unit there. His sons Hajime and Noboru took part in the foundation of Tsuburaya Visual Effects Productions, soon to be known as Tsuburaya Productions or Tsuburaya Pro. Tsuburaya would also bring his young disciples Koichi Takano, Minoru

Nakano and Kazuo Sagawa on board. He also welcomed a young screenwriter named **TETSUO KINJO** (1938-1976) into the fold. Only in his mid-20s, Kinjo was a native Okinawan who had survived the Battle of Okinawa. Mentored by Shinichi Sekizawa, he would in time become a skilled writer. Through Sekizawa, Kinjo had met Hajime and Noboru Tsuburaya.

Tsuburaya Productions

Eiji Tsuburaya had long been eager to branch into television. His family had been among the first Japanese to own a TV. Neighbors would often come to the Tsuburayas' house to marvel at their television set. At his new company, Tsuburaya began to develop a novel concept for a science fiction TV show entitled *Woo*. *Woo* was to involve a nomadic giant alien creature coming to Earth and forming an alliance with humanity, defending the planet from malevolent space monsters. Soon, Shigeru Komatsuzaki had created some striking conceptual art and story meetings commenced. As Woo itself was cloud-like in form, Tsuburaya knew he'd need state-of-the-art optical printing technology to bring it to life. He thus ordered an Oxberry 1200 series printer from Hollywood at immense cost. *Woo* wound up canceled in pre-production. Its potential station, Fuji TV, thought the project was getting too expensive. Tsuburaya was even asked to cancel his order for the Oxberry printer, but it had already been shipped. He would order another Oxberry 1900 unit for use at Toho later that year. Regardless, the concept of *Woo* would become the basis for a more iconic Tsuburaya property a few years down the road.

In the meantime, Tsuburaya kept busy at Toho. His next film was **SIEGE OF FORT BISMARCK** [Director: **KENGO FURUSAWA** (1919-1997) - **Release Date (Japan):** May 29th, 1963]. *Siege of Fort Bismarck* is another inventive war movie spectacle on

Tsuburaya's end. A rare Japanese film set during World War I, it depicts the 1914 Battle of Qingdao that pitted Japanese forces against Imperial Germany. *Siege of Fort Bismarck* is an action-packed adventure and, unusually for an entry in Toho's war picture cycle, depicts the country on the right side of history. It was another dream project for Tsuburaya. Having grown up in awe of WWI aviators, he certainly welcomed the opportunity. His team constructed miniaturized biplanes sporting four-foot wingspans; these included the MF-11 Shorthorn and the German Rumpler Taube. For Furusawa's unit, full-scale biplanes were built. The aerial dogfights are once again well executed.

Tsuburaya's unit stages an explosive finale with a model train

The final 20 minutes of the picture are stunning, featuring spirited action direction from Furusawa and Tsuburaya's finest-caliber miniature work. There are impressively detailed miniaturized landscapes and a naval battle that looks forward to Tsuburaya's later work on *Battle of the Japan Sea* (1969). An enormous miniature set of Fort Bismarck itself was built outdoors near Mount Fuji.

Siege of Fort Bismarck also features some of Tsuburaya and gunpowder master Kyuzo Yamamoto's best-coordinated pyrotechnic work. The explosive finale was shot with multiple cameras, with Sadamasa Arikawa once again manning an airborne camera from a helicopter. As with Honda and Matsubayashi, Tsuburaya's unit maintains an excellent creative synergy with director Furusawa in the picture's climax.

Daiei's next special effects production was **WIND VELOCITY 75 METERS** [**AKA: TYPHOON REPORTER** - **Director:** Shigeo Tanaka - **Release Date (Japan):** July 13th, 1963], produced at their Tokyo branch. The special effects unit was once again managed by Yonesaburo Tsukiji. It is far more Shigeo Tanaka's picture, a melodramatic political thriller involving an intrepid reporter (*Super Giant*'s Ken Utsui), dealing with corporate intrigue and gangsters. Tsukiji's work on *Wind Velocity 75 Meters* is fairly invisible throughout, limited to an exploding building. The contributions of Tsukiji's FX unit only kick in during the final ten minutes.

Executive Masaichi Nagata (right) visits the miniaturized Ginza district to be deluged

In the last five, it rips through director Tanaka's melodrama like the typhoon itself tears through Tokyo's Ginza district. Dominating *Wind Velocity 75 Meters*' final five minutes is a masterfully executed tokusatsu hurricane sequence with spectacular miniature work. To create the typhoon, Tsukiji's unit dropped a whopping 15 tons of water onto the miniaturized Ginza. *Wind Velocity 75 Meters*' finale would be the finest special effects sequence ever staged at Daiei's Tokyo branch. Yonesaburo Tsukiji shows himself to be a master of miniatures, though monsters would prove more challenging.

Next from Toho came **MATANGO** [**AKA: ATTACK OF THE MUSHROOM PEOPLE** - **Director:** Ishiro Honda - **Release Date (Japan):** August 11th, 1963]. The tale of castaways washing ashore a deserted island populated by mutagenic mushrooms, *Matango* is a hallucinogenic horror film dominated by Honda's unit. Like *The Human Vapor*, it is among the most actor driven of Honda's genre pictures. Writer Takeshi Kimura and actors Akira Kubo, Kenji Sahara and Kumi Mizuno all considered *Matango* a favorite of the films they worked on. Ishiro Honda was insecure about the film's editing between its location shooting and sets on the Toho backlot, but came around to *Matango* in later years. Honda longed to make a darker picture; a film mocking the materialism now seen in post-war Japan.

Eiji Tsuburaya (right) and Ishiro Honda (center right) co-direct actors Kenji Sahara, Yoshio Tsuchiya, Akira Kubo and others

Like *Godzilla*, *Matango*'s genesis was inspired in part by news headlines. A group of wealthy youths had taken a parent's yacht and sailed it too far into the Pacific Ocean. Lost at sea, they wound up needing rescue. Reports of ships vanishing in the Bermuda Triangle also got Honda and screenwriter Kimura's imaginations going. Loosely based on a 1907 short story by William Hope Hodgson entitled *A Voice in the Night*, *Matango* is a misanthropic yarn evoking Sartre's *No Exit* and Golding's *Lord of the Flies*. *Matango* was not the first adaptation of *A Voice in the Night*, however: it had been previously adapted into a 1958 episode of the American anthology series *Suspicion*.

Ishiro Honda would mainly shoot his half on location at Oshima and Hachijo islands, wherein the cast and crew had to contend with the scourges of venomous snakes and giant centipedes. Tsuburaya and members of his unit would occasionally accompany Honda to the island locations for background plates. For *Matango*'s shoot, the distinction between Honda and

Tsuburaya's units was less clear. Many sequences were largely co-directed by the pair. Fresh off *Siege of Fort Bismarck*, Eiji Tsuburaya launched straight into work on *Matango*. He creates atmospheric, phantasmagorical images rivaling Euro horror maestros like Terence Fisher, Mario Bava and Jacques Tourneur. The effects team were allowed to expand into more experimental territory on *Matango*, working hard to elevate it beyond its perceived B-picture status.

Matango was one of Tsuburaya's first films to use front projection rather than rear. The old process would project an image onto a screen behind the camera. This process uses a projector placed in front of the screen and closer to the camera. Combined with better screens made of road sign material, the result is brighter and crisper. An early scene featuring the film's ensemble cast aboard a yacht was filmed on Toho's soundstage with footage of the ocean front projected behind them. The result is stellar for the 1960s. On *Matango*, Tsuburaya would also employ his newly purchased Oxberry printer. The optical printer is used for many fanciful composites, including a stunning shot where the castaways eye a derelict ship wrecked on the island's shore. This shot mixed footage filmed on Oshima Island by Honda with a miniature, background plates and matte work. A miniature was also built for the castaways' yacht the *Albatross*. It was large and actually sailable, its scenes shot in Toho's Big Pool. Tsuburaya's team also built a miniaturized Tokyo cityscape for the wraparound scenes shot by Honda's unit of Akira Kubo's character confined to a psych ward.

Matango's conceptual designs were created by Shigeru Komatsuzaki. Komatsuzaki came up with the visual motifs for the fungus monsters themselves, combining the aesthetics of atomic horror and traditional *yokai*. *Matango*'s production design is superb. Both units' art directors Shigekazu Ikuno and Akira Watanabe kept in good communication throughout to make sure their work was visually consistent. The derelict ship's walls were made to appear fungus covered with rubber glue spiked with acetone. This mixture was later diluted and used to make the spores which fill the air in later scenes. Ishiro Honda instructed the film's actors to pretend the sets smelled awful. Indeed, between the magnificently disgusting sets and the actors' convincing performances, the viewer can very nearly smell the dank, stagnant aroma of mold and rust. For sequences deep in the island's jungle, Fuchimu Shimakura painted some of his best, most lifelike backdrops.

The Matango themselves were named after the *mamadango,* an edible strain of earthstar mushroom native to Tsuburaya's own Fukushima Prefecture. Teizo Toshimitsu modeled and built the on-set mushrooms, creature suits and prosthetics. Toshimitsu and his modeling team worked feverishly for ten days to complete them. Actors Kenji Sahara and Yoshio Tsuchiya thought the mushrooms on set looked ridiculous but were sold when they saw the finished picture. The Matango prosthetics and suits were constructed entirely of latex and, depending on the complexity of the designs, some were made in four pieces with others made in one.

Kuichiro Kishida's team lights a moody scene

The largest Hero Matango suit inhabited by Haruo Nakajima was a whopping ten feet tall. It was, however, one of the lighter Toho monster suits and weighed under 70 pounds per its latex build. The head was based on the *shimeji* mushroom, which is popular as a delicacy in Japan. The Matango suits were finished with a solution made from melted Scotch tape and fluorescent paint. Toshimitsu was particularly proud of his work on the "Skulking Transitional Matango" as portrayed by actor **HIDEYO AMAMOTO** (1926-2003). Amamoto, well known for his Marxism and love of Spanish culture, had lunch at Toho's cafetaria fully made up, giving the staff quite the fright. The FX and modeling staff were at a loss with how best to disfigure actor Kumi Mizuno. They felt guilty at making such a beautiful actress look ugly. It was Ishiro Honda who suggested that rather than turn grotesque, Mizuno's character Mami Sekiguchi should become more beautiful and seductive. Tsuburaya loved the idea and said "Honda! That's it!".

The shots of the mushrooms burgeoning from the ground are the Tsuburaya unit's greatest showstopper. They were a difficult technical feat. At first, the effects director considered using cotton candy-style spun sugar but his team found the best results with a liquid nylon solution. Poured into cans, this mixture produced mushroom-like shapes. Smaller mushrooms were made with soft drink cans, medium fungi with corned beef cans and the largest with paint cans. The solution expanded very quickly and was shot at a high frame rate. The edible mushrooms consumed by the actors were *mochi* rice pastries. The mochi itself was made by a local confectionery shop who were confounded by the special effects staff's continuous orders. It was then hand-crafted into mushrooms by the modeling team. They added flavors to the mochi as a playful prank and often stole some for dessert after lunch. *Matango* was a critical and commercial failure. As a result, Toho would abandon more horror-oriented fare featuring *kaijin* (human-sized monsters) and double down on giant beasts. It was also, sadly, Ishiro Honda's final horror movie. *Matango*, however, would go on to develop a strong cult status in both Japan and the United States.

At Toho, Tsuburaya next tackled the adventure picture **SAMURAI PIRATE [AKA: THE LOST WORLD OF SINBAD - Director:** Senkichi Taniguchi - **Release Date (Japan):** October 26th, 1963]. An Arabian Nights-inspired tale with Toshiro Mifune as Sinbad-like pirate Sukezamon, Tsuburaya's contributions are subtle early on. There's a stormy shipwreck sequence early on similar to a recent scene in *Matango*. This is along with fanciful process shots, a life-like castle and miniature ships shot in Toho's Big Pool. *Samurai Pirate* features clever optical wizardry as an evil witch (Hideyo Amamoto) turns her victims into stone, Medusa-style. Creative optical animation is also employed for a shapeshifting old wizard (Ichiro Arishima) and his transformations. The best executed scene features a chase between the wizard and witch who have transformed; the former into a fly, the latter into an airborne spiked ball. This was achieved by combining optical animation and traveling mattes.

Another sequence where the effects work takes center stage is an impressive segment where Sukezamon flies into the castle on a kite-like glider. This scene feels like a demonstration of Tsuburaya's new Oxberry printer and its capabilities. His fledgling company would also take their first freelance commission around this time for **ALONE ACROSS THE PACIFIC** [Director: **KON ICHIKAWA** (1915-2008) - **Release Date (Japan):** October 27th, 1963], released a day later by Nikkatsu. Based on Kenichi Hori's book about his boat voyage to San Francisco the previous year, Tsuburaya Productions created a maritime storm sequence for the film.

Eiji Tsuburaya (right) and crew lens models

As *Samurai Pirate* was released, the assiduous Eiji Tsuburaya was already shooting his next project for Toho: **ATRAGON** [Director: Ishiro Honda - **Release Date (Japan):** December 22, 1963]. Loosely based on Shunro Oshikawa's 1899 novel *The Undersea Warship, Atragon* began production in September with rushed but extensive story meetings between Honda and Tsuburaya. Honda's half boasts some of his most quintessential humanist subtext with an earnest commentary on Japanese nationalism. Called an "adult fairytale" by assistant director Koji Kajita, *Atragon* explores the specter of Japan's former wartime aggression in a sincere and apologetic fashion. In *Atragon*, the Earth is threatened by the villainous ancient Mu Empire, inspired by the works of English occult author James Churchward. All that stands in their way is a super-submarine built by patriotic navalman Hachiro Jinguji (Jun Tazaki), an Imperial "holdout" who bitterly refuses to accept that Japan lost the Pacific War.

In spite of its lavish production values, *Atragon* was a hectic production, slated for Toho's New Years' holiday slot. Due to this rushed schedule, Tsuburaya split special effects shooting into three subunits. The main unit, "A", was overseen by Tsuburaya himself. For the second unit, "B", he recruited his old friend Keiji Kawakami. Shochiku was giving Kawakami little work and as their contractual obligations were less strict than Toho's, he was allowed to participate. The third unit, "C", was entrusted to young Teruyoshi Nakano, who shot background plates at various locations. Tsuburaya's team impresses with eye-popping composites and more of their best miniature work. There's an especially stunning wide process shot of an exploding ship composited against reacting extras. Made with a miniature ship and live elements filmed on Oshima Island by Honda, it beautifully shows off what Tsuburaya's Oxberry printer can do.

A miniature Tokyo - soon to be demolished

The film's titular undersea warship, the *Atragon* or *Goten-go,* was designed by Shigeru Komatsuzaki. Four miniatures were constructed: one-foot, three-foot and six-foot models along a whopping 15-foot mini-submarine built from metal and wood. The six-foot miniature was used the most and the 15-foot model had radio controlled miniature parts. For the scenes where the submarine discharges its "Zero Cannon," an aeresolized smoke was fired from the model's nozzle. Shots of the *Goten-go* diving are particularly beautiful, executed by actually submerging the miniature in water. A short scene of the *Goten-go* destroying a Muan warship was shot but left on the cutting room floor.

Manda, the giant sea serpent worshiped by the Muans, was added at the insistence of producer Tomoyuki Tanaka a la *Gorath*'s Maguma. Tanaka wanted a dragon-like monster in *Atragon* as it was due to be released in the New Year's holiday season for 1964, the Year of the Dragon. Manda was brought to life via two wire-controlled marionettes. Designed by Akira Watanabe, the puppets were modeled by Teizo Toshimitsu. They were filmed on a dry miniature seabed. For these shots in *Atragon*, the Tsuburaya unit perfected a soon-to-be classic tokusatsu technique. Light was reflected through water tanks to give the footage an undersea texture.

The most jaw-dropping sequence in *Atragon* features downtown Tokyo "imploding" from an attack by the Mu Empire. Another of the grandest miniature scenes ever engineered by Tsuburaya's unit, Yasuyuki Inoue was responsible for most of its planning. It was accomplished by collapsing support beams placed beneath the miniatures, built from easily crumbling plaster. As with the anti-gravity scene in *Battle in Outer Space,* explosives aided in the process and it required precise mathematical calculation. The set was constructed about six feet from the ground and had to be built and secured carefully so as to not fall on and injure crew members. By this time, Yasuyuki Inoue practically ran Toho's FX art department. Tsuburaya would often go straight to him - bypassing department head Akira Watanabe. This often caused conflicts between Inoue and Watanabe.

Atragon's climactic explosion where the Mu Empire blows sky high was once again created by using the classic "cloud tank" method, in which paints were dumped into a water tank and the image flipped vertically upon printing. The picture did modestly successful business at the Japanese box office and would prove to be one of Toho's more influential classic tokusatsu films.

Daiei's Tokyo branch also planned an effects film for the New Years' holiday. Inspired by the success of *King Kong vs. Godzilla*, Masaichi Nagata was keen to produce a monster picture to rival Toho's output. Their first attempt was *Giant Rat Horde Nezura* with Mitsuo Murayama slated to direct and Yonesaburo Tsukiji in charge of the special effects. *Nezura* would wind up unfinished with its production infamous in tokusatsu industry lore. The film's concept, to feature giant rats enlarged through a chemical foodstuff menacing Tokyo, drew influence from Alfred Hitchcock's recent *The Birds* and H.G. Wells' *The Food of the Gods*, later adapted in 1976 by Bert I. Gordon. With stop motion considered too expensive, Tsukiji's unit opted to employ live rats crawling over miniatures. There was also to be a giant Nezura monster, portrayed through suitmation and modeled by Ryosaku Takayama.

The lab rats purchased by the effects crew proved too docile, so captured sewer rats were used. This proved a logistical and hygienic nightmare. The rats were difficult to wrangle, carried fleas, lice and ticks and frequently bit members of the crew. They engaged in cannibalism, escaped often and bred on the Daiei backlot. The crew had to be masked on set and the miniatures sprayed down with pesticides daily. Effects crew member Michio Mikami developed an allergic reaction from a rat-borne tick bite and nearly died. Shinsuke Kojima, who acted as Tsukiji's AD, was bitterly opposed to the use of live rats.

Yonesaburo Tsukiji on the set of the aborted *Nezura*

Before long, the production of *Nezura* caused a vermin outbreak. Neighbors complained and Daiei's union, chaired by effects AD Shinsuke Kojima, formed picket lines. Tokyo's health department finally ordered production of *Nezura* shut down and the rats exterminated by immolation. Kojima was so disgusted by the debacle that he quit Daiei's special effects division, joining P-Productions and becoming Tomio Sagisu's right-hand man. Perhaps owing to shame over the production's animal cruelty, Kadokawa later destroyed all surviving elements of *Nezura* when they acquired Daiei's holdings in 2002. *Nezura*, however, would not be Daiei's last attempt at a monster picture.

IX.
1964
昭和三十九

According to the Chinese Zodiac, 1964 was the Year of the Dragon; fittingly, the year would see the release of two Godzilla entries. Moreover, the Olympics were to be held in Tokyo in September and Japan's economy was booming. Thanks to excitement over the looming broadcast, most Japanese families now owned television sets. These factors combined to make the Year of the Dragon a particularly busy one for Eiji Tsuburaya.

Toho's first film in 1964 to make use of Tsuburaya's FX unit was **WHIRLWIND** [**Director:** Hiroshi Inagaki - **Release Date (Japan):** January 3rd, 1964]. A sequel to Inagaki's *Daredevil in the Castle*, Tsuburaya's contributions are limited to the picture's first and last reels. The opening makes use of stock footage from *Daredevil in the Castle*. In *Whirlwind*'s final 10 minutes, a tornado, stunningly orchestrated by Tsuburaya's unit, shows up as retribution for the baddies' misdeeds. The miniature work is top tier as usual with the villains' forts reduced to flying rubble by Tsuburaya's strongest effects fans; it's very much like a classic Toho monster sequence sans the monster. On this or another film soon after heavily using the special effects fans, AD Teruyoshi Nakano would have to get one of his fingers reattached following an accident with one.

Modeling master Fuminori Ohashi (left), known for his talent in making ape suits

At the same time, Tsuburaya continued development of a new series at his company with writer Tetsuo Kinjo. Kinjo's concept was called *Unbalance* and influenced by the popular *The Twilight Zone* and *The Outer Limits*. The program would involve the appearance of monsters, triggered by the "unbalance" of humanity's disruption of the natural order. Tokyo Broadcasting Service (TBS) agreed to sponsor the show and development continued. In February of 1964, however, Tsuburaya Productions was almost beaten to the punch in creating an early giant monster-themed show on television.

AGON: THE ATOMIC DRAGON [AKA: PHANTOM MONSTER AGON - Television Run (Japan): January 2nd - January 8th, 1968] was a four-part miniseries produced by Nippon TV with Toho scribe Shinichi Sekizawa as writer and showrunner. It revolved around a giant, radioactive, Uranium-eating dinosaur attacking Japan. The show was directed by Norio Mine and Fuminori Ohashi with Ohashi handling the special effects unit and suit modeling. Ohashi's FX work is less polished than Tsuburaya's but boasts experimental and atmospheric flourishes. Agon's suit is not as sleekly modeled as Teizo Toshimitsu's work but has expressive touches such as a moving throat. The miniatures are elaborate and the show's unique feel is aided by an atmospheric, albeit unrefined, sound design more in line with an American independent genre picture than a Toho theatrical feature. *Agon* was not the first monster-themed program to be created for Japanese television, however. A show entitled **MARINE KONG [Television Run (Japan):** April 3rd - September 25th, 1960] had come years before it on Fuji TV.

Agon: The Atomic Dragon was set to be broadcast in fall of 1964 and beat Tsuburaya's *Unbalance* to the airwaves. Toho, however, felt the concept was too similar to their own Godzilla. They accused Sekizawa of violating the no-compete clause in his contract and Ohashi, as he had worked on the original Godzilla suit, of plagiarizing the design. As a result, the network dropped *Agon: The Atomic Dragon*. (Toho would finally allow the miniseries to air in 1968.)

UPA's Henry Saperstein, one of tokusatsu cinema's biggest advocates in Hollywood

The popularity of Japanese special effects works was now ascending not only in Japan, but overseas as well. Just two decades after the war and the bitter anti-Japanese sentiment it brought, Toho's monster films played to packed drive-ins in rural America. Hollywood and its players took note of what, to them, were peculiar but also inventive and competently made Japanese special effects movies. While some, like Ray Harryhausen, believed their own works superior, others like **HENRY G. SAPERSTEIN** (1918-1998) were impressed with the ability of Japanese technicians to create polished pictures with less time and money than it took in LA. Saperstein ran United Productions of America (UPA), best known for animated works like Mr.

Magoo and *The Gay Purr-ee* (1962). Having heard that Toho makes the best science fiction films overseas from a librarian at the Academy of Motion Picture Arts and Sciences, Saperstein even took classes on Japanese business etiquette. With the dollar strong against the yen, U.S./Japanese co-productions soon came into being.

The first major American production to hire a Japanese effects team was **FLIGHT FROM ASHIYA** [**Director:** Michael Anderson - **Release Dates:** March 25th (**U.S.**) - March 28th, 1964 (**Japan**)]. *Flight from Ashiya*, starring Yul Brynner, is a convoluted and propagandistic picture glorifying the U.S. Navy. As the film centered around American navalmen stationed in Japan, producer Harold Hecht partnered with Daiei's Masaichi Nagata. Filming was done at military bases in Japan along with Daiei's Kyoto branch. Though uncredited, the miniature effects were helmed by Yoshiyuki Kuroda; his first gig as full-fledged FX director.

Kuroda's work in *Flight from Ashiya* is subtle but plentiful in the first and final reels with Toho-quality miniature work. There are jaw-dropping model-driven scenes that are intercut seamlessly with genuine military aircraft, along with an impressive avalanche sequence that very much looks forward to the work of Kuroda's unit on the Majin films. This scene was shot in a Self-Defense Force training base and used over a ton of fake styrofoam as snow. Another stunning shot features an HU-16 *Albatross* hydroplane setting down onto a stormy sea, capped by a rainbow.

The crew's American side was impressed with the ingenuity and craftsmanship of the Japanese team, particularly production manager **GILBERT KURLAND** (1904-1978). The Hollywood end included none other than *The Beast From 20,000 Fathoms'* and *Gorgo*'s director Eugene Lourie as production designer. The blue-screen shots' quality suffered as the Hollywood labs, according to cinematographer Fujio Morita, did not color time the compositions properly.

At the same time, Toho were hard at work on development of another Godzilla entry after the success of *King Kong vs. Godzilla*. A direct follow-up was considered, as was a film pitting Frankenstein's Monster against Godzilla. Toho decided that pairing Godzilla with Mothra was the best bet. The result was **MOTHRA VS. GODZILLA [AKA: GODZILLA VS. THE THING** - **Director:** Ishiro Honda - **Release Date (Japan):** April 29th, 1964]. Shinichi Sekizawa began work on the script in late 1963. It was originally more of a direct sequel to

Mothra, but Sekizawa revised it under the guidance of Honda. The story was to involve Godzilla's body, thought dead, put on display by a greedy exhibitor. This was changed to Mothra's giant egg, which, at the suggestion of Honda, ultimately hatches into twin monsters. *Mothra vs. Godzilla* is one of the finest Godzilla films; a rare sequel which successfully expands on not one but two predecessors. It effectively combines the anti-nuclear themes and monster-on-the-loose tropes of *Godzilla* with the magical realism of *Mothra*. Sekizawa's screenplay has a darker-than-usual satire on corporate greed.

The Tsuburaya unit shoots a monster battle (left) - Teizo Toshimitsu at work sculpting (right)

Mothra vs. Godzilla is a classic example of a monster picture where Honda and Tsuburaya's units are in perfect synergy. In spite of the budget being lower than *Mothra* or *King Kong vs. Godzilla,* Tsuburaya's team shines with some of their most creative work. The film's tempestuous opening credit sequence was created by Tsuburaya's unit in Toho's Big Pool. This is followed by an impressive typhoon scene which allows Tsuburaya the opportunity to compete with his protégé Yonesaburo Tsukiji's recent work on *Wind Velocity 75 Meters*. A jaw-dropping miniature shot appears early in the film: an expansive, eagle's-eye vista of Mothra's egg as a fleet of small fishing boats sail towards it. This is followed moments later by another striking wide shot of a crowd thronged around the egg on the beach. This used a matte painting printed with the Oxberry Optical Printer onto a wide plate of the gathered masses. This is just one of many stunning shots in the film enhanced by Tsuburaya's recent purchase. Tsuburaya and Hiroshi Mukoyama show more ease in using this printer with *Mothra vs.*

Godzilla. It is used in Honda's end of the film to almost seamlessly integrate Emi and Yumi Ito's Twin Fairies in with the regular-sized actors. The Fairies are better executed in scale than in *Mothra* with oversized sets combined with Oxberry composites. The printer is used to composite Godzilla into real-world environments with the greatest fidelity yet, further enhancing the picture's realism.

Eiji Tsuburaya (right)

Akira Watanabe's new Godzilla suit design for *Mothra vs. Godzilla* is among the finest. By this time, Teizo Toshimitsu's modeling team had gotten monster suit construction down to a science and all the future *Showa* series Godzilla suits would be manufactured similarly. As usual, the head was the realm of Toshimitsu, with Eizo Kaimai and the Yagi Brothers sculpting the body. Keizo Murase crafted the teeth and claws. It was the most lightweight Godzilla suit yet; made with input from Haruo Nakajima. Nakajima often came to the modeling department and allowed the unfinished suit to be fitted to him. Here he gives a signature Godzilla performance with a distinctive, almost feline mischievousness. Assistant director Teruyoshi Nakano and Nakajima improvised a memorable moment where Godzilla, having emerged from seaside mudflats, shakes the sand from its skin.

Godzilla's rampage through Nagoya is among the best in the series, effectively mixing miniatures with location footage and background plates. A detailed model of Nagoya Castle was constructed for this sequence over the span of a week. Like the Osaka Castle miniature in *Godzilla Raids Again*, it was built so well that Nakajima couldn't destroy it. The structure was repaired, weakened and another take was ordered with the sequence well salvaged in the edit using both takes. Nakajima also had difficulty destroying the miniature incubator around the Mothra's egg prop. The finished scene took coordination between Nakajima and the wire staff like Fumio Nakashiro, **AKINORI TAKAGI** (1940-) and **KOJI MATSUMOTO** (1933-2005). Close-ups of the incubator being smashed were done with a separate tail prop which was quite heavy and required two stagehands to operate.

One Godzilla scene filmed but cut from the Japanese version features an American-led naval force attacking the monster with "Frontier Missiles". The pyrotechnic shots were filmed at the Nakatajima sand dunes at Hamamatsu. The reason for this scene's deletion is unclear, but it would be reinstated in the U.S. version, *Godzilla vs. the Thing*. The footage may have been intended exclusively for American audiences, though a snippet appears in the Japanese trailer. As Ishiro Honda's personal copy of the script had this scene crossed out, however, it's possible that he ordered it edited. Perhaps Honda felt insecure about how post-war audiences would react to a display of American military might on Japanese soil. *Mothra vs. Godzilla* is indeed one of the more military-heavy Godzilla pictures, though by this time the involvement of the Self Defense Force was lessening. The JSDF brass had started to wonder if these depictions of constant defeat were good for their image. *Mothra vs. Godzilla* thus uses entirely miniature tanks from Tsuburaya's unit. They were not built from scratch but modified from models bought at a local toy store with the addition of blender motors.

For the execution of Mothra, the prop from 1961 was reused in some scenes, mainly the shots on Infant Island. Imago Mothra was scaled down considerably from the original film to match Godzilla's size. A new, larger and better-constructed prop was built by Teizo Toshimitsu for its battle with Godzilla. This giant marionette was almost twice as large as the first, with a body measuring eight feet in length and an impressive 15-foot wingspan. The puppet was given radio-controlled parts to move the legs and head. A motor, coupled with another Y-shaped wire brace, was used to make its wings flap more quickly and realistically.

Imago Mothra's battle with Godzilla is among Tsuburaya's masterworks as special effects director. Dynamically shot by Sadamasa Arikawa, it is a kinetic, Eisensteinian sequence with creative use of suits, marionettes, puppets and miniatures. As Mothra ferociously battles Godzilla, it destroys an extensive miniature set decked with bonsai trees similarly to Tsuburaya's recent work on *Whirlwind*, once again utilizing powerful fans. With the monsters realistically manipulated, high-speed and fast motion shooting is integrated to create a chaotic effect. One wide shot is particularly striking: combining actors on location with a miniature terrain and the Mothra prop and Godzilla suit. Guignol puppets, though mismatched, are used for more fierce battle moments. Arikawa objected to the use of the Godzilla puppet in some instances but Tsuburaya was steadfast. This led to one of the most heated arguments of their long working career, with Arikawa almost quitting on the spot. Much more footage of the puppet was filmed for *Mothra vs. Godzilla* but most wound up cut.

Kyuzo Yamamoto (left) creates the effect of spraying cocoon silk

For the shots of Mothra's egg hatching, a second egg prop was constructed. It was built by molding glue and a calcium powder made from oyster shells around a styrofoam orb. The styrofoam was then removed with a hot wire, creating a hollow shell that was easy to crack. Two-foot hand puppets were used to portray the larvae as they hatched. For most of the film's finale, the twin Mothra larvae were portrayed with two sets of mechanical props. The first were built for the land shots and radio controlled, though they were also augmented with piano wire puppetry. The second were for the water scenes and had a built-in motorized rotating conveyor belt created by engineer **SOJIRO IIJIMA.** This created a self-propelled up-and-down motion as the larvae swam.

For the climatic sequence where the larvae cocoon Godzilla, the silk was made from the same recipe as in *Mothra*. For offscreen shots of Godzilla being hit with the sticky substance, the mixture was poured into a cup with small holes on its top and placed inside an effects fan. It would shoot out and solidify in the air as the fan spun. For close-ups of the material fired from the larvae's mouths, a compressed air dispenser was built into the puppets' beaks a la silly string. Due to the silk's sticky and corrosive nature, the Godzilla suit had to be soaked in gasoline after shooting. For some water shots, particularly the cocooned Godzilla plunging into the ocean at the climax, the suit from *King Kong vs. Godzilla* was used. *Mothra vs. Godzilla* was not the mega-hit that *King Kong vs. Godzilla* was but did spirited business. Among fans on both sides of the Pacific, it has long been a favorite.

As Tsuburaya continued development on *Unbalance*, his next monster spectacle with Toho was **DOGORA [AKA: DAGORA, THE SPACE MONSTER - Director:** Ishiro Honda **- Release Date (Japan):** August 11th, 1964]. Featuring the first giant Japanese monster hailing from space, the project was conceived by novelist **JOJIRO OKAMI** (1918-2003) as *Space Mons*. *Space Mons* was to be an ambitious project with international scope crossing Toho's space opera films and its monster cycle. The plot wound up simplified and the budget cut. Honda's half of the movie is not his strongest, throwing a gaggle of cartoony gangsters into the mix with less effectiveness than in *The H-Man*.

By contrast, Eiji Tsuburaya dominates the picture with strong footage. His unit goes to inventive lengths to depict the titular monster, a jellyfish-like mutant space cell that grows by eating diamonds and coal. Dogora itself was designed by Shigeru Komatsuzaki. Komatsuzaki developed the jellyfish motif in his conceptual art for *Space Mons* years prior. Dogora's single-celled early form was created by shining light through ground glass sandwiched between two panels. Once again, Tsuburaya and Hiroshi Mukoyama put the Oxberry printer to work with one dream-like composite after another. There are stunning shots early on of a satellite falling toward Dogora. Another early sequence of the monster devouring coal at a coalyard was achieved by dropping black sand in fast motion. The miniature smoke-stacks lifted by the monster were shot by dropping them at a high frame rate. Both were then printed in reverse.

Dogora's highlight sequence is the monster's mid-film attack on Kitakyushu. It is a tour-de-force combining optical printing, miniature work, a water puppet for the monster and even anime flourish. The Dogora puppet was built by Keizo Murase from a translucent vinyl material. It was an extremely delicate prop, a crucial part of why it was decided to film it in water. It was hung in an aquarium and moved with fishing line. Jets of water were also shot at the puppet from inside. Air bubbles were a problem and, thanks to the chlorination of Tokyo's tap water, the tank would get cloudy. A stunning shot shows Dogora hovering near the top of the frame over an industrial area. For shots of the monster grabbing the recently built Wakato Bridge, the tentacles were brought to life with cel animation created by Sadao Iizuka. Iizuka also fleshed out Dogora's design and drew the movie's storyboards. There's also an impressive composite near the picture's end, created with the Oxberry, of the villains flattened by a falling, crystalized portion of the monster. In the United States, badly processed TV prints were the bane of the film's existence. *Dogora* deserves a reappraisal for its unique concept and innovative FX work.

As the October Tokyo Olympics drew closer, Eiji Tsuburaya continued development of his upcoming program *Unbalance*. It was gifted the largest budget yet in Japanese television history, which allowed it to be shot on 35mm rather than 16mm as usual for Japanese TV. In his typical Hakuraku fashion, Tsuburaya gathered a top-tier stock of behind-the-camera talent for this ambitious venture. For directors, he enlisted the talents of his son Hajime Tsuburaya and Ishiro Honda's favorite assistant, Koji Kajita, along with TV journeymen and newcomers like **SAMAJI NONAGASE** (1923-1996), **TOSHIHIRO IIJIMA** (1932-2021), **HARUNOSUKE NAKAGAWA** (1931-2018) and **KAZUHO MITSUTA** (1937-). For the special effects unit, he recruited old friends Keiji Kawakami from Shochiku and Toru Matoba, who had recently left Daiei. Sadamasa Arikawa and Honda's favorite DP **HAJIME KOIZUMI** (1926-) would also helm the FX unit. Cameras rolled on the first episode, *"The Mammoth Flower"* in September of 1964, directed by Kajita with FX sequences by Kawakami. Tsuburaya could not shoot at Toho, so he rented studio space at the Tokyo Art Center.

A month later, on October 10th, the Tokyo Olympics commenced. Television sets had now found their way into 90% of Japanese households and the 1964 Olympics were the first to be broadcast by satellite. Between 600 and 800 million people watched the games worldwide. The Olympics served as proof to the other nations that Japan had gone from aggressive international pariah to Asia's economic success story.

With the Tokyo Olympics, many Japanese felt that the post-war miracle was here to stay, even as conflict brewed simultaneously in nearby Vietnam.

One notable takeaway from the 1964 Olympics was Gymnast Yukio Endo winning three gold medals and one silver with his "Ultra-C" parallel bar maneuver, resulting in the word "Ultra" becoming a popular buzzword in Japan. To cash in on the trend, TBS demanded that Tsuburaya change the name of his show from *Unbalance* to something using the word "Ultra". The show thus became known as *Ultra Q*. The "Q", standing for "Question", likely came from the popular anime program *Obake no Q-taro*.

Eiji Tsuburaya (right)

Though Eiji Tsuburaya was so occupied with his own company that he was barely sleeping, he managed to cram one last monster film for Toho into his schedule: **GHIDORAH, THE THREE-HEADED MONSTER** [**Director:** Ishiro Honda - **Release Date (Japan):** December 20th, 1964]. Bringing Toho's giant monster stars Godzilla, Rodan and Mothra together to battle a novel foe, *Ghidorah* was an early example of a franchise crossover film long before Marvel's *The Avengers* (2012). Like *Atragon*, it had a hectic shooting schedule. Akira Kurosawa's *Red Beard* had been intended for release in the 1964-65 holiday season but the director's obsessive perfectionism delayed production. Toho needed a film for *Red Beard*'s spot on the release slate, so another Godzilla entry was rushed into production. The hurried nature of *Ghidorah*'s shooting does show compared to *Atragon* or *Mothra vs. Godzilla*. The work of the effects team is more plentiful but less polished. There are, however, a handful of standout sequences. During principal photography of *Ghidorah*, Newsweek would visit Toho's backlot and cover Tsuburaya's special effects unit.

The Godzilla suit from *Mothra vs. Godzilla* was reused, though with modifications. These were mainly to soften the look to a less villainous one and included a tongue and new wooden eyes that could be moved by radio control. A new Rodan suit was built by Teizo Toshimitsu and the Yagi Brothers and given remote-controlled eyes and a mouth. A pair of miniature flying Rodan models were made as well. *Ghidorah, the Three-Headed Monster* makes particular use of Guignol hand puppets. New Godzilla and Rodan puppets were made for battle scenes between the two beasts. A mechanical larva Mothra prop from the previous film was also reused for much of the creature's footage.

Unsung heroines - a group of women put the finishing touches on model buildings

The most difficult and extensive construction was required for the film's villain: the three-headed space dragon King Ghidorah. The iconic Ghidorah, fittingly conceived in the Year of the Dragon, was designed by Akira Watanabe and modeled by Toshimitsu and the Yagis. The creature was based on the iconic Yamata no Orochi with motifs of the lion-like Kirin expressed in its faces. The staff, having worked on a Yamata no Orochi suit for *The Three Treasures*, were less green this time around; Ghidorah stands among the finest suits ever built by Teizo Toshimitsu's team. The suit weighed around 180 pounds and each plaster scale was cut with scissors and attached by the modeling department one by one. Ghidorah's necks were made from urethane tubes. The creature was first painted a blue-green with rainbow-colored wings, as evidenced by early stills. At the suggestion of Keiko Suzuki, Tsuburaya decided to have Ghidorah painted gold to connect the creature to the planet Venus, which figures prominently in its backstory.

The role of Ghidorah was shared by stuntmen **KOJI URUKI** and Shoichi Hirose. The inside of the suit had a metal bar to help them balance. The heads, wings and tails were, at the same time, controlled by the wirework crew headed by Fumio Nakashiro, **SHO OGAWA** and Akinori Takagi. It took ten operators to control Ghidorah alone. The impressive finale where the four monsters do battle took 25 staff members to operate the wires. As with Orochi on *The Three Treasures*, Ghidorah's necks would often tangle if the wireworkers weren't in good coordination. Wires would also get snagged in the scales.

Preparing a miniature set for demolition

The miniature work in *Ghidorah* is considerable. A large miniaturized downtown Tokyo was built for a scene where Godzilla and Rodan battle in the city. Much of its footage was left on the cutting room floor. The model Mount Fuji set used in *Ghidorah*'s climax was a particular achievement. According to David Kalat's *A Critical History and Filmography of Toho's Godzilla Series*, it took 12,000 man hours to build. Bonsais were again used as miniature trees on this 1/25th scale set. Fuchimu Shimakura painted a fanciful "horizont" of Fuji's summit.

There are two standout sequences in *Ghidorah*. The first is where King Ghidorah is explosively birthed from a fallen meteorite. This scene masterfully combines suitmation, ingenious pyrotechnics, miniature photography and cel animation composited with the Oxberry. Tsuburaya's biggest influence for this segment was the Id Monster scene in *Forbidden Planet* (1956). Another highlight shows Ghidorah raining apocalyptic hellfire with its gravity beams on Tokyo and Yokohama. Originally, this sequence was to take place in New York City to give the film an international scope but was changed as a cost-cutting measure. The staff, led by Yasuyuki Inoue, spent two months building the miniatures for Ghidorah's rampage. They were blown apart with gunpowder at a high frame rate with optical beams added later. Tsuburaya's unit shot an alternate take that is available on Toho's 1986 *Special Effects Outtake Collection* documentary. This version is longer but clumsier and the need for a retake is apparent. As usual, Sadao Iizuka was responsible for the optical animation in both, which are among Tsuburaya's very strongest. Once again, there are stunning vistas created with the Oxberry. These include panoramic shots integrating a battling Godzilla and Rodan into the actual Japanese countryside as residents flee at the bottom of the screen. Another amazing cut of *Ghidorah* features the titular monster destroying a *torii* gate as terrified onlookers cower.

Ghidorah, the Three-Headed Monster was the first film to overtly humanize Godzilla, something Ishiro Honda had reservations about. Illustrating this is a silly sequence where, as the Ito Sisters' Fairies translate, larval Mothra parlays with Godzilla and Rodan to fight alongside her for the Earth's sake. This humanization of the monsters began a new direction for the series. It was the final nail in the coffin, for now, of Godzilla as a fearsome metaphor for nuclear destruction. As if to punctuate this more lighthearted approach, in the United States, *Ghidorah* was double-billed in many cities with the Elvis Presley musical *Harum Scarum* (1965), bringing the King of the Monsters and the King of Rock together. Perhaps due in part to the sharp turn in tone, *Ghidorah, the Three-Headed Monster* performed better at the box office than *Mothra vs. Godzilla*, sending the Year of the Dragon off with an explosive bang.

X.
__1965__
昭和四十

Japanese poster for *None But the Brave* (1965)

As shooting and development of *Ultra Q* continued, Hollywood came knocking on Eiji Tsuburaya's door; the U.S./Japanese co-production **NONE BUT THE BRAVE [Director: FRANK SINATRA (1915-1998) - Release Dates:** January 15th **(Japan)** - February 25th, 1965 **(U.S.)]** would enlist the services of his effects unit. Starring and directed by the legendary Frank Sinatra, *None But the Brave* is a riveting World War II drama with themes of universal brotherhood. The picture features an American garrison stranded on an island occupied by Imperial Japanese troops. At first the two groups make war before coming to a tenuous truce. The film looks forward to later Pacific War-themed co-productions such as John Boorman's *Hell in the Pacific* (1968), Nagisa Oshima's *Merry Christmas Mr. Lawrence* (1983) and Clint Eastwood's *Letters From Iwo Jima* (2006). *None But the Brave* even features an early score by John Williams, though it is little used over Tsuburaya's effects footage.

Though less extensively used in this picture, the effects team's miniature shooting in *None But the Brave* is reminiscent of their work on *Storm Over the Pacific* and *Attack Squadron*. It includes panoramic shots of the island, an aerial dogfight and an impressive crash sequence. The largest-scale effects scene depicts a typhoon pummeling the island where the troops are marooned. It is another of Tsuburaya's best-staged flood sequences. Engineered by Yasuyuki Inoue, it was created in one take by pouring a copious amount of water down a slope towards a large miniature set of the island's coastline. During the shoot for *None But the Brave*, Tsuburaya and his team would scold Inoue when the mechanical propeller of a miniature plane wouldn't stop spinning.

The following year, Paramount would approach Tsuburaya to helm a lavish recreation of the 1906 San Francisco earthquake for a film adaptation of William Bronson's book *The Earth Shook, the Sky Burned*. To be shot at Toho, Tsuburaya was planning to build an impressive apparatus to shake his miniature sets and do location shooting at Kasumigaura. For reasons unknown, though Tsuburaya even met with executive Howard Koch, this next collaboration with Hollywood never came to pass.

Due to his involvement in TV productions, Eiji Tsuburaya and his FX unit were assigned only three major projects at Toho in 1965, The first was a rekindling of Toho's war film cycle, **THE RETREAT FROM KISKA [Director: SEIJI MARUYAMA** (1912-1989) - **Release Date (Japan):** June 19th, 1965]. *The Retreat From Kiska* is another fervently anti-war picture about one of the few Japanese garrisons to survive World War II. With parallels to Dunkirk at the European theater, in mid-1943 the Japanese Imperial Navy slipped through an American blockade under the cover of fog. They then evacuated a battalion from the Aleutian island of Kiska. Opening with a remorseful memorial to Japan's war dead, the film boasts luminous monochrome cinematography.

Tsuburaya's work on *The Retreat From Kiska* is plentiful with its strikingly staged aerial bombardment sequences a highlight. These impressively shot, constant warfare scenes give *Kiska* a feel like a tokusatsu *Paths of Glory* (1957). The picture drags a bit but has a remarkable opening and finale. *Kiska* boasts more of the Tsuburaya unit's finest miniature FX cinematography in its final reel. This final sequence took Tsuburaya's team two months to film. It was necessary to shoot using an indoor FX pool, as outdoor filming would prove impractical per the fog machine required. The striking shots of the Imperial fleet slipping past Kiska's rocky shore were accomplished by placing large rails at the bottom of the pool, wiring them, and running the miniatures across them; this allowed for meticulous steering. As with *Submarine I-57: Will Not Surrender,* Tsuburaya shot the picture's composites in color to make use of superior bluescreen technology.

The chief assistant director on *The Retreat From Kiska* was **YOSHIMITSU BANNO** (1931-2017). Born in Ehime Prefecture, Banno had joined Toho in 1955. Not long after, he served as AD on Akira Kurosawa's *Throne of Blood* (1957). As he had a scuba-diving license, Banno was often enlisted for underwater photography sequences at Toho. By 1967, Banno would be allowed to direct the underwater shooting on *Young Guy in the South Pacific.*

When *The Retreat From Kiska* was completed, a screening was arranged for Kiska's survivors. They cheered throughout the film. *The Retreat From Kiska* also garnered Eiji Tsuburaya another "Special Technology Award" from the Japan Movie Association.

Toho's next monster mash was **FRANKENSTEIN CONQUERS THE WORLD [AKA: FRANKENSTEIN VS. BARAGON - Director:** Ishiro Honda - **Release Date (Japan):** August 8th, 1965]. Featuring Hollywood star Nick Adams in a leading role, it was the first Japanese monster film co-produced with American companies. These were United Productions of American and its subsidiary Benedict Pictures, headed by producer Henry G. Saperstein. *Frankenstein Conquers the World* was another project seeded from the sale of Willis O'Brien's *King Kong vs. Prometheus* to Toho. While they had opted to substitute Godzilla for Frankenstein in *King Kong vs. Godzilla,* they still entertained the notion of producing a Frankenstein movie.

Toho first considered matching Frankenstein with the Human Vapor. Later, they developed *Frankenstein vs. Godzilla.* Based on a treatment by American writer Jerry Sohl, the script was by Takeshi Kimura, who was so tired of writing monster movies by this time that he started using the pseudonym "Kaoru Mabuchi" to distance himself from the genre. *Frankenstein vs. Godzilla*'s story would form the basis for the completed film with Godzilla substituted by novel foe Baragon.

Frankenstein Conquers the World is a distinctively Japanese vision of Mary Shelley's iconic creation. Ala Godzilla, the monster is reimagined in the shadow of World War II as a literal *hibakusha* (A-bomb survivor). Yet Ishiro Honda and screenwriter Kimura's subtext is in line with Shelley's. Frankenstein's Monster, like Godzilla and the atomic bomb, is a prime example of misuse of science. *Frankenstein Conquers the World* is an entertaining and endearing though uneven Honda/Tsuburaya collaboration, a rare film whose strengths belong to the former more than latter. The first half is an effective atmospheric horror film where Honda's unit shines. The second is a sillier kaiju picture dominated by Tsuburaya that doesn't quite measure up.

Nick Adams (right) visits the FX unit and meets Haruo Nakajima (left)

The opening is a highlight as the undying heart of Frankenstein's Monster is smuggled out of Nazi Germany during the Fall of Berlin and sent by U-boat to Imperial Japan. An impressive miniature shot of the German countryside under siege opens the picture. Shortly thereafter, as army doctors examine the heart in Hiroshima, Little Boy falls on the city, irradiating it. Pre-bombing Hiroshima was created by combining background plates of the modern city with miniatures and matte paintings created by the FX art department. The bombing scene consists of a few newly filmed shots and stock footage from *The Last War*. There's a well executed earthquake sequence at an oil rig caused by Baragon. To show the monster's glowing horn beneath the water, a light was shone from underneath the surface of the FX pool. This light had to be heavily waterproofed to keep it working.

The latex Frankenstein makeup, first worn by child actor Sumio Nakao and then by main player **KOJI FURUHATA** (193?-?), was modeled by Keizo Murase. A member of Honda's unit who specialized in wigs for *jidai-geki* films applied it. Furuhata, a member of a theater troupe, was deaf and mostly mute, making him an ideal choice for the tragic role. *Frankenstein Conquers the World* was his last film; he retired from acting shortly after. Furuhata wore green contact lenses to give him a more Caucasian appearance and enlarged prosthetic feet. The makeup was changed from scene to scene, at first subtly and then significantly, to show the monster's growth. Early scenes featuring the Frankenstein Monster boast strong overtones of horror and are well directed with a similar synergy between Honda and Tsuburaya's units as *Matango*. Both directors wanted Frankenstein to feel more human and empathetic than their typical monsters.

Eiji Tsuburaya's FX work in the middle act is subtle and well crafted. By this time, The effects staff had grown comfortable in their roles and duties. His crew enjoyed working on these sequences and building their miniatures at a larger scale; along with the challenge of creating sympathetic monster scenes where the creature interacted with Honda's actors directly. Sadamasa Arikawa and Honda's DP Hajime Koizumi had to coordinate the actors' eyelines closely. These sequences put similar scenes of giant humanoids in Bert I. Gordon's films like *The Amazing Colossal Man* (1957) and *Village of the Giants* (1963) to shame. Honda was particular about the composite shots where Frankenstein interacts with human characters and these prove to be the film's best. Blue screen shooting and the Oxberry printer were used heavily in *Frankenstein Conquers the World*. There's a stunning Oxberry composite of a growing Frankenstein breaking out of his holding cell as a TV crew and scientist Dr. Kawaji (Tadao Takashima) attempt to flee.

Another striking composite depicts Frankenstein seen though scientist Sueko Togami (Kumi Mizuno)'s apartment window. The miniatures of Sueko's apartment were built at a large scale by Yasuyuki Inoue as Frankenstein is only 20 feet tall in this segment (due to radiation, he is constantly growing). Frankenstein's escape, a well-staged scene, was shot late into the night. Honda and

Tsuburaya's units shot their ends of the sequence concurrently and the crew were exhausted by morning.

On Honda's unit, Nick Adams performed his lines in English, working from a different script than his Japanese co-stars. Adams was quite smitten with leading lady Kumi Mizuno, though whether they had a genuine affair is unknown. Adams indeed proposed to Mizuno at some point; she turned him down as she was already engaged to actor Manabu Yamamoto. On August 22nd, 1965, Nick Adams would reflect on his experiences making *Frankenstein Conquers the World* in Japan in a *Los Angeles Times* article. He heaped particular affection on Ishiro Honda and Eiji Tsuburaya, saying, "These two geniuses have earned the well deserved title of the world's greatest directors of science fiction films."

For a sequence involving Frankenstein's severed hand, a motorized prop was built. This was pulled across the floor with piano wire and a motor inside which moved the fingers. A scene where Frankenstein emerges at Lake Biwa before a ship filled with partygoers was shot in Toho's Big Pool. The miniature ship was fairly large; built at 1/12th scale and the segment is staged similarly to a sequence in *Godzilla*. The bubbling water was, as usual, created by tubing from an air cylinder placed underwater.

Another memorable scene involves Frankenstein chucking a tree at a vulture. The Oxberry is again put to excellent use when the tree smashes a miniature hut, its residents fleeing in the foreground. For DP Sadamasa Arikawa, this scene was difficult to shoot per its sizing and perspective. He found Frankenstein's scale confusing for certain sequences and often guessed. The wild boar chased by Frankenstein was a wire controlled puppet. For a shot that ends the sequence, the SDF soldiers' greenish-blue uniforms were difficult to bluescreen. The trees in these scenes were made of living miniature Japanese cedars. These had unseen roots added for realism, just in case one happened to be torn out by a monster. As they tended to wither under the studio lights, these cedars had to be replanted daily. Miniature cedars would also be used in *Frankenstein*'s sequel, *The War of the Gargantuas* (1966).

The film's second half introduces the dopey but lovable rabbit-eared kaiju Baragon as an adversary. From this point, *Frankenstein Conquers the World* develops a charming ludicrousness. Baragon was designed by Akira Watanabe and played by Haruo

Nakajima. As usual, Teizo Toshimitsu constructed its head and the Yagi Brothers built the body, with Keizo Murase putting touches on both. Murase shaped its distinctive indented back and horned forehead. Baragon was built lighter than the average Godzilla suit and an electric bulb was placed inside its horn. The mouth and eyes could be moved through radio control. The ears were initially given an armature of wire mesh, but this could not stand up against the rough fight scenes. As a result, they were remade with a thick cloth as base.

A horse puppet, used by Tsuburaya rather than a composite of a real horse, as in his words it was **"more fun"**

There's a stunning sequence where Baragon attacks a mountain lodge with stellar composite shots. A darkly comic moment features Baragon attacking a farm and devouring livestock. This scene uses a miniature horse doll rather than a genuine horse. Some crew members suggested using a composite of an actual horse, but Tsuburaya was steadfast on using the doll. There was also a pragmatic reason according to Sadamasa Arikawa: the horse doll was used so that Nakajima's Baragon could destroy the entire stable in one shot without cutting. Compositing in a genuine horse would have required additional shots. Arikawa found shooting Baragon's consistent scale easier than Frankenstein's.

The climactic battle between Frankenstein and Baragon is overlong. From a cinematic perspective, the image of Furuhata's Frankenstein, an actor in makeup, grappling with Nakajima's suitmation Baragon doesn't quite hold up. Baragon was given a heat ray a la Godzilla, drawn by Sadao Iizuka with assistance from Koichi Kawakita. The creature's ability to leap great distances was accomplished by attaching the suit to piano wire and then running them into a pendulum-like pulley that lifted the suit. Tsuburaya, who choreographed the fighting, relished these scenes, though Honda was less enthused. Tsuburaya, already developing another show to follow *Ultra Q*, had so much fun shooting the climax of *Frankenstein* that it influenced the direction of his TV project. The dynamic of an agile humanoid battling kaiju came to dominate his iconic *Ultraman*. During a short break in the battle, there is a stellar, Hollywood-grade composite of the giant Frankenstein setting a rescued Dr. Kawaji down before the car of Dr. Bowen (Nick Adams) and Dr. Togami. This is among the finest in Tsuburaya's entire career.

The U.S. version of *Frankenstein Conquers the World* features additional FX shots as Hollywood producer Henry Saperstein wanted a more aggressive monster. In the American cut, Frankenstein tramples a policeman during his escape, throws a post at a police car and hurls the cruiser itself, causing it to explode. The police cars used in this sequence were miniatures. Saperstein would visit Tsuburaya's set at various points and in his own words, he "felt like Paul Bunyon! Tsuburaya had a stage that was a block and a half long. And when you walked in there, there were–in miniature–cities, mountains, and highways, the traffic lights worked, the cars moved, the water flowed in the river. It was fascinating to see!".

Frankenstein Conquers the World features an alternate ending, shot at the behest of U.S. producer Saperstein. It was filmed in a rush as a pick-up to principal photography. This ending was not included in the Japanese version as shooting could not be completed quickly enough to polish and include it by August 8th. Director Ishiro Honda also found it daft. In it, a giant octopus inexplicably shows up to drag Frankenstein into a lake. The prop was modeled by the Yagi Brothers with assistance from Keizo Murase. It was built from sponge and its slimy coating was made from a mixture of sawdust and latex. The prop isn't well executed and the crew had difficulty manipulating the legs. Due to the rushed modeling, Tsuburaya also felt the prop didn't look "slimy" enough. The sequence's highlight is a strikingly composited wide shot. The scene wound up rejected by the American producers and excluded in its overseas release as well. The ending was something of an enigma for fans until Toho used it in a 1980s TV broadcast, whereupon it became a popular alternate version of the film. The octopus prop would be used effectively the following year in *The War of the Gargantuas*.

Daiei Tokyo, still reeling from the failure of *Nezura*, next produced the war drama **ZERO ACE** [**Director:** Mitsuo Murayama - **Release Date (Japan):** September 4th, 1965]. Released to compete with Toho's *The Retreat From Kiska*, *Zero Ace* is similar in approach to the rival company's war film cycle. It is more bleak and nihilistic compared to the heroic but fatalistic tone of Toho's pictures. It is closer, however, to Toho's war movies in style than the coming Gamera films would be to the classic Godzilla series. Yet like the Noriaki Yuasa-directed Gamera films versus Ishiro Honda's best Godzilla entries, *Zero Ace* is a tier below Toho's lavish war pictures in production value and quality.

Yonesaburo Tsukiji supervised the special effects unit, helming the aerial battle sequences. Due to Tokyo Daiei's smaller facilities and its FX division's fewer staff, Tsukiji's team could not produce the model planes required for the film in enough time. Tsukiji thus went to his old friend Eiji Tsuburaya and asked to borrow some miniature Zeros used in his Toho productions, to which the latter was happy to oblige. Tsukiji's sequences boast striking, explosive images but lack the majesty of Tsuburaya's. *Zero Ace* is a similar film to the following year's *Zero Fighter* from Toho, but Tsuburaya would thoroughly outstage Tsukiji. Wartime stock aviation footage is used to cut costs but feels like a cop-out. Shortly after his work on *Zero Ace* concluded, Tsukiji was brought aboard Daiei's next stab at a monster film to be released a few months later.

At the same time Toei's Nobuo Yajima would found the Tokusatsu Research Institute. Still in operation today, it was a freelance firm that provided its special effects skills to a variety of film and television productions. It was also a collective headed by Yajima that refined experimental film techniques in the art of Japanese special effects. They were mainly hired by Toei, who were more lax in their contractual rules than Toho, but in the years ahead, a wider variety of clients began to pursue Yajima. He had a more experimental sensibility than the effects staff at Toho or Daiei and the lower budget medium of television gave Yajima and his team a good arena in which to try out new ideas. As television's aesthetic standards were less strict, Yajima could afford to film FX shots that weren't always perfectly executed but that could lead to his team shooting better footage. The first TV show to hire Yajima and his Tokusatsu Research Institute for effects contributions was the Bondian **SPY CATCHER J3** [**Television Run (Japan):** October 7th, 1965 - March 31st, 1966], produced by Toei and first broadcast on NET.

Eiji Tsuburaya, meanwhile, as he prepared *Ultra Q* for airing, took part in **CRAZY ADVENTURE** [**Director:** Kengo Furusawa - **Release Date (Japan):** October 31st, 1965]. The film was an entry in Toho's *Crazy Cats* comedy series. The Crazy Cats were a jazz and comedy troupe headed by the beloved Hajime Hana and Hitoshi Ueki. While monster pictures had their place, Toho's comedy films were more profitable, making them the studio's true bread and butter. As actor Yu Fujiki would say in *Monsters Are Attacking Tokyo*: "That's where the studio made its money, which was then given to people like Kurosawa to make their movies.". Toho's comedy series such as the *Salary Man*, *Crazy Cats*, *Company President* and *Train Station* films alleviated the average urban office worker's burn-out in workaholic post-war Japan. This subgenre had a name: the *salaryman* comedy, partially named after the franchise that started it. *Ghidorah, the Three Headed Monster*'s success is partially attributable to its sharing a double bill with such a film, *Samurai Joker* (1964), a spin-off comedic period drama featuring the core members of the Crazy Cats.

Crazy Adventure was one of the first Toho comedies to use Tsuburaya's unit. They had done miniature shots on films like *Paradise Island Story* and *Salary Man: Advancement Section Chief No. 1* (1959) but this was Tsuburaya's first credit as special effects director in a comedy. The Peanuts appear early on as lounge singers in an amusing cameo. The picture revolves around its oafish protagonists stumbling upon a Neo-Nazi conspiracy aiming to bring a still-living Adolf Hitler (Andrew Hughes) back to power. The effects work is subtle until late in the picture. There are a handful of process and miniature shots and the FX team assisted in some of the more outlandish stunts. As was often the case for non-FX-centered films, Tsuburaya and company aren't really let loose until *Crazy Adventure*'s final reel, including a miniature submarine and a spectacular sequence of the Nazis' secret island being destroyed by atomic missiles. It foreshadows a similar island destruction scene staged by Tsuburaya and his protégé Sadamasa Arikawa in *Ebirah, Horror of the Deep* the following year.

Daiei's president Masaichi Nagata was still reeling from the disastrous failure of *Nezura* and eager to make another monster picture. This led to **GAMERA [Director: NORIAKI YUASA** (1933-2004) **- Release Date (Japan):** November 27th, 1965]. A la Tomoyuki Tanaka, Nagata claimed to have had a vision of a giant turtle soaring through the air as he flew home in an airliner from abroad. The truth is that Tomio Sagisu's P-Productions had been pitching a TV show featuring a variety of stop motion animated shorts called *STOP!*. One episode, screened at Daiei, involved a flying turtle. Nagata, known for being a prickly man with ties to the Japanese underworld, likely "borrowed" the concept.

Masaichi Nagata (left) - Noriaki Yuasa (center right) and child actor Yoshiro Uchida (right)

Nagata formed a production committee with producer Yonejiro Saito, who brought in writer **NIISAN TAKAHASHI** (1926-2015). Gamera was originally to be called "Kamera" (*kame* is Japanese for "turtle"). It was realized, however, that the *katakana* was identical to "camera". Daiei's veteran directors, Mitsuo Murayama included, passed on the project thanks to how *Nezura* had fared. Nagata thus hired young director Noriaki Yuasa. A jolly man of only 32, he came from a show business family: Yuasa's father was actor Hikaru Hoshi and his grandmother *Meiji*-era stage actress Hideko Azuma. Yuasa joined Daiei in 1957 where he worked as an AD under esteemed directors like Teinosuke Kinugasa and Umetsugu Inoue. *Gamera* was only his second film, his debut being the musical comedy *If You're Happy, Clap Your Hands* (1964). It was critically skewered, leaving Yuasa's career on life support. Many believed he was assigned *Gamera* as a form of humiliation. Yuasa, however, would come to be as synonymous with the future Gamera series as Honda and Tsuburaya to Godzilla.

Yuasa's direction on *Gamera* is more pedestrian than Honda's. Yet the film feels starker and more atmospheric than its sequels, enhanced by moody monochrome cinematography by Nobuo Munekawa. Principal photography on *Gamera* did not commence until September of 1965 and concluded only two weeks prior to its debut. The budget was slashed, which is the main reason it was filmed in black and white when most Japanese effects films were now in color. *Gamera* was a trying shoot for Yuasa. Equipment broke down, props exploded and lighting fell into the effects pool, almost killing the person inside the Gamera suit. Yuasa often faced heckling from executives as rushes were screened.

Shooting an early sequence

The special effects sequences were supervised by Yonesaburo Tsukiji, but unusually, Yuasa opted to co-direct them, Hollywood-style. He was among the first main unit directors on a tokusatsu production to do so. This enraged Tsukiji's staff who thought Yuasa should have stuck to directing the actors. At one point, one of them yelled "Do you really think you're going to be the next Tsuburaya?!".

Tsuburaya was revered even at Daiei as he was Tsukiji's mentor and Yuasa taking creative control over the FX sequences was seen as disrespectful. Daiei's brass grew so irritated by *Gamera*'s frequent production problems that they considered hiring staff from Tsuburaya's unit at Toho to do the FX scenes instead.

Yuasa and Tsukiji's special effects work in *Gamera* is decent, if below Toho quality. The black and white cinematography hides its less polished quality better than in future entries. As it was a specialty of Tsukiji's, the miniature work is the film's strong suit and largely on par with that produced by Tsuburaya's team. A ten-foot model was used for the icebreaker *Chidori Maru* in early sequences. Gamera himself was designed by **AKIRA INOUE** (1929-2017), who would go on to be the art director for future installments.

As with Godzilla, multiple Gamera suits and props were constructed. They were created by the Yagi Brothers from Tsuburaya's modeling team, with assistance from Kanju's son **MASAO YAGI** (1926-2008). Masao had helped his father and uncle model Godzilla in 1954. He joined Daiei in 1956 and aided Toru Matoba on *The Invisible Man vs. the Human Fly*. Yagi had been offered work on *Nezura* two years prior to assist in the suit for the rats' giant leader. He declined due to his disgust with the production's hygiene practices. His father Kanju Yagi sadly died shortly after *Gamera* and Toho's *Invasion of Astro-Monster* were released. From his sickbed, Kanju ordered Masao about, advising him on ingredients and materials. The Yagis balanced making Gamera turtle-like with building a viable monster suit an actor could move in. The costumes were mainly built from foam rubber and latex. The final suit was six-and-a-half feet tall. It was lighter than Toho's Godzilla suits, but still quite heavy at around 120 pounds.

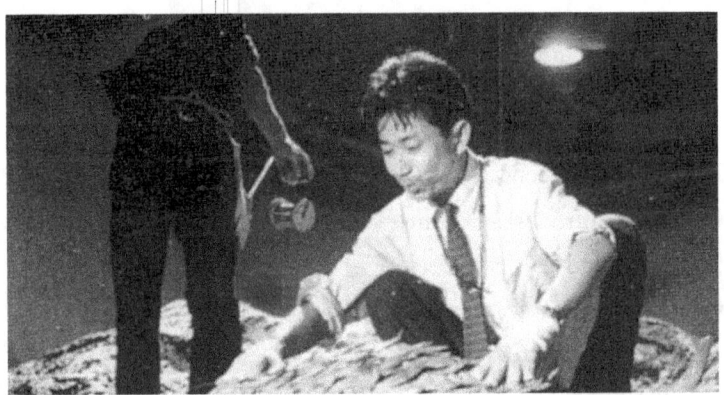

Yonesburo Tsukiji

Unlike Godzilla's often optically animated heat ray, Gamera's flame breath was made using a propane torch. It was Keizo Murase who created Gamera's fire-breath apparatus, using a cooking torch for crisping tofu that was injected with gasoline. The suit had to be padded and heat-proofed to protect the actors inside which added to its weight. A lighter suit was built for the non-fire breathing scenes. In contrast to Godzilla, Gamera was portrayed by a multitude of actors. Noriaki Yuasa first recruited college weightlifters, but none lasted more than three days in the suit. By the end of *Gamera*'s grueling production, members of the FX staff were drawing straws each day to see who had to get inside.

An early sequence where Gamera saves a boy (Yoshiro Uchida) from falling at a lighthouse strongly evokes *The Beast From 20,000 Fathoms*. *Gamera* comes alive a bit more in later scenes. The creature's flying sequences were challenging to stage. Gunpowder was used to create the flames igniting from inside the creature's shell. Only a certain type of gunpowder produced the desired effect and had to be specially ordered. Four Gamera shell props were built. The extra props were necessary as the pyrotechnics inflicted such damage that the shells could not be repaired in time. These shell props were also constructed by Keizo Murase. Oftentimes, the gunpowder didn't ignite properly. The shell's spinning effect was created with piano wires affixed to the prop and attached to a motor. It had to be done carefully or the wires would snap, which they often did, causing the prop to fall to the ground mid-take. The motor was unwieldy and difficult to turn on and off, so timing was difficult. Yuasa was worried audiences would find the concept of a giant flying turtle ludicrous but these scenes are easily *Gamera*'s highlight.

Gamera's nighttime attack on Tokyo is another good sequence mimicking Godzilla's 1954 rampage, but lacking its pathos. The best shot, mimicking the original *Godzilla*, is of Gamera, cloaked in flames, hovering over a miniature city freeway with moving cars. The scene where Gamera knocks over Tokyo Tower was almost ruined and considered an "NG". The miniature tower was pulled over too quickly, but Yuasa filmed an insert, saving the moment as in *Mothra vs. Godzilla*. To build the miniature, it is rumored that Daiei's FX team used the Tokyo Tower blueprints made by Tsuburaya's unit for *Mothra*, either stolen or leaked from Toho by industrial spies. Miniatures left over from *Nezura* were also used. Others were newly built from plaster, with reinforcement bars built into them so they could crumble more realistically. Yuasa and Tsukiji's unit did their pyrotechnics for the later bits of this sequence more crudely than Tsuburaya's, soaking rags in a mixture of kerosene and metallic powder. A portion of these scenes had to be shot outdoors thanks to the toxic smoke.

After *Gamera*, Yonesaburo Tsukiji quit Daiei's FX division and went freelance, working on television and educational films. Tsukiji was frustrated by what he felt was Yuasa's usurping of his creative control and felt Daiei did not understand special effects. Noriaki Yuasa would thus become the de facto head of Daiei Tokyo's FX division. Yuasa screened the final cut of *Gamera* to Masaichi Nagata and Daiei's brass. As the lights went up, Nagata wryly remarked "Amusing", filling Yuasa with anxiety.

However, *Gamera* was a hit, billed with the Kyoto film *New Kurama Tengu: Duel at Gojozaka*, a Raizo Ichikawa vehicle directed by Yoshiyuki Kuroda. It was noted that the lighthouse sequence with Gamera saving the boy protagonist screened particularly well with children. The sequels would be increasingly tailored to a child audience, though the first would be a Toho-style A-picture for adults. *Gamera* was released in the U.S. in 1966 as *Gammera, the Invincible*. Similarly to *Godzilla, King of the Monsters!*, it featured new American sequences shot by director Sandy Howard with genre stalwarts Brian Donlevy (*The Quatermass Xperiment*) and Albert Dekker (*Doctor Cyclops*). A bit longer than its Japanese counterpart, this version even features alternate FX shots.

At the same time, Toho were at work on their next Godzilla picture. **INVASION OF ASTRO-MONSTER [AKA: MONSTER ZERO - Director:** Ishiro Honda **- Release Date (Japan):** December 19th, 1965]. Another classic Godzilla sequel representing the Honda and Tsuburaya teams in top form, it was once again co-produced by Saperstein's UPA and starred Hollywood actor Nick Adams, who would tragically die only three years later. *Invasion of Astro-Monster* successfully combines the pulpy sci-fi trappings of Honda and Tsuburaya's prior space pictures like *The Mysterians* with the city-smashing theatrics of their monster classics. A rare Toho creature feature where Honda's unit dominates, it boasts stunning space scenes and iconic alien antagonists in the Xiliens, led by the scheming Commandant (Yoshio Tsuchiya). As in Hollywood's *Earth vs. the Flying Saucers* (1956), they are destroyed by sound.

Eiji Tsuburaya's effects end features some of Akira Watanabe's finest retro-futuristic designs and elaborate miniatures. The P-1 spaceship, which explores the mysterious Planet X behind Jupiter in the first reel, is beautifully crafted and shot. Designed by Watanabe and Yasuyuki Inoue, it was inspired by NASA's then-current *Gemini* program. An enormous ten-foot tall miniature of the P-1 was built along with a smaller one-foot model for certain wide shots. As in *Battle in Outer Space*, to shoot the P-1's launch back to Earth from Planet X, Inoue dug a hole in the studio floor. He got in a little less trouble this time around. *Invasion of Astro Monster*'s space sequences strongly recall prior Honda/Tsuburaya collaborations such as *Battle in Outer Space* and *Gorath*. There are particularly striking Oxberry composites of the P-1 soaring through space and past Jupiter. To create the effect of stars in space, tiny light bulbs were attached to the backdrop. This would become another tokusatsu tradition. Fuchimu Shimakura paints among the most gorgeous "horizons" in his career for the Planet X segments. Nearly every image looks like it could be an illustration in a pulp sci-fi magazine.

Actor Keiko Sawaii visits the FX art department and touches a model flying saucer

Invasion of Astro-Monster features more of Tsuburaya's grandest miniature work, particularly in the Planet X sequences. The Xiliens' prominent flying saucers were again designed by Watanabe and Inoue. Made from Fiber Reinforced Plastic, several were built, all three feet in diameter. The saucers were filled with electrical wiring so that they could light up, with a power cord cleverly hidden and painted into the piano wire suspending the models from above. When the saucers rise from a lake mid-picture, dry ice was used for the frothing steam effect. A wide shot where a saucer lands before a terrified crowd is another striking Oxberry composite. The space ray cannon used to free Godzilla and Rodan from their force fields on Planet X was a repurposed Atomic Heat Ray Cannon from *Mothra*.

The Rodan and King Ghidorah suits from *Ghidorah, the Three-Headed Monster* were reused with repairs and renovations. Rodan was given a larger wingspan and portrayed by stuntman **MASAKI SHINOHARA** (1926-2018) while Ghidorah was again played by Shoichi Hirose. For Godzilla, however, the suit from *Mothra vs. Godzilla* and *Ghidorah* was in poor shape as it had been modified into the monster Gomess on *Ultra Q*. A new Godzilla suit was thus built by Teizo Toshimitsu and the Yagi Brothers. While similar to the previous costume with a head made from the same mold, some notable differences in sculpting are apparent. The eyes were new and using techniques perfected on Baragon earlier that year, had the best radio-controlled movement yet. This is notable in an expressive close-up where a downed Godzilla darts its eyes about upon suddenly coming to its senses. A large-scale Godzilla foot was built for shots of the monster flattening miniature buildings. This foot was used effectively, though it wasn't easy to control, resulting in quite a few "NGs".

Core members of the Godzilla series' creative team (from left to right): Eiji Tsuburaya, Ishiro Honda, Tomoyuki Tanaka and Shinichi Sekizawa

The overt humanization of Godzilla continued with *Invasion of Astro-Monster*. The creature was midway in its journey from foreboding villain to monster superhero. After defeating Ghidorah on Planet X,

Godzilla celebrates by dancing a jig (called the *"Gojira shie"* in Japanese). This moment was opposed by Ishiro Honda, but he was a company man and tended to have little choice in his concessions to Tomoyuki Tanaka and Tsuburaya's creative wishes. Tanaka's decision to take Godzilla's characterization in a lighter-hearted direction was influenced by American producer Henry G. Saperstein. It was Saperstein who convinced Toho the character would be more marketable as a "good guy".

The film introduces futuristic weaponry in the form of the A-Cycle Light Ray cannons which sever the aliens' electromagnetic control over the monsters in the finale. These were designed by Mutsumi Toyoshima, now an apprentice of Yasuyuki Inoue with a skill for futuristic mechanical creations. Two large A-Cycle car miniatures were built along with five smaller ones. Iodine car lamps were used in the bases of larger models to make them light up. They could not move on their own and had to be pulled with piano wire. Sadao Iizuka's optical animation is particularly prevalent in *Invasion of Astro-Monster*. The A-Cycle Light Ray's fluidly animated beams were created with the help of Iizuka's young apprentice, Koichi Kawakita. This was along with the hefty optical elements when the aliens transport Godzilla and Rodan to Planet X in electromagnetic capsules. Kawakita developed a love of animated rays from his years of work with Iizuka.

Invasion of Astro-Monster features perhaps the Tsuburaya unit's finest Oxberry composites. Once again the monsters are printed into real world environments with near-seamless clarity. There are striking wide shots juxtaposing Godzilla, Rodan and King Ghidorah amongst fleeing masses of villagers and pedestrians. The most stunning of these images, near the end of the picture, features all three monsters off in the distance as soldiers mobilize near the bottom of the frame. The destruction scenes are quality, though there's an overabundance of stock footage from *Rodan*, distractingly cropped to the 'scope ratio. The budget was slashed and, to Honda's chagrin, stock shots had to be used. *Invasion of Astro-Monster* was also the last Toho tokusatsu film to employ the core special effects team who worked on the original *Godzilla*. The staff began to be cut and the crew downsized as the years drew on and the budgets allocated to the unit became more paltry. This was art director Akira Watanabe's final picture with Tsuburaya. Watanabe would soon leave Toho to start his own freelance company, Nihon Special Effects Co, Ltd.

Invasion of Astro-Monster, however, represents a zenith for 1960s Japanese science fiction and Toho's special effects cycle. The American VHS cover from Paramount aptly describes the film as a "Japanese monster movie fan's ecstasy". *Invasion of Astro-Monster* was a box-office disappointment with substantial attendance drop-off compared to *Ghidorah, the Three-Headed Monster*. *Astro-Monster*'s dismal gross likely influenced the change in direction the Godzilla series would soon take. Regardless, the release of *Invasion of Astro-Monster* within weeks of Daiei's rival production *Gamera* was notable. Japanese schoolboys would soon have the option of seeing monsters on the small screen, too.

XI.
__1966__
昭和四十一
(Part 1)

Eiji Tsuburaya and some fans

In January of 1966, after years of development, **ULTRA Q [Television Run (Japan): January 2nd - July 3rd, 1966]** finally hit the airwaves via TBS. The show opened with an iconic logo: the title's words swirling into clarity like paint. This was optically animated by Minoru Nakano. The first episode to air, "*Defeat Gomess!*," was actually filmed quite late in production. The titular monster was created by modifying the 1964 Godzilla suit; its phoenix-like foe Litra was likewise a repurposed Rodan prop from *Ghidorah, the Three-Headed Monster*.

The first episode of *Ultra Q* drew fantastic ratings. Throughout its run, the show's viewership averaged over 30% of the Japanese public.

At the beginning of most episodes, radio personality and actor Koji Ishizaka would calmly read foreboding narration akin to Rod Serling's in *The Twilight Zone*. As the credits rolled and Kunio Miyauchi's haunting music blared from TV sets, Ishizaka would say "For the next 30 minutes, your eyes will leave your body and enter into this strange moment in time." The show centered around reporter

Yuriko Edogawa (Hiroko Sakurai) and pilots Jun Majome (Kenji Sahara) and Ippei Togawa (Yasuhiko Saijo). Each week, the three, hunting for stories, encounter a different monster; some prehistoric, others extraterrestrial. The show's 28th episode, *"Open Up!"*, was cut from the schedule per its lack of monsters to allow for a preview of Tsuburaya Productions' next show. *"Open Up!"* would finally air in December of 1967 during *Ultraseven*'s run.

Ultra Q featured a large menagerie of monsters. Many were portrayed by recycled Toho monster suits that Tsuburaya's company was allowed access to. Besides Godzilla, the King Kong suit from *King Kong vs. Godzilla,* Baragon from *Frankenstein Conquers the World* and Maguma from *Gorath* would also be repurposed for Goro, Pagos and Todola, respectively, The Manda prop from *Atragon* and octopus prop from *Frankensetin* were also reused. Even the mechanical belt used for larval Mothra in *Mothra vs. Godzilla* and *Ghidorah, the Three-Headed Monster* was recycled into the slug monster Namegon. Toho even allowed Tsuburaya Productions the use of stock footage from their films.

Ultra Q (1966-67) title card

Other monsters were made from scratch, designed by Toru Narita and modeled by Ryosaku Takayama and **AKIRA SASAKI** (193?-). Eiji Tsuburaya had been impressed with a sea turtle sculpture that Takayama had created for the newly opened amusement park Yomiuri Land and was adamant on hiring him. Sasaki was a classmate of Toru Narita at Musashino Art College. He would bring to practical life many of Toru Narita's drawings, including one of Tsuburaya and Narita's most emblematic creations: Ultraman.

Flying ice monster Peguila (played by **YUKIHIRO KIYONO**) appears in two episodes and was the first of many Ultra monsters to be designed by Toru Narita and modeled by Takayama. Another distinctive Narita and Takayama creation was Garamon, an android space monster played by suit actor **MINORU TAKAHASHI** that appears in another pair of episodes. The pair also created Kanegon, a coin-eating monster that a greedy young boy is transformed into and the Gill Man-like Ragon, the latter played by **BIN FURUYA** (1943-).

Suit modeler Ryosaku Takayama at work

The best episodes were directed by Ishiro Honda's protégé Koji Kajita, who channels his mentor. Those with effects by Keiji Kawakami also shine. Some were influential on future productions helmed by creators who saw the show in childhood. Shades of *"The Mammoth Flower"* can be found in *Godzilla vs. Biollante* (1989) and *Gamera 2: Advent of Legion* (1996) decades later. The episode features an impressive use of stop motion, a matter Tsuburaya was very particular about, demanding numerous retakes from Keiji Kawakami. *"Grow! Turtle"*, directed by Harunosuke Nakagawa with effects by Hajime Koizumi, is strongly echoed in 2006's *Gamera: The Brave*. A unique installments is *"Baron Spider"*, which takes on gothic horror stylings like a Japanese Ricardo Freda movie. Also striking is *"Balloonga."* Directed by Samaji Nanagase, Kawakami provided the imaginative effects work. Balloonga itself, created by Akira Sasaki, is an unusual monster akin to Dogora.

"Kanegon's Cocoon", directed by Harunosuke Nakagawa with effects by

Toru Matoba, is another standout. It depicts a child-like sense of surreal fantasy more effectively than Noriaki Yuasa's Gamera films. Thrifty Kaneo (Satoshi Tsujisawa)'s Kafka-esque transformation into a coin-guzzling beast is unsettling; juxtaposing the absurd and mundane (Kaneo and Kanegon are both puns on *kane* - the Japanese word for money). Exemplifying this is a scene which depicts Kanegon walking through a crowded city street. According to AD Kazuho Mitsuta, this was shot guerilla style with random pedestrians and no permits. Moments like this look forward to independent maverick Shinya Tsukamoto's *Tetsuo: The Iron Man* (1989). The then-six-year-old Tsukamoto saw *Ultra Q* and was enraptured by it.

During *Ultra Q*'s run, Eiji Tsuburaya at one point overheard the neighbors' children talking about how happy they were that they could see monsters at home without having to go to the theater. Fan letters from tykes rolled in, a few dramatized in the documentary *The Father of Ultra Q:* "Mr. Eiji Tsuburaya, thank you so much for the *Ultra Q* postcard! It has a picture of a giant monster, six facts about the monster and a signature of Mr. Eiji Tsuburaya as well! I was so happy to receive it! I'm looking forward to watching your next monster film! What I really wish for is a picture of the movie, pictures of the monsters and an invitation ticket to the premiere. Every week, I look forward to watching *Ultra Q*!". Another, bolder one reads: "I love *Ultra Q*! It's popular all over the world! What do you think of my drawing? If it's possible, could you put the monster in my drawing in one of your movies?". Tsuburaya's legacy was realized and the "Monster Boom" in full swing: a time when big and small monsters flooded movie theaters and airwaves in Japan. *The Outer Limits,* a heavy influence on the show, was even aired in Japan as *The Ultra Zone* due to *Ultra Q*'s success to better ratings than its original run.

Daiei, meanwhile, wasted little time in challenging Toho and Tsuburaya Productions as the fledgling Monster Boom took hold. Their next special effects release was a monster-themed double feature released in April. The double bill contained Daiei Tokyo's first Gamera sequel, **GAMERA VS. BARUGON [Director:** Shigeo Tanaka **- Release Date (Japan):** April 17th, 1966], directed by Shigeo Tanaka alongside the Daiei Kyoto production **MAJIN [Director: KIMIYOSHI YASUDA** (1911-1983) **- Release Date (Japan):** Ibid]. Yoshiyuki Kuroda was promoted to *Majin*'s special effects director after his work on *Flight From Ashiya*.

Released six months after the original, *Gamera vs. Barugon* was given an "A-picture" budget by Masaichi Nagata and lensed in color. The film was at first to be called *Gamera vs. the Space Ice Men* and would have involved Gamera thwarting an alien invasion by a race of ice people and their humanoid giant. A more conventional story was instead chosen, though elements of the concept would be kept. Gamera's foe, the freezing reptile Barugon, came out of the idea of an ice monster and Kyoto's *Majin* was born from the script's motif of a giant humanoid.

Tykes in line to see Daiei's monster-themed double bill - a duo feature of two creature films was unheard of at the time; Toho considered it impossible as Tsuburaya could not make two special effects films at once

Niisan Takahashi's script for *Gamera vs. Barugon* was altered heavily and Noriaki Yuasa was not rehired as director. Instead, Yuasa was put in charge of the special effects unit in light of Yonesaburo Tsukiji's recent departure. Daiei's dependable hitmaker Shigeo Tanaka was instead hired as main director. Tanaka and Yuasa clashed somewhat as Tanaka wanted to emphasize the human drama whereas Yuasa wanted a focus on his special effects scenes. The two often strongly disagreed on the film's editing.

For *Gamera vs. Barugon*, an adult tone was taken with darker plot threads and not a child actor in sight. Of the vintage Gamera films, it has the most Toho-like vibe. Gamera's adversary Barugon is discovered on a South Pacific island a la *Mothra*. The picture also features a similar cooperation between scientists and the military as Ishiro Honda's works with lengthy army operations to destroy the new nemesis. *Gamera vs. Barugon*'s flaw is that it is overlong at a whopping 101 minutes. The American television cut, *War of the Monsters*, rectifies this as it is around 15 minutes shorter. Indeed, children who were interviewed by the studio said they were often bored. Yuasa was thus put back in charge of future entries and the series began to cater more toward children's attention spans.

Noriaki Yuasa

By this time, Masao Yagi had started his own suitmaking company, Equis Productions, with colleagues Keizo Murase, Toru Suzuki and Michio Mikami. A new Gamera suit optimized for color shooting was constructed by Equis for *Gamera vs. Barugon*. Yuasa wanted a more animalistic look and as a result, Gamera spent much of the film on all fours. Once again, several shell miniatures were made; the bigger ones were three feet in diameter and the smaller' used for wide shots, were one foot. For this film, Gamera now had a regular suit actor - frequent Ultra monster stuntman **TERUO ARAGAKI**. Aragaki would go on to reprise the role several times. Like at Toho, shooting the water sequences in the Gamera films tended to be brutal for the suit actors. As the Gamera movies were often released in spring, they were shot in the dead of winter and the water in the effects pools was bitingly cold.

Barugon, designed by Akira Inoue using motifs such as crocodiles and monitor lizards, was built by Ryosaku Takayama. Equis put the finishing touches on the suit, however, and molded its skin. This was because Takayama had to go to Kyoto to make Majin for *Gamera vs. Barugon*'s co-feature. Three-foot Guignol puppets were also made for Gamera and Barugon. These are used more effectively and seamlessly than by Tsuburaya's unit at Toho.

The work of Noriaki Yuasa's unit on *Gamera vs. Barugon* is among his best and a big step up from the first *Gamera*. These are among the often clunky Yuasa's finest staged tokusatsu sequences with nearly Tsuburaya quality segments and strikingly beautiful images. The effects are not hurt by the more revealing medium of Eastman color. An early sequence where Gamera attacks and destroys Kurobe Dam is the most impressive in a *Showa* Gamera film. A large miniature of the dam was built from plaster. For the dam's striking flood as it is broken by Gamera, a gigantic wooden tank filled with twelve tons of water was placed behind it. This tank was opened with propeller-controlled double doors and the resulting flood was shot at around 240 frames per second to stunning effect.

There's a remarkable sequence showing a goo-covered Barugon hatching from what was thought to be a large gem as it is hit by an infrared lamp. This scene is Tsuburaya quality and Yuasa was proud of it. The newborn creature is brought to life via a hand puppet, enhanced with cigarette smoke and a mucus made with a lubricant imported from the United States. Yuasa was less satisfied with a segment where Barugon knocks down the Port Tower in Kobe with its tongue. The miniature was built too sturdy and could not be knocked over. The film then ran out before the miniature fully collapsed. As with Gamera pulling over Tokyo Tower in the first film, this scene was saved in the edit by cutting to a wide shot of the tower falling and exploding. A large miniature of Osaka Castle was built by Akira Inoue and the staff had difficulty getting these miniature sets inside Daiei's smaller soundstages.

While the effects budget was higher than in the previous film, it was still below what Eiji Tsuburaya was working with at Toho. Daiei did not have access to state-of-the-art tech like the Oxberry Optical Printer, so Yuasa tried to pull off as many in-camera practical effects as he could. An eye-catching shot features figures fleeing from inside an inn as Barugon advances through the frame. This was created by projecting a 16mm loop inside the miniature. Rather than use an animated ray, the freezing liquid Barugon spews from its tongue came from a fire extinguisher. Barugon's destructive "rainbow", however, required expensive optical animation, done at Toyo Photo Lab's facilities.

Model helicopters are flown

The shot of Osaka Castle thawing was a particular challenge. Yuasa and his team shot it in time lapse over the course of a night. When he played the film back, it looked too choppy. Yuasa rectified this by having each frame optically blended together to create a smoother transition. The effect of water trickling from Gamera as he thaws was created by tilting the set, along with a bolted-down camera. For the segment where villain Onodera (Koji Fujiyama) is eaten by Barugon, a full-sized version of the monster's tongue was built for Tanaka's unit.

This would be the first instance in a kaiju film where a monster devours a human being outright. Toho's *The War of the Gargantuas*, released three months later, would feature similar segments.

A notable aspect of Yuasa's work in the Gamera films is that his monster battles are surprisingly gruesome. This was in stark contrast to Tsuburaya who angrily shot down suggestions by crew to make his monsters bleed. Yuasa, however, gave the monsters outlandishly colored blood so as to frighten children less. This makes the graphic monster-on-monster violence feel slapstick akin to a *Looney Tunes* or *Tom and Jerry* cartoon. This was encouraged by Masaichi Nagata and his son Hidemasa as they wanted to differentiate the Gamera films from Toho's product.

Majin's creative team - director Kimiyoshi Yasuda (top left), special effects director Yoshiyuki Kuroda (top right) and cinematographer Fujio Morita (bottom)

The other feature in the double bill, *Majin*, was the first kaiju film made at Daiei Kyoto. *Majin* successfully combined the *jidai-geki* period theatrics they were known for with Tsuburaya-style tokusatsu monster mayhem. The two branches of Daiei had a different corporate culture and in general, the works of this arm of the studio were regarded as higher quality than the Tokyo branch's. *Majin* is one of the finest Japanese monster films of the 1960s. It is an atmospheric and well made fantasy film on par with what

Honda and Tsuburaya were making at the time and in some ways more creative and inventive. Kimiyoshi Yasuda, a major player in the popular *Zatoichi* and *Nemuri Kyoshiro* series, directs the period theatrics with stylistic flair. The character of Majin, a ferocious stone idol that comes to life to punish a wicked warlord (Ryutaro Gomi), was a carryover from the "ice giant" in the scrapped Gamera proposal. Another major influence was the Hebrew myth of the Golem, especially as depicted in the French/Czech co-production *Le Golem* (1936), directed by Julien Duviver.

Yoshiyuki Kuroda, unlike prior effects directors at Daiei, was given the "special effects director" credit next to director Yasuda a la Tsuburaya. This is a testament to his talent, mainly reserved for the stunning final reel. Another major player was veteran cinematographer Fujio Morita. As a child, Morita had grown up near Nikkatsu's Kyoto studio, engendering an interest in cinema from an early age. Morita would sneak into the backlot to watch scenes being shot and film processed. He started working at Daido Films before it was merged with Daiei. Morita soon helped Eiji Tsuburaya himself create the striking optical effects in *The Invisible Man Appears*. Another of Morita's mentors was Kohei Sugiyama under whom Tsuburaya also apprenticed. By this time, Morita was considered the greatest DP at Daiei's Kyoto branch.

Kuroda and Morita, like Tsuburaya, had an affinity for the science of visual effects. After *Flight From Ashiya*, they spent years studying and perfecting blue screen technology. For *Majin*, Masaichi Nagata acquired a massive blue screen lit by iodine bulbs. These shots in *Majin* best those created by Tsuburaya's unit. Tsuburaya's were often tinged with subtle blue artifacts, whereas Kuroda's are cleaner. Kuroda and Morita were also keen on filling their shots with atmospheric particles like mist and smoke. Dried potato, cigarette smoke, cork dust and charcoal were blown onto the set with an industrial fan. Morita felt the air in Tsuburaya's effects scenes was too "clean" and that the mayhem and desolation of destroyed and burning buildings should abound with smoke and dust.

Fujio Morita's techniques were ingeniously complex. Majin's statue in the picture's early moments is seamlessly superimposed into the Kanban waterfall in Okayama. As Kuroda's unit did not have the luxury of Tsuburaya's Oxberry, old-school masking and double exposure was used. This was also to avoid the quality degradation inherent in film-based compositing. A full-scale Majin statue was built for scenes which called for interaction with actors. A 1/25th scale miniature statue was also made. The shot of Majin coming to life before heroine Lady Kozasa (Miwa Takada) and a boy (Shizuhiro Izoguchi) was also created with double exposure on raw film. Majin's stone face turning to Riki Hashimoto's glaring scowl was shot with a dual camera magazine designed for double exposure. Majin's hand was shot prior in the front magazine and a mask was made of that footage which aided in a cleaner transition.

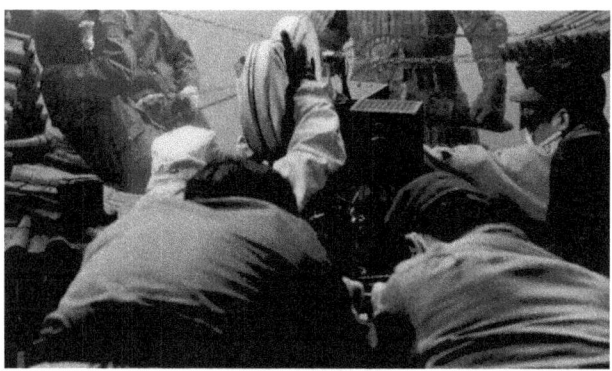

Lensing a sequence

The suit for Majin himself was created by Ryosaku Takayama, who traveled to Kyoto shortly after working on the Barugon suit in Tokyo. His main inspiration was the *haniwa*. *Haniwa* were terracotta clay figures which were buried with warriors in ancient Japan. Initially, Takayama built the suit with artificial eyes lit with bulbs. The head proved too big and bulky and so Takayama built a sleeker head that allowed actor Hashimoto's eyes to shine through. The monster god was portrayed by baseball star-turned-stuntman **RIKI HASHIMOTO** (1933-2017). Hashimoto would, years later, be known for playing Mr. Suzuki, the "final boss" opposite kung fu superstar Bruce Lee in *Fist of Fury* (1972). As the suit was built to accommodate Hashimoto's eyes, Majin throws an unblinking, chilling stare at everything in his path. The bloodshot nature of Majin's eyes was at first by a happy accident. This was due to Kuroda ordering Hashimoto to not blink during takes and DP Morita's penchant for filling each shot with particles. As a result, Hashimoto's eyes became irritated, resulting in a visual effect which Kuroda liked.

The last 15 minutes of *Majin* are astounding as Kuroda's unit takes the stage and the ferocity of a wrathful god is unleashed. This sequence is Tsuburaya quality but with a haunting visual beauty. Being longtime colleagues, Yasuda and Kuroda coordinate their units' footage with a synergy seldom seen even with Honda and Tsuburaya. It was of benefit to the production that, unlike at Toho where the drama and effects units typically had separate DPs, Fujio Morita shot for both and brought along the same camera and lighting crew. Morita himself was conscious of this and felt a flaw in the original *Godzilla* was that the two units lacked visual cohesiveness. In *Majin*, the actors are so closely integrated with the effects elements that it's clear Yasuda and Kuroda co-directed many shots. It also helps that Majin is only 20 feet tall, allowing for highly detailed miniature fortresses and other structures. The effects sequences in *Majin* were shot at around 60 frames per second, lower than the rate normally used at Toho, but equally effective given Majin's size.

Actor Miwa Takada and a statue prop under construction

Some composites are astounding, including a shot where Majin stomps toward the warlord's fort as his men look on in dread. Fujio Morita would always shoot the miniatures first, followed by the actors. Another stunning wide shot features Majin composited among a swath of actors, conveying an excellent sense of scale. Another arresting image is a wide view of Majin standing amongst a sea of burning brush that the warlord's samurai hope will halt his advance. Yet another grand composite features Majin, pacified by Kozasa's tears, collapsing into dust. The collapsing statue was built by Takayama. It took many takes and considerable trial and error to get it to crumble to Kuroda's liking. For the final take, used in the film, compressed air was shot at it from above the set.

In general, *Majin* features a more fluid execution of its practical effects than Noriaki Yuasa's simultaneous work on the Gamera films at Daiei's Tokyo branch. The sole flaw in this impressive climactic sequence is the use of an unconvincing full-sized Majin hand, looking like a similar prop in *Attack of the 50 Foot Woman* (1958). A full-sized Majin leg was also built and used more effectively. *Majin* is a cinematic tour de force combining the best of the tokusatsu and *jidai-geki* worlds. In spite of a strong box office performance, Daiei's double bill was not a financial success. Nagata had spent too much money on the two films and their robust business still left Daiei in the red. For upcoming Gamera entries, the budgets were slashed considerably.

Not long after, Toho followed with **ADVENTURE OF TAKLAMAKAN [AKA: ADVENTURE IN KIGAN CASTLE - Director:** Senkichi Taniguchi - **Release Date (Japan):** April 28th, 1966]. *Adventure of Taklamakan* is a similar film to *Samurai Pirate*, though Eiji Tsuburaya's contributions are more subtle. Both feature Toshiro Mifune as a Sinbad-like adventurer along with actors Ichiro Arishima and Hideyo Amamoto as a wizard and witch, respectively. Taniguchi's unit did location shooting in Iran which aids in a feeling of realism. Tsuburaya was quite busy at his company developing and shooting his next show, so his work is limited to process, miniature and optical shots.

The witch sequences are again imaginative in their use of optical compositing. The Oxberry-driven optical work is the picture's highlight. There's a striking segment wherein the witch summons fire from her staff. These optical scenes were mainly handled by veteran engineer **KAZUNOBU SANPEI** (1922-). During World War II, Sanpei had flown in the attack on Pearl Harbor. After the war he joined Toho and aided in the composite work for Tsuburaya's unit. *Taklamakan* also boasts a giant condor similar to one seen later that year in *Ebirah, Horror of the Deep* along with well-executed miniature work in the finale. *Adventure in Taklamakan* is, however, a more pedestrian film than *Samurai Pirate*.

The next effects driven Japanese film production was **WATER CYBORG**

[AKA: TERROR BENEATH THE SEA - Director: HAJIME SATO (1929-1995) - **Release Date (Japan):** July 1st, 1966]. Boasting a mixed Japanese and Western cast, *Water Cyborg* was made with the cooperation of Italian company RAM Films for airing on American television, though it would not hit stateside airwaves until 1971. Nobuo Yajima's Special Effects Research Institute was hired to provide the FX work. Despite having helmed several tokusatsu films, director Sato was a private man and little is known about him. A cousin of another Toei director, Junya Sato, he graduated from Keio University with an economics degree. Sato joined Toei in 1952 before directing his first film in 1960. Hajime Sato's first genre production was the Ricardo Freda/Mario Bava-inspired *Ghost of the Hunchback* (1965), which was popular when exported to Italy.

Behind the scenes of *Water Cyborg* (1966)

Water Cyborg was shot with three units: one headed by director Sato, a tokusatsu unit headed by Yajima and an underwater photography group run by Akira Tateishi. *Water Cyborg* is an overall uneven affair but at its strongest when Sato channels his beloved Italian genre directors. It boasts a psychedelia akin to Mario Bava films like *Planet of the Vampires* (1965) or *Danger: Diabolik* (1968). Sato's aesthetic is unique, combining Toei's house "action" flavor with Antonio Margheriti-like stylings. If not for its star Shinichi (not yet Sonny) Chiba and Yajima's distinctively Japanese FX work, *Water Cyborg* could be mistaken for a European genre film.

Yajima's miniature submarine shots, created on dry stages, are less effective than Tsuburaya's, though there are impressive moments. His best miniature work involves a model plane flying above the ocean's surface. On Sato's end, a scene of the protagonists being abducted by the titular water cyborgs evokes Bava. These *Creature From the Black Lagoon*-like beasties, along with the submarines and miniature underwater city, were designed by Toru Narita. Narita, however, per his contracts with Tsuburaya Productions and Toho, was obliged to use a pseudonym.

A stand-out in *Water Cyborg* is a sequence where the monsters are shown being created through gruesome surgery. Here, director Sato's Bava-esque horror stylings and Yajima's experimental filmmaking methods come into synergy. Yajima creates imaginative stop motion shots of human skin transforming into scales. Sato's end of *Water Cyborg* is just as strikingly filmed with a shot of ingenue Jenny (Peggy Neal) screaming with a kaleidoscopic funhouse effect. Furiously paced later scenes recall old school Republic serials. A water cyborg suit would later appear in an episode of the Toei show **LI'L DEVIL** [**Television Run (Japan):** October 6th, 1966 - March 30th, 1967], which began airing later in the year.

Three days later, **AMBASSADOR MAGMA** [**Television Run (Japan):** July 4th, 1966 - June 26th, 1967] began airing on Fuji TV. This new show beat out Tsuburaya's upcoming *Ultraman* to the airwaves by 13 days, making it the first color Japanese special effects program. Based on a recent manga by Osamu Tezuka, it was the first successful TV project from Tomio Sagisu's P-Productions. Sagisu had been trying to get a television show off the ground for years, having pitched a stop motion-themed variety show called *STOP!*. In 1965, Sagisu and former Daiei special effects technician Shinsuke Kojima produced a pilot called *Adventures of Club Kimi,* based on a manga by Reiji Aki. This pilot did not see full fruition, but it was screened at Osamu Tezuka's fledgling anime studio Mushi Production. Present at the screening was TV producer, Kazuo Ueshima, who proceeded to take the *Adventures of Club Kimi* pilot to confectionery manufacturer Lotte. Lotte was keen on sponsoring a show from P-Productions, but wanted more familiar subject material. Sagisu thus asked Osamu Tezuka for permission to create a tokusatsu adaptation of *Ambassador Magma*. Tezuka was hesitant as he had not been happy with previous live-action adaptations, but relented.

Ambassador Magma, which ran for 52 episodes, concerns the invasion of Earth by brutish alien warlord Goa (Toru Ohira). Goa, with an army of prehistoric monsters at his disposal, is opposed by Ambassador Magma (Tetsuya Uozumi). Magma, a benevolent cosmic golden giant who has the ability to transform into a rocket, has befriended Earth boy Mamoru (Toshio Egi). Unlike Tsuburaya's shows, which tended to feature self-contained single episode stories in which a "monster of the week" is defeated, *Ambassador Magma* has lengthier story arcs ala the BBC's *Doctor Who*. These would often stretch out into four episodes with each ending in a cliffhanger. Each episode cost around five million yen (roughly $50,000), which irritated sponsors. Towards the show's finale, the arcs were pared down to two episodes each, which was easier to budget.

Ambassador Magma (1966-67) title card

The effects work on *Ambassador Magma* brings Tezuka's manga panels to pantomime tokusatsu life. It is in many ways more creative and fanciful than what was being done at Tsuburaya Productions simultaneously. Like Nobuo Yajima, Tomio Sagisu and effects director Shinsuke Kojima had an experimental sensibility but their execution is often more polished. Some of the best shots are nearly theatrical quality. Per Sagisu's manga background, the show boasts heftier amounts of optical animation than in *Ultraman*. In some episodes, it's so extensive that it resembles Terry Gilliam's animations in *Monty Python's Flying Circus*. Much of this was handled by Yoshio Watanabe. The most elaborate animations were created by early anime luminary Kenzo Masaoka.

The show's assortment of monsters were built by Fuminori Ohashi, who reuses the Agon suit in the first episode. Ohashi also supervised the modeling of Ambassador Magma himself and villain Goa. The show's pilot had a different look for Magma: actor Tetsuya Uozumi's real face was covered with gold paint. This irritated his skin, so Ohashi and Eizo Kaimai opted to depict the character's face through a mask made from FRP. Magma's hair was a wig made from imported Chinese yak fur. As it was damaged by water, several extra wigs were kept on hand. Magma's body was made from latex and urethane foam. The gold paint caused the torso of the suit to deteriorate, leading to the body having to be periodically reconstructed.

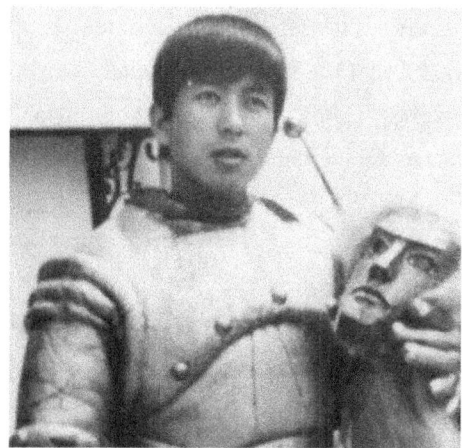

Actor Tetsuya Uozumi takes a break

Yoshio Irie, formerly of Tsuburaya's unit at Toho, supervised construction of the miniatures. Though Sagisu was now one of his biggest rivals, Eiji Tsuburaya respected his former apprentice. He made occasional visits to the set of *Ambassador Magma*. Young staff who also worked for his units at Toho and his company would hide when Tsuburaya came to set, worried they may be violating the companies' strict contractual terms. Tsuburaya was impressed that Shinsuke Kojima was producing quality effects footage in facilities far inferior to those at Toho or his own company. Sagisu and P-Productions began work on another show, *The Monster Prince*, which was being filmed in Kyoto. As the program was understaffed and experiencing production problems, Kojima was sent to Kyoto to take over its special effects. The remaining work on *Ambassador Magma* was handled by Takeo Sakai. In the United States, the show was purchased for syndication and retitled *The Space Giants*.

All the while, Eiji Tsuburaya remained absurdly busy, balancing film assignments with the launch of his next TV program. One of his few films for

Toho in 1966 was their next war drama, **ZERO FIGHTER [Director: SHIRO MORITANI (1931-1984) - Release Date (Japan):** July 13th, 1966]. Moritani, a Tokyo native, had been an assistant director for Mikio Naruse and Akira Kurosawa. For Kurosawa, he acted as AD for *The Bad Sleep Well* (1960), *Yojimbo* (1961), *Sanjuro* (1962), *High and Low* (1963) and the recent *Red Beard* (1965). Moritani's direction of *Zero Fighter* is strong for what was his directorial debut. Revolving around an air squadron stationed in New Guinea in 1943, headed by dashing aviator Lt. Kudan (Yuzo Kayama), it is similar to *Colonel Kato's Falcon Squadron* and *Farewell Rabual*. Yet there is a self-aware, sardonic humor that a wartime propaganda picture like *Colonel Kato* wouldn't have dared. The tone is also less dour than Ishiro Honda's somber *Rabaul*.

Eiji Tsuburaya (left) and Shiro Moritani (right)

Zero Fighter features Tsuburaya's finest air battle sequences thanks to the Oxberry. His unit took care to create footage that matched better with Moritani's than in previous Toho war movies. The less revealing medium of black and white also aids in more realism than prior color films. *Zero Fighter* is laden with stock footage, however, much of it from *Farewell Rabaul* but some going as far back as *Battle Troop*. A nighttime aerial battle is among the most stunning war film sequences produced by Tsuburaya's unit. There are haunting shots of Zero formations gliding across the horizon. Later scenes involving the squadron flying low and attacking American targets are equally impressive. As a former Imperial aviator himself, DP Sadamasa Arikawa clearly took his war movie work to heart. His shooting is among his most innovative in *Zero Fighter*.

Zero Fighter is another shining example of the Tsuburaya unit's finest miniature shooting. With Akira Watanabe running his own company, Yasuyuki Inoue stepped into the role to head Toho's special effects art department. As art director, he would always start by reading the script and then work on concept art. Inoue also designed the blueprints and chose materials. He would then produce small mock-ups of the miniature sets. Inoue would largely remain in this position for over 20 years and design numerous monsters and mecha. Inoue would even make estimates for the cost of set construction while going over the script. He soon began to storyboard the special effects sequences for Tsuburaya and later Sadamasa Arikawa and Teruyoshi Nakano. Tsuburaya meanwhile, had been developing another television show at his company which was due to begin airing just four days after *Zero Fighter* hit theaters.

XII.
1966
昭和四十一
(Part 2)

Ultraman (1966-67) title card

In mid-July of 1966, **ULTRAMAN** **[Television Run (Japan):** July 17th, 1966 - April 9th, 1967] found its way to Earth's airwaves via TBS. Subtitled "A Special Effects Fantasy Series", the show would become as seminal an institution in Japan as Godzilla. Development of this much-anticipated hit show began in the late summer of 1965. TBS was preparing *Ultra Q* for air and already wanted another show from Tsuburaya Productions, but in color. TBS wanted this program to focus on monster battles and star a "good monster". To establish a premise, Tsuburaya called on writer Tetsuo Kinjo for ideas. They channeled the original treatment for *Woo*, their initial TV proposal which featured a benevolent alien creature doing battle with monsters.

The original concept for *Ultraman*, proposed in fall of 1965, was called *Scientific Investigation Agency Bemler*. This would combine a peacekeeping organization called the Scientific Investigation Agency and a benevolent monster named Bemler who battled malicious alien creatures. Bemler's design motif was a mix between the Garuda of Hindu lore and the Japanese *yokai* Karasu Tengu. TBS executive Takeshi Kakoi worried audiences might be confused by Bemler's monstrous appearance and the notion of a good monster battling evil ones. It was thus decided to take the series in a different direction. Ultraman's first foe, however, was named Bemler as a nod to this original concept. Tsuburaya had immensely enjoyed the making of *Frankenstein Conquers the World*, in which a giant humanoid does battle with a dinosaurian kaiju; he decided to bring a similar dynamic to the new show, an approach Kakoi was quicker to accept.

Shooting an episode

The project was retitled *Science Investigation Agency Redman* and the character of Bemler changed to a crimson-armored alien named Redman. DC Comics' Superman was a major influence as Tsuburaya wanted Japan to have its own equivalent to the Man of Steel. Further elements that would become iconic tropes of *Ultraman* originated in *Redman*. Redman, fleeing from the destruction of his home planet, was to have accidentally collided with the protagonist Sakomizu's aircraft, killing him. Redman thus merges with this man. This keeps them both alive and grants Sakomizu the ability to transform into Redman in times of need triggered by the appearance of giant monsters.

Two concepts pivotal to *Ultraman* were also introduced with *Redman*. The first was that Redman could only operate in Earth's atmosphere for a few minutes, creating a time limit for the monster battles. This served two purposes - amping up the narrative stakes while keeping the battles' runtimes at a budget-friendly level. The other trope was giving Sakomizu a device that allowed him to transform into Redman, first called the Flash Beam and then the Beta Capsule. Takeshi Kakoi, however, was still not totally happy with the proposal and asked for a changed design. The project thus became *Ultraman*. The name *Redman*, however, would be reused for a short kiddie program in 1972.

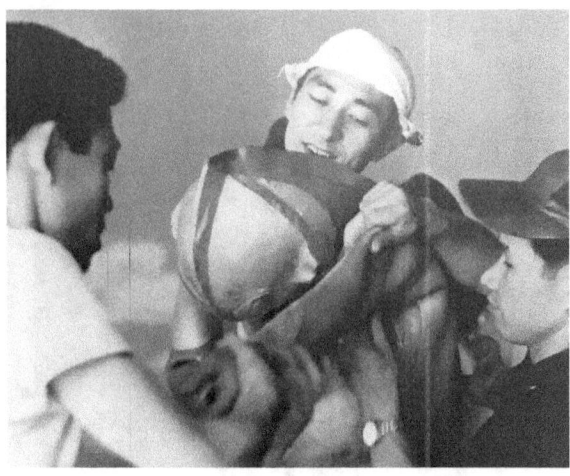

Bin Furuya (center)

Toru Narita got to work on designing this soon-to-be iconic superhero. Narita drew influence from around the world including gods of Greek mythology, legendary Japanese swordsman Musashi Miyamoto and statues of Buddha and Kanon. Akira Sasaki got to work sculpting a maquette of Ultraman and building the suit. It was decided to use a scuba wetsuit to form the basis of the body as this had been effective for the Kemur aliens in *Ultra Q*. The lightweight nature would allow the actor to move quickly and aggressively, making for exciting fight sequences. Stuntman and bit player Bin Furuya (who, incidentally, had played the aforementioned Kemur) was chosen to portray Ultraman. Furuya was young, energetic, tall for a Japanese and had a good physique, all of which made him ideal for the role. Ultraman's head was closely fitted and tailored to a plaster mold of his face to fit snugly. A late addition, opposed by Narita, was the Color Timer, a light which flashed as the hero's energy dwindled during monster battles, powered by a small blinking light bulb. Ultraman was also given a Specium Beam, which actor Furuya would summon through a distinctive hand gesture that remains an essential part of his convention appearances across the globe. Sadao

Iizuka, from Tsuburaya's unit at Toho, composed the optical animation.

The head of the first Ultraman suit, called "A" in Japan, was made from FRP with a latex skin. Additional parts, such as a vertical fin, were added to the suit to make it appear more "alien". This fin obscured the wetsuit's zipper on camera. Painting the first Ultraman suit was difficult as there were no paints in Japan that could stick to a neoprene surface. Rubber-based adhesives, silver paint and metal powder were thus mixed. After shooting the rowdy monster battles that Ultraman engaged in week after week, suit "A" would lose much of its paint job. The suit had to be repainted at least once an episode. Two more Ultraman suits were constructed throughout the show's production, each sleeker and better built than the last. "B" was used in the midrange and "C" was used for the show's final ten episodes. The second and third suits were given superior paint jobs as well. The red stripes mixed into Ultraman's metallic body became more vivid.

As the suit was being crafted, some story changes were made. Sakomizu became Hayata and the female Fuji (played by *Ultra Q*'s Hiroko Sakurai) was added to the Scientific Investigation Agency team, also called the Science Patrol. Eiji Tsuburaya was keen on A-list Toho actor Akira Kubo playing Hayata. Kubo turned the role down, unsure if he could handle balancing his film commitments with a show. Thus B-list player Susumu Kurobe was cast. Actor and singer Susumu Ishikawa was initially cast as Ide, the show's comic relief, but left production on short notice. Thus Masaharu Nihei was cast at the last minute.

Koichi Takano - promoted to FX director on *Ultraman*

Cameras began to roll on *Ultraman* in March of 1966. In contrast to *Ultra Q*, the show had a hectic production schedule. Cost factors and quick production of episodes necessitated the use of 16mm film, though 35mm was used for optical compositing. The use of 16mm cameras meant that Tsuburaya's trademark high frame rate photography could not be used. At the same time, the lower production standards of television allowed for more creative, experimental filmmaking than Tsuburaya would be permitted to do at Toho. For *Ultraman*, Eiji Tsuburaya promoted Koichi Takano, one of his favorite pupils, to special effects director. Takano would run the FX unit on the bulk of the episodes, particularly in the latter half. Support came from Toru Matoba, Hajime Tsuburaya and Sadamasa Arikawa. Takano's footage tends to be hit or miss, resulting in many impressive moments alongside less successful ones.

The menagerie of colorful beasts that Ultraman battles episode after episode were built by Ryosaku Takayama with occasional work by Akira Sasaki, **YASUHI SATO** and Equis Productions. Unlike in *Ultra Q*, most of the suits were newly built, with only Neronga, Gabora and Jirass made from Toho costumes. Baragon from *Frankenstein Conquers the World* was again used for both Neronga and Gabora. For Jirass, the head of the 1965 Godzilla suit was borrowed from Toho during production of *Ebirah, Horror of the Deep*. It was then paired with the body of the '64 suit. Some *Ultra Q* suits were also reused. The monster Ragon reappears in giant form. The suit for "Peter" became the aquatic reptile Gesura. The Garamon suits became the human-sized monster Pygmon and Peguila was reinvented as Chandler. Suits from earlier episodes were occasionally reused. The first episode's Bemler was made into the monster Gyango and Red King's suit became Aboras.

The monsters' names were decided at board meetings, with the writers and designer Narita given relative free reign to envision outlandish creatures. Narita often had to balance his imagination with the episodes' budgets and constraints of 1960s practical FX. Of the novel beasts, the most iconic is surely alien Baltan. The creature was designed by Toru Narita with the first suit being built by Yasuhi Sato and the second by Akira Sasaki. Another notable creature is the skull-headed dinosaur Red King, a Narita-Takayama creation. Other memorable monsters birthed by this fruitful partnership are Kemular, a four-legged beast with a toxin-spewing flower on its back and the subterranean dinosaur Telesdon.

Appearing in the show's only two-parter is the dinosaur Gomora, one of Takayama's best suits. The alien monster Dada is another memorable creation by Narita. With a surreal, psychedelic black and white pattern on its skin, it was named after the Dadaist modern art movement. These monsters were portrayed by a variety of stuntmen that included Haruo Nakajima, Teruo Aragaki and Kunio Suzuki.

Once cameras began to roll on *Ultraman*, the shoot was again divided into three groups, each handling various episodes. Group "A", helmed episodes #2, #3 and #5 and was directed by Toshihiro Iijima with the effects unit run by Toru Matoba. These were the first episodes shot. The production ran into many technical issues. The miniature for the Jet Beetle, the Science Patrol's *Thunderbirds*-like battle vehicle (a modified VTOL model from *Gorath*), smashed into a horizont backdrop and both had to be repaired, which delayed shooting. The second group, "B", was handled by director Samaji Nonagase with effects by Koichi Takano and shot episodes #4, #6, #7 and #9. Group "C" was directed by Tsuburaya's son Hajime and covered episodes #1 and #8.

It did not help matters that TBS decided to cut *Ultra Q*'s monsterless final episode from the slate and demanded that *Ultraman*'s pilot be aired a week earlier than scheduled. They also wanted the show out faster to compete with *Ambassador Magma.* This put tremendous pressure on Eiji Tsuburaya and his company. As group "A" had fallen behind, group "C" was given priority over "B" so the first episode would be ready quickly. The rental fees for the studio and equipment were close to bankrupting Tsuburaya Productions and by June of 1966, it was feared that episode #1 would not be ready in time. Takeshi Kakoi and Tsuburaya came up with the ingenious idea to air a TV special in lieu of a first episode, setting up the character of Ultraman. Directed by **AKIO JISSOJI** (1937-2006) and **YUZO HIGUCHI** (1935-), this special got the job done, buying *Ultraman*'s crew just enough time to complete *"Ultra Operation No. 1"*. It was handed in to TBS only four days before air.

For directors, Tsuburaya enlisted the aid of *Ultra Q* veterans like his son Hajime, Toshihiro Iijima, Samaji Nonagase and Kazuho Mitsuda. He also brought in newly promoted players including Jissoji, Higuchi and **TOSHITSUGU SUZUKI** (1934-20??). Akio Jissoji's episodes were always a highlight. Jissoji was a Tokyo native, though his family relocated to Japanese-occupied

Qingdao when he was young. Following Japan's defeat, his family returned to Tokyo. After graduating from Waseda University, Jissoji joined what would become TBS as an assistant director in 1959. Jissoji had a quirky, distinctive style and experimental sensibility that often got him into trouble. In 1963, Jissoji, now promoted to directing soap opera-style shows and live performances, was nearly fired. He filmed superstar Hibari Misora in a peculiar, unflattering way that appalled her fans. Eiji and Hajime Tsuburaya, however, liked this eccentric young man and saw potential in him. The incident with Misora perhaps reminded Eiji of his fights with actors in the Imperial era who complained that he wasn't shooting them in a complimentary fashion.

Akio Jissoji

Jissoji had conceived *Ultra Q* proposals that weren't produced and directed a TV documentary on Eiji Tsuburaya prior to *Ultraman*'s airing. This special, entitled *The Father of Ultra Q*, is an amazing portrait of Japanese special effects cinema's greatest luminary. The documentary features behind-the-scenes footage of the currently shooting *The War of the Gargantuas*. *The Father of Ultra Q* takes the viewer up close and personal with the mythic Tsuburaya, with whom little other film footage exists.

Seeing candid shots of Tsuburaya as a real person is almost surreal: speaking, directing and ordering his crew around along with attending weekly Sunday mass. In a highlight, Jissoji cuts together footage of Tsuburaya editing film stock by hand to a classical soundtrack: a sequence that feels transcendent.

With a European sensibility akin to Jean Luc Goddard, Akio Jissoji spoke French and was obsessed with classical music. He did things differently from

Ultraman's other directors. Jissoji supervised both the drama and special effects. Like Noriaki Yuasa, this brought him into conflict with special effects staff, particularly Koichi Takano and Minoru Nakano. Jissoji's episodes always contained unconventional and beautiful imagery. Even his unit's horizons looked like expressionistic paintings. The Science Patrol's HQ is lit in an atmospheric and foreboding fashion, far removed from the warm look of other episodes. Jissoji shoots actors' faces unflatteringly with wide angle lenses, a technique later employed by spiritual protégé Hideaki Anno.

Two of Jissoji's most memorable episodes are *"My Home is Earth"* and *"The Monster Graveyard"*. *"My Home is Earth"* features a formerly human monster, Jamila (Teruo Aragaki). Once an astronaut, Jamila became a giant beast upon exposure to the atmosphere of an alien planet. This downbeat installment recalls the British/U.S. co-production *First Man Into Space* (1959). Jissoji shows compassion for his monsters in a way that even Ishiro Honda never did, personally empathizing with them as outcasts. He treats them like somber Shinto spirits; elements of nature gone wrong. *"The Monster Graveyard"* is a similar episode that is as existentially disturbing as it is unique. It features an undead beast named Seabouz (Kunio Suzuki) which emits a haunting wail that no doubt echoed in the nightmares of youngsters on both sides of the Pacific. Seabouz desperately wants to return to the eponymous Monster Graveyard in space where its soul can rest in peace. The creature is treated with the pathos of a frightened child and is one of the most sympathetic portrayals of a monster in the tokusatsu medium.

Broadcast weekly, *Ultraman* was a tremendous hit on Japanese airwaves. It proved an even greater ratings giant than its predecessor, reaching as high as 42% of the Japanese public. An entire generation of children were inspired by the show, including a six-year-old boy from Yamaguchi Prefecture named **HIDEAKI ANNO** (1960-). Its final episode, *"Farewell Ultraman,"* takes on a decisive tone as the Science Patrol's HQ is directly attacked by aliens. This foreshadows the next series, *Ultraseven*, which features entirely extraterrestrial menaces. Ultraman then meets his match in the hulking alien killing machine Zetton (Teruo Aragaki). Seeing Ultraman's limp body on the ground, his color timer blinking as he dies, gave Japanese monster kids the same healthy trauma as the shooting of the title character's mother in Disney's *Bambi* (1942). Zetton is, incidentally, brought down by the human characters and not Ultraman, demonstrating that perhaps humanity has reached the point where it can defend itself against monsters on its own. The episode's final shots, of Ultraman and his superior Zoffy (Hikaru Urano) flying toward the Land of Light are beautiful, cathartic and among special effects director Takano's best work.

Ultraman was picked up for American distribution shortly after it started airing by United Artists and was syndicated on U.S. television until the 1980s. So grand was the show's success that Toho was keen on making a feature-length *Ultraman* film with Tsuburaya. For reasons unknown, the project didn't make it to green light. Toho settled for a compilation movie edited from episodes that played with their *King Kong Escapes* the following summer.

Watari, the Ninja Boy was shown on a double-bill with the anime film *Cyborg 009*

Toei, meanwhile, would release another special effects extravaganza - **WATARI, THE NINJA BOY,** [Director: **SADAO FUNATOKO** (1932-1972) - **Release Date (Japan):** July 21st, 1966] produced at their Kyoto branch. Funatoko was no stranger to the tokusatsu genre, having directed episodes of *Moonlight Mask* and *Ambassador Magma*. The plentiful effects were supervised by **JUNJI KURATA** (1930-2002). Based on a manga by Sanpei Shirato, it concerns the adventures of Watari (Yoshinobu Kaneko), a wily young ninja boy in Warring States Japan. *Watari* features elaborate optical composite work. To compete with Eiji Tsuburaya, Toei's next generation president **SHIGERU OKADA** (1924-2011) ordered an Oxberry printer from the United States. Special effects director Kurata doesn't achieve the same level of mastery as Tsuburaya, but for the mid 1960s, the picture's optical effects are fanciful. *Watari* features a fair amount of miniature and pyrotechnic work along with cel animation by Toei's anime division.

The production of *Watari* was expensive and manga author Shirato was at first unhappy with the footage he was screened. However, when it was released for the summer Toei Manga Festival on a double bill with the anime feature *Cyborg 009,* it was one of Toei's most successful films that year. Shigeru Okada ordered the production of two more period films with special effects flourishes, including a film about legendary ninja Jiraiya. Seeing Toei release a successful effects film would also spur Nikkatsu and Shochiku to action. Those two companies began planning tokusatsu monster films for the following year.

Watari's co-feature, *Cyborg 009,* had been based on a popular manga by **SHOTARO ISHINOMORI** (1938-1999), then only in his 20s and one of Osamu Tezuka's most notable protégés. Born Shotaro Onodera, he would eventually take the name of his hometown, Ishinomori in Miyagi Prefecture. He adored cinema as a boy and longed to be a movie director. In elementary school, he encountered Osamu Tezuka's post-war manga debut *New Treasure Island* and was floored. From that point on, young Ishinomori began to draw manga. He befriended Tezuka and published his first manga in 1954 while still a high school student. Ishinomori would go on to be an iconic luminary of tokusatsu as well as anime.

Amazingly, as Eiji Tsuburaya began production on *Ultraman* at his company, he was also at work on another classic monster mash at Toho - **THE WAR OF THE GARGANTUAS** [Director: Ishiro Honda - **Release Date (Japan):** July 31st, 1966]. *The War of the Gargantuas,* a loose sequel to *Frankenstein Conquers the World,* was put into production by Tomoyuki Tanaka in early 1966. Tentatively titled *The Frankenstein Brothers,* it was Toho's third collaboration with Henry G. Saperstein's United Productions of America and subsidiary Benedict

Pictures. Much of *Frankenstein*'s creative team from both sides of the camera returned.

Nick Adams, unable to reprise his role, was to be replaced by Tab Hunter. Hunter was also unavailable, so *West Side Story* (1961) and *The Haunting*'s Russ Tamblyn was cast. Whereas Nick Adams had been respectful to and friendly with the Japanese cast and crew, Tamblyn caused difficulty on Honda's side. Tamblyn holed himself up in his hotel room with his wife, did not socialize with his Japanese fellow cast and took little of Honda's direction. Partially due to his bitter experience with Tamblyn, Honda was never fond of *The War of the Gargantuas*. The film's script, co-written by Honda and Takeshi Kimura, is weak with little character development. Being the final Toho monster film for decades to receive direct support from the Self-Defense Force, it is perhaps fitting that the military spectacle is the highlight of the live-action segments; unfortunately, there is otherwise little of interest on Honda's end of the picture. *The War of the Gargantuas* is also hampered by a ridiculous bit where a foreign lounge singer (played by Kipp Hamilton, Saperstein's mistress) belts out an embarrassing pseudo-Burt Bacharach song.

Assistant director Teruyoshi Nakano (center right) claps the slate, startling Keiko Suzuki (left) as Tsuburaya (center) directs

Yet somehow *The War of the Gargantuas* succeeds entirely through memorably outlandish creatures and tokusatsu spectacle. In contrast to *Frankenstein Conquers the World*, *The War of the Gargantuas* belongs to Tsuburaya, who clearly took it to heart. Despite the fact that he was occupied preparing *Ultraman* for air, the effects director helms his finest monster sequences since *Mothra vs. Godzilla*. The film opens in atmospheric fashion with a battle between aquatic Frankenstein monster Gaira (Haruo Nakajima) and a giant octopus, a nod to the prior picture's unused ending. The octopus prop, fresh from use on *Ultra Q*, was renovated and is used more effectively, with lights added to its eyes.

Eiji Tsuburaya amidst one of his miniaturized worlds

The film's unique monsters were designed by Toru Narita. The production team was inspired by a Japanese myth of warring brother gods Umihiko and Yamahiko: one residing in the ocean and another the mountains. Born from the cells of the first film's creature is the ogre-like Gaira, one of the Tsuburaya unit's most ghoulish creations. Sanda, played by **YU SEKITA** (1932-), is largely the previous picture's Frankenstein Monster, though given a more feral, ape-like appearance.

The two suits were modeled by Teizo Toshimitsu and Yasuei Yagi. Toshimitsu created expressive masks that were molded more closely to the actors' faces. Perhaps taking a cue from rival Ryosaku Takayama's work on *Majin*, the masks used the actors' genuine eyes. This allowed Sekita and Nakajima to give more expressive and even disturbing performances. Gaira would become one of Nakajima's favorite roles until his dying day. To strengthen the impression of an aquatic creature, Eizo Kaimai glued seaweed and water flowers on Gaira's fur. The hair on Sanda's body was made from hemp. For Honda's unit, the modeling team built a suit for Baby Sanda (Yasuhiro Komiya) as seen in a flashback. A full-sized Gaira hand, similar to the one built for King Kong in 1962, was also constructed for sequences of the monster snatching human prey.

The Gargantua suits were far lighter than any of Toho's reptilian monsters. This allowed for faster-paced battles. Indeed, Sanda and Gaira whale on each other like a pair of drunken brawlers. The monsters even turn whatever objects their immediate environment provides into projectiles and blunt implements. When Sanda finds out about his brother's "people food" diet, he pulls up a tree, roots and all, and whacks Gaira with it. Later, during the climatic Tokyo brawl, Sanda smashes a boat over Gaira's head. There's a certain grotesque freakishness to the Gargantuas not present in prior Toho kaiju. In a flourish uncharacteristic of the bloodshed-hating Tsuburaya, Gaira has the grisly habit of eating humans and is depicted doing so on several occasions. Like a tokusatsu take on Francesco Goya's *Saturn Devouring His Son,* these moments were considered unsettling by Japanese audiences. They no doubt sewed some night terrors into the subconscious of monster-loving kids.

A superb shot early on, of Gaira looking hungrily from under the waves at a pair of fishermen unfortunate enough to stray into his waters, is like a nightmarish moment from a fairy tale. This was accomplished by filming actor Nakajima through a water tank. Another stunning segment, made possible by the Oxberry printer, features fishermen on a coastline fleeing as Gaira is caught in the net they were hauling in. The scene of Gaira attacking Haneda airport is one of the Tsuburaya unit's very best monster sequences. The most impressive Oxberry shot in the entire film features Gaira advancing down the airport runway in the distance towards its terminals.

Thanks to the Gargantuas' smaller size compared to Godzilla and company, the miniatures on *The War of the Gargantuas* could be built at a larger scale. Special effects art director Yasuyuki Inoue's sets are among the most realistic the Toho FX team achieved. The artificial forests, valleys and cities were built with a particular attention to detail. Once again, miniature Japanese cedars played the role of pines and unseen roots were added for realism in case the suit actors tore them out. Inoue even built a miniature city for Honda's unit, used for the exterior of a hotel room set.

This was used for an eye-catching scene in which Dr. Stewart (Russ Tamblyn) opens the curtain to reveal a blacked-out Tokyo in the midst of lighting up.

Eiji Tsuburaya (right)

The War of the Gargantuas, the last film where the JSDF gave Honda's unit support, features the military mounting an intricate defense. They attempt to kill Gaira with giant death ray cannons called Type 66 Masers. These were not present in the original script and were added at Honda's suggestion. The Masers were designed by Mutsumi Toyoshima and bring elements to synthesis of previous beam weapons in *The Mysterians, Mothra* and *Invasion of Astro-Monster.* Akinori Takagi, by now specializing in the electrical engineering of models, installed iodine lamps to light the cannons from the base. The rays were once again animated by Sadao Iizuka with assistance from Koichi Kawakita. The maser attack sequence is a dazzling spectacle with superb miniature work. Often via stock footage from *The War of the Gargantuas,* they would return in many Toho monster films to come.

Another pair of stunning wide Oxberry composites come later on of an advancing Gaira juxtaposed against feeling villagers. By the picture's finale, the effects team has well and truly taken over. Sanda and Gaira's brutal Tokyo brawl stands among Tsuburaya's best kaiju battle sequences. *The War of the Gargantuas* is capped in a tragic finale in which the two beasts are wiped out by an impressively executed underwater volcano. The picture was originally to end more elaborately with the eruption engulfing Tokyo. This ending would have made it clearer that the Gargantuas and their cells had been completely destroyed. In the end, Tomoyuki Tanaka decided that an extra destruction sequence would push the film over budget, though stock shots from *The Last War* were to supplement Tsuburaya's footage.

The War of the Gargantuas has since become a cult classic worldwide. It would also prove influential, inspiring such future works as *Gamera: Guardian of the Universe* (1995), Quentin Tarantino's *Kill Bill Vol. 2* (2004), *Crank 2: High Voltage* (2009), Guiliermo Del Toro's *Pacific Rim* (2013) and the *Attack on Titan* franchise. In the United States, it didn't hit drive-in screens until 1970, on a double bill with *Invasion of Astro-Monster*. The U.S. version is longer and contains additional and alternate footage. References to *Frankenstein Conquers the World* were removed, however, with the monsters passed off as Yeti-like cryptozoological horrors rather than giant Frankensteins.

Released two weeks later was Daiei Kyoto's **RETURN OF MAJIN** [**Director:** Kenji Misumi - **Release Date (Japan):** August 13th, 1966]. Once again, Yoshiyuki Kuroda helmed the special effects unit and Fujio Morita shot both. *Return of Majin* is a standard *jidai-geki* with striking cinematography by Morita. This time the Majin statue resides on an island at a lake as another nasty warlord (Takashi Kanda) conquers and oppresses two neighboring territories. The villains show more craftiness this time around and succeed in destroying the statue. Kuroda matches the quality of his work in the first film, hitting another home run with Morita and the FX unit. The scale of their sequences was determined using precise mathematical calculations.

A full-sized Majin statue was again built for the lake set with its rocky surroundings made from steel. Morita's penchant for atmospheric particles went on full display once more as heavy fog, made from paraffin, was dispersed throughout the sets with giant fans. The destruction of the Majin statue was done on a full-sized set with explosives in steel cylinders. This approach differs from the course Eiji Tsuburaya would have taken, with miniatures, high frame rate shooting and gunpowder. The Majin suit from the first film was given heavy renovations by Keizo Murase as *Return of Majin* called for more mobility from the monster god.

As Majin comes to life, he parts the lake a la Charlton Heston's Moses in *The Ten Commandments* (1956), among other intriguing Judeo-Christian images. Yoshiyuki Kuroda, who had ghost-directed the similar "Divine Wind" finale in *Nichiren and the Great Mongol Invasion*, stuns here. Among the best tokusatsu water sequences ever filmed, it looks better than John P. Fulton's work in *The Ten Commandments,* yet was made on a far slimmer budget. Gas cylinders with compressed nitrogen were pumped into the water to create the effect of Majin emerging from the lake. A genuine waterfall was filmed from both sides and composited into the scene. Kuroda had to go to Tokyo Daiei and use their optical printer to create this, as none were to be found at the Kyoto branch and the shot was too complex to create through masking and double exposure. Kuroda and particularly Morita were actually disappointed with this sequence. Morita felt the straight lines on top of the water were unconvincing. They also wanted a sequence that was more frightening than visually beautiful.

Kenji Misumi

Another arresting shot features Majin tearing down the wall of the warlord's fortress, revealing Misumi's live action set. This was Fujio Morita's idea. The miniature work is also stellar. The shots of Majin destroying a model castle had to be re-filmed as they didn't crumble properly. Kuroda's crew worked through the night to rebuild and repair it. The effect of muskets being fired at Majin was created with firecrackers encased in rubber bullets, which suit actor Riki Hashimoto found quite harrowing. Other shells, to explode in midair, were executed via medicine capsules filled with gunpowder. These were lit and shot upward through small cylinders. Morita was frustrated by errors in scale with the final shots of Majin gazing at heroine Lady Sayuri (Shiho Fujimura). He had also wanted the water to bubble up and consume Majin. This effect proved too time-consuming to execute, so a simple optical wipe was used instead. Overall, *Return of Majin* lacks the novelty of the first. Once again, however, the final reel is jaw-dropping. Kenji Misumi had helmed several entries in the Zatoichi franchise and would later be known for directing most of the *Lone Wolf and Cub* series.

In the meantime, Eiji Tsuburaya had incredibly been at work on developing yet another TV series at his company since March. Like American puppet master **JIM HENSON** (1936-1990), who developed *The Muppets* for older children and *Sesame Street* for preschoolers, Tsuburaya was keen on creating a TV program for kids not quite old enough for his Godzilla or Ultraman franchises. The show, **BOOSKA THE FRIENDLY BEAST** [Television Run (Japan): November 9th, 1966 - September 27th, 1967], was intended to start airing on Nippon TV in October of 1966, but wound up being postponed until November. *Booska, the Friendly Beast* partially sprang from the popularity of the more child-oriented *Ultra Q* episodes, particularly *"Kanegon's Cocoon."* It concerns a boy named Daisuke Tonda (Tomohiro Miyamoto) who feeds his pet iguana an experimental substance. The lizard becomes the friendly, human-sized monster Booska and hijinks ensue. Booska, played by a variety of suit actors, is powered by an element called "Booskanium". This can only be replenished via a diet consisting of ramen noodles.

This black-and-white show was originally to be 26 episodes long, but due to stellar ratings among children, Nippon TV ordered 21 more episodes. Toru Matoba often supervised the special effects, with support from Sadamasa Arikawa and **ATSUSHI OKI** (1940-1996). Oki had worked as an assistant director for both Tsuburaya Productions and P-Productions and was promoted to special effects director on *Booska*. Like the ensemble of *The Muppets* or *Sesame Street,* the character of Booska is still beloved among young audiences in Japan.

By December of 1966, the Monster Boom was in full swing. Monster-loving Japanese boys, for their New Years' holiday break from school, had their pick of an unprecedented four special effects films on the big screen. These boys included the six-year-old Hideaki Anno from Ube, the now 11-year-old Shusuke Kaneko, the seven-year-old **KEITA AMEMIYA** (1959-) from Chiba Prefecture and a quirky young boy celebrating his seventh birthday named **SHINYA TSUKAMOTO** (1960-). The available choices included a third Majin film, a new Godzilla entry and a double feature headed by a movie about ninja hero Jiraiya. If they saved their allowances cunningly, perhaps they could see them all. On television, they could watch Ambassador Magma defend the Earth from Goa, Ultraman beat on the monster of the week and Daisuke and Booska engaging in their divers. The Monster Boom would leave an indelible mark on all four of these children, who would grow up to become noted genre figures themselves.

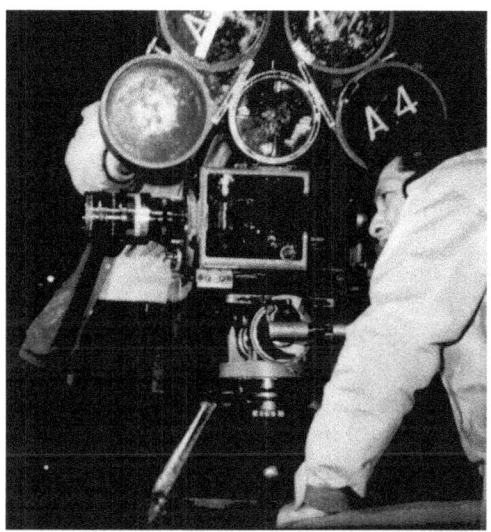

Fujio Morita (right) and one of his favorite weapons - the dual camera magazine

The first of the 1966 holiday releases was **MAJIN STRIKES AGAIN** [Director: Issei Mori - Release Date (Japan): December 10th, 1966]. For this entry, a more child-oriented approach was taken as a quartet of boy protagonists figure heavily into the plot. The most ambitious but uneven of the films, *Majin Strikes Again* often feels like an old-school live action Disney movie. The direction of the child actors is better than Noriaki Yuasa's on the *Showa* Gamera films. Behind the scenes, Mori, who had no children of his own, handled them in a stern, grouchy manner. In all three films, the music of Akira Ifukube lends the same level of grandeur as in any Toho production.

Catering to the shorter attention spans of youngsters, the film opens with an impressive effects scene which features a well-staged flood and astonishing miniatures. The opening sequence of *Majin Strikes Again* made use of Daiei Kyoto's giant effects pool built for *Nichiren and the Great Mongol Invasion*. The shot of parched soil splitting was created by placing dirt and sand atop plastic tenting. This was then dried and pulled to create the effect. An early shot of Majin materializing was created through a process called negative rubbing which was done directly on the film stock.

The bulk of shooting took place in August and September of 1966. Per the more rushed schedule, Fujio Morita would share DP duties with colleague Hiroshi Imai, the latter focusing on director Mori's side. Their cinematography is lush with moments of visual beauty. The location scenes, the most stunning in the trilogy, tended to be shot first and the on-set and effects shots were done afterward, adjusted to the location's weather for continuity. This was a big challenge for Morita. Another problem that put pressure on an already behind-schedule production was that a good portion of negatives were scratched during processing, rendering a swath of both units' footage unusable. The crew scrambled to pull off reshoots in rural Tateyama.

Kuroda's unit supplies another impressive divine rampage for the finale, extended in runtime. Kuroda repeats visual motifs from the first two films and the sequence lacks a little novelty. In keeping with DP Morita's predilection for air particles, the sequence is aided by snowfall fluttering through the air. Styrofoam was used as snow and freon gas was released onto the set. This was to make the styrofoam particles appear lighter in mass like snowflakes. The sequence is, however, on par with Toho's subsequent work and contains stunning segments such as Majin wading through a torrent of cannonfire. Cement was often mixed into the explosives to give them more volume.

Another stunningly executed bit in the final moments features Majin turning to snow as the sky clears. This effect was engineered by Keizo Murase. Kuroda was impressed with it; his crew nailed it in one take. *Majin Strikes Again* is the weakest of the three pictures but technically polished and entertaining in a way the subsequent Gamera films made at Daiei Tokyo seldom were. *Majin Strikes Again* makes one wish that Yoshiyuki Kuroda had been brought in to handle the FX work there which was sadly impossible due to corporate politics within Daiei.

The next holiday monster release was put out a week later: **EBIRAH, HORROR OF THE DEEP [AKA: GODZILLA VS. THE SEA MONSTER - Director:** Jun Fukuda - Release Date (Japan): December 17th, 1966] from Toho. For *Ebirah*, the Godzilla series took a different creative approach. Tomoyuki Tanaka and the brass at Toho opted for a change of scenery for this entry, both in front of and behind the camera. Ishiro Honda stepped aside and Fukuda was made director. Since directing *The Secret of the Telegian*, his career had come a long way. Having just completed the popular dark comedy spy flick *Ironfinger* (1965), he had established himself as a specialist in action programmers.

Eiji Tsuburaya (left) and Jun Fukuda (right)

Eiji Tsuburaya was also too absorbed in supervising *Ultraman* and *Booska* to take on yet another film at Toho that year. His hard-driving work schedule rushing back and forth between his company and Toho, which often left him sleeping in a desk chair, was taking its toll. Sadamasa Arikawa was thus placed in charge of the FX unit for *Ebirah, Horror of the Deep*. Tsuburaya was still given "special effects director" credit and made frequent visits to the set. Furthermore, to keep the budget lower and eliminate the need for model cities, the locale was changed to the exotic South Pacific. Further highlighting the change in direction, Akira Ifukube was even substituted with Masaru Sato, whose cues give the film a more playful and lighthearted tone. *Ebirah* is an underrated entry and a lot of fun. Fukuda's direction is livelier than Honda's clinical sensibility with stylistic flair per his action background. The script by Shinichi Sekizawa also has one of the more engaging human plots in the Godzilla series.

Ebirah, Horror of the Deep began life as *Operation Robinson Crusoe*, which was to have featured King Kong in place of Godzilla. Toho was eager to make another Kong film while they still held the rights from their deal with RKO a few years prior. Rankin-Bass, to co-produce *Operation Robinson Crusoe*, were not happy with the script and adamant that Ishiro Honda direct the picture. As Honda was occupied with the romantic comedy *Come Marry Me*, the project was retooled to star Godzilla. Apart from this character swap, essentially no adjustments were made in the script; Godzilla, sometimes bewilderingly, behaves in a Kong-like manner. The creature is awakened by electricity a la *King Kong vs. Godzilla* and even takes a visible interest in native girl Dayo (Kumi Mizuno). Toho would take another crack at a Kong film with Rankin-Bass the following year.

The Godzilla suit from *Invasion of Astro-Monster* was reused for *Ebirah, Horror of the Deep*. The suit's face oddly changes appearance dramatically in later sequences. This was because, as Arikawa's unit was filming, Tsuburaya asked for use of the suit's head in episode #10 of *Ultraman*. The cut-off head was sent to Tsuburaya Productions and used to portray Jirass. As it had been repainted by Ryosaku Takayama's modeling team, the head required extensive repairs by Teizo Toshimitsu before being reattached. Damage from the water sequences also likely contributed.

Ebirah, a mantis shrimp-like monster crustacean with lobster claws, was played by Yu Sekita. The creature was designed by Yasuyuki Inoue using motifs of various crustaceans and arthropods. The well-constructed suit was built mainly by Yasuei Yagi with its claws made from FRP. The suit's shell-like coating was again created by mixing latex and sawdust. For shots of Ebirah's claw rising from the ocean, a large prop was constructed by Toshimitsu. Mothra also appears in Imago form and acts as a deus ex machina. Time-worn props left over from *Mothra* and *Mothra vs. Godzilla* were used. One sequence, a nod to the pteranodon scene in *King Kong*, features Godzilla battling a giant condor. A Rodan prop from *Ghidorah, the Three-Headed Monster*, having served as Litra in *Ultra Q* a year prior, was again redressed.

Arikawa, under Tsuburaya's supervision, handles the FX unit well, starting with an impressive typhoon at sea that heralds Ebirah's appearance. His work is more hit or miss than his mentor Tsuburaya's, but he was well trained in staging the same style of effects sequences. There are frequent, stunning Oxberry composites combining the actors and giant monsters with impressive intricacy. One segment midpicture even features briefly glimpsed rowing puppets on boats capsized by Ebirah.

The monster brawling, shot in Toho's Big Pool, is the most physical yet with shots of realistic underwater photography using the suits. Typically, underwater monster battles were shot on a dry set with atmospheric lighting (filtered through water tanks) to convey the deep sea effect. Arikawa was the first to have the actors in their suits battle underwater; filming them through an aquarium-like glass window. As one might expect, this was quite dangerous, as the monster suits absorbed water; actors Haruo Nakajima and Yu Sekita were obliged to use an aqualung between takes. Guignol puppets were also used effectively in certain shots.

Wrangling a monster bird prop

One exciting highlight is found in a sequence in which Godzilla does battle with a squadron of jets sent by the communistic villains. This scene certainly ranks among the former aviator Sadamasa Arikawa's greatest achievements as special effects director. Shots from it were pilfered for future Godzilla entries. *Ebirah, Horror of the Deep* is, however, not devoid of flaws. Parts of the film, particularly the Infant Island sequences, look cheap compared to Toho's glory days in the first half of the '60s. In one shot, a crew member's put-out cigarette can even be seen on Mothra's head. Also somewhat underwhelming is a brief, awkwardly staged battle pitting Mothra against Godzilla, which fortuitously leads to two of the film's best moments. There's a strikingly lifelike Oxberry composite of the film's cast running towards a landed Mothra. The destruction of the South Pacific island in the final moments is another spectacular highlight; recycled almost wholesale in *Godzilla vs. Megalon* (1973). It stunningly blends Yasuyuki Inoue's ingeniously engineered miniatures with Kyuzo Yamamoto's pyrotechnic alchemy.

Days later, Toei unleashed a special effects-laden double bill just in time for the New Years' holiday. It consisted of **GRAND DUEL IN MAGIC [AKA: THE MAGIC SERPENT - Director: TETSUYA YAMAUCHI (1934-2010) - Release Date (Japan):** December 21st, 1966] and **THE GOLDEN BAT** [**Director:** Hajime Sato - **Release Date (Japan):** Ibid]. Toei president Shigeru Okada had ordered the production of two more special effects laden period pieces after the massive success of *Watari, the Ninja Boy*. The first was **GOLDEN THIEVES** [**Director:** Tadashi Sawashima - **Release Date (Japan):** December 13th, 1966], containing only subtle tokusatsu effects. The story of Jiraiya, a legendary ninja said to transform himself into a monster frog, was a natural choice for the second, *Grand Duel in Magic*. Popular actor Hiroki Matsukata was cast as the iconic hero.

Director Yamauchi, a native of Hiroshima, had graduated from Chuo University's economics department before joining Toei as an assistant director in 1957. He was a relatively new director, having made his debut in 1964 with the popular *Ninja-Gari*. For *Grand Duel in Magic*, he was not granted the luxury of a special effects director and helmed both the main and FX units himself. This is a double-edged sword for *Grand Duel in Magic* but the film does feel more cohesive as a result. Despite the lack of a special effects director, these scenes are lavish. *Grand Duel in Magic* sports a strong synchronicity between the FX and actor shots.

A magical realist fantasy with Eastern fairy tale overtones, early scenes feature a well-executed Chinese dragon, the monster form of villain Orochimaru (*Watari*'s Ryutaro Otomo). There's also a giant eagle that looks much like the bird monsters created by Tsuburaya's unit. The miniature sets are well made and the optical work is often striking, though sometimes crude. An early sequence features Jiraiya removing and reattaching his head, created through trick photography and an optical printer. Another memorable scene features the film's evil warlord (Bin Amatsu) confronted by the ghosts of Jiraiya's parents; turning from color to black-and-white. More firmly on the live-action side of things, anachronistic lounge music played over a traditional Japanese dance lets the viewer know

Grand Duel in Magic is a Toei production. *Grand Duel in Magic* being a ninja movie, unlike in a tokusatsu show, Jiraiya and Orochimaru cross swords on a beach at the climax after the latter's dragon form is defeated.

In the original story and Shozo Makino's silent version, Jiraiya and Orochimaru's monster forms are the size of large animals. In keeping with the times, for this film the two transform into kaiju and do battle, *Ultraman*-style. In the folktale, Tsunade (Tomoko Ogawa), turns into a monster slug. For *Grand Duel in Magic*, this changed to a giant spider which she merely summons, as Toei worried that transforming the popular Ogawa into a slug would anger her fans. Keizo Murase of Equis Productions constructed the monsters.

Jiraya and Orochimaru's monster forms are constructed

The special effects work in *Grand Duel in Magic* is overall uneven and below the quality of Tsuburaya or Kuroda. The monsters, suits with rod puppet enhancements, are a little awkwardly manipulated. The giant spider is weaker in execution than Toho's Kumonga, to appear in the following year's *Son of Godzilla*. There are fanciful moments, however, such as Jiraiya's frog form and Orochimaru's dragon exchanging fire and water. This uses live pyrotechnics rather than optical beams as other special effects directors would employ.

The success of *Watari, the Ninja Boy* and *Grand Duel in Magic* would lead to Toei's TV series **RED SHADOW** [**Television Run (Japan)**: April 5th, 1967 - March 27th, 1968], based on a manga by Mitsuteru Yokoyama. Tetsuya Yamauchi would go on to direct episodes and the monster suits from *Grand Duel in Magic* were reused. Yamauchi would next travel to Taiwan and helm the *wuxia* picture **LIST OF THE GODS [Directors:** Lin Chung Kuang, Tetsuya Yamauchi - **Release Date (Taiwan):** October 10th, 1969], which features a giant dragon similar to the one in *Grand Duel in Magic*, also modeled by Equis Productions.

The other film on Toei's double feature, the black-and-white *The Golden Bat*, was based on the world's very first superhero. Predating Batman and Superman by close to a decade, *The Golden Bat* began as a *kamishibai* show in 1931, a type of traveling street theater popular in pre-war Japan. This involved a streetside narrator similar to a silent film benshi displaying and verbally elaborating upon a series of pictures. Eventually, *The Golden Bat* became a popular manga. The Aztec-themed hero got his first film adaptation in 1950 from the independent studio Shin Eiga, though without much in the way of tokusatsu effects.

Toei's adaptation is pulpy fun but uneven in execution, one of director Hajime Sato's weaker, more eclectic films. Highly episodic, *The Golden Bat* often feels like a cross between a Republic serial and Fox's then-current *Batman* show. The picture is laden with sci-fi and tokusatsu flourishes not present in earlier adaptations. Per much of director Sato's work, the most effective moments are of Freda and Bava-esque foreboding atmosphere. Toei's version seems to have held some influence for young manga artist Go Nagai, soon to turn heads in the early '70s with edgy manga and anime icons like *Devilman* and *Cutie Honey*. An anime version of *The Golden Bat* would debut only four months later in April.

The effects unit was handled by veteran Sadao Uemura. *The Golden Bat* features excellent miniature work, though most of it only approaches the level of Tsuburaya and company. Some scenes strongly evoke Uemura's work on the Super Giant films for Shin Toho. The heroic Golden Bat's archnemesis is Nazo (Koji Sekiyama). A mad scientist in the original story, he's now an evil space alien with a goofy but endearing puppet-like appearance. *The Golden Bat*'s climax features elaborate model shooting with Nazo's tower-like fortress being the most interestingly executed. *The Golden Bat* would be one of Sadao Uemura's last tokusatsu films, though he would continue with occasional TV work.

With four releases in theaters and three TV shows to choose from, the New Years' holiday season of late 1966 to early '67 was the peak of the Japanese Monster Boom. The fad would simmer for the next two years. 1967 would be another delight for monster-loving boys like Shusuke Kaneko, Keita Amemiya and Hideaki Anno. Four of the "Big Five" studios would release monster pictures and as *Ultraman* and *Ambassador Magma* concluded that spring and summer, an even higher volume of special effects shows would swarm the airwaves. Kaiju and tokusatsu cinema and television were big business in Japan. An Associated Press article on Japan's Monster Boom run in local American newspapers throughout mid-1967 put it this way: "For a people who love the delicate beauty of flower arranging and tea ceremonies, the Japanese can dream up some of the most nightmarish monsters ever projected on movie screens. The reasons are simple: monster films are hits and great moneymakers."

XIII.
<u>1967</u>
昭和四十二

Thunderbirds' Gerry Anderson would befriend Eiji Tsuburaya over their shared passion for shooting miniaturized craft

By 1967, the Monster Boom was far from over. *Ultraman* and its sequel reigned supreme on the airwaves and the studios continued to pump out special effects pictures. All of the "Big Five" released monster media in '67. Toho put out both King Kong and Godzilla films while companies that had never dabbled in kaiju movies such as Shochiku and Nikkatsu got their feet wet. While Toei did not produce a live-action theatrical monster film, they produced several special effects shows including the creature-laden *Giant Robo* and released the fittingly named anime film *Cyborg 009: Monster Wars*. Even Japan's adversary South Korea took notice of these movies' domestic popularity and imported Japanese technicians to help them make a similar film.

Eiji Tsuburaya started the year with a much-deserved vacation. After his breathless work in 1966 developing and working on several shows and films, he went abroad for several months starting late that year. Tsuburaya visited the United Kingdom where he met *Thunderbirds* producer **GERRY ANDERSON** (1929-2012), whom he had befriended. Tsuburaya visited Anderson's set and the two bonded over their mutual enthusiasm for miniature effects. Tsuburaya was inspired by what he saw at Century 21 Productions. Anderson's elaborate, intricately constructed miniaturized worlds no doubt reminded Tsuburaya of his own. Tsuburaya would in turn feature a greater number of Andersonian flying vehicles in his coming shows *Ultraseven* and *Mighty Jack*. He had also been chosen to create an exhibition in the upcoming 1970 Osaka World Expo, so was eager to see Expo '67 in Montreal. Tsuburaya also visited the U.S., where he appeared as a guest on *The Ed Sullivan Show*. As his incessantly hardworking lifestyle was beginning to affect his health, the coming year would see him at the helm for only one film at Toho.

Noriaki Yuasa

In mid-March, **GAMERA VS. GYAOS** [**Director:** Noriaki Yuasa - **Release Date (Japan):** March 15th, 1967] was released by Daiei. Both Yuasa's best directed Gamera entry and the finest *Showa* Gamera picture, *Gyaos* represents a peak for a series that would sink to embarassing lows. While *Gamera vs. Gyaos* marks the point where Gamera officially becomes "the friend to children", it strikes a balance between the darker tone of the previous two films and the silliness to come. The bat-like Gyaos was inspired by Stoker's Count Dracula, a direction insisted upon by Masaichi Nagata. Designed by Akira Inoue, Gyaos was made by Equis Productions; sculpted by Masao Yagi and painted by Keizo Murase. It comes off rather like a pastiche of Toho's monsters: the creature flies like Rodan, shoots beams like Ghidorah and is a nocturnal hunter with a taste for people food like

Gaira. It even destroys Nagoya Castle as Godzilla did.

While the output of Noriaki Yuasa's FX team doesn't quite match that of their Toho rivals, the effects are among his strongest with striking images throughout. There are gorgeous composites, such as child protagonist Eichi (Naoyuki Abe) optically printed onto Gamera's hand. Some of the FX shots make use of old-school rear projection, others with dual camera magazines similar to those employed by Fujio Morita in the Majin films. Gyaos' attack on Nagoya and subsequent battle with Gamera is perhaps the finest sequence directed by Yuasa. It is loaded with impressive optical composites that approach Tsuburaya level. Among the best of these features Gyaos flying over a moving plate of Tokyo at high altitude.

Gamera suit actor Teruo Aragaki

Gamera vs. Gyaos is again surprisingly gruesome in contrast to Tsuburaya's work. A memorable bit features Gamera biting and dragging Gyaos with its teeth as the latter's Pepto Bismol-like blood gushes profusely. Though future entries would be more child-oriented, Yuasa's comical monster gore would only intensify. *Gamera vs. Gyaos,* double-billed with the Japanese/Soviet co-production *Little Fugitive*, netted good box office. Ishiro Honda, ever the gentleman, even sent screenwriter Niisan Takahashi a congratulatory card as it had outperformed Toho's *King Kong Escapes* and he had personally enjoyed the film.

Export poster for *The X From Outer Space* (1967)

At the same time, executive Shiro Kido, still in power at Shochiku, was keen for his company to produce more special effects films. The company was known internationally for having produced many of Yasujiro Ozu's films, and Kido perhaps felt that it was time to expand their export market, as Japanese sci-fi and monster movies had seen success abroad as well. On March 25th, 1967, Shochiku released their first monster picture, **THE X FROM OUTER SPACE [Director:** Kazui Nihonmatsu **- Release Date (Japan):** March 25th, 1967]. While the film is endearing in its ineptitude, it is overall the poorest quality monster picture produced in Japan in the 1960s. *The X From Outer Space* is entertaining akin to "so-bad-their-good" classics like *Robot Monster* (1953) or Ed Wood's *Plan 9 From Outer Space* (1956). There are also a few fanciful effects unit moments, however.

Nihonmatsu's direction is humdrum and the script so terrible it's hard to believe it took three people to write it. The opening moments feature an embarrassing gaffe involving a helicopter door not being closed properly, boding ill for the cinematic experience ahead. Although Shochiku had a special effects unit headed by Keiji Kawakami, it was largely out of commission due to the former's involvement in freelance projects and Tsuburaya Productions. Thus, while Tsuburaya acolytes Kawakami and Akira Watanabe lent supervision, the FX were helmed by newcomer **HIROSHI IKEDA**. Ikeda's effects work is often television quality, particularly once the ridiculous monster shows up. Quite a few effects staff members from Toho and Tsuburaya Productions, including Fuchimu Shimakura who painted the horizons without credit, quietly took part in *X*'s production. While scouting locations near Mount Fuji, they ran into a production unit from Tsuburaya Pro and were caught violating their contracts. As a result, they were temporarily fired.

The X From Outer Space combines monster movie and space opera tropes as, thanks to the progress on NASA's flight to the moon, interstellar motifs were popular again. Early scenes in this vein, such as an impressive spaceship launch, fare best of all. *The X From Outer Space* is most entertaining when it revels in campy '60s style retro-futurism like an episode of *Lost in Space*. It boasts similar moonbase imagery to Stanley Kubrick's then-in production *2001: A Space Odyssey*, but the two films feel from alternate universes. *The X From Outer Space,* featuring an awful score by Taku Izumi, is even bookended by two inappropriate romantic ballads.

The monster Guilala, looking like a giant reptilian chicken, is spawned from spores released by an alien spacecraft resembling a cosmic hamburger. It was named in a contest Shochiku held with schoolchildren. The winner was a 12-year-old girl and her prize was a trip to Europe. The Guilala suit was created by Eizo Kaimai, who had gone freelance from Toho's modeling department and started his company Kaimai Productions.

The creature's rampage scenes are inept and soundly fail to match the work being done by Tsuburaya, Kuroda or even Noriaki Yuasa. Little if any high frame rate cinematography is in evidence. An air battle with Lockheed R-104 Starfighters, seldom used at Toho, is a highlight in an otherwise clunky sequence which includes not one but two planes inexplicably crashing directly into Guilala's face. There are laser beam cannon weapons, an obvious nod to *The War of the Gargantuas*.

Nighttime scenes fare better, in particular a segment of Guilala turning itself into a flying fireball, which very nearly makes the grade. Another good scene features Guilala chasing after heroes Sano (Toshiya Wazaki) and Miyamoto (Shinichi Yanigisawa) in a jeep as they lure it away with atomic rocket fuel. This exciting bit features a good synthesis between the main and FX units and dynamic editing by Yoshi Sugihara. Another striking and decently executed sequence occurs at the climax, where Guilala, coated in space gel, shrinks back into a gonad-like spore. It's possibly the most imaginative moment. *The X From Outer Space* was Shochiku's sole monster film in the *Showa* era but a trio of better special effects pictures would follow a year later. The Guilala suit would go on to make a cameo in the rockabilly comedy *A Little Snack* (1968).

Hiroshi Ikeda (right) directs the FX sequences in *The X From Outer Space* (1967)

Ultraman finished its run on April 9th, 1967. As the show's end approached, its station TBS had a problem. They wanted to start airing the next show immediately in its wake, but Tsuburaya Pro's follow-up to *Ultraman* was not ready. TBS thus went to Toei, who agreed to produce a filler program, **CAPTAIN ULTRA** [Television Run (Japan): April 16th - September 24th, 1967], not to be confused with the Marvel superhero introduced in the 1970s, Nobuo Yajima and his Tokusatsu Research Institute would handle the show's special effects. *Captain Ultra* is fairly uninspired, a hodgepodge of everything that was popular on genre TV back in 1967.

It features hero Captain Ultra (Hirohisa Nakata) doing battle with space monsters ala Ultraman and the Science Patrol. The show is also set in a spacefaring future akin to Gene Roddenberry's then-on-the-air *Star Trek*. Other moments evoke the high camp of Fox's *Batman* series or the pulpy unreality of Gerry Anderson shows like *Thunderbirds* or *Captain Scarlet and the Mysterons*. Unfortunately, the monster suits are distinctively amateurish. Of better quality are the miniature spacecraft, looking forward to Yajima's future work on *Message From Space* (1978). While *Captain Ultra* was below the quality of Tsuburaya Productions' fare, it kept Japanese schoolboys occupied as Tsuburaya readied his next show, *Ultraseven*.

Nikkatsu next threw their hat into the kaiju ring with **GAPPA, THE TRIPHIBIAN MONSTER [AKA: MONSTER FROM A PREHISTORIC PLANET - Directors:** Haruyasu Noguchi, Hiroshi Hashimoto, Isao Hayashi - **Release Date (Japan):** April 22nd, 1967]. As a studio, Nikkatsu was best known for its crime-themed action potboilers with stars like Yujiro Ishihara and Tetsuya Watari. By this time, however, they had fallen into financial straits. So with a generous government grant that was barely spent on the movie itself, they began development of their sole *Showa*-era monster and tokusatsu movie in 1966.

Just as *Godzilla* began life as a pair of giant whale and octopus-themed proposals, the form of Nikkatsu's monster changed as it was developed. First the creature was to be an alien spider named Gigant and then a giant squid named Architius, which was to do battle with a Nazi U-Boat. Nikkatsu also considered proposals involving a giant flying squirrel and a monster manta ray named Reigon. The latter came closest to being produced, but was dropped due to cost. For *Gappa*, Akira Watanabe, Yukio Manoda and their Nihon Special Effects Co. were brought on board to handle the effects.

At first glance, *Gappa* has strong parallels with the British production *Gorgo* (1961), with both involving parent monsters wreaking destruction while seeking out their kidnapped offspring. Incidentally, the King Brothers had contemplated making *Gorgo* in Japan with Eiji Tsuburaya's involvement, but such plans fell through. Yet *Gappa*'s screenwriters **RYUZO NAKANISHI** (1932-2013) and Gan Yamazaki, in Stuart Galbraith's *Monsters Are Attacking Tokyo*, swore to have never seen *Gorgo*. The picture is also evocative of *Mothra*.

Gappa is a step up from Shochiku's *The X From Outer Space,* but still lacks the magic of a Toho production. Akira Watanabe's special effects footage is expertly lensed. Watanabe, like Sadamasa Arikawa, has learned the technical skill of his mentor Tsuburaya. Yet there's a certain creative flourish that is lacking. Under Watanabe's direction, the top-tier miniature work is the brightest spot. A crumbling stone statue during an earthquake is well executed and realistic. Given Watanabe's background in art direction, *Gappa* is quite atmospheric. The suits, built by Eizo Kaimai, are a step up from his work on *The X From Outer Space* and on par with Ryosaku Takayama's monsters in *Ultraman*.

Putting finishing touches on a monster suit

Overall, *Gappa*'s above-average FX job makes it worth watching despite the picture's clunkiness. The final third is surprisingly strong as Watanabe's unit takes the stage with wall-to-wall tokusatsu sequences. The monsters' attack on Atami City is well staged. There are visually beautiful shots, including a composite of the parent monsters glowering behind a genuine waterfall. There's another dynamically filmed sequence in which the Gappas do battle with a fleet of F-104 Starfighter jets before Atami Castle, previously destroyed in *King Kong vs.*

Godzilla. A Self-Defense Force attack on the Gappas at Lake Kawaguchi followed by a masterfully executed tidal wave is the highlight. These moments are close to Tsuburaya quality. Less successful is an oil refinery attack.

The longer international export version that languished on late night television in the United States contains quite a few additional FX shots, though at the cost of weaker pacing. The monster parentage angle, touchingly driven home in the climax as the kidnapped baby Gappa is reunited with its parents, was perhaps an influence on Toho's upcoming *Son of Godzilla*. Oddly, *Gappa* got better than usual reviews from Western critics, including a rave review in industry trade *Variety*. Footage from *Gappa* later found its way into a 1991 episode of the BBC sci-fi show *Red Dwarf*.

Eiji Tsuburaya (right) and assistant director Teruyoshi Nakano (left) inspect a model

Eiji Tsuburaya's sole special effects director job at Toho in 1967 was **KING KONG ESCAPES** [**Director:** Ishiro Honda - **Release Date (Japan):** July 22nd, 1967]. After the retooling of *Operation Robinson Crusoe* into *Ebirah, Horror of the Deep*, Toho began development of another Kong film with Rankin-Bass before their rights expired. Producer **ARTHUR RANKIN** (1924-2014) had a history of and affinity for collaborating with

Japanese filmmakers. His company, first called Videocraft, produced legendary stop-motion animated works such as *Rudolph the Red-Nosed Reindeer* (1964) and *Mad Monster Party* (also 1967). These were actually created in Japan by stop-motion pioneer Tadahito Mochinaga. Arthur Rankin and partner Jules Bass would go on to work with several anime studios such as Mushi and Topcraft. They would later also co-produce the historical adventure *Marco* (1973) in Japan and collaborate several times with Tsuburaya Productions.

King Kong Escapes uses plot elements from the concurrent *The King Kong Show* cartoon, itself animated at Toei. There was friction between Arthur Rankin (who credited himself as director in American prints) and the staff at Toho. According to the film's Hollywood lead, Rhodes Reason (brother of *This Island Earth*'s Rex Reason), Rankin was worried that Honda and Tsuburaya would make the film too "silly", having Reason "keep an eye on things". Rankin and Reason often demanded Honda's sets be redecorated as they reportedly found the Japanese style of set decoration too cluttered.

King Kong Escapes was a dream project for Eiji Tsuburaya, so obsessed with the original *King Kong* that he owned a 35mm print. Especially as the 1933 classic had so powerfully influenced *Godzilla*, it was fitting that the final monster picture Honda and Tsuburaya made together would be a Kong movie. Though Tsuburaya was given a large budget, his effects work is more of a mixed bag than in *The War of the Gargantuas*. Like *Gargantuas*, it is more Tsuburaya's film than Ishiro Honda's, whose direction is not at its most inspired. The miniature work is a strength and on par with Tsuburaya's war films. Atmospheric mock underwater shots of the heroes' submarine, the *Explorer*, filmed on a dry set, outshine Nobuo Yajima's similar work on *Water Cyborg*. The *Explorer* was designed by Mutsumi Toyoshima and two large miniatures in a 1/10th and 1/15th scale were produced.

As with *King Kong vs. Godzilla*, *King Kong Escapes* is marred by a poor ape suit only subtly better than the one in '62. It's a shame that Fuminori Ohashi, the best ape-suit specialist in Japan, wasn't consulted for either of Toho's Kong films. Built by Teizo Toshimitsu and Yasuei Yagi, the new suit was, at least, designed to look more gorilla-like. The King Kong suit is inhabited by Haruo Nakajima, who gives a more ape-like performance than Shoichi Hirose in *King Kong vs. Godzilla*. Nakajima remains the only actor to have portrayed both King Kong and Godzilla, unless one counts Andy Serkis' consulting for *Godzilla* (2014).

Two Kong masks were again built: one for close-ups with radio-controlled eyes and mouth and one for action shots. The body of the 1962 Kong suit was also used for water scenes and a Guignol puppet was utilized for some close-ups. A miniaturized puppet was built by Nobuyuki Yasumaru for the shots of Kong being airlifted by Dr. Who's helicopters. The full-scaled hand of Gaira from *The War of the Gargantuas* was modified for Honda's scenes of Kong carrying leading lady Susan Watson (Linda Miller).

Eiji Tsuburaya directs a highlight sequence

Kong's foe Mechani-Kong (played by Yu Sekita) was again made by Toshimitsu and Yagi. The suit was built from a urethane material used in bath mats. As with the 1962 Kong suit, two pairs of arms were made, long and short, which were changed out depending on the level of action required by the scene. The bulb of an 8mm film projector was installed in its eyes to make them light up brightly. A one-foot miniature Mechani-Kong was also built for the finale at Tokyo Tower, along with a full-sized hand.

For a sequence early on, Eiji Tsuburaya crafts a loving tokusatsu recreation of the Allosaurus battle in *King Kong*. He even copies a shot verbatim, of Kong and the dinosaur tussling in the corner of the frame while the ingenue looks on in terror from a tree in the foreground. The dinosaur foe, Gorosaurus (also Yu Sekita), was the first suit made by Toshimitsu's assistant Nobuyuki Yasumaru. Toho's modeling department was too occupied producing the Kong and Mechani-Kong suits, so originally it was to be outsourced to Ryosaku Takayama. Takayama got halfway through modeling but the team at Toho were unsatisfied with his work, so Yasumaru took the job. It was among the first Japanese monster suits made with styrofoam instead of wire mesh. Tsuburaya popped into the modeling department and took a lot of interest in Yasumaru's new technique of using styrofoam molding. He was incredulous but impressed by Yasumaru's novel approach as it was explained to him.

When Kong snaps Gorosaurus' jaw similarly to the 1933 film, Iwao Mori and the American backers wanted Tsuburaya to make the dinosaur's mouth ooze blood. Eiji Tsuburaya was dead set against this. Mori backed off when Ishiro Honda sided with Tsuburaya, who instead had Gorosaurus froth at the mouth. A scene shortly after where Kong battles a sea serpent is executed clumsily. The prop, built by Toshimitsu and Yagi, was about 12 feet long. A highlight of *King Kong Escapes* is a sequence where villain Dr. Who (Hideyo Amamoto) and his forces capture King Kong on his home of Mondo Island and airlift him to the North Pole. The miniature and pyrotechnic work is particularly impressive. The sequence features one of Tsuburaya and Hiroshi Mukoyama's finest Oxberry composites with superb scaling: Dr. Who and his men, in the background of the frame, examine a knocked-out Kong in the foreground.

The finale again makes use of the Tokyo Tower blueprint made for *Mothra*. The Tokyo Tower miniature in *King Kong Escapes* was built at a larger scale and made of reinforced steel to allow the suit actors to grapple on it. After Mechani-Kong's fatal plunge from the tower, Tsuburaya wanted the smashed wreckage to look cluttered with a myriad of mechanical parts. TV boards and parts of former miniatures including *Mothra*'s Atomic Heat Ray Cannon and the Maser truck from *The War of the Gargantuas* were added.

King Kong Escapes was not a success. It received scathing reviews on both sides of the Pacific. In Japan it was a fair flop, with even Shochiku's *The X From Outer Space* doing better business. The box office failure of a big-budget King Kong film co-produced with Hollywood was the first sign that Japan's Monster Boom was ebbing.

Although things were cooling off at home, the success of Japanese-style monster films would even be noted around this time in South Korea. Here anti-Japanese sentiment was so bitter that media from Japan of any sort was banned until 1998. Korean studio Keukdong wanted to produce a Japanese-style monster film in Korea.

To that end, staff from Equis Productions in Japan including Masao Yagi and Toru Suzuki were recruited for this production: **YONGARY, MONSTER FROM THE DEEP** [**Director:** Kim Ki-duk - **Release Date (South Korea):** August 13th, 1967]. Like Godzilla, the monster is a theropod-style dinosaur awakened by nuclear testing and defeated by a young scientist's chemical compound. The creature also shows an affinity for an annoyingly precocious boy (Kwang Ho Lee) a la Gamera. *Yongary* is a poor film and less polished than a Japanese production but not without redeeming value.

Yongary, Monster From the Deep (1967)

The miniatures were designed and created by Toru Suzuki and are the picture's strongest point. The miniaturized sets are not quite Toho quality but on par with the other FX units in Japan. The Yongary suit, built by Masao Yagi and inhabited by stuntman Cho Kyoung-min, is weaker, it more or less matches the level of Japanese television. Embarrassingly, in certain shots, the nozzle of a propane torch is visible through the mouth. Masao Yagi acted as the de facto effects director, with assistance from producer

Lee Byoung-woo, though the crew was mainly Korean. Unfortunately, the Korean crew doesn't shoot or edit the miniatures and monster suit as well as a seasoned Japanese unit. The shots are often clunky in execution and the cutting awkward. There's the occasional Tsuburaya-style optical composite, but *Yongary*'s bad shots outweigh the good. Some moments feel distinctively Japanese, such as the highlight: a missile attack on Yongary. Though not executed to the standard of a Japanese production, it has visual beauty.

A bit where Yongary dances in front of the precocious boy protagonist is as embarrassing as the most cringeworthy moment in a Noriaki Yuasa film. The climax of *Yongary* is a ghastly affair. There's a poor composite of a jeep swerving under Yongary's legs. Worst is the creature's grotesque death: Yongary expires twitching in agony as it bleeds from its anus into a river. It is a disturbing moment, unbefitting a monster movie, that Eiji Tsuburaya would have been appalled by. *Yongary*'s effects and production values fare better, however, than other Korean monster movies like the same year's *Monster Wang Ma Gwai* or the atrocious *A*P*E* (1976), both produced without Japanese involvement.

Back in Japan, a trio of effects shows would hit the airwaves in October in ferocious competition for ratings. First, Tsuburaya Pro's long awaited next program began airing on TBS: **ULTRASEVEN [Television Run (Japan):** October 1st, 1967 - September 8th, 1968]. Before *Ultraman* was off the air, Eiji Tsuburaya had begun development of a follow-up show. As the airing of Toei's *Captain Ultra* bought them time, this new program was fleshed out. Initially, Tsuburaya and writer Tetsuo Kinjo drafted a proposal entitled *The Ultra Garrison* which would have featured a space garrison doing battle with monsters and no giant superhero. Considered too similar to *Captain Ultra*, this proposal was rejected. Kinjo thus got to work on another draft called *The Ultra Eye*.

The Ultra Eye added a hero and once again drew influence from Tsuburaya's unproduced *Woo*. The Ultra Garrison concept was kept but turned into an Earth-based organization called the Ultra Guard. The protagonist was now a boy named Dan Moroboshi who was secretly an alien, once again named "Redman." Redman would battle space monsters attempting to invade Earth. When unable to transform, young Moroboshi used benevolent "capsule monsters" to fight the various alien creatures. This concept would look forward to Satoshi Tajiri's juggernaut *Pocket Monsters (Pokemon)* video game and anime franchise.

With *The Ultra Eye*, Tetsuo Kinjo wanted to cover darker, more philosophical ground than previous shows. As an Okinawan, considered a second-class citizen by the Yamato (mainland) Japanese, he empathized with the character of Dan Moroboshi, a Christ-like alien outsider walking amongst humanity. With more creative freedom allowed his company per the success of *Ultraman*, Tsuburaya encouraged Kinjo to include more political diatribe and anti-war themes. Gene Roddenberry's then-popular *Star Trek* was likely an influence and indeed, many of Kinjo's best scripts feature a similar melding of sci-fi and social commentary to Harlan Ellison's work.

Title card #1 for *Ultraseven* (1967-68)

The concept was changed slightly to its final form, *Ultraseven*, with the character of Dan Moroboshi (Koji Moritsugu) now a fully grown man. The motif of *"Seven"*, signifying Dan as the seventh member of the Ultra Guard, was a carryover from *The Ultra Seven*, a nearly-produced comedic proposal Kinjo had been working on. Another major contributor to *Ultraseven*'s scripts was **SHOZO UEHARA** (1937-2020), a friend of Kinjo's and fellow Okinawa native.

Unlike Kinjo, Uehara was lucky enough to have been evacuated from Okinawa to Taiwan before the U.S. invasion. Uehara would go on to write for numerous Tsuburaya Productions shows, eventually taking part in programs for Toei and others as well.

Again, Toru Narita handled the design of Ultraseven along with the Ultra Guard's vehicles. The "Ultra Hawk" drew particular influence from Gerry Anderson's *Thunderbirds*. Ultraseven's design took inspiration from Mayan culture and European knight armor. Narita had wanted Seven to be silver and blue. At the urging of the visual effects staff, blue was changed to red per the usage of blue-screen composites. Four Ultraseven suits were made during the run, though these were more uniform than Ultraman's. From episode #11 on, the third and fourth suits were used alternatively.

Toru Narita wanted Bin Furuya to return as Seven's stuntman. Furuya, however, had been cast in the main unit role of Amagi and there was no way he could play both. Thus stuntman **KOJI UENISHI** (1938-20??) was hired and would portray Seven in most episodes. To transform into Ultraseven, rather than the Beta Capsule, Dan Moroboshi uses the Ultra Eye, a headset resembling a pair of glasses. Seven also has novel weapons which include the "Eye Slugger," a boomerang-like device kept on his head. This can be thrown to slice, dice and decapitate monsters. In keeping with the show's darker tone, *Ultraseven*'s monster battles are considerably more violent than its predecessor's.

Cameras began to roll on *Ultraseven* in May of 1967. Much of the behind-the-camera staff from *Ultraman* returned. *Ultraseven*'s directors included Hajime Tsuburaya, Samaji Nonagase, Akio Jissoji and Toshihiro Ijima. Younger directors Toshitsugu Suzuki and Kazuho Mizuha were assigned more episodes in *Ultraseven*. The effects unit was helmed by Koichi Takano with support from Toru Matoba, Atsushi Oki and Sadamasa Arikawa. Again, *Ultraseven* had to be rushed to air earlier than anticipated, as *Captain Ultra*'s run was cut short by two episodes. This time, however, Tsuburaya Productions had less trouble meeting the deadline. *Ultraseven* is perhaps Eiji Tsuburaya's TV masterwork with its only flaw too much filler as its run was extended to 49 episodes. With greater artistic liberty granted by TBS, *Ultraseven* was allowed to be more experimental and yet reaches the highest heights of any Ultra show.

Ultraseven boasts a collection of extraterrestrial monsters more outlandish than the saurian menagerie of *Ultraman*. Narita's design team, alongside Ryosaku Takayama's modeling crew, was allowed to produce a multitude of unorthodox creations. Unlike *Ultra Q* and *Ultraman*, which reused suits from Toho films and prior shows, *Ultraseven* features more newly constructed monsters. At this point, Eiji Tsuburaya was realizing that the more novel foes he created for Seven to battle, the more toys he could license. Toho and Tsuburaya Productions were among the first media firms to merchandize their properties, predating the heavy toy marketing of Hollywood high-concept films like *Star Wars* (1977). After episode #31, Narita would leave the show to work on Tsuburaya Pro's next program *Mighty Jack,* leaving his assistant **NORIYOSHI IKEYA** (1940-2016) to design the rest of the show's monsters.

 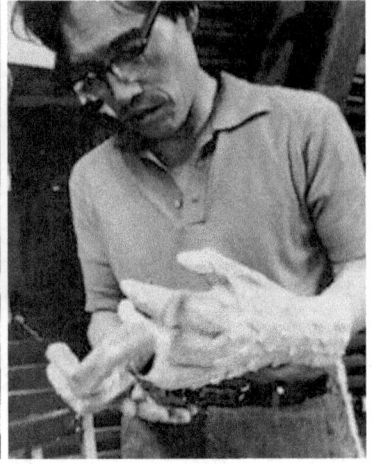

Designer Toru "Tohl" Narita (left) - modeler Ryosaku Takayama (right)

One of the most well-known *Ultraseven* monsters is Eleking, appearing in *"The Secret of the Lake"* and controlled by two girlish alien women, looking forward to the Kilaaks in the following year's *Destroy All Monsters*. Another memorable foe is King Joe, appearing in the two-parter *"Westward: Ultra Guard!"*. Played by Haruyoshi Nakamura, the mechanical creature is a "Super Robot" made of combined smaller machines, foreshadowing and predating Go Nagai's *Getter Robo*. King Joe, who manages to bring Seven to his knees, is believed to be named after writer Tetsuo Kinjo. The concept of Seven having capsule monsters from earlier drafts was kept. Bringing back prior Ultra monsters was considered, but in the end three new creatures were designed: the robotic Windam, the alien Miclas and the dinosaur-like Agira. A handful of episodes, including *"The Invading Dead"*, *"The Stolen Ultra Eye"* and *Nightmare on the Fourth Planet,* feature no giant monsters at all. A dip in ratings resulted, with children being frustrated by the lack of monster battles.

Koichi Takano's FX have improved since the previous show, as evidenced right out of the gate by a magnificent oil refinery explosion in the pilot episode, *"The Invisible Challenger."*

The miniature work in many episodes is impressive for television and on par with that of Gerry Anderson. *"The Devil That Dwells in a Flower,"* features one of veteran Toru Matoba's best sequences and is obviously inspired by Fox's recent *Fantastic Voyage* (1966). By the finale, Koichi Takano's FX work begins to rival that of Nobuo Yajima on the simultaneous *Giant Robo*.

Ultraseven features more philosophical, morally complex themes than its predecessor in line with authors like Isaac Asimov and Harlan Ellison. The show's alien invaders tend to have sinister motives and the Ultra Guard and Seven are thrust into complicated moral situations. *"The Dark Zone"* features Seven committing the mass genocide of an alien race to save humanity. *"Super Weapon R1"*, darkly satirizes the Cold War and arms race. *"Nightmare of the Fourth Planet"*, directed by Akio Jissoji, darkly looks forward to the futurist phenomena of artificial intelligence and automation.

Besides Tetsuo Kinjo and Shozo Uehara, *Ultraseven*'s darker direction was no doubt influenced by Jissoji. Once again, his episodes no doubt led to a few twisted nightmares among its young viewership. One of Jissoji's signature *Ultraseven* installments is *"The Targeted Town"*, a gritty affair shot on high speed film stock. It features a disturbingly sociopathic alien scheme in line with the machinations of *The Dark Knight*'s Joker. One of the finest episodes in the Ultra franchise, its themes are existentially terrifying for a kids' show.

Another of Jissoji's episodes is *"From A Planet With Love"*. Years later, it would spark serious controversy. Featuring radiation-poisoned aliens covered in keloid scars, they were called the "Hibakuseijin" in a 1970 publication. *"Hibaku"* means "atomic bomb survivor" and this was a tone-deaf mistake on Tsuburaya Pro and the publisher's part. It was seen by the teenage daughter of the Atomic Bomb Victims Association's head. The *Asahi Shimbun* ran an article sympathizing with the Atomic Bomb Victims Association's claims that the episode depicts atomic bomb survivors as monsters and protest ensued. Tsuburaya Productions would thus treat *"From a Planet With Love"* as a "missing episode". It is omitted from official books, not aired in re-runs and has never been released to home video.

Ultraseven concluded in a tense, two-part finale, *"The Greatest Invasion in History"*, aired on September 1st and 8th, 1968. Seven becomes sickly from having depleted his energy battling monsters. The Ghose, an alien race with plans to exterminate humanity, seizes upon this opportunity to make their invasion. This apocalyptic final episode fittingly makes use of footage from *The Last War*. With Ultraseven's fate left somewhat unclear, it is a more dour and bittersweet finale than the previous show's. On average, *Ultraseven*'s ratings didn't reach the heights of its predecessor but remained strong, outshining those of its rivals. One factor was the decline of Monster Boom by mid-1968.

Child actor Mitsunori Nomura and one of Fuminori Ohashi's props

A day after *Ultraseven* started airing on TBS, another monster-themed show appeared on Fuji TV, **THE MONSTER PRINCE [Television Run (Japan): October 2nd, 1967 - March 25th, 1968]** from P-Productions. Modeling expert Fuminori Ohashi had made connections in Hollywood and Screen Gems and producer Sidney Shelton wanted a dinosaur-themed show from him. In Japan, Ohashi's concept was taken up by producer Kazuo Ueshima of Tokyu Agency and Tomio Sagisu at P-Productions.

The show was to be called *The Giant Monster Operation*, but a more child-friendly angle was established. Ohashi had worked on an unaired program entitled *The Jungle Prince* and influence was drawn from it, along with the manga *Kenya Boy* by Soji Yamakawa. *The Monster Prince* centers around Takeru (Mitsunori Nomura), who as a baby was stranded on an island after a plane crash. Raised by brontosaurus-like dinosaurs, Takeru becomes a Mowgli/Tarzan-like wildboy.

Shot in Kyoto, *The Monster Prince* was a troubled production. The show began shooting in October of 1966 in the wake of *Ambassador Magma*'s premiere, with P-Pro's staff running back and forth between both programs. The creature modeling in *The Monster Prince* was done by Fuminori Ohashi with support from Ryosaku Takayama and Eizo Kaimai. The special effects unit was mainly helmed by Shinsuke Kojima, whose FX work is similar to his output on *Ambassador Magma*. The pyrotechnics and miniatures are strong, though Ohashi's dinosaurs look stiff in a way that foreshadows his work on *Legend of the Dinosaur and Monster Bird* (1977). The show was allotted substantial funds for early episodes, but as production dragged out, the FX staff had to bolster the budget with money raised from exhibitions at local department stores with the monster suits.

The Monster Prince was to start airing in July of 1967, but its production problems delayed the debut. Unfortunately, the Monster Boom was by then deflating and the show's ratings were marginal. Production on *The Monster Prince* wound up cut short at 26 episodes and two dinosaur suits built by Ryosaku Takayama wound up unused. Screen Gems also passed on the program for U.S. airwaves, dashing the staff's hopes of future Hollywood collaborations. *The Monster Prince* proved damaging to Fuminori Ohashi's career, as blame for the production problems and poor ratings was placed squarely on him. The following year Ohashi would go abroad and work on Fox's *Planet of the Apes*, directed by the Japanese-born Franklin J. Schaffner. The iconic ape prosthetics in those films were partially the brainchild of Ohashi and his modeling skill. He won the job thanks to his ape suit work on *The Jungle Prince,* which finally aired in the summer of 1970.

Just over a week later, yet another special effects show started its run on TV Asahi: **GIANT ROBO [Television Run (Japan):** October 11th, 1967 - April 1st, 1968]. Produced by Toei, it was based on a manga by Mitsuteru Yokoyama. Encouraged by *Red Shadow*'s good ratings, Toei was eager to make another show with Yokoyama. *Giant Robo* boasts a similar concept to Yokoyama's *Tetsujin No. 28*, featuring a boy with an even larger giant robot at his disposal. The villains are an evil organization called Big Fire, led by diabolical alien overlord Emperor Guillotine (Hirohiko Sato). The show's kid protagonist Daisaku Kusama

(Mitsunobu Kaneko) joins the Science Patrol-like "Unicorn" organization. Big Fire's henchmen, with fascistic wardrobe motifs, often engage in comically bloodless gun battles with the heroes that would not fly on children's programming today. The surprising violence, fascist baddies and other edgy elements foreshadow the blatant transgressiveness of Toei's coming *Kamen Rider*.

Each week, Daisaku sends his robot into battle against a new pantomime beast from Emperor Guillotine. These include Dakolar, a sea monster, along with Gloval, a giant globe creature, the leonine beast Ligon and Gammons, an enormous eye. *Giant Robo* successfully combines the "boy and his robot" premise of *Tetsujin No. 28* with the "defeat the monster of the week" formula of *Ultraman*. The show's directors include **MINORU YAMADA** (1926-1995), **KOICHI TAKEMOTO** (1928-1993), **ITARU ORITA** (1934-2006) and **KATSUHIKO TAGUCHI** (1931-2020). Most of these men would go on to play integral roles in *Kamen Rider*. Toei's brass had wanted Hajime Sato and dependable B-movie director **KINJI FUKASAKU** (1930-2003) to helm episodes of *Giant Robo*, but they had to pass due to scheduling conflicts.

Giant Robo (1967-68) title card

The special effects on *Giant Robo* were handled by Nobuo Yajima and his Tokusatsu Research Institute. The effects are imaginative and a major step up from *Captain Ultra*'s. They often equal Tsuburaya Productions' in quality, if slightly more raw. There is the occasional theatrical-grade composite, all the more impressively done in the lower resolution of 16mm. The monster suits and modeling are a huge improvement over those in *Captain Ultra*. The Giant Robo's suit in particular is excellently made; designed after the Egyptian sphinx and portrayed by Toshiyuki Tsuchiyama.

Toru Suzuki and **SHIGERU INOUE** handled most of the suit modeling. The show's final episode aired on April 1st, 1968. In it, Giant Robo sacrifices itself to save Earth, breaking the hearts of schoolchildren nationwide. *Giant Robo* even found its way to the United States in 1969 under the title *Johnny Sokko and His Flying Robot*.

In contrast to the previous year, the 1967-1968 New Year's season was nearly devoid of special effects movies. Toho, however, released their next Godzilla entry in December, **SON OF GODZILLA** [**Director:** Jun Fukuda - **Release Date (Japan):** December 16th, 1967]. Tomoyuki Tanaka decided to center this film around a baby monster. Along with pleasing his growing child audience, Tanaka wanted to draw in a "date crowd," hoping a baby monster would tap into young Japanese women's mothering instincts. **KAZUE KIBA**, a female writer, was brought in to assist Shinichi Sekizawa in developing the concept. Kiba had submitted a proposal to Toho called *Two Godzillas: Japan S.O.S* in which the idea of a baby Godzilla originated.

Son of Godzilla would be the most overt step in Godzilla's humanization. No longer was the monster burning civilians to ash; the nuclear horror was now rearing an adorably monstrous kid. Like Shochiku's Guilala, Godzilla's son "Minilla" was named in a contest held by Toho which received submissions from over eight thousand children. *Son of Godzilla* is an odd film that sounds embarrassing on paper. Yet its creative execution makes it a standout entry; it is both enchanting and underrated. Taking the exotic locale of *Ebirah, Horror of the Deep* a step further, location scenes were lensed in Guam, adding a touch of realism. Composer Masaru Sato creates another breezy score and it's hard to even imagine Akira Ifukube scoring *Son of Godzilla*. Sadamasa Arikawa returned to helm the effects unit in place of Tsuburaya. Eiji Tsuburaya, preoccupied with *Ultraseven* and *Mighty Jack,* visited the set less frequently. Arikawa was granted more money and artistic license, neither of which were wasted; *Son of Godzilla* is the finest effects job of his career. There are fanciful composites throughout and Yasuyuki Inoue's miniatures are top quality.

For *Son of Godzilla*, a new Godzilla suit was made by Teizo Toshimitsu and Yasuei Yagi. It was built larger to make Godzilla look towering next to its child. The suit wound up too large for Haruo Nakajima and the part was recast for this entry. His replacement was **SEIJI ONAKA** (1934-201?), a professional baseball player. Midshoot, however, Onaka broke his fingers during a game. Thus the dependable Yu Sekita stepped into the role for the remainder of the scenes. Haruo Nakajima did portray Godzilla in a handful of water scenes wearing the suit from the previous two films. Godzilla emerging off the coast of Solgell mid-film is among the creature's more memorable entrances and was difficult to stage. Nakajima needed an oxygen tank and was pulled from Toho's Big Pool with a rope attached to a car.

Sadamasa Arikawa

For Minilla, a two-foot puppet was built for the infant creature's early scenes. Once it becomes mature enough to walk, it is played by actor **MASAO FUKUZAWA** (1921-2000), better known as "Little Man Machan". Fukuzawa, a little person who was a professional wrestler and cabaret performer, had difficulty moving in the suit, often wobbling. Arikawa, however, thought this enhanced Fukuzawa's performance and made it convincingly toddler-like. Arikawa wanted Minilla's atomic breath to resemble a *shuriken* (ninja star). It was Eiji Tsuburaya, while visiting the set, who suggested that the baby monster should puff atomic "smoke-Os".

Son of Godzilla's arthropod antagonists, the mantis monsters Kamakiras and the giant spider Kumonga, were intricate marionettes. Both designed by Yasuyuki Inoue, their sequences are the Toho FX unit's best under Arikawa. Inoue made sketches of live mantises as foundation for his design of Kamakiras. While the Kamakiras, built by Nobuyuki

Yasumaru, are impressive in their own right, Kumonga is among the best executed puppet-monsters in the tokusatsu medium. Modeled by Teizo Toshimitsu, the prop was a whopping 18 feet long. Controlled by piano wire, it required 20 puppeteers, headed by Fumio Nakashiro, in many shots. Each leg alone called from two operators who worked from a platform above the stage. Arikawa would assign each staff member a number and call the numbers out to help coordinate the movements. Kumonga's webbing was the polystyrene recipe used for Mothra's cocoon silk; a similar dispenser was installed in the puppet's mouth. A full-size Kumonga leg was also built to interact with the actors on Fukuda's unit. Kumonga's sequences are so well conceived that they're even unnerving.

Son of Godzilla's final sequence is surprisingly poignant. In it, Godzilla and Minilla go into hibernation as the tropical island is frozen during a weather control experiment. For among the first times in a Toho monster picture, one feels genuine pathos for the monsters. The artificial snow used by Arikawa's unit was a mix of styrofoam and paraffin. Arikawa liked paraffin as it melted similarly to snow. This scene was originally longer with more narrative tension. Godzilla was to contemplate abandoning Minilla and begin wading into the ocean before having a change of heart. A portion of this extended sequence can be seen in Toho's original trailer. It was wisely deleted, probably for making Godzilla too unlikable. As the film reaches its bittersweet final moments, Godzilla and Minilla cuddle together amidst a torrent of snowfall.

Despite its creative energy and admirable execution, *Son of Godzilla* was a box-office disappointment. With the Monster Boom having reached its end, Toho's brass began to contemplate retiring Godzilla for the time being.

XIV.
1968
昭和四十三

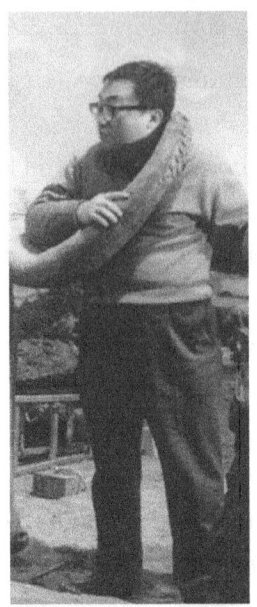

Noriaki Yuasa

While *Ultraseven, Giant Robo* and *The Monster Prince* aired on TV, the next special effects productions wouldn't come until March 1968 when Daiei again released a monster-packed double bill. The top half was **GAMERA VS. VIRAS** [Director: Noriaki Yuasa - **Release Date (Japan):** March 20th, 1968], produced at the Tokyo branch. Second was **ONE HUNDRED MONSTERS** [Director: Kimiyoshi Yasuda - **Release Date (Japan):** Ibid], from Daiei Kyoto.

Gamera vs. Viras signals the point where the Gamera series would drop off in quality and production value. The film is a marked step down from *Gamera vs. Gyaos,* which struck a better balance between kiddie silliness and impressive monster sequences.

Noriaki Yuasa directed both the special effects and main units in only 25 days. The picture's budget was slashed. Perhaps due to the paltry budget, Yuasa decided to fully embrace a child audience. Daiei was also working with their American distributor, American International Pictures, who had been releasing the Gamera sequels to stateside TV. One part of the deal required that one of the film's leading children be American; thus Carl Craig, the half-Japanese son of a U.S. army official stationed in Japan, was cast as a lasso-wielding Boy Scout.

Lifting a model

Gamera vs. Viras' highlight is its miniature work. A three-foot model of the imaginative alien ship was built, designed by **SHIGEO MANO**. An early scene where Gamera is captured underwater by a bubble-like alien force field is the best. The transparent bubble was made of acrylic cloth. While filming a sequence of the spaceship landing on Chigasaki Beach, Yuasa and his crew ran into trouble when the miniature kept wobbling, preventing a convincing touchdown. Yuasa wound up having the staff lift the miniature upwards with piano wire and had the footage printed backwards.

The Gamera suit from the previous film was reused, again inhabited by Teruo Aragaki. Viras, a giant alien squid, is uninspiring. Designed by Shigeo Mano, a suit and a miniature puppet were made by Equis Productions with Masao Yagi leading the modeling. Yuasa wanted the suit to be flexible and Yagi was unsure of which material to use. In the end, he chose urethane as its soft, spongy appearance reminded him of the flesh of a squid. For some shots, six crew members were required to operate the monster's tentacles.

Yuasa's direction of both the drama and FX scenes feels more flat-footed than previous entries. The effects work is unrefined and the tone more juvenile than prior films. *Gamera vs. Viras* boasts surprisingly grisly moments that foreshadow the grand guignol of the next entry. The Viras aliens' human forms are decapitated and Gamera is gruesomely impaled. The Viras monsters merging together into giant form to battle Gamera in the climax is a striking composite, at least at first. It is ruined by cutbacks.

One major flaw is an overabundance of runtime-padding stock footage. A stipulation of Daiei's agreement with AIP also involved the film running 90 minutes while Yuasa's cut for Japanese theaters was only 72 minutes long. Thus close to 20 minutes of recycled monster battle sequences from *Gamera vs. Barugon* and *Gamera vs. Gyaos* were included as a "flashback" in export versions. For Gamera's rampage through Tokyo, the film even uses mismatched black-and-white stock destruction scenes from the first *Gamera*. Using monochrome footage in a color film is an aesthetic low even the effects unit at Toho in the lean years to come never sank to. Nonetheless, *Gamera vs. Viras* was profitable per its cheapness and Toho would move in a similar direction with their Godzilla entries.

Again, the Daiei Kyoto-produced period co-feature, *One Hundred Monsters,* boasted better production values. While giant monsters were falling out of favor with kids, a more traditional form of creature was becoming popular with the 1965 publication of the manga *GeGe no Kitaro* by Shigeru Mizuki. This "Yokai Boom" would intensify when a TV anime adaptation of *Kitaro* from Toei began airing in January of 1968. Like Western vampires and werewolves, *yokai* are supernatural, old-world monstrosities far removed from the atom age terrors of Godzilla or Gamera. Whimsical forces of nature, these Shinto entities range from mischievous to malevolent to benign, with each region in Japan having its own distinctive local yokai.

Daiei sought to tap into the popularity of *GeGe no Kitaro* with *One Hundred Monsters.* The film centers around the *Hyaku Monogatari Kaidankai,* a storytelling game popularized in the Edo period. In it, a group of people gather and light one hundred candles before telling one hundred ghostly stories. With the *Hyaku Monogatari* as a backdrop, *One Hundred Monsters* tells a similar story to Yasuda's previous *Majin*. Once again, a supernatural force liberates the common people from oppression. This time it's crooked landowners trying to demolish a shrine to build a brothel. Fittingly, the leader and his right-hand man are played by Ryutaro Gomi and Takashi Kanda, both of whom played warlords in the *Majin* films.

Yoshiyuki Kuroda returns from the *Majin* trilogy to handle the plentiful effects phantasmagory, along with Fujio Morita. Much of *One Hundred Monsters* was co-helmed by directors Yasuda and Kuroda. Yasuda was passionate about this project as he loved yokai. He storyboarded the entire film himself in an office filled with drawings of yokai as inspiration. *One Hundred Monsters* feels closer in tone to an early J-Horror film like the works of Nobuo Nakagawa than a tokusatsu monster movie. Nonetheless, the use of tokusatsu FX and trick photography is even more plentiful than in the *Majin* films.

Director Kimiyoshi Yasuda (right) and a monster marionette

Kuroda's best contributions feature a phantasmal splendor. Early in the picture, the viewer is treated to a scene featuring a *rokurokubi* (played by **IKUKO MORI** [1933-?]), a woman who can stretch her neck to serpentine lengths. This effect is stunningly executed and the sequence features some of Kuroda and Morita's most inventive trick photography. Actress Mori's debut was in 1957's *The Invisible Man vs. the Human Fly*; after *White Snake Beauty* (1957), she became a popular screen siren associated with snakes.. Her *rokurokubi* role was a throwback to this. Tragically, after appearing in 1969's *The Haunted Castle*, she stabbed her lover to death, with whom she had an out-of-wedlock child. The first active high-profile actress to commit murder in Japan, Mori's trial was among the *Showa* film industry's grandest scandals. She was released on parole in 1977; her fate remains unknown.

Another good sequence features Bava-esque colored lighting and the *Nopperabo* (No Face), a ghostly spirit with no eyes, nose or ears. A distinctive creation that appears mid-picture is the *Karakasa* or *Kasa Obake*, a one-eyed, one-legged goblin taking the form of an umbrella. Created with an intricate marionette manipulated with piano wire, it feels concocted from the combined sensibilities of Jim Henson, the Krofts, and Tim Burton. The puppet took six people to operate. Certain scenes called for cel and optical animation, which was provided by Tomio Sagisu's P-Productions. Their most memorable contribution is a series of shots depicting an animated painted *Karakasa* on a sliding door.

One Hundred Monsters finale, where a gaggle of yokai converge on the landowner, is weaker in execution than *Majin*'s. Whereas the Majin films felt dynamic, this scene is a bit pedestrian, as evidenced by a static shot that goes on for around half a minute. In many ways, however, this ungainly execution is forgivable, as a hundred yokai are a more ambitious FX goal than one giant monster. The strongest bits feature the *Okubi* (or Big Head, played by **KEIKO KOYANAGI** [1926-]), a gigantic floating female head making use of the blue screen processes perfected in *Majin*. Its well-executed monster humanoid grotesquery looks forward to the popular *Attack on Titan* franchise. The final moments are the strongest and most hallucinatory as the yokai parade in a macabre funeral procession before the crack of dawn.

The *yokai* themselves are intriguing. Building a hundred apparitions was quite a challenge for Masao Yagi and Equis Productions who were otherwise occupied with modeling for *Viras*. To ease the burden, old costumes from *Suzunosuke Akado* (1957) and *Buddha*, made by Fuminori Ohashi, were used for certain yokai. *Tsuchikorobi*, a giant hairy cyclops, was made from a hemp-like material created from the Philippine abaca plant. The suit contained three performers. Also on display is *Kappa*, a famed Japanese river sprite and *Karasa Tengu,* a legendary flying crow monster. Another memorable yokai is *Abura Sumashi*. Played by child actor **TOSHIYASU BEPPU**, he's a short humanoid with gray skin and straw clothing. Another worth mentioning is the *Aobozu* ("Blue Priest"), a blue-skinned creature in Buddhist ecclesiastical garb. Using a remodeled costume from *Suzunosuke*

Akado, the role was taken on by **SHINJIRO AKATSUKI**.

The double bill of *Gamera vs. Viras* and *One Hundred Monsters* was a surprise hit for Daiei and the immature trend of the Gamera series would proceed unchecked. Masaichi Nagata would ask Noriaki Yuasa if he could make two Gamera films a year instead of one to which the latter declined. Yoshiyuki Kuroda, however, would be at work on a follow-up to *One Hundred Monsters* before the year was out.

Days later in the United States, the special effects medium was brought to new heights with the premiere of **2001: A SPACE ODYSSEY** [**Director**: Stanley Kubrick - **Release Date (U.S.)**: April 2nd, 1968]. Released in Japan only days later, its images of lunar space stations and psychedelic stargates were the most lifelike put to film. *2001: A Space Odyssey* very nearly transcended any and all limitations of the cinematic art form. **DOUGLAS TRUMBULL** (1942-2022), only in his 20s, would help Kubrick pioneer and realize these groundbreaking miniature and visual effects. While the Japanese studios cranked out one monster movie and effects show after another, Kubrick had been working on this massively budgeted 70mm feature since early 1965. Like *A Trip to the Moon*, *Metropolis*, *King Kong* and even *Godzilla*, *2001: A Space Odyssey* remains among the most influential genre films in cinema history, inspiring nearly every future luminary.

Sadly, however, *2001* marked the beginning of the end of Japan's successful competition with Hollywood. Before Kubrick and Trumbull, Eiji Tsuburaya's effects unit at Toho was among the best in the world. His only major competition came from the likes of George Pal, Ray Harryhausen and a few others. Stanley Kubrick had shown moviegoers a level of cinematic realism never thought possible with visual effects. The unreality of Japanese effects films thus began to be regarded by Americans as shoddy and inferior. Ironically, Kubrick himself had drawn influence from Japanese sci-fi, being fond of *Warning From Space* and taking aesthetic cues from Tsuburaya works like *Gorath*. *2001*, for better and worse, would take genre cinema in a new direction. This direction would be accelerated nine years later by the release of another space-themed Hollywood movie.

Japanese poster for *2001: A Space Odyssey* (1968)

Tsuburaya Productions, meanwhile, had been working on yet another TV series, this time for Fuji TV. **MIGHTY JACK** [Television Run: April 6th - June 29th, 1968]. Unlike the Ultra shows, it was for an hour-long timeslot and geared at adults. *Mighty Jack* owes its origins to a scrapped Toho project called *The Flying Battleship* written by Shinichi Sekizawa in 1966. Intended as a loose follow-up to *Atragon*, it was to have been directed by Ishiro Honda. Toru Narita had created some impressive mechanical designs and Tsuburaya was disappointed that the film wasn't made. He thus fought to develop the concept into a TV show.

By this time in the 1960s, spy movies and shows were extremely popular. The James Bond films dominated the box office. The then-most recent 007 entry, *You Only Live Twice* (1967), was set and partially filmed in Japan with the involvement of actors Tetsuro Tanba, Mie Hama and Akiko Wakabayashi. The British show *The Avengers* was also quite successful. On American airwaves, a multitude of secret agent-themed shows reigned supreme, including *The Man From U.N.C.L.E.*, *Mission: Impossible* and *Get Smart*. Even in Japan, Toei's *Spy Catcher J3* was popular and *Key Hunter*, another spy show from Toei, started airing on TBS the same day as *Mighty Jack*. Such Gerry Anderson works as *Stingray* and *Thunderbirds* were undoubtedly an influence on *Mighty Jack* as well.

Mighty Jack concerns a clandestine organization of the same name battling the SPECTRE-like international terrorist group Q (NOO in Sekizawa's *Flying Battleship*). The show stands out from its Western counterparts for its prominent giant warships depicted in miniatures. The most memorable is Mighty Jack's signature craft the *MJ*. Designed by Toru Narita, it can travel on land, sea and air, much like *Atragon*'s *Goten-go*.

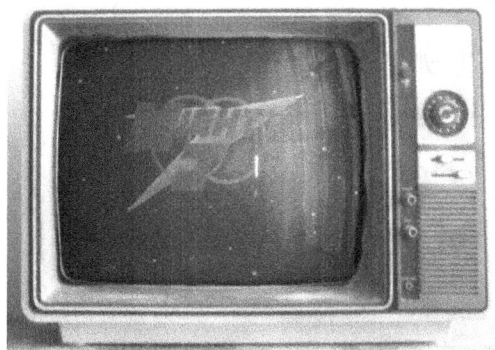

Mighty Jack (1968) title card

Mighty Jack was an expensive endeavor. Out of pocket, Tsuburaya purchased a new 35mm Mitchell camera for the special effects sequences. There was friction between Tsuburaya, the staff and the show's star Hideaki Niitani, who wanted the program to focus more on its characters than special effects. As the show went on, it suffered from rushed shooting and production cutbacks, so the episodes were of inconsistent quality. Regardless, Tsuburaya was particularly proud of *Mighty Jack*.

The series was helmed by directors Kazuho Mitsuta, Samaji Nonagase, and Toei veteran Tsuneo Kobayashi. Atsushi Oki and Kazuo Sagawa were placed in charge of effects, as Koichi Takano was occupied with *Ultraseven*. Sagawa, newly promoted to effects director, shows talent, particularly in the execution of miniatures. Thanks to his work on *Mighty Jack*, as effects director Sagawa would specialize in the dynamic depiction of mechanical craft. His nickname became "Flying Sagawa" as he had a particular affinity for staging scenes of miniature craft in flight.

For the mecha designs, Toru Narita's assistant was the 24-year-old **AKIHIKO IGUCHI** (1943-). Born Akihiko Takahashi in Matsumoto, Nagano Prefecture, Iguchi had been an underclassman of Narita's older assistant Noriyoshi Ikeya. Iguchi would become a rising designer at Tsuburaya Productions and eventually Toho. Yoshio Suzuki would also make his debut as art director for the main unit of *Mighty Jack,* handpicked by Tsuburaya himself. Suzuki had worked as a modeling assistant to Eizo Kaimai on *Godzilla* and *Godzilla Raids Again* and had moved to Toho's art department by 1961.

Mighty Jack's miniature work is a major highlight with striking shots of the *MJ*. The use of 35mm for the effects sequences allows for high frame rate shooting, often missing from other, 16mm-lensed shows. From a special effects perspective, *Mighty Jack* is Tsuburaya Pro's best show yet. It features the most dynamic miniature battle sequences on tokusatsu television to date. A stunning shot includes the *MJ*'s dock being flooded with water, made possible only through high-speed shooting. Another remarkable shot features a miniature helicopter, landed by hand with piano wire work. *Mighty Jack*'s miniature work is nearly theatrical quality. Unfortunately, *Mighty Jack*'s ratings were poor. After 13 episodes, the brass at Fuji TV ordered its premise reworked. The sequel show, called **FIGHT! MIGHTY JACK [Television Run (Japan):** July 6th - December 28th, 1968], was made more child friendly than its predecessor and reduced to a half-hour time slot.

Fight! Mighty Jack features a new cast of characters and producer Yoshiyuki Shindo was brought on board, along with director **KEINOSUKE TSUCHIYA** (1924-?). Both had worked on a popular Toei series called *Phantom Agents* that aired from 1964 to '66. Tsuchiya had also directed episodes of *Ambassador Magma* and *The Monster Prince*. To further draw in children, monsters began to appear midway through the series. The octopus prop from *Frankenstein Conquers the World* and *The War of the Gargantuas* was again dusted off for use in episode #14. Another monster, "Packy" from episode #16, was originally made for a shelved comedy program proposed by Tetsuo Kinjo. There's even a scene spoofing *Ultraseven* featuring actor Koji Moritsugu. **SHOHEI TOJO** (1939-) would also make his directorial debut on a pair of episodes. Tojo, a native of Fukushima and classmate of Kazuo Sagawa, would become one of Tsuburaya Pro's trusted directors, making his mark at Toei as well.

Toho, meanwhile, had realized that the Monster Boom was now over, displaced by a "Sports Boom" kicked off by the March 1968 airing of *Star of the Giants*, a sensationally popular baseball-themed anime series. Their next Godzilla film **DESTROY ALL MONSTERS** [**Director:** Ishiro Honda - **Release Date (Japan):** August 1st, 1968] was planned by Tomoyuki Tanaka to be the final entry. A proto-cinematic universe ensemble piece made half a century before *Avengers: Endgame*, *Destroy All Monsters* was to send off the Monster Boom in epic style. This all-out monster assault also recalls Universal horror ensemble films like *House of Frankenstein* (1944).

Destroy All Monsters was originally titled *Giant Monster Chushingura*, a nod to the beloved folktale of the 47 Ronin. Conceived in 1967, early scripts were ambitious. In addition to the final cast of 11 monsters: King Kong, Mechani-Kong, Maguma, Ebirah, Sanda and Gaira were considered. Tanaka decided to make Kazue Kiba's proposal instead into *Son of Godzilla*, though *Giant Monster Chushingura*, soon retitled *Monster Advance Order*, was kept in development. The number of monsters was cut to make the picture easier to produce. As assistant effects director Teruyoshi Nakano would say, it was a concept perfect for the splendor of the Cinemascope format. The entire cast of monsters could be laid out in grand style across the expansive frame like actors on a kabuki stage.

For *Destroy All Monsters*, the budget was increased and Ishiro Honda was brought back. Honda brings similar pulp sci-fi elements to the table as in *The Mysterians*, *Battle in Outer Space* and *Invasion of Astro-Monster*. Perhaps drawing influence from *Star Trek*, *Destroy All Monsters* is one of the first explicitly futuristic Japanese monster movies, set near the end of the 20th century, then quite a ways off. The science-obsessed Ishiro Honda brings futurist concepts to the table. These include the monsters being imprisoned via force field in Monsterland, a sanctuary to keep humanity safe from them, along with undersea farming and a moonbase in the fashion of *2001: A Space Odyssey*. Some ideas were discarded due to budget concerns: Honda wanted to delve deeply into the ocean farming of the monsters' food and feature "hybrid" monsters that had been bred and genetically engineered. Eiji Tsuburaya was again too busy to direct the effects work as production on *Admiral Yamamoto* overlapped. Sadamasa Arikawa thus stepped into the effects director chair again.

A new Godzilla suit was constructed by Teizo Toshimitsu and Yasuei Yagi for *Destroy All Monsters*. This would be the final Godzilla suit built by Toshimitsu. Haruo Nakajima returned to play the monster and the suit was designed to look more anthropomorphic. With Nikkatsu action hunks like Yujiro Ishihara and Tetsuya Watari exceedingly popular, Godzilla, too, was made into something of a handsome leading man. The 1965 suit was also used for water sequences such as Godzilla attacking the United Nations Building in New York City.

From left to right: Sadamasa Arikawa, Ishiro Honda, Eiji Tsuburaya and Tomoyuki Tanaka

The only other novel suit made was for Anguirus, as the costume from *Godzilla Raids Again* had long since decayed. Built by Nobuyuki Yasumaru, the new Anguirus suit had fangs and horns made from FRP and its shell was urethane. The thorns on the shell were carved balsa wood with a polyester resin. The suits for Rodan (Teruo Aragaki), Minilla (Masao Fukuzawa), Gorosaurus (Yu Sekita), Baragon and King Ghidorah (Susumu Utsumi) were all refurbished from previous appearances, along with the Mothra and Kumonga props. The Manda puppet from *Atragon* received renovations with its horns and whiskers removed. In the case of Varan, the suit from 1958 was not in usable shape. A new, three-foot doll was built and a repaired Guignol puppet from the original film was used. Miniature puppets for several of the monsters were also built for wide, bird's-eye view shots. As promotion, the Nichigeki Dance Team, known for their sexy stage shows at Toho's now-defunct theater of the same name, did a swimsuit-clad photoshoot at a hotel pool with the monster suits.

Destroy All Monsters is a mid-range Godzilla entry. With a barebones script co-authored by Honda and Takeshi Kimura, it feels formulaic and painted by numbers. Honda had covered similar ground better in earlier films like *The Mysterians* and *Astro-Monster*. The FX work of Arikawa's unit is uneven but again he does a good job mimicking his mentor's style. *Destroy All Monsters* does, however, reach a level of spectacle the series had yet to depict, though the film feels too ambitious in concept for its budget.

A notable error in the film is that Gorosaurus is shown destroying the Arc de Triomphe in Paris. The monster, not known to burrow, is shown surfacing from underground. It is referred to in the following scene by a newscaster (Saburo Iketani) as "Baragon". Baragon was indeed intended to be used in that sequence. Rumor has swirled that the Baragon suit had been too damaged from its usage in *Ultra Q* and *Ultraman* episodes, but that was two years prior and the suit had since been repaired. The truth is that Arikawa was concerned that Baragon's ears would break off while shooting this sequence. As the Arc was an expensive miniature and the tight budget made rebuilding it difficult, Arikawa could not afford any "NGs". Thus, he chose to use the more durable Gorosaurus suit. By this time, Ishiro Honda's unit had already shot the newscaster sequence with Iketani.

The miniature work in *Destroy All Monsters* is its strongest suit with prevalent contributions from Yasuyuki Inoue. The work of the Toho effects unit under Arikawa reaches its greatest heights with a sequence which sees Godzilla, Mothra, Rodan and Manda all converging upon a futuristic Tokyo. Alongside Godzilla's original rampage in '54 and destruction of Nagoya in *Mothra vs. Godzilla,* it is among the best urban rampages in the *Showa* films. Miniature cars appear on miniature roads, looking like a view from an airplane. The Manda prop's execution is less adroit than would have been the case under Tsuburaya's direction, but the pyrotechnics are the most intricate yet. A few shots are sublime, such as Godzilla advancing from afar behind a building shrouded in smoke. The images of Godzilla and Manda gleefully marching through Inoue's facsimile Tokyo, swarmed by exploding gunpowder, rounds take the series to its grandest spectacle yet. A short deleted segment has Godzilla tussling with Manda; this was improvised by Nakajima but was removed, possibly because of the awkward appearance of the Manda prop, or simply because it was narratively confusing. The Tokyo destruction sequence is capped by similar shots of smoldering, decimated buildings as in *Godzilla*.

Another stand-out sequence is the U.N. Defense Force's attack against the monsters near the Kilaak aliens' base. An explosive, dynamic scene, it features some of the Showa series' very finest miniaturized war machines. Among the most amazing miniature shots in the film is subtle. With a camera pan, it stunningly blends, all in-camera, one of Fuchimu Shimakura's best horizons of the summit of Mount Fuji with an intricate miniaturized Aokigahara forest, now tragically known for its suicides, from Inoue. There are some particularly striking optical Oxberry composites in *Destroy All Monsters*, especially one blending an advancing Godzilla with the fleeing actors in Aokigahara.

Shooting a miniaturized space battle craft

Gerry Anderson's influence continues to be felt with the *Moonlight* SY-3, designed by Mutsumi Toyoshima. The SY-3 is a crewed super spacecraft in sleek miniature form, one part exploration rocket, the other part space battleship. In the opening scene, it launches from a base at Iwo Jima, which had been returned to Japan just a month prior to release. Toy maker Marusan had a hand in its design. The miniatures were mainly built from balsa wood and three of varying scales were made. As with the *Battle in Outer Space* SPIPs and *Astro Monster*'s P-1, shooting its launch was difficult. As usual, Arikawa's unit had to dig a hole in the studio floor. Without Tsuburaya there to talk them out of trouble, extra pains were taken to give Toho's guards the slip. The lunar attack on the Kilaak base is as far removed from Kubrick's NASA realism in *2001* as can be imagined, evoking George Pal and

Gerry Anderson, along with Tsuburaya's work on *Battle in Outer Space*. A nifty optical composite is seen when the barrier of the Kilaak base is burned through by the crew of the SY-3. The inside of the base turns into a black-and-white image as it is petrified by the change in temperature and air pressure, followed by the foreground.

Destroy All Monsters' climax features an army of monsters led by Godzilla teaming up for a brawl against King Ghidorah. Requiring dozens of crew people to man the wires, it is an operatic *Cirque du Soleil* of stuntmen in monster skins, piano wires and radio-controlled mechanics. As Ghidorah gruesomely bleeds from its mouths while Godzilla curb stomps its heads, it's clear Arikawa was at the helm and not Tsuburaya. In the final moments, the SY-3 battles a Kilaak saucer disguised as a "fire dragon", featuring Sadao Iizuka's most elaborate optical animation. The Kilaak saucers, of which three were constructed, were three feet wide and made of FRP. A wide shot of a saucer flying into a portal inside the spacious alien base features some of the most intricate wire work ever pulled off at Toho. Piano wires were rigged through the tunnel and the ship was guided through with a winding pulley.

Destroy All Monsters' last scene feels like a sublime send-off to both the Monster Boom and the Godzilla series; it amounts to a curtain call depicting the monsters living happily in peace in Monsterland. Godzilla is in his Heaven and all right is with the world. Had *Destroy All Monsters* been Toho's final monster picture, this would have felt fitting, though Tomoyuki Tanaka decided against such plans. *Destroy All Monsters*, shown on a double bill with an edited version of *Atragon*, would gross even lower than *Son of Godzilla*. While the higher budgeted *King Kong Escapes*, *Son of Godzilla* and *Destroy All Monsters* had flopped, the child-oriented *Gamera vs. Viras* made at Daiei had been a surprise hit. Tanaka thus decided to continue making monster films at Toho, albeit with a similar formula aimed at a child audience. Incidentally, in 1973 in the U.S., *Destroy All Monsters* would form the namesake for an experimental Detroit-area rock band.

Eiji Tsuburaya, meanwhile, had been hard at work on **ADMIRAL YAMAMOTO** [Director: Seiji Maruyama **Release Date (Japan):** August 14th, 1968]. The film is the second entry in Toho's "8/15" series: Starting with *Japan's Longest Day* (1967), directed by Kihachi Okamoto, Toho would release a war movie each summer to commemorate the day of

Japan's surrender. This 1968 entry was a biopic of legendary Imperial navalman Isoroku Yamamoto. The role of Yamamoto is tackled by Toshiro Mifune, who brings a gravitas to the role not unlike his performances for Akira Kurosawa, with whom he had fallen out due to the long and difficult production schedule of *Red Beard* (1965).

The Tsuburaya unit lensing more naval warfare in miniature form

Tsuburaya had revered Yamamoto during the war and took this film to heart, passing on *Destroy All Monsters* to take on the project. *Admiral Yamamoto* again features some of the best miniature work to come from his team, boasting no fewer than 156 miniature ships and planes made. Amazingly, art director Yasuyuki Inoue engineered and directed construction of the miniatures while already occupied with *Destroy All Monsters*. *Admiral Yamamoto* is, however, not a peak Tsuburaya war film and like *Destroy All Monsters*, it suffers from a smaller budget than its ambition demands.

Times were changing. Script supervisor Keiko Suzuki, now married, would leave Toho's FX department after working on *Destroy All Monsters* and *Admiral Yamamoto*. She felt the quality of the films was declining. When she joined Toho in the late 1950s, Eiji Tsuburaya was typically given four months to shoot his effects sequences. By now, that relatively luxurious schedule had been reduced to two months. Thus, *Yamamoto* contains a fair share of stock footage, particularly from *Storm Over the Pacific*, with the Pearl Harbor attack reused wholesale. Similarly, the use of footage from *Attack Squadron* for the Midway sequence results in Shiden fighters being jarringly mismatched with newly-shot Zeros. Many of *Storm Over the Pacific*'s Midway shots are reused as well.

The newly filmed footage is, nonetheless, quite impressive. There's one of Tsuburaya's most jaw-dropping aerial shots, a lifelike swarm of miniature planes seen over tiny ships in a gelatin sea. The sequences dealing with the 1942-43 Battle of Guadalcanal are a highlight, consisting of newly filmed shots. Stunning composites, once more made possible with the Oxberry Optical Printer, juxtapose Imperial Army soldiers trying to swim to safety with anchored warships. The Guadalcanal segments feature some of the Tsuburaya unit's most spectacularly staged aerial bombardment scenes. Other memorable shots feature Zeros flying in formation against a setting sun, a motif evoking Japan's impending defeat. The mournful final sequence, in which Yamamoto's plane is shot down over Rabaul, boasts intricate miniature work. It is a stunning scene with aviator's-eye compositions of Yamamoto's aircraft explosively crashing over Inoue's meticulously crafted miniaturized jungle. Unlike *Destroy All Monsters*, *Admiral Yamamoto* was a big hit that year.

The same day came a new special effects release from Shochiku, **GOKE, BODY SNATCHER FROM HELL** [**Director:** Hajime Sato - **Release Date (Japan):** August 14th, 1968]. *Goke*'s concept came from a tokusatsu pilot that was being shopped around by P-Productions' Tomio Sagisu. It involved a benevolent alien that could transfer to humans battling a monster, "Gokemidoro," spawned from alien-possessed airline food. An episode was produced as proof of concept and a hairy Gokemidoro suit with multiple arms was modeled by Ryosaku Takayama. This pitch would, at best, only vaguely resemble the finished product. Like Godzilla, the name "Gokemidoro" was a clever portmanteau. It came from "Golgotha", the biblical site of Christ's crucifixion, along with the English word "chemical" and Japan's Midoro Pond, a locale known for its ghost stories. Sagisu took this pitch to Shochiku, who decided to make it into a feature. *The X From Outer Space* had been a sleeper hit and Shochiku's president Shiro Kido was eager to make more such films.

Screenwriter **KYUZO KOBAYASHI** (1935-2006) began work on a new script for *Goke*. As director, Toei's Hajime Sato was hired at Kobayashi's suggestion. Unlike Toho or Daiei, Toei allowed its directors to do freelance work for other studios. Sato, in turn, brought in screenwriter **SUSUMU TAKAKU** (1933-2009), a prolific writer on the popular *Key Hunter* TV series. Largely departing from the original pitch's concept, Sato and Takaku opted for a horror-oriented film without a kaiju. Setting the story in a mental hospital was considered, but in the end a plane crash was decided on. Sato drew inspiration from Nostradamus' famous prediction that in 1999 "A great King of Terror will come from the sky". Frederic Brown's 1961 sci-fi novella *The Mind Thing* was also influential on its alien mind control trope. P-Productions would stay on board for the special effects, with Shinsuke Kojima at the unit's helm. *Goke* was shot mainly at a quarry that would later become a familiar sight to viewers of Toei's special effects shows.

Goke (1968) export poster

Goke, Body Snatcher From Hell melds J-Horror with tokusatsu sci-fi theatrics, along with a hearty dose of apocalyptic nihilism. It concerns survivors of a plane crash who must contend with a vampiric assassin (chanson singer Hideo Ko) possessed through a suggestively shaped gash in his skull by amoeba-like aliens bent on exterminating humanity. Sato's direction is stellar with excellent production design. Complementing the surreal weirdness of the picture are a pair of Salvador Dali paintings which appear early on.

A miniaturized airplane crash

Hajime Sato was versed in the work of his contemporaries and at any moment, *Goke* can bring to mind films by better known directors. Its tropes and bleak ending remind one of Don Siegel's *Invasion of the Body Snatchers* (1956). Sometimes *Goke* evokes the grotesque imagery and outlandish lighting of Nobuo Nakagawa's *Sinner to Hell* (1960). The opening, involving suicidal birds splattering against airplane windows, brings to mind Alfred Hitchcock's *The Birds* (1963). Its story of marooned survivors turning on each other while facing a monstrous threat suggests Ishiro Honda's *Matango*. The gruesome, phantasmagorical images and space vampire concept are similar to Mario Bava's *Planet of the Vampires* (1965). Finally, its apocalyptic atmosphere and sense of rage over the Vietnam war parallels George A. Romero's *Night of the Living Dead*, released in the U.S. only a month and a half later. A la the misanthropic Romero, *Goke* suggests that perhaps the space creatures are giving humanity what it deserves. Sadly, *Goke* was director Hajime Sato's final theatrical film.

The work of Kojima's effects unit on *Goke* is also inventive. Support came from Michio Mikami, along with Yoshio Watanabe who handled the optical animation. The footage is at times unpolished with embarrassing shots involving unrealistic dummies blown up and thrown off cliffs, but the miniature work is effective and nearly on par with Tsuburaya's. *Goke* stuns from its opening shot, later copied verbatim by Quentin Tarantino in *Kill Bill Vol. 1* (2003). A miniaturized jetliner flies through a blood-red, crimson sky. Shortly thereafter, Kojima and company create the finest plane crash in tokusatsu to date. The Gokemidoro's glowing miniature spaceship is strikingly executed and the sequences of the aliens entering and exiting the skulls of their human hosts through vagina-like gashes are rather incredible. Condoms were melted and pumped out of realistic replicas of actors Hideo Ko and Masaya

Takahashi's heads. The footage was printed backwards for the effect of the aliens entering. Another inventive segment, of a vampire's dead body turning to dust and blowing away, exceeds the vampiric disintegration scenes in any Hammer Dracula film.

Goke's final moments are another miniature marvel as an armada of saucers descend upon a conquered Earth. Through simple lighting and optical fading, the planet's atmosphere is destroyed in moments and Earth turns into a dead planet. *Goke, Body Snatcher From Hell* was released on a double feature with Kinji Fukasaku's pulpy, transgressive heist flick *Black Lizard*. The theatrics of lead Akihiro Miwa, a proto-drag queen who is something of Japan's Divine, together with a chanson singer being face-raped by alien goo must have made for a mind-melting night at the movies in '68. After finishing *Black Lizard*, Fukasaku would get to make a space gunk-themed sci-fi movie of his own.

With *Ultraseven* ending, Tsuburaya Productions' next TV show was **OPERATION: MYSTERY** [Television Run (Japan): September 15th, 1968 - March 9th, 1969], which saw air on TBS during *Seven*'s former timeslot. For this program, TBS had asked Tsuburaya Pro to create a different kind of show. Instead of giant monsters, the focus in *Operation: Mystery* would be on supernatural phenomena. This was in part inspired by Japan's "Yokai Boom". Originally entitled *Challenger: Horror Science Series,* the title *Operation: Mystery* was a nod to *Mission: Impossible.* Again, Tetsuo Kinjo headed the writing team. The program would involve yet another scientific organization, the SRI (Science Research Institute), who help the police solve baffling crimes that appear to have supernatural causes. In some episodes, these crimes are indeed unexplainable. In others, the cunning SRI is able to expose these misdeeds as hoaxes using scientific reasoning.

Operation: Mystery is in line with Tsuburaya's earlier work on *kaijin* films such as *The H-Man*. Prolific use was made of opticals and the distinction between the drama and FX units blurred with regular-sized phantoms. Atsushi Oki and Kazuo Sagawa handled the visual effects on various episodes. The show would be a breakout for Shin Kishida, a distinctive character actor. One of Kishida's most notable later roles was that of a Japanese Dracula in *Lake of Dracula* (1971) and *The Evil of Dracula* (1974).

As with *Ultraseven*, one of the episodes, *"The Lunatic Man,"* is now under a self-imposed studio ban at Tsuburaya Productions. In 1995, a laserdisc set was recalled because it contained the episode. The exact reason for the episode's suppression is unknown, but its insensitive depiction of mental illness is suspected. *Operation: Mystery* got decent if not spectacular ratings, so the show ended after 26 episodes. Tsuburaya Pro's next show would also be horror themed: **UNBALANCE: HORROR THEATER [Television Run (Japan):** January 8th - April 2nd, 1973], which began production in 1969. Due to Eiji Tsuburaya's untimely death and a backlash against "scary" content on TV, it would wind up unbroadcast until years later.

Meanwhile, Shochiku was quick to follow *Goke* with a downbeat double feature of genre pictures: **GENOCIDE [AKA: WAR OF THE INESECTS - Director:** Kazui Nihomatsu - **Release Date (Japan):** November 9th, 1968] and **THE LIVING SKELETON [Director:** Hiroshi Matsuno - **Release Date (Japan):** Ibid]. Keiji Kawakami directed the effects for both films nearly simultaneously with support from Akira Watanabe's Nihon Special Effects Co. *Genocide*, written by *Goke*'s Susumu Takaku, boasts a similar bleakness. The political commentary, which draws aggressively on a number of hot-button issues, is quite radical for a Japanese studio picture. *Genocide*, opens with an American B-52 bomber downed by a swarm of bees fictitious island (standing in for Okinawa). It drew inspiration from the Palomares incident. In January of 1966, an American B-52 carrying several nuclear weapons had similarly crashed near the Spanish fishing village of Palomares. Thanks to two of the bombs paritially detonating, the area suffered nuclear contamination. *Genocide*, shot on Hachijojima, also explores raw topics like Vietnam, U.S. foreign policy and even the Holocaust with nihilistic glee.

The work of Keiji Kawakami's FX unit is prevalent in *Genocide*'s first and final reels. The effects shots are imaginative with stellar miniatures and optical composites. Most impressive are shots of the model B-52 sparking as it is swarmed by the deadly bees, which were realized using a mix of on-set particles and optical animation; these images strongly resemble Tsuburaya's work. Another eye-catching wide process shot shows the bees ominously swarming in the sky as characters look on.

Genocide's final reel is a hallucinogenic trip with elaborate optical animation and queasy macro-lens close-ups of the bees stinging and biting their victims. It was planned to feature human-sized monster bugs as well, but the concept was discarded as the first monster suit took too long to construct. As

Kawakami's unit was understaffed and also dealing with work on *The Living Skeleton*, construction on the suits necessary for the scene could not be finished in time. The sole completed monster suit was used in footage created exclusively for the trailer.

Genocide is capped in a doomsday climax ala *Goke*. The film's pregnant ingenue, played by Emi Shindo, cowers in a canoe as an enormous mushroom cloud hovers on the horizon - created, as usual, in Tsuburaya's style with paint in a water tank.

Shochiku's theater program for *Genocide* (right) and *The Living Skeleton* (left) - the right-to-left reading of Japanese print media suggests the former was shown first

The Living Skeleton was written by *Goke*'s other screenwriter, Kyuzo Kobayashi. With a dourness akin to Herk Harvey's *Carnival of Souls* (1962), it boasts similar haunting monochrome images. *The Living Skeleton* involves a group of murderous smugglers haunted by a ghost ship and the siren-like spectre of one of their victims (Kikko Matsuoka). From the opening shot of a miniaturized ship in a gelatin sea, Keiji Kawakami copies his mentor Eiji Tsuburaya's techniques so closely that it could pass for the latter's work. Director Hiroshi Matsuno's unit dominates the picture, however, and *The Living Skeleton* skews more toward J-Horror than tokusatsu. The Eurasian-featured Matsuoka, with jet-black hair, a pale face and deathly stare, resembles a classical Japanese *yurei* with shades of *Black Sunday*'s Barbara Steele. She is a memorable screen siren who looks forward to the many vengeful female ghosts to haunt

J-Horror audiences in films like *Ring* (1997).

Sequences aboard the ghost ship, shot in a genuine cargo steamer anchored at Yokosuka, evoke European horror films with a sense of gothic horror akin to the work of Ricardo Freda or Mario Bava. Several of these are unnerving and well directed. A twisted later scene involves mad scientist Nishizato (Ko Nishimura), who lives aboard the ghost ship and keeps his wife's mummified corpse fresh with blood transfusions while listening to tapes of feminine moans. This sequence features memorable optical and stop motion effects. There are uneven elements such as unrealistic prop skeletons and unconvincing bats hung on wires. The skeletons look better later on, however, when they're creepily pulled from the ocean, along with the dead body of a diver.

Kawakami's FX unit lets loose in the *House of Usher*-like final moments, which see the ghost ship dissolved into nothingness by an acid released onboard. *The Living Skeleton* is atmospherically directed from both units and a memorable melding of moody horror and tokusatsu. Amusingly, after shooting, the owner of the cargo ship used was appalled by the film's gruesome content and lodged a complaint. Shochiku, much to screenwriter Kobayashi's annoyance, had some gore scenes edited down prior to release. Keiji Kawakami's work on *Genocide* and *The Living Skeleton* would be among his last before his death in 1973, only a few years after his mentor's.

Toei, meanwhile, had been at work on their next international co-production with Hollywood's MGM and Italy's RAM Films: **THE GREEN SLIME [AKA: GAMMA 3: BIG SPACE OPERATION - Directors:** Kinji Fukasaku, Katsuhiko Taguchi - **Release Dates:** December 1st **(U.S.)** - December 19th, 1968 **(Japan)]**. The picture was made as an in-name-only follow-up to Anthonio Marghereti's Gamma One series which began with 1966's *Wild, Wild Planet*. Kinji Fukasaku, a native of Mito, had been promoted to director in 1961 with a quartet of hour-long action pictures featuring Shinichi (Sonny) Chiba. He was brought in per his action background and reputation for budget efficiency.

The Green Slime, its script written by Batman co-creator Bill Finger, revolves around the titular space gunk which American VHS copy describes as looking like "Godzilla squashing the Blob under its rather large reptilian foot". It is found on an asteroid and accidentally brought aboard space station Gamma III where it grows into a tentacled, one-eyed thingamajig. The monster feeds on electricity and lethally jolts passersby. Attacks only cause it to replicate and soon the station is overrun with creatures.

The Green Slime (1968) U.S. poster

Director Fukasaku wanted to spin the story as a subtle Vietnam parable while the film's backers wanted an artless programmer. This would be far from Fukasaku's last genre film, however, and he would one day better meld sci-fi and Cold War anxieties in the later U.S/Japanese co-production *Virus* (1980). Fukasaku would also later share the burden with **TOSHIO MASUDA** (1927-) for the Japanese sequences of Fox's *Tora! Tora! Tora!* (1970) after the departure of Akira Kurosawa. *The Green Slime* took about six weeks to shoot and Fukasaku was under a lot of pressure to bring it in under budget.

The Hollywood studio brought in Western star Robert Horton along with *The Dirty Dozen*'s Richard Jaekel while the Italian side supplied actress Lucinana Paluzzi (*Thunderball*). Horton was impressed by the grit of the Japanese crew as they hefted gigantic lights in bare feet. Serving as supporting characters and extras are a who's who of Japan's expat community. This included William Ross, whose studio, Frontier Productions, dubbed many tokusatsu films into English and his frequent collaborators Robert Dunham and Budd Widom. Among the other extras were a number of Israeli Defense Force recruits fresh from the Six Day War.

The plentiful special effects were helmed by none other than Akira Watanabe and Yukio Manoda from Nihon Special Effects Co. *The Green Slime*'s images of miniaturized interstellar rockets, space stations and giant asteroids are quite reminiscent of Watanabe's work on *Gorath* and *Invasion of Astro-Monster*. The miniature work is intricately executed and close to Toho grade. Watanabe's biggest contribution to *The Green Slime* is a sequence in which an asteroid threatening Earth, Flora, is blown up; using an effective blend of optical work, miniature photography and pyrotechnics. *The Green Slime*'s most stunning shot takes place in its final reel and mixes Fukasaku and Watanabe's units via bluescreen. As the miniature space station Gamma 3 plummets out of its orbit behind them, a space-suited Rankin (Robert Horton) holds on to a dead Elliot (Richard Jaeckel).

Kinji Fukasaku

Inventive visual trickery is used for the "slime effects," such as stop motion and a rotating set, a concept Watanabe likely adapted from his time on *The H-Man*. Green-dyed soap suds were also used to create the effect of the slime proliferating. The monsters themselves, mainly shot by Fukasaku and Taguchi, don't fare as well. The suits were occupied by a mix of crew members and schoolchildren headed by child actor **MASANORI MACHIDA** (1955-). Diminutive, cycloptic beasties who look like Sid and Marty Krofft show rejects, they're only a nudge less silly than Guilala. The modeling team was likely headed by Eizo Kaimai per his prior work with Watanabe's firm.

The U.S. version is significantly longer. In Japan, the film was released in an alternate, faster-paced version to the Toei Manga Festival on a double bill with the anime *Pinocchio in Space*. Actor Robert Horton, a New Yorker, copped a viewing of *The Green Slime* with his wife when it played at a local grindhouse. Horton fled the scene before the movie ended, fearing he might be recognized.

Another effects-oriented double feature from Daiei was in the cards for the New Years holiday season, pairing the Tokyo branch's **SNAKE GIRL AND THE SILVER HAIRED WITCH** [**Director:** Noriaki Yuasa - **Release Date (Japan):** December 14th, 1968] with Kyoto's **SPOOK WARFARE** [**Director:** Yoshiyuki Kuroda - **Release Date (Japan):** Ibid]. *Snake Girl and the Silver Haired Witch*, based on manga by **KAZUO UMEZU** (1936-) is a child-oriented J-Horror film with tokusatsu flourishes. It sports a different aesthetic to Yuasa's Gamera films with spooky monochrome visuals throughout.

Spook Warfare, by contrast, is an even more elaborate follow-up to *One Hundred Monsters*. Like the prior film, it draws from Mizuki's *GeGe no Kitaro*. *Spook Warfare* takes its main concept from a 1966 storyline in which Kitaro recruits an army of Japanese yokai to battle a gang of Universal-style foreign monsters that include a vampire, a werewolf and Frankenstein. Toho's recent *Destroy All Monsters* was also an influence. Whereas *One Hundred Monsters* had a stronger J-horror sensibility, *Spook Warfare* is heavier on the tokusatsu monster theatrics.

Spook Warfare is, overall, the highlight of the Yokai films - reaching the highest heights of the three. Director Yoshiyuki Kuroda handles both the effects and drama in one unit and as a result, the ghoulish pantomime beastliness is well integrated with *jidai-geki* melodrama. The special effects are improved from the first with imaginative trick photography that represents Kuroda at the top of his form. Fujio Morita did not return for *Spook Warfare*, however, but Kuroda's work with DP Hiroshi Imai is just as impressive. The film's opening, which boasts top-tier miniature work, provides a monumental introduction for the villain, vampiric Babylonian demon Daimon. Played by *Majin*'s Riki Hashimoto, the creature resembles a cross between Count Dracula and *The Exorcist*'s Pazuzu. Indeed, Riki

Hashimoto's trademark dead stare is as unsettling as Christopher Lee's.

Spook Warfare features an even larger army of yokai than *One Hundred Monsters'*. Once again, Masao Yagi's Equis Productions was kept busy. Many of the yokai from the first film returned, along with their costumes. *Abura Sumashi* (Toshiyasu Beppu), *Aobouzu* (Shinjiro Akatsuki), the umbrella-like *Kasa Obake*, the bird-like *Karasa Tengu* and *Rokurokubi* (Ikuko Mori) all reunite. The last is even more impressive than in the first movie, once again executed through in-camera FX. A new costume for the *Kappa* (**GEN KUROKI**), who plays a more prominent role, was made. A new monster is introduced in *Ungaikyo* (**HIDEKI HAMAMURA**), a fox-like beast with a mirror in its belly. This effect was created with a film projector. Another is *Futakuchi Onna*, played by **KEIKO YUKITOMO**. Otherwise a normal young woman, *Futakuchi Onna* has a monstrous face on the back of her head. The creatures, who did not speak in *One Hundred Monsters*, are humanized and given voice. The *Rokurokubi* (Long Necked Woman) once again is executed through in-camera FX that is even more impressive than in the first movie.

The climax, where Daimon grows to a giant size while battling the yokai, features Yoshiyuki Kuroda's most sophisticated process and optical work and feels phantasmagorical in its intensity. The double exposure processes pioneered by Daiei Kyoto's FX unit on films like *The Invisible Demon* are combined with the blue-screen monster effects perfected on *Majin*. The results are sensational with complex and multi-layered visual effects shots and optical processing as advanced as Tsuburaya's. As with the Majin films, there's an excellent sense of scale with giant Daimon claws and feet employed. Overall, *Spook Warfare* is a practical effects marvel.

As the decade of the 1960s drew to a close, so too would the dominance of domestic films at the Japanese box office. For Japan's film business, hard times lay ahead. The "Big Five" studios would never again relive the glory days when production, profit and creativity were at their peak. Additionally, a month into the new decade, the film and TV industries would lose one of their greatest luminaries. Eiji Tsuburaya's workaholic lifestyle was beginning to take a serious toll on his health.

AN EXPRESSION OF EXISTENCE: THE MUSIC OF TOKUSATSU

by Tyler Martin

It was the winter of 1949. During the production of Hiroshi Inagaki's *I Am a Bodyguard*, actor Ryunosuke Tsukigata was spending the evening with the film's composer at a restaurant in Kyoto. They were soon joined by an unannounced guest who proceeded to make himself comfortable, engaging them in lively conversation while enjoying a few drinks at Tsukigata's expense. The actor did not bother to introduce the men, perhaps assuming they knew each other already, as both were involved in the movie business. A number of times thereafter, the two ran into each other by chance in Kyoto bars and enjoyed pleasant chats, with the composer covering the tab; still, they never learned one another's names.

A few years later, they found themselves at a press conference held to introduce the creative staff for an upcoming monster movie in which they were both involved, the first of its kind in Japan: *Godzilla*. The men were delighted to meet again in such an unexpected setting. In short order, it was revealed that the beneficiary of those free drinks had been none other than Eiji Tsuburaya, the master of Japanese special effects; the benefactor, **AKIRA IFUKUBE** (1914-2006), who would soon prove himself master of Japanese special effects music.

Due to the film's novel nature, Ifukube had great difficulty conceiving music for the titular creature. He asked Tsuburaya to show him the rushes, but the effects director balked; a famously stubborn man, he refused to share the footage with the composer. However, after persistent requests from his former drinking buddy, Tsuburaya relented, and the immortal sound of Godzilla was born. Although his love was mainly for classical music and he worked in a variety of motion picture genres, for many, Ifukube would become most closely associated with special effects films.

Born and raised in Hokkaido, the northernmost of Japan's main islands, Akira Ifukube was largely self-taught as a musician. From a young age, he had a deep-seated affinity for the natural world, due in large part to his exposure to and mingling with the Ainu, the aboriginal people of the region, to whom nature is an object of worship. The music of the Ainu would have a profound influence on the man and his work; he channeled this in combination with dense orchestration and rhythmic patterns derived from Russian influences like Stravinsky and Mussorgsky to craft a truly singular sound. After graduating from university, he took work as a forestry officer in the wilds of Hokkaido, living in isolation, often for weeks at a time. During this period, says Ifukube's longtime student and friend, pianist **REIKO YAMADA**, he became more intimate with the vast physical and spiritual power of nature, which far exceeds the control and comprehension of human beings; this would be crucial broadly in the development of his character and compositional style, and more specifically in the case of his signature sound for *kaiju eiga* and other tokusatsu epics, which are rooted in such themes. He used music not merely to accompany flashy special effects, but to channel the inner life of the creatures and characters depicted. Indeed, his keen sensibilities lent themselves very well not only to the horror and grandeur of giant monsters, but also to the tenderness and tragedy of human figures like *Godzilla*'s Dr. Serizawa and *Terror of Mechagodzilla*'s Katsura Mafune; the imagined musical traditions of fictitious cultures; the sublime majesty and mystery of space and the natural world; and, of course, the tremendous show of (frequently impotent) military might.

For his later films, Ifukube would screen footage for the musicians in his orchestras so that they would understand the need to "play with appropriate force;" otherwise, the sound they produced would be more well suited to a concert hall than a scene of mass mayhem. This recalls his initial insistence on seeing Tsuburaya's rushes for *Godzilla*: Such extraordinary spectacle requires an extraordinary sound.

However, Akira Ifukube was far from the only composer to realize this principle and bring "appropriate force" to the table; indeed, no history of tokusatsu is complete without mention of its peculiarly strong musical tradition. As the spirit of the tokusatsu craft lies not in photorealism but in creating something more spectacular, and, indeed, more interesting than real life, so must the music seek to instill in these images an "expression of existence" that transcends everyday reality. An impressively broad range of craftsmen and craftswomen have ably met this challenge and created soundscapes befitting the unique visual flavor of this medium.

Akira Ifukube

For 1955's *Godzilla Raids Again*, an up-and-coming young musical voice named **MASARU SATO** (1928-1999) was brought on board to score. Though his music for that picture gives little indication of the liveliness that he would soon become known for (late in life, he would muse that "it sounds like a child learning"), it was the first step in a cycle of very notable contributions to SFX film.

Also hailing from Hokkaido, Sato was a protégé of the great Fumio Hayasaka, a longtime friend of Akira Ifukube (both of whom he considered "gods"). Hayasaka was also a good friend of the director Akira Kurosawa, with whom all three composers worked at various points; after Hayasaka's untimely death in 1955, Sato became Kurosawa's principal composer for the next ten years.

In contrast to the headstrong primitivism of Ifukube, Sato readily embraced modern music and popular Western influences, most notably jazz. Unlike his mentor, Sato expressed no interest in writing for the concert stage, preferring to work exclusively in motion pictures. His prolific output and versatility led to comparisons with Ennio Morricone. His wide-ranging ability could produce varying sounds depending on what was called for by a given film or scene, though the discerning ear can distinguish certain components that remain largely consistent. For example, arranger and performer **MAKOTO INOUE** (1956-) has observed that Sato excelled at complementing the swagger of tough, masculine characters like Toshiro Mifune's nameless ronin in *Yojimbo* and effectively provided Godzilla with a similar musical identity.

Riichiro Manabe

Bringing a markedly different approach to bear, **RIICHIRO MANABE** (1924-2015) made a conscious effort to set his sound wholly apart. A pupil of Akira Ifukube, Manabe went on to study film music under Angelo Francesco Lavagnino (whom genre fans may know for his work on 1961's *Gorgo*, a British take on kaiju eiga). His early motion picture assignments included two *Super Giant* features; later, he would contribute to the Godzilla series and Michio Yamamoto's "Bloodthirsty" trilogy. Active in film, television, and classical music, Manabe was never one to shy away from experimenting with unusual tonalities and instrumentation. Much of his special-effects work is characterized, for instance, by unapologetically harsh dissonances and diverse applications of the guitar (both acoustic and electric), which he particularly adored.

Apart from Akira Ifukube's *"Main Title"* from *Godzilla*, perhaps the most widely recognized piece of music in tokusatsu film is the *"Song of Mothra,"* executed to perfection by twin pop sensations **EMI ITO** (1941-2012) and **YUMI ITO** (1941-2016) and composed by **YUJI KOSEKI** (1909-1989). Hailing from Fukushima Prefecture, Koseki was a beloved writer of classical, pop, film, and, during the war years, martial music. This last would somewhat ironically inform his work on the Honda/Tsuburaya epic *Eagle of the Pacific* (1953), which carries an anti-war subtext. In the following decade, he imbued his score for *Mothra* (1961) with a luxuriant magic and mystery quite unique in tokusatsu.

SHUNSUKE KIKUCHI (1931-2021) was a conspicuously powerful force in feature films and (especially) television. Marked by a decidedly blunt implementation of the distinctly Japanese fusion of traditional pentatonic and modal scales, Kikuchi's work can be heard in a number of Gamera entries as well as a slew of superhero programs such as *Kamen Rider, Robot Detective,* and *Jumborg Ace*. Though his heroic themes are typically rendered in major ("happy-sounding") keys, an abundance of minor ("sad-sounding") chords are interspersed throughout, giving singer **ICHIRO MIZUKI** (1948-) the impression of a hero's anguish—he fights only because he must, not because he wants to. Though incredibly prolific and stupendously successful, Kikuchi is remembered as a kind, humble man who disliked being addressed with lofty honorifics.

Naturally, when the discussion turns to tokusatsu television, mention must also be made of **KUNIO MIYAUCHI** (1932-2006), who lent his talents to Tsuburaya Productions' seminal kaiju series, *Ultra Q*, and its legendary follow-up, *Ultraman*; though subsequent Ultra series would become the territory of **TORU FUYUKI** (1935-), it was Miyauchi who established the sound of the franchise in its infancy. One of Miyauchi's first film assignments was 1960's *The Human Vapor* for Ishiro Honda, with whom he would work again on *All Monsters Attack*. In both instances, he gives an impressive account of himself. Like Sato, Miyauchi was versatile and drew a great deal of inspiration from jazz, though his music is often quite a different beast from the work of the former.

As with most musical talent to take part in such productions, tokusatsu was but one facet in the varied career of **TOSHIAKI TSUSHIMA** (1936-2013). Taking a free hand with his work and catering to the needs of each individual project, Tsushima would come to develop his own hard-hitting spin on the pentatonic/modal sound typical of Japanese film and TV music in the 1960s and '70s. Especially known for period pieces, action films, and some memorable collaborations with director Kinji Fukasaku, his SFX credits include *The Magic Serpent, Army of the Apes, Zero Pilot,* and *The War in Space*.

The reader will by this point have grasped that tokusatsu encompasses not only monsters and superheroes but other genres as well, including war films, which proved key in its development. A number of Japan's greatest war pictures are given musical life by **IKUMA DAN** (1924-2001), a celebrated composer of symphonic and operatic works. Splendorous and sentimental, Dan's film music carries powerful Western influences and recalls the sounds of old Hollywood, evoking the likes of Erich Wolfgang Korngold. This style effectively enhances the surging hope and tragic inevitability of films like *Storm Over the Pacific* and *The Last War*.

As witnessed by such examples as the Tsuburaya dynasty and the Yagis of Equis Productions, tokusatsu often runs in the family. At times, this has extended to the musical sphere as well. The son of P-Productions founder Tomio Sagisu (also known as Soji Ushio), **SHIRO SAGISU** (1957-), has left his mark on such titles as *Attack on Titan* (2015) and *Shin Godzilla* (2016), the latter a collaboration with Hideaki Anno, with whom he also worked on the tokusatsu-influenced *Neon Genesis Evangelion* franchise — as with many composers to work in the medium, he boasts extensive anime credits as well. In this vein, **MICHIAKI "CHUMEI" WATANABE** (1925-), whose music accompanies a profusion of classic Toei superhero programs and other projects as recent as 2020's *Nezura 1964*, is father to **TOSHIYUKI WATANABE** (1955-), known for his excellent work on the 1990s *Mothra* trilogy and a myriad of other ventures. Noted composer Ryoichi Hattori did not contribute directly to tokusatsu but beget progeny who would do so: his son **KATSUHISA HATTORI** (1936-2020) provided musical backdrops for the *Planet Prince* series and Shue Matsubayashi's final war epic *Imperial Navy*; Katsuhisa's son, **TAKAYUKI HATTORI** (1965-), has scored no fewer than five Godzilla entries.

The task of creating music suitable for tokusatsu productions is not always simple. Composers are frequently given little guidance by directors, requiring them to draw deeply from the well of inspiration. For *The Return of Godzilla* (1984), **REIJIRO KOROKU** (1949-) sought to go beyond the "monstrous" to express the greater "existence" of the character, evoking a mysterious, even religious kind of grandeur. To this end, he employed a number of techniques, including pedal point (named for the foot pedals of an organ), in which a low, continuous tone is sustained unchangingly to support the melody, resulting in a powerful sound not unlike church music. When scoring the opening of *Gamera 3: Revenge of Iris* (1999), **KOW OTANI** (1957-) turned his copy of the film's script upside down and transcribed the text as he saw it, which was then set to music and sung by a choir. **MICHIRU OSHIMA** (1961-), the first female composer in kaiju eiga, cleverly devised a Spanish-flavored theme for the final duel in *Godzilla vs. Megaguirus* (2000), which at points strongly resembles a bullfight, with Godzilla standing his ground against a constantly charging foe.

Ko Otani (left) - Michiru Oshima (right)

When performed in concert, apart from its original context, the greatest tokusatsu music takes on a life of its own. In the early 1980s, bowing to popular demand, Akira Ifukube wove some of his most memorable SF themes into the *Symphonic Fantasia* cycle, which was met with acclaim and has since rattled concert halls across the globe. His pupil, pianist Reiko Yamada, is a strong advocate of his work and has given many performances of his compositions in Japan and the United States; though these focus almost exclusively on classical music, fans will note a great deal of cross-pollination between the maestro's film and concert work. Musician Makoto Inoue created electronic arrangements of classic Toho cues for a series of albums entitled *Godzilla Legend*, which he and his ensemble have performed live numerous times. American conductor **JOHN DESENTIS** has deftly brought the work of Ifukube, Masaru Sato, and Kow Otani to the stage in a series of concerts held in Chicago, Illinois. Michiru Oshima participated in the most recent of these, in 2019, personally conducting her own Godzilla music; for this event, she also composed an entirely new piece, *"Godzilla in Chicago"*, to the delight of the audience.

Though the "Golden Age" now lies behind us, tokusatsu history continues to be written. The filmmakers, effects artists, and performers active in the medium today remain ever conscious of the massive shoulders on which they stand, and so, too, do the musicians. Fans and researchers may not know what they have to look forward to, but, as the present volume illustrates, there is plenty to look back upon with wonder and admiration. Wherever the future may lead, the origins of tokusatsu remain set in stone — and in sound.

*The author of this article wishes to thank **Reiko Yamada** for her kind cooperation and insight and **Maki Yamada** (no relation) for her invaluable assistance.*

XV.
1969 - 1970
昭和四十四 - 四十五

With the Monster Boom at an end, the 1969 release slate for special effects productions in Japan was more sparse than in previous years. Giant monsters had left the airwaves, though theatrical Godzilla and Gamera features were still produced with an increasingly younger audience in mind. Eiji Tsuburaya was now pushing 70 and his health was in decline, though against doctors' orders he took part in several effects productions that year.

Daiei started the 1969 special effects film cycle with another double bill featuring the Tokyo-produced **GAMERA VS. GUIRON** [Director: Noriaki Yuasa - **Release Date (Japan)**: March 21st, 1969] and the Kyoto-made **ALONG WITH GHOSTS** [**Directors**: Kimiyoshi Yasuda, Yoshiyuki Kuroda - **Release Date (Japan)**: Ibid]. The budget for this next Gamera installment was as low as that for *Gamera vs. Viras*, but *2001: A Space Odyssey* and NASA's moon mission were fueling a surge in space media; thus, an alien planet setting was decided upon.

Gamera vs. Guiron, again made with American television in mind, is among the poorest of the old school Gamera films. Here, Noriaki Yuasa's directing style begins to take on a feverish, Ed Woodsian strangeness. The special effects work by Yuasa is clunky and TV grade. In fact, the television work being done by Tsuburaya Productions, P-Productions and Nobuo Yajima's Tokusatsu Research Institute was often superior. There's the occasional good shot, but the composites are particularly poor.

Novel foe Guiron (named after the guillotine) was designed by Akira Inoue, who was quite fond of this creation. Design motifs for the blade-headed monster included the *deba* knife, used in Japan for sashimi, along with types of flatfish. The suit was built by Eizo Kaimai and Guiron wound up one of Inoue's favorite creations. A new Gamera suit was constructed by Equis Productions as well. The creature was portrayed by **UMENOSUKE IZUMI,** an Ultra monster veteran who would play

Gamera in the following film. Smaller Guignol puppets of Gamera and Guiron were built for some shots, such as Guiron attacking Gamera's shell with its bladed head.

Gamera vs. Guiron, however, is worth a watch for some twisted touches and ghoulish moments for a kids' movie. These include a Brothers Grimm-like pair of alien women (Hiroko Kai and Reiko Kasahara) with a craving for the brains of the boy protagonists (Nobuhiro Kajima and Christopher Murphy). A uniquely deranged sequence features novel foe Guiron slicing and dicing a "Space Gyaos" (the 1967 suit painted silver) with its knife=shaped head. It's a scene looking forward to the "Black Knight" gag in *Monty Python and the Holy Grail* (1975), ending with Gyaos dismembered, decapitated and then cut like a loaf of bread. Another affectionately ridiculous sequence features Gamera performing Olympic-style stunts, including swinging on a crossbar a la the famed "Ultra-C" maneuver. These gags were added because the Mexico City Summer Olympics had taken place in October of 1968. *Gamera vs. Guiron* would go on to be lampooned savagely on the popular American comedy show *Mystery Science Theater 3000.*

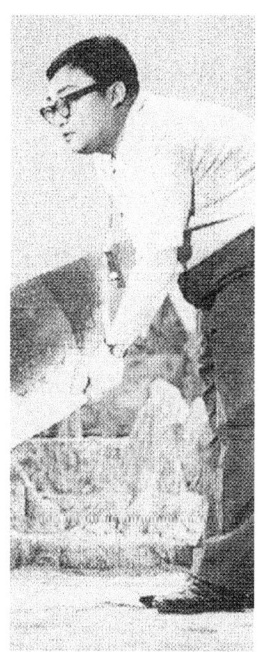

Noriaki Yuasa

Once again, Kyoto's offering was stronger. *Along with Ghosts* is a solid, character-driven kiddie J-Horror film with tokusatsu touches. Again featuring a cast of ghoulish yokai, *Along with Ghosts* is a semi-follow-up to Kimiyoshi Yasuda and Yoshiyuki Kuroda's *One Hundred Monsters* and *Spook Warfare*. Yasuda and Kuroda would this time co-direct. Taking a cue from Tokyo's Gamera series, the protagonist is a little girl named Miyo (Masami Burukido), traveling along the Tokaido Road, a famous trade route well known in Japan for its ghost stories.

Along with Ghosts is narratively engaging, with more focus on its human characters than spooks. According to director Kuroda, the intent was to focus less on the yokai themselves and create a straight-up *jidai-geki* akin to the *Zatoichi* films where the creatures happen to appear. Once again, Kuroda brings vivid phantasmal spectacle to life. A sequence where a pair of yakuza thugs pursue Miyo and a boy (Pepe Hozumi) into a haunted forest is eye-catching. Another bit, where the silhouettes of a gaggle of yokai appear behind screen doors surrounding the villains, is among the more viscerally nightmarish scenes in all three pictures.

Equis Productions and Masao Yagi would again model what characters were not reused from the previous entries. New yokai include *Hyakuya*, a creature from Suruga Prefecture with the appearance of an elderly man, played by Sumao Ishihara. There's also the *Suisha Yokai*: flying, bloody severed heads that live in water mills and attack the villains. In its final reel, *Along with Ghosts* becomes one of the most macabre kids' movies in cinema history. Seen back-to-back with the dementedness of *Gamera vs. Guiron*, it must have given Japanese tykes a few night frights.

Toho's newest Crazy Cats comedy would feature tokusatsu flourishes: **CRAZY BIG EXPLOSION [Director:** Kengo Furusawa - **Release Date (Japan):** April 27th, 1969]. The music number-laden film features the Crazy Cats getting mixed up in another caper involving an evil organization and a hydrogen bomb. The production design is evocative of Ken Adam's work on the 007 films. With Tsuburaya and Arikawa occupied on a variety of work, assistant director Teruyoshi Nakano was allowed for the first time to run the special effects unit.

Given his later penchant for explosive spectacle, it's quite fitting that Nakano made his debut on a film entitled *Crazy Big Explosion*. Nakano's work is barely noticeable until the final five minutes. Indeed, Kengo Furusawa's unit uses genuine jet fighters where in prior years, Tsuburaya would have created them with miniaturized models. The final moments of *Crazy Big Explosion* demonstrate that Nakano had learned quite a bit from his mentors Tsuburaya and Arikawa. They feature an impressively staged miniature spaceship launch and the titular explosion, created through pyrotechnics and paint in a water tank.

Daiei Tokyo's next special effects release was **GATEWAY TO GLORY** [**Director:** Mitsuo Murayama - **Release Date (Japan):** July 12th, 1969]. This naval war picture, filled with training sequences, features extensive effects helmed by Noriaki Yuasa. The film, shot for six weeks in Hiroshima, suffered production setbacks on Murayama's end: actor Raizo Ichikawa became ill and had to be replaced by Ken Utsui. *Gateway to Glory*'s Imperial military veteran assistant director taught the extras who played naval cadets proper etiquette, including how to salute.

Yuasa's often explosive images of miniaturized fighter planes are hardly Toho quality. Yet they exceed his work on the prior Gamera pictures. While not up to the standard of Tsuburaya's war films, *Gateway to Glory* features some of Yuasa's finest miniature photography with splendid aerial dogfights. James Henry of *The Japan Times* praised Yuasa's effects work: "Highlighting the film are the remarkable special effects of Noriaki Yuasa, responsible for the popular 'Gamera' series. Through the competent efforts of this talented special effects director, the attack on Pearl Harbor, the Midway naval battle and death of Adm. Isoroku Yamamoto, among other historical events, are breathtakingly recreated."

Toho's last international co-production to use Hollywood stars was **LATITUDE ZERO** [**Director:** Ishiro Honda - **Release Date (Japan):** July 26th, 1969] released days after Neil Armstrong and Buzz Aldrin walked on the moon. It would also be the final collaboration between Honda and Tsuburaya. *Latitude Zero* was based on a radio play conceived in the 1940s by writer Ted Sherdeman, known among genre fans for writing the monster classic *Them!* (1954). Don Sharp, a Hollywood TV producer, took the concept to Toho in 1967 after having unsuccessfully pitched it as a television show. There was talk of shooting the movie in 70mm Super Panavision, but importing that equipment to Japan proved too costly.

Tsuburaya (second from right) inspects a model

Alongside *The Green Slime*, *Latitude Zero* was one of the first Japanese special effects films to be shot in English. Unlike the "Tower of Babel" style used on European films with international casts where everyone spoke their mother tongue and were dubbed in post-production, here, even the Japanese actors speak English (with varying degrees of success). Hearing actors like Akira Takarada speak genuine, un-dubbed English is surreal. *Latitude Zero* features a group of Hollywood stars, including *Citizen Kane*'s Joseph Cotten, the mighty Caesar "Joker" Romero and Patricia Medina as his moll. Richard Jaeckel, fresh from his last trip to Japan battling *The Green Slime*, also appears. Jaeckel, called a "party animal" by assistant director Seiji Tani, enjoyed his time in Japan. The young, blonde Linda Haynes is also on hand, later to appear in Jack Hill's exploitation classic *Coffy* (1973).

The shoot for *Latitude Zero* began in late October of 1968. Problems arose immediately. Don Sharp's firm went bankrupt 10 days into the shoot. Production was halted for a time as Toho was forced to take up the funds and cover the cost of the Hollywood stars themselves. This resulted in a considerable budget slash for the film itself. The American co-producer and creative advisor was Sharp's partner Warren Lewis. There was creative friction with Lewis from day one as he wanted control over the project. The Japanese crew felt Lewis was being disrespectful to Ishiro Honda and Eiji

Tsuburaya, who by this time were given considerable creative freedom by Tomoyuki Tanaka. Assistant directors Teruyoshi Nakano and Seiji Tani coordinated between Tsuburaya and Honda's units. The Japanese crew, especially Nakano, felt that the American side looked down on them. Nakano felt that the Americans did not respect the efficiency and craftsmanship of Japanese filmmaking.

As the shoot droned on, there were arguments. One disagreement arose over the Japanese DPs' conservative habits in terms of how much film they exposed. This was a leftover from the war years when stock was scarce. Hollywood players disliked this practice; director Richard Fleischer would also complain about this method after working with Kinji Fukasaku and Toshio Masuda on *Tora! Tora! Tora!* (1970). Ishiro Honda at first fell in line with Lewis' demands, shooting the film with three cameras covering the actors at all times and the shot sequencing decided in editing. After a few days, however, Ishiro Honda and DP Taiichi Kankura began to shoot in the more efficient Japanese style.

Helping to smooth things over was translator Henry Okawa. Previously, Okawa had helped interpret for Nick Adams, Russ Tamblyn and Rhodes Reason. The Japanese crew was tactful with the Americans and thanks to Okawa, little was lost in translation. There were spats, however. Warren Lewis wanted actress Linda Haynes to appear naked onscreen which Honda was dead set against. The two clashed over a later sequence where Joseph Cotten's Nemo-like Captain Mackenzie was to use Patricia Medina's Lucrecia as a human shield against Romero's Malik. Lewis thought it was unacceptable for a "good guy" to do this.

Eiji Tsuburaya's end of *Latitude Zero* features more of his unit's finest miniature and process work. The first reel alone contains his best use of the "cloud tank" method, this time to simulate an underwater volcano. Yasuyuki Inoue created a specially-made water tank for the effect. Miniature submarine and mock underwater photography techniques refined by Tsuburaya on *Atragon* and *Mighty Jack* are put to good use. A thrilling nautical battle sequence features elaborate miniature work and plentiful optical animation. To add the effect of diffusion and depth to many underwater miniature shots, smoke was used.

There's further Gerry Anderson influence with lengthy segments of similar miniaturized crafts. The super-submarine *Alpha*, sleekly designed by Inoue, was represented by three models. The largest was over 20 feet long, the second was ten feet and the smallest four. They were built from wood and the largest had doors that could open and close. The villains' submarine, the *Black Shark,* was designed by Mutsumi Toyoshima and ten-foot and four-foot versions were built. Other notable models include the Japanese research vessel *Fuji,* which appears in the early moments along with a bathysphere. The miniaturized *Fuji*'s was a whopping 45 feet long and powered by a Chrysler engine. In the shooting of miniatures, Tsuburaya shows absolute mastery. Amusingly, the American side of *Latitude Zero*'s production even criticized Tsuburaya's use of them. According to AD Teruyoshi Nakano, someone (probably Warren Lewis) said "Miniatures look cheap. I don't want you to make this film with things that look like toys."

Underwater sequences, such as where the protagonists are rescued in a sunken bathysphere, were shot in a giant water tank used for underwater ballet at Yomiuri Land amusement park. For miniature explosions shot underwater, the chemical CFC was directly injected and detonated. In scenes where Captain MacKenzie and crew use their levitation belts on Malik's hideout of Blood Rock, dolls are used with surprisingly effectiveness. There are impressive optical composites blending human extras with elaborate miniatures. Some were created with the Oxberry and aided with rotoscoping, others with old-fashioned mattes.

Unfortunately, the monsters in *Latitude Zero* don't fare as well. These pitiable creatures seem to have borne the brunt of the budget cuts, looking like something Sid and Marty Krofft might pass on. The most prominent is a giant Gryphon (Haruo Nakajima) which Malik creates by transplanting the brain of a human woman, Kuroiga (Hikaru Kuroki), into a lion with grafted condor wings. The suit's mane was made with bear fur from China. A two-foot miniature was constructed for the shots of Kuroiga in flight. Human-sized "bat men" also appear and are hampered by visible piano wire use during MacKenzie's climactic battle against Malik. The suits allow the actors' eyes to show through, which makes them intimidating in some shots. Though five bat monsters appear, only three costumes were made due to cost. More effective are a gaggle of giant rats. A neanderthal-like creature which was to die gruesomely in a pool of acid never came to be due to budget constraints; humorously, the

FX staff had nicknamed it "Warren." In addition to the Gryphon, Nakajima also took on the parts of a rat and a bat monster. Other monster skins were occupied by Yu Sekita, Teruo Aragaki, Haruyoshi Nakamura, and Susumu Utsumi. Teizo Toshimitsu, along with Yasuei and Hirotoshi Yagi, built the Gryphon and bat monsters. Equis Productions constructed the giant rats, headed by young sculptors **NORI MAEZAWA** (1942-) and **AKIRA TAKAHASHI** (1938-).

The final battle between the *Alpha* and the *Black Shark* on the shores of Blood Rock is another Tsuburaya tour-de-force of miniature photography, optical animation and Kyuzo Yamamoto's most elaborate pyrotechnics. The bird's-eye view shot of Blood Rock exploding was challenging. Due to the size of the explosion, it had to be shot in the open air at Toho's Big Pool. Rails were laid under the pool with a 20 foot scaffold for the camera. Tsuburaya's unit had contacted the fire department beforehand, but the explosion was so loud they showed up at Toho's lot anyway.

Sadly, *Latitude Zero* was a flop at the Japanese box office, making back less than half of its budget. It was a sign of the times: the Japanese film industry was experiencing stiff competition from television and theater attendance was in decline. In the United States, the American backers had hoped *Latitude Zero* would be picked up by a major studio, but had to settle for a smaller release in late 1970 through grindhouse outlet National General. *Latitude Zero* was unavailable on home video for decades thanks to the troubled production's rights entanglements. These were finally settled in the mid 2000s.

Toho's following special effects release was **BATTLE OF THE JAPAN SEA** [**Director:** Seiji Maruyama - **Release Date (Japan):** August 13th, 1969], their third entry in the "8/15" series and Eiji Tsuburaya's final feature film. Set during the Russo-Japanese War and starring Toshiro Mifune as Admiral Heihachiro Togo, *Battle of the Japan Sea* climaxes with the May 1905 Battle of Tsushima. The film is a fitting swansong for Tsuburaya. It is set in the *Meiji* era of his childhood and features heavy reliance on miniature warships, the shooting of which Tsuburaya had spent his life perfecting.

Using Toho's Big Pool almost exclusively, the miniature shots in *Battle of the Japan Sea* are plentiful and among Tsuburaya's most life-like. A modeling team of 60 people constructed the whopping 107 model ships, many at various scales for perspective. The largest was the legendary warship *Mikasa*, another mammoth 45-foot miniaturized vessel powered by a diesel engine and operated by a crew of two; in effect, a true ship. Akinori Takagi created the electrical components.

Building an armada of miniaturized turn-of-the-century steamships

Battle of the Japan Sea boasts one stunning naval battle sequence after another. A composite early on with surviving navalmen swimming from a freighter destroyed by a Russian attack is striking. This beautifully combines elements shot by Maruyama and Tsuburaya using a matte. Establishing shots of the Imperial fleet anchored at dusk and dawn also feel painterly.

The Battle of Tsushima is a triumphant symphony of spectacle with Maruyama and Tsuburaya's units in good synergy, combining miniature photography, optical printing and intricately coordinated pyrotechnics. Freon gas was used to create the effect of water droplets splashing throughout. Few elderly directors manage to make one last masterwork before passing. In that spirit, Eiji Tsuburaya's work on *Battle of the Japan Sea* feels like a magnum opus: a tokusatsu *Battleship Potemkin* and a last hurrah for Japan's greatest special effects director. The production of *Battle of the Japan Sea* was difficult for Tsuburaya, who still, in spite of his frail health, was going back and forth between Toho and his company. While on location shooting background plates at Gotemba near Mount Fuji, art director Yasuyuki Inoue fell behind the group due to his prosthetic foot. He noticed something odd - the usually energetic Tsuburaya was also lagging behind and had to rest. Inoue asked Tsuburaya if he was alright. The effects director quickly changed the subject and said "Look at how beautiful Mount Fuji is."

Daiei Tokyo followed with a war picture of their own - **THE FALCON FIGHTERS** [**Director:** Mitsuo Murayama - **Release Date (Japan):** November 1st, 1969]. The picture is a biography of Tateo Kato, this time portrayed by Makoto Sato. Unlike Toho's wartime *Colonel Kato's Falcon Squadron*, *The Falcon Fighters* feels darker, fatalistic and deconstructive. As with *Gateway to Glory*, Noriaki Yuasa handled the special effects unit. Yuasa's work on *The Falcon Fighters* is passable and among his better effects jobs. In the second half, his handiwork becomes prevalent with thrilling air raid sequences. There are imaginative touches. The cockpits of the Hayabusa fighters feature tiny puppet pilots that move. By far, the best executed miniature effect is a squad of IJA paratroopers launching with tiny parachutes from a model plane. This moment is the greatest achievement in Noriaki Yuasa's career as special effects director. His composites, however, are sloppily done and mar otherwise decent FX footage.

By this time, the Japanese film industry was beginning its impending decline. Movie theaters were closing and theater attendance was plummeting due to the competition of television. Toho's previous monster films, *King Kong Escapes, Son of Godzilla, Destroy All Monsters* and *Latitude Zero,* had all been flops. Tomoyuki Tanaka turned to rival companies Daiei and Toei for inspiration. Though he had contemplated ending the Godzilla series with *Destroy All Monsters*, Tanaka decided to take the films in a similar direction to Daiei's Gamera series. They would be budgeted lower, necessitating the use of stock footage from previous films. These new Godzilla entries would also be aimed at a child audience. Tanaka also drew influence from Toei's popular Manga Festival which had featured *Watari* and *The Green Slime*. Toho would create their own rival: the Champion Matsuri Festival.

As with the Toei Manga Festival, workaholic Japanese parents could drop off their tykes at the local theater. There the children could feast upon a heaping helping of anime, tokusatsu and comedy. The first Champion Matsuri Festival was held in December. Its program was headed by a new Godzilla entry, **ALL MONSTERS ATTACK [AKA: GODZILLA'S REVENGE - Director:** Ishiro Honda -

Release Date (Japan): December 20th, 1969]. It was shown with the comedy **KONTO 55: GREAT OUTER SPACE ADVENTURE** [Director: Jun Fukuda - Release Date (Japan): Ibid], along with a *Star of the Giants* anime feature to keep more athletic boys entertained.

Ishiro Honda directs the special effects unit for the first and only time in his career

All Monsters Attack is possibly the most reviled Godzilla movie. Michael J. Weldon, in his *Psychotronic Encyclopedia of Film*, calls it a "Godzilla film for six-year-olds" when "most of them are aimed at 10-year-olds". This is apt as both a criticism and fact. Unusually character driven for a Godzilla entry, *All Monsters Attack* revolves around Ichiro (Tomonori Yazaki), a monster-loving boy with wage-slave parents who are loving but neglectful. A latchkey kid, he daydreams about hanging out with Minilla on Monster Island while watching a medley of stock footage from prior Godzilla entries.

All Monsters Attack was both Toho's lowest budgeted and quickly produced monster picture to date, beginning shooting in October 1969. By this time, Eiji Tsuburaya's health was on the decline and his doctor advised him against participating in more film productions. Tsuburaya was also occupied with his work on the Mitsubishi Pavilion at the upcoming Expo '70. Sadamasa Arikawa was also unable to participate as he was helping Tsuburaya with the Mitsubishi exhibit. These factors combined led to Ishiro Honda directing both the live action and special effects sequences under one unit with the same camera and lighting crew. This was albeit with assistance from AD Teruyoshi Nakano, now seasoned in Tsuburaya's techniques. Tsuburaya was still, however, given a "special effects director" credit out of respect despite doing no work on the film.

While the direction is influenced by the Gamera series, Ishiro Honda brings more pathos and introspection to the film than Noriaki Yuasa would have. Shot in the industrial town of Kawasaki, *All Monsters Attack* is at its strongest outside of its awful monster scenes. The character-driven scenes showcasing Ichiro's alienation in a bleak, urban industrial hellscape are the highlight. The monster sequences by contrast are embarrassing, a TV-style "clipshow" with heavy stock footage from *Ebirah, Horror of the Deep, Son of Godzilla* and *Destroy All Monsters*. New footage features Minilla being bullied by the *oni*-like Gabara, retconned as a "mutated toad" by Toho. These scenes were lensed on limited soundstages by Honda and Nakano and look cheap.

All Monsters Attack begins the trend of Godzilla's appearance changing dramatically from scene to scene thanks to heavy stock footage use, obvious to nearly every child in the audience. For the suits, the Godzilla suit from *Destroy All Monsters* was reused in the newly filmed footage. The Minilla suit made for *Son of Godzilla* was given repairs and modifications to allow for more expression. For close-up shots of Minilla speaking to Ichiro, a full-sized upper body puppet was constructed. Godzilla and Minilla were again portrayed by Haruo Nakajima and Masao Fukuzawa. Gabara, named by screenwriter Shinichi Sekizawa after Che Guevara, was modeled by Teizo Toshimitsu and Yasuei Yagi. Stuntman **YASUHIKO KAKUYUKI** portrayed Gabara in his suit acting debut. Kamakiras also appears in one novel shot, hovering over a pit that Ichiro has fallen into. The sole surviving model from *Son of Godzilla* was used. The more effective special effects shots involve Gabara using his ability to conduct electric bolts on Minilla and then Godzilla. These were created by Koichi Kawakita.

All Monsters Attack is most tolerable when not viewed as a monster movie. Like Val Lewton's *The Curse of the Cat People* (1944), it's an unusual film not without merit. In truth, Ishiro Honda intended it as a movie set in the real world, a place devoid of giant monsters, about a boy using his love of them as escapism. The climax, involving Ichiro cleverly battling a pair of bumbling robbers (Sachio Sakai and Kazuo Suzuki), looks forward to *Home Alone*

(1990). Overall, *All Monsters Attack* is not a high point in Honda's career or Toho's monster cycle. Yet who reading this can't relate to a lonely, bullied kid using monster movies to escape our banal world?

All Monsters Attack's co-feature, *Konto 55: Great Outer Space Adventure,* also had tokusatsu elements. Starring Konto 55, a comedy duo composed of Kinichi Hagimoto and Jiro Sakagami, the humor is more juvenile than the Crazy Cats'. The plot features Hagimoto and Sakagami as a pair of samurai, who, along with a geisha (Noriko Takahashi), are whisked through time by an alien (Hiroshi Kawaguchi). Yoichi Manoda ran the tokusatsu unit with art direction by Mutsumi Toyoshima and optical work from Kazunobu Sanpei. Their contributions are subtle but effective. The miniature flying saucer prop is well executed and looks like it belongs in a better movie. The tokusatsu unit is employed for some of the visual gags, including miniaturized laundry hung to dry on the UFO. The longest FX sequence consists of the saucer battling a ketchup bottle flying an American flag. There are even striking shots of the saucer flying over a shoreline.

While the humor in *Konto 55* is childish in the extreme, it takes an amusingly dark turn in the final reel as the samurai duo's warlike ways destroy the alien time traveler's utopian civilization. For this sequence, Manoda attempts the "ink-in-a-water tank" explosion effect. The execution is ruined by a single air bubble that betrays the illusion. Like its co-feature, *Konto 55: Great Outer Space Adventure* features swaths of Tsuburaya-era stock footage from films as varied as *The Three Treasures, The Last War* and *Latitude Zero*. The first Champion Festival, thanks to its lower budget content, made a better return on investment and Toho continued the program. Nineteen Champion Festivals would eventually be held, with the last in spring of 1978. For future Champion screenings, a number of older monster pictures from Toho's library would be reissued in edited versions.

As *All Monsters Attack* was being produced, Eiji Tsuburaya was, unbeknownst to him, nearing the end of his life. Along with helping develop *Horror Theater: Unbalance,* his final project would be his work for the Mitsubishi Pavilion at the coming Expo '70. The exhibition was directed by Yoshimitsu Banno and Tsuburaya spent months shooting plates. He had been diagnosed with angina and took this project on against his doctor's wishes. Tsuburaya also took part in editing of *All Monsters Attack,* advising the team to truncate certain shots and scenes.

In November of 1969, as Ishiro Honda finished work on *All Monsters Attack*, Tsuburaya paid him a visit. The two excitedly talked of future collaborations, including a dream project about Japan's WWI-era aviators Tsuburaya wanted Honda to direct. The two were itching to create a special effects picture that didn't involve monsters. In Tsuburaya's own words, "Let's make special effects films not just about monsters destroying buildings but something more fantastic and entertaining to give children dreams and hope." The effects director was also keen on making a new adaptation of *Tale of the Bamboo Cutter* with Yoshiyuki Kuroda at the helm. By January of 1970, as the new decade rang in, Eiji Tsuburaya was eager to get back to work. He was due to take part in Toho's next monster movie, *Space Amoeba*, and continued outlining his aviation-themed project.

Yasuyuki Inoue, helping out on the Mitsubishi Pavilion attraction, had a melancholy dream about Tsuburaya in January. The special effects director smiled at him and gave encouraging words. As Tsuburaya wrapped shooting on the Expo '70 pavilion, he stayed at his villa on the Izu Peninsula with his wife Masano. He was due to return to Tokyo on January 26th to start working on projects at Toho and his company. However, all of these plans were not to be. His heart had given all it had to give. At 10:15 p.m on January 25th, Eiji Tsuburaya breathed his last; mercifully, he passed away in his sleep. He was 68.

OBITUARIES

EIJI TSUBURAYA

Eiji Tsuburaya, (real name Eiichi), film special effects expert and president of Tsuburaya Production Co., died of a heart ailment at 10:15 p.m. Sunday at his villa in Ito, Shizuoka Prefecture. He was 68.

Tsuburaya was born in Sukagawa, Fukushima Prefecture. He started his career in the cinema world in 1919 as a cameraman and entered the Kyoto film studio of Shochiku Co. in 1925. He later moved to Toho Co., Ltd. where he built his fame in special effects filming.

His works include "New Soil," "The Battles of the Hawaii and Malaya Seas," "Gojira," "Radon," "Global Defense Forces," and "Battle of the Japan Sea."

Two dozen of his "monster" series films featuring Gojira, Radon and others have been exported to the U.S. and Southeast Asian countries.

Funeral services will be held at Toho Movie Studio in Setagaya Ward, Tokyo at 1 p.m. Feb. 2.

Eiji Tsuburaya's obituary in *The Japan Times* (1970)

The Japanese film industry was sent into a state of shock. His wake was held at his home on January 27th. Two days later, a Catholic funeral service was held and Eiji Tsuburaya was laid to rest. Another service was held on February 2nd at Toho by executive Sanezumi Fujimoto. Between all three, numerous friends, colleagues and protégés attended. Tetsuo Kinjo and Ishiro Honda gave beautiful speeches. Minoru Nakano, who loved Tsuburaya like a father, loudly wept over his coffin. In his own words: "When he died, I didn't know how to live". Hajime Tsuburaya, now the head of Tsuburaya Productions, berated Nakano. Eiji Tsuburaya had been a good father, but he was also a workaholic who was seldom home and there was resentment. Hajime said to Minoru Nakano: "How could you do what we sons could not!". Sadao Iizuka and his wife, whose marriage Tsuburaya had acted as matchmaker for, also cried at his passing. In their minds they could hear the old effects director scolding "Don't cry." Eiji Tsuburaya's grave can be visited at the Catholic Cemetery in the Fuchu district of Tokyo.

Osaka's Expo '70 - at the top of the stairs is Taro Okamoto's still-standing Tower of the Sun

While the special effects world was still reeling from this tragic loss, Expo '70 opened in Osaka on March 15th with a lavish ceremony attended by Emperor *Showa* himself. Osaka had been chosen as the site for the '70 World's Fair in 1965, in the wake of the Tokyo Olympics. It was formally awarded in 1966 and construction began shortly after. Science fiction author **SAKYO KOMATSU** (1931-2011), known for his bleak novels *Japan's Apaches* and *Resurrection Day*, was involved in the Expo's planning committee.

The exposition, designed by architect Kenzo Tage and boasting contributions from 77 countries, was flanked by the now iconic Tower of the Sun created by Taro Okamoto. Inside the still-standing Tower of the Sun was the Tree of Life featuring creatures designed at Tsuburaya Productions. All the newest science and tech was on display including proto-mobile phones, conveyor belt sushi and a lunar rock collected by *Apollo* 12 the previous year. If the Olympics had shown Japan to be Asia's economic miracle, Expo '70 presented the country as a new center of science and technology.

The late Eiji Tsuburaya's final work was on vivid display at the Mitsubishi Pavillion. Inside, spectators would move along a walkway surrounded by panoramic images created by

Tsuburaya's unit, giving the impression of being inside a Toho special effects film. They were projected on the walls and mirrors were used to enhance their depth. The first room was said to be the most impressive, featuring striking images of floods and volcanic eruptions as the music of Akira Ifukube blared loudly around spectators.

Other immersive films were shown including the first 70mm IMAX short, *Tiger Child*. For monster fans, there was even a *Godzilla vs. Gamera* stage show held daily, to date the only official crossover between Toho and Daiei's properties. Haruo Nakajima appeared live in the Godzilla suit and Minilla, Gorosaurus and Space Gyaos were part of the show. Osamu Tezuka, who also created the Fujipan Robot Pavilion, drew up "Expora," an Expo '70-themed kaiju illustration. Expo '70 would run until September and attract over 64 million visitors from all over the world.

Daiei's next double feature was released only days after Expo '70 opened. It consisted of the Tokyo-produced **GAMERA VS. JIGER [AKA: GAMERA VS. MONSTER X - Director:** Noriaki Yuasa - **Release Date (Japan):** March 21st, 1970] and the Kyoto-made **THE INVISIBLE SWORDSMAN [Director:** Yoshiyuki Kuroda - **Release Date (Japan):** Ibid]. *The Invisible Swordsman* features subtle tokusatsu elements making use of the impressive in-camera effects and the optical printing processes refined by Kuroda over the years. Kuroda would soon abandon special effects filmmaking, focusing instead on helming main units. He would go on to direct non-special effects sequences in episodes of *Mirrorman* and *Jumborg Ace*, along with the *Lone Wolf and Cub* entry *White Heaven in Hell* (1974).

Gamera vs. Jiger is, fittingly, set amidst the Expo, though Yuasa was not allowed to depict the destruction of any pavilions due to corporate pride. Early moments feel like an in-movie commercial for Expo '70. The budget was increased slightly and the effects work, more elaborate this time around, is a nudge above the prior two entries, though it's still weaker than the higher budgeted, resourceful work done by Yuasa on *Gamera vs. Barugon* and *Gamera vs. Gyaos*. The miniature shooting is the strongest suit and the composites are improved.

There's a striking matte mixing Gamera, a miniature set and a wide, distant plate of the actors. Jiger's death ray is a fanciful optically animated flourish with Defense Force soldiers turned to skeletons, a macabre touch that anticipates similar moments in Toho's *Godzilla vs. Hedorah* (1971). Most impressive is a long take, around a minute in length, panning through a miniaturized version of the Osaka Bay Power Plant as Gamera retreats to the shore. It feels like another of Yuasa's finest achievements as an effects director. Noriaki Yuasa went directly to Masaichi Nagata and begged him for more money to stage this scene on a full-scale special effects set.

The monster action is rather ungainly. The Gamera suit from the previous picture was reused, though its head was replaced and its face made a little friendlier by Equis Productions. Jiger was designed by **TOMOHISA YANO** with a demon motif. Screenwriter Niisan Takahashi wanted to bring occult elements to *Jiger*'s script with the Wester Island statue's curse, foreshadowing the "Occult Boom" that would kick off in the wake of *The Exorcist* (1973). Jiger's suit was constructed by Eizo Kaimai. Small miniature puppets of both Gamera and Jiger were also made.

Staging a volcanic eruption in miniature

Jiger proves Gamera's most formidable foe: the creature can spit spears and impregnates its opponent *Alien*-style. To create the effect of Gamera's face and hands becoming transparent after being implanted with Jiger's parasitic offspring, the head and arms were replaced with a transparent polyvinyl which was lit from inside. The most elaborate gimmick is a clear nod to Fox's *Fantastic Voyage* (1966). The usual precocious boy protagonists (Tsutomu Takakuwa and Kelly Varis) enter Gamera's mouth in a small submarine where they find Jiger's offspring inside. A second, smaller Jiger suit was built for this scene. The inside of Gamera's body looks cheap; the lung walls are clearly inflated balloons.

One of the weirdest moments is a *mondo* movie-style touch that feels deranged in a kids' movie. To demonstrate Gamera's plight, a scientist (Jutaro Hojo) screens disgusting footage of surgery on an elephant's trunk to remove parasitic worms. This was not genuine but created by the special effects unit with a prosthetic and pig roundworms. Yuasa had it printed in black and white to make the scene less shocking. Sadly, while filming *Gamera vs. Jiger,* a member of the lighting staff collapsed from a cerebral hemorrhage. He survived, but died in the hospital after the film's completion.

Toho's special effects crew would make subtle contributions to the horror picture **THE VAMPIRE DOLL [Director: MICHIO YAMAMOTO (1933-2004) - Release Date (Japan):** July 4th, 1970**]**. With box office receipts dwindling, Tomoyuki Tanaka drew influence from UK studio Hammer's horror cycle and screened *Goke, Body Snatcher From Hell* for Toho's staff. *The Vampire Doll* concerns Yuko (Yukiko Kobayashi), a vampire girl, cursed by her mother's pact with Satan, who prowls a spooky mansion seeking victims. Kobayashi had to wear gold contact lenses which impaired her vision, resulting in a number of accidental bumps in the night.

Atmospheric vistas of the spooky house were miniatures obviously staged by Toho's effects team. Optical effects, created by Kazunobu Sanpei, appear here and there. Toho would produce two more vampire films directed by Yamamoto: *Lake of Dracula* (1971) and *The Evil of Dracula* (1974). Both also feature subtle contributions from Toho's effects unit. These include an impressive optical process shot at the opening of *Lake*, occasional miniatures and elaborate vampire disintegration sequences akin to Hammer's.

Toho followed *The Vampire Doll* with a more effects-heavy production in **SPACE AMOEBA [AKA: YOG: MONSTER FROM SPACE - Director:** Ishiro Honda **- Release Date (Japan):** August 1st, 1970**]**. *Space Amoeba* would headline Toho's third Champion Matsuri Festival alongside several anime. It had begun development 1966 as a more ambitious proposal, *The Space Monsters*, to be an international co-production with Henry Saperstein's UPA. By this time, with recent Godzilla entries having flopped, Toho was eager to try their hand at a new kaiju film without their flagship monster.

Eiji Tsuburaya had long been attached to the project. Upon his planned return to Tokyo, Tsuburaya was due to take a supervisory role over effects director Sadamasa Arikawa. Two days after *Space Amoeba* began principal photography, Tsuburaya died. Therein lies *Space Amoeba*'s biggest flaw: it feels like a classic Toho special effects picture devoid of the man who gave them their magic. To Ishiro Honda's frustration, the budget was slashed, ending plans to shoot in Guam as with *Son of Godzilla*. Instead, *Space Amoeba* was shot on Hachijojima. The setting, Sergio Island, was named after Italian Spaghetti Western king Sergio Leone, whose films were becoming popular in Japan.

Space Amoeba was released in the U.S. in 1971 with the Lovecraft-inspired title *Yog: Monster From Space*

Space Amoeba centers around the popular trope of alien gunk attaching itself to a space probe. The cosmic microbes go on to possess a squid, crab and turtle, transforming them into kaiju. The screenplay by **EI OGAWA** (1930-1994), who also wrote Michio Yamamoto's vampire films, is such a formulaic parade of tired tropes that it feels satirical. *Space Amoeba* is, however, noteworthy as one of the final productions made with Toho's old guard under the classic studio system. Yet the absence of Eiji Tsuburaya's ingenuity is noticeable and significant. Sadamasa Arikawa's effects unit for *Space Amoeba* often felt that they wished the Old Man was there, giving them the creative drive and inspiration he was known for. Arikawa's effects work is unremarkable and spotty, if a nudge above TV quality or the work Noriaki Yuasa was doing at Daiei. Even the Oxberry printer is used with less skill by Hiroshi Mukoyama sans Tsuburaya's supervision.

The miniature art direction by Yasuyuki Inoue is the strongest suit. It is arresting in the opening scene depicting the launch of space probe *Helios* 7 against a crimson sunset. The rocket miniature was close to ten feet tall and the capsule around 20 inches. Tomoyuki Tanaka, often going back and forth between Toho and Expo '70 for work on the Mitsubishi Pavilion, visited Arikawa's effects unit when this was being shot and demanded that more smoke come from the launch. Just as *Space Amoeba* was wrapping production, the *Apollo* 13 incident took place in April of 1970.

The monsters don't fare as well. As an effects director, Sadamasa Arikawa's specialty was wirework. His team tries their best to use this strength, but the execution is mixed. First is Gezora, a giant squid based on the kisslip cuttlefish, a popular sushi delicacy in Japan. Its name comes from the Japanese word *geso*, for squid tentacles. Gezora, played by Haruo Nakajima with support from the wire team, was one of the last suits built by Teizo Toshimitsu with assistance from Yasuei Yagi. It looks impressive in some shots, ridiculous in others. Gezora's light-up eyes were supposed to move but the mechanism broke and Arikawa's unit did not have the time or money to repair it. This situation would have been different had Eiji Tsuburaya been overseeing things. A pair of full-sized tentacles, puppeteered by piano wire, were constructed by the modeling department for Honda's unit.

One of *Space Amoeba*'s best sequences is an underwater attack by Gezora on heroes Kudo (Akira Kubo) and Dr. Miya (Yoshio Tsuchiya). Yoshimitsu Banno likely did underwater second unit shooting for this sequence with two stunt actors. Gezora's attack on Selgio Island's native village resembles a shoddy, lower budget remake of Tsuburaya's superior octopus attack in *King Kong vs. Godzilla*. The shots are wildly inconsistent in quality. There are superb vistas such as a high angle composite of Gezora hovering before an altar and praying shaman (Tetsu Nakamura); or the monster standing in the destroyed, smoke-filled village in a wide shot. Others are embarrassing, such as optically animated tentacles that stick out like a sore thumb. The decision to use a performer in a suit rather than an intricate puppet is what dooms these sequences in execution.

Giant crab Gamines appears next, also portrayed by Haruo Nakajima. Its design was based on the rubble crab and the suit was modeled by Nobuyuki Yasumaru. Sadamasa Arikawa asked Yasumaru to make the Gamines' mouth frightening and have it disturbingly gurgle bubbles. A mechanism was installed in the suit for the bubbles and its jaws and eyes could move via radio control. The creature is less awkward than Gezora in execution, but still more unwieldy than prior Arikawa creations like Ebirah or Kamakiras. There are striking composite shots putting actors Akira Kubo and Atsuko Takahashi in the same shot as Gamines and its explosive death.

The third monster is Kamoebas, a giant turtle inspired by the *mata mata*. Portrayed by Haruyoshi Nakamura, the suit was also modeled by Nobuyuki Yasumaru. It's the best executed though least memorable of the three monsters. The creature's neck pops out; this was done by engineering a contracting metal spring into the neck and blasting compressed air through a bicycle pump. Suit actor Nakamura was startled by the loud sound, inches from his head, of the neck popping out. Kamoebas and another Gamines duke it out so the movie can give its child audience an obligatory monster battle. The sequence, though still unrefined, is the best monster scene in the movie. There are striking visuals such as wide shots of bats in the sky encircling the monsters. The final volcanic eruption, however, lacks the destructive grandeur of a Tsuburaya symphony.

Sadamasa Arikawa found working on *Space Amoeba* frustrating to the point that he disliked talking about it in interviews. His unit was not given the time or money needed, thanks to Tsuburaya not being there to lobby on his behalf. Arikawa pushed for the film to open with a title card memorializing Eiji Tsuburaya. Toho's brass would not allow this, which he found enraging. The final straw was that, after shooting for *Space Amoeba*'s effects scenes wrapped in March 1970, Tanaka formally dissolved Toho's special effects department. Arikawa thus quit Toho and went freelance. From hereon, he'd do special effects work for television and supply his Japanese filmmaking ingenuity to movies in Hong Kong and Taiwan.

Due to the financial strain of a film industry in decline, Toho would abolish its studio system completely. Employees were laid off, contracts terminated and the company reordered into over 70 subsidiaries under the umbrella corporation "Toho Eizo." Toho's special effects unit still existed in principal, but they were no longer unionized employees but contractors. Numerous members of Toho's effects staff would follow Arikawa's lead and pull out. Veterans like Teizo Toshimitsu, Hiroshi Mukoyama and Kyuzo Yamamoto would retire. Others would go freelance. But there was also opportunity in this new order. Toho's staff were no longer bound by contractual restrictions; they could take work at other studios and for television, which many did. Ishiro Honda even temporarily retired from making films at Toho after *Space Amoeba* and occupied his time with television jobs. The death of Eiji Tsuburaya and the dismantling of the special effects department at Toho, which he had spent decades creating, marked the end of an era.

Sadamasa Arikawa

Toho's "8/15" film that year was **THE MILITARISTS** [**Director:** Hiromichi Horikawa - **Release Date (Japan):** August 13th, 1970], a biography of the fascist Hideki Tojo (Keiju Kobayashi) and his rise to power in Imperial Japan. The tone is mournful and the film is bleak and earnest in depicting the collective madness of Imperial Japan. In contrast to Shunya Ito's later *Pride* (1998), its depiction of Tojo is damning. *The Militarists* featured only subtle contributions from Toho's effects staff. There are a few novel miniature and process shots, but the lion's share are stock footage cuts from prior war movies like *Storm Over the Pacific* and *Admiral Yamamoto*.

As if to mourn Eiji Tsuburaya, the rest of 1970 was devoid of special effects productions. The airwaves, once saturated with monsters, swelled with sports anime. The 1970-71 holiday season had no new monster movies in theaters, save for an edited version of

Mothra vs. Godzilla at the winter Champion Matsuri Festival. However, a second boom was soon to ignite, sparked off by a trio of popular shows with Tomio Sagisu's P-Productions leading the way.

XVI.
<u>1971</u>
昭和四十六
(Part 1)

Title card for *Spectreman* (1971-72), originally released as *Space Ape Man Dr. Gori*

The dry spell of monster content in Japanese theaters and television was broken by the release of a new show from Tomio Sagisu's P-Productions: **SPECTREMAN [Television Run (Japan):** January 2nd, 1971 - March 25th, 1972]. The development of *Spectreman* began back in August of 1967. In the wake of *Ambassador Magma* and during production of *The Monster Prince*, P-Pro had created a 15-minute proof-of-concept short entitled *Jaguarman*. Directed by Sadao Funatoko, the effects footage by Shinsuke Kojima is among his finest.

Jaguarman's brisk 15 minutes are packed with the elaborate, fanciful and experimental effects work P-Pro was known for, combining suitmation, miniatures, optical work, stop motion and anime touches. Jaguarman is a caped superhero who bears a golden, metallic feline face. He battles monsters sent by the underground "mantle people" and their devil-like commander Sigma. The show was nearly greenlit at Fuji TV, but shelved after the ratings failure of *The Monster Prince*. *Jaguarman*'s concepts, however, would be recycled by creator Tomio Sagisu for two upcoming shows: *Spectreman* and *Lion Maru*.

Sagisu next submitted another pilot to Fuji TV and its suit **TAKAHARU BESSHO** (1935-2006): *Elementman*. The *Elementman* pilot was closer to *Spectreman*, though with major differences. Elementman looked similar to Spectreman but had a different design and its arch-villain Gori was more gorilla-like. The gorilla suit built for *Elementman* would be reused in *Spectreman*. Shinsuke Kojima had since left P-Productions, so Tomio Sagisu enlisted the aid of veteran special effects director Toru Matoba to create its FX work. The pilot previewed well enough that Besho ordered development continued. Ultimately, *Spectreman* was greenlit thanks to the premature cancellation of the TV drama *Red Lightning*. P-Productions had only 25 days to bring their first episode to air and it was a fight against time.

Spectreman's grittiness and hectic production schedule (even more so than Tsuburaya Pro's output) only enhances The early episodes' use of environmentalist themes predated Toho's *Godzilla vs. Hedorah* by six months. The first monster was even called "Hedron". By the early 1970s, thanks to its rapid post-war economic development, pollution had reached nightmarish levels in Japan. Public scandals involving the populace being poisoned by industrial activity were commonplace. This began to reach public awareness in the 1960s after multiple outbreaks of "Minamata disease": a rash of congenital deformities caused by mercury poisoning released by heavy industrial activity. By the early '70s, particularly in industrial areas, children were now developing severe asthma and having to go to school in surgical masks.

It is against this backdrop that *Spectreman*'s *Planet of the Apes*-inspired villain Dr. Gori (**TAKENOBU TOYA** [1946-]) arrives. Gori is an extraterrestrial simian with a genius IQ, exiled from his peaceful home planet for using his cunning to create weapons. Gori is disgusted with humanity's environmental abuse and wishes to conquer Earth to save humans from themselves. One of the greatest villains in the history of tokusatsu, Dr. Gori, aided by his dim witted accomplice, General Rah, is not a flamboyant force of evil like *Kamen Ride*r's Shocker. Gori is complex, charming and even somewhat sympathetic. This green-faced, blond-haired space ape is a villain whose motives can be understood even as the monster attacks he commands cause destruction and suffering.

Gori's arch-nemesis is Spectreman, the Ultraman-like android agent of the peacekeeping Nebula 71. Spectreman embodies all the best aspects of his direct rivals Ultraman and Kamen Rider. Like Rider, he sometimes battles monsters and aliens in human size. Of course, he possesses the ability to grow gigantic to slay tougher kaiju. Like *Ultraseven*, Spectreman walks the Earth in human form, that of Joji Gamo (Tetsuo Narikawa). In a sign of the times, the show's equivalent to the Science Patrol is basically a local Tokyo EPA branch called the "Pollution G-Men". When the pollution focus of the show was toned down and removed, however, they became a monster fighting organization.

Dr. Gori - one of tokusatsu's greatest villains

The show ran in the same time slot as the beloved *Star of the Giants* and there was little faith *Spectreman* would see great success. However, by episode #15, the show's ratings began to eclipse *Star of the Giants'*. *Spectreman* would air on Japanese television in three arcs. For the first 20 episodes, it was called *Space Ape Man Dr. Gori*. These episodes are serious, brooding and feature pollution as a theme, but sponsors soon soured on the environmentalist message. The last straw came when Nippon Paper

Industries, a massive corporation, complained about images of one of their paper mills spewing toxic filth. They also didn't understand why the program was named after the villain and not the hero. The show was thus retitled *Dr. Gori vs. Spectreman,* with greater emphasis on the monster battles. For the final arc, it was changed to *Spectreman*. The focus was shifted further. As Dr. Gori had created every manner of colorful monster, he began to team up with fellow aliens instead. Throughout, the episodes tended to run in two-part arcs.

The special effects on *Spectreman* are offbeat, if at times clearly born of lesser financial means. Toru Matoba handled the effects unit on early episodes. The FX unit in the show's mid-range was mainly supervised by Takeo Sakai. Many episodes feature no special effects director credit and it is known that Keinosuke Tsuchiya and assistant director **KOICHI ISHIGURO** ran the unit on episodes when Matoba or Sakai were not available. For the show's second half, P-Productions enlisted the aid of effects director Nobuo Yajima and his Tokusatsu Research Institute. Yajima would helm the effects almost entirely for the final third. His effects footage on *Spectreman* is similar to his work on *Giant Robo*. Yajima fittingly made his debut with episode #27, featuring one of his best-staged monster battles to date. Once again, typical of Sagisu's manga background and strong ties to the animation industry, there are anime garnishes, plentiful optical work and striking matte paintings, which were primarily the work of Yoshio Watanabe. Stop motion animation is even featured, such as in episode #3 with Midron, a dragon-like creature created in the Dynamation style by **SEIYO FUJIMORI**. The results are mixed with some shots looking amateurish and others approaching the level of David Allen.

The lion's share of the monster suit modeling was done by Ryosaku Takayama and his firm Atelier May. *Spectreman*'s monsters are colorful and outlandish, if rubbery. Gori's prosthetics were made by Takayama, as was the Rah suit, a better gorilla costume than either of Toho's Kongs. Spectreman's modeling was entrusted to Toru Suzuki and Shigeru Inoue as Takayama was busy with the monsters. They completed their first clay maquette of the mask from scratch in less than a day. The mask and suit were initially made of FRP, but the body was changed to wetsuit fabric as mobility proved difficult. Spectreman and Rah were both portrayed by *Ultraseven*'s Koji Uenishi. Uenishi even went to Tokyo's Ueno Zoo to watch the gorillas and study their movements, much like

Haruo Nakajima in preparation for *Godzilla*. Genius art director Yasuyuki Inoue also joined the effects staff following the production of *Godzilla vs. Hedorah*. On sabbatical from Toho, he had just founded his company Alpha Project. Inoue designed certain monsters and oversaw the creation of miniatures. Gori's spaceship itself was created from a Gokemidoro saucer model left over from the production of *Goke, Body Snatcher From Hell*.

Spectreman is strongest in its darker early episodes and loses some steam at its end. Regardless, it is an offbeat classic tokusatsu show with an engaging story. In *Spectreman*'s finale, Dr. Gori refuses to surrender to humanity and live in peace. Like an IJA soldier in the previous summer's *Battle of Okinawa*, he detonates a grenade-like charge and commits suicide. *Spectreman* would be exported to the United States later in the decade by producer Richard L. Rosenfeld, airing on TBS Superstation. It was even more popular in Europe and Latin America. The young Hideaki Anno was particularly enraptured by *Spectreman*. Years later, he would admit to empathizing with Dr. Gori as a character.

By the late 1960s, Japanese effects technicians began going abroad to other East Asians countries to share their filmmaking ingenuity. In Taiwan, where anti-Japanese sentiment was mild, numerous films were made enlisting Japanese talent behind-the-camera. One of the more memorable is **THE FOUNDING OF MING DYNASTY** [**Director:** Hsu Ta-Chun - **Release Date (Taiwan):** February 18th, 1971], co-produced by Foo Hwa Cinema Company and Tsuburaya Productions. While director Hsu helmed the Mandarin drama and martial arts action, Koichi Takano commanded a Japanese special effects unit, his first outside of the small screen. Yoshio Suzuki acted as art director and designed the film's monsters; the dragon puppetry was done by **SADAO TSUKAMOTO**. Another Japanese player was **GOZO MATSUI** (1934-2001), who acted as DP. Matsui was an expat who had been working on Taiwanese productions as a cinematographer since the mid '60s. Perhaps inspired by working with Takano, he would act as a special effects technician on more films in Taiwan, later creating tokusatsu-style monster sequences on *King of Snake* (1987).

Taiwanese poster for *The Founding of Ming Dynasty* (1971), featuring FX footage by Koichi Takano

The Founding of Ming Dynasty is a standard fantasy *wuxia* (Chinese swordplay film), as was common in Taiwan. The contributions of Koichi Takano are frequent, including plentiful opticals. Takano's Japanese unit takes the stage in the final reel when a kaiju-sized, red-bearded armored demon is brought to life and goes on the rampage. It then does battle with a white monkey who grows gigantic, Ultraman-style. The monster costumes are decent, with the actors' eyes shining through like Majin and Gaira, whom the demon resembles a cross between. A golden Chinese dragon whom the heroes ride on as it joins the fray is also well modeled, looking like a mix of Manda and *The Neverending Story*'s Falcor. The monsters' roars are, amusingly, straight from Toho's stock sound effects library; the giant demon has the voice of Godzilla and the dragon the roar of Rodan.

Koichi Takano creates his most impressive effects sequence to date, seizing the opportunity to use 35mm high frame rate shooting and employ impressive Tsuburaya-style composites. Takano channels his late mentor in this sequence, a thrilling finale that elevates an otherwise routine film. The final moments of the bad guys' fortress being destroyed by the dragon's pyrotechnic breath and a divine flood is distinctively Japanese. Takano proves himself a worthy effects director: even successfully staging a miniature flood, a rite of passage in the tokusatsu industry. *The Founding of Ming Dynasty* and its magnificent ending beg to be seen in its original anamorphic widescreen. Koichi Takano would next return to Taiwan for **THE DEVIL FROM THE BOTTOM OF THE SEA [Director:** Yu Han-Hsiang - **Release Date (Taiwan):** November 11th, 1975], featuring a well-executed water monster resembling a giant *Creature From the Black Lagoon*. Stock footage from both *The Founding of Ming Dynasty* and *The Devil From the Bottom of the Sea* would be used prominently in another *wuxia* film: *The Fairy and the Devil* (1982).

In April of 1971, *Spectreman* was joined on the air in Japan by two more superhero shows, ushering in the new monster boom, called the "*Henshin* (Transformation) Boom." The first of these was Tsuburaya Productions' **RETURN OF ULTRAMAN [Television Run (Japan):** - April 2nd, 1971 - March 31st, 1972], which began airing on TBS for 51 episodes. During his last days, Eiji Tsuburaya had been eager to create a third Ultraman show that was a more direct sequel to the first than *Ultraseven*. The initial idea was that the first Ultraman would return, fuse with a new human host and battle monsters once more.

Tsuburaya's death delayed development but by 1970, Tsuburaya Productions was under the leadership of Hajime and the sponsors were anxious for another Ultra show. The first three programs were rebroadcast in 1970 and had achieved surprising ratings. Monster toy sales were also heating up, particularly from the companies Bullmark and Marmit. Thanks to the influence of the toy companies, it was decided to create a new Ultraman character, Jack, so new figures could be sold, though with a design more closely resembling the original Ultraman than was used than *Ultraseven*.

Fittingly, as if to signal the beginning of the new monster boom, *Return of Ultraman*'s debut episode is called "*Destroy All Monsters*" and directed by Ishiro Honda, recently having made the switch to helming TV. Honda's creative hand in the series and strong direction keeps the show narratively engaging. *Return of Ultraman* is among the most popular Ultraman shows in Japan and with good reason; it's more character driven than its predecessors.

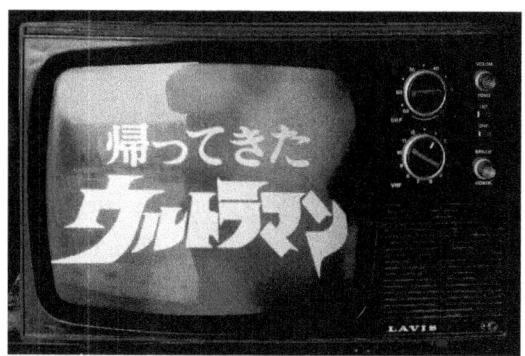

Return of Ultraman (1971-72) title card

Its protagonist is Hideki Go, a young race car driver played with pathos by the handsome half-American Jiro Dan. Go sacrifices his life to save a boy and dog but is resurrected by Ultraman Jack. Go starts off brash, impulsive and arrogant but as the show goes on becomes wizened and mature. Unlike with Hayata, Ultraman Jack does not always allow Go to transform if his reasons are selfish. The Science Patrol's successor in *Return of Ultraman* is called the Monster Attack Team or MAT. They are perhaps the most popular Earth Defense Force-style team in the franchise. MAT even has an undersea base ala Irwin Allen's *Voyage to the Bottom of the Sea* and Gerry Anderson's *Stingray*.

On the special effects end, early episodes were mainly overseen by Koichi Takano, who shows more confidence in the wake of his mentor's death and stages flashier FX sequences. Later on, Kazuo Sagawa, Atsushi Oki and Yoichi Manoda directed the effects unit. The design and modeling for *Return of Ultraman* was difficult as the art staff who often worked with Tsuburaya Pro were occupied on projects like *Spectreman* and *Godzilla vs. Hedorah*. As a result, quite a few art directors and designers participated.

Ultraseven's Noriyoshi Ikeya only did a little design work for *Return of Ultraman* as he was occupied with film projects. Much of the responsibility fell on younger art director Akihiko Iguchi, along with Yoshio Suzuki and Toho's **TOSHIRO AOKI** (1936-2018). Aoki had been a longtime assistant to Akira Watanabe and Yasuyuki Inoue. By the following year's *Godzilla vs. Gigan,* he'd be in charge of the art for the Godzilla series. Assistant producer **KEN KUMAGAI** (1937-2018) was also involved in designing the monsters. Kumagai, who had served as an assistant director under the esteemed Yasujiro Ozu, had a background as an art assistant at Toho. He then joined Tsuburaya Pro during production of *Ultra Q*. Kumagai would soon become influential as a producer there.

Many of *Return of Ultraman*'s popular mecha designs were handled by young conceptual artist **TETSUZO OSAWA** (1946-2010). A protégé of Toru Narita and Noriyoshi Ikeya, Osawa would become a prominent art director and monster and mechanical designer and work for Tsuburaya Productions, Toei and Toho in the years to come. The miniature work on *Return of Ultraman* is among the finest done at Tsuburaya Productions so far. *Return of Ultraman* also features striking optical work and improved animation from Minoru Nakano and Sadao Iizuka. There's phantasmagorical beauty to its images, such as Hideki Go's eyes brightly shining and a stunning optical animation of Ultraman Jack merging with a dead Go in the debut.

The show's monsters are less memorable than in the first three shows, a more generic parade of creatures and extraterrestrials. Ryosaku Takayama and his Atelier May were busy with *Spectreman*, but they still managed to create several of the most popular beasts including Gudon and Twin Tail. Nobuyuki Yasumaru's team at Toho also contributed a few suits such as Takkong, as did Tsuburaya Pro's in-house modelers. Much of the suit modeling on *Return of Ultraman* was done by Eizo Kaimai's company, however. Kaimai's firm now operated out of a barn-like building in a rice field near Toho's backlot. The floor in his studio was strewn with materials and half-made monster bodies like the laboratory of a mad scientist in a program Kaimai would be hired to build something for. Children often stopped in to pay witness to the monsters' construction. By this time, Kaimai also took work making monster suits for TV commercials.

Ultraman Jack's suit actor was **EICHI KIKUCHI** (1942-), a versatile stuntman and martial artist proficient in karate. When actor Koji Uenishi was unavailable for a pair of episodes in *Ultraseven*, Kikuchi had doubled for him. This led to Kikuchi getting the job as Jack. Jack's monster opponents were often played by Takanobu Toya, who was a college classmate and friend of Kikuchi's. As Toya was also portraying Dr. Gori on *Spectreman*, he was quite busy going between Tsuburaya and P-Pro. Occasionally the schedules for the two shows would conflict and he'd be unavailable. When this happened, crew members were imprisoned in the suits, particularly director and frequent AD Shohei Tojo.

Storm Over the Pacific and *The Last War*'s director Shue Matsubayashi even helmed a pair of engaging and thought-provoking episodes near the show's end. Episode #49 features a pair of warring space aliens who look like a cross between the salt vampires on *Star Trek* and "Trumpy" from the infamous Spanish production *Extra Terrestrial Visitors,* aka *The Pod People* (1983). This episode also evokes *The War of the Gargantuas*. The finale, *"The Five Ultra Oaths"*, is a somber tearjerker well directed by Ishiro Honda. Here, Hideki Go and Ultraman Jack battle a revived Zetton, sent by the nefarious "Bat Aliens" who are waging war against the Ultra family. Unlike in *Ultraman*'s finale, Jack is able to overcome the super monster. The final moments are bittersweet, though Hideki Go would return in future shows. *Return of Ultraman* was a ratings phenomenon for TBS, with the final episode reaching around 29.5% of Japanese television audiences. The Ultraman franchise was successfully revived and for now here to stay with a new show yearly.

Kamen Rider (1971-73) title card

While Toei's prior special effects shows such as *Li'l Devil, Red Shadow, Captain Ultra* and *Giant Robo* had achieved decent ratings, they had not matched the success of their rival Tsuburaya's Ultraman franchise. Toei's tokusatsu cycle would at last hit its stride with **KAMEN RIDER [AKA: MASKED RIDER - Television Run (Japan):** April 3rd, 1971 - February 10th, 1973], debuting on NET one day after *Return of Ultraman*. Alongside Godzilla and Ultraman, Kamen Rider would become one of the most iconic pop culture properties from Japan. *Kamen Rider* proved so tremendously popular that it ran nonstop for close to two years, only ending to make room for the follow-up *Kamen Rider V3*. *Kamen Rider* would also codify the style and tropes of Toei's tokusatsu programs for decades to come.

Shotaro Ishinomori, the beloved manga artist and apprentice to Osamu Tezuka, was tasked with its development. Toei's *Cyborg 009* anime films and show, based on a manga by Ishinomori, were extremely popular, so he was an ideal choice to help Toei's brass create a tokusatsu program to rival *Ultraman*. *Kamen Rider* shares a similar premise to *Cyborg 009*. Both revolve around young men kidnapped and turned into super-powered cyborgs by fascist organizations bent on world domination with the aim of using them to further their dastardly plots. Cyborg 009 and Kamen Rider alike then turn on their creators and vow to defend the world from these evil orders. As *Kamen Rider* aired, Ishinomori created a similarly popular serialized manga version. Another player in *Kamen Rider*'s development was veteran writer Masaru Igami. Igami had written episodes of *Red Shadow* and *Giant Robo*, worked with Ishinomori on *Cyborg 009*'s anime show and would even write a few episodes of *Return of Ultraman* at Tsuburaya Productions.

Development on *Kamen Rider* began in 1970 under TV producers **TORU HIRAYAMA** (1929-2013) and **YOSHINORI WATANABE** (1930-2019). The popularity of *Cyborg 009* and another manga-based anime show from Toei, *Tiger Mask*, inspired the show's concept of a masked cyborg. Working titles included *Maskman K* and *Masked Angel*. It was then decided to have the hero ride a motorcycle into combat, likely due to the popularity of *Easy Rider* (1969). The program was to then be called *Crossfire* and many elements from this treatment survived.

Kamen Rider himself was designed by Ishinomori, with a grasshopper influence. Toei's brass wanted a skull motif to the design. This frustrated Ishinomori as he felt it was redundant; he had recently worked on the skull-themed anime film *Flying Phantom Ship* (1969). Ishinomori made close to 50 designs for Kamen Rider and showed them to his son Joe to get a child's input. Joe liked the grasshopper-themed design most. Shotaro Ishinomori also thought that a grasshopper-styled hero brought environmentalist undertones to the character. Kamen Rider's ability to jump impressive heights during his battles was also inspired by grasshoppers. The character also boasts a red scarf: a manga-like trademark that feels distinctively Ishinomori.

Yoshinori Watanabe liked the design, though Toru Hirayama was skeptical of an insect motif as he felt heroes should be mighty and tiny insects are weak. Hirayama came around, however, and the final design was approved. Marvel's *The Incredible Hulk* also provided inspiration, specifically on Kamen Rider's direct physical transformations. Vivid *henshin* (transformation) sequences would become a Toei tokusatsu trademark and even influence anime like *Sailor Moon*. Originally, ala Ultraman, Kamen Rider and his monster adversaries were to grow gigantic and do battle. Ishinomori talked the producers out of this as he wanted the show to be more distinct and preferred human-sized superheroes. Toei's brass were sold, as having to build fewer miniature sets kept production costs low. Indeed, in *Kamen Rider*, as he battles Shocker's "regular sized" monsters, there is far less distinction between the units than in Tsuburaya and P-Pro's shows.

As a studio, Toei had a more "grindhouse" sensibility than its rivals. As other Japanese film and television studios went bankrupt or downscaled their productions, Toei thrived in the 1970s. Being closely associated with actor and martial artist Sonny Chiba's Japan Action Club, they were known for their action-based fare. In the '70s they produced numerous crime, exploitation and martial arts films that, though low budget, were creatively made. *Kamen Rider* fits snugly into this "edgy" mold, making Tsuburaya Productions' output feel downright wholesome. The show was shot at Toei's newly opened Ikuta Studio in Kawasaki where most of their 1970s tokusatsu programs would go on to be lensed.

There's a more transgressive quality to *Kamen Rider*. Twisted for a children's show, it features villains that are bonafide fascists. With the JAC involved in the show's choreography, the action sequences are flashier and better staged than other tokusatsu shows, feeling somewhat like a Hong Kong production. Also on-brand with Toei, the show is lensed in grottier locales than Tsuburaya Pro's programs, such as abandoned warehouses and other dilapidated structures. As *Kamen Rider* aired its first episode "*The Mysterious Spider Man*", children who heard its catchy theme song, first sung by actor Hiroshi Fujioka and later by prolific anime and tokusatsu song vocalist **MASATO SHIMON** (1944-) knew they were in for a fun half hour.

The first Kamen Rider is the suave Takeshi Hongo (Hiroshi Fujioka), a motorcycle racer who is kidnapped by the depraved neo-fascist organization Shocker and turned into a battle cyborg. Escaping before he can be brainwashed, Hongo dedicates his life to fighting them. Founded by a former Nazi, Shocker are about as nice as Pol Pot's Khmer Rouge. Called "Hell's Army" in the opening theme song's lyrics, they live up to that in ghoulish evil. Throughout the show, Shocker commits a litany of atrocities that includes slavery, bio-warfare, medical experimentation, torture of animals, frequent attemped murder of children and terrorism. Their enigmatic leader even wears Ku Klux Klan-style robes. The average Ultraman franchise alien is trying to save its dying planet by conquering Earth. Dr. Gori in *Spectreman* is trying to liberate humanity from what he views as its own stupidity. Shocker, by contrast, are nihilistic sociopaths. There's an occult element to Shocker, perhaps paying reference to the Nazis' obsession with it. Yet their actions are also rooted in a Joker-like nihilism. The fascistic depravity of Shocker no doubt kept *Kamen Rider* off the airwaves in the United States, though Toei would one day have grand success exporting their tokusatsu fare stateside.

**Manga and tokusatsu legend
Shotaro Ishinomori**

Kamen Rider's first 13 episodes are considered the best by Japanese fans. These episodes, lensed in gritty locales on grimy 16mm with experimental film-like FX cuts, feel the most quintessential in Ishinomori's vision for *Kamen Rider*. Shocker has gaggles of soldier grunts which Kamen Rider defeats easily. "Grunt battles" became another Toei tokusatsu trademark for decades hence. Even the sound design of Shocker's monsters and grunts is unsettling and must have echoed in the nightmares of young Japanese Boomers and Gen-Xers. They're given high pitched cackles that sound almost demonic.

The special effects on *Kamen Rider* were not often shot with a separate unit but featured strong input from a Tsuburaya apprentice, Michio Mikami, who became the show's art director. Mikami recruited his colleagues at Equis Productions to assist in the modeling and effects work. His main assistants were Akira Takahashi and **TSUTOMU YAGI** (1951-), the son of Masao Yagi and grandson of Kanju. Kamen Rider and his suits and helmets were modeled at Equis, as were the show's numerous monsters. Keizo Murase was also involved in sculpting the original helmet. At first, Kamen Rider's helmet was darker but, after the appearance of the second Rider, Ichimonji, it was decided to change the mask to a brighter shade of green to help it stand out in night sequences. The team at Equis avoided making Kamen Rider's body with a wetsuit to differentiate the character from Ultraman. They also made two sets of masks. For close-ups and non-action scenes: hard FRP masks were created. For the action sequences which tended to be more punishing for the stuntmen than other shows, soft vinyl and latex masks were made.

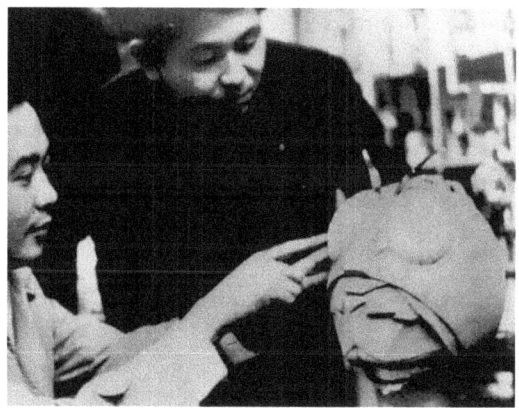
Modeling a superhero mask

Other stylistic flourishes abound including stop motion animation cuts and occasional miniature shots, mainly for pyrotechnic effects. These were shot by Takahashi, Yagi and propsmaster **MASAMITSU SAKUMA**. Doll duplicates of Kamen Rider are occasionally used for wide miniature shots, particularly in later episodes as his motorcycle becomes able to glide through the air. Kamen Rider's "transformation" sequences are more visually elaborate than Ultraman's. They feature probable contributions from Toei's animation division.

In Toei's special effects hero shows from hereon, the human actors seldom if ever played their costumed counterparts. These sequences were shot with a separate "stunt unit" and had stuntmen in the costumes. At first, Hiroshi Fujioka donned the costume and did his own stunts. Toei would soon realize this was a liability. Early in production on *Kamen Rider*, disaster struck. While filming an episode, Hiroshi Fujioka was injured in a motorcycle accident. Toei were sent into a panic. A few more Takeshi Hongo episodes were squeezed out through the use of stock footage and more screen time for transformed Kamen Rider. Young stuntman **MASARU OKADA** (1950-) portrayed the first Rider in most episodes from hereon. There was no way around it, however, something had to be done as Fujioka was in recovery and unable to shoot for some time.

The character of Hayato Ichimonji was thus created, played by Takeshi Sasaki. Ichimonji, a photojournalist, is kidnapped by Shocker to become a second Kamen Rider and defeat the first. However, the Hongo Rider rescues him and like his predecessor, Ichimonji decides to use his powers to battle Shocker. Toei's leader and creative team thought about killing off the Hongo Rider but such a move was considered too grim for a children's show. It was thus decided that Hongo should go to Europe and hand the baton to Ichimonji. By episode #13, Hongo spends the entire time in Kamen Rider form save for a little stock footage per Fujioka's accident and fittingly battles an army of prior monsters as a send-off. An expository dialogue explanation by Ichimonji that Hongo and love interest Ruriko (Chieko Morikawa) "went to Europe" feels contrived. Nonetheless, considering the circumstances, the changeover between protagonists is well handled.

Once Fujioka recovered, Hongo made occasional appearances on the show to aid Ichimonji. Eventually, for the show's later arcs and with Fujioka able to do action again, Takeshi Hongo was again made the protagonist with Ichimonji making guest appearances. The iconic trope of a henshin "transformation pose" was introduced with Sasaki's Ichimonji. This pose was devised by the show's action director **KAZUTOSHI TAKAHASHI** (1943-1991). The low-angle shots of Kamen Rider leaping into the air, thrilling to children, were created with trampolines.

Kamen Rider's monsters are more humanoid than *Ultraman*'s, being medically and cybernetically modified people. Amusingly, Kamen Rider's first two foes are named "Spider Man" and "Bat Man". Another memorable villain is Sabotegron, a monster from Mexico who sends exploding cactus bombs to the heroes in the mail, Unabomber-style. In the first Ichimonji arc, Shocker "commanders" are introduced. They include the Gestapo officer-like Colonel Zol (Jiro Miyaguchi). Then comes Dr. Death, played by Toho villain actor Hideyo Amamoto in a Dracula cape, along with the sphinx-like Ambassador Hell (Kenji Ushio). All three turn out to be Shocker monsters in disguise. With Ambassador Hell's defeat, Shocker finally disbands in episode #79. They reform in the next episode, merging with another neo-fascist organization, Geldam, to become the more formidable Gel-Shocker. Gel-Shocker's commander is the Kaiser Wilhelm-lookable General Black (Matasaburo Niwa). Gel-Shocker keeps its grunts obedient by hooking them on drugs that kill them from withdrawal in a matter of hours; probably the most deranged thing in a kids' show ever.

Regardless, *Kamen Rider* was a ratings sensation and would be here to stay in various forms as one of Toei's most popular franchises. Similarly to DC and Marvel stateside, Toei and Tsuburaya Productions would become the two biggest rivals in the creation of Japanese superheroes and the production of media themed around them.

XVII.
__1971__
昭和四十六
(Part 2)

Kihachi Okamoto (center)

The guns of war sounded that summer with Toho's "8/15" entry for the year, **BATTLE OF OKINAWA [Director: KIHACHI OKAMOTO (1924-2005) - Release Date (Japan):** July 17th, 1971]. A similar film to Okamoto's prior *Japan's Longest Day* (1967), *Battle of Okinawa* is a fatalistic and darkly satirical retelling of Imperial Japan's doomed defense of Okinawa and its environs at the end of the Pacific War. If Kurosawa was Japan's John Ford, Kihachi Okamoto could be called its Sam Peckinpah. One of Toho's top directors, Okamoto disliked working with special effects and *Battle of Okinawa* remains his only film to begrudgingly employ an FX unit, run by Teruyoshi Nakano. It's far more Okamoto's film and Nakano's contributions are subtle. Tomoyuki Tanaka had wanted Okamoto for years to helm a special effects picture but he fervently refused. (Teruyoshi Nakano would notably not take part in Okamoto's later sci-fi film *Blood Type: Blue* (1978), which deliberately uses minimalist special effects to depict its UFOs. The next "8/15" film, *Eternal Cause* (1972), directed by Tadashi Imai, would also feature minimal at best contribution from Toho's effects staff.)

For his footage, Nakano uses his mentor Tsuburaya's tricks of the war movie trade, though on a limited budget. These include vistas of the *Yamato* and Imperial fleet, made with tiny ships placed on gelatin sheets as usual. There are impressive miniature shots, including of the *Yamato* and Okinawa from high above as American planes descend upon them. These look forward to Nakano's stunning "god's-eye-view" shots in *Submersion of Japan* (1973). Nakano or his pyrotechnician **TADAAKI WATANABE** (1940-2021) also likely helped Okamoto's unit stage full-scale pyrotechnics in some shots. It was likely on *Battle of Okinawa* that Teruyoshi Nakano became aware of his particular talent in staging explosions.

Battle of Okinawa is a well-directed picture rife with Peckinpah-like cinematic chaos. The film uniquely combines the shock value of a '70s Japanese cult movie with the effects flair of a tokusatsu unit. Its high-profile production suffers only a little from the post-studio system 1970s cheapness. This is evident when the IJA brass watch a kamikaze attack composed of Pacific War stock footage. There are mild historical inaccuracies such as Type 61 Self Defense Force tanks doubled for American Shermans, likely thanks to a lowered budget.

Some slightly cheap looking battle sequences and obvious sets also mar realism. Yet they also lend an unreal theatricality and enhance the feeling of dark satire as does the use of Toho's stock sound effects library. Recreations of explosions and gunfire that killed real people and caused genuine suffering are rendered with sound effects associated with the childlike fantasy of Toho's tokusatsu monster films. Okamoto even satirically depicts the invading Americans as a kaiju-like force of destruction. While subversive, this is no right-wing film. *Battle of Okinawa* is about Japan's agony and shame and contains plenty of pointed, if subtle, jabs at the Imperial era's collective psychosis. *Battle of Okinawa* is capped with a stunningly brutal cinematic montage set to an elderly Okinawan woman's native chant as she's run down by an American tank. This is a similar chaotically violent climax to those refined by Okamoto in bleak period pieces like *Samurai Assassin* (1965) and *The Sword of Doom* (1966). From the doomed samurai warriors in his sword films to the Imperial Japanese Empire in *Japan's Longest Day* and *Battle of Okinawa*, Kihachi Okamoto is a director fond of loser narratives that conclude in a torrent of bloodshed.

Imperial warships on an *agar* (gelatin) sea, the FX staff often had to wear elevated *geta* (Japanese-style sandals) to avoid slipping or breaking the surface

One of the top grossing domestic films that year, a young Hideaki Anno saw *Battle of Okinawa* and was traumatized and transfixed by its gruesome images as it became his favorite film. Anno was particularly moved by a grisly moment of civilians on the island of Tokashiki commiting mass suicide via grenade. It made him better understand the collective nightmare that Japan's wartime generation had lived through. According to a story in Galbraith's *Monsters Are Attacking Tokyo*, Kihachi Okamoto was at work on his next picture later that year when some local children approached him. *Kamen Rider* was popular on the air, which starred Okamoto's close friend Hideyo Amamoto as Shocker commander Dr. Death. Amamoto was often said to look like Okamoto's brother. The children mistook Okamoto for Amamoto and kept asking him "Are you Dr. Death?" The kids would not let up and finally, a frazzled Okamoto exclaimed "Yes, I am Dr. Death! Now leave me alone!"

Daiei's next and (unbeknownst to them) final special effects production of the 1970s was **GAMERA VS. ZIGRA [Director:** Noriaki Yuasa **- Release Date (Japan):** July 17th, 1971**]**, released the same day as Toho's *Battle of Okinawa*. Though more tolerable in the polished format of widescreen and Japanese, *Gamera vs. Zigra* is a depressing affair and the worst *Showa* Gamera film. In the badly panned-and-scanned and English dubbed format heckled on *Mystery Science Theater 3000*, it is almost unwatchable. Shot on location at Kamogawa Sea World, Yuasa's direction of both its drama and tokusatsu units is uninspired.

The miniature photography is among his weakest, a step down from Yuasa's work on *The Falcon Fighters* and *Gamera vs. Jiger*. An opening where the film's monster, Zigra, attacks a moonbase features cheap-looking models which would barely pass muster on television. Static master shots tend to linger on screen for up to a minute with no cutaways or insert coverage. Yuasa's effects aren't all bad, however. There are a few good sequences including a Starfighter attack on Zigra's spaceship with above-average miniature work. A fairly imposing three-foot model of Zigra's ship was used for shooting.

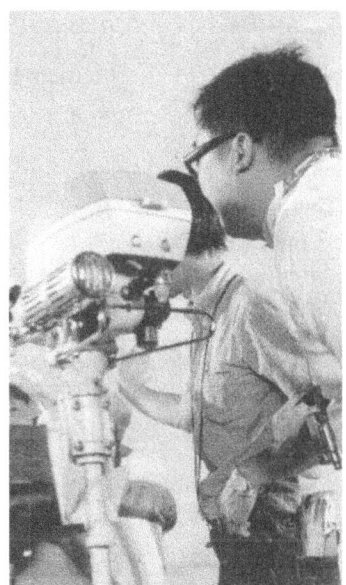

Noriaki Yuasa (right)

The Gamera suit from the previous film was reused with minor repairs. Zigra was designed by Tomohisa Yano with a deep sea goblin shark as inspiration. The suit was built by Equis Productions with Nori Maezawa handling its construction. Keiichi Noda, an anime voice actor who also provided the vocals of Gokemidoro in *Goke, Body Snatcher From Hell*, voiced Zigra. Noda at least makes the creature sound intimidating as he announces his existentially terrifying plans to factory farm human beings for food as in Peter Jackson's *Bad Taste* (1987). Zigra's first battle with Gamera is pedestrian in staging. Gamera somehow uses his fire underwater in blatant defiance of the most basic laws of physics.

Gamera vs. Zigra's flaws can be summed up in the fact that at one point, Zigra sets off the largest earthquake in Tokyo's history. With the exception of a few images on TV sets, this momentous event is mentioned entirely in passing, putting the paltry budget on display. Again, Gamera is knocked unconscious and requires revival by annoying children. Gamera's final underwater showdown with Zigra is staged with some degree of dynamic action, yet it is followed by among the most embarrassing moments in kaiju movie history: Gamera plays his theme song by hitting a rock against Zigra's fins like a xylophone. *Gamera vs. Zigra* features particularly shallow anti-pollution subtext, likely shoehorned in per *Spectreman*'s success and as Toho was making *Godzilla vs. Hedorah* at the same time. There were plans to make one more Gamera entry to be filmed at the Ueno Zoo in Miyazaki Prefecture, but Daiei's financial woes were now a lot worse than anyone knew.

Only a week later, Toho released **GODZILLA VS. HEDORAH [AKA: GODZILLA VS. THE SMOG MONSTER** - **Director:** Yoshimitsu Banno - **Release Date (Japan):** July 24th, 1971], screened at the 6th Champion Matsuri Festival. The film represented a dramatic departure for the Godzilla series in style and tone.

With Eiji Tsuburaya gone and Ishiro Honda now focusing on directing TV, their replacements at Toho were proteges Nakano and Banno. By this time, Teruyoshi Nakano was the de facto head of what was left of Toho's effects department. He had his own, very 1970s way of doing things with a defining love for pyrotechnics. The deafening boom of explosions could be heard across the Toho backlot from his effects set and his crew's ears rang from the cacophony. Whereas Tsuburaya was known as "The Old Man", Nakano's team gave him a different nickname: "Bomber Nakano".

The very busy man who created the pyrotechnics for Nakano's unit was Tadaaki Watanabe. A native of Fukushima and protege of both Akira Watanabe and Kyuzo Yamamoto, Tadaaki Watanabe would become Toho's go-to gasoline and gunpowder technician for decades. Nakano and Watanabe had a specific recipe they liked to use for their distinctive orange-green conflagrations. They mixed high octane leaded gasoline with copper sulfite. In a fiery form of alchemy, Nakano and Watanabe also liked to mix different types of gunpowder together. Nakano's infamous penchant for heavy pyrotechnics was partially borne out of the low budgets he was forced to work with. As they could not afford to build extensive miniature sets and had to be sparing in their use of optical composites, this was Nakano and his crew's '70s way of making their FX footage look visually stunning at low cost. Nakano includes a signature explosion sequence in *Godzilla vs. Hedorah* with impressive shots of miniature oil refineries blowing sky high.

Yoshimitsu Banno (left) and
Teruyoshi Nakano (right)

Yoshimitsu Banno, by contrast, had an auteurist tack quite different from Honda's "company man" attitude. The popularity of his work on the Mitsubishi Pavilion at Expo '70 got him the job to direct the next Godzilla picture, the first after Tsuburaya's death. For *Godzilla vs. Hedorah*'s development, Tomoyuki Tanaka gave Banno relative free reign. Banno chose to focus strongly on ecological horror as he felt it was a similar existential threat as nuclear weapons. Banno remembered a visit to a disgustingly polluted beach near the industrial center of Yokkaichi where the very air smelled like rotten eggs. He was also obsessed with Rachel Carson's 1962 *The Silent Spring*. A recent news story additionally sparked his imagination: High school girls in Tokyo collapsed during physical education due to smog from a nearby factory. Direct homage is paid to this in *Godzilla vs. Hedorah* with a sequence of Hedorah flying over a group of exercising schoolgirls, nearly asphyxiating them.

Godzilla vs. Hedorah was allotted another low budget and director Banno was given only 35 days to shoot the entire film. The funding only allowed for one unit, so like Noriaki Yuasa on the Gamera films and Ishiro Honda on *All Monsters Attack,* Banno helmed both the drama and special effects scenes. The latter, however, was with close collaboration and strong creative input from Teruyoshi Nakano. Yoichi Manoda served as DP for both the drama and effects shots. In spite of the paltry budget, Banno was determined to include imagery and aesthetic never before seen in the Godzilla series. In contrast to Honda or even Jun Fukuda's more conventional directing styles, *Godzilla vs. Hedorah* features unusual camera angles, staccato editing and lots of "far out" cinematic technique. These include multi-screen montages, trippy anime sequences, manipulation of color saturation and use of fish-eye lenses.

Godzilla vs. Hedorah feels closer in many ways to surrealist works like Seijun Suzuki's *Branded to Kill* (1967), Toshio Matsumoto's *Funeral Parade of Roses* (1969) or Shunya Ito's *Female Prisoner Scorpion: Jailhouse 41* (1972) than *King Kong vs. Godzilla*. In spite of blatant low budget flaws like a poverty row Self-Defense Force that consists of a dozen soldiers, *Godzilla vs. Hedorah* contains an impressive level of atmosphere. In a rarity for Toho's normally set-bound films, much of the actor footage was shot on location. This gives *Godzilla vs. Hedorah* a grittier feel.

Like a kaiju *Pink Floyd's The Wall* (1982), *Godzilla vs. Hedorah* is a psychedelic "head film" as much as a monster picture. It switches stylistic gears whenever it pleases and features surrealistic images throughout like a fever dream. A mannequin, looking like a mangled corpse, lies atop in sludge-filled waters. Male hero Yukio (*Silver Mask*'s Toshio Shiba), probably tripping out on the best acid one could get in Japan back then, hallucinates that his friends in the "Go Go Club" have fish heads. The club's unorthodox aesthetic drew influence from both a Tokyo discotheque and an American gay bar. A kitten is left behind in Hedorah's wake, mewing as it sits covered in toxic sludge. A quartet of men playing mahjong die shrieking as a chunk of Hedorah comes flying through the window. Another arresting bit features among the most graphic civilian casualty scenes in the kaiju genre. In a wide shot, an airborne Hedorah soars over a dock as people flee. The civilians all drop to the ground from the monster's noxious fumes. Banno cuts to a close-up of a man as his face burns to a crisp and turns psychedelic colors with optical printing. Later, as Yukio and his hippie crew party before a bonfire at Mount Fuji, a group of elderly people with stern expressions, played by local farmers, watch them from afar.

Like Toho's later, Banno-penned *Prophecies of Nostradamus* (1974), *Godzilla vs. Hedorah* is grim in its worldview. Human attempts to stop pollution are depicted, as Shakespeare would say, "Full of sound and fury, signifying nothing". *Godzilla vs. Hedorah* features unusual anime sequences that add to its bizarro-world psychedelia. Banno had wanted manga artist Yoshiharu Tsuge to create them, Tsuge had drawn a pollution-themed manga called *Salamander* which Banno loved. Tsuge, however, turned Banno down as he had social anxiety and did not want to animate in a group. Instead, the animation was created by animator Etsuro Yasui who had worked on Banno's Expo '70 exhibit. Production designer Yasuyuki Inoue, unusually, also supervised the art direction for the drama scenes and storyboarded the entire film.

Preparing an unsettling image - the infant was the gaffer's son

The effects work is mixed but Banno and Nakano clearly learned a lot from each other. The two were frustrated that they were not given the same amount of studio space to erect miniature sets as Tsuburaya had been. Despite the limitations they faced, some impressive visuals are on display.

The disgusting shots of a polluted bay that open and close *Godzilla vs. Hedorah* are not genuine. They were created by the special effects staff at one of the FX pools. Dead fish and garbage were mixed into the water and the stench was almost unbearable as the fish spoiled under the lights.

The Godzilla suit created for *Destroy All Monsters* was again used. Haruo Nakajima returned for what would be his penultimate turn as Godzilla, who is put through unusually gruesome torments battling the sadistic Hedorah. Similarly to Noriaki Yuasa and in contrast to his mentor Tsuburaya, Nakano had no qualms hurting his monsters. The costume from *Invasion of Astro-Monster* was used one last time; for the water sequences and a bit where the creature is almost drowned in a bath of toxic sludge by Hedorah. The suit was so badly damaged from filming the sequence that it was never used again.

Hedorah, originally named Hedoron, is an impressive creation which takes various forms, all designed by Yasuyuki Inoue. The shape of Hedorah's distinctive eyes was inspired by the human vagina. The toy companies were not happy with Inoue's Hedorah design as they felt it was too difficult to make figurines from. Inoue also created the miniature electrodes used to "dry out" Hedorah, based on an idea suggested by popular science fiction writer Masami Fukushima. They were based on a toaster in shape. After *Godzilla vs. Hedorah*, Yasuyuki Inoue would soon go freelance from Toho. He'd be back soon, however; fittingly for 1973's prestige production *Submersion of Japan*.

With Teizo Toshimitsu and Yasuei Yagi both retired, Nobuyuki Yasumaru was now in command of the modeling department. While up against deadlines, Yasumaru would guzzle a hidden bottle of whiskey to relieve his stress. Two Hedorah suits, as well as multiple puppets for the monster's tadpole and flying forms, were constructed by Yasumaru. With unsettlingly dead eyes, Hedorah's final form was one of the bulkiest monster suits ever built, created entirely from foam rubber. The hulking costume was worn by a young actor named **KENPACHIRO SATSUMA** (1947-). Satsuma (aka Kengo Nakayama), a former Kagoshima steel worker whose real name remains unknown, had been a stuntman at Nikkatsu. After the studio began to switch from their conventional gangster fare to softcore erotica or "Roman Porno", he moved to Mifune Productions. There he was discovered by Teruyoshi Nakano, who needed a stuntman to play Hedorah. During the shoot, Satsuma would suffer acute appendicitis while inside the monster skin. The small "tadpole" Hedorahs were portrayed by live fish and the sulfuric acid mist flatulently sprayed by the monster throughout was made with freon gas. Hedorah possesses the ability to fire a laser beam from its eyes. This was created by Koichi Kawakita, who can also be seen reveling amongst the dancers in the "Go Go Club".

As time and money wore thin, Banno and Nakano shot frantically on the special effects stage, filming 30 to 50 shots per day. A reference to the *Ultraman* franchise was included: Godzilla does Ultraman's iconic "specium beam" pose before being hit, ironically, by Hedorah's beam. Another segment, cut from the finished film, was a nod to *Kamen Rider*. The Godzilla suit was hung with piano wire and used to do a "Godzilla kick" on Hedorah. A similar gag would be staged in *Godzilla vs. Megalon* (1973). Yoshimitsu Banno went over budget with *Godzilla vs. Hedorah* before shooting could be finished. A furious Tomoyuki Tanaka ordered production halted. It was Ishiro Honda who intervened on Banno's behalf, agreeing to watch a rough cut of the film and give the younger director his feedback. Thanks to Honda's mediation, it was successfully concluded with an extended deadline.

Tomoyuki Tanaka had to be briefly hospitalized at the end of *Godzilla vs. Hedorah*'s shoot. While Tanaka was in the hospital, Banno decided to add a scene that wasn't in the script. He and Nakano felt that the picture's tone was getting too grim and should be offset by something lighthearted. Thus they filmed Godzilla flying by propelling itself into the air with its ray. Inspired by the swimming motion of a seahorse, this effect was created with a two-foot Guignol puppet left over from *Invasion of Astro-Monster* and freon gas. This preposterous sequence is a major flaw, stopping *Godzilla vs. Hedorah* cold. Banno and Nakano had deliberately shot it so it could be cut from the film if Toho's suits weren't happy. They even shot alternate footage of Godzilla chasing Hedorah on foot instead that can be glimpsed in Toho's trailer.

Banno got permission from most of Toho's brass, save for Tanaka. By the time Tanaka was discharged from the hospital, it was too late to edit out the scene. Contrary to popular belief, Tanaka was not so much enraged by the segment itself. He was angry that Banno went around him to get approval, a disrespectful faux pas in the Japanese business world. In Tanaka's words: "Banno will never direct a special effects film again". That statement proved prophetic.

Godzilla vs. Hedorah did better than expected business, however. In the United States, it was often shown on a double bill with another eco-horror flick: *Frogs* (1972). Amusingly, *Frogs* features a few seconds of Toho's polluted bay footage from *Hedorah*. Banno was keen on making follow-ups set in Africa and Okinawa, but Tanaka was lukewarm on these proposals. In the 2000s, Banno would eagerly try to get another follow-up made, a short film to be produced in 70mm IMAX entitled *Godzilla 3-D: To the Max*.

In December, another show from Tsuburaya Productions joined *Return of Ultraman*, *Kamen Rider* and *Spectreman* on Japanese airwaves: **MIRRORMAN** [Television Run (Japan): December 5th, 1971 - November 26th, 1972]. Fuji TV had wanted to produce a *Pippi Longstocking* anime show, but negotiations with author Astrid Lindgren fell through, leaving them with a time slot but no program to fill it with. Writer Tetsuo Kinjo had submitted a proposal in 1969 called *Mirrorman*. A pilot version was produced by Tsuburaya Productions in June to July of '71. This pilot episode had a mostly different cast and wound up reshot. With *Pippi Longstocking* off the table, Fuji TV greenlit *Mirrorman* for its replacement. *Mirrorman* is a similar superhero show to the Ultraman franchise but is differentiated by a darker and edgier quality. Once again, director Ishiro Honda leant his pedigree to a number of early episodes.

The story revolves around the half-alien, half-human Kyotaro Kagami (*kagami* meaning "mirror" in Japanese) played by Nobuyuki Ishida. Like Ultraman, he can transform into a gigantic superhero, this time an interdimensional being. While *Mirrorman* does employ the "monster of the week" format, a la *Ambassador Magma*, *Spectreman* and *Kamen Rider*, the monsters are sent by regular villains. The fiendish "Invaders" are indeed a nod to the popular American TV show created by Larry Cohen. Throughout *Mirrorman*, Kagami struggles with his hero status more than Hideki Go or Takeshi Hongo. *Mirrorman*, like the Ultraman shows, features a Science Patrol-like organization that combats the Invaders: the Science Guard Members (SGM). Unlike the Ultraman teams, the SGM don't get their Gerry Anderson-style flying craft until later episodes.

Mirrorman (1971-72) title card

To transform, Mirrorman must stand before a reflective surface and flash the "mirror pendant" given to him by his alien father. Like Hideki Go, Kagami grows as a character throughout the run, which climaxes in a tense, apocalyptic two-part finale. The Invaders, in a last-ditch effort, decide to obliterate the Earth by smashing their planet into it *Gorath*-style. Though Kagami had his heart set on living as a human once the Invaders were defeated, he gives up these dreams for duty and returns to his father's planet.

Mirrorman is another above-average '70s tokusatsu show that features top tier talent behind the camera. Besides Ishiro Honda, another player in the show's success was none other than Yoshiyuki Kuroda. Despite their corporate rivalry, Eiji Tsuburaya had been enraptured with Kuroda's work on the Majin films. He'd wanted Kuroda to direct his planned *Princess Kaguya* adaptation. Hajime Tsuburaya was keen on getting the project off the ground to honor his father with Kuroda at the helm, who had just left the Daiei, which was fast approaching bankruptcy. Hajime's death, sadly soon to come, likely put an end to *Princess Kaguya*'s development.

In preparation for this project, which wound up shelved until the 1980s, Kuroda was brought aboard *Mirrorman*, not as a special effects director but in charge of the main unit for many episodes. Kuroda's episodes are more engagingly directed than Honda's, filled with his trademark flair for atmospheric visuals. Moments in certain episodes almost evoke Mario Bava's work. There's even a blatant nod to Daiei's Yokai films in his first episode featuring a spooky forest with a "No Face" in Buddhist garb. Kuroda brings a quirky attention to detail and his involvement is betrayed particularly by the preponderance of atmospheric particles. Kuroda also appears to have had input into the special effects sequences. Koichi Takano shows markedly stronger work in the Kuroda episodes to which he contributed. There are even phantasmagorical kaleidoscope effects in one episode that resemble the finale of *Spook Warfare*. Kazuho Mitsuda, Shohei Tojo and Toshitsugu Suzuki also helmed installments.

If *Return of Ultraman* had the most empathetic protagonist and *Kamen Rider* the best action, *Mirrorman*'s major strength is in its special effects sequences. Takano was in charge of the unit for the most episodes. His effects work had improved noticeably since his return from Taiwan. Occasional support came from Yoichi Manoda, Kazuo Sagawa and Atsushi Oki. Being based around an interdimensional, mirror-themed alien hero, the optical effects, supervised by Minoru Nakano, are plentiful and innovative for television. Mirrorman himself was designed by **YOSHIHIRO MORITO** (1944-2000), an artist entrusted to draw manga versions of Tsuburaya Pro's shows. The costume was modeled by Eizo Kaimai's firm, as were many of the monsters. As Kaimai Productions was understaffed and didn't have sufficient workspace to make all the monsters, Yoshio Irie and Ryosaku Takayama also did suit modeling for the show. The creatures were often designed by **KAKO YONETANI** who had worked on *Return of Ultraman*, with support from Noriyoshi Ikeya, Tetsuzo Osawa and Ahihiko Iguchi.

Starting in episode #16, Tsuburaya Productions would bring none other than Nobuo Yajima and his Tokusatsu Research Institute on board to helm the effects sequences. Eiji had seen talent in Yajima and wanted him as an apprentice back in the '50s. Toru Narita had also tried to recruit Yajima for *Mighty Jack*. Yajima would go on to handle the special effects on numerous episodes of *Mirrorman*. He directs some of his best sequences here, a nudge above his work on *Spectreman*. Yajima's miniature work is particularly improving in quality. His scenes are often imaginatively directed and both *Spectreman* and *Mirrorman* feature Spaghetti Western-style "face off" shots from a low angle. For the series finale, Yajima stages impressive floods and earthquakes, though supplemented with Tsuburaya-era Toho stock footage.

Mirrorman's ratings were decent, though not as good as *Return of Ultraman* or *Kamen Rider*'s. *Mirrorman* was in direct competition with another show that aired on TBS at the same slot: **SILVER MASK [Television Run (Japan):** November 28th, 1971 - May 21st, 1972]. *Silver*

Mask's lead, Toshio Shiba, had portrayed Mirrorman in the unaired pilot. Though the show featured early episodes directed by Akio Jissoji, *Silver Mask* airing at the same time as *Mirrorman* proved its undoing; the ratings were abysmal. At first, *Silver Mask* was a "regular sized" hero a la Kamen Rider. It was decided to give him the ability to grow to giant size and battle monsters to better compete with *Mirrorman*. This gave the show an uptick in ratings at first, but they soon slipped again to single digits. The show only lasted 26 episodes as a result and was seldom rebroadcast. Atsushi Oki was in charge of the special effects unit and frequently went back and forth between the two rival productions.

Daiei, meanwhile, was in dire financial straits. The company had suspended its operations on November 29th and on December 21st, Daiei declared bankruptcy, unable to honor 18 million yen in checks for its employees. Many of Daiei's workers quietly suspected that Masaichi Nagata had run the company into the ground on purpose because its employees had been unionizing and lobbying for better salaries. Nagata himself wound up hospitalized with hypertension. Daiei's end put the kibosh on *Gamera vs. the Two-Headed Monster W*. New suits had even been built. As Daiei liquified without giving its workers the final bonuses they were promised, angry employees destroyed all the monster suits in storage. Allegedly, an embittered Noriaki Yuasa was among them, slashing up his own Gamera suits in a fit of sorrow. Daiei was now out of the game, though the company's assets would be acquired in 1974 by publishing mogul **YASUYOSHI TOKUMA** (1921-2000), who would begin to rebuild the studio.

In another sign of the desperate times Japan's film industry now faced, a day after Daiei's liquidation, Akira Kurosawa attempted suicide. Depressed at his removal from Fox's *Tora! Tora! Tora!* and the box office failure of his recent *Dodes'kaden* (both 1970), Kurosawa slashed his arms and neck with a razor. Kurosawa's suicide attempt even caused tension in his friendship with Ishiro Honda, who viewed his behavior as petulant. The two, however, would soon reconcile. For Japanese special effects cinema, things were going to get worse before they got better, though the airwaves continued to swarm with programming in the next year.

XVIII.
1972
昭和四十七

As 1972 rang in, Toho's next Godzilla entry was **GODZILLA VS. GIGAN [Director:** Jun Fukuda - **Release Date (Japan):** March 17th, 1972], released at the 8th Champion Matsuri Festival. *Godzilla vs. Gigan* is an early example of franchise "course correction". The seasoned Fukuda was put back in the director's chair and the tone redirected to escapist fantasy. *Godzilla vs. Gigan* is among the weaker *Showa* entries, awkwardly combining the "hip" ecological subtext of *Godzilla vs. Hedorah* with classic alien invasion tropes. It began life as a treatment called *Godzilla vs. the Space Monsters* which was writer Takeshi Kimura's final contribution to kaiju cinema. Kimura's proposal was more ambitious in scope than the finished movie, pitting Godzilla, Anguirus and a Majin-inspired stone idol against King Ghidorah and novel foes Gigan and Megalon. Shinichi Sekizawa rewrote the concept into *The Return of King Ghidorah* which was developed into the finished film.

Though the prior two Champion Godzilla entries had abandoned the two-unit shooting style, it was resumed with *Godzilla vs. Gigan*. The units, however, did not shoot concurrently and used much of the same below-the-line crew, with Fukuda's main unit shooting their scenes first and Nakano's effects sequences being shot afterward. Teruyoshi Nakano was not yet credited as "special effects director". Amazingly, even after the damage it endured at Yoshimitsu Banno's hands, the 1968 Godzilla suit was used one last time. By now, it's in ratty shape with visible tears in the arms and bits flying off in shots. *Godzilla vs. Gigan* would be Haruo Nakajima's final, bittersweet outing as Godzilla. For water sequences, the suit from *Son of Godzilla* was used and worn by Nakajima, likely cut in two. In addition to Nakajima, wire expert Fumio Nakashiro would also depart Toho's effects unit following *Godzilla vs. Gigan*.

The new monster Gigan is an intriguing creation. Illustrator **TAKAYOSHI MIZUKI** designed

Gigan, brought in by Nakano to introduce some "new blood". Mizuki incorporated such varied elements as eagles, elaborate kimonos, and even actor Yujiro Ishihara into the design. Gigan's suit was built by Nobuyuki Yasumaru who even installed an electric conveyor belt inside for its abdominal buzzsaw. Kenpachiro Satsuma inhabited the suit. Fittingly for FX director Nakano, Gigan comes to life in an explosion. The Anguirus costume from *Destroy All Monsters* was reused with a new paint job. The original King Ghidorah suit was also used once again, though with renovations and repainting by Yasumaru. Wooden "flying props" of Ghidorah and Gigan were also constructed, though these turned out rather poorly. With Yasuyuki Inoue temporarily freelance from Toho, his apprentice Toshiro Aoki was now in charge of art direction for the Godzilla series. The miniature set for Children's Land, an amusement park from which human-sized alien cockroaches from a polluted planet are trying to conquer Earth, is the most impressive. Among Aoki's greatest creations is the Godzilla Tower, a miniature marvel also crafted by Nobuyuki Yasumaru from plaster. Nakano's unit even contributes subtle miniature effects to a Fukuda sequence where the heroes escape the Godzilla Tower.

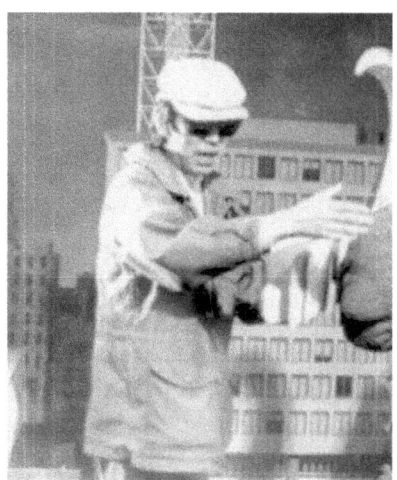

Teruyoshi Nakano

Overall, the work of Teruyoshi Nakano's unit is uneven; it would take a few more films for the effects director to find his feet. By the second half, his unit dominates *Godzilla vs. Gigan* with wall-to-wall monster mayhem. Nakano's best scene features Gigan and Ghidorah torching a miniaturized Tokyo. The most striking miniature shot evokes *Mothra* with a mannequin-filled storefront, viewed from inside, smashed by Gigan's clawed foot. There's a stunning wide shot showcasing a ship engulfed in conflagration by Ghidorah's rays as Gigan's rampages in the background. Nakano fittingly has Godzilla and Anguirus battle Gigan and Ghidorah in an oil refinery amidst a torrent of flames. It's a fun but at times clunky sequence. The finale is clumsily staged save for one effective segment where Godzilla is mowed down by the G-Tower's beam. Godzilla and Anguirus freely gush crimson blood when cut by Gigan's saw, a touch that Tsuburaya would not have tolerated.

Godzilla vs. Gigan's undoing is a bevy of stock footage that pads the runtime. As with the anime industry's decades-long practice of recycling animation, the use of stock shots from earlier films was common in thrifty Japanese studio filmmaking. Even Eiji Tsuburaya employed this method surprisingly often. *Godzilla vs. Gigan*, however, features minutes-long stretches that consist of stock footage from a variety of previous special effects films. These include *The Last War, Ghidorah, the Three-Headed Monster, Invasion of Astro-Monster, The War of the Gargantuas, Destroy All Monsters* and even the previous year's *Godzilla vs. Hedorah*. Nakano reuses the oil refinery explosion from that film and cuts away a frame before Hedorah shows up on screen. The heavy use of stock shots in *Godzilla vs. Gigan* feels lazy, distracting and makes one wish they were watching the superior Tsuburaya-era films from which the scenes were lifted.

Another grating aspect of *Godzilla vs. Gigan* is that Godzilla and Anguirus "talk" to each other. In the Japanese version, this is depicted more tolerably with manga-style speech balloons. The English dubbed version was recorded by a small firm in Hong Kong that produced thousands of cheap dubs for Greater Chinese and Japanese studios. It dispenses with this and has the monsters talk out loud in guttural voices, making the outfit's owner, Ted Thomas, perhaps the only person to have served as Godzilla's voice in a non-comedic context.

Less than a week later came the Toei Manga Festival which screened **KAMEN RIDER VS. SHOCKER** [**Director:** Minoru Yamada - **Release Date (Japan):** March 18th, 1972]. *Kamen Rider vs. Shocker* was a new, though short length, theatrical Kamen Rider adventure. A re-edited *Kamen Rider* episode had been screened at the previous summer's Toei Manga Festival on July 18th, 1971 as *Go Go Kamen Rider*. 35mm 'scope blow-ups were done on a handful of 16mm Toei tokusatsu show episodes for the Manga Festival. These were reminiscent of the company's grungy yakuza films which often featured 16mm-lensed sequences. Producer Toru Hirayama attended one of the screenings and saw the tremendous impact it had on the assembled children, who began to belt the theme song in chorus. Hirayama and Yoshinori Watanabe thus decided to start producing Kamen Rider shorts exclusively for theatrical exhibition of the Toei Manga Festival. Kids could now see occasional *Kamen Rider* episodes on the big screen in the crisp splendor of 35mm Cinemascope.

Poster for *Kamen Rider vs. Shocker* (1972)

Shot in three days simultaneously with the show, *Kamen Rider vs. Shocker* is a fun half-hour piece of kinetic tokusatsu cinema. The production values are more polished than the show's and the cinematography stronger than on television. The Takeshi Hongo and Hayato Ichimonji Riders both appear. This time around, Dr. Death and the dastardly Shocker kidnap a little girl (Hiroko Saito) from her own birthday party as bait to get her father's anti-gravity device. Dr. Death then lures the two Riders into a trap in Hell's Valley. Fittingly, it's the quarry also used in *Goke, Body Snatcher From Hell*. Hongo and Ichimonji battle an army consisting of every previous Shocker monster they've defeated, dusting off all the costumes Toei had in storage. Toei unveiled another Kamen Rider short at the following summer Manga Festival. **KAMEN RIDER VS. AMBASSADOR HELL** [Director: Minoru Yamada - **Release Date (Japan):** July 16th, 1972], reaches the highest heights of spectacle in the franchise thus far. There's even a sequence with Shocker grunts on horseback, the horses probably loaned over from a *jidai-geki* production at Toei's Kyoto branch.

P-Productions weren't far behind with their next TV series, **LION MARU** [**Television Run (Japan):** April 1st, 1972 - April 7th, 1973], which ran for 54 episodes. *Lion Maru* also draws influence from Tomio Sagisu's unmade *Jaguarman* with a feline-themed superhero. Unlike P-Productions' earlier programs however, *Lion Maru* is set in Japan's past, combining *Sengoku*-era *jidai-geki* theatrics with tokusatsu stagecraft. The result is a unique program that bests Toei's prior *Red Shadow*. Airing a half-hour prior to *Kamen Rider*, *Lion Maru* clearly takes inspiration, inventively moving its tokusatsu hero tropes to medieval Japan.

The show centers around Shishimaru (Tetsuya Ushio), a young man, orphaned in old Japan's incessant civil wars and taken in by legendary ninjutsu sorcerer Kashin Koji (Shin Tokudaiji). After the death of his master at the hands of Demon King Goshun's forces, Shishimaru inherits Koji's magic abilities. With the help of a mystical sword gifted to him by Koji, he is able to transform himself into Lion Maru and battle Goshun who is trying to conquer Japan from a Mario Bava-styled lair. Lion Maru often rides a flying horse, summoned with a flute, into battle, executed with fanciful miniature mock-ups. As in *Kamen Rider*, the monsters Goshun sends to battle Lion Maru are human-scaled, though old world-themed yokai rather than cyborgs. Lion Maru's mask was modeled by Ryosaku Takayama, its mane created with yak hair.

Overall, *Lion Maru* is another blast of a show from P-Productions. As with *Spectreman*, Nobuo Yajima, now splitting his time between various programs at P-Productions, Toei and Tsuburaya, was heavily involved on the special effects end. His effects work on *Lion Maru* features some of his most imaginative trick photography: looking forward to his work on Kinji Fukasaku's later fantasy *jidai-geki* like *Samurai Reincarnation* (1981) and *Legend of the Eight Samurai* (1983). A follow-up Lion Maru series, **LION KNIGHT** [Television Run (Japan): April 14th - September 29th, 1973], would follow for 25 more episodes. The company's next major TV program would follow a week after *Lion Knight*'s end: **TIGER SEVEN** [Television Run (Japan): October 6th, 1973 - March 30th, 1974]. *Tiger Seven* also featured a feline-themed superhero, though set this time in the modern day. *Tiger Seven*'s ratings were poor and the show ended after only 26 episodes.

A day after *Lion Maru*'s premiere came **SUPERHUMAN BAROM-1** [Television Run (Japan): April 2nd - November 26th, 1972] from Toei, based on a manga by *Golgo 13*'s **TAKAO SAITO** (1936-2021). *Superhuman Barom-1* was nearly made into an anime show at Toei Animation. Thanks to the popularity of *Kamen Rider*, however, Toei suit Yoshinori Watanabe decided to turn it into a live action special effects program instead. *Barom-1* revolves around two young men: Takeshi Kido (Hitoki Izuka) and Kentaro Shiratori (Hiroyuki Takano). Lifelong friends born on the same day, the two are attacked by Okozeruge, a fishman monster. They are given the ability to transform into the hero Barom-1 by joining hands. Their adversary is the demonic Dolge (Hideo Murota), whose monstrous henchmen naturally pose a weekly threat.

Kamen Rider directors Katsuhiko Taguchi, Itaru Orita and Minoru Yamada primarily helmed the show. The design and form of Barom-1 was changed from its manga incarnation, though Saito himself was in charge of the redesign which was given a bird motif. Modeling for the suit and monsters of *Superhuman Barom-1* was first handled by Equis Productions. As the Yagis and their staff were also working on *Kamen Rider* and soon became occupied with *Transforming Ninja Arashi* as well, the modeling responsibilities were handed over to Keizo Murase's Twenty. The show's art and monster designs were handled by Equis' Michio Mikami.

Unfortunately, *Superhuman Barom-1* would generate bad PR for Toei and TV company Yomiuri. In August of 1972, an expat German professor living in Kobe claimed that his son was being bullied by local children due to the family's surname, which happened to be the same as the show's villain: "Dolge". This individual attempted to file a legal injunction against the producers of *Barom-1* to stop the use of the name. As name and likeness laws were stricter in Germany, he even tried using his embassy's own legal jurisdiction to get the show off the air. The controversy stirred up by this incident stunted *Superhuman*

Barom-1's ratings and the show ended prematurely after 35 episodes. When shooting the final episodes, a point was made for the name "Dolge" to be mentioned as little as possible.

Transforming Ninja Arashi (1972-73) title card

Beginning its run days later was **TRANSFORMING NINJA ARASHI** [Television Run (Japan): April 7th, 1972 - February 23rd, 1973] from Toei. Once again, Shotaro Ishinomori was hired to develop the concept and design the main character. Like *Lion Maru, Transforming Ninja Arashi* transplants the henshin hero formula to old Japan. Much of *Kamen Rider*'s staff was brought on board, including writer Masaru Igami and director Minoru Yamada. Young ninja Hayate (Tatsuya Nanjo) is taught the ability by his father to transform into Arashi (meaning "Storm" in Japanese) a birdlike ninja hero. His enemies, the Blood Wheel Clan, much like a *Tokugawa*-era answer to Shocker, are aiming to plunge a unified Japan into civil war once again. Arashi looks quite like an old world Kamen Rider thundering on the back of his noble steed Hayabusao. Striking images abound, such as Arashi riding across the horizon of Mount Fuji. The plan was to shoot *Transforming Ninja Arashi* at Toei's Kyoto studios but the show wound up being filmed in the Kanto region instead.

Later in the show's run, the Blood Wheel Clan begins enlisting the aid of Western-style monsters, including Dracula, to conquer Japan. A la the Ichimonji Rider, another transforming ninja appears at the show's halfway point: Hayate's brother Fuyute (also played by Nanjo), who can become the heroic Tsukinowa. In the action scenes, Arashi was portrayed by stuntman **BUNYA NAKAMURA** (1946-2001), who quit *Superhuman Barom-1*'s production after the first two episodes to take part. Again, Sonny Chiba's Japan Action Club handled the punishing stunts. *Transforming Ninja Arashi* would run for 47 episodes. It struggled with ratings as it aired in the same time slot as the newest show by Toei's biggest competitor in tokusatsu television.

Ultraman Ace (1972-73) title card

Airing in the same Friday evening slot as *Transforming Ninja Arashi* was Tsuburaya Productions' next Ultraman show: **ULTRAMAN ACE [Television Run (Japan):** April 7th, 1972 - March 30th, 1973]. *Ultraman Ace* is a big step down from *Return of Ultraman*, though the program has its highlights. MAT's successor is TAC (Terrible-Monster Attack Crew). *Ultraman Ace* takes a cue from Tsuburaya Pro's prior *Mirrorman* and the popularity of *Kamen Rider*, both of which featured consistent arch-villain "overlords". For *Ultraman Ace*, the disparate "Monster of the Week" formula is altered and the show's monsters, super kaiju called "*choju*" (terrible monsters), are sent by evil interdimensional alien beings called Yapool.

Ultraman Ace also tries a new concept, perhaps influenced by *Barom-1*, having its Ultra hero Ace merge with the bodies of two earthlings rather than just one, delivery boy Seiji Hokuto (Keiji Takamine) and nurse Yuko Minami (Mitsuko Hoshi). The two are given "Ultra Rings" which they must touch together to summon Ace. This concept proved unpopular with the show's male audience, so in episode #28, the character of Yuko was written out. She's revealed to be the descendent of a race of lunar-based humans and departs the cast. Amusingly, Minami remains mentioned in the lyrics of the program's opening song until its end.

Ultraman Ace himself was designed by art director Yoshio Suzuki. Monster and mecha designs were handled by Akihiko Iguchi and Toshiro Aoki. Many of the "terrible monsters" were modeled by Eizo Kaimai's firm and others by Keizo Murase's Twenty. Ace was portrayed by **TADASHI NAKANISHI** in early episodes, followed subsequently by **MASAHARU TAKEUCHI**. The monsters tended to be portrayed by young stuntmen **TORU KAWAI** (194?-1996) **MAMORU KUSUMI** (1950-) and **ISAO ZUSHI** (194?-), all of whom would participate in upcoming Godzilla entries. The special effects unit on *Ultraman Ace* was mainly run by Kazuo Sagawa and Koichi Takano. The miniature work on the show is outstanding and nearly silver screen quality. For *Ultraman Ace*, Toho allowed Tsuburaya Productions the use of its special effects stages for many episodes. There are surprising moments of extreme monster battle gore in *Ultraman Ace* that Eiji Tsuburaya himself might have found excessive. In episode #8, its FX unit directed by Kazuo Sagawa, a resurrected Muruchi from *Return of Ultraman* is brutally torn apart by Terrible-Monster Doragory with early Peter Jackson movie ferocity. Later in the episode, the offspring of the Metron Alien from *Ultraseven* is cleaved down the middle by the Ace's guillotine attack, its organs gruesomely falling out of its body.

Ultraman Ace is most significant as being the debut of rising talent and future Godzilla luminary Koichi Kawakita. He would act as special effects director on close to a dozen episodes. Kawakita shows immediate promise in this capacity: His direction is dynamic and visually striking. Kawakita's first episode, #21, features a Princess Kaguya-inspired alien, perhaps a nod to his mentor Tsuburaya. As Kawakita had specialized in creating animated beams for a decade now, his episodes are filled with optical animation and lasers. As a character, Ultraman Ace would be particularly known for his beam attacks, no doubt thanks to the creative influence of Kawakita. *Ultraman Ace* is overall an ambitious but minor entry in the long-running TV franchise. The ratings were a nudge below *Return of Ultraman*'s, but decent enough to continue with the more juvenile *Ultraman Taro*.

As *Kamen Rider* dominated the airwaves, Toei came out with another Shotaro Ishinomori-created show, **ANDROID KIKAIDER [Television Run (Japan):** July 8th, 1972 - May 5th, 1973]. *Android Kikaider* played on NET in the time slot directly after *Kamen Rider*. For monster-loving Japanese kids, Saturday nights were fun in mid to late '72 as *Lion Maru*, *Kamen Rider* and *Android Kikaider* aired in the evening from 7 pm to 8:30, followed by Go Nagai's anime *Devilman*.

Drawing inspiration from *Pinnochio*, *Android Kikaider* again shares similar tropes to Ishinomori's *Cyborg 009* and *Kamen Rider*. Another evil organization, this time called Dark and run by the nefarious Professor Gil (Mitsuo Ando), creates an android super soldier that turns against them. Unlike Cyborg 009 and Kamen Rider, who are former humans modified with cyborg enhancements, Kikaider is entirely robotic. Created by kidnapped engineer Dr. Komyoji (Hajime Izu), Kikaider can disguise him into the human form of Jiro (Daisuke Ban), who carries around a guitar like a Spaghetti Western antihero. In the fashion of Kamen Rider, Kikaider rides around on a motorbike, this time with a sidecar. Masaru Igami again helped develop the concept and wrote early episodes, though he had to drop out midway for development of *Kamen Rider V3*.

Android Kikaider is a more lighthearted show than the edgy *Kamen Rider*. The show feels more like a live action manga with beautifully outlandish designs that smack of Ishinomori. The very busy Tokusatsu Research Institute, with Nobuo Yajima at the helm, oversaw special effects with engineering help from Equis Productions member and Tsuburaya apprentice Toru Suzuki. The modeling on *Kikaider* was the responsibility of Eizo Kaimai and Keizo Murase's firms. The Kikaider suit has impressive electrical engineering inside its head, likely the work of Suzuki. In the special effects sequences, Kikaider was portrayed by **TOSHIAKI KIKUCHI**.

Android Kikaider gets goofier and loses steam at the halfway point but perks up with the arrival of Hakaider, another android created by Dark. Introduced in episode #37, Hakaider has a knock-down, drag-out brawl with Kikaider. Unlike the Ichimonji Rider, Hakaider remains Kikaider's adversary. The character, who gets his own theme song with lyrics, would prove as popular as Kikaider himself. Hakaider was portrayed by young stuntman **TETSU MASUDA** (1954-2021). Though ratings were at first sluggish, they perked up when Hakaider was introduced.

Android Kikaider ended its run and succeeded by a follow-up, **KIKAIDER 01 [Television Run (Japan):** May 12th, 1973 - March 30th, 1974]. This time, Haikaider was made the main villain. After surviving the defeat of Dark, he starts his own evil organization called Shadow. Haikaider is later revealed to be housing the brain of Professor Gil. Kikaider 01, another android created by Dr. Komyoji, prior to the events of the first show, awakens to battle Shadow. As with his predecessor, Kikaider 01 has a human form as disguise, that of a young man named Ichiro (Shunsuke Ikeda). Often, as in *Kamen Rider*, Daisuke Ban's Jiro/Kikaider from the previous show would appear to lend a hand to Kikaider 01. Yajima's Tokusatsu Research Institute again provided the effects unit work, with assistance from Kazufumi Fujii, who had been Noriaki Yuasa's FX cameraman on many Gamera entries. Ratings for *Kikaider 01* dropped off and plans for a third Kikaider show were abandoned.

Patrick Macias says it best in a *Tokyoscope* column in *Animerica*: *Godman* is like the Eastern concept of God in that he's simultaneously the greatest and worst Japanese superhero ever

A popular, *Sesame Street*-like variety show for kids in Japan was *The Good Morning! Kids Show* on Nippon TV. Airing in the early morning on weekdays, small children watched it before school. Starting on April 24th, 1972, it began airing a five minute mini-tokusatsu segment. The first of these bite-sized programs was **REDMAN**, named after the scrapped early name for Ultraman. The show, lensed on 16mm reversal film, was a cheap bit of business with the eponymous hero, portrayed by Mamoru Kusumi, battling a usual monster. All the suits Tsuburaya Pro had stored away from the Ultra series and Mirrorman were rolled out to depict these creatures. *Redman* is below the quality of Tsuburaya Pro's full-length programs but boasts a creative exuberance the company was known for.

Redman's successor on *The Good Morning! Kids' Show,* which began airing on October 5th, 1972, was **GODMAN**. While *Redman* was far from the best tokusatsu TV program, it seems like a television masterpiece compared to *Godman*. Produced by Toho, *Godman* is a depressingly poor affair. The series makes the studio's upcoming *Godzilla vs. Megalon* look like a Stanley Kubrick production. *Godman* features flatly directed, artlessly shot monster battles between a low rent Ultraman knock-off and decaying suits from Toho's storehouse. These include the Gargantuas, Gabara and Gorosaurus. Only Godman Himself, modeled by Nobuyuki Yasumaru, was newly created. This show scarcely meets even the low standards of kiddie programming, feeling more on par with an amateur film. Yet there's an ironic, trainwreck-like 1970s charm to *Godman*.

Godman would be followed by **GREENMAN** on *The Good Morning! Kids Show* beginning on November 12th, 1973. *Greenman* is a step up from *Godman* with improved production values. Unlike *Redman* and *Godman* which were plotless monster battle segments, *Greeman* has an ongoing narrative, albeit a thin one. Influenced by the *Devilman* and *Exorcist*-fueled "Occult Boom", *Greenman* features demented Judeo-Christian and occultist themes. Its villain is a tokusatsu version of Satan, desperately trying to collect the blood of children for his resurrection. Greenman himself is an angelic *kyodai* (giant) hero sent by God to protect kids from Satan. *Greenman* is a more polished and elaborate mini-show than *Godman*, though old Toho costumes are still used, including the Minilla suit. Greenman's suit was created by Keizo Murase's firm Twenty. Following *Greenman* on *The Good Morning! Kids' Show* was **GO! KOTARO USHIWAKA,** which aired from November 1974 to April 1975. It takes the monster battle formula and transplants it to old Japan with a ninja hero and yokai-themed adversaries.

Another Toho-produced tokusatsu program was **ASSAULT! HUMAN!! [Television Run (Japan):** October 7th - December 30th, 1972], which aired for only 13 episodes. It was a *Kamen Rider*-style series with designer Toru Narita as main art director. *Assault! Human!!* aired in the same slot as *Kamen Rider* and as a result suffered miserable ratings. In a first for tokusatsu, the program was shot on videotape rather than film and broadcast live with entirely in-camera stage effects. Sadly, *Assault! Human!!* is lost as the master tapes were recorded over by accident.

Besides *Assault! Human!!*, three other tokusatsu programs found their way to the airwaves in the month of October 1972, with **THUNDER MASK [Television Run (Japan):** October 3rd, 1972 - March 7th, 1973] coming first. *Thunder Mask* was to be a live action adaptation of Osamu Tezuka's 1959 manga *The Devil Garon*. Tezuka's company was to produce it in an attempt to break into tokusatsu television. A pilot was produced in 1971, but it was not greenlit and later taken over by a smaller company, Hiromi Productions. Elements from *The Devil Garon* would be used but the story changed.

Thunder Mask is an underappreciated and underrated gem of a show employing top talent. As with the 1959 *Mighty Atom*, it represents another collaboration between Tezuka and a *Godzilla* luminary, this time Ishiro Honda who directed several episodes. Toru Narita was to act as the special effects art director but was occupied with *Assault! Human!!* and couldn't participate. Though already busy with *Kamen Rider*, Michio Mikami assumed the duty for *Thunder Mask*. Equis Productions took on the modeling of the various monsters, though they had to mobilize all their staff to do so.

Thunder Mask features a complex, well-written backstory and world building. The hero, Thunder Mask, travels to Earth to halt the invasion of the evil Dekanda. Due to Newtonian time dilation traveling from his distant planet to Earth, he arrives on our world in the stone age. Thunder Mask thus has to go into hibernation until the present day, when he's awakened by the heroes. He walks the Earth in the human form of Koichi Inochi (Kazutaka Sugawara). There's the usual Science Patrol organization and the villain Dekanda, basically a devil lizard from hell, looks like a *Star Trek* Gorn via the Master in *Manos: The Hands of Fate* (1966). Thunder Mask, as with Spectreman, can battle in both human-sized and giant kyodai forms. Like the eponymous hero in *Zone Fighter*, in which Ishiro Honda also had a hand, Thunder Mask goes through a second round of transformation for his kyodai hero form.

Thunder Mask was designed by **HIROSHI UEYAMA**. Dekanda, himself a pawn of the devilish Bem King, was created by manga artist and former Mushi animator **MAKIHO NARITA** (1945-), who also designed the show's monsters. The effects unit was run by a little-known director named **KEIJI KANEDA** who is granted the full-fledged "special effects director" credit. *Thunder Mask* features heavy miniature work for TV with FX footage as good as that being done at Tsuburaya Productions. In kyodai form, Thunder Mask himself was portrayed by Kenpachiro Satsuma.

Thunder Mask was popular in Japan and got good ratings but the program ended after 26 episodes. With its limited staff, it was becoming too difficult to produce. Osamu Tezuka was also allegedly unhappy with it. *Thunder Mask* was never released on home video because of rights disputes between Hiromi Productions and co-producer Toyo (currently Sotsu) Agency. A good portion of *Thunder Mask*'s episodes are now believed to be lost.

Three days after *Thunder Mask*, another tokusatsu show from Toho began airing on NET: **WARRIOR OF LOVE: RAINBOWMAN** [Television Run (Japan): October 6th, 1972 - September 28th, 1973]. *Rainbowman* was a comeback for *Moonlight Mask* and *Messenger of Allah*'s creator Kohan Kawauchi. It centers around a professional wrestler named Takeshi Yamato (Kunihisa Mizutani) who develops the ability to transform into a superhero form after studying in India with legendary yogi Devadatta (Shobun Inoue). Inspired by Indian, Chinese and Islamic motifs, Rainbowman boasts seven different costumes inspired by various elements which he later develops the ability to combine. Rainbowman's enemies are the "Die Die Gang" headed by Mr. K (Akihiko Hirata), a terrorist group attempting to punish Japan for its atrocities in World War II.

Warrior of Love: Rainbowman (1972-73) title card

The show boasts plentiful optical animation and occasional miniature effects including a Guignol-style puppet of the hero. The special effects end on *Rainbowman* was mainly supervised by Sadamasa Arikawa, who was often at odds with Kohan Kawauchi. Regardless, Arikawa enjoyed the challenge of creating special effects and miniature photography on a television budget. *Rainbowman*'s numerous costumes were created by Eizo Kaimai's company. His team, composed of art college interns, wanted to use leather in the costume's construction, but the budget could not provide for such a luxury. Kaimai himself thus went to a Tokyo tailor shop and purchased the best vinyl imitation leather he could find, even having the shop begin sewing the costumes.

Rainbowman aired for 52 episodes. Its ratings were decent and the manga adaptation by Mitsuru Adachi was even more popular. *Rainbowman* would be an influence on the following year's popular anime and manga series *Cutie Honey* by up-and-coming Go Nagai. Kohan Kawauchi's follow-up tokusatsu TV program would be **DIAMOND EYE** [**Television Run (Japan):** October 5th, 1973 - March 29th, 1974], also produced by Toho for NET. Kawauchi's final significant effects show was **CONDORMAN** [**Television Run (Japan):** March 31st - September 22nd, 1975], produced at Toei and ran on NET for 24 episodes. Nobuo Yajima and his Tokusatsu Research Institute would anonymously participate. Kawauchi would soon become a prominent government official for the Liberal Democratic Party. His love of other cultures made him a valuable advisor in foreign affairs.

Two days later, another new show joined *Rainbowman* and *Assault! Human!!* on Japanese airwaves: **IRON**

KING [Television Run (Japan): October 8th, 1972 - April 8th, 1973]. *Iron King* was ad agency Senkosha's second tokusatsu show after the failure of *Silver Mask*. *Iron King* was successful with a spirited performance at first. The series, conceived by frequent *Ultraman* scribe Mamoru Sasaki, featured directorial contributions from Gamera's Noriaki Yuasa. Primarily overseeing the effects work was Koichi Takano with support from **KIYOSHI SUZUKI** (1942-). Suzuki had gotten his start at Tsuburaya Productions, helping Eiji shoot his contribution to Kon Ichikawa's *Alone Across the Pacific*. Suzuki had acted as assistant director and cameraman on many of Tsuburaya's shows from *Ultra Q* on.

Iron King is an entertaining show with surprising creative flourish. The villains are the Shiranui Clan, a secret society descended from Japan's earliest peoples plotting to punish the Yamato Japanese for having persecuted them. Our heroes are the Spaghetti Western-style lone wolf Gentaro Shizuka (Shoji Ishibashi) and the comic relief sidekick Goro Kirishima (Mitsuo Hamada). To combat the Shiranui's ancient robots, the goofy Kirishima transforms into the giant hero Iron King. This is often with the assistance of Shizuka who possesses an "iron belt" that can be used as a weapon against the monsters. The Shiranui clan is defeated in episode #10, replaced by the anarchistic Phantom Militia and then the alien Titanians. *Iron King*'s action scenes have a low budget martial arts film-like madness and its tokusatsu sequences are inventively lensed for television. Unfortunately for Senkosha and TBS, a popular new anime show, the Go Nagai-created *Mazinger Z*, began to air during *Iron King*'s timeslot. The ratings for *Iron King* slipped and fell into the dismal single digits. Thus the show ended after only 26 episodes on April 8th, 1973.

At the 10th Champion Matsuri Festival that holiday season, **DAIGORO VS. GOLIATH** [Director: Toshihiro Iijima - Release Date (Japan): December 17th, 1972] was unveiled alongside a re-release of *Destroy All Monsters*. A collaboration between Tsuburaya Productions and Toho, the two companies had planned *Godzilla vs. Redmoon*. Set to pit Godzilla against vengeful monster parents Erabus and Redmoon in Okinawa, the project was to be directed by Shohei Tojo. Toho were even planning to send Tsuburaya Pro the Godzilla suit from *Son of Godzilla*, but *Godzilla vs. Redmoon* was canceled for reasons unknown. This failed project, however, gave rise to *Daigoro vs. Goliath*. Atsushi Oki, aided by Minoru

Nakano, was chief of the effects unit on the film.

Daigoro vs. Goliath is a cut above the recent Gamera pictures. Per Tsuburaya Pro's involvement, there's a creative whimsicality also missing from Toho's *Godzilla vs. Gigan*. Starring Hiroshi Inuzuka of The Crazy Cats, its deliberate comedy makes the absurdities an easier sell. The tone is lighthearted with similarities to *Chitty Chitty Bang Bang* (1968). Other moments feel like a live action Hayao Miyazaki film. Incidentally, *Daigoro vs. Goliath* was also co-billed with *Panda! Go Panda!:* written and designed by Miyazaki. Atsushi Oki's work on *Daigoro vs. Goliath* is surprisingly solid with fanciful composites for the picture's budget.

Modeling veteran Ryosaku Takayama with a rotting monster head

The baby monster Daigoro himself is a stupid but adorable creation, sharing a name with wandering samurai Ogami Itto's son in Kazuo Koike's popular manga *Lone Wolf and Cub*. Daigoro is well manipulated with animatronic parts in the suit's head. Echoes of the character can be seen in *Godzilla vs. Spacegodzilla* (1994)'s Little Godzilla, with similar execution and some nearly identical shots. Daigoro, his mother and dinosaurian alien foe Goliath were all designed by Kako Yonetani. The suits, mainly built by Ryosaku Takayama, are well made.

The final showdown between Daigoro and Goliath is a fun sequence with odd moments of visual majesty. Overall, *Daigoro vs. Goliath* is an above-average children's film. It does, however, end with Daigoro taking a literal monster shit in a giant water closet, an idea even Noriaki Yuasa might have cringed at. *Daigoro vs. Goliath*'s lighthearted tone and childlike humor would no doubt influence Tsuburaya Productions' next Ultra show, *Ultraman Taro*.

With Eiji Tsuburaya gone and Daiei liquidated, only a handful of Japanese special effects films were being made for theatrical distribution. Yet monsters along with *henshin* and *kyodai* heroes were in vogue again on TV and Tokusatsu cinema would soon be revitalized by the production of a hit film from the apocalyptic mind of novelist Sakyo Komatsu.

XIX.
1973
昭和四十八

The first 1976 English pressing of Sakyo Komatsu's novel *Japan Sinks* (1973)

In 1973, the news cycle was dominated by coverage of the Watergate scandal involving U.S. President Richard Nixon's administration. The nearby Vietnam War was winding down as the U.S. began to withdraw its forces in defeat. An oil crisis was to come later in the year, hitting the Japanese economy particularly hard. A horror film entitled *The Exorcist* was released in America at year's end, terrifying audiences worldwide as it brought cinematic shock to new heights. In Japan, an apocalyptic science fiction novel by Sakyo Komatsu called *Japan*

Sinks was on the bestseller charts for months on end.

The "Henshin Boom" continued with a bang as two new Tsuburaya Productions shows began in January: **FIREMAN** [Television Run (Japan): January 7th - July 31st, 1973] and **JUMBORG ACE** [Television Run (Japan): January 17th - December 29th, 1973]. Both were similar in style and creative spirit to the prior *Mirrorman*. Hajime Tsuburaya would tragically pass weeks after their premieres at only 41. The stress of running the company had worsened Hajime's diabetes and high blood pressure. On February 9th, he developed a cerebral hemorrhage and collapsed, dying afterward in the hospital. Noboru Tsuburaya was now in charge of Tsuburaya Productions.

Fireman is another inspired offering from Tsuburaya Pro, produced in collaboration with advertising firm Mannensha which had partnered with Toho on *Rainbowman*. The program was intended as a return to a harder sci-fi aesthetic than the fantastical Ultraman shows. Involving another kyodai hero from a lost underground volcanic civilization, its subterranean dinosaur monsters foreshadow future Tsuburaya works like *The Last Dinosaur* (1977) and *Dinosaur War Izenborg*, which would use stock footage from *Fireman* in its opening. As usual, there's another Science Patrol-like organization with *Thunderbirds*-style vehicles. *Fireman*'s cast includes Shin Kishida (who also wrote episode #12) and Goro Mutsumi, both of whom would soon co-star in Toho's *Godzilla vs. Mechagodzilla* (1974).

Most impressive are *Fireman*'s special effects sequences, among the best executed on TV to date. The effects unit was mainly helmed by Atsushi Oki and Kazuo Sagawa, showing off some of their finest work. Art direction was headed by **KAZUMASA OTANI** and Noriyoshi Ikeya. *Fireman* features impressive optical VFX courtesy of Minoru Nakano and nearly theatrical quality miniature work. Unfortunately, the ratings for *Fireman* were abysmal as it shared a timeslot with popular anime sitcom *Sazae-San* and was discontinued after 30 episodes.

Jumborg Ace was more successful and ran for 50 episodes. Its origins go back as far as 1966 to a concept that Eiji Tsuburaya had been developing. Young writer **SHIGEMITSU TAGUCHI** (1944-) created a proposal in 1969. *Jumborg Ace* revolves around air delivery man Naoki Tachibana (played by an actor also named Naoki Tachibana). As his Cessna is downed during an attack from a monster sent by the evil Groth aliens, Tachibana is rescued by an Ultraman-style extraterrestrial. Tachibana is given the ability to transform his plane into Jumborg Ace, a giant humanoid robot.

Drawing influence from Go Nagai's *Mazinger Z*, Tachibana pilots Jumborg Ace from inside a cockpit with a movement-controlled suit. Starting in episode #27, Tachibana also acquires a car which turns into Jumborg 9, another giant robot. Jumborg Ace was designed by Kako Yonetani and modeled by Kaimai Productions, who embellished the head with car antennas. Tetsuzo Osawa headed the art department for the special effects unit and also designed Jumborg 9. Osawa and Yonetani also designed many of the show's monsters.

Jumborg Ace (1973) title card

Much of *Mirrorman*'s staff returned for *Jumborg Ace*, including director Yoshiyuki Kuroda who helmed a dozen episodes. Shohei Tojo and Toshitsugu Suzuki also directed. Atsushi Oki, on both *Fireman* and *Jumborg Ace*, would lead the main unit on certain episodes and the effects on others. On *Jumborg Ace*, the special effects unit was mainly handled by Nobuo Yajima and Koichi Takano. Both were now drowning in television work and going back and forth between studios. Once again, Yajima worked often with Kuroda's main unit and the two developed a better creative synergy than in *Mirrorman*. Yajima's sequences in *Jumborg Ace* are his most inventive and creatively directed yet. Support also came from Yoichi Manoda and **YOSHIYUKI YOSHIMURA**. Most impressive of all is the miniature work. Once again, there's another Science Patrol-style team, PAT (Protective Attack Team), who execute their duties in sleekly designed *Thunderbirds*-style mecha. These were the work of

SHIGEO KURAKATA, who began as a mechanical designer under Toru Narita in *Ultraman*.

Jumborg Ace would lead to Tsuburaya Pro's next co-production, this time with Thai company Chaiyo. Chaiyo's founder was named **SOMPOTE SAENGDUENCHAI** (1941-2021). Saenguenchai had been mentored by Eiji Tsuburaya himself. Years later, this would come back to haunt Tsuburaya's offspring. As a student, Saenguenchai had visited the sets of Toho films such as *King Kong vs. Godzilla* and *Son of Godzilla*. Like Run Run Shaw turning to Nihon cinematic technology for his Greater Chinese movie empire, Saenguenchai longed to bring Japanese-style filmmaking to Thailand.

On March 9th, 1973, Chaiyo released *Tah Tien*, a monster fantasy film featuring a pair of battling giants from Thai mythology: Yak Wat Jaeng and Yak Wat Pho. *Tah Tien* was a top-grossing domestic film in Thailand that year. Its success spurred a collaboration between Chaiyo and Tsuburaya Productions: **JUMBORG ACE AND GIANT [Director:** Shohei Tojo - **Release Date (Thailand):** March 16th, 1974]. *Jumborg Ace and Giant,* unreleased in Japan, teamed Jumborg Ace with Yak Wat Jaeng and Yak Wat Pho, pitting them against adversary Jumkiller. Kazuo Sagawa ran the effects team on *Jumborg Ace and Giant*.

There's an unpolished, *Turkish Star Wars*-like dementedness to *Jumborg Ace and Giant* owing to its Thai origins. Yet the effects work, distinctively Japanese in its spectacle, is well executed with elaborate optical animation and plentiful pyrotechnics. The optical photography supervisor was **TAKESHI MIYANISHI** (1942-) who had studied under Motoyoshi Tomioka at Toho and worked for Tsuburaya Pro. Miyanishi would soon take Hiroshi Mukoyama's place as head of optical effects photography at Toho starting with *Godzilla vs. Megalon*.

Toei, meanwhile, swiftly followed *Kamen Rider* up with a sequel series, **KAMEN RIDER V3 [Television Run (Japan):** February 17th, 1973 - February 9th, 1974]. This new program has tight continuity with the first and picks up where it left off. Toei's brass had contemplated creating a third Kamen Rider character in the latter half of the first show: Jiro Chiba's popular supporting character Kazuya Taki was nearly made into the third Rider. It was decided to hold off and introduce a novel character for a new series. Starting with *Kamen Rider V3*, Toei switched to a similar "yearly show" format to the *Ultraman* franchise.

The name "V3" has its origins in the English word "victory" and the fact that this new Rider is the third. The new protagonist is Shiro Kazami (Hiroshi Miyauchi), his villainous foils being Destron, reformed from the remnants of Gel-Shocker. They haven't gotten any less dementedly sociopathic though, wearing black klansman robes in the first episode and brutally butchering Kazami's family in a moment probably a little traumatic to Japanese tykes. Kazami is voluntarily transformed into the third Rider by Takeshi Hongo and Hayato Ichimonji. The two wind up temporarily departing the show after defusing a nuclear weapon at sea similarly to *The Dark Knight Rises* (2012). They would return for guest appearances.

Summer 1973 Toei Manga Festival poster

To design the red-masked V3, Shotaro Ishinomori took inspiration from dragonflies. Once again, the mask was sculpted from FRP. Later in the series' run, Destron scientist Joji Yuki (Takehisa Yamaguchi) is betrayed by General Yoroi (Bunya Nakamura) and loses his right arm. He's transformed into the cyborg Riderman and swears revenge on Destron, eventually aiding Kazami/V3. Unlike the other Riders, the bottom half of Riderman's face is exposed, giving him a distinctive appearance. The action and mix of tokusatsu theatrics and stunt work of *Kamen Rider V3* is even better executed than in the first show. The opening features a constant stream of explosions erupting every few feet around the hero, a sight that might make Teruyoshi Nakano blush. According to actor Hiroshi Miyauchi, the amount of gunpowder used in the show was threefold that of the previous program.

The crew's obsessive gunpowder use would get them into trouble when shooting the short spin-off **KAMEN RIDER V3 VS. DESTRON MUTANTS** [**Director:** Minoru Yamada - **Release Date (Japan):** July 18th, 1973]. The short was shown alongside the popular anime feature *Mazinger Z vs. Devilman* at the Toei Manga Festival. In *Kamen Rider V3 vs. Destron Mutants*, physicist Dr. Okita (Hideo Nihei) discovers the aptly named isotope "Satanium", coveted by Destron to mass produce nuclear weapons. Destron's Doktor G (Jotaro Senba), naturally, tests a sample of Satanium on human guinea pigs Unit 731-style. The short also features ample embedded marketing for the Sunflower ferry line, also featured in the upcoming *Godzilla vs. Mechagodzilla*.

Overall, *Kamen Rider V3 vs. Destron Mutants* is well directed and benefits from action sequences in the polish of Cinemascope. Moments, like V3 cruising down temple steps on his motorcycle, feel like coolness distilled. The Hongo and Ichimonji Riders make a surprise guest appearance, though not in human form. The three Riders battle another army of Destron's mutants in the usual quarry. While shooting an explosive scene at the Muroto peninsula on the locale of Shikoku Island, the crew used so much gunpowder that it cracked the cape's rocky surface, damaging the local ecosystem. The fishermen, who had given the filmmakers permission, were furious as fishing did not recover for years.

At Toho's own Champion Matsuri Festival, the newest Godzilla entry was **GODZILLA VS. MEGALON** [**Director:** Jun Fukuda - **Release Date (Japan):** March 17th, 1973]. Teruyoshi

Nakano returns to helm the effects unit and, despite the film's poor reputation, begins to find his footing and pulls off livelier work. The picture was shot in only three weeks with the lowest budget yet and was grueling on its staff. *Godzilla vs. Megalon* is a controversial entry; fans are torn over whether it's the worst, second worst or third worst Godzilla movie. In reality, it gets a worse rap than it deserves and is a step up from *Godzilla vs. Gigan*. As TV Tropes would say, it takes refuge in its audacity. By now, things are so ridiculous that it feels anarchic. As such, *Godzilla vs. Megalon* is hard to hate.

Teruyoshi Nakano's FX unit doing what it did best

Fittingly, the credits run over explosions courtesy of Nakano's unit who by now were probably suffering long-term hearing loss. An opening sequence of a draining lake is surprisingly effective with a good conformity between Nakano's miniature shooting and actor footage from Fukuda's unit shot at Mount Fuji's Lake Motosu. It was the dead of winter and the lake was frigid. As Fukuda and the crew drank spirits to keep themselves warm, little Hiroyuki Kawase was stuck in the middle of the lake in freezing agony. On Nakano's end, this scene is his best FX sequence thus far. Throughout the film, Fukuda keeps the human action going at a good clip.

The new insectoid monster Megalon was played by **HIDEO DATE**. The creature is sent to flatten Tokyo by Seatopia, an ancient civilization with dancing high priestesses in '70s lingerie. Originally conceived in Takeshi Kimura's *Godzilla vs. the Space Monsters* treatment, Megalon was built by Nobuyuki Yasumaru. Similiarly to

Hedorah, the suit was very heavy, with wings built from bath mat sponge. The veins that run across Megalon's skin were created by pasting and painting over yarn. The hand drills were hewn from FRP. With Nakano's smaller crew and the suit's weight, pulling it around on wires was particularly laborious.

The heroic robot Jet Jaguar was originally called Red Alone, named in a contest by an elementary student. Intended to cash in on the tokusatsu hero boom, the robot's grinning grill was likely a nod to the popular *Mazinger Z*. Played by **TSUGUTOSHI KOMADA** (1948-) and **MASACHIKA MORI**, its head was sculpted from FRP by Yasumaru and his new apprentice **TOMOKI KOBAYASHI** (1948-2009). The body consisted of a wetsuit similar to the Ultraman costumes. It was custom-fitted to actor Komada and fixed together with rubber cement. The feet contained lifts to make Komada appear taller. Getting the suit on took around ten minutes. For the choreography of his fight sequences, Komada would occasionally integrate karate movies.

Modeling department head
Nobuyuki Yasumaru

Small dolls for flying shots were also made for Jet Jaguar and Megalon. For what essentially amounts to a guest appearance, a new Godzilla suit was built by Yasumaru and Kobayashi. For the first time, Haruo Nakajima did not return to play Godzilla; after Tsuburaya's death, he had struggled to maintain the will to continue, finally retiring after *Godzilla vs. Gigan*. Instead, the monster was portrayed by **SHINJI TAKAGI**. Godzilla was made more "cute", with big, dog-like eyes. These were given radio-controlled operations which Nakano's team struggled with, as they refused to work properly. This mechanism would be better used in future appearances. Gigan and its suit, along with actor Kenpachiro Satsuma, returned from the previous entry with repairs and renovations. Around this time, Nobuyuki Yasumaru would also create the "Wolf Guy" in *Crest of the Wolf* (1973), based on a popular manga by Kazumasa Hirai.

The middle act of *Godzilla vs. Megalon* is ungainly, though a sequence where Megalon smashes up a dam is well executed and a highlight. Shot on an outdoor miniature set, Nakano described it as the shoot's only luxury. This replica of Ogouchi Dam at Lake Okutama is another of Toshiro Aoki's finest miniatures. A young assistant director who got his start on *Godzilla vs. Megalon*'s production was **EICHI ASADA** (1949-), who ran tasks for Fukuda and Nakano's units. According to Asada, the dam sequence was ingeniously engineered. A water-filled tank was positioned above the miniature at an angle. Pins were used to keep it from spilling and eventually the effects crew pulled a rope to release the water.

The urban destruction scenes are weak, however, relying heavily on sloppy use of stock shots. Much of the same stock footage used in *Godzilla vs. Gigan* is again cut into the movie and entire minutes of the picture are devoted to reused images from Tsuburaya-era films. Nakano's unit mainly shoots footage of pyrotechnics exploding around Megalon which is intercut with repurposed footage. There are even significant shots reused from *Godzilla vs. Gigan*. When Megalon swats at jets from *Ebirah, Horror of the Deep*, badly matched cuts of Gigan's claws are used.

Godzilla vs. Megalon's final showdown takes up a third of the film's entire runtime. It's a fun shut-off-your-brain monster slugfest for one's inner eight-year-old. There's a stunning composite courtesy of Takeshi Miyanishi with Jet Jaguar inexplicably growing in size to battle Megalon. Per the paltry budget, it takes place in a vacant countryside dotted with mini bonsai and cedar trees. In one memorable scene, Jet Jaguar and Godzilla, to quote Johnny Cash, fall into a burning ring of fire, the best that Nakano's pyromaniacal unit could conjure. The film concludes with a song by Masato Shimon which cements the "tokusatsu television on the big screen" feel. *Godzilla vs. Megalon* is not a quality entry, but it's a lively and entertaining one. Godzilla's *Kamen*

Rider-style drop kick at the climax, also bitingly lampooned on *MST3K*, is perhaps the most embarrassing moment in the series so far. By now however, things have reached such a pass that it almost works cinematically.

A flop in Japan, *Godzilla vs. Megalon* was considerably more successful in the United States. In 1976, it was marketed well by grindhouse outlet Cinema Shares with a poster, inspired by De Laurentiis' current *King Kong*, of Godzilla and Megalon atop the World Trade Center towers. It would become the most viewed Godzilla entry stateside, airing on NBC during prime time heavily cut and hosted by comedian John Belushi in a Godzilla suit. By the 1980s, it was believed to be public domain. As a result, in the words of *Videohound's Cult Flicks and Trash Pics,* it "proliferated across the land" in hordes of low-grade VHS releases. These cropped 16mm transfers did the film few favors and contributed to *Godzilla vs. Megalon*'s poor standing abroad. High-definition transfers reveal a more technically polished movie. Its finale is actually impressive viewed in Cinemascope, a far cry from the mess seen on American home video or *Mystery Science Theater 3000*.

Zone Fighter (1973) title card

Shortly after, Toho debuted their next special effects show, **ZONE FIGHTER** [**Television Run (Japan):** April 2nd - September 24th, 1973], on NTV. *Zone Fighter* revolves around an alien family from the decimated Peaceland. Peaceland's conquerors, the GWAR-like Garogas, next set their sights on Earth. The "Zone Family" thus disguises themselves as the Sakimoris, a seemingly normal Japanese family. Their father, Yoichiro (*Ultraseven*'s Shoji Nakayama), is a toymaker, a fitting toy industry tie-in as by now, tokusatsu and toy production were becoming intertwined. His three children, Hikaru (Kazuya Aoyama), Hotaru (Kazumi Kitahara) and Akira (Kenji Sato) can transform into the heroes Zone Fighter, Zone Angel and Zone Junior, respectively.

Zone Fighter is capable of transforming into Ultraman-like kyodai form to battle the Garogas' "Terror Beasts". *Zone Fighter* is similar in setup, style and tone to the concurrent Ultraman shows but with subversions. Like Ultraman and Mirrorman, Zone Fighter can only stay in giant form for a short period of time, but can be recharged mid-battle. This is often achieved by Zone Angel and Junior in their rescue ship "Smokey." During the show's development, Zone Angel was also to grow to giant size, making her the first female kyodai hero, but this was scrapped.

Principal photography on *Zone Fighter* began in February shortly after *Godzilla vs. Megalon*'s concluded. Teruyoshi Nakano and the up-and-coming Koichi Kawakita were placed in charge of the effects unit with support from Yoshio Tabuchi and Shinichi Kamisawa. *Zone Fighter* features some of Nakano's most elaborate effects work to date, all nearly theatrical quality. Nakano enjoyed shooting in standard Academy instead of Cinemascope as he felt the taller frame benefitted the giant hero and monster adversaries' scale.

Toho's monster titan Godzilla makes frequent guest appearances. Fittingly, episode #4, the first featuring Godzilla, was directed by Ishiro Honda. The FX unit on this installment was handled by Koichi Kawakita, presaging his later involvement with the Godzilla series. Kawakita's sequences are energetically directed and again show talent. *Zone Fighter* makes one wish Kawakita had gotten to collaborate with Honda on a feature film. King Ghidorah makes a guest appearance in a pair of episodes with the original suit dusted off and used one last time. Gigan also appears in an installment fittingly directed by Jun Fukuda, who refused to even discuss *Zone Fighter* in interviews. Crazy Cats comedy director Kengo Furusawa also helmed several episodes.

Much of the art and mecha designs were handled by **HIROSHI KOMURA** (1938-). Komura had joined Toho in 1961 during production of *Mothra* and stayed on in the special effects art division. Komura's work on *Zone Fighter* would get him the opportunity to head the special effects art alongside Toshiro Aoki on the next two Godzilla entries. The miniatures on *Zone Fighter* were created by **TAKASHI NAGANUMA**

(1947-). Naganuma had begun his career on *Ultraman Ace* the previous year and had also built the miniaturized version of the pedaling "dolphin" boat that sinks into the lake in *Godzilla vs. Megalon*.

Zone Fighter himself was designed by **NOBUHIRO OKASAKO** (1942-), who had been mentored under Osamu Tezuka as an animator at Mushi Production. Okasako, who had worked on Toho's *Rainbowman*, did character design and animation direction for many anime franchises including *Cutie Honey* and *Space Battleship Yamato*. His only direction came from Mannesha producer **KIMIHIKO ETO** (1930-2003), who demanded that the character be visually similar to Ultraman. Nobuyuki Yasumaru's modeling team created the Zone Fighter mask along with many of the monstrous Terror Beasts. Support came from Keizo Murase's Twenty who built Wargilgar in episode #4. Occasional monster designs also came from Akihiko Iguchi who mainly created Wargilgar and Spyler.

The Godzilla suit created for *Godzilla vs. Megalon* was used in its *Zone Fighter* appearances with minimal modifications, including repairs to the radio-controlled eyes. Zone Fighter was portrayed by Mamoru Kusumi and **TATSUMI NIKAMOTO** (1953-). Nikamoto was a young stuntman also involved in Sonny Chiba's Japan Action Club. Like Kusumi, he would go on to play monsters in upcoming Godzilla entries. In guest appearances, Godzilla, given its own cave to live in by the Zone Family, was played by Isao Zushi and Toru Kawai. Both would don the suit again in *Godzilla vs. Mechagodzilla* and *Terror of Mechagodzilla* (1975), respectively.

Zone Fighter also features quality optical work created by **TADASHI KAWANA** and Kazunobu Sanpei. Fumio Nakashiro's successor in wire operation was Koji Matsumoto. *Zone Fighter* was Matsumoto's first job heading wire works. Matsumoto would go on to serve in this capacity for Nakano and Kawakita's units in coming years. Another technician to get his start on *Zone Fighter*'s production would be **OSAMU KUME** (1944-2011). Kume would apprentice under Tadaaki Watanabe in the handling of gunpowder and explosives. Though *Zone Fighter*'s ratings started off strong, by the show's halfway point, they had dropped into the miserable single digits. As a result, *Zone Fighter* ended prematurely after 26 episodes with the story left largely unresolved.

By now a powerhouse of special effects programming, Toei premiered another series only three days after *Zone*

Fighter: **ROBOT DETECTIVE** [**Television Run (Japan):** April 5th - September 26th, 1973]. Conceived by Toru Hirayama, *Robot Detective* combines elements of Toei's tokusatsu programs with the police procedurals popular on Japanese TV at the time; in particular, the long-running *Special Mobile Investigation Corps* and *Key Hunter*, which had moved away from Bondian spy elements to hardboiled police drama.

Robot Detective (1973) title card

Robot Detective is a unique show. The titular robot detective is K, who looks straight from Ishinomori's manga panels. K assists Tokyo police detectives Go Shinjo (Jiro Chiba) and the older, hard-nosed Daizo Shiba (Kaku Takashina), using his artificial intelligence-based cunning to solve crimes. These crimes are connected to yet another Shocker-like evil organization with world domination ambitions: the aptly named BAD. The Japan Action Club was also heavily involved with Sonny Chiba himself appearing early on as Detective Shinjo's older brother. Like a police procedural, *Robot Detective* features a legal disclaimer at the end of each episode.

Robot Detective boasts occasional tokusatsu unit flourishes. Unlike in *Kamen Rider* or *Transforming Ninja Arashi*, a separate effects unit was formed and used prominently. In the drama unit, **TAKASHI NAKAJIMA** played Detective K, whereas for battle scenes he was portrayed by JAC stuntman **OSAMU KANEDA** (1949-). K takes off his distinctively Ishinomori red blazer to assume combat mode in the stunt unit sequences. Akira Takahashi modeled K's suits. Miniature work was used to create the effect of K's flying car and occasional unconvincing but charming puppet mock-up cutaways. Also achieved through miniatures is a gigantic, robotic fortress called Mother which Detective K summons to replenish his energy during battles. The fortress is inhabited by K's literal "mother" and creator, lady scientist Dr. Saori Kirishima (Yuko Kimi).

K was also one of the first tokusatsu heroes to use a firearm as a weapon, which was controversial in Japan with its strict gun control laws. Running for 26 episodes, *Robot Detective* looks forward to Toei's upcoming Metal Hero cycle which tends to feature robotic heroes in police roles. *Robot Detective* also marked Ultra scribe Shozo Uehara's first foray into a Toei show. After scripting a pair of *Ultraman Taro* episodes, Uehara would stop writing for Tsuburaya Productions for now and move to Toei's programs.

Only a day after *Robot Detective* came the premiere of Tsuburaya Productions' next installment in the Ultra franchise: **ULTRAMAN TARO** [**Television Run (Japan): April 6th, 1973 - April 5th, 1974**]. Even compared to *Ultraman Ace*, *Ultraman Taro* represented a significant change in direction and tone. *Ultraman Taro* is best described as peak 1970s Ultraman. There's a similar ridiculousness to it as Toho's *Godzilla vs. Megalon*. It's hardly the zenith of the franchise, but many episodes manage to be a lot of ridiculous '70s fun.

Once again, Toho leant its soundstages to Tsuburaya Pro for *Taro*'s production. *Ultraman Taro* was also created and developed closely with players from the toy industry such as Bullmark. The monster toys from *Mirrorman* and *Ultraman Ace* were not selling well, so the focus was changed to promoting toys of the mechanical designs and heroes. The credits are fittingly played over a montage of Gerry Anderson-style miniaturized aircraft. Many of these mecha were sold as toys but not featured in the actual show.

Ultraman Taro (1973-74) title card

The show's utter absurdity makes it a nudge more entertaining than *Ultraman Ace*. *Ultraman Taro* revolves around aspiring boxer Kotaro (Saburo Shinoda) who, like Hayata, Hideki Go and Hokuto before him, is given the ability to transform into Taro, the sixth Ultra Brother. The Science Patrol's latest successor is ZAT (Zariba of All Territory) and its members wear more colorful red and blue uniforms. The show also introduces the popular character of the Ultra Mother, the matriarch of the Ultra family who gifts Kotaro with a badge to transform. Akihiko Iguchi designed Ultraman Taro and Eizo Kaimai's firm handled the modeling. Taro's suit actor was **HIROSHI NAGASAWA.** The construction of the show's numerous monsters was carried out by Kaimai and Equis Productions.

Ultraman Taro's highlight is surprisingly stellar special effects footage. Its FX sequences tend to be better than the program's reputation suggests. *Ultraman Taro*'s miniature work is a highlight in most episodes. The program also features striking composite shots throughout that could possibly pass in a feature film. The effects unit on *Ultraman Taro* was overseen by a variety of directors including Kazuo Sagawa, Kiyoshi Suzuki, Koichi Kawakita, Eizo Yamagiwa, Koichi Takano, Atsushi Oki and, in his first Ultra show job, Nobuo Yajima. All the show's effects directors bring their own unique sensibilities to the proceedings. Sagawa's work in the pilot is among his most inventive yet and nearly theatrical quality. Koichi Kawakita's FX footage continues to impress, clearly displaying a rising talent. Nobuo Yajima does some of his most dynamic television work to date with creative staging and shooting.

The moving final episode, its effects unit helmed by Atsushi Oki, is filled with explosive, Nakano-like set pieces and exhilarating tokusatsu battles that can make an adult viewer feel eight again. In a subversion of the franchise's usual tropes. Kotaro defeats the final alien monster without the aid of his Ultraman form. *Ultraman Taro*, even when it aired, had strong detractors. Older children and teenagers who grew up on the early shows felt the program was getting too childish and stopped watching. Little kids, however, ate the show's goofy theatrics up and thus the Ultraman franchise continued.

Meanwhile, Senkosha had been working on **SUPER ROBOT RED BARON [Television Run (Japan): July 4th, 1973. - March 27th, 1974]** which saw air on NTV. While the program was conceived before

Mazinger Z hit the airwaves, the legendary anime show would influence its direction. Sharing tropes with *Mazinger Z*, a young man, Ken Kurenai (Yosuke Okada) pilots Red Baron, a giant crimson robot. The villains are the usual evil outfit: the Iron Masked Party led by Dr. Deviler (Hiroshi Ikaida) and their monster robot army. The show features yet another team of on-the-ground allies, the SSI (Secret Science Investigation). *Super Robot Red Baron* features frequent martial arts sequences. These were added at the request of Toshio Kobayashi, the president of Senkosha, per the popularity of Bruce Lee.

Designed by manga artist **RYU NOGUCHI** (1944-), the suits for Red Baron and the Iron Masked Party Robots were expensive to make. Ryosaku Takayama's Atelier May and the company Hiruma Modeling were responsible for their construction. Hiruma Modeling was run by **SHINJI HIRUMA** (1932-). Mentored by Yoshio Irie, Hiruma had already built miniatures for Daiei's Gamera and war films, along with Tsuburaya and P-Productions shows. The Red Baron suit used for the flight and launch sequences was made from fiberglass. Carbon dioxide with lighting enhancement was used for the contrail effect from the feet. The robot suits for action scenes were built more durably from rubber.

In technical quality, *Super Robot Red Baron* contains the most spectacular special effects sequences on Japanese television yet. The miniature work in particular is astounding, always creatively and innovatively lensed and well orchestrated. *Super Robot Red Baron*'s images often resemble a live-action version of the '70s anime it was made to cash in on. For *Red Baron*, a special effects director was not used and the main directors helmed both the drama and FX sequences, though the crews were different. The show's directors include Kiyoshi Suzuki, Koichi Takano and Toshitsugu Suzuki.

Super Robot Red Baron's ratings began sluggishly but by episode #9 creeped into the double digits. The show could only run for 39 episodes, however, as its airline sponsors were suffering financial hardship and could no longer afford to fund it. Senkosha thus found new backers and produced a second follow-up show, **SUPER ROBOT MACH BARON** [Television Run (Japan): October 7th, 1974 - March 31st, 1975]. The toys were selling well but the ratings were beginning to sag and *Mach Baron* ended after 26 episodes. The special effects footage in *Mach Baron* is again innovative for television with high-quality miniature engineering and optical animation. In Taiwan, *Super Robot Mach Baron*'s effects footage would be edited into a film entitled *The Iron Super Man* (1975).

Shotaro Ishinomori would develop yet another special effects hero series for Toei: **INAZUMAN [Television Run (Japan):** October 2nd, 1973 - March 26th, 1974]. Originally called *Mutant Z* and envisioned in 1972, *Inazuman* is another fun program from the amiably twisted minds of Ishinomori and Toei's production committee. The show features interesting subversions from the standard henshin hero formula. Instead of a cyborg or magic ninja, Inazuman's alter ego, a college boy named Goro Watari (*Kikaider*'s Daisuke Ban), is a mutant with latent psionic powers.

Inazuman (1973-74) title card

Unlike Kamen Rider, Kikaider or Arashi, Watari has two superhero forms and rounds of transformation. To become the superpowered mutant Inazuman, Watari must first transform into the weaker Sanagiman. Sanagiman resembles Ben Grimm's alter-ego The Thing in Marvel's *The Fantastic Four* comics but was based on a larval pupa. In a very '70s touch, during the second transformation, Sanagiman explodes into Inazuman. This final form, his design motif based on a luna moth, is more colorful in costume than Kamen Rider. The Sanagiman and Inazuman suits were both modeled at Equis Productions and worn by *Transforming Ninja Arashi*'s Bunya Nakamura.

Inazuman also has parallels with Marvel's *X-Men* franchise. There's yet another Shocker-style evil organization on the rampage, the Neo-Human Empire ruled by the ghoulish Emperor Bamba. Like Magneto, they are evil mutants who believe themselves superior and wish to enslave humanity.

Of course, they have an army of gas-masked grunts who are enhanced with unsettling sound design. Defending against them are the Youth League, a benevolent group of young mutants run by the Charles Xavier-like Captain Saler (Hideo Murota), which Goro joins. Daisuke Ban's Goro is a more troubled character than the Riders, with a dark past.

Shotaro Ishinomori would direct episode #11 of *Inazuman*. Having also helmed episode #84 of *Kamen Rider*, Ishinomori again takes a break from his grind drawing up manga panels. His involvement even mentioned in the preview, Ishinomori's episode is one of the most downbeat and visually spectacular. Emperor Bamba turns Goro Watari's long lost mother (Yuko Hamada) into his newest, rose-themed monster. This cruelly tests Goro and almost breaks him. The episode features the show's most complicated visual trickery, kinetic madness and staccato editing and is loaded with trippy optical work and VFX, with segments even switching to black and white. Ishinomori's directing style is distinctive and much like Katsuhiro Otomo's live-action works, makes one wish he had helmed more films and TV.

Besides Ishinomori, much of *Kamen Rider*'s core staff returned for *Inazuman*, including writer Masaru Igami and directors Minoru Yamada and Katsuhiko Taguchi. Scripting support also came from Susumu Takaku and Shozo Uehara. *Inazuman* features more plentiful tokusatsu effects shots than *Kamen Rider* or *Transforming Ninja Arashi*. Inazuman rides around in a flying car with teeth, executed through miniature FX, called *Raijingo*. The show's opening features almost theatrical-grade composites. The miniature unit's spirited work was mainly handled by Tsutomu Yagi with art direction by **KATSUSHI MURAKAMI** (1942-), best known for his mechanical designs in anime and for the toy industry. Murakami would one day be CEO of the monolithic Bandai.

Inazuman ended up the least successful of Toei's Ishinomori-run tokusatsu shows. By its final episode, the "Henshin Boom" was dying down. Additionally, Japan, dependent entirely on petroleum imports, was hit hard by the October 1973 oil embargo placed on the country for its support of Israel in the Yom Kippur War. This set off the worst economic crisis in Japan since the end of World War II. The cost of film and TV production, to say nothing of petrochemical-based special effects materials, was driven up in an industry already suffering financially.

Inazuman's toys were selling well, however, particularly models of the *Rajingo*, so the show continued under the title **INAZUMAN F [Television Run (Japan):** April 9th - September 24th, 1974]. *Inazuman F*, like *Kamen Rider V3*, picks up where the first show left off for the continued adventures of Goro Watari. The villains are yet another Shocker-like organization, the Desper Army. Led by the Nazi-like Führer Giesel (Mitsuo Ando), it decimates the prior Neo-Human Empire and begins its attacks after Inazuman's defeat of Emperor Bamba. In an attempt to improve ratings, *Inazuman F* was given a darker tenor and more female characters were included. Action and special effects scenes were minimized to keep the budget down. Ratings remained unsatisfactory and the program ended after only 23 episodes. Years later, Ishinomori would reveal that he believed *Inazuman* was too ahead of its time and that the Japanese special effects industry lacked the resources and technology to properly depict the supernatural elements he had envisioned.

All the while, at the top of the bestsellers list in Japan throughout 1973 was a science fiction novel entitled *Japan Sinks* by Sakyo Komatsu. Komatsu had started writing it in 1964, on the heels of his popular debut novels *Japan's Apaches* and *Resurrection Day*. It would take him the greater part of nine years to complete *Japan Sinks*. The premise is simple, involving the apocalyptic submersion of the Japanese archipelago under the Pacific Ocean, playing into its culture's collective angst over the country's natural disaster-prone status and fears of losing national identity. The novel has proved prophetic as Japan, surrounded by water, stands to lose a great deal from climate change, which could worsen its prevalent geological disasters.

Miniature skyscrapers are readied for decimation like Buddhist sand mandalas

Sakyo Komatsu mentioned the book on a TV news show in 1972. Immediately after, Daiei's Masaichi Nagata announced a film, intended to revitalize his bankrupted company, entitled *The Sinking of the Japanese Islands*. Blatantly stealing Komatsu's concept, the project never came to light, either due to Daiei's dire financial straits or legal action. At Toho, the cunning Tomoyuki Tanaka had scooped up the book's rights before it was even published. In a June 6th, 1973 *Japan Times* article entitled **"Japan Submersion Book Having Great Popularity,"** Toho announced production of a film adaptation: "The popularity of the book prompted the Toho Motion Picture Co. to decide to make it into a film. Toho plans to spend about ¥500 million on the making of the film".

SUBMERSION OF JAPAN [Director: Shiro Moritani - Release Date (Japan): December 29th, 1973] was Toho's grandest scale special effects production since Eiji Tsuburaya's death. Fittingly, it would single-handedly revitalize big screen tokusatsu filmmaking. Tanaka brought in his company's finest talent to realize Komatsu's bleak vision; veterans of both Akira Kurosawa and Eiji Tsuburaya's teams. This included director Shiro Moritani and esteemed screenwriter Shinobu Hashimoto. Teruyoshi Nakano was given a budget that dwarfed his work on prior Godzilla entries and, finally, the same "special effects director" credit as his mentor. On *Submersion of Japan*, Nakano earns the title with possibly his finest work. Yasuyuki Inoue also returned to Toho's special effects unit, bringing his ingenious miniaturized engineering to *Submersion*'s apocalyptic spectacle. Working with close to a quarter billion yen, Teruyoshi Nakano's effects are nothing short of stunning. *Submersion of Japan* manages to be arguably the greatest tokusatsu film produced in the 1970s.

Though the FX crew got started earlier, *Submersion of Japan* began lensing on September 1st, the 50th anniversary of the Great Kanto earthquake. An early scene featuring the miniaturized submarine *Wadatsumi* exploring the Japan Trench is impressive. Even this sequence is superior to anything in *Godzilla vs. Gigan* or *Godzilla vs. Megalon*. The submarine was designed by Inoue and elements look forward to his mecha the Super-X in *The Return of Godzilla* (1984). Many of the miniature sets in *Submersion of Japan* were built to vibrate and shake mechanically. This doomed miniature Tokyo was constructed on an elevated platform to allow the placement of machinery and explosives to shake and destroy it.

Submersion of Japan's highlight is a scene where a monster earthquake batters the Kanto region and obliterates Tokyo. It is the greatest sequence of destruction of Nakano's career. As with Ishiro Honda and Eiji Tsuburaya in the Tokyo rampage in *Godzilla*, there is an excellent creative harmony between Shiro Moritani and Nakano's units for this lengthy scene. Nakano brings explosive doom to Tokyo while Moritani provides darker human casualty elements. Civilians are shown burned and gruesomely maimed with an intensity akin to a nuclear war film like *The Day After* (1983) or *Threads* (1984). To domestic audiences, who still live with the collective anxiety of an inevitable Kanto earthquake, this sequence was as existentially terrifying as *The Last War*'s climax had been 12 years prior. In one disturbing bit, a glass skyscraper, the recently built Kasumigaseki Building, breaks apart, its shards gruesomely impaling the faces of hapless bystanders.

Submersion's Tokyo earthquake features ingenious miniature work from Yasuyuki Inoue, who engineered structural weaknesses into many of the models. Nakano began to call him "Breaking Inoue" due to his skill in engineering miniature buildings that realistically broke apart. Inoue's protégé **NAOYUKI YOSHIMURA**, along with Takashi Naganuma, built numerous miniaturized props for this sequence, such as airplanes, boats, cars, billboard signs and houses. Tiny cars tumble realistically off crumbling bridges. Inoue obsessively kept work notebooks by this time. For *Submersion of Japan*, he studied geology to help him better engineer the film's visions of destruction.

Perhaps best of all, Nakano's unit gets to liberally do what it does best: blow things sky high. While shooting an intense oil refinery explosion created with napalm, the first take was an "NG" as Teruyoshi Nakano felt the blast was too small. Tadaaki Watanabe and assistant director **YOSHIO TABUCHI** thus increased the amount of napalm and gasoline. While the ensuing explosion pleased Nakano, it wound up searing the top of the special effects stage. According to assistant director Eichi Asada, by the end of each shoot day, the effects crew would be covered in soot and smoke from the violent sequences of destruction they staged. A type of coal-based cement powder called fly ash was mixed into the explosions for atmosphere and according to Asada, the staff suffered respiratory problems. The effects crew would go to a restaurant every night after shooting covered in black soot, enraging the eatery's staff as they dirtied the tables and chairs.

Later sequences in *Submersion of Japan* involving volcanic eruptions and massive typhoons are inventively executed and shot. Orange glowing images of flowing lava boast similar visual brilliance to Tsuburaya's nuclear destruction of Tokyo in *The Last War*. Like those in *The Last War*, these shots would be reused as stock footage in pictures to come. For Mount Fuji's explosive eruption, a 1/1200th scale miniature mountain was built inside Toho's Studio 7. DP Motoyoshi Tomioka shot it with a telephoto lens from outside the studio to give it a realistic perspective. Director Moritani demanded the sequence be redone by Nakano's unit just as they were tearing the set down. Another stunning shot, courtesy of Takeshi Miyanishi and Kazunobu Sanpei, is a disturbing panoramic Oxberry composite of doomed people fleeing volcanic eruptions around them.

In tokusatsu industry culture, a rite of passage as a special effects director is to successfully stage a flood. Teruyoshi Nakano and company not only beautifully stage several thrilling flood sequences but sink all of Japan in the process. To create these enormous waves in Toho's Big Pool, Nakano's unit often used a giant electric fan powered by a Cessna engine. An apparatus, designed by Yasuyuki Inoue, was also placed underwater in the effects pools. Another wheeled device was pulled through the FX pools, devised by Inoue years prior on *The Three Treasures*, creating floods by displacing water. A wide composite shot of an approaching tidal wave hitting coastal dwellings is eye-popping and seamlessly blends miniatures and optical printing. It is among Nakano's most masterfully executed images. Most impressive are satellite's-eye view vistas of the Japanese archipelago as volcanoes erupt and the islands sink into the sea. These shots, brilliantly engineered by Yasuyuki Inoue, were created with a variety of dyes, liquids and materials. Beer was pumped onto the miniature mockups to create the effect of smoke from the volcanoes and land submerging. Blue dyed liquor atop glass, rather than the usual gelatin, was used to make the water around it. Beer was also mixed into the water for flood sequences to make it look dirtier and more ocean-like.

Nakano's effects in *Submersion* best the work done close to a year later by Frank Brendel and Albert Whitlock on Hollywood's similar *Earthquake*. When *Submersion of Japan* hit American screens in 1975, it was retooled to cash in on *Earthquake*, with large swaths of plot and character development excised and new scenes featuring that film's star, Lorne Greene, were shot. This version, *Tidal Wave*, was given a savage review by *The New York Times:* "Because so little time is spent in the characterization of various participants in the disaster, one never really feels any sympathy for its numerous victims. What remains is a clinical, tedious apocalypse. Children may find such a spectacle entertaining."

Shooting impressive images of Japan's geological doom

In Japan, however, *Submersion* was the top-grossing film, selling a whopping nine million tickets. As *The Exorcist* terrified American audiences with its vivid depiction of demonic evil in late 1973 to early '74, the Japanese thrilled to their own collective nightmare. An eight-year-old boy from Tokyo named **SHINJI HIGUCHI** (1965-) would see *Submersion of Japan* with his father. Young Higuchi was captivated by its array of visually stunning, apocalyptic images. This boy was certain of his future: he would work in special effects.

Due to Toho's contract with Sakyo Komatsu, *Submersion of Japan* was made into a TV series simultaneously. Half a billion yen was again invested into it. To conserve resources, 16mm B-roll for use in the show was filmed on the set of the movie. Some of this footage, amusingly, wound up edited into the film version. With the exception of Keiju Kobayashi who played the role of Dr. Tadokoro in both the movie and show, the cast was different. The program's directors included Jun Fukuda and Eizo Yamagiwa and the special effects unit was run by Koichi Kawakita, Yoshio Tabuchi and Koichi Takano. With 26 hour-long episodes that aired from October 6th, 1974 to March 30th, 1975, this TV version of *Submersion of Japan* presents an uncondensed vision of Komatsu's novel. It includes many subplots cut from the movie along with soap opera-like drama. Each episode typically revolves around a particular area of Japan being submerged. The ratings were strong as people around the country would tune in to see their own local region destroyed. *Submersion of Japan* aired right after Tsuburaya Productions' *Army of the Apes,* also conceived by Komatsu.

Tomoyuki Tanaka was eager to make a sequel to *Submersion of Japan* focusing on the surviving Japanese people scattered abroad in the wake of their country's destruction. To be directed again by Shiro Moritani, this follow-up never made it to production for unknown reasons. Thanks to *Submersion*'s stellar box office, theatrical tokusatsu filmmaking would make an explosive comeback in 1974. Nakano's unit would be granted a slight budget increase for their next Godzilla entry and two more expensive disaster pictures were just around the corner.

XX.
__1974__
昭和四十九

The Exorcist was released in Japan in 1974, igniting an "Occult Boom"

February of 1974 saw the latest iteration of Kamen Rider hit Japanese airwaves: **KAMEN RIDER X [Television Run (Japan):** February 16th - October 12th, 1974]. *Kamen Rider X* revolves around Keisuke Kami (Ryo Hayami). He is transformed into the newest Rider by his father Professor Kami (Toho actor Jun Tazaki) to battle yet another evil organization. In classic Ishinomori form, they are called "GOD". This makes the show's dialogue sound hilarious with lines like "Tomorrow, our battle against GOD begins". The requisite disposable, creepy-sounding lackeys are present, though the overall tone is more upbeat.

The show's connection to previous installments feels looser at first, though the Riders would unite for the upcoming film *Five Riders vs. King Dark*. The classic character Tobei Tachibana appears as well, played by *Ultraman*'s Akiji Kobayashi, who feels like a common thread connecting the disparate worlds of Tsuburaya and Toei tokusatsu TV. For *Kamen Rider X*'s stunt unit, the Rider role was taken over by stuntman **TETSUYA NAKAYASHIKI** (1948-).

Kamen Rider X is more visual effects heavy and features the best creature modeling in the series yet with Equis Productions' Akira Takahashi in charge of creature creation. GOD's monsters are themed around mythical beings. These include Neptune, Medusa, Icarus, Prometheus and more. Though they still gleefully engage in atrocities, GOD feels like a kinder, gentler Shocker less evocative of real-world fascism. *Kamen Rider X* is a step down from the first two shows, feeling like more of the same but without the early programs' edgy dementedness. The ratings slipped quickly as the "Henshin Boom" was now waning and being displaced by robot anime shows like *Mazinger Z* and *Getter Robo*.

Not long after, Toho unveiled their next Godzilla film, **GODZILLA VS. MECHAGODZILLA** [Director: Jun Fukuda - **Release Date (Japan):** March 21st, 1974], again shown in the Champion Matsuri Festival. The first preview had been screened at the previous winter festival headlined by an edited version of *King Kong Escapes*. It was decided to set the action at Okinawa as Expo '75 was to be held on the island the following year and Tomoyuki Tanaka, having recently visited the area, thought it would make a refreshing backdrop. The unmade *Godzilla vs. Redmoon* and a concept from Yoshimitsu Banno set in Okinawa may have also influenced this decision. Thanks to Teruyoshi Nakano and his unit's stellar work on *Submersion of Japan*, the budget was given a bump and resources left over from that production proved useful on *Godzilla vs. Mechagodzilla*'s.

An underrated entry, *Godzilla vs. Mechagodzilla* is mindless but unadulterated cinematic cool catering to one's inner ten-year-old. It's among director Jun Fukuda's best Godzilla entries and features one explosive monster battle after another from Nakano. The direction of both units is a big step up from that of the previous year's *Godzilla vs. Megalon*. Nakano was now enjoying shooting in Cinemascope, which he and other effects staff had difficulty adjusting to in earlier years.

Teruyoshi Nakano

For *Godzilla vs. Mechagodzilla*, Fukuda and Nakano wanted to take the Godzilla series back to its darker roots in honor of the 20th anniversary. Tomoyuki Tanaka was, however, adamant that Godzilla stay a protector of Earth for the sake of child audiences. Inspired by Mechani-Kong in *King Kong Escapes* and the popularity of *Mazinger Z*, the character of Mechagodzilla was created so Godzilla could battle an evil version of itself. Sequences where Mechagodzilla rampages disguised as "Fake Godzilla" were wish fulfillment on Nakano's part. In his own words in *Japan's Favorite Mon-Star:* "Mechagodzilla reminded people of the bad Godzilla of the 1960s. We couldn't have made Godzilla the bad guy, because children wouldn't have liked it, so we created Mechagodzilla and acted out our feelings through it — we transposed our feelings of going back to the origins of the Godzilla series onto Mechagodzilla."

For a scene in the early moments where the monster Anguirus is shown in Siberia, baby powder was used as snow. Fittingly for Nakano's unit, the title and monster stars are introduced with explosive aplomb via literal pyrotechnics. As effects director, Nakano believed that his films' opening and ending sequences should impress.

The eruption of Mount Fuji, from which the disguised Mechagodzilla emerges, was originally to be a longer sequence. The piano wires reflected the light of the blast, forcing Nakano and his editors to cut it short. The script also called for Mechagodzilla to do battle with American forces at Okinawa. Nakano chose not to shoot this as Okinawa had been returned to Japan only in 1972 and the continuing presence of American troops was too sensitive an issue for a children's film. Another early sequence where "Fake Godzilla" ghoulishly snaps Anguirus' jaw isn't great with obvious wires. An oil refinery battle between the disguised Mechagodzilla and the real deal is a highlight. Employing surviving miniatures from *Submersion of Japan*, this is Nakano's best monster battle yet. It doesn't reach the heights of what Nakano could do on bigger budgeted pictures like *Submersion* and the upcoming *Prophecies of Nostradamus* but some shots are striking.

The Godzilla suit created for *Godzilla vs. Megalon* was used again for "Fake Godzilla". It looks better this time around with renovations and a new paint job. Isao Zushi would portray Godzilla and likely "Fake Godzilla" in solo scenes. For some scenes and individual shots, including those of Godzilla battling the incognito Mechagodzilla, a decidedly less effective suit created for promotional appearances was used. Mechagodzilla itself, unveiled in an eye-popping optical animation where Fake Godzilla's skin is burned off *Terminator*-style, was designed by Akihiko Iguchi. To envision Mechagodzilla, Teruyoshi Nakano took a hammer to a tin Godzilla toy to eliminate its seams. Iguchi was next tasked with the design, having made a name for himself while working with assistant director Koichi Kawakita on *Ultraman Ace*. Elements of European knight armor, kabuki costumes and military tanks were all incorporated into the design. Nakano and the effects staff even went to museums to examine medieval armor as reference.

The suit was constructed by Nobuyuki Yasumaru with help from Tomoki Kobayashi. Its head was built from FRP and the mouth given radio control. Much of the body was built from a polyethylene resin used in bath mats, the same as Mechani-Kong. Yasumaru and Kobayashi strove to outdo their previous work on Jet Jaguar. The Mechagodzilla suit was enhanced with vehicle parts, including motorcycle taillights for the eyes. The Mechagodzilla suit's paint job had to be retouched constantly as Nakano and Tadaaki Watanabe's constant barrage of pyrotechnics dulled it. Inside the costume was **KAZUNARI MORI**, who had gotten his start playing various monsters in *Jumborg Ace*. Mechagodzilla's posture while walking was inspired by the *hakama*, the trousers worn by samurai. A large doll of Mechagodzilla for flying shots was built from styrofoam and the legs were made to shoot freon gas.

The Anguirus suit from *Destroy All Monsters* was also dusted off for the creature's guest appearance one last time. A new beast, Okinawan guardian King Caesar, was designed by Akihiko Iguchi based on ceremonial *shisha* statues. These statues, similar to Japanese *kirin*, are a cultural descendent of Chinese "guardian lions". King Caesar was a contribution by Shinichi Sekizawa, who wrote the original treatment. Nobuyuki Yasumaru and Tomoki Kobayashi modeled its suit from rubber. As with Mechagodzilla, Caesar's eyes were made from a vehicle's taillight; fittingly, as the guardian beast uses his own eyes to reflect the beams paid out by the villainous robot's. Goat hair, purchased from a garment shop in Tokyo, was used for fur. Anguirus and King Caesar were both portrayed by Mamoru Kusumi. Kusumi claimed that playing Caesar was easier as the suit was lightweight.

Godzilla vs. Mechagodzilla features *Planet of the Apes*-like ape villains that have tokusatsu elements. Called "Black Hole Aliens", they're headed by the dastardly Kuronuma, played by Goro Mutsumi who would essentially reprise the role in the following Godzilla entry. They feel like a pastiche of what was popular on tokusatsu television: they're green-faced space apes a la *Spectreman*'s Dr. Gori but with the sociopathic sadism of *Kamen Rider*'s Shocker. Incidentally, stuntman Takanobu Toya, who played Gori, portrays a Black Hole Alien.

A scene filmed by Fukuda's unit, though with poor day-for-night shooting, features alien agent Yanagawa (Daigo Kusano) on board a ferry attempting to steal a statue from the heroes that awakens King Caesar. Teruyoshi Nakano's FX unit provided support with the character's gruesome transformation after being shot in the face. Actor Kusano had to sit still for five hours as the makeup was slowly changed and his face shot in stop motion. For a close-up where a Black Hole Alien's hand changes to its hairy green true form, assistant director Eiichi Asada stepped in to double as the hand. Asada also had to keep his hand still, held up by nails, for hours.

A major contributor to *Godzilla vs. Mechagodzilla*'s production was uncredited assistant director, Koichi Kawakita, who practically co-directed the FX end. Having cut his teeth on the Ultra franchise and *Zone Fighter* episodes, Kawakita was especially enthusiastic for *Godzilla vs. Mechagodzilla* as he loved robots and mechanics. He directed Takeshi Miyanishi and Kazunobu Sanpei in the creation of Mechagodzilla's optically animated beams.

The FX staff poses for a group photo upon the shoot's wrap on February 23rd: director Jun Fukuda is in the center, with Teruyoshi Nakano to his left

The exhilarating finale of *Godzilla vs. Mechagodzilla*, set at Okinawa's Cape Zanpa, is crammed with explosive eye candy and cinematic ecstasy for any child-at-heart with a love for 1970s camp. Truly explosive, as in segments Nakano and Tadaaki Watanabe set off a conflagration every second. Nakano drew influence from samurai films for *Mechagodzilla*'s climax and staged the finale similarly to a sword duel. In the best bit, partially ghost-directed by Kawakita, Mechagodzilla rains a fiery torrent of missiles and laser beams on Godzilla and King Caesar. As composer Masaru Sato's Morricone-like score blares, Nakano's unit brings the heat for a tour de force of animated rays and pyrotechnics. Mechagodzilla's prism-like beam was created by placing different colored animated layers together for a filter effect. This was faster than drawing the entire prism frame-by-frame.

Mechagodzilla's finale is the most violent monster battle in the series yet as Godzilla is bloodied with nearly Peckinpah-level intensity. Influence was likely drawn from Toei's gangster pictures as Kinji Fukasaku's *Battles Without Honor and Humanity* series was ongoing and extremely popular at the time of production.

Mechagodzilla's finger missiles, at one point impaled in Godzilla's hide, were made from wood and tin coating by Takashi Naganuma. The effect of Mechagodzilla hovering in the air, defeated by Godzilla's sudden, inexplicable magnetism, was difficult; much of the FX staff had to hold the suit up together. *Godzilla vs. Mechagodzilla* wrapped shooting in late February. It did better business than its predecessor, so the series would get another installment.

The final major TV show from P-Productions was **ELECTROID ZABORGER** [Television Run (Japan): April 6th, 1974 - June 29th, 1975], which aired for 52 episodes on Fuji TV. The day of broadcast was changed three times, first airing on Saturday, then Friday, then Sunday. As P-Productions was in dire financial straits due to the failure of *Tiger Seven*, they outsourced *Zaborger* to a smaller production company. *Electroid Zaborger* is the least interesting thus far of P-Productions' shows, though it uniquely subverts the tropes of *Mazinger Z* and *Kamen Rider*, of which it often feels like a fusion. It is also notable as a rare tokusatsu credit for manga artist **KAZUO KOIKE** (1936-2019). Best known for works like *Lone Wolf and Cub* and *Crying Freeman*, Koike is credited with the show's development. According to Tomio Sagisu and scriptwriter Shozo Uehara, however, Koike was barely, if at all, involved and his name was simply added for the sake of star power.

Electroid Zaborger revolves around secret agent Yutaka Daimon (Riderman's Takehisa Yamaguchi), whose scientist father Isamu (Jun Nagami) is murdered by yet another Shocker-style evil organization: Sigma. Sigma, likely a nod to the scrapped *Jaguarman*'s villain, is led by the vicious cyborg-implanted Dr. Akunomiya (Ken Okabe), who is trying, as per tradition, to conquer the world with cyborg monsters. From his father, Yutaka inherits Zaborger, a robotic warrior. Unlike in *Mazinger Z*, *Jumborg Ace* or *Red Baron*, Zaborger and Sigma's enemy cyborgs are human-sized. Rather than pilot Zaborger, Yutaka merely shouts voice commands. In what feels like a literal recombination of *Mazinger Z* and *Kamen Rider*, Zaborger can turn into a motorcycle form that Yutaka rides into battle.

Once again, thanks to the popularity of the late Bruce Lee, *Electroid Zaborger* is filled with Hong Kong-style martial arts action. Primary responsibility for the stunts and suit work fell to Eiichi Kikuchi and Takenobu Toya with **YOSHIRO TAJIRI** portraying Zaborger. Miniature effects appear occasionally and the mechanics of Zaborger are inventively executed. The modeling was handled by Yasuyuki Inoue's Alpha Planning, Hiruma Modeling and Ryosaku Takayama's Atelier May. *Ultraman*'s Toshitsugu Suzuki and *Gamera*'s Noriaki Yuasa would direct episodes of *Electroid Zaborger*. After the defeat of Sigma, Yutaka Daimon battles the prehistoric Dinosaur Army and its dinosaurian robots. Another secret agent joins Yutaka in the fight: Ken Matsue (Tatsuya Sakada), who rides Machine Bach, a bazooka-armed motorcycle. In a probable nod to the popularity of Go Nagai's *Getter Robo,* Machine Bach can merge with Zaborger into the more powerful Strong Zaborger. This also looks forward to the merging mecha in Toei's Super Sentai franchise.

A 14-year-old junior high student named **TOMOO HARAGUCHI** (1960-) got his start on *Electroid Zaborger*, getting inside the costume of an evil henchman. Haraguchi would soon develop a passion for monster suits. *Electroid Zaborger* would prove more profitable than *Tiger Seven* as Bullmark's toys of the robot sold well. Sagisu would next produce the five-minute children's program **ADVENTURES OF ROCK BAT** (1975). That would ultimately prove to be his swansong, though Sagisu would unsuccessfully pitch a pilot for a new tokusatsu program entitled *Silver Jaguar* in 1979 to '80.

Six days later, Tsuburaya Productions' next and final Ultra show of the 1970s, **ULTRAMAN LEO [Television Run (Japan):** April 12th, 1974 - March 28th, 1975], began airing on TBS. *Ultraman Leo* was to start airing on April 5th, but a production delay resulted in an extra episode of *Ultraman Taro* to tide audiences over. Parallelling the contemporary Godzilla entries, if *Ultraman Taro* and its '70s ridiculousness can be likened to *Godzilla vs. Megalon, Ultraman Leo* is analogous to the upcoming *Terror of Mechagodzilla* (1975), which also features actress Tomoko Ai. Amusingly, Ai went to her audition for that film and met Ishiro Honda in her MAC uniform from *Leo*. The tone of *Ultraman Leo* is almost shockingly dark. This direction was inspired by criticism from fans over *Taro* along with the popularity of apocalyptic movies like *Submersion of Japan*.

Ultraman Leo himself, unlike prior characters, is not a member of Ultraman's family but a different alien species from Nebula L77 who allies with the Ultramen. His alter-ego is Gen Otori (Ryu Manatsu) who, like Dan Moroboshi, walks the Earth as a Christ-like outsider. Gen can transform into Leo with the use of a ring. Dan

Moroboshi himself returns to *Ultraman Leo* as the leader of the new Science Patrol: MAC (Monster Attack Crew). Actor Koji Moritsugu was to have played a different character, but he insisted that Moroboshi be brought back. This connection to *Ultraseven* which shares *Ultraman Leo*'s darker feel is a major strength. Seven is badly crippled in the first episode battling a pair of monsters and Dan loses his ability to transform. He thus mentors Gen/Leo and the two have a rich dynamic. Jiro Dan's Hideki Go also makes a guest appearance in episode #34. *Ultraman Leo*'s dark tone is apparent from the first episode, which features Ultraseven's leg gruesomely maimed.

Ultraman Leo (1974-75)

Leo himself was designed by Yoshio Suzuki. As with the name, the character's visual appearance was lion-based. The suit was modeled by Eizo Kaimai's firm. Initially, Leo was played by **KAZUNORI KAWAGUCHI** in his first sequence. However, stuntman Tatsumi Nikamoto, soon to appear in *Terror of Mechagodzilla* as Titanosaurus, found the suit fit him better. So Nikamoto took over the role for the finale of episode #1 and continued for the remainder of the series. Leo's surviving brother Astra was portrayed by Mamoru Kusumi.

Chiefly overseeing the special effects unit on *Ultraman Leo* were Koichi Takano, Nobuo Yajima and Atsushi Oki, all of whom pull off their finest work. Tetsuzo Osawa handled the art direction and mechanical design on many episodes and his miniatures are top notch. Osawa would join Yajima's Tokusatsu Research Institute and work on numerous Toei shows in the coming years. In the pilot, Koichi Takano stages the most visually stunning flood sequence on tokusatsu television yet. Easily the most impressive scene of destruction yet produced for Japanese TV, it pays clear homage to the recent *Submersion of Japan*. The model shooting from Takano, Oki and particularly Yajima's unit is also the best on television thus far.

Nobuo Yajima's FX footage is reminiscent of the work he would do in *Message From Space* (1978). *Ultraman Leo* also features some of Yajima's finest sequences of miniaturized mass destruction. Most impressive are tiny cars swallowed up into mechanically engineered fissures. The program also features Yajima's most eye-popping composite shots. Atsushi Oki's work is also his best, featuring dazzling optical photography, a specialty of his. Minoru Nakano's Den Films, as usual, supplied the optical animations.

Ultraman Leo's edgier vibe even rubs off onto its main unit footage with wider lenses and more staccato editing than usual. Nobuo Nakagawa, famous for his fright pictures like *Ghost of Yotsuya* (1959) and *The Sinners of Hell* (1960), even helms a pair of J-Horror flavored episodes. In these, the director's flair is apparent with fittingly nightmarish touches like Dario Argento-style lighting and funhouse-like mirror filters placed over the camera lens. The end of episode #33 becomes downright hallucinatory and must have given the tykes at home a good scare. These episodes pair Nakagawa with effects director Nobuo Yajima. Even Yajima's unit draws influence and creative direction from the legendary Nakagawa with the use of expressionistic lighting.

Ultraman Leo is a step up from *Ultraman Taro*. The program's flaw is that it goes too far in the other direction. After a cathartic arc finale pitting and reconciling the Ultra Brothers against Leo and Astra, *Ultraman Leo* goes full George R.R. Martin in its 40th episode. Written by Shigemitsu Taguchi, episode #40 makes the show too morbid for its own good. During the birthday of Haruko (Tomoko Ai), the evil Saucer Aliens begin their invasion of Earth, led by Black Commander (Takeshi Obayashi), a Coffin Joe-like space creep with a crystal ball. Every member of MAC, including Dan Moroboshi, is annihilated, along with most of Gen's adoptive family in a Red Wedding-style bloodbath that feels just mean-spirited. Even the show's adorable little girl Kaoru (future anime voice actress Miina Tominaga) is unceremoniously killed off; the death of children being something even Toei typically avoided in their shows.

This was actually a panic decision on the part of Tsuburaya Productions' brass. Thanks to the ongoing oil crisis and sagging ratings, production on *Ultraman Leo* was getting a lower return on investment. It was thus decided to change it into a home drama in its final arc and this meant getting rid of many of its characters. *Ultraman Leo* was young Hideaki Anno's least favorite of the *Showa* Ultraman programs and yet most foreshadows the fatalism of his later *Neon Genesis Evangelion*. In *Ultraman Leo*'s finale, like his mentor Ultraseven, Gen reveals his true identity to Kaoru's older brother Toru (Tsunehiro Arai). The evil Black Commander is brought down by a group of angry schoolchildren before melting Wicked Witch of the West-style. *Ultraman Leo*'s ratings did not improve, though, and the franchise was temporarily retired after this final episode. It would not return for five years.

At the Toei Manga Festival, the newest big screen Kamen Rider adventure was unveiled: **FIVE RIDERS VS. KING DARK** [**Director:** Itaru Orita - **Release Date (Japan):** July 25th, 1974]. Released with the anime short *Mazinger Z vs. the Great Dark General*, *Five Riders vs. King Dark* is another amusing half-hour bringing Japanese superhero legends together to the delight of its child audience, *Avengers*-style. The Hongo and Ichimonji Riders join X in the fight against GOD, though actors Fujioka and Sasaki only appear via stock footage. V3 and Riderman, the latter having somehow survived his apparent death, also return. Equis' Akira Takahashi would model the new monster Bat Franken. G.O.D's archfiend King Dark is an impressive full-sized mechanical puppet with electronic enhancement. Built by Masamitsu Sakuma, this set piece also appears regularly in *Kamen Rider X*.

With *Five Riders vs. King Dark*, the franchise reaches its highest, most anarchic level of tokusatsu spectacle yet. The most visually stunning of the '70s Rider shorts, it features strikingly shot and kinetically edited bits. Blighting the action scenes are occasional shots revealing the studio ceiling, as the usual trampoline cuts had to be filmed indoors owing to unexpected rain. In the glory of Cinemascope, however, *Five Riders vs. King Dark*'s climax is like a battle scene in *Avengers: Infinity War* (2018) done ten times better via Toei's unhinged lunacy. With one Rider theme song after another being piped onto the soundtrack over the chaos, *Five Riders vs. King Dark* becomes almost impossible to follow. Viewers are again advised to shut off their critical minds and let their inner kids take hold as they drink in the spectacle of five battling heroes, which presages Shotaro Ishinomori's coming *Secret Squadron Gorenger* and the franchise it spawned.

While *Japan Sinks* had already been adapted into a big-budget blockbuster, another popular bestseller in 1973 had been *Great Prophecies of Nostradamus* by journalist **BEN GOTO** (1929-2020). Goto, a Christian, was influenced by Biblical prophecy along with the dire, Malthusian predictions of the time. With the visions of much-publicized French prophet Michel de Nostredame (Nostradamus) as a backdrop, the book provides grim predictions on the sustainability of the global food supply and the likelihood of thermonuclear warfare. Serving as an advisor was none other than Shinya Nishimaru of the Japanese government's Ministry of Agriculture.

Sensing a hit much like *Japan Sinks*, Tomoyuki Tanaka scooped up the rights, this time putting the entire world in Toho's apocalyptic crosshairs with a film adaptation: **PROPHECIES OF NOSTRADAMUS** [AKA: CATASTROPHE 1999 - **Director:** Toshio Masuda - **Release Date (Japan):** August 3rd, 1974]. Masuda, once a specialist in gritty potboilers at Nikkatsu, had taken over the direction of *Tora! Tora! Tora!* (1970) from Akira Kurosawa after going freelance.

Making films for both Toei and Toho, Masuda had a strong "hitmaker" reputation. He was fresh from directing **THE HUMAN REVOLUTION** [**Director:** Toshio Masuda - **Release Date (Japan):** September 8th, 1973], a biography of controversial *Soka Gakkai* founder Josei Toda, played by Tetsuro Tanba. One of the top-grossing domestic films of 1973 alongside *Submersion of Japan*, *The Human Revolution* even featured subtle contributions from Teruyoshi Nakano and his effects team.

Prophecies of Nostradamus is a preachy and melodramatic but endearingly strange eco-horror epic boasting gleefully fatalistic doomsday spectacle. Depicting a civilization falling apart due to slow-building ecological catastrophe, its science has relevance. The main character, Dr. Ryogen Nishiyama (Tetsuro Tanba again), ferociously drives its themes home in dialog like an apocalyptic gaia cult preacher, not unlike the actor's previous role in *The Human Revolution*. Tanba himself would become infamous for his *Dai Reien Kai* (Great Spirit World) New Age movement. In his approach to *Prophecies of Nostradamus'* narrative, director Masuda, who co-wrote the script without credit, channeled the terror he had felt after the atomic bombings and during the height of the

Cold War. When Masuda married his wife post-war, he was fairly certain the world would face nuclear annihilation and felt unsure if they should even bother having children.

Another major player in *Prophecies of Nostradamus* was its main screenwriter, *Godzilla vs. Hedorah*'s Yoshimitsu Banno. His script asks similar questions as *Hedorah* but with more scope. Again Banno drew influence from news stories, in this case that of a disturbingly high percentage of deformed children being born in Niigata Prefecture. *Prophecies of Nostradamus* even links environmentalist and anti-war sentiments, theorizing that ecological disaster could disrupt the food supply chain, straining international diplomacy and causing World War III. The most accurate and chilling prophecy comes towards its end: An earthquake destroys the Fukushima Daiichi power plant and floods the nearby prefecture with radiation, staged with pyrotechnic aplomb by Teruyoshi Nakano and his FX unit. Banno's script does offer hope that humanity might solve these daunting challenges and concludes that fatalism is more part of the problem than solution. This is evidenced in the heavy-handed final moments in which the Prime Minister (So Yamamura, who took on the role more than any other Japanese actor) assuages the audience with an FDR-like speech over tranquil images.

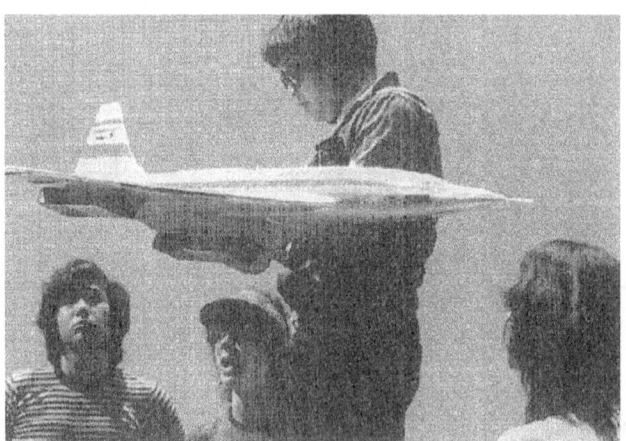

Wrangling a miniaturized SST jet, soon to be blown up

Prophecies of Nostradamus meditates on similar existential matters as Godfrey Reggio's non-narrative *Koyaanisqatsi* (1982). The difference is *Koyaanisqatsi*'s images of whizzing freeways, belching factories, war machines and urban sprawl merely suggest what *Prophecies of*

Nostradamus boldly asserts. Moments can also feel like an Italian *mondo* film with newsreel footage of genuine human suffering in Africa and second unit location shots helmed by Banno in New Guinea. Banno was enamored with the works of *Mondo Cane* creators Gualtiero Jacopetti and Franco Prosperi, particularly *Africa Addio* (1966). The voice of Kyoko Kishida, known for her title role in Hiroshi Teshigahara's *Woman in the Dunes* (1964), is heard coolly reading Nostradamus' prophecies over the apocalyptic chaos. *Prophecies of Nostradamus* also features a rocking score by Isao Tomita, soon to be best known for his synthesizer arrangements of Debussy and Holst, that perfectly compliments the picture's apocalyptic psychedelia.

Teruyoshi Nakano and his unit craft more fine scenes of destruction in *Prophecies of Nostradamus,* shot in May and June of 1974. Yasuyuki Inoue returned as art director and his miniature work is jaw-dropping, including snow-capped Egyptian pyramids and crumbling polar ice caps. The monster effects are well crafted, including chemically enlarged slugs. These were originally created by Keizo Murase, but Murase's models could not stand up to the heat from the sequence's pyrotechnics. Thus Nobuyuki Yasumaru remade them with fireproof organic glass. The monster slug models had motors installed in them to help them move and were pulled and steered with piano wire. For a scene in which mutated plants appear in Tokyo's subways, brackens and ferns were used alongside a miniature train. In the New Guinea sequence, there's an impressively executed bird-eating pitcher plant and vicious mutated bats that are more convincing than those in prior films. The effect is ruined only by a revealing still close-up of a decidedly unrealistic-looking dead bat. Wide vistas of oceans blighted with red tide and collapsing fishing stocks were created with the usual gelatin, though the coloring proved quite a challenge. Another scene depicting the freezing of the South Pacific used 25 tons of ice blocks.

A later shot of a tree and then the whole countryside browning from a torn-open ozone layer was created by spraying diluted sulfuric acid on cedar buds. Nakano was inspired by seeing trees brown in industrial areas. His crew at first tried using paint to discolor the leaves but felt it didn't look realistic enough. They also did not have time to kill the plant through dehydration. They thus tried soaking the soil under the plant with a variety of toxic chemicals including hydrochloric, sulfuric and nitric acid, all strong enough to severely burn human skin. They waited for three days and while the roots and stem had blackened, the leaves remained verdant. While the effect was finally achieved by spraying the toxins directly onto the leaves, Nakano was left somewhat horrified. As he witnessed the vitality of the plant's leaves as they clung to life, the gravity of the project's apocalyptic themes sunk in. Nakano realized just how horrific the pollution in Japan must be for trees to be dying.

Catastrophe 1974: the Tokyo fire department arrives as Toho's Studio 7 burns to the ground

While Nakano's unit shot the ensuing forest fire two days into principal photography, real-life catastrophe befell them as the blaze went out of control. Toho's entire Studio 7 burned to the ground. Nakano and his pyrotechnician Tadaaki Watanabe had finally done it. Like Icarus flying too close to the sun, their cinematic pyromania got them into a little trouble as the fire department was called to Toho's backlot. They were too late. Scores of Tsuburaya-era props and monster costumes in storage were destroyed, including the Mogera suit from *The Mysterians*. There were, thankfully, no injuries. Undaunted, Nakano's thrifty unit would shoot footage of the rubble of Studio 7 for use in a later scene. A disturbing and arresting image, it shows charred corpses amid the aftermath of the Fukushima plant's destruction as irradiated rain falls. Some of the rubble and debris was saved by Toho's prop department and used in future productions.

Nakano's highlight sequence in *Prophecies of Nostradamus* is a fiery freeway pile-up later in the picture.

Cars are jammed bumper-to-bumper with hapless civilians trying to get out of Tokyo before the apocalypse. An impatient driver crashes his car which then explodes. This starts a violent chain reaction which results in a firestorm of burning vehicles that stretches across the city. Another Eisensteinian tour de force like the Odessa Steps with metric tons of gunpowder and gasoline, it's Nakano's signature 1970s sequence. Masuda and Nakano's units are in excellent synergy with the former's end featuring full-sized stunts and brutal human casualties such as trapped children burning to death. The work of Nakano's team boasts ingenious miniature engineering from Inoue and expertly coordinated pyrotechnics courtesy of Watanabe. Nakano was certainly fond of the scene as his unit would go on to reuse its footage in future productions like *The War in Space* (1977), *Deathquake* (1980) and *The Return of Godzilla* (1984). Fittingly, *Prophecies of Nostradamus* had the most extensive use of gunpowder in a Toho movie yet, going well over its allotted budget for the explosive. Nakano often had to fight to get the amount and type of gunpowder that he needed to stage the perfect conflagrations.

Creating fiery cinematic chaos in miniature

Another disturbing segment shows a family's home catching fire and their skin burned by UV radiation from a hole in the ozone layer. The final shot, combining elements from both Masuda and Nakano's units, is hauntingly reminiscent of the World War II-era firebombings. The FX crew also stages stunningly realistic flood sequences on par with *Submersion of Japan*'s. In later scenes, Tokyo's sky, thanks to pollution refracting the sun's light, turns into a giant mirror as Tanba's Nishiyama stands gloomily on a balcony. Utilizing the most impressive process work Nakano's unit had yet achieved, these shots were created by **YOSHIO ISHII**

(1932-). They were supervised by Koichi Kawakita who found them challenging but rewarding to stage.

Prophecies of Nostradamus boasts a speculative finale that is less remarkable on Nakano's end with hefty reliance on stock images from *The Last War* and *Submersion of Japan*. There are stunning new shots, however, such as torrents of apocalyptic intercontinental ballistic missiles launching from underground silos. A plaster miniature with metal weights placed inside was used for a memorable shot of a silo door smashing open. As Nakano's team was shooting the miniaturized nuclear apocalypse on one Toho soundstage, famed Hong Kong singer Agnes Chan was filming a commercial next door. The segment is capped with disturbing visions from Masuda's main unit. A group of military men lay dead from radiation poisoning in a silo as the missiles continue to launch. Toshio Masuda would return to the theme of nuclear warfare and feature similar imagery in his anime film *Future War 198X* (1982).

Prophecies of Nostradamus' most infamous scene features a pair of post-nuke mutant children, hideously deformed like Joseph Merrick and covered in cancerous growths. The two starving creatures viciously spar over a snake they want to eat. Played by two young boys, **ISAMU SUGII** and **NOBUYUKI NAKANO**, they are called "Soft-Bodied Humans" in official press. They were designed by Akihiko Iguchi and crafted from rubber by Nobuyuki Yasumaru. The scene looks forward to the BBC's speculative nuclear holocaust drama *Threads* (1984), which also implies in its coda that after a nuclear holocaust, children will be born with horrible deformities. The sequence, though similarly staged to a tokusatsu monster scene, was actually directed by Toshio Masuda.

Though *Prophecies of Nostradamus* was less successful than *Submersion of Japan*, it was Toho's top grossing film of 1974, even holding its own against *The Exorcist* which was in release in Japan concurrently. *Prophecies of Nostradamus* came at a good time: Its predecessor *Submersion of Japan* had sparked a heyday for apocalyptic disaster movies. Simultaneously, the popularity of Go Nagai's *Devilman* along with *The Exorcist* had started an "Occult Boom" which drew public interest to Nostradamus and his prophecies.

Prophecies of Nostradamus' release soon caused controversy, however. Similarly to *Ultraseven*'s episode #12, a group of Hiroshima survivors' activists based in Osaka protested the movie. They were offended by two scenes in particular. The first features a radiation-mutated native in New Guinea gnawing on the flesh of an expedition member like a tribesman in an Italian cannibal flick. The second was the Soft-Bodied Human segment. They felt both were discriminatory against *hibakusha* (A-bomb survivors) and took the matter to Eirin, Japan's MPAA. Toho scrambled and re-released the film with cuts, even having projectionists snip out offensive scenes. A sequel was planned: *Prophecies of Nostradamus II: The King of Terror,* which would have brought back directors Masuda and Nakano. As with *Submersion of Japan*, a tie-in TV series was also in the works with 16mm B-roll shot on the special effects unit. Both were scrapped due to the controversy.

Prophecies of Nostradamus is a visually stunning film that needs to be seen in a modern transfer to be appreciated. After a final TV airing in 1980 and a failed attempt at a home video release in 1986, Toho has relegated the picture to their vaults. Interested parties must squint at a VHS-quality bootleg made from a leaked betacam tape or watch the abysmal American reedit *The Last Days of Planet Earth*. The only legal way to experience the uncut Japanese version is through a "drama CD" containing only the audio. Teruyoshi Nakano next worked with Masuda on **CONTINUING HUMAN REVOLUTION** [Director: Toshio Masuda - **Release Date (Japan):** June 19th, 1976], a sequel to *The Human Revolution.*

During this time, the *Planet of the Apes* series, based on the novel by Pierre Boulle, was popular in Japan, having concluded only a year prior with *Battle of the Planet of the Apes.* The iconic ape makeup in those films was actually developed through tokusatsu industry ingenuity. It was Fuminori Ohashi, invited to Hollywood thanks to his skill at modeling apes, who helped **JOHN CHAMBERS** (1922-2001) devise the ingenious prosthetics in the original film. After a successful airing of *Planet of the Apes* on Japanese television, TBS and Tsuburaya Productions' Kazuho Mitsuta began development of a similar TV series with sci-fi authors Sakyo Komatsu, **ARITSUNE TOYOTA** (1938-) and **KOJI TANAKA** (1941-). The popularity of apocalyptic cinema like *Submersion of Japan* and *Prophecies of Nostradamus* also played a part.

TBS and Tsuburaya Productions had to consult lawyers to make sure they wouldn't receive any threats from 20th Century Fox. The result was **ARMY OF THE APES [AKA: TIME OF THE APES - Television Run (Japan):** October 6th, 1974 - March 30th, 1975] which aired for 26 episodes. Komatsu and company made major changes such as the apes having a modern Japanese society instead of a medieval-style civilization as in the 1968 *Planet of the Apes*. This is closer to Boulle's novel in many respects. In Fox's series, the gorillas are depicted as war-like while the chimpanzees are pacifists. In real life, chimps are more aggressive than gorillas due to their human-like intelligence. Komatsu thus reversed the temperaments.

Called "*Planet of the Apes* seen through a low budget Japanese filter" by the *Mystery Science Theater 3000* crew, *Army of the Apes* concerns a female scientist named Kazuko Izumi (Reiko Tokunaga) and children Jiro (Masaki Kaji) and Yurika (Hiroko Saito). They wind up in an ape-ruled future after being trapped in cryogenic freeze. *Army of the Apes*' most impressive aspect is that it contains the best ape makeup yet achieved by the tokusatsu industry. The ape prosthetics, created by **KOSUKE TAMIYA**, are high quality and nearly on par with Fox's films. About 50 ape masks were manufactured. These were padded with rubber for the actors' comfort. Tamiya had trouble hiding the seams between the actors' eyes and masks while applying them. Actor **BAKU HATAKEYAMA** (1944-1978), who played the villain Gabor, wound up passing out from overexerting himself in the mask.

Army of the Apes also features occasional miniature unit work in episodes, handled by Kazuo Sagawa. A miniaturized flying saucer belonging to an apocalyptic Skynet-style supercomputer makes appearances. Komatsu's vision is even bleaker than Pierre Boulle's: In this world humanity used apes as soldiers before being wiped out by artificial intelligence. *Army of the Apes*' final episode features a tokusatsu version of the Stargate sequence in *2001: A Space Odyssey* (1968), created by Minoru Nakano's Den Films. *Army of the Apes* is overall a bit flatly directed but plays better in individual episodes and original Japanese rather than in its American compilation film *Time of the Apes*. The show suffered poor ratings as it aired in the same Sunday timeslot as the anime shows *Space Battleship Yamato* and *Heidi, Girl of the Alps*. Aritsune Toyota incidentally also wrote for *Yamato*.

The newest Kamen Rider program would be **KAMEN RIDER AMAZON** [Television Run (Japan): October 19th, 1974 - March 29th, 1975] which began airing two weeks after *Army of the Apes*. *Kamen Rider Amazon* revolves around the Tarzan-like Daisuke Yamamoto (Toru Okazaki), a Japanese wildman who was lost in the Amazon *Kenya Boy*-style. Adopted by an Amazon tribe, they are massacred by the Ten-Faced Demon Gorgos. The leader of Gedon, yet another evil organization, Gorgos is a nightmarish giant monster head filled with smaller heads. The tribe's Incan-descended shaman Bago (Ushio Akashi) gifts Daisuke with an ancient amulet and performs a ritual on him. Daisuke is sent to Japan with the ability to transform into Kamen Rider Amazon to battle Gedon and its "beastman" monsters. Amazon, no longer a cyborg but a magical hero, had his various suits and masks modeled at Equis. Rider Amazon was designed by Shotaro Ishinomori and Michio Mikami and portrayed by young stuntman **KAZUO NIIBORI** (1955-) with support from Bunya Nakamura and Tetsuya Nakayashiki.

Kamen Rider Amazon (1974-75) title card

In stark contrast to the tamer *Kamen Rider X*, *Kamen Rider Amazon* takes Toei's trademark madness to an apex. In creating a more primitivist vision of Kamen Rider, Ishinomori drew influence from John Boorman's *Zardoz* (1974). The Ten-Faced Demon Gorgos in particular was influenced by that recent film. Daisuke/Amazon himself was also informed by the popularity of Bruce Lee. The show features heavier miniature and trick photography inserts than usual for the Kamen Rider franchise, but little about the FX crew is known.

Kamen Rider Amazon has a mondo movie flavor with a level of graphic gore that is conspicuous even for a Toei show. This direction may have been due in part to the popularity of mondo-style films which were successful in Japan such as Umberto Lenzi's *The Man From Deep River* (1972). *Kamen Rider Amazon* would be the final Kamen Rider show broadcast on NET and the shortest in the franchise at 24 episodes. The program was cut short as TBS, the property's soon-to-be new home, wanted another new series. Regardless, *Kamen Rider Amazon* would gain a cult following on both sides of the Pacific thanks to its offbeat tone and gruesome violence.

Sompote Saengduenchai

Tsuburaya Productions and Sompote Saengduenchai's Chaiyo would meanwhile collaborate on another Japanese/Thai co-production, **THE SIX ULTRA BROTHERS VS. THE MONSTER ARMY [AKA: HANUMAN VS. 7 ULTRAMAN - Directors:** Shohei Tojo, Sompote Saengduenchai - **Release Date (Thailand):** November 26th, 1974]. Both Tojo and Saengduenchai are credited as exclusive directors in Japanese and Thai versions respectively. The Japanese FX unit was headed by Kazuo Sagawa whose sequences are the most tolerable aspect. *The Six Ultra Brothers vs. the Monster Army* pairs the Ultras: Zoffy, Ultraman, Ultraseven, Jack, Ace and Taro with simian Hindu god Hanuman. Hanuman, closely related to the Chinese Son Goku, is fused with Koh (Ko Kaeoduendee), a Thai boy killed by treasure looters.

Saengduenchai's half of the picture is characterized by a deranged, Ed Woodsian strangeness. The picture betrays its Thai origins with a level of ghoulish violence far beyond that found in Japanese children's media. Koh is gruesomely shot by the robbers, one of whom is then crushed to a bloody pulp in the palm of Hanuman's hand. Majestic Oxberry composites of giant Hanuman chasing the looters are ruined by the villains comically running in fast motion. Hanuman and the Ultra Brothers' adversaries are a gaggle of five monsters: *Ultraman*'s

Gomora, *Mirrorman*'s Dustpan and *Ultraman Taro*'s Astromons, Tyrant and Dorobon, who are introduced in a pyrotechnics storm that would make Teruyoshi Nakano proud. The Gomora suit appears to be the same one from the original show and has seen better days.

Thai poster for *The Six Ultra Brothers vs. the Monster Army* aka *Hanuman vs. 7 Ultraman* (1974)

Kazuo Sagawa's effects unit work is a mixed bag but shows improvement. There's genuinely inventive miniature cinematography depicting celestial bodies in space and a smoking sun. Sagawa and his DP Sadao Sato, however, shoot another miniature set in a shallow focus, ruining the illusion. Also on hand is trippy optical animation that again feels like a tokusatsu vision of *2001: A Space Odyssey*'s climax. It's also created by Minoru Nakano who really lets loose with his best work. Inventive photography abounds such as the camera following jets attacking the monsters in midair. Flying miniature scenes being a specialty of Sagawa's, these look foreshadow the dynamic staging of Shinji Higuchi. The widescreen Cinemascope frame feels well suited to the premise of seven heroes battling five monsters. *The Six Ultra Brothers vs. the Monster Army*'s highlight is an explosive monster attack on a rocket launch site. Again, the pyrotechnics evoke Teruyoshi Nakano's work at Toho, though staged with less precision. There are also striking low angle shots of Gomora lurking behind palm groves.

Saengduenchai displays his mondo-style influence during the final battle; it's viciously brutal in a way that would have enraged Eiji Tsuburaya. Two of the monsters are gruesomely decapitated. Dorobon has its skin flayed from bone like a scene in the infamous Chinese propaganda picture *Man Behind the Sun* (1988). Gomora is brutally beaten with a baseball bat-like weapon while being held down akin to a gangland assault. Though popular in Thailand, *The Six Ultra Brothers vs. the Monster Army* would not be released in Japan until March 1979.

Sompote Saengduenchai would next seek to collaborate with Toei and Ishinomori Productions on a Hanuman crossover film with the Kamen Riders. Toei declined Chaiyo's offer. Saengduenchai, undaunted, illegally produced the movie anyway. *Hanuman and the Five Riders* (1975) was the result, which consists largely of stock footage from *Five Riders vs. King Dark.* For the scenes where the Riders interact with Hanuman, Chaiyo made their own counterfeit Kamen Rider costumes. Hanuman would later return again in Chaiyo's *The Noble War* (1984). Kazuo Sagawa would also collaborate with Saengduenchai on *Crocodile* (1978), a a Thai/Korean blend of *Jaws* and *Godzilla* chock-full of revolting animal cruelty.

Years later, relations between Tsuburaya Productions and Chaiyo disintegrated as Saengduenchai proved crooked. By the mid 1990s, Chaiyo claimed outright to own the international rights to the Ultraman franchise. Sompote Saengduenchai boasted that he had helped Eiji Tsuburaya conceive Ultraman when the two were looking at Buddhist statues in Thailand. Saengduenchai even went as far as to forge the Tsuburaya family's *hanko* (family seal) on a fake contract. Litigation lasted for decades and was not resolved until 2018 when a Los Angeles court finally ruled in favor of Tsuburaya Productions.

Toho, meanwhile, followed *Submersion of Japan* with another Sakyo Komatsu adaptation, **ESPY [Director:** Jun Fukuda - **Release Date (Japan):** December 28th, 1974]. Based on Komatsu's 1965 novel of the same name and short for "Esper Spy", *ESPY* concerns an organization of spies with psychic powers. They are opposed by Counter-ESPY, another group of psychics aiming to destabilize the world. Toho had planned to produce an adaptation in 1967, also to be directed by Fukuda. The project was put on hold as planned star Akiko Wakabayashi's contract at Toho was not renewed. The success of *Submersion* and a visit by Uri Geller to

Japan convinced Tomoyuki Tanaka to revive *ESPY*. Teruyoshi Nakano was again put in charge of the special effects unit.

ESPY is a more Jun Fukuda film with occasional offerings from Nakano. It features a bigger budget and superior production values to Fukuda's concurrent '70s Godzilla films. *ESPY* is dynamically shot and edited; its DP, **MASAHARU UEDA** (1938-). would go on to help lens Akira Kurosawa's later films from *Kagemusha* (1980) on. Ueda had worked as a camera assistant to Hajime Koizumi on *Mothra*. *ESPY* also sports impressive international location shooting in Turkey and Switzerland by a second unit run by **KENJIRO OMORI** (1938-2006). The contributions of Teruyoshi Nakano's FX unit are understated, limited mainly to optical work akin to Tsuburaya *kaijin* films such as *The Human Vapor*. These were, as usual, the work of Takeshi Miyanishi and Kazunobu Sanpei. Nakano's unit only takes the stage in a thrilling aerial sequence that employs well-executed miniature work. Six model jetliners were built at varying scales by Takashi Naganuma. The work of Nakano's crew in the finale is also subtle, consisting of miniature and process shots including the villains' exploding hideout made from plaster. Director Jun Fukuda was to helm a similar project to follow *ESPY* entitled *The Invisible Man vs. the Human Torch*, but it never materialized.

The following year would be a watershed for the tokusatsu industry, seeing the Godzilla, Ultraman and Kamen Rider franchises all temporarily retired. Box office grosses and TV ratings were down and high oil prices battered Japan's economy, making film production a riskier endeavor.

XXI.
1975 - 1976
昭和五十・五十一

Japan, however, would not see *Jaws* until Christmas time

Oil prices continued to cripple Japan's economy. In April 1975, the Vietnam War concluded with the fall of Cambodia to the Khmer Rouge and Saigon to the Vietcong; by now, Americans were largely indifferent. On the silver screen, an iconic blockbuster film entitled **JAWS [Director: STEVEN SPIELBERG** (1946-) - **Release Date (U.S.):** June 20th, 1975], based on a novel by Peter Benchley, kept people off beaches that summer. The film's mechanical shark was made by specialist **ROBERT A. MATTEY** (1910-1993). It worked poorly, so Spielberg and his crew had been forced to rely on a minimalistic approach and keep their monster offscreen. This turned *Jaws* into a critically acclaimed masterpiece that stayed in American theaters for months and birthed the modern blockbuster cycle.

Meanwhile, Toho's last Godzilla entry for the time being was **TERROR OF MECHAGODZILLA** [Director: Ishiro Honda - **Release Date (Japan):** March 15th, 1975], released in the 16th Champion Matsuri Festival. Tomoyuki Tanaka was planning to give Yoshimitsu Banno another shot at directing a Godzilla film but was as usual unenthused by Banno's offbeat pitches. Ishiro Honda was thus coaxed out of semi-retirement. A more conventional entry and direct sequel to *Godzilla vs. Mechagodzilla* was decided on. The studio held a story contest and the winner was **YUKIKO TAKAYAMA** (1945-). A talented writer and the daughter of painter Tatsuo Takayama, Yukiko Takayama would pen the darkest, most ambitious Godzilla story yet. Her original script featured two dinosaur "Titans" who merge together for the climax. With the input of director Honda (likely with budget constraints in mind), the Titans were changed to a single giant monster: Titanosaurus.

Teruyoshi Nakano again returned to helm the effects unit, taking full advantage of resources left over from the previous summer's *Prophecies of Nostradamus,* which came in handy. Like *All Monsters Attack* and *Godzilla vs. Hedorah*, the shoot for *Terror of Mechagodzilla* was done without the traditional concurrent two-unit shooting style. While Ishiro Honda directed the drama scenes and Nakano the special effects, DP Motoyoshi Tomioka shot the entire movie with the same camera crew.

In many ways an even better film than its predecessor, *Terror of Mechagodzilla* is another highlight of the 1970s Godzilla cycle. *Godzilla vs. Mechagodzilla* and *Terror* make for interesting companion pieces. The two pictures boast similar sequences, yet Jun Fukuda and Ishiro Honda bring markedly different sensibilities to the table. Honda contributes a somber tone to *Terror of Mechagodzilla* hearkening back to the original 1954 film, the effect aided by Akira Ifukube's first original Godzilla score since *Destroy All Monsters.*

Most interesting on Honda's end is the character of Katsura Mafune (Tomoko Ai), a cyborg girl. Thanks to writer Takayama, she's one of the best-written and most compelling female characters in a Japanese special effects picture. In one scene, she's shown with (prosthetic) bare breasts while being repaired and turned into a Mechagodzilla control unit by the Black Hole Aliens. Trimmed from American prints, this is a shocking moment for a kiddie programmer. There are elements of transhumanist fetishism to this sequence akin to future robotic anime and manga characters like *Ghost in the Shell*'s Motoko Kusanagi. While shooting it, Tomoko Ai kept falling asleep: the young actress was lulled by the warmth of the studio lights.

Creating an impressive in-camera lighting effect

Teruyoshi Nakano, whose name appears in the opening credits over an explosion, had now cut his teeth with stellar work on *Submersion of Japan* and *Prophecies of Nostradamus*. Nakano crafts his finest monster sequences yet with a mastery not present in earlier Godzilla entries. *Terror of Mechagodzilla* boasts a strong opening of the newest threat, Titanosaurus, attacking an underwater submarine, the *Akatsuki*. It strongly resembles the *Wadatsumi* scene in *Submersion*. In Godzilla and Titanosaurus' first nighttime tussle, surviving miniatures from the freeway explosion sequence in *Prophecies of Nostradamus* were used. The scene is among Godzilla's most memorable entrances: during a bleak sunrise, the monster's face slowly illuminates from the darkness as Ifukube's thrilling notes rise. This effect was created with a flaming torch held off-camera by a stagehand.

The Godzilla suit from *Godzilla vs. Megalon* was again brought back with another round of renovations to make it look ferocious. This time, Toru Kawai inhabited the mighty monster's skin. The Mechagodzilla costume from the previous entry was reused for "Mechagodzilla II" with repainting and the code "MG2" added to its arms. A new suit was also constructed with slightly redesigned arms. Kazunari Mori again wore the costume. Titanosaurus was designed by Akihiko Iguchi with the suit built by Keizo Murase and his firm Twenty. A colorful aquatic dinosaur with a seahorse-like head, it is among Murase's finest achievements as a suit maker. Murase used some of the newest pigments available to give the Titanosaurus its vivid color. Mechanical parts were also added to allow the mouth and tail fins to open and close. Tatsumi Nikamoto, fresh from playing Ultraman Leo, portrayed the beast. A large doll prop of Titanosaurus was built for shots of it diving through the ocean. A Guignol puppet of the monster's head was also used for close-up shots. Miniature alien spaceships appear briefly in the film - the Black Hole Aliens attempt to escape in them before they're blasted by Godzilla. These resemble the ships from *The Mysterians* and *Battle in Outer Space*, but were newly made by Toshiro Aoki's art department. They measured around 15 inches.

Teruyoshi Nakano

Terror of Mechagodzilla marks a return to heavier urban mass destruction than previous entries. It also boasts impressive, though sometimes poorly scaled, composite shots. Teruyoshi Nakano at first holds back on his beloved pyrotechnics a little more than usual, but ignites another grand hellstorm in the finale. In one of its most impressive sequences, Mechagodzilla II lets loose a *Prophecies of Nostradamus*-like torrent of conflagration, rendering a miniaturized Tokyo to a pyrotechnic pulp. There's an edgy, *Ultraman Leo*-style moment where two boys are squished by Titanosaurus right as Godzilla shows up, re-edited in American prints to look like they were saved. Godzilla's brawling with Mechagodzilla and Titanosaurus is staged creatively. Low-angle suit shots taken outdoors in natural light are effectively intercut with FX stage footage. As Godzilla wades through Nakano and Tadaaki Watanabe's most ferocious barrage of pyrotechnics yet, it becomes so intense that the suit catches on fire. This happy accident is gleefully left in the movie by Nakano and his editors.

Sadly, *Terror of Mechagodzilla* was the lowest grossing Godzilla entry yet. Tomoyuki Tanaka thus put the series on temporary hiatus. As Godzilla, in the form of the gnarly-looking promotional suit, wades off into the Big Pool one last time in the final moments, it was going into a decade-long hibernation. Tanaka made multiple attempts to revive Godzilla in the coming years. Some came close to fruition, but the creature would not return to movie screens until late 1984. *Terror of Mechagodzilla* would also mark Ishiro Honda's final film. The esteemed filmmaker would next assist his friend Akira Kurosawa on production of the latter's films, starting with *Kagemusha* (1980). Honda would, however, provide creative input to and largely co-direct *"The Tunnel"* segment in Kurosawa's *Dreams* (1990), said to be based on a recurring nightmare of his.

On the small screen, Toei's next and, for now, last Kamen Rider show would be **KAMEN RIDER STRONGER** [**Television Run (Japan):** April 5th - December 27th, 1975]. The program had switched networks from NET to TBS. Originally called *Kamen Rider Spark, Stronger* is by far the least interesting program in the franchise thus far. In contrast to the more provocative approaches taken by *Ultraman Leo* and *Kamen Rider Amazon, Stronger* has a shockingly lighthearted tone compared to the gritty original. Toei's Toru Hirayama initially had the idea for the program to feature a team of five Riders. Hirayama was opposed by the TV brass, who wanted to stick to the conventional "one-hero, one-show" formula. Undaunted, Hirayama and Shotaro Ishinomori would develop another concurrent program for NET.

Kamen Rider Stronger's smug, suave protagonist is Shigeru Jo (Shigeru Araki). He casually walks into the laboratory of Shocker, Destron and GOD's successor Black Satan and volunteers to be turned into a cyborg.

Secretly plotting revenge against Black Satan for their murder of his friend, Shigeru is able to resist brainwashing and becomes Kamen Rider Stronger. He rescues another victim of Black Satan, a young woman named Yuriko Misaki (Kyoko Okada). Yuriko can also transform into a cyborg, the Riderman-like Tackle. In keeping with the show's lighter sensibility, Tackle becomes Stronger's sidekick. Black Satan's grunts are given googly eyes like a monster in Larry Buchanan's Z-grade cheapies. Stronger, at least, got a novel design, modeled after American football gear. Nori Maezawa of Equis created the suit and took over art direction for the show as Tsutomu Yagi was recruited for *Gorenger*. According to stuntman Tetsuya Nakayashiki, the visibility was poor in the Stronger costume.

Like Ishinomori's *Inazuman*, later in the show's run to combat sagging ratings, Stronger gains the ability to change himself into a tougher form: Charge-Up Stronger. Tackle, who tragically dies in episode #30, was designed with a ladybug motif. It was decided to try a female hero after Toru Hirayama and Shotaro Ishinomori received a surprising amount of letters from girls who wanted a female character to play "henshin hero" with the boys. Actress Yuriko Misaki portrayed Tackle in most scenes, but for the roughest stunt unit sequences, stuntwoman **MAKI KIYOTA** of the Ono Kendo Club acted as her double.

Kamen Rider Stronger's ratings were the worst yet. The program was slated to run for a full year's slot of 52 episodes. The ratings were so dismal that the show ended prematurely after only 39. Two days after Christmas, the final episode of the Kamen Rider franchise for four years would air. Like a low-budget 16mm-lensed 1970s *Avengers: Endgame* (2019), *Kamen Rider Stronger* goes all-out in spectacle for its swansong, co-directed by Minoru Yamada and Shotaro Ishinomori. In it, all seven Riders unite to battle the last remnants of Black Satan's spin-off the Delza Army. The actors Hiroshi Fujioka, Takeshi Sasaki, Hiroshi Miyauchi, Akira Yamaguchi, Ryo Hayami and Toru Okazaki all returned to reprise their roles. Getting every Rider alumnus together with their busy schedules in film, TV and even music was no easy task. Only a single day could be allotted for group scenes. The end of *Kamen Rider Stronger* was tough for kids who relished tokusatsu; Godzilla and Gamera were out of theaters and Ultraman and Kamen Rider off the air. It wouldn't be forever, though, and more properties arrived to take their place.

Premiering the same day as and airing in the tim -slot after *Kamen Rider Stronger* was another Ishinomori-run Toei show: **SECRET SQUADRON GORENGER [Television Run (Japan):** April 5th, 1975 - March 26th, 1977]. Like *Kamen Rider, Gorenger* would become a pop culture phenomenon in Japan. It would spawn another popular franchise: Sentai, which spread abroad decades later as *Power Rangers*. The word *sentai* can be translated into English as "Task Force" or "Squadron". During the war it was used to refer to elite army units. The concept for *Gorenger* came out of Shotaro Ishinomori's rejected proposal for *Kamen Rider Stronger* which would have involved a team of Riders. Ishinomori's prior manga and anime series *Cyborg 009* also influenced *Gorenger*'s inception as it featured a team of cyborgs. TV station NET was happy to take on the concept as the Kamen Rider franchise had moved to TBS. It was decided to make a five-hero team by Toei's Yoshinori Watanabe, inspired by the five-actor kabuki play *Benten Kozo*.

Secret Squadron Gorenger (1975-77) title card

At first, the entire team was to be costumed red. It was decided, especially as color TVs were now commonplace, that each squad member or "Ranger" should have their own distinct color. Red was reserved for the leader, Akarenger (Naoya Makoto). Other members of the original team included the blue Aorenger (Hiroshi Miyauchi), the green Midorenger (Yukio Ito) and the yellow Kirenger (Baku Hatakeyama). The Rangers were named after their colors with one exception: Momorenger (Lisa Komaki), the sole female member. Despite her pink wardrobe, in Japan, the word "pink" was associated with erotic films so *momo* (peach) was substituted.

Kiiranger, as his human alter ego Daita Oiwa, makes an impression as the comic relief. The chubby Daita likes to gorge himself on curry rice, much to the annoyance of the squad's leader, Gonpachi Edogawa (Toshio Takahara). The five-member group all belonged to EAGLE, a benevolent organization formed to combat the evil Black Cross Army. Black Cross sent monsters to each Japanese branch, leaving only one survivor at each location; these survivors became the rangers. Now they unite, armed with cybernetic battlesuits, to stop Black Cross. The Rangers even pilot a *Thunderbirds*-style mecha battleship called *Variblune*, eventually destroyed and replaced by the more powerful *Varidorin*. These ships foreshadow the giant robots that later sentai teams would pilot starting with *Battle Fever J*.

As with *Kamen Rider*, Shotaro Ishinomori's vision for the franchise can best be seen in early episodes of *Gorenger*. The transgressive '70s Toei tone is almost shocking when contrasted with the franchise's commercialized future. Like the Riders, the Rangers ride around on motorbikes and even the human cast's wardrobe feels Ishinomori-inspired. The Rangers themselves look as much like the Mysterians as the later iconic team in *Zyuranger* whose stunt footage formed the basis for *Mighty Morphin' Power Rangers*. They look manga-influenced per Ishinomori's background with flowing capes, although these were discarded fairly quickly. Yet there's a more "real world" feel to *Gorenger* than future Sentai shows.

The Black Cross Army is yet another fascistic evil organization. They are as depraved as Shocker, if not more so with a leader called "Fuhrer" dressed like a Klan grand wizard. In the first episode alone, they reach a nadir in nihilistic sociopathy by strapping bombs to a bus full of kindergartners. American parents who wouldn't let their kids watch *Mighty Morphin' Power Rangers* because it was "too violent" would have suffered from aneurysms had their children been watching an average episode of *Gorenger*. Yet there are strong hints of the tropes and imagery that led to *Power Rangers'* popularity on American airwaves. *Gorenger* feels purer than future shows which over-complicated things with magical elements and giant super robots.

Gorenger's directors and creative team, along with many of its stuntmen, were veterans of *Kamen Rider* and prior Ishinomori shows. These include Koichi Takemoto, Minoru Yamada and Katsuhiko Taguchi. The stunt unit was made the work of the Ono Kendo Club in the first 66 episodes and Sonny Chiba's JAC in the following 18. Kazuo Niibori, Tetsuya Nakayashiki and Bunya Nakamura all played rangers and monsters along with newcomers **HIROSHI UEDA** (1952-) and **HARUHIKO HASHIMOTO**. The teenage **RYOJI KURIHARA** (1956-), who doubled as the Momoranger, would later become known for his roles in adult films. Equis Productions handled modeling for most of the ranger and monster suits with Nori Maezawa heading construction.

Gorenger features a stronger FX unit presence than *Kamen Rider*. It particularly comes into play with sequences featuring *Variblune* or *Varidorin*. Nobuo Yajima and his Tokusatsu Research Institute were employed to create these shots. Toru Suzuki, now often working for Yajima's unit, engineered them. Their work tends to be more intricate and plentiful in some episodes. When the *Varidorin* comes into play with its chariot-like land pod the *Varitank*, the miniature work takes the stage. In the best episodes, particularly *"Fire Mountain's Last Big Explosion"*, Yajima's unit shines with nearly theatrical quality work.

Baku Hatakeyama's character, Daita Oiwa, would step out of the role of Kiirenger later on in the show's run. This was because Hatakeyama was given a supporting role in Sadao Nakajima's gangster flick *Okinawa Yakuza War* (1976) and could not balance it with his part in *Gorenger*. The mantle of Kirenger was thus taken up by another character: Daigoro Kumano (Jiro Daruma). When Hatakeyama was finished shooting *Okinawa Yakuza War*, Daruma's Kumano was unceremoniously killed off and Hatakeyama's Oiwa made Kirenger again. Hatakeyama had difficulty coping with the stardom thrust upon him by the show's runaway success. He felt typecast by the role of Kirenger and had difficulty getting work after *Gorenger* ended. On July 13th, 1978, Hatakeyama comitted suicide by hanging at 34.

Gorenger's ratings were outstanding and the program did well with toy sales. The show would air for close to two years and as with *Kamen Rider*, episodes of *Gorenger* were blown up to 35mm 'scope and shown at the Toei Manga Festival. A short spin-off film made exclusively for theatrical screening at the festival was also produced: **SECRET SQUADRON GORENGER: THE BOMB HURRICANE** [**Director**: Minoru Yamada - **Release Date (Japan)**: July

18th, 1976]. The film's climactic set piece involves the Ranger Squad executing their titular "Bomb Hurricane" attack, an explosive game of football, against monster Steel Sword Dragon. The Cinemascope frame is a good fit for the five-person sentai squad and the miniature FX, created mainly by Toru Suzuki, look better lensed in 35mm. *Gorenger: The Bomb Hurricane* was shot in Shikoku, whose fishing trade had already suffered damage at the hands of Toei's stunt unit with *Kamen Rider V3 vs. Destron Mutants*. *Gorenger* thus began the popular Sentai franchise with shows released in a nearly unbroken yearly cycle to this day.

Export poster for *The Bullet Train* (1975)

As American audiences thrilled to the maritime horror of *Jaws*, in Japan the summer of '75 saw the release of two competing disaster spectacles, both involving terrorists threatening to set off deadly explosions. Shigeru Okada at Toei had begun production on the massively-budgeted, Irwin Allen-style disaster flick **THE BULLET TRAIN** [Director: **JUNYA SATO** (1929-2019) - **Release Date (Japan)**: July 5th, 1975]. With parallels to Jan De Bont's *Speed* (1994), it revolves around the Tokyo bullet train being booby trapped with an explosive device that will detonate if the train drops below a certain velocity. It drew influence from a scrapped picture

Akira Kurosawa had tried to make in Hollywood called *Runaway Train*, which would eventually be produced ten years later.

The Bullet Train features extensive miniature work by **SHOZO KONISHI** and Tsuburaya designer Toru Narita. The miniatures were constructed outdoors in a large courtyard in Toei's lot. The model for the *Shinkansen Hikari* 109 alone was close to 80 feet long and enormous miniaturized train tracks were constructed. These would later be used in an episode of Tsuburaya Productions' *Ultraman 80*. To stretch the budget, Narita used colorized photographs printed onto panels to simulate a distant cityscape. Toru Narita's FX unit would also use a snorkel lens camera, which could get up close to the models and maintain wide focal length and deep focus, to shoot these miniatures. These same cameras were next used by John Dykstra's visual effects team on *Star Wars* (1977). The Tokyo *Shinkansen* tried to stop the release of *The Bullet Train* as they feared real-life criminals could take cues from the film. They were unsuccessful and no one was inspired by the movie to booby trap their trains with explosives. *The Bullet Train* paved the way for more big budget Toei effects films to come.

Toho also produced a disaster epic that was released a week later: **CONFLAGRATION [AKA: HIGH SEAS HIJACK - Director: KATSUMUNE ISHIDA** (1932-2012) - **Release Date (Japan):** July 12th, 1975]. *Conflagration* was based on the novel *Critical Explosion* by Koji Tanaka, who had visited the special effects set of *Prophecies of Nostradamus* (1974). There he watched Nakano's unit stage a miniaturized oil refinery explosion which got his creative juices flowing. On November 9th, 1974, the oil tanker *Yuyo Maru* No. 10 collided with cargo ship *Pacific Alice* in Tokyo Bay. As the sea caught fire, the Self-Defense Force had to be dispatched. In light of this sensational news story, Tomoyuki Tanaka greenlit a film adaptation of Koji Tanaka's novel. *Conflagration* almost feels like it was written for Teruyoshi Nakano's effects unit to a comical degree. A character based on Nakano, a special effects director named Susumu Wakabayashi, even appears, played by actor Akio Satake. Nakano was originally to play the role himself but was too busy directing the picture's FX sequences.

Conflagration revolves around the *Arabian Light,* an oil tanker sea-jacked by a band of African revolutionaries (actually African-American expats living in Tokyo), led by Simba (Kay Amore). Their plans are to blow it up in Tokyo Bay unless the Japanese government destroys an oil refinery. The explosion of the *Arabian Light* and its metric tons of flammable hydrocarbons would result in the complete annihilation of Tokyo. Yet in typical anarchic '70s Japanese cinema fashion, the viewer feels sympathy for these foreign terrorists despite their misdeeds as they revealed to be radicalized victims of the developed world's exploitation of their countries. While not without its strengths, *Conflagration* is talky and a step down from the apocalyptic splendor of *Submersion of Japan*.

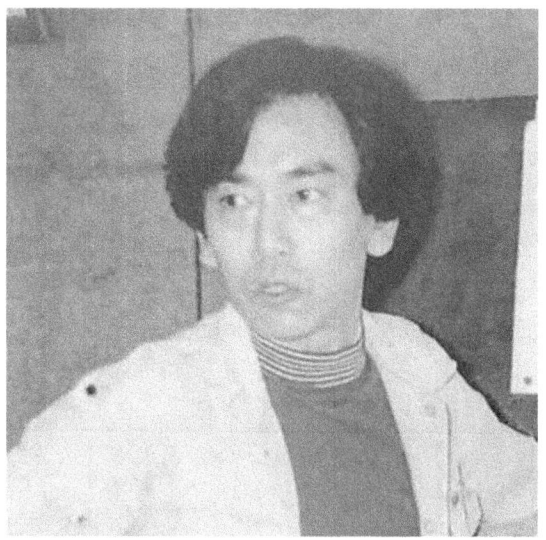

Teruyoshi Nakano, whose pyromaniacal antics inspired the story of *Conflagration* (1975)

FX art director Yasuyuki Inoue led the construction of the *Arabian Light* miniature. He clashed with Tomoyuki Tanaka who wanted the model built at a smaller scale to save money. Inoue ignored this and built a 24-foot model. Nakano's most striking contribution is a speculative Tokyo destruction sequence as impressively bleak as anything in *Submersion of Japan*. It boasts brilliantly executed pyrotechnic miniature destruction and striking optical composites by Takeshi Miyanishi. Shots were later reused in *Godzilla vs. King Ghidorah* (1991) and *Godzilla Against Mechagodzilla* (2002).

Conflagration is at its best when it turns into a dark parody of tokusatsu filmmaking. Rather than give in to the revolutionaries, the Japanese government and Self-Defense Force hire a tokusatsu unit to stage a mock refinery explosion on live television with miniatures and gunpowder. The viewer sees a model refinery being built and horizon backdrops painted. In the nihilistic '70s antithesis of Giuseppe Tornatore's *Cinema Paradiso* (1988), tokusatsu filmmaking and its inherent variables just make the situation worse. Nakano and his team of pyromaniacs take the stage as Toho's FX department lampoons themselves in a self-deprecating way.

To create this live explosion, the pyrotechnic miniature footage is video composited onto the horizontal painted matte at another location. Simba and his revolutionaries are almost fooled but then a torrential rainstorm hits the outdoor horizon, ruining their suspension of disbelief and forcing the SDF to clean up the mess with special ops. As Nakano's explosive images created with gunpowder and toxic chemicals thunder on TV screens across Japan, a reporter (Fumio Watanabe) exclaims "That's from *Earth 1999*, the tokusatsu film I covered!". A nod to *Prophecies of Nostradamus* and author Koji Tanaka's visit to the set, hearing the word "tokusatsu" uttered in a tokusatsu film is the most meta moment in any *Showa*-era Toho special effects movie.

Sir Run Run Shaw, knighted by the Commonwealth in 1977 for his contributions to HK's film industry

Japan's special effects hero shows were also popular on Cantonese airwaves in Hong Kong, particularly the Kamen Rider franchise. Run Run Shaw of the monolithic Shaw Brothers was thus eager to cash-in on their popularity. Run Run and his brother **RUNME**

SHAW (1901-1985) in 1957 had purchased 46 acres of land in Clearwater Bay. By 1961, Shaw Brothers was the largest scale film production company in the world. When looking to push the company's technological capabilities forward, Run Run Shaw well understood the merit of neighboring Japan's filmmaking ingenuity. Cinematographer Tadashi Nishimoto, who had shot *Emperor Meiji and the Great Russo-Japanese War* and Nobuo Nakagawa's *Ghost of Yotsuya* (1959), acted as a technical consultant to this fledgling Greater Chinese movie factory. It was Nishimoto who convinced Shaw to start shooting and releasing his films in anamorphic Cinemascope, branded "Shawscope." Nishimoto spent years in Hong Kong, shooting many of Shaw Brothers' classic films for directors like Yueh Feng, Li Han-Hsiang and King Hu and training Hong Kong crews in sophisticated cinematography techniques.

Though his company's films often featured Japanese villains per local populism, Run Run Shaw even drew influence from Japan's film industry in how he structured his business operations, particularly favoring the model of Iwao Mori and Tomoyuki Tanaka at Toho. Like Toho, Shaw Brothers owned its own line of movie theaters in Hong Kong with a distinct house style. A la the "Big Five" in '60s Japan, the actors, directors, writers and craftspeople were exclusively contracted to Shaw Brothers. Shaw even hired Japanese directors to make his films, including the prolific Umetsugu Inoue, Akinori Matsuo, *The Falcon Fighters*' Mitsuo Murayama and *Warning From Space*'s Koji Shima. By their 1970s peak, Shaw Brothers was putting out dozens of pictures per year. They were best known for their formulaic, stagey but polished martial arts films. The most famous abroad included *King Boxer* aka *The Five Fingers of Death* (1972), *The 36th Chamber of Shaolin* and *The Five Venoms* (both 1978). Yet they produced films in every genre from romantic comedy to gruesome East-Asian horror. In total, Shaw Brothers put out over a thousand pictures in their decades of operation.

The Shaws' first major attempt at a Japanese-style special effects film was **THE SUPER INFRAMAN [AKA: INFRA-MAN - Director:** Hua Shan - **Release Date (H.K.):** August 1st, 1975]. Seen by Westerners as a Hong Kong Ultraman rip-off, *The Super Inframan* owes more to Shotaro Ishinomori's henshin creations than Eiji Tsuburaya's kyodai heroes. There is a Science Patrol-like organization and at one point Inframan and a bug monster grow gigantic and battle each other, kyodai-style. Yet Inframan himself has more in common with Kamen Rider and Kikaider, his human alter-ego played by popular actor Danny Lee, who later starred in John Woo's *The Killer* (1989). The colorful, human-sized monsters are also more in line with *Kamen Rider*'s.

DP Tadashi Nishimoto (left) and production manager Chua Lam (right), Chua also befriended Keizo Murase

To give *The Super Inframan* a *Kamen Rider*-style aesthetic, the Shaw Brothers hired Michio Mikami, that show's production designer. An apprentice of Tsuburaya and friend of Ishinomori who had worked for most of Japan's FX units, Mikami was ideal. He designed Inframan, along with villainess Princess Elzebub (Lau Wai-Yue), her gaggle of monsters and Shocker-style grunts and the sets. Mikami and his newly founded company Cosmo Productions even modeled the monster suits, but to his frustration, director Hua Shan rejected them. To the Chinese end, Mikami's suits were too delicate for the rough and tumble of the Hong Kong stunts and so were remade by art director Johnson Tsao. Several more monsters were designed and constructed than appear in the finished film and one additional creature even had footage shot.

The Super Inframan is like aerosolized high camp and is ferociously entertaining. Once transformed, Inframan takes on creature after creature in one off-the-wall action sequence after another. The mayhem is breathlessly choreographed by stuntman **TANG CHIA** (1937-), a veteran of dozens of the Shaws' martial arts productions. *The Super Inframan* also boasts Japanese-style miniature work likely supervised by Mikami and even stock footage from Toho's *Submersion of Japan*. *Inframan* effectively combines the phantasmagorical splendor of tokusatsu television with the kinetic action of HK martial arts cinema.

Inframan's cinematographer was none other than Tadashi Nishimoto. In 1972, Nishimoto had worked with Bruce Lee on *The Way of the Dragon*. The memorable finale, a brawl between Bruce Lee and Chuck Norris in the stray cat-filled Roman Colosseum, was no doubt Nishimoto's partial brainchild. In *The Super Inframan*, Nishimoto's compositions are always striking. Roger Ebert said it best when *Inframan* was released in the United States by Joseph Brenner in 1976: "When they stop making movies like *Infra-Man* (sic), a little light will go out of the world."

While *The Super Inframan* was a flop in its native Hong Kong, it would not be the last time the Shaw Brothers sought out the expertise of Japan's tokusatsu industry. **THE SNAKE PRINCE [Director:** Lo Chen - **Release Date (H.K.):** July 31st, 1976] featured a trio of monster snake puppets modeled by Keizo Murase's Twenty. *The Snake Prince* is, unsurprisingly, about a prince (popular martial arts star Ti Lung) who can turn into a giant, fire-breathing monster snake. Up until that point a lighthearted musical with romantic overtones, *The Snake Prince* turns into a tokusatsu creature bloodbath in its finale.

Back in Japan, with *Gorenger* on the air, Shotaro Ishinomori developed several more special effects shows, though none had the enduring popularity of *Kamen Rider* or *Gorenger*. The next two, like *Gorenger*, revolved around groups of heroes. First came **AKUMAIZER 3 [Television Run (Japan):** October 7th, 1975 - June 29th, 1976]. With influence from Alexandre Dumas' *The Three Musketeers*, *Akumaizer 3* boasts a trio of heroes: Xavitan, Evil and Gabra, all of the Demon Clan, an ancient empire of demonic cyborgs who inhabit a "hollow Earth." *Akumaizer*'s motif was influenced by the still-active "Occult Boom". The villain Mezalord is one of the best and most frightening demon characters in the tokusatsu medium, drinking wine made from human blood.

As the "Henshin Boom" had now passed, the three heroes have no human forms, don't transform and are played entirely by stunt performers. These included **TOSHIMICHI TAKAHASHI** (1951-), **JUNICHI**

HARUTA (1955-), **YOSHINORI OKAMOTO** (1955) and Tetsu Masuda. Masuda had first played Hakaider on *Kikaider* and then *Condorman* earlier in 1975. An 18-year-old stuntman named **TSUTOMU KITAGAWA** (1957-) got his start on *Akumaizer 3*. Kitagawa would rise as a stuntman in coming Toei shows through the next two decades and win the role of a certain iconic monster at Toho. With no human counterparts, the Akumaizer 3 were dubbed by anime voice actors including Makio Inoue, best known as Captain Harlock, and Joji Yanami, to someday voice Dr. Briefs and King Kai on *Dragon Ball*. Employing anime voice actors was not uncommon for tokusatsu shows. Shocker, Destron and Black Satan's enigmatic leader was voiced by Goro Naya, known for dubbing Inspector Zenigata on *Lupin III* and Captain Okita on *Space Battleship Yamato*.

Akumaizer 3 (1975-76) title card

Nobuo Yajima's Tokusatsu Research Institute was brought on board *Akumaizer 3* and produced impressive miniature work for television with the help of art director Tetsuzo Osawa, who had become acquainted with Yajima through their work at Tsuburaya Productions. Tsuburaya's old-school technique of a high-altitude gelatin sea was used. The Demon Clan's underground kingdom resembles a miniaturized tokusatsu hell, looking forward to Yajima's work on *The Inferno* (1979). *Akumaizer 3* also features a prominent space galleon reminiscent of Ishinomori's designs on *Flying Phantom Ship* (1969) and foreshadowing his work with Yajima on the coming *Message From Space* (1978). This galleon, controlled by the Demon Clan, is commandeered by the Akumaizer 3 and can turn into a form resembling a mechanical shark.

Akumaizer 3's production struggled to find adequate studio space at Toei as they were already making *Kamen Rider Stronger* and *Gorenger* on most of the soundstages. Shooting on *Akumaizer 3* thus tended to take place in the wee hours of night to morning. *Akumaizer 3,* running for 38 episodes, was popular enough to get a follow-up: **CHOJIN BIBYUN** [Television Run (Japan): July 6th, 1976 - March 29th, 1977]. *Chojin Bibyun* resurrected the characters' souls into human hosts who become demonic henshin heroes and battle the evil Yokai King Galver. It was decided to return to the "henshin" tradition at the request of the sponsors. *Chojin Bibyun* aired for 36 episodes.

Shotaro Ishinomori's following program with Toei was **SPACE IRONMEN KYODAIN** [Television Run (Japan): April 2nd, 1976 - March 11th, 1977], which aired for 48 episodes. Once again, *Space Ironmen Kyodain* featured a hero team. As *Gorenger* had featured five heroes and *Akumaizer* a trio, *Kyodain* featured a duo of robotic brothers: Skyzel and Grounzel. *Space Ironmen Kyodain* is Ishinomori's most unusual and experimental show. It's strange even by the standards of Ishinomori, whose universe is like a Japanese Frank Miller's where heroes undergo two rounds of transformations, squads of proto-Power Rangers play explosive football and there's one fascistic terrorist organization with a flamboyantly evil name on the rampage after another. This time, at least, the villains are alien invaders from the Planet Dada, sharing a namesake with the *Ultraman* monster. Extraterrestrial antagonists were insisted upon by the network as Yoshinobu Nishizaki and Leiji Matsumoto's anime show *Space Battleship Yamato* was gaining popularity in Japan.

Skyzel and Grounzel are created by the kidnapped Dr. Hayama (*Mirrorman*'s Junya Usami). Forced by the Dada aliens to help them advance their robotics, Hayama infuses the Kyodain (*kyodai* means "brothers" in Japanese) with the personalities of his sons Joji (Yusuke Natsu) and Ryuji (Takeshi Sasaki). When Dada's Robot Army attacks Earth, the Kyodain appear to defend humanity and protect their younger brother Kenji (Satoshi Furukawa). With outlandish designs by Ishinomori, the suits for Skyzel and Grounzel were modeled by Michio Mikami and his newly founded Cosmo Productions. Moments featuring the brothers' faces on TV monitors atop the robot suits' heads are fanciful and nightmarish. Skyzel was portrayed by frequent Kamen Rider stuntman Tetsuya Nakayashiki. Granzel was played by **HIROO KAWARAZAKI** (1953-), another young stuntman who had cut his teeth on prior Toei/Ishinomori Productions shows.

Space Ironmen Kyodain, a la *Robot Detective*, could be considered a proto-Metal Hero show. Though intended to be more child-friendly than *Kamen Rider*, it features surprising experimental filmmaking techniques. Particularly in fight sequences, pixelation is used to disorient and distort time. In its hyperkinetic filmmaking and metallic heroes and villains, *Space Ironmen Kyodain* oddly foreshadows Shinya Tsukamoto's *Tetsuo: The Iron Man* (1989). *Kyodain* also boasts comical miniature effects sequences with heavy use of Guignol-style puppetry. These were handled by Nobuo Yajima's Tokusatsu Research Institute. At first, the Kyodain transform into a gigantic mecha. Due to budget issues, this was written out of the show and mostly excluded after episode #7 with the climaxes handled by the stunt unit. Yajima's effects work, however, continued to make frequent, though more sparing, appearances.

Koichi Takano would again venture to Greater China to handle the effects sequences for the Taiwanese **THE WAR GOD** [**Director:** Chen Hung-Min - **Release Date (Taiwan):** July 24th, 1976]. Though Taiwan had many talented filmmakers like Pai Ching-jui, by now its industry had developed a reputation for pumping out low-rent martial arts cheapies. Even by the standards of contemporary Taiwanese cinema, *The War God* is strange. Unlike prior Taiwanese-Japanese co-productions, *The War God* boasts a contemporary setting and science fiction elements. A gaggle of giant albino insectoid Martians lay waste to Hong Kong. A statue of Chinese folk hero Guan Yu, introduced in a *Kwaidan*-like flashback, comes to life and becomes gigantic Majin-style to defend the city.

Originally, the carnage was to take place in Taipei, but the *Kuomintang* (Republic of China) government objected to the capital being destroyed. All cinema produced in Taiwan had to fall in line with the *Kuomintang*'s agenda of reclaiming the Chinese mainland. Officials feared a Taipei under attack by aliens would make them appear weak to the communists. At one point early on, Carl Douglas' "*Kung Fu Fighting*" plays on the soundtrack, a colorfully self-referential moment for a '70s Taiwanese flick. Director Chen uses bonafide avant-garde techniques to disorient the audience as the aliens show up, including footage printed in reverse, staccato editing and a trippy warping visual perspective.

Once Koichi Takano's unit takes the stage, the film becomes stylistically inconsistent as the Japanese and Taiwanese units' footage doesn't cut well. Takano brings a distinct tokusatsu spectacle to *The War God*, marred by the unwatchable quality of current transfers. It's an impressive monster brawl sequence loaded with pyrotechnic and optical work, though some moments fall to the level of television. Best are striking composites reminiscent of the work of Teruyoshi Nakano's team at Toho.

The War God (1976) - another Taiwanese film with FX by Koichi Takano

The War God's finale effectively combines the Japanese tokusatsu and Greater Chinese *wuxia* cinematic traditions: a flashy martial arts duel created with monster suits in a model city. The sequence also boasts some of Takano's best miniature work yet including tiny cars smashed on tiny HK streets. The final shots, of Guan Yu amongst a smoldering, miniaturized Hong Kong, feel majestic. Only available in cropped, VHS-quality transfers, *The War God* cries out for a full-scale restoration.

Back in Japan, a unique new program from Tsuburaya Productions began airing in October: **DINOSAUR EXPEDITION BORN FREE** [**Television Run (Japan):** October 1st, 1976 - March 25th, 1977]. *Born Free* was the first of two nearly experimental attempts to meld the disparate anime and tokusatsu mediums. The concept was first proposed by Tsuburaya Productions in 1974 with the proof-of-concept short *Giant Beast Planet*. The show was greenlit when dinosaurs and cryptozoology became popular again due to recent fossil discoveries. This new "Dinosaur Boom" in Japan also influenced Toei with *Legend of the Dinosaur and Monster Bird* (1977) and Toho with their aborted *Nessie*. Depicting the human characters with *Thunderbirds*-like doll marionettes was considered, but cel-driven anime was decided on. One of the anime studios who worked on *Born Free* was Sunrise, soon to be famous for animating Yoshiyuki Tomino's *Mobile Suit Gundam*. The anime half of *Born Free* is pedestrian with limited, low frame rate animation. One of the characters, engineer Akira Gonda, was modeled after Masato Shimon, who sang the show's theme song.

Born Free proposes an idea that could be better executed by future filmmakers. The concept of the "drama unit" rendered in anime form and juxtaposed with a miniaturized tokusatsu world is unique. Yet it often feels like two disparate Japanese cinema flavors that don't always blend. *Born Free* feels odd, like *Thunderbirds* via *Speed Racer* meets Sid and Marty Krofft's then-popular *Land of the Lost*. The dinosaurs are executed via stop motion, an idea first experimented with by Tsuburaya Productions in another proof-of-concept short: *The Time Tunnel* (1974). The stop motion effects are the weakest link. They tend to be jerky and a tier below that of Japanese stop motion master Tadahito Mochinaga. These are heavily supplanted with mismatched Guignol puppet close-ups. Due to the difficulty creating quality stop motion on the hectic schedule of TV production, *Born Free*'s successor, *Dinosaur War Izenborg*, would employ suitmation instead.

Born Free's highlight is its model shooting by **SHINICHI OKA** (1947-) who had started his career unpretentiously lensing Tsuburaya Productions' *Redman* shorts. Once again, the miniaturized mecha strongly evokes Gerry Anderson. This is spottier in the water sequences with a slight "toys in a bathtub" look, but wide shots of the models are majestic. Koichi Takano handled the bulk of direction on *Born Free* and his flair for miniature photography shows. Support came from Atsushi Oki and Kiyoshi Suzuki. *Born Free* would only last 25 episodes, likely due to the difficulty in producing it. At the same time, Tsuburaya Productions would create another partially animated program entitled **PRO-WRESTLING STAR AZTECASER** [Television Run (Japan): October 7th, 1976 - March 31st, 1977]. This program, co-produced with Mannensha, was created by anime/manga luminary Go Nagai and his close associate **KEN ISHIKAWA** (1948-2006). In it, the hero Aztecaser transforms his live action surroundings into anime to execute wrestling stunts that are easier to pull off in animation.

Toho's sole major special effects film in 1976 was **ZERO PILOT** [AKA:

SAMURAI OF THE SKIES - Director: Seiji Maruyama - **Release Date (Japan):** October 2nd, 1976]. *Zero Pilot* is based on the memoirs of Imperial aviator Saburo Sakai. One of the few flying aces to survive World War II, Sakai had shot down dozens of American planes in combat. *Zero Pilot*'s opening features interview footage with Sakai that precedes the Toho logo. The film was partially funded by *Tenka Ikka no Kai*, an infamous pyramid scheme that Sakai was embroiled in.

Zero Pilot feels akin to the Imperial flying ace films that came before it such as *Colonel Kato's Falcon Squadron*, *Farewell Rabual*, *Zero Fighter* and *The Falcon Fighters*. Yet its tone is more contemporary like a fatalistic wartime *Top Gun* (1986). Director Maruyama's end is a well-directed character study of Sakai, portrayed by *Kamen Rider*'s Hiroshi Fujioka. Fujioka's Sakai is a more '70s, anti-establishment flying ace who resists suicide missions and the Imperial brass' view of pilots as expendable cannon-fodder but can't fight the tide.

The effects unit on *Zero Pilot* was helmed by Koichi Kawakita, his debut on a feature film. Kawakita was only 33 at the time, a young age for promotion to full-fledged effects director. Not yet credited with the official title, Kawakita proves himself a force to be reckoned with. Alongside *Submersion of Japan*, *Zero Pilot* is among the grandest Japanese special effects films of the 1970s. It boasts some of the most visually stunning flying sequences in the tokusatsu medium yet. Kawakita loved mechanics and engineering; he drew particular fascination from the wartime Mitsubishi Zero. His engineer skills beget an arresting sense of realism. Kawakita's side of *Zero Pilot* boasts the best staged aerial battle and bombardment sequences in a Toho war film to date. Kawakita was determined to make an impression on Toho's brass. He insisted stock footage be kept to a minimum and all airplanes be built from scratch, the responsibility of Yasuyuki Inoue. Besides Inoue, most of Nakano's crew worked under Kawakita for *Zero Pilot* including DP Motoyoshi Tomioka, engineer and wireman Koji Matsumoto and pyrotechnician Tadaaki Watanabe. Kawakita, known for being particular in his directing style, helms them with better precision than Nakano.

Zero Pilot features mainly radio-controlled Zeros as opposed to the traditional method of hanging and flying model planes with wire. They were piloted in some shots in open skies by crew with controllers, others against facsimile high altitude landscapes. This proved a logistical challenge as they frequently crashed and had to be repaired. Most difficult were the shots combining the RC models with pyrotechnics which had to be timed to the second. Kawakita would continue to employ the highest tech RC-powered models in future films such as his Godzilla entries. Kawakita's miniaturized Zeros, made by Yasuyuki Inoue's modeling team and given electrical life by Koji Matsumoto, even retract their wheels in midair via RC. This was something Eiji Tsuburaya could never pull off.

Lensing dynamic miniaturized aerial combat

Zero Pilot boasts a kinesis to its masterfully executed sky battles like a top-tier anime film or John Dykstra's upcoming work on *Star Wars*. These aerial sequences feature lifelike cloud effects and their realism is aided further by energetic camerawork from Tomioka. Genuine high altitude photography is also mixed in, blurring the distinction between the units. There's a haunting shot: a wide vista of an Imperial bomber exploding in midair admist a contrail plume. Courtesy of Takeshi Miyanishi and optical animator Yoshio Ishii, *Zero Pilot* features the most realistic process work done at Toho thus far. Most memorable is a stunning shot of a Zeros squadron flying over an army hospital as the love interest (Naoko Otani) looks on.

Zero Pilot's finale sports some of the best action filmmaking Toho had yet achieved. There's good synthesis and striking cinematography from both Maruyama and Kawakita's units. There is even a Hollywood-grade use of moving front projection shots, seldom employed in Japan. Kawakita's mentor Tsuburaya would have been proud. Though Godzilla and Ultraman stayed in hibernation for now, tokusatsu film production would ratchet up in the following year. This was partially spurred by a new, influential film from Hollywood that stunned moviegoers in May of 1977.

XXII.
__1977__
昭和五十二

Vigilante Zubat (1977) title card

The 1977 tokusatsu cycle began on February 2nd with another Shotaro Ishinomori show, this time on TV Tokyo: **VIGILANTE ZUBAT** [**Television Run (Japan):** February 2nd - September 28th, 1977]. *Vigilante Zubat* would be among Ishinomori's most unique creations, changing up the henshin hero formula intriguingly. Though the arty cinematography makes its Toei origins obvious, *Zubat* has a markedly different tone from Ishinomori's other creations. In the manner of a tokusatsu hero show directed by Quentin Tarantino, *Zubat* draws thematic and aesthetic influence from Spaghetti Westerns, particularly *Django* (1966) by Sergio Corbucci. The films of directors like Corbucci and Sergio Leone were popular in Japan, where they were called "Macaroni Westerns". Inspiration was also drawn from the *Wataridori* "Rambler" series made at Nikkatsu. Beginning with *The Rambling Guitarist* (1959), they featured heartthrob Akira Kobayashi as a guitar-toting wanderer similar to *Zubat'*s titular hero.

Ken Hayakawa (Hiroshi Miyauchi) is a private detective with the fashion sense of a typical Macaroni Western protagonist. Hayakawa's scientist friend Goro Asuka (Jiro Okazaki) is murdered by *another* nihilistically sociopathic secret society. In the first episode alone, they try to run over schoolchildren on a field trip with a car, beat the children with a whip, brutally assault Goro's sister Midori (Nobuko Oshiro), strap bombs to the kids' schoolbus and then blow up a hospital *Dark Knight*-style. Hayakawa uses Goro's research in a powerful space suit and battle car to transform himself into the hero Zubat. He then begins his vengeful, Macaroni Western-fashioned journey.

In a subversion of Ishinomori's usual tropes, a la Batman, Hayakawa doesn't transform. Though the suit's design is Sentai-like, Hayakawa merely puts on the Zubat suit which he keeps in his guitar case. A tokusatsu answer to Leone and Clint Eastwood's Man With No Name, Hayakawa/Zubat often wanders from town to town. Unlike *Kamen Rider* or *Gorenger*, rather than a monster of the week, Zubat's adversary tends to be a *yojimbo* (bodyguard), an enforcer for the criminal organization akin to a rival gunslinger. Perhaps taking a cue from from *Ultraman*, Hayakawa can only fight in the Zubat suit for a matter of minutes. The modeling for Zubat was handled by Kaimai Productions and the suit worn by Bunya Nakamura in stunt unit sequences. *Vigilante Zubat* has a lighter miniature unit involvement than recent Ishinomori shows like *Gorenger* or *Kyodain*. Regardless, the Tokusatsu Research Institute was brought in and contributed shots of a miniaturized Zubat flying through the air in his "Zubat Car".

Vigilante Zubat was popular in Japan and got strong ratings. The problem was that the darker, more mature themes and Spaghetti Western influence drew a high school and college age audience rather than children. As a result, toy sales were poor and *Vigilante Zubat* was ended after only 32 episodes though it would achieve cult status. One of its school-aged viewers was a then-17 Hideaki Anno, whose Daicon Film (later Studio Gainax) would go on to create several fan shorts inspired by *Zubat* in the 1980s starting with the 15-minute **VIGILANTE NOTENKI** (1982). *Notenki* meaning "scatterbrain", the character was played by future Gainax producer and director Yasuhiro Takeda.

Premiering on U.S. television later in February was **THE LAST DINOSAUR** [Directors: **TSUGUNOBU KOTANI** (1935-2020), Alexander Grasshoff - **Release Dates:** February 11th (**U.S.**) - September 10th, 1977 (**Japan**)]. It was the first of several international collaborations between Tsuburaya Productions and Rankin-Bass distributed in the states as TV movies. *The Last Dinosaur* was later released to Japanese theaters by Toho.

The Last Dinosaur is an underrated monster picture boasting a mostly American cast led by Richard Boone. Boone's performance as Trumpian oil empire heir and big game hunter Masten Thrust is strong. Boone had also voiced the dragon Smaug for Rankin-Bass in *The Hobbit* (also 1977), animated in Japan by Topcraft. Comic book author William Overgard's script is engaging. It follows the literary tradition of classic lost world stories by Jules Verne, Sir Arthur Conan Doyle and Edgar Rice Borroughs' but with '70s twists.

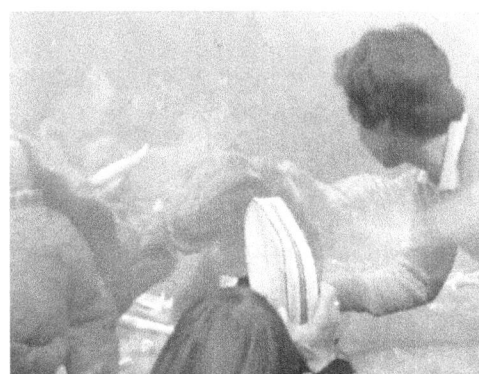 

Shooting prehistoric mayhem - special effects director Kazuo Sagawa (right)

Made in English, *The Last Dinosaur* was a trying shoot for director Kotani. Richard Boone, only a few years from his death, was a severe alcoholic whose massive hangovers occasionally halted shooting. Boone would play Commodore Matthew Perry for Tsuburaya Pro and Rankin-Bass' *The Bushido Blade*, released after his death in 1981 and also directed by Kotani. The mountainous Kamikochi region in Nagano Prefecture served as *The Last Dinosaur*'s prehistoric world and the weather was often uncooperative as it was the rainy season. The film's tribe of cave people were portrayed by Japanese actors which is oddly effective. The footage taken on location at Kamikochi is integrated well with the special effects unit's work and the climax in particular is thrillingly cut.

Supervising *The Last Dinosaur*'s effects unit was Kazuo Sagawa. Tsuburaya Productions had contemplated using stop motion a la *Born Free,* but settled for the suitmation techniques their artisans were seasoned in. *The Last Dinosaur*'s FX footage is similar to Roger Dicken's work on Amicus' recent Burroughs adaptation *The Land That Time Forgot* (1974). Sagawa's work is spotty, though some of it matches the level of Teruyoshi Nakano's work at the time. The miniature shooting, as per Sagawa's background on Tsuburaya Pro's shows, is a strength.

The Polar-Borer, used by Thrust and his expedition to travel to the picture's lost world, was designed by Rankin-Bass with its miniatures constructed by Hiruma Modelcraft. Three Polar-Borer models were built: a large-sized one made from plywood, a medium of FRP and small-scaled aluminum craft. Sagawa's unit went to particular lengths to make the miniature sets look lived in. Smoke machines were used to obscure wires and talcum powder was scattered onto the Tyrannosaurs' boneyard. Most impressive is a miniature helicopter landing done manually with wires, a trademark of Sagawa's since *Mighty Jack*.

The eponymous dinosaur is a very Godzillian Tyrannosaurus Rex. Its roar is even a re-mixed version of Godzilla's and the suit inhabited by Toru Kawai who played the monster in *Terror of Mechagodzilla*. *The Last Dinosaur*'s highlight sequence is a gory battle between the Tyrannosaurus and a Triceratops that makes good use of wirework. The dinosaur suits were crafted from foam rubber and the Triceratops is executed pantomime horse-style with two actors inside headed by Tatsumi Nikamoto. It's among the more effectively realized suits done in this style. *The Last Dinosaur*'s Tyrannosaurus costume would be reused soon after in *Dinosaur War Izenborg* and *Dinosaur Corps Koseidon*.

The Last Dinosaur is among the first tokusatsu films since the 1950s shot with spherical lenses rather than anamorphic. These lenses would soon become standard again in Japanese films. *The Last Dinosaur,* unlike many spherically lensed Japanese films which tended to be "hard matted", was shot open matte using the full academy ratio frame. This came in handy when the film was shown on American television. Producers Arthur Rankin and Jules Bass were keen on *The Last Dinosaur* being exhibited theatrically, but the picture failed to entice a distributor stateside and so was aired on ABC.

Soon after, Toei premiered yet another Ishinomori-run show in March: **DAITETSUJIN 17 [Television Run (Japan): March 18th - November 11th, 1977]**. *Daitetsujin 17* is like an edgier '70s version of Mitsuteru Yokoyama's *Tetsujin 28* and *Giant Robo*. Inspired by the popularity of Go Nagai's *Mazinger Z* and *Getter Robo*, Ishinomori was ordered to develop a live-action giant robot show for Toei and TBS. Thanks to its eponymous robot, *Daitetsujin 17* is the most tokusatsu-reliant of Ishinomori's programs. The robot itself was designed by Ishinomori with adjustments made by Katsushi Murakami, who would apply similar motifs to designs in *Mobile Suit Zeta Gundam*, the second TV installment of Yoshiyuki Tomino's landmark franchise. The modeling for the robot and its monster adversaries was done at Equis Productions with **YOSHITO KOMATSU** at the head. Komatsu would later model similar robots in future Super Sentai series.

Nobuo Yajima

Daitetsujin 17 manages to be another underrated gem in Ishinomori's television oeuvre. As usual, writer Masaru Igami and director Minoru Yamada were involved in many episodes. The villain, "Brain", is an evil A.I. supercomputer with an army of literal Nazis. Brain can manufacture giant monster robots, one of whom kills the family of young Saburo Minami (Masahiro Kamiya) on his sister's wedding day. Saburo winds up stumbling into Brain's secret base. Like Shotaro Kaneda and Daisaku Kusama before him, he gains control over one of these robots: Daitetsujin 17. Even the opening for *Daitetsujin 17* is impressive, featuring Saburo commanding 17 (pronounced "One Seven") and transforming into the title card.

The special effects unit on *Daitetsujin 17* was run by Nobuo Yajima and his Tokusatsu Research Institute. Wire work, engineering and pyrotechnics were handled by Toru Suzuki and Toho unit veteran Osamu Kume. Stuntman

Kazuo Niibori played 17 while Toru Kawai tended to play its adversaries. Yajima's FX footage is his best for TV yet. It's similar in style to his work in *Giant Robo* ten years prior but more sophisticated. With excitingly staged, shot and directed sequences of imaginative destruction, Yajima started to hit his stride as effects director on *Daitetsujin 17*. It was with this program that Yajima and his unit began to refine the style that they would use in shows to come, particularly the Super Sentai franchise.

The Self-Defense Force appears to have been heavily involved with *Daitetsujin 17*, as it is big on military spectacle with a prominent military organization, the Red Scarves, figuring into the plot. The end credits of early episodes even resemble a JSDF recruitment film. The ratings began to suffer with children and so the tone was lightened to a more comedic one. A second, benevolent supercomputer, Big Angel, along with another robot, Daitetsujin 18, were introduced in later episodes.

Simultaneously, Ishinomori was developing the second Sentai show, which began airing shortly after *Gorenger*. Entitled **J.A.K.Q. BLITZKRIEG SQUAD** [Television Run (Japan): April 9th - December 24th, 1977]. This time, the show and its team were themed after playing cards. The title, *J.A.K.Q*, stands for the four heroes, who are based on the cards Jack, Ace, King and Queen, a powerful hand of trump cards. Like Cyborg 009 and Kamen Rider, the four members of J.A.K.Q. are cybernetically enhanced. Rather than the usual motorbikes, they ride around in race cars or "buggies". They have a bigger armada of mecha at their disposal than the Gorengers, including a flying ship and amphibious tank. The deranged bad guys this time around are a criminal cabal unpretentiously called Crime, led by Rasputin-like Slavic oligarch Iron Claw (Masashi Ishibashi). As his name portends, he has an iron claw prosthetic for a hand. The good-guy outfit fighting Crime is ISSIS, not to be confused with another organization who are like real-life versions of villains from an Ishinomori show.

J.A.K.Q. was given a darker, more police procedural-like tenor than its predecessor and its ratings began strong. Once again, the Japan Action Club covered the stunts with a heavier emphasis on action than *Gorenger*. The effects unit for the miniature sequences was as usual handled by Nobuo Yajima and Toru Suzuki of the Tokusatsu Research Institute and the modeling on the ranger costumes and monster suits by Equis Productions. Sadly, ratings on *J.A.K.Q*. slipped as children were less interested thanks to its crime show vibe. As a result, *J.A.K.Q.* was lightened up a bit.

Starting in episode #23, the ranger squad is joined by a fifth member and the franchise's first "white ranger": the suave and cybernetically enhanced Sokichi Banba (*Key Hunter*'s Hiroshi Miyauchi), who becomes the commander of ISSIS' Japan branch. A la Tuxedo Mask in the Sentai-influenced *Sailor Moon*, he shows up when the going gets tough and wields deadly roses. These measures failed to boost ratings, however, and *J.A.K.Q.* was canceled after 35 episodes. 1978 would be the only year to this day since *Gorenger*'s debut without a Sentai show on the air in Japan. *J.A.K.Q.*, however, has a strong cult following thanks to its edgier tone. It was also the final Sentai program with Shotaro Ishinomori as showrunner.

Another dinosaur-themed tokusatsu production that year was **LEGEND OF THE DINOSAUR AND MONSTER BIRD** [**Director:** Junji Kurata - **Release Date (Japan):** April 29th, 1977]. *Legend of the Dinosaur and Monster Bird* was inspired by Steven Spielberg's *Jaws*. Toei's CEO, Shigeru Okada, had been floored by the Hollywood blockbuster, and with the same year's *The Bullet Train* having been a hit, he was eager for Toei to start producing theatrical special effects films that could be exported abroad. There was also a "Cryptozoology Boom" at the time and Okada's rival Tomoyuki Tanaka at Toho was planning *Nessie* with England's Hammer. Okada thus greenlit production on three films including *Legend of the Dinosaur and Monster Bird* and another, space horror-themed monster picture called *Devil Manta*. He also approved a remake of Nobuo Nakagawa's *The Sinners of Hell* (1960) per the "Occult Boom", revitalized by *The Omen* (1976). Like *The Bullet Train*, *Legend of the Dinosaur and Monster Bird* would be the most expensive Japanese movie up to that time. It was dethroned by *Message From Space* a year later.

Legend of the Dinosaur and Monster Bird is a mess but taken in its original Cinemascope aspect ratio is fun; revealing a movie with good production values. Toei's gritty cinematic "house style" is apparent. *Legend of the Dinosaur and Monster Bird* is laden with tilted "dutch angle" shots and offbeat cinematography seldom seen in Toho's output. The atmospheric opening of *Legend of the Dinosaur and Monster Bird* is superbly executed and stylishly directed by Kurata. Shades of *Jaws* are apparent with the "cardboard fin" gag even recycled wholesale.

As in *Jaws*, there's inventive underwater photography peppered into the monster attacks. Toei built a giant effects pool like Toho's just to stage these water sequences. The picture also employed the most state-of-the-art front projection to date. An FPC-101 unit from Cinema Productions Corporation in Hollywood was acquired at immense cost. *Legend of the Dinosaur and Monster Bird* was also the first tokusatsu film to employ video technology. In Toei fashion, it is grislier than *Jaws* and features sexual content, all censored in American prints.

Fuminori Ohashi fabricates prehistoric reptile heads

Legend of the Dinosaur and Monster Bird's biggest flaw is subpar and unconvincing FX work for its budget. There's just one beautiful FX shot: a wide composite of the Rhamphorynchus attacking villagers. The titular Plesiosaur and Rhamphorynchus were built by Fuminori Ohashi. It took Ohashi's team four months to construct four Plesiosaurus puppets along with a full scale head and fins much like his work on *The Whale God*. They also built a puppet and a full-sized head for the Rhamphorynchus. Ohashi would handle the physical execution of the monsters, though director Kurata was in charge of the unit. Ohashi was a master at fabricating hominids, but his work on dinosaurs falls short.

The FX footage in *Legend of the Dinosaur and Monster Bird* is TV quality at best; FX directors such as Nobuo Yajima and Koichi Takano were in fact doing better work in that medium. The Plesiosaur and Rhamphorynchus puppets look stiff and awkwardly manipulated. The final reel features the Plesiosaur and Rhamphorynchus doing battle in Aokigahara forest as Mount Fuji erupts. This is a singularly inept sequence that crashes and burns the entire picture, well set up in early sequences. There's at least an amusing coda of Toei nihilism as the protagonists' fates are left ambiguous. It's a shame as *Legend of the Dinosaur and Monster Bird* would be a minor genre masterpiece with polished effects footage. Sadly, the film was Fuminori Ohashi's swansong as an FX modeler.

In May, American audiences lined up outside their local theaters to see a new space-themed film with heavy visual effects sequences: **STAR WARS** [**Director: GEORGE LUCAS** (1944-) - **Release Date (U.S.):** May 25th, 1977]. Lucas, though cut from the cloth of his "New Hollywood" auteur contemporaries, wanted to make something unique. The shoot was trying for Lucas, who suffered a bout of hypertension, and *Star Wars* was expected to be a failure. The film was saved and enriched in the edit and through its visual effects sequences by **JOHN DYKSTRA** (1947-). Dykstra pioneered computer-controlled motion camera technology more sophisticated than Douglas Trumbull's, who had passed on the project.

Obsessively tweaked by its copyright holders in years since, *Star Wars* shines most in its less polished theatrical form. To people in 1977, *Star Wars* looked almost real: like a window into another world. Its images feel magical: a timeless fairy tale that happens to have technological flourish. *Star Wars* brought cinematic FX full circle from Méliès to Kubrick and Trumbull, drawing influence from everything in between including *Metropolis*, *The Wizard of Oz* (1939) and even Eiji Tsuburaya's work on *Battle in Outer Space*.

In addition to taking *Star Wars'* narrative from Akira Kurosawa's *The Hidden Fortress* (1958), George Lucas drew on monomythical elements from all over the world, including Japan. He would go on to produce Kurosawa's *Kagemusha* (1980). The iconic villain Darth Vader's design was influenced by samurai armor and, (allegedly), certain baddies from Shotaro Ishinomori's series. Lucas even courted Toshiro Mifune to play Obi Wan Kenobi or Darth Vader, which the legendary actor turned down. *Star Wars* is pure cinematic storytelling that is so universal and timeless that it feels transcendent - bridging the ancient and futuristic along with Arthurian myth and samurai drama. Luke Skywalker could be a medieval prince or ronin swordsman. Darth Vader could be a fearsome black knight or ruthless samurai warlord. Obi Wan would be an elderly wizard or a wizened *ninjutsu* master. *Star Wars* is an ingeniously assembled collection of visual motifs and mythical tropes innovatively executed. Moments feel timeless yet decades ahead of their time.

American audiences in line to see a new space picture

Star Wars evokes the fanciful spectacle of Japanese tokusatsu cinema but with Hollywood realism, filtering childlike wonder through cinematic hyper-believability. With similar kinetic, Eisensteinian editing to Tsuburaya's, the Battle of Yavin and destruction of the Death Star is the grandest visual effects sequence in cinema thus far. *Star Wars'* unreal, manufactured sound design by Ben Burtt even evokes Toho's tokusatsu oeuvre. Humorously, an early audience reaction sheet handed to producer Gary Kurtz after a test screening read "This is the worst film I have ever seen since *Godzilla vs. the Smog Monster* (sic)!" It's a shame Eiji Tsuburaya did not live to see *Star Wars,* as he no doubt would have adored it.

Star Wars' success was a double-edged sword. It led to commercial cinema abandoning story for spectacle. Every studio wanted to make a paint-by-numbers replica of the film and for decades hence, they've tried. In Japan, *Star Wars* was not released until June of 1978 and filmmakers and filmgoers alike were enraptured. It came at a good time, too, coinciding with the popularity of the *Space Battleship Yamato* anime franchise. Toho's Tomoyuki Tanaka and Toei's Shigeru Okada both shelved monster movies at their respective companies to prioritize tokusatsu *Star Wars* cash-ins.

Both were squeezed out before *Star Wars* was even in Japanese theaters.

The Japanese and Taiwanese film industries would meanwhile cross paths again on the war epic **HEROES OF THE EASTERN SKIES** [**Director:** Chang Tseng-Chai - **Release Date (Taiwan):** July 7th, 1977]. *Heroes of the Eastern Skies* revolves around a legendary group of Chinese aviators during the outbreak of the Sino-Japanese war in 1937. Though the film concerns a painful time in Japan-China relations, Japanese tokusatsu ingenuity was again employed. As Taiwan's native effects industry could not produce the necessary miniaturized aerial battle sequences, industry veterans Toru Suzuki, Michio Mikami and **RYUJI KAWASAKI** were brought in from Japan. Suzuki would helm the effects unit and direct construction of 360 miniature planes. The miniature footage is indeed distinctly Japanese, though Chang's main unit creates full-scale battle scenes with David Lean-style spectacle. *Heroes of the Eastern Skies'* extensive tokusatsu aerial battles are reminiscent of Noriaki Yuasa's work on *Gateway to Glory* and *The Falcon Fighters* (both 1969). They also resemble Koichi Kawakita's footage on the then-recent *Zero Pilot*, minus his engineering genius. *Heroes of the Eastern Skies* was extremely successful and won Best Film at the Golden Horse Awards.

In the wake of *Star Wars*, another film released the summer of '77 in Japan would ignite a smaller cinematic revolution: **HOUSE** [**Director: NOBUHIKO OBAYASHI** (1938-2020) - **Release Date (Japan):** July 30th, 1977]. Obayashi had directed the avant-garde short film *Emotion* (1966) and since then had become a successful director of TV commercials. His most famous was a spot for the perfume "Mandom" featuring Hollywood's Charles Bronson, but he worked with many other stars as well including Sophia Loren, Ringo Starr, Kirk Douglas and Katherine Hepburn. Obayashi found the transition to commercials from art films surprisingly easy, treating his spots as micro-movies. It was good training for him as TV ads tended to boast higher production values in Japan than films.

As with *Legend of the Dinosaur and Monster Bird, House* was developed thanks to *Jaws*. Obayashi and writer Chiho Katsura created a proposal inspired by ideas from his daughter Chigumi with a haunted house eating people rather than a shark. Chigumi herself was inspired by trips to her grandparents' in the country and an injury sustained during piano lessons.

The horror stories of English writer Walter de La Mare were also influential. Obayashi purposely gave the film an English title, taboo in the Japanese film industry. To Obayashi's surprise, Toho greenlit *House* within a few hours of proposal. The film languished in production hell for two years as their entire stock of directors passed on it and Toho were hesitant to hire an outsider like Obayashi. Obayashi thus put his advertising skills to work in a PR blitz which built anticipation in Japan, even creating a soundtrack ahead of time. Most of the film's supporting female cast were pulled from various commercials Nobuhiko Obayashi had directed during *House*'s development.

Actor Miki Jinbo (left) and director Nobuhiko Obayashi (right)

Toho reneged and allowed Obayashi to helm the film. Their veteran directors were livid that an outsider with no AD experience was being handed a feature film. Kihachi Okamoto, however, a friend and mentor of Obayashi's, defended him. Obayashi was only allowed to use Toho's biggest sound stages as he had made commercials there. Rather than use a seasoned Toho DP, Obayashi insisted that **YOSHITAKA SAKAMOTO** (1942-), who worked on his commercials, shoot the movie. Toho's gaffers were resistant to working under Sakamoto, but in time Obayashi won them over. A la Sergio Leone, Obayashi had the film's soundtrack played on set to inspire his ingenues.

House, though more J-Horror than classical tokusatsu, is hallucinogenic cinema with cult status on both sides of the Pacific. *House*'s cinematic fever dream boasts an absurd unreality like a manic brew of *The Wizard of Oz* (1939), *Kwaidan* (1964), a live-action anime film, the best Italian horror pictures of Mario Bava or Dario Argento and the effects work of Eiji Tsuburaya. *House* combines the flavor of Japan's native ghost stories and Western gothic horror with arresting power. Other moments predict the hyperkinesis of Shinya Tsukamoto's *Tetsuo: The Iron Man* (1989). The bad trip really kicks in midway. There's one disturbing sequence of grotesque phantasmagoria after another as the film's young cast is devoured by the eponymous house, possessed by the spirit of the lead's love-starved aunt (Yoko Minamada).

For *House*'s visual effects, Obayashi strived to rebel against the realism of contemporary Japanese and Hollywood cinema. To do this, he used an arsenal of cinematic techniques learned from his commercial work. This includes surreal sets with painted backdrops, expressionistic lighting, rapid-fire staccato editing, tokusatsu-style miniatures, optical animation and unsettling sound design. Nobuhiko Obayashi was offered the opportunity to work with Teruyoshi Nakano's FX unit by Toho but opted to direct the picture's effects end himself with input from DP Yoshitaka Sakamoto. Obayashi felt he could handle it because of his long history using VFX in commercials. He wanted his images executed differently in a more unreal fashion than Toho's FX team would have given him. Several frequent members of Nakano's unit, however, worked on *House* including optical composite specialists Takeshi Miyanishi and Yoshio Ishii. *House*'s painted backdrops resemble both Masaki Kobayashi's *Kwaidan* and the "horizons" of Eiji Tsuburaya's tokusatsu set pieces. These were created by none other than Fuchimu Shimakura, Tsuburaya's veteran backdrop painter. The miniature set of the "house" itself was another contribution from Toho's FX staff. *House* was shot full frame with spherical lenses rather than in anamorphic Cinemascope, likely due to its ease in VFX compositing.

Obayashi and Sakamoto were experimental in their approach with a shooting process that was almost improvisational. Obayashi avoided using storyboards, an extreme rarity for a VFX heavy film. With a childlike creative spirit, Obayashi aimed to combine old-school techniques with innovative, Hollywood-style filmmaking. The crew were sometimes flummoxed. They had little idea what the finished images they were working on would look like. Obayashi makes his mentality clear in this quote from an interview conducted by Criterion: "The power of cinema lies not in the explainable, but in the strange and inexplicable".

The astonishing peak of *House* is a sequence where one of the girls, Melody (Eriko Tanaka), gets chewed and devoured by a grand piano as she plays it. The scene renders its graphic carnage with intricate optical animation. It's capped in a close up shot of severed fingers playing the piano keys so well executed as to be arresting. *House* was another one of the first Japanese films to employ video technology. To depict the body of another girl, Professor (Ai Matsubara), being dissolved in water near the climax, blue paint was poured onto the naked actress and the element lensed on video. In the film's downbeat but hauntingly beautiful final moments, the lead Gorgeous (Kimiko Ikegami) devours her father's new lover (Haruko Wanibuchi) as an upbeat song by pop band Godiego plays. This is concluded with a stunning shot of the two women facing each other as the white feline mascot trots across the frame.

House was controversial with critics. It made good money, however, and launched Obayashi's directing career; this film netted him the Blue Ribbon Award for Best New Director. Obayashi would in 1979 propose a bizarro-world Godzilla project to Toho entitled *A Space Godzilla*. Promoted in a two-part article in Japanese Starlog magazine illustrated by rising manga star Katsuhiro Otomo, it would have made *Godzilla vs. Hedorah* look tame. Tomoyuki Tanaka was particular about the character of Godzilla, a likely reason it went unmade.

The Shaw Brothers in Hong Kong would also enlist the expertise of Japanese special effects staff again for their cash-in on Dino De Laurentiis' *King Kong* (1976): **THE MIGHTY PEKING MAN [AKA: GOLIATHON - Director: HO MENG-HUA** (1923-2009) - **Release Dates:** August 11th, 1977 **(H.K.)** - March 11th, 1978 **(Japan)]**. Director Ho had directed a film at Shaw Brothers that was surprisingly epochal in Greater Chinese popular culture: *The Flying Guillotine* (1974). Ho was likely chosen for *The Mighty Peking Man* as he could handle special effects-laden pictures - he had previously directed gruesome Southeast Asian horror films like *Black Magic* (1975) and *The Oily Maniac* (1976). *The Mighty Peking Man*'s production was troubled. The Shaw Brothers began planning it in early 1975 and were originally going to make the film as a straight-up King Kong movie, but this was deemed too legally risky. They wanted to release *The Mighty Peking Man* before De Laurentiis' *King Kong* hit theaters in Hong Kong but these production problems halted such plans. As Ho's unit shot on location in Mysore, India, they could not stand the regional cuisine and barely ate until they found a Chinese restaurant.

Japanese poster for *The Mighty Peking Man* (1977)

Modeler Keizo Murase of Twenty was among the first Japanese staff enlisted for *The Mighty Peking Man*. During production of *The Snake Prince*, Murase had become friendly with production manager **CHUA LAM** (1941-) who offered him a job on *The Mighty Peking Man*, then-in development. The Shaw Brothers decided to hire an entire Japanese effects unit this time. Initially, Yoshiyuki Kuroda was first chosen as effects director for *The Mighty Peking Man*. The Shaw Brothers were fond of *Majin*, as evidenced by their frequent resampling of Akira Ifukube's music cues in many of their *wuxia* films.

The shooting for Kuroda's unit wound up delayed and the Japanese end's visas expired. Sadamasa Arikawa was thus chosen as Kuroda's replacement and with him came an entirely new staff from Toho. This included longtime veteran DP Motoyoshi Tomioka along with Koichi Kawakita, who acted as Arikawa's assistant director. Also accompanying Arikawa to Hong Kong was pyrotechnician Osamu Kume, given much to do in *The Mighty Peking Man*'s fiery finale. *The Mighty Peking Man* was an expensive production for Shaw Brothers, costing six million HK dollars. Front projection technology never before employed in Hong Kong was utilized, though the process work in *The Mighty Peking Man* is quite spotty. Arikawa's Japanese unit stayed in the Shaws' dormitories at Clearwater Bay for over four months. According to Koichi Kawakita, Arikawa was a strict taskmaster and demanded the crew be on their best behavior abroad. There was friction between Arikawa and director Ho. Ho had shot much of his end and wanted the effects sequences filmed more quickly, whereas Arikawa felt he was not being given the necessary time to produce quality footage.

Utam, the Peking Man himself, was made by Keizo Murase with the direction of Michio Mikami and his firm Cosmo Productions. Equis' Akira Takahashi designed the monster. There were two designs and respective suits made, with the first being scrapped due to Kuroda's departure. This first costume was made of goat's hair. For the second and final suit, Murase used genuine human hair which was donated by local women. A Guignol puppet of Utam was employed for close-up shots. Additionally, full-sized hands, arms and chests for Utam were built. The full-sized ape hand is awkwardly executed, but the Utam suit is one of the best ape costumes in tokusatsu history. Throughout much of the film, Utam was portrayed by **YUEN CHEUNG-YAN** (1957-), a martial arts stuntman and the brother of famed fight director Yuen Woo-Ping.

Director Ho Meng-Hua's end of *The Mighty Peking Man* is marred by mondo-style animal cruelty and a love montage so corny it looks directed by Trey Parker and Matt Stone. Though among the best East Asian pseudo-tokusatsu films, the work of Sadamasa Arikawa's unit on *The Mighty Peking Man* is a mixed bag. His team took the film and its King Kong influence to heart and Arikawa's footage is better directed. It is a nudge below what Arikawa could pull off in Japan, however, and not edited cohesively with the footage of Ho's unit. Some of the composite shots are poor as Arikawa did not have access to the same equipment as in Japan and could not supervise these shots as his visa ran out. Many front projection shots are not color timed properly with noticeable contrast disparities between foreground and background elements.

The miniature photography by Arikawa's unit is stronger and more atmospheric. An exhaustively detailed, miniaturized version of Hong Kong was created. These models were built by local Chinese carpenters and Keizo Murase was awed by their craftsmanship and attention to detail. Murase was also impressed with how no expense was spared with the production in contrast to thriftier Japanese filmmaking. Hong Kong's many quirks are well captured in these miniatures such as storefronts, hanging laundry, apartment spaces, commercial streets and even tiny air conditioning units.

The Mighty Peking Man's final third is more fun than Ho's sleazier first half as Arikawa's unit takes the stage and the picture takes on Japanese tokusatsu flair. His work is plentiful in these sequences. There are striking vista composites during Utam's King Kong-style rampage through Hong Kong. The highlight is a thrillingly staged battle sequence between British army helicopters and the monster. These boast high altitude, aviator's eye view shots, a speciality of Arikawa's. Amusingly, the Hong Kong British army commissioner is played by entrepreneur Ted Thomas, whose HK-based firm dubbed numerous tokusatsu movies into English (ironically, his voice is dubbed by another actor in all versions of *The Mighty Peking Man*).

The Mighty Peking Man's grim finale features Utam gruesomely bloodied by explosives and set aflame atop the Jardine House, Hong Kong's tallest skyscraper at the time. It's like the ending of *King Kong* filtered through the nihilism of '70s HK cinema. Stuntman Yuen refused to shoot this sequence as he felt it was too dangerous and the production's insurance didn't adequately cover it. The shoot halted for a week. With time short, the Shaws and director Ho frustrated and the Japanese crew's visas running out, Murase got inside the suit. He was pelted with exploding gunpowder, set on fire with oil and had to fall off the miniaturized Jardine House. Production manager Chua Lam felt so bad for Murase that he bought him an expensive gold watch.

The visas of Arikawa's unit wound up expiring before they could finish every shot. Murase himself would direct a single special effects sequence in the film: a well-staged miniature air crash during a storm. *The Mighty Peking Man* made good money and was more successful in Hong Kong and Taiwan than *The Super Inframan*. Sadly, the Shaw Brothers' fortune would shift, and they would eventually cease film production in 1986 before more collaborations with Japanese filmmakers could take place, marking the end of an era in Hong Kong cinema.

U.S. VHS sleeve of *Attack of the Supermonsters*, an edited feature version of *Dinosaur War Izenborg* (1977-78)

Back in Japan, Tsuburaya Productions would attempt one more program melding anime and tokusatsu: **DINOSAUR WAR IZENBORG [Television Run (Japan):** October 7th, 1977 - June 30th, 1978]. *Izenborg* was to be a direct sequel to *Born Free* with that show's protagonists battling hostile dinosaurs instead of rescuing them. However, connections to the prior series were discarded. To produce the anime scenes, Studio Deen was employed this time. Deen, a dominant studio to this day, was founded by ex-Sunrise animators and would go on to work with luminaries such as Mamoru Oshii and Rumiko Takahashi. *Izenborg*'s first episode opens in a collage of stock footage from Toho films and Tsuburaya shows such as *Fireman* and *Ultraman Leo*. The miniature work tends to be clunkier as Koichi Takano and Kazuo Sagawa were not involved. *Izenborg* was mainly directed by Kazuho Mitsuta and Shohei Tojo.

This time, the monstrous dinosaurs are created through suitmation. In *Izenborg*, an army of sentient, intelligent dinosaurs have formed yet another evil organization. They're led by Ururu, brought to life with the Tyrannosaurus suit from Tsuburaya Pro's prior *The Last Dinosaur*. Ururu is later revealed to be a pawn of Gottes, an evil alien, and killed by the Izenborg. There's clear influence from Tatsunoko's popular *Gatchaman* in the character designs. Protagonists Ai and Zen Tachibana can unite *Ultraman Ace/Barom-1* style to become Izenborg, a cyborg that pilots another Andersonesque battle vehicle. With its "Izencross" circular blades, it can slice and dice monsters. Later on, the two develop the ability to become a gigantic kyodai hero who battles the dinosaurs in the manner of Ultraman. Tatsumi Nikamoto filled the role of Izenborg's hero form and Toru Kawai again portrayed many of the monsters. *Dinosaur War Izenborg* features more shots mixing live action and anime elements than *Born Free*. Japanese media mixing anime with live action is still rare, with notable exceptions being Hiroaki Yoshida's *Twilight of the Cockroaches* (1987) and moments in Hideaki Anno's *Evangelion* films.

Izenborg proved extremely popular in the Arab world, where none other than former Saudi crown prince Muhammad bin Nayef has counted himself a fan. In 2016, Tsuburaya Productions partnered with a Saudi company to produce *The Return of Izenborg,* a documentary with a new tokusatsu sequence directed by Kiyotaka Taguchi. Tsuburaya Productions' next program was also dinosaur-based and reused the Tyrannosaurus costume from *The Last Dinosaur:* **DINOSAUR CORPS KOSEIDON [Television Run (Japan):** June 7th, 1978 - June 29th, 1979]. Unlike *Born Free* and *Izenborg*, the show was entirely live action. Thanks to the influence of *Star Wars*, it boasted stronger space-themed elements.

For their News Years' holiday release, Toho put out a space film of their own intended to beat *Star Wars* to the punch in Japan: **THE WAR IN SPACE [Director:** Jun Fukuda - **Release Date (Japan):** December 17th, 1977]. Earlier in the year, Tomoyuki Tanaka had gone to Hawaii to see *Star Wars* and returned with immediate plans for a space opera. Toho came close to producing a pair of monster movies that year. The first was *Rebirth of Godzilla*, a new Godzilla entry to feature the monster battling terrorists at a nuclear power plant. The second was *Nessie*, a Loch Ness Monster-themed co-production with England's Hammer Films. Both projects were put on the backburner where they wound up unproduced to make way for Tanaka's *Star Wars*-style proposal.

The War in Space was a hectic production, greenlit in October and released in theaters two months later for the New Years' holiday. *The War in Space*'s Japanese title *"Wakusei Daisenso (Great Planetary War)"*, was originally to be the title for *Star Wars* in Japan. George Lucas rejected this as he wanted every version of his film to be called *Star Wars* per his company's branding plans. Maligned among fans, *The War in Space* is more rewarding when viewed as a '70s answer to Toho's Tsuburaya-era space operas than a Japanese *Star Wars* ripoff. The picture is a soft remake of *Battle in Outer Space* with elements of *Atragon*. Aspects of Yoshinobu Nishizaki and Leiji Matsumoto's popular *Space Battleship Yamato* anime franchise are also clearly integrated. Besides prominently featuring a space warship, *The War in Space*'s crew uniforms and the blueish-green skin of the nasty aliens appear rather *Yamato*-influenced. A *Space Battleship Yamato* compilation film had been released the previous summer. Its success driven by the international *Star Wars* buzz, *Space Battleship Yamato* wound up outperforming Lucasfilm's offering at the Japanese box office.

Technicians hang miniature spacecraft

The War in Space is silly and far from the best Japanese special effects production of the 1970s, but it still manages to be exhilarating. At its heights, the film is like a live-action *Space Battleship Yamato* movie made in the classic Toho mold by the staff behind *Godzilla vs. Mechagodzilla*. *The War in Space* offers few new tropes and Jun Fukuda's end is among his least inspired. Yet Teruyoshi Nakano's half of *The War in Space* is solid, especially if one avoids comparing it to John Dykstra's work. This is not a trailblazing production like *Star Wars* but a traditional tokusatsu flick where the spaceships are hung with piano wire in front of lightbulbs representing a starfield.

The War in Space boasts eye-catching composites mixing actors with miniatures in the *Gohten*'s docking bay similar to shots in Nakano's prior Mechagodzilla movies. Takeshi Miyanishi and Kazunobu Sanpei were in charge of the film's optical work as usual. Of course, to remind the viewer that it's the 1970s and the budget was tight, the aliens' rampage consists almost entirely of a stock footage montage with shots from *The Last War* and *Prophecies of Nostradamus*. The *Gohten*'s launch is a thrilling scene, however. Once the crew reaches Venus, *The War in Space* comes alive. The most visually extraordinary sequence features the *Gohten* descending through Venus' orange atmosphere.

The picture's final third features some of the Nakano unit's finest miniature shooting. Many impressive models were created for *The War in Space* with art director Yasuyuki Inoue at the department's helm. The *Gohten*, named after the *Goten-go* from *Atragon*, was sleekly designed by Inoue. Executed with ten and four-foot models, it even features a gunbarrel-style revolving launcher that spits out space fighters like bullets. This is the sort of fun that tokusatsu cinema is all about. Nakano deliberately had the *Gohten* fly in straight and curved lines to differentiate it from the entirely straight flight paths of the Imperial Star Destroyers in *Star Wars*.

The Yomi aliens' Roman-style ship, the *Daimakan*, was inspired largely by Roman warships and Asian pirate vessels. Leiji Matsumoto's manga *Space Pirate Captain Harlock,* which had an anime TV adaptation on the way, was also an influence. Nakano had Inoue add laser-firing oars to the design. The modeling department built a four-foot miniature of the *Daimakan* that was made to look ancient and lived-in, though they felt they didn't have enough time to get it just right. Larger sections of the ship were also built for close-ups.

For the *Gohten*'s jet-like Space Fighters and the Yomi aliens' Hell Fighters, a variety of miniatures were built at various sizes, all designed by Yasuyuki Inoue. The Space Fighters were made to resemble bullets as they are fired from the *Gohten*'s revolver barrel-like airlock. The Hell Fighters were constructed from FRP with the largest miniatures around ten inches. Jun Fukuda jokingly called them "spinning eggs." Inoue's department also built a *Gohten* Land Rover and Hovercraft at two-foot and tiny four-inch scales from wood.

Despite the distinctly Japanese flourish of *The War in Space*, the art department paid some homage to Hollywood, particularly on Fukuda's end. The spacesuits worn by the cast are patterned after the suits in *2001: A Space Odyssey* and there's a Chewbacca-inspired Space Beastman who acts as a guard dog for the Yomi aliens. The suit modeled by Nobuyuki Yasumaru, the Beastman was portrayed by professional wrestler **MAMMOTH SUZUKI** (1941-1991).

Teruyoshi Nakano

For the Venus sequences, Nakano's unit explosively takes the stage, literally and figuratively. It resembles Nakano's '70s answer to Eiji Tsuburaya's and Sadamasa Arikawa's respective moon battle sequences in *Battle in Outer Space* and *Destroy All Monsters*. It was Teruyoshi Nakano who persuaded the writers to set the climax on Venus. His reasoning was simple. Nakano wanted a final battle on a planet with an atmosphere that would allow for liberal use of his beloved explosions. Ground glass and sprayed water was used to make the Venusian terrain look natural. Coal-based fly ash, a favorite tool of Nakano and Tadaaki Watanabe's for mixing into their gunpowder, was strewn through the air in these sequences to create the effect of Venus' toxic atmosphere. This was mixed with colored cement and by the shoot's end the FX staff's skin had begun to change color.

The War in Space was the first film of Nakano's to employ **TAKESHI**

YAMAMOTO (1949-) as head FX cinematographer. The son of Tsuburaya-era pyrotechnician Kyuzo Yamamoto, he had helped Motoyoshi Tomioka shoot *Godzilla vs. Mechagodzilla* and *Prophecies of Nostradamus*. *The War in Space*'s final, symphonic explosion of Venus was actually shot with a spherical lens akin to the title plate in *Nostradamus*. Nakano wanted the explosion to stretch out to the corners of the frame in an interesting way. *The War in Space* would be among the last Japanese special effects films shot in anamorphic Cinemascope. By this time, the Japanese film industry was trending toward spherical lenses again. Jun Fukuda was unhappy with *The War in Space* as he felt he wasn't given enough time and it wound up his final theatrical film. Nakano, however, was more proud of it. In his own words, predicting the sentiments of his future apprentice Shinji Higuchi, he said "I wanted to make a movie that was visually appealing. So I created image after image built on each image to create the overall visual appeal of the picture".

After *The War in Space,* Toho nearly put *Nessie* into production, but the project was scrapped due to Hammer's financial woes. *Nessie* came closer to production than most of Toho's abandoned projects. Bryan Forbes, who had helmed *The Stepford Wives* (1975), was hired as director with Nakano set to lead a tokusatsu unit in Japan. Yasuyuki Inoue designed the monster and built maquettes as lavish trade ads were put out in *Variety*. The project would likely have been more fruitful than Hammer's collaborations with Shaw Brothers like *Legend of the 7 Golden Vampires* (1974). Hammer soon went belly up after producing a remake of Alfred Hitchcock's *The Lady Vanishes* (1979).

Soon after, Teruyoshi Nakano's unit would contribute FX footage to **THE FIREBIRD [AKA: HINOTORI - Director:** Kon Ichikawa - **Release Date (Japan):** August 19th, 1978]. Based on the manga by Osamu Tezuka, *The Firebird* was an expensive prestige production mixing anime and live-action elements. It was met with harsh critical reviews and its high production costs did not justify a second part adapting more of Tezuka's manga. Instead, an anime adaptation, *Phoenix 2772,* was released in 1980.

While Godzilla hibernated and interest in interstellar spectacle reigned supreme, effects director Nobuo Yajima would be kept particularly busy with the production of numerous films and television shows at Toei.

XXIII.
1978 - 1979
昭和五十三 - 五十四

In late January, the next collaboration between Rankin-Bass and Tsuburaya Productions aired on American television: **THE BERMUDA DEPTHS** [Director: Tsugunobu Kotani - **Release Date (U.S.):** January 27th, 1978]. *The Bermuda Depths* swaps out the lost world tropes of *The Last Dinosaur* for Melvillian nautical horror. With Kotani's main unit on location in Bermuda, the picture features an entirely Hollywood cast. This includes Leigh McCloskey, *The Greatest American Hero*'s Connie Sellecca as Calypso-like sea siren Jennie Haniver, *Rocky* and *Predator*'s Carl Weathers and the Santa Claus-like Burl Ives. Described as "more like a harlequin romance than a Gamera movie" by Stuart Galbraith, the film is indeed dull, though it has moments of lyrical beauty with idyllic Bermuda locales. *The Bermuda Depths* feels like a step down from its predecessor *The Last Dinosaur*.

The effects unit on *The Bermuda Depths* was helmed by Kazuo Sagawa and lensed in Japan. Save for some miniature shots, Sagawa's contributions are fairly invisible in early scenes. Sagawa and company take over for the final 20 minutes, recalling *Jaws* with a maritime hunt for Jennie's pet monster sea turtle. The creature executed mainly through suitmation and puppetry, these scenes are a highlight and feature impressive miniature shooting. Sagawa's FX footage is not well matched, however, with the Bermuda-shot main unit. *The Bermuda Depth*s is capped in a downbeat ending in which several major characters die. Besides this and its effects end, the picture is fairly forgettable.

At the Toei Manga Festival in March, the crossover short **J.A.K.Q. VS. GORENGER** [Director: Katsuhiko Taguchi - **Release Date (Japan):** March 18th, 1978] was unveiled. For Toei's second-to-last mini-film of the 1970s, influence was drawn from the success of *Five Riders vs. King Dark*, along with the Go Nagai anime crossover *Great Mazinger vs. Getter Robo* (1975). A crossover with *Daitetsujin 17* was considered, but in the end Toei decided to bring the two Shotaro Ishinomori-created Sentai squads together. The two squadrons team up to battle a resurgent Crime and the evil Iron Claw. With the help of his Big Four: Captain UFO (Mitsuo Ando), Baron Iron Mask (Kenji Ushio), General Sahara (Hideyo Amamoto) and Hell Boxer (Osamu Kaneda), Iron Claw is planning to plunge the world into chaos by dropping atomic bombs on major cities.

J.A.K.Q. vs. Gorenger (1978)

J.A.K.Q. vs. Gorenger is another of the better Toei short subject-tokusatsu films with arresting cinematography and staccato editing. The film amusingly reveals that all of the Ishinomori hero shows are set in the same warped universe with mentions made of Kamen Rider V3 and Kikaider. Lisa Komaki's Peggy Matsuyama is the sole Gorenger to appear on-screen in actor form. Audio loops from *Gorenger* were used to create the vocal performances of Akaranger and Midoranger as their actors were not available. As Nobuo Yajima and his Tokusatsu Research Institute were occupied with pre-production on *Message From Space,* the miniature work is unusually patchy. The stunt unit's work on *J.A.K.Q. vs. Gorenger*, however, is sublime. The two Sentai teams battle the armies of Crime in a hyperkinetic finale at the usual quarry. Crime's Big Four combine into a tank-like robot monster and only a coordinated attack from the Gorengers and J.A.K.Q. can bring it down. *J.A.K.Q. vs. Gorenger* is another action-loaded gem in Toei and Ishinomori's oeuvre far more entertaining than any recent superhero media from Hollywood.

Star Wolf (1978) soundtrack by Norio Maeda

Tsuburaya Productions' following major program was **STAR WOLF [AKA: FUGITIVE ALIEN - Television Run (Japan):** April 2nd - September 24th, 1978]. Based on a series of novels by American science fiction author **EDMOND HAMILTON** (1904-1977), *Star Wolf* was produced to celebrate the 15th anniversary of Tsuburaya Productions. It drew inspiration from the contemporary popularity of space operas like *Star Wars* and *Space Battleship Yamato*. Stylistic influence from *Star Wars* is apparent in the program's first moments with Star Destroyer and X-Wing-inspired mechanical designs to the alien craft. *Star Wolf* is also stylistically similar to Universal's *Battlestar Galactica*, which started its run in the U.S. just as its Japanese counterpart was leaving the airwaves. *Star Wolf* was aimed at older audiences than the average Tsuburaya Productions show and this was its undoing.

Kazuo Sagawa was the series' special effects director and *Star Wolf* is his masterwork. Though lacking polish in some instances, *Star Wolf* features the finest visual effects on Japanese television to date. Minoru Nakano and his Den Films were heavily involved in the visual effects, which proved challenging, as he was also busy with *Message from Space*. *Star Wolf* uses Hollywood-style VFX techniques, though on a '70s Japanese TV budget. Some shots are easily theatrical quality and a few *Battlestar Galactica*-grade. *Star Wolf* is loaded with imaginative compositions beautifully blending models, optical animation and matte paintings along with visually stunning miniature shots. A highlight is the heroes' ship the *Bacchus* III traveling through a Black Hole; not unlike a tokusatsu version of the climax of *Interstellar* (2014). Also memorable is an exploding star with contributions from Minoru Nakano along with brilliantly coordinated pyrotechnics going off as the camera moves through a tunnel.

Star Wolf boasts prominent miniature work. The extensive mechanical designs were handled by **OSAMU YAMAGUCHI** (1946-). Yamaguchi got his start on *Silver Mask* in 1971 and designed the Izenborg hero form in *Dinosaur War Izenborg*. Art support came from Akihiko Iguchi and Shinichi Kamisawa. For *Bacchus III*, a trio of miniatures were produced including a four-foot model. The Star Wolf command ship was a two-foot piece and the X-Wing-like Wolf Claw attackers had four types of miniatures made. Larger models for close-ups were made from metal, while smaller miniatures were made from FRP. Tiny models for long shots were produced at a nearby toy factory. The young Tomoo Haraguchi assisted in modeling many of the miniatures. Though its visual effects were dazzling, *Star Wolf*'s ratings were poor. In Japan, the show was seen as too serious for children but too silly for adults. Starting with episode #14, the title was changed to *Space Hero Star Wolf* and the tone lightened. These changes made little difference in ratings and *Star Wolf* ended after 24 episodes.

Later in April, Toei would unleash their own answer to *Star Wars* two months before it was released in Japan: **MESSAGE FROM SPACE** [Director: Kinji Fukasaku - **Release Date (Japan)**: April 29th, 1978]. *Message*

From Space was spawned from the redevelopment of Toei's planned space monster film *Devil Manta*. As with *Legend of the Dinosaur and Monster Bird*, *Devil Manta* was planned to revitalize big screen tokusatsu filmmaking at Toei. It was to be director Hajime Sato's first film in almost a decade. Nobuo Yajima was due to helm the special effects unit and Shotaro Ishinomori contributed monster and mecha designs. With the release of *Star Wars*, however, development on *Devil Manta* was halted. Toei's Shigeru Okada, frustrated that Toho and Tomoyuki Tanaka had beaten him to the punch with *The War in Space,* changed the project's direction to a space opera.

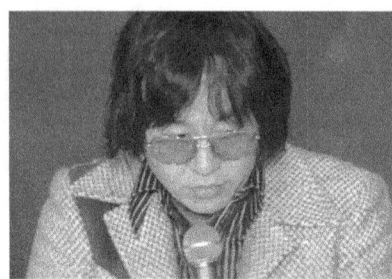 

Shotaro Ishinomori (left) - Kinji Fukasaku (right, center)

Though Ishinomori and Yajima were kept on, Hajime Sato was taken off the project and replaced with Kinji Fukasaku. Since directing *The Green Slime* and supporting Toshio Masuda on the Japanese segments of *Tora! Tora! Tora!* (1970), Fukasaku had become known for his gritty and arrestingly helmed gangster pictures at Toei. Fukasaku directed *Message From Space* in-between two *jidai-geki* movies in 1978: *Shogun's Samurai* and his *Chushingura*-adaptation *The Fall of Ako Castle*. Okada liked Fukasaku's idea that this new space opera film should be a "*jidai-geki* in space". The dependable director was thus hired while still at work on *Shogun's Samurai.*

Screenwriter **HIROO MATSUDA** (1933-), after returning from a *Star Wars* screening in Hawaii with Nobuo Yajima, decided to make the story an intergalactic adaptation of Bakin Tozawa's classical novel *Satomi Hakkenden* to differentiate it. Fukasaku tried to avoid seeing *Star Wars* before the shoot as he was worried he might copy its style too much, but he wound up attending a screening. As with *The Green Slime*, Fukasaku again directed Hollywood actors. *Message From Space* stars the tragically late Vic Morrow (*Dirty Harry, Crazy Larry*) and young actors Phillip Casnoff and Peggy Lee Brennan, though the supporting cast was Japanese. Like *Legend of the Dinosaur and Monster Bird*, the budget was the highest yet in Japanese film history. It would be quickly dethroned by another Fukasaku film: *Virus* (1980).

Message From Space is an exuberant, aesthetically eclectic picture that revels in affectionate ridiculousness. Patrick Macias says it best in *Tokyoscope: The Japanese Cult Film Companion*: "At any moment, it can change gears". At points, its cinematography by Toru Nakajima has an unconventional feel in line with Fukasaku's *yakuza* movies with dutch angles and handheld camerawork far removed from Gilbert Taylor's shooting of *Star Wars*. A tavern sequence evokes the Mos Eisley cantina via the dance club in Fukasaku's prior *Black Lizard* (1968). The ever-faithful Toei quarry naturally stands in for several alien planets. One of them, where the heroes encounter Prince Hans (Sonny Chiba), has its footage tinted crimson akin to *The Angry Red Planet* (1959).

Fukasaku's main unit was imbued with a strong tokusatsu industry presence in the form of art director Michio Mikami and contributions from Shotaro Ishinomori. Mikami's expressionistic sets, seen throughout the film, give the film the feel of a manga panel brought vividly to life. The sequences with the villainous Gavanas, headed by the silver-faced Rockseia (Mikio Narita, who often played yakuza dons for Fukasaku), echo his work on *The Super Inframan*. Michio Mikami would later incorporate similar design motifs into his coming show *X-Bomber*.

With *Message From Space*, Kinji Fukasaku, Shotaro Ishinomori and Nobuo Yajima craft Toei's finest tokusatsu feature since *Grand Duel in Magic*. Nobuo Yajima's special effects unit shot furiously from February to early April of 1978. At one point, they produced 500 effects cuts in the span of five days. Yajima's FX footage is less refined but more creative and fanciful than Teruyoshi Nakano's in *The War in Space*. Shotaro Ishinomori produced 500 designs for the film and SFX art director Tetsuzo Osawa headed the construction of numerous intricate miniatures. Fittingly per Ishinomori's design sensibility, the Gavanas' ships have devil horns like their helmets. Toru Suzuki handled model building, wirework and pyrotechnic rigging alongside Osamu Kume. Yajima's crew numbered 50 and there was a shortage of special effects staff as Tsuburaya

Productions' *Star Wolf* was shooting concurrently.

With *Message From Space,* Kinji Fukasaku and Nobuo Yajima would become Toei's edgier answer to Ishiro Honda and Eiji Tsuburaya. The two respected each other and had worked together on one of Fukasaku's very first films. Fukasaku allowed Yajima complete creative freedom in his effects sequences and gave him little direction.

Yajima's team made novel use of high-tech equipment. These included a Hollywood-grade snorkel lens, used to mimic Dykstra's Star Destroyer shots with Gavanas' warships flying close to the camera. There were only three in the world at that time and the rental price was one million yen per day. Even the starscape horizons were high tech, consisting of over 1500 tiny light bulbs outfitted with a "dimmer" to control their brightness according to the shot's needs.

Nobuo Yajima

Also used was the new Totsu Inc. ECG System which Yajima's effects unit took a liking to. It was a video-based optical system that was cheaper to use and could composite unlimited layers, unlike film-based compositing. Video previews could also be viewed on set, a convenience Kinji Fukasaku especially enjoyed. The system's drawback was that the film footage had to be transferred to analog video with a fuzzier-looking end result. Yajima would utilize the system better in Metal Hero shows like *Space Sheriff Gavan* where the quality difference was less apparent on the lower resolution of TV. In the Japanese special effects industry, the ECG System would be supplanted by high definition HiVision equipment by the late 1980s. Nonetheless, Yajima achieves some impressive sequences with it in *Message From Space* such as the "space firefly" scene and the climactic "chicken run". Minoru Nakano and Den Films, who had worked with Yajima at Tsuburaya Productions, were involved in *Message From Space* with dazzling optical animations throughout. Tsuburaya unit veteran Sadao Iizuka even contributed animated rays and the stunning painted starscapes in the opening credits were created by P-Productions' Yoshio Watanabe.

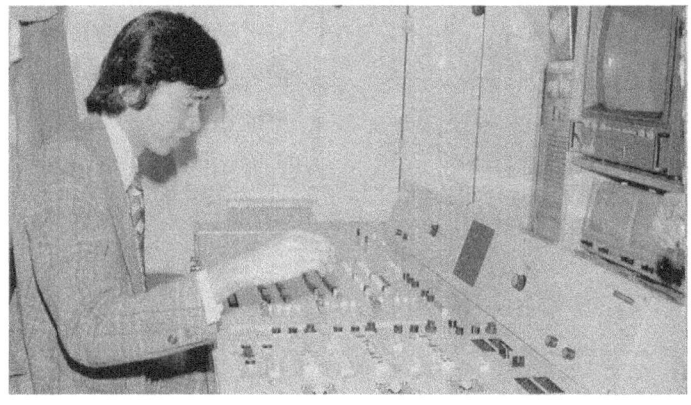

The Totsu ECG system, first used in *Message From Space* (1978), was used often by the tokusatsu industry in the next half-decade including on *Gamera: Supermonster* (1980) and Toei's Metal Hero shows

A standout sequence with Yajima at the top of his form as effects director is the Earth military's attack on the Gavanas' fortress. Its pyrotechnics from Osamu Kume foreshadow the distinct conflagrations he would create for Koichi Kawakita at Toho. Yajima's masterwork as special effects director is the Eisensteinian "chicken run" through the Gavanas' castle. The later Death Star II run through in *Star Wars: Return of the Jedi* (1983) is almost cut-for-cut identical. *Message From Space*'s final shot showing its Jillucian space galleon departing through a sea of stars is stunning, likely the work of Minoru Nakano. Yajima's regret with *Message From Space* was its short production schedule. He wanted to include more effects sequences and further polish those he had.

Message From Space was profitable and released in the U.S. later that year. Often playing on a double-bill with Luigi Cozzi's *Starcrash* (also 1978), it made money though received savage reviews from American critics. Roger Ebert and Gene Siskel chose it as a "Dog of the Week" on their show with Ebert calling Yajima's effects "trashy". *The Boston Globe* was even more vicious: "The fallout from *Star Wars* space garbage continues to litter the motion picture screen". The popularity of *Message From Space* would give rise to a TV series, **MESSAGE FROM SPACE: GALACTIC WARS** [Television Run (Japan): July 8th, 1978 - January 27th, 1979], which began airing on TV Asahi. Also starring Sonny Chiba's pupil Hiroyuki Sanada, the show features heavy stock footage from the movie along with 16mm B-roll lensed on set. For the few novel special effects shots, Yajima's Tokusatsu Research Institute was again recruited. Ratings sagged and *Message From Space: Galactic Wars* ended after 27 episodes. In the United States, episodes were compiled into the feature *Swords of Space Ark*, often airing (bizarrely) on evangelist Pat Robertson's Christian Broadcasting Network.

Produced as a result of a licensing agreement with America's Marvel Comics, Toei's next televised tokusatsu offering was destined to be quite unique: **SPIDER-MAN** [Television Run (Japan): May 17th, 1978 - March 14th, 1979], which began airing on TV Tokyo. *Spider-Man* indeed features **STAN LEE** (1922-2018) and Steve Ditko's iconic creation but with a decidedly Japanese spi,: filtering Marvel's all-American property through Toei's house style. This is as fun as it sounds and Toei's *Spider-Man* has earned a well-deserved fan following. Stan Lee even went to Japan and met with Toei's brass. Toei was originally going to use Spider-Man as only a supporting character for a time-slipped Yamato Takeru. As *Spider-Man* aired in Japan, the more conventional *The Amazing Spider-Man* was being broadcast stateside. A production practice from *Spider-Man* would even wind up influencing its American counterpart: *The Amazing Spider-Man*'s crew began to use hidden ropes to create the scenes where the title character scales buildings just like Toei's stunt unit.

Toei's *Spider-Man* is more fun with the Marvel incarnation of the character put out of one's mind. The protagonist's name is not Peter Parker but Takuya Yamashiro (Shinji Todo). Instead of the death of Uncle Ben, Takuya is spurred by the demise of his professor father (Toho actor Fuyuki Murakami). Rather than being bitten by a radioactive spider, he gets his "spider powers" from an injection with an alien extract by Garia (Toshiaki Nishizawa), a refugee from Planet Spider, a world wiped out by Professor Monster (Mitsuo Ando) and his Iron Cross Army. They employ the usual grunts, this time with duck noses.

Spider-Man (1978-79) title card

Spider-Man has web-shooters but unlike Peter Parker, he exclaims "Spider String!" every time he uses them. Spider-Man's "spidey sense" translates to full-on, *ESPY*-style psychokinetic powers. Like the Ishinomori heroes, he rides around in his own flying car, the Spider Machine GP-7. Also unlike Peter Parker, Spider-Man has a spacecraft at his disposal inherited from Garia called the Marveller. This can turn into a giant robot named Leopardon, something Peter Parker might wish he had in the usual battle with Doc Ock. Needless to say, Aunt May, Mary Jane and J. Jonah Jameson are nowhere to be seen in Toei's *Spider-Man*. If not for the use of the unmistakable Marvel design, *Spider-Man* could easily be another Shotaro Ishinomori-created henshin hero show. The Spider-Man jumpsuit was mainly inhabited by Japan Action Club stuntman **HIROFUMI KOGA** (1954-), who had previously played the title character in *Chojin Bibyun*.

Kamen Rider and Sentai veterans Koichi Takemoto and Katsuhiko Taguchi helmed most episodes though **YOSHIAKI KOBAYASHI** (1936-) directed much of the second half. On hand for the special effects work was the Tokusatsu Research unit. Yajima's team takes the stage in episodes where the robot Leopardon battles the monster of the week who often grows to giant size. These sequences foreshadow the mecha-monster battle scenes in the Super Sentai franchise starting with *Battle Fever J*. Leopardon was designed by Katsushi Murakami with Equis Productions' Nori Maezawa modeling the suit from FRP.

In the U.S., Stan Lee found the show highly amusing after Toei sent him videotapes of it. In his own words in an interview conducted by Toei, "I liked the way they did it in a Japanese style. It wasn't really like the American version. It had its own flavor. It was so different from the way we do them in the United States that it was fun". Lee was impressed by the practical effects and stunts: "Whatever you saw on the screen was really being done by human beings". Stan Lee and Yoshinori Watanabe planned a follow-up show written by Lee combining the American and Japanese styles but these plans never materialized. Marvel executive **MARGARET LOESCH** (1946-) later wanted to export Toei's *Spider-Man* to United States airwaves, though this too did not come to pass. Loesch would become head of the Fox Kids' Network in 1990 and be instrumental in the launch of *Mighty Morphin' Power Rangers*. Toei's Spider-Man would go on to appear in Disney/Marvel's computer-animated *Spider-Man: Across the Spider-Verse (Part One)* (2022).

Toei soon released a specially made theatrical Spider-Man short via their Manga Festival. **SPIDER-MAN** [**Director:** Koichi Takemoto - **Release Date (Japan):** July 22nd, 1978] was shown opposite a *Space Pirate Captain Harlock* compilation. Likely the last tokusatsu film shot in anamorphic Cinemascope, moments of *Spider-Man* are refined cinematic awesome. The contributions of Nobuo Yajima's unit, however, are disappointing for the big screen. These feature the robot Leopardon shot in separate close-ups from the monsters. Yajima was forced to employ this tactic increasingly, along with stock footage, as the show went on. The Leopardon suit had been stolen from Toei's lot and a replacement could not be made with the budget.

October saw the debut of a landmark special effects series on Nippon Television:, **MONKEY** [**Television Run (Japan):** October 1st, 1978 - April 8th, 1979]. Initially planned as a feature film, the program is a lavish adaptation of the beloved Chinese folktale *Journey to the West*. This had been tackled by numerous Japanese filmmakers in the past, including Eiji Tsuburaya and his mentor Yoshiro Edamasa. Additionally, Japanese and Chinese relations were improving with the end of the Maoist Cultural Revolution and the signing of the Treaty of Peace and Friendship Between Japan and China. *Monkey* was made as a commemorative production to the healing of the two cultures' painful histories. Isao Tomita was originally to score *Monkey*, but he was replaced by rock band Godiego, who performed the wildly popular theme song in English. *Monkey* and its sequel series were also the final directing jobs for both Yoshiyuki Kuroda and Jun Fukuda.

Monkey features strong tokusatsu contributions and elaborate effects footage for television. In the first series, staff from Tsuburaya Productions were employed. The effects unit was headed by Koichi Takano with support from Kazuo Sagawa and Kiyoshi Suzuki. Akihiko Iguchi oversaw the show's special effects art direction and Minoru Nakano's Den Films created the sophisticated optical animations. The opening, minute-long segment, which depicts Son Goku (Masaki Sakai) hatching from a stone egg, is a nearly theatrical-grade sequence. This scene alone took two months to shoot and Tatsumi Nikamoto doubled as Goku, pulled upwards by piano wire.

Monkey was extremely successful in Japan with its final episode watched by a remarkable 27.4% of the populace. This led to production of a sequel program: **MONKEY II [Television Run (Japan):** November 11th, 1979 - May 4th, 1980]. Retaining the cast from the first series, *Monkey II* was even partly shot in the now reopened People's Republic of China. The show was given more action and Son Goku often battled supernatural adversaries like a classical Chinese tokusatsu hero. Tsuburaya Productions' staff like Kazuo Sagawa and Kiyoshi Suzuki again ran the FX unit with support from Toho veterans like Teruyoshi Nakano and Koichi Kawakita. *Monkey* and *Monkey II* were popular abroad as both programs were dubbed into English and shown on the BBC in the United Kingdom. The English folk band Monkey Swallows the Universe drew its name from an episode of *Monkey*.

Sadamasa Arikawa would again venture to Greater China to helm an effects unit for the Taiwanese/Japanese/U.S. co-production **THE PHOENIX [AKA: WAR OF THE WIZARDS - Director:** Chang Mei-Chun - **Release Date (Taiwan):** October 20th, 1978]. Arikawa, billed as "Sam" Arikawa in American prints, again utilizes many techniques learned from Tsuburaya. Motoyoshi Tomioka acted as DP once more. The work of Arikawa's unit is subtle in most of the picture, limited to process and miniature shots. *The Phoenix*, blending traditional *wuxia* theatrics with tokusatsu-style fantasy flourish, is the best Taiwanese collaboration with the tokusatsu industry. There's a plethora of optical animation created by the Japanese staff. The process shots are handled better than in *The Mighty Peking Man* with the exception of some poor video-based composites.

In the United States, *The Phoenix* was released in 1983 as *War of the Wizards*

Arikawa's unit takes charge with the arrival of the eponymous giant phoenix achieved via a Mothra-style puppet with the monster's call on the sound mix. Arikawa commands the picture's final third and channels his mentor with a style akin to Tsuburaya's work on *The Three Treasures*. This aesthetic is aided by the use of Toho stock sound effects. A highlight midway is a fantastical battle sequence between the Phoenix and villainess Flower Fox (Betty Pei-Tei). There's a flood scene executed so similarly to the climax of *Madame White Snake* that it might as well be stock footage. The hero (Terry Hu) possesses a solar-powered magical sword that fires a Toho space opera-style laser beam. There's even a monster battle, not unlike those previously staged by Arikawa, between the phoenix and a stone giant played by a stuntman in a suit.

Being a *wuxia* rather than *kaiju* film, however, *The Phoenix* concludes with a magical martial arts showdown. Richard Kiel, fresh from playing Jaws in *The Spy Who Loved Me* (1977), plays Flower Fox's big boss and brawls with the hero Chuck Norris-style. Even this Chinese-style mystical sword mayhem features contribution from Arikawa's unit and tokusatsu flourish.

The Phoenix is another film that begs to be seen in its original aspect ratio. Sadamasa Arikawa would retire after *The Phoenix* and go on to teach special effects techniques at vocational colleges in Japan.

That Christmas, another influential blockbuster was released to American theaters: **SUPERMAN** [Director: **RICHARD DONNER** (1930-2021 - Release Date (U.S.):** December 15th, 1978]. Like *Star Wars*, *Superman* is another milestone in Hollywood's high-concept formula. With the biggest budget in film history, it was the first prestige comic book movie of many. *Superman* again features the most dazzling visual effects sequences in cinema yet. Its cinematography by **GEOFFREY UNSWORTH** (1914-1978) is arresting.

Japanese poster for *Superman* (1978), released in Japan on June 30th, 1979

Superman is another film that Eiji Tsuburaya would have loved. It boasts a similar visual effects spectacle to his. Using the most sophisticated bluescreen and rear-projection techniques to create its extensive flying sequences, *Superman* also employs a Japanese-style miniature unit. This was run by **DEREK MEDDINGS** (1931-1995), who had worked with Gerry Anderson. There are even miniaturized dam break, flood and rockslide sequences that evoke Tsuburaya's work. *Superman*'s success pushed Tsuburaya Productions to revive Ultraman; the franchise would soon be back on Japanese airwaves with *The Ultraman*, which saw broadcast in April 1979 and was an animated show created by Sunrise. Tsuburaya Pro also planned a big-budget collaboration with Hollywood to be called *Ultraman: The Jupiter Effect*, but plans fell through.

Toei's next Sentai program and the first without the involvement of Shotaro Ishinomori was **BATTLE FEVER J [Television Run (Japan):** February 3rd, 1979 - January 26th, 1980]. *Battle Fever J* also sprang out of Marvel's collaboration with Toei. Originally, it was to be a Captain America show and then a Japanese answer called Captain Japan. In the end, it was decided to make the program a sentai show with a national motif. It was named *Battle Fever J* due to the popularity of *Saturday Night Fever* (1977). Tonally different from Ishinomori's edgy *Gorenger* and *J.A.K.Q.*, the franchise's more lighthearted, commercial approach would begin with *Battle Fever J*. Following the lead of *Spider-Man*'s Leopardon, the show began the long tradition of including a giant robot that the sentai squad summons to battle enlarged monsters. The franchise would be retitled "Super Sentai" from *Battle Fever J* on, the "super" added to emphasize the giant mecha and monster battles. The tropes and production style of future shows running all the way to the present day would be established with *Battle Fever J*.

Battle Fever J (1979-80) title card

This time, the team consisted of five members led by Masao Den (Hironori Tanioka) or "Battle Japan". Japan Action Club stuntman **KENJI OBA** (1955-) played the Black Panther meets Kenya Boy-like Shiro Akebono or "Battle Kenya". Oba, a protege of Sonny Chiba, got his start on *Kikaider* and *Robot Detective*. Though it was considered a liability, he was the first actor since Hiroshi Fujioka in the original *Kamen Rider* to portray both his human and hero forms. Oba's pre-transformation action sequences tended to be more aggressive than the other actors per his stunt background. Lisa Komaki, who had portrayed Peggy Matsuyama in *Gorenger*, would play pink ranger "Miss America" in the stunt unit sequences. As the costume was more revealing and feminine than usual, a male stuntman could not double. The first Miss America was Diane Martin, played by model Diane Martin. Though half-Japanese, Martin was raised in the United States and spoke only English, so Komaki dubbed her voice. When Martin had to leave the show, Maria Nagisa (Naomi Hagi) became the second Miss America. The show's country-based hero motif would be influential on the fan film *Patriotic Sentai Great Japan* (1982), created by the future members of Gainax. Anime voice actress Noriko Hidaka, then only 17, would appear in *Battle Fever J*.

The shooting schedule for *Battle Fever J* was tight and not helped by the recent closure of Toei's Ikuta Studio, where their special effects shows had been shot. Once again, the effects unit was helmed by Nobuo Yajima and members of his Tokusatsu Research Institute. Tetsuzo Osawa oversaw the effects art direction while Toru Suzuki executed the wire work. Again, Yajima and the Tokusatsu Research Institute take the stage whenever the squad's giant robot, Battle Fever Robo, appears. The robot was to show up in the first episode but wound up introduced later in episode #5. This was because the suit could not be completed in time as Katsushi Murakami's design was slow to be approved. Murakami's design motifs for Battle Fever Robo were mainly samurai and Western knight armor. The modeling was done at Equis Productions and the mechanical transport ship Battle Shark was made by Hiruma Modelcraft.

Japan Action Club member Osamu Kaneda was responsible for the fight direction of both the stunt unit and the tokusatsu shooting, choreographing Battle Fever Robo's fights. Nobuo Yajima delegated his special effects role, as he had been hired for Masahiro Shinoda's *Demon Pond* (1979) and could not work on both productions at once. Tsuburaya Productions' Kazuo Sagawa was thus recruited as support for Yajima. *Battle Fever J* ran for 52 episodes. Ratings were good and the franchise has continued uninterrupted to this day.

Throughout 1978 and '79, Toho produced no special effects or genre films with the exception of Kihachi

Okamoto's *Blood Type: Blue* (1978). Director Okamoto, who held tokusatsu in low regard, decided against using an effects team in favor of deliberately minimalist VFX for the film's alien spacecraft. Toho was, however, somewhat active on television. In May, **MEGALOMAN** [Television Run (Japan): May 7th - December 24th, 1979] premiered on Japanese TV, their first special effects program since *Zone Fighter*, as well as the little-known **SAUCER WAR BANKID** [Television Run (Japan): October 3rd, 1976 - March 23rd, 1977]. Megaloman, his human alter ego Takashi Shishido (Yuki Kitazume), is a half-human, half-alien *kyodai* hero. Standing nearly 500 feet tall, he remains the largest-scaled Japanese superhero ever. *Megaloman* and its concepts use much of what was popular with superhero media, both in Japan and abroad. Besides *Ultraman*, the show recalls Toho's prior *Zone Fighter* in that Takashi has human-sized hero and kyodai forms. Like Toei's popular Sentai franchise, Takashi's friends are recruited by his alien mother (Yukiko Takabayashi) to join him as a superhero team. Taking a cue from *Superman*, the characters wear capes and Takashi/Megaloman can fly through the air. There are even Kamen Rider/Sentai-style lackeys complete with creepy vocalizations. Like Toei and Ishinomori's *Inazuman*, Takeshi's superhero form "explodes" into Megaloman.

The effects unit on *Megaloman* was mainly run by Yoichi Manoda with later support from Koichi Takano and Shinichi Kamisawa. *Megaloman* was among Manoda's final works as FX director. Akihiko Iguchi was responsible for the art direction and hero and monster designs. Megaloman's suit was created at Kaimai Productions by Eizo Kaimai and a young apprentice named **SHINICHI WAKASA** (1960-). As with Kaimai's previous work on Ambassador Magma, yak hair was used for Megaloman's mane. The show features beautifully crafted miniatures and heavy optical work, especially for Megaloman's fire-based attacks, pulled off with aplomb by Takeshi Miyanishi. Megaloman was portrayed by **JUN MURAKAMI** (1956-), a stuntman from the Japan Action Club who had gotten his tokusatsu start on episodes of *Akumaizer 3* and *Gorenger*. Tsutomu Kitagawa would also appear as a handful of monsters.

Koichi Kawakita was put in charge of the effects footage for a single episode, which is among the series' best. It features Kawakita's most elaborate TV work yet with extensive miniature shooting. This installment also boasts Kawakita's most complex monster battle sequences along with heavy VFX opticals depicting a glowing monster. Megaloman spends most of the episode in kyodai form. Toho's brass were furious at Kawakita, however, as he spent the budget of two episodes, even making an enormous volcanic cavern set. While he would not be brought back for future episodes, Kawakita's work was well received by viewers. *Megaloman* ended after 31 episodes. The show has yet to be released on home video due to a complicated string of rights entanglements.

Alien (1979) Japanese poster, it was released there in July

In the summer of '79, another soon-to-be-iconic effects-laden Hollywood blockbuster hit screens: **ALIEN [Director: RIDLEY SCOTT** (1937-) - **Release Date (U.S.):** May 25th, 1979]. Like *2001: A Space Odyssey* and *Star Wars*, *Alien* advanced cinematic worldbuilding with new levels of filmmaking ingenuity. Akin to *The Exorcist* and *Jaws*, *Alien* also brought cinema to a new height of terror. *Alien* is an almost perfect genre film with one visually arresting image after another - utilizing well worn science fiction tropes with a novel and realistic execution. Many of its effects techniques were not unlike those employed by Japanese filmmakers. The space trawler *Nostromo* was created through exhaustive miniature shooting headed by **BRIAN JOHNSON** (1939-) and **NICK ALIDER** (1943-). The iconic Xenomorph designed by **H.R. GIGER** (1940-2014) was brought to vivid life with suitmation and puppetry by **CARLO RAMBALDI** (1925-2012). *Alien*'s climax is among the most thrilling, suspenseful and masterfully directed in any genre film.

As American audiences thrilled to the interstellar horror of *Alien*, **THE INFERNO [AKA: HELL - Director: TATSUMI KUMASHIRO** (1927-1995) - **Release Date (Japan):** June 3rd, 1979]** was released in Japan by Toei. A big-budget remake of Nobuo Nakagawa's *The Sinners of Hell* (1960), it was first greenlit thanks to the Occult Boom's revitalization per the success of Richard Donner's *The Omen* (1976). Besides its action and crime fare, Toei was known for producing distinct exploitation pictures starting in the late 1960s. Called "pinky violence" as they combined hefty amounts of sexual content and brutality, the best known of these films include Shunya Ito's *Female Prisoner 701: Scorpion* (1972) and its sequels. Other stand-out Toei exploitation titles are Norifumi Suzuki's *Sex and Fury* (1973) and the works of Teruo Ishii such as *Bohachi Bushido: Code of the Forgotten Eight* (also 1973). While these transgressive movies often contained graphic depictions of sexualized violence, they also mixed in radical political commentary and stylish filmmaking removed from the lower-rent production values of Hollywood exploitation.

The Inferno (not to be confused with Dario Argento's 1980 *Inferno*) is much in line with Toei's exploitation lineage, though it was marketed as a prestige picture. Teruo Ishii was to direct but his vision of hell was considered too expensive. Ishii would later get a crack at the subject material with *Japanese Hell* (1999). Nikkatsu *roman porno* veteran Tatsumi Kumashiro was instead brought on board. *The Inferno* is every bit as transgressively surreal as Nobuo Nakagawa's original but more lurid in its sexuality and carnage per its '70s Toei vintage. Director Kumashiro and DP Shigeru Akatsuka's images are painterly, though as with many '70s exploitation films there are depictions of sexual violence that may be uncomfortable for viewers. At times, *The Inferno* is as visually stunning as Akira Kurosawa's *Dreams* (1990). *The Inferno*'s brutal sequences of torture and body horror feel in line with the sadomasochistic visions of Clive Barker. Actress Meiko Harada, later to appear in Kurosawa's *Ran* (1985), plays a dual role as a mother and daughter who wind up condemned to the eponymous inferno for their sins.

The Sinners of Hell had only minor tokusatsu industry involvement. Like the works of Mario Bava, most of the visual effects were accomplished through in-camera techniques and lighting by Nobuo Nakagawa's main unit. In stark contrast, *The Inferno* has major contributions from special effects director Nobuo Yajima and his Tokusatsu Research Institute, including psychedelic process shots throughout. For the final third, Yajima's unit takes the reins in epic fashion as the cast of sinners are crushed by a divine tokusatsu landslide, including Harada's lead as she engages in incestous sex. This is a moment that feels quintessentially Toei.

The hellish climax is Nobuo Yajima's best visual effects footage to date with good synergy between his and director Kumashiro's units. A tokusatsu industry "Last Judgment", it resembles an old-school Japanese Buddhist hell scroll brought to vivid cinematic life. Much of Yajima's team from *Message From Space* returned for *The Inferno* including Toru Suzuki and art director Tetsuzo Osawa. One of Yajima's finest sequences features masses of sinners being swallowed into a fiery crevasse and engulfed in conflagration, accomplished through both video and film-based compositing, miniatures and heavy pyrotechnics. There are giant *oni* reminiscent of Nobuo Nakagawa's *The Adventures of Tobisuke* that also foreshadow *Attack on Titan*. They feed transgressors into an enormous flesh-grinding contraption powered by fellow tortured souls like a Nihon Hieronymus Bosch painting. These shots are marred only by occasional bluescreen elements.

The Inferno is not as masterfully executed as Nakagawa's classic *The Sinners of Hell*, nor does it reach the phantasmagorical heights of Nobuhiko Obayashi's *House*. Yet it is a worthy remake with a spectacularly grotesque finale. In Japan it was a critical and box office failure as the "Occult Boom" had died down and did temporary harm to actress Harada's career. Nobuo Yajima would also take extensive part in Shochiku's big-budget fantasy film **DEMON POND [Director: MASAHIRO SHINODA** (1931-) - **Release Date (Japan):** October 20th, 1979]. Yajima's unit staged a climactic flood sequence with the extensive use of wave machines. *Demon Pond* was tied up in rights issues, preventing its official home video release for years. These were resolved and a 4K remaster was issued in 2021.

Thanks to the popularity of science fiction and fantasy works worldwide and *Space Battleship Yamato* in Japan, Toei decided to resurrect the Kamen Rider franchise after three years off the air. **SKYRIDER [AKA: KAMEN RIDER NEW - Television Run**

(Japan): October 5th, 1979 - October 10th, 1980] thus ran on Friday nights on Mainichi Broadcasting. Though Shotaro Ishinomori was less involved, *Skyrider* would reunite much of the original franchise's core talent. This included producer Toru Hirayama, writer Masaru Igami, director Minoru Yamada, composer Shunsuke Kikuchi and the Ono Kendo Club for stunts. *Skyrider* is a highlight in the franchise.

Like similar contemporary productions such as *Ultraman 80* and Toho's *The Return of Godzilla* (1984), it hearkens back to the franchise's origins but also succeeds as a sleeker modern update. The second half of *Skyrider* features frequent guest appearances by all the past Riders. Suzuki Motors would partner with Toei for the production of *Skyrider* and supply the motorbikes used.

Skyrider (1979-80) title card

Once again, a young man, this time the athletic, glider-loving Hiroshi Tsukuba (Hiroaki Murakami) is transformed into a Kamen Rider cyborg. Shocker has reformed as Neo-Shocker and their leader, though apparently a different character, is still voiced with the angry snarl of Goro Naya. They're still psychopathic neo-fascists, though driven by Malthusian convictions rather than the original group's Joker-like desire to cause human suffering for the hell of it. The first commander is the aptly named General Monster (Shinzo Hotta), another former Nazi who, according to Toei's lore, ran the gas chambers at Auschwitz. Like *Battle Fever J*, *Skyrider* is tamer in its violence than earlier shows, though the intricate stunts are impressive. Toei's softening of their usual flamboyant brutality likely came out of having worked with Marvel and a desire for marketing their shows abroad.

Skyrider features a stronger tokusatsu industry involvement than prior Kamen Rider programs. Per his name, Hiroshi Tsukuba's Skyrider can fly, an obvious nod to *Superman*. These flying scenes make use of the Totsu ECG system, used similarly the following year in *Gamera: Supermonster*. Nobuo Yajima was once again on hand for the effects unit work on many episodes. The art direction on *Skyrider* was handled by Akira Takahashi and the modeling by Michio Mikami and his Cosmo Productions. *Skyrider* features the best FX modeling yet, particularly for the monsters. It's far superior to the subsequent work being done at Toho on *Megaloman*. Thanks to advances in FRP, the material was now lighter, and so the use of a latex Kamen Rider "action mask" was ended with *Skyrider*. The suit's arms were made of leather. Once again, Tetsuya Nakayashiki played the role of Skyrider in the stunt unit sequences, with support from Kazuo Niibori. In keeping with its tone hearkening back to the original show, classic villains are recreated in *Skyrider*, including Spider Man, Scorpion Man and Cobra Man. *Skyrider* doesn't reach the peak of the edgy original show from Ishinomori, but it is a worthy update of the property. *Skyrider*'s ratings were decent but not quite what Toei had hoped. The show ran for 54 episodes whereupon another entry in the franchise would begin.

By 1980, the production of Japanese special effects films and television would begin to boom again. Ultraman followed Kamen Rider in its return to the air. This was along with a new Gamera entry and a big budget disaster picture from Toho. In the coming years and decades, Hollywood would continue to produce a myriad of visual effects intensive films. All the while, Japan's special effects industry battled, in its own ingenuitive way, to keep up while maintaining some of its core traditions.

つづく

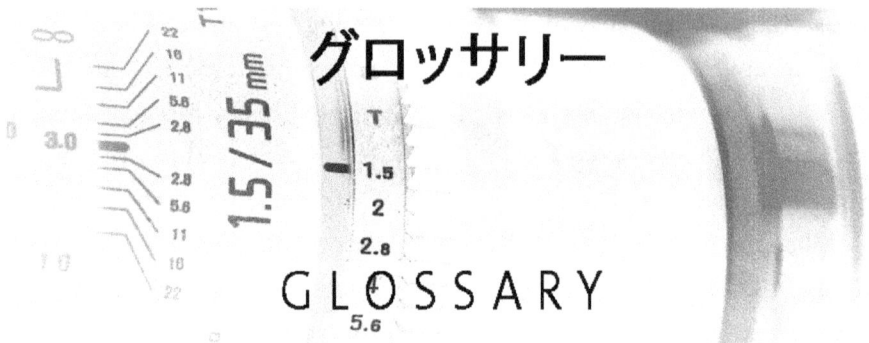

グロッサリー
GLOSSARY

ABOVE-THE-LINE - Members of a film production that are considered quintessential to a movie's vision: mainly the screenwriter, producers, director and lead actors. A term derived from the "line" in old school film budget sheets, these are essentially the players given emphasis on advertising materials.

ACADEMY RATIO - An early aspect ratio standard of 1.37:1 adopted in 1932 by the Academy of Arts and Sciences. This is the aspect ratio of a 35mm frame with a 4-perf pulldown. It was commonly used in the Japanese film industry until the late 1950s.

AD - Industry slang for "assistant director", the AD mainly helps organize a shoot and coordinate between the various departments involved. In the Japanese film industry, being an assistant director was a career path toward directing and many ADs were mentored by the directors they were working under.

ANAMORPHIC - A style of camera lens that compresses a 2.35:1 widescreen image onto a film or video frame. In projection, the image is decompressed. The Japanese studios mainly shot their films with these lenses from the late 1950s to '70s.

APERTURE - Also called the "iris", this is the opening in which light passes into a camera's lens to expose an image.

ART DIRECTOR - Also called a production designer, the art director heads the art department which is in charge of designing and building the film's sets along with decorating them.

ASA - A measure of film stock's light sensitivity created by the American Standards Association. Low values indicate little sensitivity and high values indicate more. Supplanted by the ISO system.

ASSET - An element or resource of an edited work.

BACKGROUND PLATE - A background element typically shot separately and often used as the bottom layer in a composite.

BELOW-THE-LINE - Members of a film crew with unsung contributions little understood to those outside the industry. With the producers, director, writers and actors considered above-the-line, below-the-line is typically everyone on a shoot from the cinematographer on down.

BENSHI - An entertainer employed during the silent era in Japan to provide live narration. The tradition is still kept alive today by a small handful of modern benshi who narrate silent film screenings in Japan.

BLOCKING - The act of choreographing the onscreen (and offscreen) elements of a film shot before the camera rolls. Some directors are more experimental and do little blocking while others are meticulous in their planning. Tokusatsu film directors tend to fall into the latter category.

COLOR TIMING - Also called "color grading". Whether film or digital, raw, ungraded shots often have subtle lighting and color/white balance inconsistencies.

Color timing fixes this and makes shots look uniform, along with often applying a subtle (or not so subtle) aesthetic "look" to the footage. In the old days, color timing was done by the processing labs. Today, both film-shot and digital movies are graded with computers. The staff member in charge of the film's color timing is called a "colorist".

COMPOSITE - A shot where multiple separately filmed elements are put together. They are a major part of tokusatsu and kaiju filmmaking. In the black and white days, they were done by filming foreground elements in front of black backgrounds. With the advent of color, blue backgrounds began to be used. Green screens are now most commonly used. Before computer technology, composites were done by film printing. Today, they are done with computers and programs like Adobe After Effects.

COPY - Commercial writing most commonly used in advertising.

COVERAGE - Coverage is the amount and manner of angles and footage shot for a scene or sequence in a film. Some directors and DPs like to "cover" a scene from as many angles as possible for a visually dynamic sequence. Others like to shoot more limited coverage. Some do both depending on the type of scene they're shooting. Japanese special effects directors tend to fall into the first category.

CUT - A single shot in an edit. In the film industry, editing is called "cutting". In the old days, movies were physically cut on film. Today, computer applications like Adobe Premiere, Sony Vegas, AVID or Final Cut Pro are used for the vast majority of films, whether digital or shot on celluloid.

DEPTH OF FIELD - In both still photography and cinematography, depth of field is how sharp and in focus a shot is from the foreground to background. It is influenced by the distance of objects, by lens focal length and by aperture f-stop. In general, wider lenses with high f-stops have deeper focus. Long lenses with lower f-stops create shallower depth of field.

DIGITAL INTERMEDIATE - Used in both digitally filmed and celluloid-shot movies, digital intermediate is where a film is polished and given color grading and VFX. Film negatives are often scanned into a computer using a system like Cineon, this gives a greater amount of creative control in post-production.

DP - Industry slang for "director of photography" or cinematographer. The DP is in charge of capturing the film's images. WIth input from the director, the DP decides lens selection, lighting conditions and what film stock or digital settings are to be used. The gaffer and key grips work closely with the DP as well.

DYNAMIC RANGE - The amount of visual bandwidth between the blackest of an image's shadow details and the whitest of its highlights. Whether working on digital or film stock, capturing images with quality dynamic range is important in professional filmmaking.

FAST - Fast film stock has a high ASA or ISO and is more light sensitive, requiring less artificial or natural lighting to be legibly exposed. The main drawback to fast film stock is that it tends to have more visible grain.

FOCAL LENGTH - Focal length is the distance from the center of a camera lens to its focal point. It is measured in millimeters. Lenses with low focal lengths are wider and higher focal lengths are "telephoto".

FOCUS RING - The manual control for a camera lens' focus settings. On older or higher quality lenses, the distance measurements are printed on the ring. On smaller shoots, the DP works the ring themselves. On large shoots, a "focus puller" is hired to handle this.

FOREGROUND - The foreground is the spacial area closer to the camera. It is typically the main focus of a shot, though not always.

FRAME RATE - In both film and digital video, the frame rate is how many frames per second are being captured/exposed or projected. The higher the frame rate, the more smooth the motion is. The standard frame rate for film projection is 24 frames per second. Tokusatsu sequences are often shot at around 60-120 frames per second and slowed down to 24 which allows miniatures to crumble more like real buildings.

F-STOP - The measure of how wide a camera lens' aperture is opened. The lower the number, the more light the aperture is allowing in.

GAFFER - Industry slang for the head of a film's lighting and electrical department or lighting director. The gaffer works closely with the DP on determining the exact lighting set-ups to be used.

GAUGE - A strip of film's precise size. Popular gauges include 8mm, 16mm, 35mm and 70mm.

GRAIN - Grain is the optical texture of processed film stock. Each grain, containing particles of silver halide, captures a tiny portion of the image. Less light sensitive stocks have finer grains that are less visible in projection. Light sensitive stock has coarse grain that is more apparent on screen. Today, many movies shot on film are given grain removal.

GUIGNOL - A hand puppet, typically used for close-ups of monsters that require more expression than the suit.

HARD MATTE - When the entire four perf 35mm frame is exposed, but a matte is used in camera to mask the image to 1.85:1. Japanese studios tended to do this when shooting in spherical Vista size.

HERO - A minor, non-speaking role in a group of extras but with significant screen time, often in makeup.

HISTOGRAM - A graph on many digital cameras that shows the dispersion of an image's data from the highlights to shadows.

HORIZONT - The painted backdrop to a tokusatsu set.

INTERPOSITIVE - An orange-based film print with a positive image made from the camera negative. It is an intermediate in creating the final positive print for exhibition. Tsuburaya and others often did their optical work using the interpositives as they have better color reproduction and lower contrast. Interpositives are also used the most often for film transfers as they are typically in the best condition.

HIGH CONCEPT - A story idea for a film seen as profitable and having potential mass appeal. Many Japanese special effects films in their native country are actually seen as high concept pictures.

KEYFRAME ANIMATION - In both 2-D and 3-D animation and video editing: key frames mark the beginning and end of an animation. In anime they are typically made first by key animators and "inbetweeners" fill in frames.

KEY GRIP - A key grip has a wide variety of responsibilities, but is generally in charge of the set's equipment and the logistical management of it.

LOCK - Industry slang for the point at which audio and visual editing have been completed and no more alterations can be made.

LOG - Short for "logarithmic". An image profile used in many digital cinema cameras designed to preserve a high dynamic range similar to film stock. It shoots with very low contrast which preserves data in the highlights and shadows. It also does not record pixels in a linear top to bottom manner, more similar to the grain of film.

LONG LENS - A camera lens with a high focal length. These lenses often boast shallower depth of field and no image distortion. As they have a more flattering effect, they are often used for shooting close-ups of actors.

LONG TAKE - A shot where the camera lingers on its subject and does not cut away for a lengthier period of time than is typical. These are rare in tokusatsu films as they require a lot of coordination between the crew to be executed properly.

LUT - Short for "look up table", these are pre-set mathematical values typically used as templates for color grading.

MASTER SHOT - A shot used for the main, basic coverage of a sequence, typically a wide angle..

MAYA - A computer program developed by Autodesk used for CGI modeling and animation. It is extremely popular in Hollywood. First used on Disney's *Dinosaur*, it has been used in the Japanese film industry.

MECHA - Japanese style mechanical designs, particularly in anime, tokusatsu and video games.

MODELING - Modeling is generally the sculpting process that takes place during the production of practical effects such as miniatures, monster suits, puppets and animatronics. It is now, however, also used for the similar digital creation of computer generated elements.

MULTIPLE EXPOSURE - When film is exposed and run through a camera more than once. Eiji Tsuburaya was fond of this process for composite shots before he acquired his Oxberry printer.

NEGATIVE - As with professionally still photography, movies shot on film typically use negative stock. Negative film stock maintains higher exposure latitude and dynamic range by exposing the darkest areas as the brightest and brightest and the darkest. This is fixed when "positive" prints are made.

NEGATIVE CUTTING - The process of conforming the edits to a film's camera negative so that high quality prints can be struck from it. As most films are finished digitally, this is rarely done today.

NG - Japanese film industry slang for an unusable take, short for "no good".

OPEN MATTE - Open matte is when a "Vista size" film is shot using the entire four perf film frame. Japanese studios tended to hard matte their films in the 1980s once spherical lenses were used. Hollywood, however, tended to prefer exposing the entire frame as it made the unmatted film easier to show on TV with no image loss.

PERF - Short for "perforation" and also known as sprocket holes, these are the holes in film stock that camera and projection equipment uses to move and "pull" it through. Different shooting methods can use different amounts of perfs for exposure and different stocks can have different shapes. A standard 35mm frame has four perfs, but some processes, like Super 35 or Techniscope, can use fewer to conserve film. VistaVision, which is horizontally run through the camera, uses eight.

PICK UPS - Pick-ups are shots or sequences that are filmed after principal photography. This is often at the request of studio executives or due to feedback from test screenings.

POST-PRODUCTION - The period of a production after the shoot (principal photography) has been wrapped. This generally involves completing the editing and polishing the work's technical aspects until it is ready for distribution.

PUSH PROCESSING - Push processing is the practice of "pushing" the exposure of prints created from an underexposed negative.

PULLDOWN - Pulldown is essentially the manner in which film stock is "pulled down", measured in its perforations. Most pulldowns for motion picture film are vertical. Horizontal pulldown is used mainly for IMAX 70mm. With 35mm, VistaVision and still cameras use horizontal pulldown.

PULL PROCESSING - Pull processing involves "pulling back" the exposure when developing a print from an overexposed negative. This can often save footage from being considered "unusable".

PRE-PRODUCTION - The period of production in which the details of a film's shoot are planned and coordinated. This typically involves casting the actors, hiring the crew, rewriting the script for filming and devising the execution of the special or visual effects.

PRINT - A copy of a movie that has been printed on film for theatrical distribution via projection. The practice of making film prints is now on its last legs as films are exhibited from digital files instead of physical prints.

PRINCIPAL PHOTOGRAPHY - Principal photography is the period in production where the film is being actively shot. Shoots can vary from taking a day to well over a year like *Apocalypse Now* or *The Lord of the Rings* trilogy. Japanese tokusatsu films were often shot in one to several months.

PYROTECHNICS - Pyrotechnics are physical explosive effects on set. They always require a specialist to be executed safely and legally.

RACK FOCUS - The practice of pulling focus from one area of a shot to another during a take. This is often done with precision on manual focus rings.

REEL - Feature film prints are split into multiple reels as they are too long to keep on one. A single 35mm film reel is around 20 minutes in maximum runtime.

REVERSAL - Reversal film, unlike negative film, is stock that requires no additional printing as it directly produces a positive image after processing, straight from exposure in the camera.

SHUTTER - In photography and cinematography, the shutter is an apparatus that allows light to pass onto film stock frames or a digital sensor to "expose" an image. The shutter is typically open for only a fraction of a second. Low shutter speeds produce blurred motion while a fast shutter produces extremely crisp and smooth motion. As tokusatsu typically involves high frame rate shooting, fast shutter speeds are used such as 1/120th of a second.

SLOW - Slow film stock is not light sensitive and needs to be exposed under heavy lighting or daylight. The advantage, however, is that properly exposed slow stock has spectacular crispness and dynamic range. The early color film stock used by Japanese studios was extremely slow which required strong lighting.

SPEED - Speed is industry slang for the light sensitivity of film stock.

SPHERICAL - A standard lens with a spherical curve, in contrast to anamorphic lenses, these expose an image with no visual compression onto the center or film frame.

SPOT - Industry slang for a TV, radio or internet commercial.

SUPER 35 - A process of shooting a film intended for anamorphic projection with more versatile spherical lenses. This is often done by exposing an entire four or three perf film frame.

STEADICAM - A steadicam is a device that stabilizes a camera to allow for more fluid handheld shooting. Stabilizing devices had been used for decades prior but the film to revolutionize Steadicam shooting was Stanley Kubrick's *The Shining* (1980).

STOCK - Industry term for physical, material motion picture film.

STORYBOARD - Employed heavily in animation and special/visual effects heavy films worldwide, particularly in Hollywood and Japan, storyboarding consists of planning shots using a series of ordered sketches or drawings. Today, some technophile directors have scrapped using physical drawings in favor of digital 3-D animatics created by computer while others still prefer theirs hand-drawn the old-fashioned way.

TAKE - Essentially a single camera rolling

"session" where part of a scene is covered with a (typically) one camera set-up. Most directors have multiple takes done for nearly everything. This is often because it can take some run-throughs for the crew and actors to get in synergy with the filmmaker's vision. Other directors simply like to have variety for their edit.

TUNGSTEN - Incandescent light bulbs made with the element tungsten are still commonly used in the film industry and were standard for over a century. They are only now being supplanted by more ecologically friendly LED lighting. When shooting on film, they require a special "tungsten" stock for the light's color and white balance to accurately be exposed.

UNIT - Industry term for a specific film crew. In Hollywood-style production, there is often a main unit headed by the director. Shots or sequences not considered essential are shot by a second unit for scheduling purposes. Oftentimes there are even third or fourth units on very large productions. Tokusatsu productions tended to use two units: one run by the director and the other by the special effects director.

VIDEO ASSIST - With the advent of video technology, filmmakers in Hollywood began shooting and recording their takes on video along with film for better quality control as the shots could be instantly rewatched. By the 1990s, Japanese tokusatsu units started doing it as well, starting with Koichi Kawakita and Shinji Higuchi.

VISTA SIZE - Also called "standard" or "standard widescreen", Vista size is typically around 1.85:1 in its width, right between anamorphic cinemascope and academy ratio. Japan's film industry transitioned to this ratio starting in the late 1970s. Since the 1990s, the TV industry has conformed to this size as well.

WHITE BALANCE - White balancing is the process of calibrating a camera to properly capture an image's color temperature. In any setting, a photographer or DP wants their raw images with pure highlights to whites and life-like tones.

WIDE LENS - A wide lens has a short focal length that shows a wider image perspective with deeper depth of field. They are often used for shooting vista and establishing shots. They also tend to work better for handheld camera work.

ZOOM LENS - A zoom lens allows its user to select a focal length. Old school zoom lenses are entirely manual and must be zoomed by hand. Modern zoom lenses are motor-operated and many high end ones have both capabilities.

BIBLIOGRAPHY

BOOKS (ENGLISH)

The Dinosaur Scrapbook (1980) by Donald F. Glut

The Japanese Film: Art and Industry (1982) by Joseph L. Anderson and Donald Richie

The Psychotronic Encyclopedia of Film (1983) by Michael Weldon

Videohound's Cult Flicks and Trash Pics (1995, 2001) by Carol A. Schwartz

The Psychotronic Video Guide (1995) by Michael Weldon

The Mystery Science Theater 3000 Amazing Colossal Episode Guide (1996) by Trace Beaulieu, Paul Chaplin, Jim Mallon, Kevin Murphy, Michael J. Nelson and Mary Jo Pehl

The Age of the Gods (1997) by Guy Mariner Tucker

Stanley Kubrick: A Biography (1997) by John Baxter

A Critical History and Filmography of Toho's Godzilla Series (1997, 2nd edition 2010) by David Kalat

Japan's Favorite Mon-Star: The Unauthorized Biography of "The Big G" (1998) by Steve Ryfle

Monsters Are Attacking Tokyo (1998) by Stuart Galbraith IV

Tokyoscope: The Japanese Cult Film Companion (2001) by Patrick Macias

The Emperor and the Wolf: The Lives and Films of Akira Kurosawa and Toshiro Mifune (2002) by Stuart Galbraith IV

Eiji Tsuburaya: Master of Monsters (2007) by August Ragone

The Toho Studios Story: A History and Complete Filmography (2008) by Stuart Galbraith IV

The Big Book of Japanese Giant Monster Movies (2016) by John LeMay

Ishiro Honda : A Life in Film, from Godzilla to Kurosawa (2017) by Steve Ryfle and Ed Godziszewswki

The Big Book of Japanese Giant Monster Movies: The Lost Films (2017) by John LeMay

Kaiju for Hipsters: 101 "Alternative" Giant Monster Movies (2018) by Kevin Derendorf

BOOKS (JAPANESE)

Fantastic Collection P-Pro Special Effects Video World (1980)

The Complete History of Toho Special Effects Movies (1983)

Daiei Tokusatsu Collection: Majin (1984)

All Monsters and Phantoms (1990)

All About Daiei Special Effects Films From Gamera to Daimajin (1994)

Birth of Godzilla - Showa 29 (1994) by Hideyuki Inoue

TV Magazine Special Edition 40th Anniversary of the Birth of Godzilla Complete Works (1994) by Toshiaki Iwabatake

Great Godzilla Picture Book Vol. 1 (1995)

Great Godzilla Picture Book Vol. 2 (1995)

Japanese Heroes Dominate the World (1995) by Eiji Oshita

Giant Monster Gamera Encyclopedia (1995)

The Ultraman Encyclopedia (1996) by Masami Yamada

Our Beloved Monster Godzilla (1996) by Koichi Kawakita

Gamera Pictorial Daiei Movie Treasures: 55 Years of History (1996)

Complete Japanese Special Effects and Fantasy Movies (1997) by Hiroshi Ishii

1970s Special Effects Hero Complete Works (1998) by Masumi Kaneda

The Making of Prophecies of Nostradamus (1998)

The Truth of Kamen Rider and Takeshi Hongo (1999) by Hiroshi Fujioka

Movie Director, Naval Officer, Jodo-Shinshu Buddhist Minister (1999) by Shue Matsubayashi

Spectreman vs. Lion Maru: The Art of Tomio Sagisu and P-Pro (1999) by Tomio Sagisu

Secret Squadron Gorenger Encyclopedia (2001) by Yoichi Iwasa

Eiji Tsuburaya's Realm of Tokusatsu (2001)

Ultraman Pictorial: The Warrior of Light 35 Years of History (2002)

The Men Who Created Monsters and Heroes: Special Effects Film Study Group (2002)

Kinji Fukasaku: Film Director (2003) by Sadao Yamane

Toho Tokusatsu Mechanical Designs (2003)

Resurrection! Yokai Movie Collection (2005)

Godzilla: Final Wars Super Complete Works (2005) by Satoshi Matsui

Super Sentai Complete Works (2007) by Naohito Mamiya

Showa Tokusatsu Encyclopedia (2008)

The Soul of Tokusatsu by Koichi Kawakita (2010)

Nostalgic Toei x Ishinomori Hero Encyclopedia (2010)

Daiei Tokusatsu Movie Encyclopedia (2010)

Kamen Rider Super Dictionary (2011)

Mothra Movie Encyclopedia (2011)

Complete Works of Toho Special Effects Movies (2012) by Kazuhiro Matsunomoto, Kazuyasu Asai, Nobutaka Suzuki and Masashi Kato

The Toei Tokusatsu Story (2014) by Nobuo Yajima

Godzilla Toho Champion Festival Perfection (2014)

Kamen Rider 1971-1984 (2014)

Keizo Murase's Monster Treasures (2015) by Yuji Nishimura and Shinichi Wakasa

The Birth of Ultra Q (2016) by Masahiko Shiraishi

Sadamasa Arikawa: Son of Godzilla and Eiji Tsuburaya (2018)

DOCUMENTARIES

The Father of Ultra Q (1966)

Behind the Scenes of The Last Dinosaur (1977)

Toho Special Effects Outtake Collection (1986)

Bringing Godzilla Down to Size (2008)

VIDEO INTERVIEWS

Ishiro Honda (1990), Director's Guild of Japan

Akira Ifukube (2000), Criterion

Teruyoshi Nakano (2003) on *Matango* (1963), Toho Video

Teruyoshi Nakano (2003) on *The War in Space* (1977), Toho Video

Seiji Tani and Teruyoshi Nakano (2006) on *Latitude Zero* (1969), Toho Video

Stan Lee (2008) on *"Spider-Man,"* Toei Video

Nobuhiko Obayashi (2010) on *House* (1977), Criterion

Haruo Nakajima (2011) on *Godzilla* (1954), Criterion

Yoshio Irie and Eizo Kaimai (2011) on *Godzilla* (1954), Criterion

Fujio Morita (2013), Kadokawa

Pat Saperstein and Allyson Adams (2020), Kaiju Masterclass

Makoto Inoue (2021), Kaiju Masterclass II

Reijiro Koroku (2021), Kaiju Masterclass II

Reiko Yamada (2021), Kaiju Masterclass II

COMMENTARY TRACKS

Godzilla (1954) with David Kalat, Criterion

Godzilla Raids Again (1955) with Stuart Galbraith, Classic Media

The Mysterians (1957) with Koichi Kawakita and Shinji Higuchi, Toho Video

Varan (1958) with Keizo Murase, Toho Video

Mothra (1961) with Steve Ryfle and Ed Godziszewswki, Sony

The Last War (1961) with Shue Matsubayashi, Toho Video

Matango (1963) with Akira Kubo, Toho Video

Atragon (1963) with Koji Kajita, Toho Video

Mothra vs. Godzilla (1964) with Steve Ryfle and Ed Godziszewswki, Classic Media

Frankenstein Conquers the World (1965) with Sadamasa Arikawa, Toho Video

Gamera (1965) with August Ragone, Shout! Factory

Invasion of Astro-Monster (1965) with Stuart Galbraith IV, Classic Media

Goke, Body Snatcher from Hell (1968) with Shinji Higuchi and Jun Miura, Shochiku Video

All Monsters Attack (1969) with Richard Pusateri, Classic Media

Space Amoeba (1970) with Fumio Tanaka, Toho Video

Godzilla vs. Hedorah (1971) with Teruyoshi Nakano, Toho Video

Submersion of Japan (1973) with Sakyo Komatsu, Koji Hashimoto and Teruyoshi Nakano, Toho Video

Godzilla vs. Mechagodzilla (1974) with Teruyoshi Nakano, Toho Video

NEWSPAPERS, MAGAZINES AND OTHER

Freedom of Information Act: Masters of Deceit, J. Edgar Hoover (1959)

The Influence of Traditional Japanese Aesthetics on the Film Theory of Sergei Eisenstein by Steve Odin; The Journal of Aesthetic Education Vol. 23 (1989)

From the Opium War to the Pacific War: Japanese Propaganda Films of World War II

by David Desser; Asian Cinema No. 1 Vol. 7 (1995)

The 1970 Osaka Expo And/As Science Fiction by William O. Gardner; Review Of Japanese Culture And Society. Vol. 28 (2011)

American Cinematographer

Animerica

Associated Press

Cinemascore

Famous Monsters of Filmland

Fangoria

G-FAN

The Japan Times

Japanese Giants

NHK Radio Magazine

Pacific Stars and Stripes

Shaw Brothers Southern Screen

Soundtrack Magazine

South China Morning Post

The Times

Variety

Battle of Okinawa liner notes by Hideaki Anno, Toho Video

The Super Inframan liner notes by August Ragone and Damon Foster, Image Entertainment

Symphonic Fantasia: The Music of Japanese Monsters liner notes

WEBSITES AND BLOGS

Educational Arts Limited: Life is Music

Kaiju Conversations (http://www.davmil.org/www.kaijuconversations.com)

Henshin Online (Archived)

Sci-Fi Japan

Vantage Point Interviews

Maser Patrol

Toho Kingdom

Pinoy Kollector

次回予告

Japanese Special Effects Cinema: Godfathers of Tokusatsu Vol. 2 continues the exhaustive history of Japan's special effects filmmaking and television. In the wake of one sophisticated Hollywood visual effects production after another, Japan's special effects industry struggles to maintain the international appeal it once had. As the *Heisei* era dawns, a new generation of filmmakers begins to inherit the mantle of Eiji Tsuburaya. The first with the luxury of studying the classics on home video, these young special effects wizards integrated their country's filmmaking tradition with state-of-the-art technology from America to bring novelty to the medium of tokusatsu cinema.

Learn about the directorial geniuses behind modern Japanese special effects films from veterans like **Koichi Kawakita** to new wave trailblazers including **Keita Amemiya** and **Shinji Higuchi** to today's rising talent such as **Kazuhiro Nakagawa** and **Daisuke Sato**. Discover the contributions of unsung below-the-line talent such as genius miniature engineer **Toshio Miike** or FX modeling artisans like **Fuyuki Shinada** and **Shinichi Wakasa**. Take an intimate look at the production of modern Japanese special effects movies and television, from modern classics like *The Return of Godzilla* (1984) and *Gamera 3: Revenge of Iris* (1999), cult films like *Tokyo: The Last Megalopolis* (1988) and *Mechanical Violator Hakaider* (1995), independent productions like *The Eight-Headed Serpent Strikes Back* (1985) and *Howl From Beyond the Fog* (2019) and everything in between from war epics to live action anime adaptations.

Spanning from 1980 to the present day, **Japanese Special Effects Cinema: Godfathers of Tokusatsu Vol. 2** takes you on a thrilling journey through the continuing history of a distinct cinematic art form.

ABOUT THE AUTHOR

Jules L. Carrozza (1986-) is a writer, filmmaker, film historian, video editor and general crazy person. Japanese special effects films have long been a passion of his. As a boy, he wore out dubbed VHS copies of his favorite Godzilla movies. In school, he was more interested in learning about Ishiro Honda and Eiji Tsuburaya than reading, writing and 'rithmetic. Carrozza is also fond of horror movies, classic anime and Hong Kong cinema.

Carrozza has written for numerous websites and publications. These include *Toho Kingdom, Otaku USA, Monster Attack Team* and *Kaiju Ramen*. He has directed a handful of independent films including *Little Red Riding Hood* (2006), *Eater* (2016) and *Fungus* (2019). This is his second book, his first being *SF: The Japanese Science Fiction Film Encyclopedia* (2021). *Japanese Special Effects Cinema: Godfathers of Tokusatsu Vol. 2* is due to be released in March 2023. Carrozza is also at work on a biography of *Evangelion* creator Hideaki Anno.

Some of Carrozza's favorite movies include *2001: A Space Odyssey* (1968), *Alien* (1979), *Blade Runner* (1982), *Star Wars* (1977), *Godzilla* (1954), *Akira* (1988), *The End of Evangelion* (1997) and *Pink Floyd's The Wall* (1982). His favorite recording artists include Pink Floyd, David Bowie, Nine Inch Nails and Emerson, Lake and Palmer. Carrozza currently lives in Boston, Massachusetts with his cats but plans a move to Japan soon.

www.ingramcontent.com/pod-product-compliance
Lightning Source LLC
Chambersburg PA
CBHW080405230426
43662CB00016B/2322